Socially Responsible Investment Law

BENJAMIN J. RICHARDSON

Socially Responsible Investment Law:

Regulating the Unseen Polluters

OXFORD
UNIVERSITY PRESS

2008

Oxford University Press, Inc., publishes works that further Oxford University's objective of excellence in research, scholarship, and education.

Oxford New York
Auckland   Cape Town   Dar es Salaam   Hong Kong   Karachi   Kuala Lumpur   Madrid   Melbourne
Mexico City   Nairobi   New Delhi   Shanghai   Taipei   Toronto

With offices in
Argentina   Austria   Brazil   Chile   Czech Republic   France   Greece   Guatemala   Hungary   Italy   Japan
Poland   Portugal   Singapore   South Korea   Switzerland   Thailand   Turkey   Ukraine   Vietnam

Library of Congress Cataloging-in-Publication Data
Richardson, Benjamin J.
  Socially responsible investment law: regulating the unseen polluters/Benjamin J. Richardson.
  p. cm.
     Includes bibliographical references and index.
     ISBN 978-0-19-533345-9 (alk. paper)
1. Investments—Law and legislation—Moral and ethical aspects. 2. Environmental law. I. Title.
  K1112.R53 2008
  346'.092—dc22

                                                                          2008010851

1 2 3 4 5 6 7 8 9

Printed in the United States of America on acid-free paper

Note to Readers
This publication is designed to provide accurate and authoritative information in regard to the subject matter covered. It is based upon sources believed to be accurate and reliable and is intended to be current as of the time it was written. It is sold with the understanding that the publisher is not engaged in rendering legal, accounting, or other professional services. If legal advice or other expert assistance is required, the services of a competent professional person should be sought. Also, to confirm that the information has not been affected or changed by recent developments, traditional legal research techniques should be used, including checking primary sources where appropriate.

*(Based on the Declaration of Principles jointly adopted by a Committee of the
American Bar Association and a Committee of Publishers and Associations.)*

You may order this or any other Oxford University Press publication by
visiting the Oxford University Press website at www.oup.com

CONTENTS

Preface　vii
Acknowledgments　ix
About the Author　xi
Abbreviations　xiii

CHAPTER I:　**The Potential and Limits of SRI**　1

　　　I.　"Unseen Polluters": A Lacuna in
　　　　　Environmental Law　1
　　　II.　SRI: Evolutionary or Revolutionary?　12
　　　III.　SRI Governance Themes　27
　　　IV.　Plan of the Book　37

CHAPTER 2:　**Corporate Financiers and the SRI
　　　　　　　Movement**　43

　　　I.　The Era of Finance Capitalism　43
　　　II.　Corporate Financing　52
　　　III.　Types of Financial Institutions　62
　　　IV.　The SRI Movement　73

CHAPTER 3:　**SRI's Challenges and Impact**　103

　　　I.　Business-as-Usual or a Shift to
　　　　　Sustainability?　103
　　　II.　What Has Modern SRI Achieved?　120
　　　III.　Doing Good While Doing Well?　159

CHAPTER 4:   Obstacles to SRI: Investment Regulation   187

    I.   Introduction   187
    II.   Financial Markets Regulation   188
    III.   Fiduciary Duties of Institutional Investors   205
    IV.   Fiduciary Duties of Pension Funds   221
    V.   Investment Duties of Other Financiers   234
    VI.   Participation in Investment Management   246
    VII.   Conclusions   278

CHAPTER 5:   SRI Regulation   281

    I.   The Impetus to SRI Governance   281
    II.   Regulatory Design for Sustainability Challenges in Financial Markets   287
    III.   Informational Mechanisms   303
    IV.   Financial Incentive Mechanisms   332
    V.   Environmental Liability of Financial Sponsors   345
    VI.   Investment SRI Mandates and Restrictions   358
    VII.   Conclusions   376

CHAPTER 6:   SRI Governance Beyond the State   379

    I.   Governing SRI Through Market Forces   379
    II.   Normative Frameworks for SRI   394
    III.   Process Standards   411
    IV.   Management Systems   425
    V.   Rating Mechanisms   432
    VI.   Verdict   447

CHAPTER 7:   The SRI Agenda: Climate Change and Indigenous Peoples   453

    I.   Introduction   453
    II.   Protecting Indigenous Peoples Through SRI   456
    III.   Finance in a Climate of Change   478
    IV.   Comparisons   505

CHAPTER 8:   The Path to Ethical Investment for Sustainability   509

    I.   Renewing the Promise of SRI   509
    II.   SRI—Adding Values, Not Just Value   520
    III.   Governance Reforms   533
    IV.   Finale   567

Index   571

PREFACE

"Money should never be separated from mission. It is an instrument, not an end. Detached from values, it may indeed be the root of all evil. Linked effectively to social purpose, it can be the root of opportunity."

Rosabeth M. Kanter, "Money is the Root ..." *Harvard Business Review,*
May/June (1991): 9.

"The superior man seeks what is right; the inferior one, what is profitable ..."
Confucius (551–479 BC)

ACKNOWLEDGMENTS

The research and preparation of this book is indebted to the ideas and support of colleagues and students at Osgoode Hall Law School. Among my colleagues, I wish to thank Professors Mary Condon, Aaron Dhir, Cynthia Williams, Stepan Wood, and Peer Zumbansen, who gave their time to discuss their perspectives about this topic. Also, I am grateful for the support of students who assisted immensely with the research and editing of the manuscript, namely: Alyssa Brierley, Linda Chiasson, Nicholas Dobbek, Irene Kim, Shauna Parr, Seema Shah, and Janet Wong. The generous financial support of Canada's Social Sciences and Humanities Research Council is also gratefully acknowledged. I am also indebted to the many individuals working in the SRI industry whom I interviewed for their ideas and advice. Finally, I wish to thank Kiri, just because . . .

ABOUT THE AUTHOR

Benjamin J. Richardson is a law professor at Osgoode Hall Law School of York University, Toronto, Canada. Previously, he lectured at the law faculties of the Universities of Manchester (UK) and Auckland (New Zealand). Beyond academia, he has also worked for the National Parks and Wildlife Service in Australia and the IUCN in Kenya and Nepal. Professor Richardson is active in various environmental law associations, particularly the IUCN Academy of Environmental Law. Apart from his scholarly interests in environmental law, he teaches and researches Indigenous legal issues, and is co-director of Osgoode's Intensive Program in Aboriginal Law.

ABBREVIATIONS

ACSI	Australian Council of Superannuation Investors
ASIC	Australian Securities and Investments Commission
ASN	Algemene Spaarbank voor Nederland
ASrIA	Association for Sustainable and Responsible Investment in Asia
BCBS	Basel Committee on Banking Supervision
BIS	Bank for International Settlements
CalPERS	California Public Employees' Retirement System
CCX	Chicago Climate Exchange
CDM	Clean Development Mechanism
CDP	Carbon Disclosure Project
CERCLA	Comprehensive Environmental Response, Compensation, and Liability Act
CERES	Coalition for Environmentally Responsible Economies
CIS	Collective investment scheme
CO_2	Carbon dioxide
CPP	Canada Pension Plan
CRA	Community Reinvestment Act

CRAs	Credit rating agencies
CSR	Corporate social responsibility
DJSIs	Dow Jones Sustainability Indexes
EBRD	European Bank for Reconstruction and Development
EC	European Commission
ECA	Export credit agency
EI	Economic instrument
EIRIS	Ethical Investment Research Service
EMAS	Eco-Management and Audit Scheme
EMS	Environmental management systems
ESG	Environmental, social, and governance
EPs	Equator Principles
EPA	Environmental Protection Agency
ERISA	Employee Retirement Income Security Act
ETI	Economically targeted investment
EU	European Union
Eurosif	European Social Investment Forum
FTSE	Financial Times Stock Exchange
GAAP	Generally Accepted Accounting Principles
GATS	General Agreement on Trade in Services
GATT	General Agreement on Tariffs and Trade
GDP	Gross domestic product
GHG	Greenhouse gas
GRI	Global Reporting Initiative
HNMI	High net-worth individual
HSBC	Hong Kong Shanghai Banking Corporation
IASB	International Accounting Standards Board

ICCR	Interfaith Center on Corporate Responsibility
ICJ	International Court of Justice
IFC	International Finance Corporation
IFRS	International Financial Reporting Standards
IIGCC	Institutional Investors Group on Climate Change
ILO	International Labor Organization
INCR	Investor Network on Climate Risk
IOSCO	International Organization of Securities Commissions
ISO	International Organization for Standardization
IUCN	International Union for Conservation of Nature
JI	Joint Implementation
JPMC	JPMorgan Chase
KAIROS	Canadian Ecumenical Justice Initiatives
KLD	Kinder, Lydenberg, and Domini
LSIF	Labour-sponsored investment funds
MBI	Mission-based investment
MDB	Multilateral development bank
MPT	Modern portfolio theory
NAFTA	North American Free Trade Agreement
NAPF	National Association of Pension Funds
NCP	National contact point
NGO	Nongovernmental organization
NRTEE	National Round Table on the Environment and the Economy
NZSF	New Zealand Superannuation Fund
OECD	Organization for Economic Cooperation and Development
PAS	Public accountability statement

PDS	Product disclosure statement
RBC	Royal Bank of Canada
RIAA	Responsible Investment Association Australasia
S&P's	Standard and Poor's
SAM	Sustainable Asset Management
SEC	Securities and Exchange Commission
SHARE	Shareholder Association for Research and Education
SI	Sustainability indicator
SIF	Social Investment Forum
SIO	Social Investment Organization
SRI	Socially responsible investment
STT	Securities transaction tax
TCCR	Taskforce on the Churches and Corporate Responsibility
TIAA-CREF	Teachers Insurance and Annuity Association, College Retirement Equities Fund
TNC	Transnational corporation
TRI	Toxics Release Inventory
UK	United Kingdom
UKSIF	United Kingdom Social Investment Forum
UN	United Nations
US	United States
USS	Universities Superannuation Scheme
UNEPFI	United Nations Environment Program Finance Initiative
UNFCCC	United Nations Framework Convention on Climate Change
UNGC	United Nations Global Compact
UNPRI	United Nations Principles for Responsible Investment

VCF	Venture capital finance
WBCSD	World Business Council for Sustainable Development
WWF	World Wide Fund for Nature
WTO	World Trade Organization

CHAPTER I

The Potential and Limits of SRI

I. "Unseen Polluters": A Lacuna in Environmental Law

A. THE FINANCIAL SECTOR'S SIGNIFICANCE

Imagine. A bank declines finance to a profitable mining company, as its new venture is fraught with unacceptable environmental risks. A pension fund increases its investment positions in agricultural businesses that specifically adhere to leading international labor standards. And a mutual fund boycotts a lucrative pharmaceutical company infringing Indigenous medicinal knowledge. While we know that these decisions are not currently ordinary, everyday occurrences in the financial world, how much closer would we be to a socially just and ecologically sustainable economy if they were?

Encouragingly an ebullient movement known as "socially responsible investment" (SRI) is rising in international financial markets. Having evolved from its obscure beginnings of church-based, single-issue activism, it now represents a broad constellation of interests campaigning for socially, ethically, and environmentally responsible financing.[1] Unlike philanthropy, SRI seeks its desired changes through investments. Among SRI adherents are pension plans interested in sustainable, long-term investment, mutual funds selling

---

1 R. Sparkes, "A Historical Perspective on the Growth of Socially Responsible Investment," in *Responsible Investment*, eds R. Sullivan and C. Mackenzie (Greenleaf Publishing, 2006), 39.

SRI portfolios to households, and banks requiring that their borrowers' projects minimize environmental degradation.[2]

While no authoritative definition of SRI exists, and investors often market the concept promiscuously, SRI has become increasingly recognized as primarily a means to further sustainable development.[3] The relationship between SRI and sustainable development is the underlying theme of this book. Sustainable development, the most widespread concept in modern environmental law and policy, seeks to ensure that economic growth does not diminish the capacity of the natural environment to meet the needs of future life.[4] Sustainability, as the ultimate goal, is a fundamentally necessary element of healthy natural and human systems.[5] It concerns the integrity of natural systems (global climate, evolutionary viability of ecosystems, and other vital life-supporting services) and societal and economic issues that may impinge upon environmental management (e.g., health, human rights, poverty). As explained by the International Court of Justice (ICJ) in the case concerning the *Gabčikovo-Nagymaros Project (Hungary/Slovakia)*,[6] implementation of the concept of sustainable development requires integration of ecological considerations into all aspects of economic decision-making, including presumably financial markets. SRI is a potential way to meld environmental, social, and economic considerations in investment decisions, raising them to a higher sustainability standard.

However, although maturing quickly, the SRI sector is still relatively insubstantial, likely below 10 percent of the capital markets of major economies.[7] Further, much finance masquerading as SRI hardly contributes to

---

2 See M. Jeucken, *Sustainable Finance and Banking: The Financial Sector and the Future of the Planet* (Earthscan, 2001); S. Labatt and R.R. White, *Environmental Finance: A Guide to Environmental Risk Assessment and Financial Products* (John Wiley and Sons, 2002).

3 For an early perspective, see S. Meeker-Lowry, *Economics as if the Earth Really Mattered: A Catalyst Guide to Socially Conscious Investing* (New Society Publishers, 1988).

4 A. Djoghlaf, "The Concept of Sustainable Development," *Environmental Policy and Law* 36(5) (2006): 211: K. Bosselmann, *The Principle of Sustainability: Law and Governance* (Ashgate Publishing, 2008).

5 For introductions, see P. Harrison, *The Third Revolution: Population, Environment and a Sustainable World* (Penguin, 1992); G.C. Daily, *Nature's Services: Societal Dependence on Natural Ecosystems* (Island Press, 1997).

6 (1997) I.C.J. Rep. 92.

7 Social Investment Forum (SIF), *2005 Report on Socially Responsible Investing Trends in the United States: A 10-Year Review* (SIF, 2006); European Social Investment Forum (Eurosif), *Socially Responsible Investment among European Institutional Investors* (Eurosif, 2003); Corporate Monitor, *Sustainable Responsible Investment in Australia—2005* (Ethical Investment Association, 2005).

sustainable development, further diminishing its influence. But if its quality were improved and it were entrenched as the dominant consideration in financing decisions, SRI could transform capital markets into a means for sustainable development. To achieve such a change, legal reform of financial markets is required to mitigate numerous market and institutional barriers to SRI.

Financial institutions have systemically been remote to the environmental and social consequences underlying their decisions to provide corporate capital. Traditionally, financiers have not been held accountable for the downstream impacts of the transactions they fund. Similarly, on the upstream side, individuals who invest in mutual funds, make deposits in banks, or take part in pension plans typically have little knowledge about the kinds of projects or companies they support, and even less about any ensuing environmental harm. Investment is thus pervasive—"unwittingly or otherwise, we participate in, benefit from, and fund institutions many of which act immorally."[8] Causal relationships between finance and environmental impacts are separated widely across time and space, frequently obscuring holistic responsibility for the degradation. Hence, we may legitimately construe financial institutions as unseen polluters, who wittingly or unwittingly contribute to environmental and social problems they sponsor and profit from.

The general structure of financial markets does not motivate investors to act for the public good.[9] Certainly, sometimes financiers can exert positive influence, by stimulating business dialogue about social and environmental issues, pricing environmental risks that hurt the bottom line, and facilitating the transfer of knowledge and technology for sustainable development. Yet, given that the exclusive profit motive is traditionally seen as intrinsic to the concept of investment,[10] ultimately banks, mutual funds, and other financial institutions are commercial entities mandated to earn private profit rather than sustaining environmentally sound development for the public good. Governance of financial markets has exacerbated this situation. Past attempts at reforms to spur SRI have been generally too isolated, non-systemic, and superficial to engender significant and lasting change. A substantial chasm

---

8 A. Kolers, "Ethical Investing: The Permissibility of Participation," *The Journal of Political Philosophy* 9(4) (2001): 435, 442.

9 M.A. White, "Environmental Finance: Value and Risk in an Age of Ecology," *Business Strategy and the Environment* 5 (1996): 198.

10 D.R. Fischel, "The Corporate Governance Movement," *Vanderbilt Law Review* 35 (1982): 1259, 1280.

remains between much of the aspirations of SRI and the professional objectives of financiers.[11]

The time has come for regulation to address this lacuna and target the financial sector. The domain of environmental law is not intuitively associated with banks, pension funds, and other financiers, the economy's unseen polluters. Authorities typically connect ecological and social problems only to those companies that visibly exploit, consume, and pollute nature,[12] despite the fact that these activities are often only made possible by the capital support of the financial sector. A committee appointed by the Norwegian Government to propose ethical guidelines for the Government Petroleum Fund advised:

> Even though the issue of complicity raises difficult questions, the Committee considers, in principle, that owning shares or bonds in a company that can be expected to commit gross unethical actions may be regarded as complicity in these actions. The reason for this is that such investments are directly intended to achieve returns from the company, that a permanent connection is thus established between the Petroleum Fund and the company, and that the question of whether or not to invest in a company is a matter of free choice.[13]

Environmental issues are not the only subject of connection between financial institutions and their culpability for social problems. Take for example the litigation ensued by Holocaust survivors against Swiss and German banks for their collusion with the Nazis' expropriation of Jewish property.[14] Yet another example is Black South Africans' lawsuit brought under the United

---

11 Friends of the Earth (FoE), *Ethical Investment in a Neo-Liberal Economy* (FoE, 2005); World Wide Fund for Nature (WWF) and BankTrack, *Shaping the Future of Sustainable Finance: Moving from Paper Promises to Performance* (WWF, 2006).

12 Few environmental lawyers and policy-makers until recently, have realized that corporate social responsibility hinges considerably on reforming the finance sector as well: e.g., Mineral Policy Institute (MPI), *The Buck's Gotta Stop Somewhere: Social and Environmental Accountability in the Financing of Mining* (MPI, 1998).

13 Graver Committee, *The Report from the Graver Committee* (Norwegian Ministry of Finance, 2003), s. 2.2.

14 P. van der Auweraert, "Holocaust Reparation Claims Fifty Years After: The Swiss Banks Litigation," *Nordic Journal of International Law* 71(4) (2002): 557.

States (US) *Alien Tort Claims Act* against international financiers for supporting the former apartheid regime.[15]

To attain sustainability in a finite biosphere, we must address the role of capital markets premised on infinite economic growth. The financial sector operates at a strategic level, because it is foundational to "wholesale" decisions regarding future development. The increased globalization of markets in recent decades has contributed to the financial-sector behemoth, and public accountability mechanisms have not kept pace with this exponential growth. Other factors in this growth are government policies of international deregulation and more liberalized markets.[16] Private financial institutions—a diverse group of banks, pension plans, mutual funds, credit unions, and others—hold far more development capital than governments.[17]

The biggest environmental impact of financiers is not their own direct ecological footprint, but indirect effects of allocating capital to the corporate sector.[18] Financiers' capital is transformed, through scale, time, and location into an instrument of development. As corporations are rarely always financially self-sufficient, they turn to capital markets to assist growth and new investments.[19] Financiers can also gain further influence through ownership

15 J.G. Frynas, "Social and Environmental Litigation against Transnational Firms in Africa," *Journal of Modern African Studies* 42 (2004): 363.

16 Other factors include technology advances, underlying income growth, and demographic changes resulting in more savings for retirement: P.L. Davies, "Institutional Investors in the United Kingdom," in *Contemporary Issues in Corporate Governance*, eds D.D. Prentice and P.R.J. Holland (Clarendon Press, 1993), 69, 72–73; H. Blommestein and N. Funke, "Introduction to Institutional Investors and Institutional Investing," in *Institutional Investors in the New Financial Landscape*, eds H. Blommestein and N. Funke (OECD, 1998), 15–16.

17 Organization for Economic Cooperation and Development (OECD), *Financial Assets of Institutional Investors as a Percentage of GDP* (OECD, 2005); R.G. Hubbard, *Money, the Financial System, and the Economy* (Pearson and Addison-Wesley, 2005).

18 J. Rada and A. Trisoglio, "Capital Markets and Sustainable Development," *Columbia Journal of World Business* 27(3/4) (1992): 42; W.L. Thomas, "The Green Nexus: Financiers and Sustainable Development," *Georgetown International Environmental Law Review* 13 (2001): 899.

19 A. Hackethal and R.H. Schmidt, *Financing Patterns: Measurement Concepts and Empirical Results*, Working Paper (University of Frankfurt, 2003); J. Corbett and T. Jenkinson, "How is Investment Financed: A Study of Germany, Japan, the United Kingdom and the United States," *The Manchester School Supplement* (1997): 69.

stakes in companies.[20] Pressure from financial markets to maintain strong profitability obliges public companies to report financial results several times during the year. The economic growth this spurs and its social and environmental sequelae are thus intertwined with the caprices of the financial sector.

The investment community continues to downplay inclusion of environmental and social criteria for consideration in corporate financing decisions. In the public sector, the World Bank and multilateral development banks (MDBs) were the first financiers to introduce environmental impact assessment and public consultation procedures in project financing, and that only after a long campaign fought by nongovernmental organizations (NGOs) and other critics during the 1980s.[21] As for private sector financiers, despite their growing rhetoric about responsible financing, they have variously sought to thwart reforms aimed to make them accountable beyond the bottom line. In 1996, the US banking industry successfully lobbied Congress to amend the Superfund legislation to obtain a safe harbor from lender liability suits for cleanup costs of contaminated lands.[22] Also, the mutual fund industry in North America fiercely resisted regulations to make it disclose how it votes as a shareholder.[23] In the United Kingdom (UK) and Australia, the pension fund sectors initially opposed or doubted proposed legislation to make them disclose publicly their policies on ethical investment.[24] These vignettes generally reveal what really motivates many financial institutions—an unencumbered market to be able to achieve the highest returns for its investors.

It is therefore noteworthy that some SRI networks such as Canada's Social Investment Organization (SIO) and the UK Social Investment Forum (UKSIF) have lobbied authorities for regulatory reform as a means to leverage

20 S.L. Gillan and L.T. Starks, *Relationship Investing and Shareholder Activism by Institutional Investors*, Working Paper (University of Texas, 1995).

21 Z.J.B. Plater, "Multilateral Development Banks, Environmental Diseconomies, and International Reform Pressures: The Example of Third World Dam-Building Projects," *Boston College Third World Law Journal* 9(2) (1989): 169; R. Muldoon, "The International Law of Ecodevelopment: Emerging Norms for Development Assistance Agencies," *Texas International Law Journal* 22(1) (1987): 1.

22 *Asset Conservation, Lender Liability and Deposit Insurance Protection Act*, 1996, Pub. L. No. 104-208, 110 Stat. 3009.

23 S. Davis, J. Lukomnik, and D. Pitt-Watson, *The New Capitalists. How Citizen Investors are Reshaping the Corporate Agenda* (Harvard Business School Press, 2006), 73.

24 D. Smith, "Pension Funds to Adopt Ethical Investment Policy," *The Times*, June 25, 2000, 2; Association of Superannuation Funds of Australia (ASFA), *Development of ASFA Policy on 'Ethical Investment'* (ASFA, October 2000).

change in capital markets. The UKSIF was one of the loudest voices for reforms to instill greater transparency among pension funds in their SRI policies.[25] Likewise, in the US, in 2007 many SRI groups petitioned the Securities Exchange Commission to abandon its plans perceived as curbing shareholders' rights to file advisory resolutions.[26]

SRI thus faces immense hurdles to influence significant systemic changes within financial markets. Appropriate laws and public policies will be crucial for improving the quality, extent, and impact of SRI.

B. SRI LAW AND GOVERNANCE

Law plays a critical although often poorly acknowledged role in shaping SRI. The legal system can facilitate, discipline, and coordinate financial markets in ways that both hinder and help SRI. Indeed, without legal ordering, markets of any sort, even the so-called "deregulated" ones, would hardly exist.[27] Much of the SRI literature has unfortunately only glossed over the legal system, characterizing the law as just an occasional umpire.[28] This stance may partly reflect faith in SRI's capacity to provide alternative standards to the fragmented and ineffectual controls of official regulation.

While SRI interfaces with formal legal governance systems, it is itself conceivable as "governance." It can be considered a form of self-regulation. SRI includes norms, institutions, and procedures that seek to achieve social and environmental changes through financial market governance. This web of governance is dynamic and heterogeneous; it encompasses guidance by voluntary codes of investment conduct, ordering via market indexes, and publicized pressure from SRI activists. These governance forces intersect with official laws, addressing for instance corporate environmental reporting standards, tax incentives for green investment, and the evolving fiduciary obligations of investment institutions. In the context of globalization, with fragmenting state authority and increasing corporate power, governance is

---

25 See, e.g., UKSIF, *Responsible Business: Sustainable Pension* (UKSIF, October 2007).

26 Social Investment Forum (SIF), "Record 22,500 Investors Speak Out Against Potential SEC Curbs on Shareholder Resolutions, Role in Board Nominations," Press release, October 10, 2007.

27 M. Moran and M. Wright, "Conclusion: The Interdependence of Markets and State," in *The Market and the State: Studies in Interdependence*, eds M. Moran and M. Wright (Macmillan, 1991), 239.

28 E.g., R. Sparkes, *Socially Responsible Investment: A Global Revolution* (John Wiley and Sons, 2002); J.J. Bouma, M. Jeucken, and L. Klinkers, eds, *Sustainable Banking: The Greening of Finance* (Greenleaf Publishing, 2001).

increasingly perceived as grown beyond the activities of governments (if ever it was thus confined).[29] The norms and processes that coordinate and discipline markets emanate from a diversity of actors beyond the state, such as NGOs and business groups, materializing as various unofficial and "private" norms. These norms can be just as influential as state legislation in overseeing market behavior.[30]

As a means of governance, SRI performs two distinct functions. In one, SRI acts as *surrogate* regulation: enlisting banks, mutual funds, and other financiers to disseminate environmental and social standards to the wider economy. SRI harnesses financial intermediaries as the instruments to convey norms and to discipline financed companies, other organizations, and individuals. One illustration of this is corporate governance reforms enabling institutional shareholders to exert more pressure on corporate management. Alternatively, voluntary codes could expect their signatories to assess the environmental risks of projects prior to granting finance or by making financing conditional on operational changes to remediate any identified deficiencies. Financial institutions acting as surrogate regulators in this fashion has existed before in other contexts, such as banks being required to report suspicious transactions as an adjunct to money laundering controls.[31]

In its second role, SRI governance seeks to directly control or influence financiers. This may involve imposing the liability of corporate sector environmental harms on its lenders, imposing fiduciary duties on pension funds to promote sustainable development, or requiring financial institutions to disclose their policies regarding criteria for investment and whether they include firms' environmental performance. While the primary function of this type of governance is to make the financial sector accountable in its own right, it is hoped that such techniques will ultimately influence the environmental and social behavior of the companies they finance.

The distinction between both governance-type functions is critical. The danger lurks in that SRI could become a self-congratulatory spectacle, in which financiers laud themselves for changing the behavior of others—those

---

29 By way of introduction, see M. MacNeil, N. Sargent, and P. Swan, eds, *Law, Regulation and Governance* (Oxford University Press, 2003).

30 See M. Rein, "The Social Structure of Institutions: Neither Public Nor Private," in *Privatization and the Welfare State*, eds S.B. Kamerman and A.J. Kahn (Princeton University Press, 1989), 49; U. Mörth, ed., *Soft Law in Governance and Regulation: An Interdisciplinary Analysis* (Edward Elgar Publishing, 2005).

31 E.g., the US's *Bank Secrecy Act*, 1970, Pub. L. No. 91-508, 84 Stat. 1118.

they explicitly fund—without acknowledging their own culpability, which the second form of governance addresses. Sustainability demands that we recognize financial institutions' amorphous and often obscured influence, as institutions that fund and profit from projects and enterprises that sometimes injure the environment and communities.

Presently, SRI governance is patchy and underdeveloped, failing to provide an adequate platform to transform the financial sector towards sustainability. Dominant governing norms tend to frame SRI as an investment evaluation of business risk inextricably linked to financial opportunity. From this constrained perspective, SRI is viable only through better economic incentives, information, and technical analyses enabling "efficient" incorporation of social and environmental variables into investment considerations. There is little room in this paradigm for evaluation of unadulterated ethical principles divorced from financial goals: whether the financial system actually contributes to sustainability, what ethical principles should guide any transformation required, and on what basis those principles should be determined. Arguably, SRI must include an *ethical* approach to achieve sustainability through new forms of corporate finance. While financial markets are economic systems, propelled by pragmatic business considerations, they, like other sectors of society, must operate within fundamental societal norms. Articulated through new legal procedures and standards, ethical investment based on safeguarding the environment can help to keep financial markets within those normative boundaries.

C. THE ETIOLOGY OF UNSUSTAINABLE DEVELOPMENT

Corporate environmental harm, with its many facets, can be traced to several cardinal problems.[32] To fully understand SRI's potential as well as its limits, we must decipher the etiology of unsustainable development in relation to the financial sector and the companies it funds.

First, it is no surprise that harms occur when businesses seek to maximize profits through exploiting market failures. A market failure generally means inadequate factoring of the full costs or benefits in prices and economic decisions. Such failures often arise in relation to the environment, either because the applicable property rights are ill-defined (e.g., biodiversity) or because

---

32 For background, see I. Bernier, *Consumer Protection, Environmental Law, and Corporate Power* (University of Toronto Press, 1985); S. Beder, *Global Spin: The Corporate Assault on Environmentalism* (Chelsea Green Publishing, 1998).

the environmental characteristics are so-called public goods (e.g., atmosphere). Ecological economics literature highlights many related systemic market failures, including the under-valuation of ecosystems,[33] the taking of excessive risks,[34] and myopic decision-making.[35] Without targeted government regulation or stiff social sanctions to correct these market defects, they may be taken advantage of by businesses operating in a competitive market place.

Moreover, because financiers have traditionally been perceived as removed from, and by implication, not responsible for environmental harms connected to the development activities of companies they fund, they may face even fewer social or regulatory restraints to behave ethically. However, if such harms affect investors' bottom line, they have incentives to consider the wider ramifications of their investments. Regulation of corporate polluters that dramatically impacts on profitability can motivate those firms' financiers wishing to protect shareholder value or to avoid bad debt write-offs and losses.

Second among the cardinal problems, the nature of the corporation inhibits accountability. The corporation is a "legal fiction," constituted as a distinct legal personality with economic objectives primarily for the benefit of its shareholders. The modern corporation is not conceived, as it once was, as an entity constituted by special charter for some public purpose to which limited liability was attached as a privilege.[36] Today, the corporate form has mushroomed into large conglomerates run by professional managers, as intermediary bodies for deploying capital for the purposes of generating private profit. The original altruistic public good at its formation is symbolic at best. Similarly, many financial organizations are structured as corporations (e.g., banks and investment companies), and other organizations such as pension trusts have similar economic purposes via their fiduciary obligations. Historically, managers and financiers of corporations have been profit-centered and shareholder-focused, rather than holistically operating within the broader environment, taking account of their decisions, and being stakeholder focused. Unsurprisingly, the result has often been environmental pillage.

Agency problems exacerbate the issue. Internal governance in widely held public corporations engenders agency problems where the interests of

---

33 R. Costanza, et al., "The Value of the World's Ecosystem Services and National Capital," *Nature* 389 (1997): 253.

34 J. von Amsberg, "Excessive Environmental Risks: An Intergenerational Market Failure," *European Economic Review* 39 (1995): 1447.

35 See M. Common, *Environmental and Resource Economics* (Longman, 1996).

36 See especially A. W. Fraser, *Reinventing Aristocracy: The Constitutional Reformation of Corporate Governance* (Ashgate Publishing, 1998).

corporate management and shareholders diverge.[37] The Enron, Parmalat, and Worldcom scandals demonstrate the shocking costs that may ensue when unscrupulous managers put personal financial interests ahead of those of the company and its shareholders.[38] Agency problems also inhere in financial organizations, particularly in the relationships between asset managers, fund custodians, and beneficiaries. Further, they can result in corporate management being lax on environmental standards to advance immediate financial interests. For example, systemically litigation against a company for pollution may not occur for years. This would appear only as a contingent liability in the notes of the financial statements. The delayed accounting can presumably appear to better the actual bottom line in the short term and thus enhance the company's reputation and as a corollary, executive remuneration. The temptation to delay accounting of true environmental costs and the possibility of over-accounting for what could be a very limited cost liability creates a tension that few managers resolve well. This tension is aggravated by short-term market demands for quarterly performance results, all of which affect share value. It is a vicious circle.

Harm can also ensue from management's incompetence or an inability to project short-term decisions into long-term implications. The concept of "bounded rationality" is advanced in the scholarly literature to describe this situation.[39] Essentially, companies, like other organizations and individuals, are not wholly knowledgeable or perfectly rational. They make mistakes. When firms are led with incompetence, it can result in errors producing wider social impacts, such as expensive pollution "accidents."[40] Thus, even where companies or their financiers have incentives not to exploit market failures and where the interests of corporate managers and shareholders, or fund managers, trustees and investors, are aligned, boundedly rational managers can fail to understand and thereby resolve complex environmental problems. In the financial sector, investment managers also

---

37 See K. Eisenhardt, "Agency Theory: An Assessment and Review," *Academy of Management Review* 12(1) (1989): 57.

38 See M.M. Jennings, "A Primer on Enron: Lessons from a Perfect Storm of Financial Reporting, Corporate Governance and Ethical Culture Failures," *California Western Law Review* 39 (2003): 163.

39 See H. Simon, *Reason in Human Affairs* (Stanford University Press, 1983); J. Elster, *Sour Grapes: Studies in the Subversion of Rationality* (Cambridge University Press, 1983).

40 C. Mackenzie, "The Scope for Investor Action on Corporate Social and Environmental Impacts," in *Responsible Investment*, eds R. Sullivan and C. MacKenzie (Greenleaf Publishing, 2005), 20.

face acute difficulties in understanding how to incorporate social and environmental factors into their financial analysis.[41] Bounded rationality may result in corporate irresponsibility to the extent that insufficient resources and effort are applied to ameliorate such issues. Systemically, understanding how their decisions undermine sustainable development has often not been rewarded.

Can SRI make a difference? According to Gro Harlem Brundtland, former head of the World Commission on Environment and Development, "[s]ustainable development cannot be achieved without socially responsible investment."[42] The Brundtland Commission put the concept of sustainable development into the consciousness of the masses. If we had perfect environmental regulation and policies, presumably there would be little need for SRI. In a sense, SRI responds to the failures of front-line regulation. Although many governments have greatly improved environmental laws and regulation in recent decades, none has engineered a truly ecologically sustainable economy.[43] Different pathways to sustainability must be evaluated and considered, such as via the financial sector. But interactions of various ideological, financial, and institutional factors can inhibit SRI, as the following section explains.[44]

II. SRI: Evolutionary or Revolutionary?

A. THE BUSINESS AND ETHICAL MOTIVATIONS OF SRI

1. Business-case SRI

SRI reflects a potpourri of investment philosophies and methods, not all of which may be ambitious enough to address sources of corporate environmental harm. There are two primary forms, of which one is merely evolutionary, and the other is perhaps revolutionary. They are the business case and the ethical

---

41 National Round Table on the Environment and the Economy (NRTEE), *Capital Markets and Sustainability: Investing in a Sustainable Future. State of the Debate Report* (NRTEE, 2007), 31.

42 SIO, "Sustainable Development Depends on SRI: Dr. Gro Harlem Brundtland," at http://www.socialinvestment.ca/News&Archives/news-0607-Brundtland.htm.

43 See B.J. Richardson and S. Wood, eds, *Environmental Law for Sustainability: A Reader* (Hart Publishing, 2006).

44 World Economic Forum (WEF), *Mainstreaming Responsible Investment* (WEF, 2005), 23–27.

case for SRI. The business case caters to value-seeking investors. The ethical case serves values-based investors. Both reflect a similar division in the motivations for corporate social responsibility (CSR) found at the corporate level.[45]

The dominance of the business case partly reflects how investment companies, pension trusts, banks, and most other financial institutions view their legal fiduciary obligations solely for their financial performance. Even SRI retail investors, investing for themselves without fiduciary obligations to others, commonly prioritize short-term financial goals. Without coincidence, ethically-motivated SRI is more likely to prosper in institutions more closely tethered to civil society, such as churches, charitable foundations, credit unions, and cooperative banks, where the governing legal principles and prevailing culture more readily accommodate non-financial considerations.

Pragmatic business case investors tend to treat social, environmental, and corporate governance issues as factors that can affect the financial condition of companies, rather than as valuable ends in their own right. Specifically, the business case considers environmental and social issues primarily to the extent that they are perceivable as financially "material."[46] Materiality is assessed by significant financial risks or investment opportunities in relation to other financial measures. For example, an environmental hazard priced at $1 million may be immaterial to a multi-billion dollar corporation. It is a relative measure. These risks and opportunities range from the tangible (e.g., litigation and regulatory sanctions) to the intangible (e.g., reputational risks and damage to brand names). While business case SRI may be construed as "ethical," in the sense that ultimately all human decisions including investment choices reflect some set of social values, this form of SRI implies a narrow "homo economicus" conceptualization of individuals:[47] the human agent is a rational utility maximizer with a restricted and predictable range of predominantly economic interests. This concept of financial materiality informs a range of financial governance mechanisms, including fiduciary responsibilities, financial accounting, and corporate reporting systems.

45 D. Vogel, *The Market for Virtue. The Potential and Limits of Corporate Social Responsibility* (Brookings Institution Press, 2005).

46 United Nations Environment Program Finance Initiative (UNEPFI), *The Materiality of Social, Environmental and Corporate Governance Issues in Equity Pricing* (UNEPFI, 2004).

47 O. Perez, "Facing the Global Hydra: Ecological Transformation at the Global Financial Frontier: The Ambitious Case of the Global Reporting Initiative," in *Constitutionalism, Multilevel Trade Governance and Social Regulation*, eds C. Joerges and E.U. Petersmann (Hart Publishing, 2006), 459.

Most business case SRI involves light-touch screens that filter out only the most pernicious companies where it is financially advantageous, polite engagement with corporate management, and technical assessments revealing financial risks and profitable opportunities inhering in corporate social and environmental behavior. In the post-Enron world of corporate scandals, investors seek better ways to identify risk, and to this end, SRI is increasingly relied on as a key strategy. There is however no bright-line distinction between "ordinary" investment and business case SRI. Conventional investment practices certainly consider financially acute environmental, social, and governance (ESG) issues. The main difference with business case SRI is that such matters should be taken into account routinely, and such investors should actively seek out ESG information and thereby enhance financial analysis. Such investors may see SRI as a way to achieve "alpha"—a measure of the incremental return added by a fund manager through active management.[48] Business case SRI thus takes some cues from the philosophy of ecological modernization, which sees a synergy between environmentally efficient and frugal businesses and enhanced profitability.[49]

There is abundant evidence of the financial drivers for SRI. To illustrate, the Institutional Investors Group on Climate Change (IIGCC) proclaims its goal to:

- Promote better understanding of the implications of climate change amongst our members and other institutional investors.
- Encourage companies and markets in which IIGCC members invest to address any material risks and opportunities to their businesses associated with climate change and a shift to a lower carbon economy.[50]

The United Nations Environment Program Finance Initiative's (UNEPFI) recent report, *Show Me the Money*, acknowledges ethical and sustainable development goals for SRI. Given its blatant title, it is not surprising however that the report touts:

The first—and arguably for investors the most important—reason to integrate ESG [Environmental, Social and Governance] issues is, simply,

---

48 E.g., Innovest, *New Alpha Source for Asset Managers: Environmentally-Enhanced Investment Portfolios* (Innovest, 2003).

49 See E.U. von Weizsacker, A.B. Lovins, and L.H. Lovins, *Factor Four: Doubling Wealth, Halving Resource Use* (Earthscan, 1998); R.J. Romm, *Cool Companies: How the Best Businesses Boost Profits and Productivity by Cutting Greenhouse-Gas Emissions* (Island Press, 1999).

50 Http://www.iigcc.org.

to make more money. There is a hypothesis, which we support, that a more thoroughgoing and systematic approach to integrating ESG issues in portfolios will, over time and in general, result in better financial performance.[51]

In another UNEPFI report, financial analysts are cautioned to "[c]ommunicate on issue-specific, proven, quantifiable, material links to business value; ... [and to] avoid moral arguments."[52]

Catering to retail investors, the mutual fund sector also habitually appeals to the bottom line.[53] Thus, the Pax World Funds (once strongly affiliated to faith-based investment principles and use of ethical screens) proclaims:

> Today, socially responsible investing is less about what you don't invest in and more about what you do invest in .... We want Pax World's social screens to help us identify financially strong, socially responsible companies. We believe that companies meeting higher standards of corporate social responsibility are better long-term investments, and we want our shareholders to benefit from investing in these forward thinking companies.[54]

Financiers are not alone in advancing business case arguments for SRI. Unusually, a 2007 report by the eminent International Union for Conservation of Nature (IUCN)[55] also argues for a business case to protect biodiversity.[56]

Economy-wide adoption of these approaches to SRI could reduce some of the most egregious social and environmental problems traceable to the financial sector. Unlike zero tolerance ethical screens, business case SRI sometimes takes a more nuanced view of corporate behavior and opens up possibilities for investors to engage with recalcitrant firms to seek change. SRI-driven financiers are motivated by evidence of a correlation between improved

---

51 UNEPFI, Asset Management Working Group, *Show Me the Money: Linking Environmental, Social and Governance Issues to Company Value* (UNEPFI, 2006), 4.

52 UNEPFI, *Generation Lost: Young Financial Analysts and Environmental, Social and Governance Issues. Executive Summary* (UNEPFI, 2004), 5.

53 R. Lowry, *Good Money: A Guide to Profitable Social Investing in the 90s* (W.W. Norton, 1991); B.N. Rosen, D.M. Sandler, and D. Shani, "Social Issues and Socially Responsible Investment Behavior: A Preliminary Empirical Investigation," *Journal of Consumer Affairs* 25(2) (1991): 221.

54 "Pax World Modernizes Social Investing Criteria," News Release, October 26, 2006, from http://www.paxworld.com.

55 Formerly known as the World Conservation Union.

56 I. Mulder, *Biodiversity, the Next Challenge for Financial Institutions?* (IUCN, 2007).

corporate sustainability performance and shareholder value.[57] Under widespread effects of such SRI, offending companies would presumably be penalized through higher capital costs.[58] Investors would be motivated to target unscrupulous corporate managers who place their own interests above the long-term interests of shareholders. Thus, this type of SRI could also address agency problems. Responsible investors may use shareholder advocacy strategies in order to change inappropriate corporate policies and practices.[59] Shareholders can encourage their firm to voluntarily comply with industry codes of conduct, even without any existing environmental regulation benchmarks.[60]

Another novel argument about why some financiers may practice SRI derives from the sheer breadth of their investments and loans. In *The Rise of Fiduciary Capitalism,* James Hawley and Andrew Williams herald the institutional investor (or "universal owner") as a new force for corporate responsibility.[61] The growth of large and diverse institutional investment holdings has, they believe, spawned the conditions for a new kind of responsible investment. Hawley and Williams contend that universal owners with broad stock portfolios have an interest in the health and long-term sustainability of the entire economy. By contrast, an investor in just one company or one economic sector will not be as broadly focused and will presumably care only about the financial performance of that narrow interest and not necessarily about the costs it may impose on others.

It is doubtful however whether universal owners such as large pension plans can coordinate their investments to keep economic growth within ecological limits. In the context of market capitalism, it is difficult to imagine

57 S.J. Feldman, P.A. Soyka, and P.G. Ameer, "Does Improving a Firm's Environmental Management System and Environmental Performance Result in a Higher Stock Price?" *Journal of Investing* 6(4) (1997): 87.

58 E. Sjöström, *Investment Stewardship: Actors and Methods for Socially and Environmentally Responsible Investments* (Project report for the Nordic Partnership in collaboration with the Stockholm School of Economics, January 2004).

59 See D.D. Guercio and J. Hawkins, "The Motivation and Impact of Pension Fund Activism," *Journal of Financial Economics* 52 (1989): 293; M.P. Smith, "Shareholder Activism by Institutional Investors: Evidence from CalPERS," *Journal of Finance* 51 (1996): 227.

60 J.E. Parkinson, *Corporate Power and Responsibility: Issues in the Theory of Company Law* (Clarendon Press, 1995), 50–55.

61 J.P. Hawley and A.T. Williams, *The Rise of Fiduciary Capitalism* (University of Pennsylvania Press, 2000).

institutional investors steering toward a "steady-state economy."[62] The market contains no mechanism to scale the economy within the environmental carrying capacity of the planet. In the absence of state-imposed restraints, such as a cap on the economy's carbon emissions, universal investors face great hurdles in working collectively to resist economic growth imperatives. There is also an underlying assumption that investors today would be motivated to forego financial return on their future pensions in order to ensure sustainable growth for the benefit of posterity.

Institutional investors have little direct control over their investments, but act through intermediaries. This further weakens the universal investor hypothesis.[63] The investment portfolio of large institutional investors is commonly distributed over several asset management companies, so that each portfolio may consequently be narrower than the original "universal" portfolio.[64] Asset or fund managers' reward system and short-term investment mandates encourages narrow and myopic investment decision-making.[65] They are often assessed quarterly, and those who repeatedly fail to meet performance targets risk dismissal. Consequently, tracking the long-term environmental performance of companies is outside of their mandate and may not be the most financially viable investment selection criterion.

Business case SRI may lessen bounded rationality by enhancing knowledge and analysis of the financial significance of social and environmental conditions.[66] Where capital markets undervalue uncertain and intangible long-term environmental costs, improved investment analysis that measures the costs of unsustainable development can help correct this type of systemic failure. In practice, so far, the financial sector tends to lack the institutional competence and expertise to integrate environmental information into investment decision-making. Development of sustainability market indexes, SRI consultancy services, and other corporate rating mechanisms have helped to make sustainability performance considerations more mainstream. Still,

62 H.E. Daly, *Toward a Steady-State Economy* (W.H. Freeman, 1973).

63 P.L. Davies, "Institutional Investors in the United Kingdom," in *Contemporary Issues in Corporate Governance*, eds D.D. Prentice and P.R.J. Holland (Oxford University Press, 1993), 69, 72.

64 Mackenzie, note 40, 22.

65 K.D. Krawiec, "Accounting for Greed: Unravelling the Rogue Trader Mystery," *Oregon Law Review* 79 (2001): 301.

66 Many specialist consultancy organizations have emerged in North America and Europe to provide SRI advice and research to investors, such as Enhanced Analytics, http://www.enhanced-analytics.com, and KLD Research and Analytics, http://www.kld.com.

problems remain.[67] The rating systems focus too heavily on formal management systems rather than on the inherent environmental risks of a company's business. Furthermore, environmental and financial analyses tend to apply at the company level rather than economy-wide. This hampers the breadth of perspective necessary for "universal investing."

In this framework, ethical issues may be considered if they affect the bottom line, but normally they will not directly motivate financial institutions. Social or environmental concerns may be too nebulous for workable financial quantification. For example a recent report on the North American financial sector commented that, "[t]o the mainstream financial community, particulate matter emissions are not yet a big factor, as investment professionals believe that these do not have a significant impact on a company's finances."[68] And too much attention to "non-economic" criteria may competitively disadvantage a financier. A survey of European banks in 2002 noted: "the application of unrealistically high environmental criteria, in isolation of its competitors, the market and the regulators, would leave [the bank] out of the game."[69] Thus, investors can be utterly silent when corporate behavior raises broader, politically-imbued questions of social and environmental injustice.[70]

Although ethical issues may not be readily financially quantifiable, sometimes "reputational risks" may be of sufficient consequence to financiers to make them pay attention. Given that somewhere between 50 to 70 percent of major public companies' value is intangible, including brand name and goodwill, risk to a company's reputation can induce more ethical behavior.[71]

---

67 J. Walker and E. Farnworth, *Rating Organisations—What is Their Impact on Corporate Sustainable Strategy?* (URS Corporate Sustainable Solutions, 2001); Å. Skillius and U. Wennberg, *Continuity, Credibility and Comparability: Key Challenges for Corporate Environmental Performance Measurement and Communication*, Report to the European Environment Agency (Lund University, 1998).

68 S. McGeachie, M. Kiernan, and E. Kirzner, *Finance and the Environment in North America: The State of Play of the Integration of Environmental Issues into Financial Research* (Environment Canada, 2005), 57.

69 ISIS Asset Management, *A Benchmarking Study: Environmental Credit-Risk Factors in the Pan-European Banking Sector* (ISIS Asset Management, 2002), 11.

70 B. Brown, "Deafening Silence from Ethical Funds on Hardie," *The Weekend Australian,* November 27–28, 2004 (discussing the liability claims filed by thousands of workers against James Hardie, the Australian asbestos miner).

71 Remarks, N. Purcell, Group General Manager, Westpac (UNEPFI Global Roundtable, Melbourne, Australia, October 24–25, 2007); D.C. Courts, M.G. Leiter, and M.A. Loch, "Brand Leverage," *The McKinsey Quarterly* 2 (1999): 100.

THE POTENTIAL AND LIMITS OF SRI | 19

Unethical conduct can negatively affect a financier's reputation, which is particularly significant in the high-profile banking sector.[72] Even if such conduct does not directly affect share value, it may have secondary consequences such as affecting a firm's ability to attract and retain a higher-quality workforce. Shell's reputation was hurt in this way by its involvement in badly managed oil projects in Nigeria[73] A pioneering report by the World Resources Institute argues that the poor and marginalized can benefit from the business case approach only in cases where financiers find that their projects need community consent and legitimacy,[74] such as where, without such consent, conflicts may arise to harm a financier's reputation and thereby affect the bottom line. Large mining and energy projects conducted with large capital commitments in the short-term with long-term payback periods are particularly vulnerable to such risks. Nonetheless, reputational risk to financiers is not an echo for all underlying societal concerns, as sometimes the most disadvantaged groups and victims of environmental hardship lack the means to publicize their plight and challenge the corporate sector.

Thus, while business case SRI can be beneficial in various contexts, it faces structural limitations.[75] It creates an additional layer of prudential checks on lending and investment, without revolutionizing the economic status quo. ESG factors may remain incidental rather than core considerations in investment policy-making. Christoph Butz and Jean Laville explain:

> Financial professionals and mainstream investors are now willing to take sustainability issues into account if (but only if) they can be reasonably assumed to influence the bottom line. On the other hand, by adopting the concept of financial materiality, the sustainable investment community is tacitly abandoning any aspiration to convey the global challenges of sustainability to the companies they invest in.[76]

---

72 Personal communication, Kim Brand, Senior Manager, Corporate Social Responsibility, Scotiabank (Toronto, September 26, 2007).

73 R. Beele, H. Fabig, and D. Wheeler, "Shell, Nigeria and the Ogoni. A Study in Unsustainable Development: II. Corporate Social Responsibility and Stakeholder Management versus a Rights-Based Approach to Sustainable Development," *Sustainable Development* 9(3) (2001): 121.

74 S. Herz, A. Vina, and J. Sohn, *Development without Conflict: The Business Case for Community Consent* (World Resources Institute, 2007).

75 J. McMurtry, *The Cancer Stage of Capitalism* (Pluto Press, 1998); H. Daly, *Beyond Growth: The Economics of Sustainable Development* (Beacon Press, 1996).

76 C. Butz and J. Laville, *Socially Responsible Investment: Avoiding the Financial Materiality Trap*, Ethos Discussion Paper No. 2 (Ethos Foundation, June 2007).

Constrained by the focus on financial materiality, business case SRI fails to see that "the ecological crisis constitutes a potentially insurmountable obstacle to modernity's dream of infinite material growth."[77] The natural environment is belatedly and partially recognized as an ingredient in the successful growth of financial capital. But the market that governs the financial sector has not accepted responsibility to build and protect natural capital.

The sheer gravity of our impact on the planet, as outlined by the UN's Millennium Ecosystem Assessment report and countless other research of its kind, demands a much more ambitious agenda for SRI and its governance.[78] As Paul Hawken once said of the challenge, "striving to attain the highest return is a direct cause of social injustice and environmental degradation.. . . How the SRI industry came to believe that it could use the same standard to reverse those ills may have more to do with marketing than philosophy."[79] The principal limitation of the business case to drive this transformation to sustainability is that sometimes there is no business case. What then?

2. Ethical Investment

The main alternative style of SRI is principally a matter of ethical necessity and a means of social and political change.[80] In some sectors, the ethical case for SRI is also known as mission or values-based investing. Consequential motives in ethical investment treat SRI as a means to change the criteria of capital allocation and motivate firms to improve their environmental and social behavior. It is associated with teleological ethics. This contrasts with the traditional deontological (or self-referential) type of ethical investment, involving investors who do not want to profit from unethical activities rather than placing a priority on leveraging change through investment. Critics of both forms of ethical investment describe them as negative and defensive in style, narrow in scope, and insufficiently linked to financial performance.[81] While these observations are certainly problematic, their influence is a key reason why ethical investment is waning. References to "ethical" in the SRI discourse are becoming scarcer, such as in 2007 when Australia's Ethical

77 M.E. Zimmerman, *Contesting Earth's Future: Radical Ecology and Postmodernity* (University of California Press, 1994), 11.

78 Millennium Ecosystem Assessment Board (MEAB), *Living Beyond Our Means: Natural Assets and Human Well-Being. Statement from the Board* (MEAB, 2005).

79 P. Hawken, *Socially Responsible Investing* (Natural Capital Institute, 2004), 5.

80 A.T. Marlin, "Social Investing: Potent Force for Political Change," *Business and Society Review* (1986): 96.

81 E.g., presentation by J. Keefe, CEO, Pax World Funds (2007 Canadian Responsible Investment Conference, Montreal, May, 27–29, 2007).

Investment Association renamed itself as the Responsible Investment Association of Australasia.[82]

Ethical investment has the potential to more fully align the financial system with the requirements of sustainable development. In the ethical approach, investors (and corporations) have a moral obligation to act in ethically responsible ways, which should not be constrained by profit motives. It sees investors as having concerns beyond enhancing their private economic welfare. These concerns include North-South inequalities, climate change, labor rights, and Indigenous peoples' land claims. Also among the concerns are the traditional objections to tobacco, armaments, and pornography.

The ethical case however does not ignore the bottom line nor discard the business case justifications for SRI, as financial considerations often remain of vital concern. Ethical investors are not donating to charity but investing in enterprises which seek to create wealth while protecting and enhancing the social values of investors. Yet, ethical investment diverges from business case justifications by insisting on the consideration of ethical issues for their own sake, and not only for financial benefit. It presumes that an individual or organization remains moral when faced with any decision, including financial management: there is no dichotomy. While the market may value ethical conduct when embodied in regulation or social pressures expressed through the lens of reputational risk, ethics has not traditionally been integral to investment decisions. Just as we expect individuals to respect various ethical standards as members of society, regardless of any individual benefit, so too corporations and financiers should behave with regard to broader social values beyond their immediate financial self-interest.[83]

These considerations are not attractive to most financial institutions. Such institutions that invest on behalf of thousands or millions of investors have often dismissed calls that they should choose investments on ethical grounds, contending that as their fund members likely hold such diverse ethical views on social and environmental issues, it would be impossible to achieve a consensus of values to guide financial decision-making. Alternatively, the maximization of financial returns is considered a clear and easily measurable benchmark to which fund managers should be held accountable. This stance relegates ethics to a matter of subjective, personal taste, compared to the supposed hard objectivity of financial returns. Certainly, there will always be some room for individuals to choose lawful investments according to their

---

82 Http://www.eia.org.au/html/s01_home/home.asp.
83 W. Cragg, "Business Ethics and Stakeholder Theory," *Business Ethics* 12(2) (2002): 113.

own moral scruples, such as eschewing financial ties to companies that engage in activities they find personally offensive, whether it be manufacturing alcohol or operating a casino. But where financial institutions manage the assets of many people and have the capacity to exert huge economic influence and potential social and environmental harm, the ethical investment movement demands adherence to specific social standards.[84]

Protection of critical ecological values should not be a discretionary option for financial institutions, but rather an essential ethical standard necessary to avert looming environmental threats such as climate change. Many scientists, policy-makers, and others see progress toward sustainable development as dependent upon challenging the anthropocentric and instrumental values of industrialized, capitalist society.[85] An ethical view helps us to understand and improve human behavior towards nature. Theorists have debated various alternative ethical frameworks, which commonly aim to broaden the moral community beyond human beings to encompass all living creatures and their ecosystems.[86] Such a "biocentric ethic" recognizes the ecological reality that humankind is interwoven into the "web of life."[87] In this vein, current imperatives suggest that we reject the view of "ethical" investment as catering only to chartered organizations (e.g., charitable investors) or individual investors managing their own portfolio. Everyone, especially large institutional investors, should act ethically in relation to the environment.

Religious institutions were the first to invest ethically.[88] They addressed social and environmental concerns not for their financial advantages, but for the moral desire and commission to improve the world we live in. The churches used their financial muscle to campaign against apartheid in South Africa, contributing to the regime's eventual demise. Today, some religious-based

---

84 N. Gunningham, R.A. Kagan, and D. Thornton, "Social License and Environmental Protection: Why Businesses Go Beyond Compliance," *Law and Social Inquiry* 29 (2004): 307.

85 See generally A. Light and H. Rolston III, eds, *Environmental Ethics: An Anthology* (Blackwell, 2003); C. Soskolne, ed., *Sustaining Life on Earth* (Lexington Books, 2007).

86 For an overview, see P.W. Taylor, *Respect for Nature: A Theory of Environmental Ethics* (Princeton University Press, 1986).

87 F. Capra, *The Web of Life. A New Scientific Understanding of Living Systems* (Anchor Books, 1996).

88 N. Kreander, K. McPhail, and D. Molyneaux, "God's Fund Managers: A Critical Study of Stock Market Investment Practices of the Church of England and UK Methodists," *Accounting, Auditing and Accountability Journal* 17(3) (2004): 408.

investors again lead a radical and ambitious agenda. Contrast the IIGCC statement on climate change above with the following goals of the Interfaith Center on Corporate Responsibility's (ICCR) Global Working Group:

- Encourage companies to report on their global warming emissions "footprints," as well as disclose global warming related risks and opportunities to shareholders; and
- In recognition of future limits on global warming pollutants, encourage companies to behave proactively by reducing greenhouse gas emissions to sustainable levels.[89]

The ICCR, which coordinates SRI among religious investors, goes further than the IIGCC by stressing the priority of reducing carbon emissions. Its aim is to prevent or mitigate global warming for its own sake, rather than as a concern merely tied to shareholder value.

Apart from religious investors, ethically shaped investments are also found in the credit union sector, such as Canada's pioneering VanCity credit union; in the banking sector, such as the Cooperative Bank and Umweltbank;[90] in public-sector pension funds, such as the UK's Universities Superannuation Scheme (USS);[91] and in some mutual funds that offer robust ethically screened portfolios, such as Domini Social Investments.[92] Community investing schemes to promote affordable housing, job creation, and other benefits for disadvantaged communities also constitute a form of ethical investment, as sometimes these investors accept below-market rates of return in order to achieve social policy goals.[93] All of these institutions have sought to make social well-being and environmental protection integral parts of their missions, alongside financial goals. Business case perspectives still feature in their policies, but they are softened by a stronger recognition of ethical and sustainable development goals as intrinsically valuable.

This ethical approach is expressed even more strongly in some of the SRI governance standards advocated by civil society groups. The Collevecchio Declaration of Financial Institutions, drafted by a coalition of NGOs in 2003, proclaims:

Financial institutions must expand their missions from ones that prioritize profit maximization to a vision of social and environmental sustainability. A commitment to sustainability would require FIs to

---

89 See http://www.iccr.org/issues/globalwarm/goalsobjectives.php.
90 See http://www.co-operativebank.co.uk and www.umweltbank.de.
91 See http://www.vancity.com and www.usshq.co.uk.
92 Domini Social Investments (DSI), *Global Investment Standards* (DSI, 2006).
93 See J. Nixon, et al., *The Double Bottom Line Handbook: A Practitioner's Guide to Regional Double Bottom Line Investment Initiatives and Funds* (Ford Foundation, 2007).

fully integrate the consideration of ecological limits, social equity and economic justice into corporate strategies and core business areas (including credit, investing, underwriting, advising), to put sustainability objectives on an equal footing to shareholder maximization and client satisfaction, and to actively strive to finance transactions that promote sustainability.[94]

While such statements can help inform the ethics behind SRI, ethics should not be merely about principles derived from international instruments. Including a deliberative process within the financial sector can allow ethical practices to reflect institutionally specific situations and to adapt to investors' changing understanding of the world. A process of ethical deliberation is an educative process. Values that shape ethical investment must incorporate a democratic process providing a forum for ethical deliberation. Without dialogue and openness to new ideas, ethical investing may degenerate into an expression of narrow, intolerant values not any more conducive to sustainability.[95]

Undemocratic governance of corporations and financial institutions limits such ethical deliberation. Contrary to the predictions of Peter Drucker in *Unseen Revolution: How Pension Fund Socialism Came to America*,[96] pension funds and other financial institutions are not kernels of democratic decision-making. Fund managers, to whom financiers commonly delegate investment mandates, wield far more power than pension plan members.[97] Even specialist ethical mutual funds are often managed much like a regular mutual fund, with few mechanisms to consult investors about investment policy. Barriers to shareholder democracy in ordinary corporations do not need elaboration.[98]

B. STRENGTHENING SRI

What sort of policy changes could make ethical SRI for sustainability more widespread and thereby more influential? Of the various reforms canvassed in this book, some of the particularly critical approaches are foreshadowed here.

---

94 Http://www.foe.org/camps/intl/declaration.html.
95 Consider, for instance, the investment policies of fundamentalist Christian mutual funds: e.g., Timothy Plan funds, at http://www.timothyplan.com.
96 P. Drucker, *Unseen Revolution: How Pension Fund Socialism Came to America* (Harper and Row, 1976).
97 R.A.G. Monks and N. Minow, *Power and Accountability* (HarperCollins, 1991), 201–2; A. Harmes, *Unseen Power: How Mutual Funds Threaten the Political and Economic Wealth of Nations* (Stoddard, 2001).
98 Parkinson, note 60, 168–69.

First, the state should set an example with regard to public finance; second, it should generally assert more influence over financial markets; and third, it should address strategic environmental issues such as climate change where the countervailing economic pressures may mute any ethically motivated investment. National pension funds provide a significant pool of capital whose financial power could be harnessed to challenge or influence an increasingly polluted and violent world, without sacrificing the financial needs of retirees. Already, national pension funds of Norway, Sweden, France, and New Zealand are legislatively mandated to invest ethically and responsibly. States must also cooperate to strengthen international law for SRI to thereby set more meaningful and legitimate controls on global financial markets. Existing transnational standards for SRI, such as the UN Principles for Responsible Investment (UNPRI), while helpful, appear unlikely to engender significant changes in the behavior of financiers over the near term.

Second, financial organizations must operate more transparently and democratically, not only to reduce agency problems, but also to promote more informed, ethical decisions. SRI needs legitimacy, particularly in determining what is "ethical" or "responsible" in local or specific contexts. If SRI is simply a fungible concept at the discretion of fund managers or unelected trustees, its legitimacy will be undermined, and it risks degenerating into another example of corporate "greenwash." Responsible financing must be based on democratically-determined norms that can be widely respected in society. Presently in the financial sector only credit unions are democratically structured (in theory), and the most critical debates about SRI are coming from NGO groups such as BankTrack. Legal reforms must aim to create conditions for participatory ethical deliberation underpinning SRI decisions, such as member nominated representatives and greater transparency in fund management.

Third, the fiduciary duties of financial institutions should extend consideration to the wider public impacts of private investment. However, there are formidable difficulties to recasting fiduciary duties to make them sufficiently clear and enforceable. A mere obligation to "promote sustainable development" would be too vague. Reforms like this are not unprecedented: the UK recently reformulated corporate directors' duties to include regard to community and environmental interests.[99] Legal commentators posit that in some jurisdictions existing statements of fiduciary duties incorporate a range

---

99 *Companies Act*, 2006, s. 172(1); see discussion in C.A. Williams and J.M. Conley, "Triumph or Tragedy: The Curious Path of Corporate Disclosure Reform in the UK," *William and Mary Environmental Law and Policy Review* 31(2) (2007): 317, 354–55.

of social and environmental stakeholder interests.[100] Advances in social accounting and sustainability indicators could help provide necessary metrics for a credible fiduciary standard of ethical investment, whereby the social and ecological costs and benefits of investment are quantified (in the case of social accounting) or performance standards are set to keep investors on a sustainable development course, based on indicators of sustainability. For residual social and environmental values too difficult to measure by either means, environmental policy standards such as the precautionary principle could help to ensure that investment choices respect ecological integrity.

These are not the only policy and governance reforms needed to embolden SRI but they are among the most vital. Collateral measures include better economic incentives (e.g., tax concessions for green investment), more robust corporate sustainability reporting standards, and even in some situations environmental liability for negligent financing decisions. These are reforms that would also strengthen the prospects for business case SRI, but more importantly could help financiers to find ways to meet ethical standards for sustainability.

Underlying these proposals is the belief that financial investments are not pure private property interests that the state should protect above other policy considerations, as some assume. Rather, regulation of investment decisions to counter harmful side-effects and promote community benefits is legitimate public policy. While individual investors' interests in their long-term economic welfare should be respected, private property rights should also be recognized as part of a web of reciprocal relations. In this vein, investors' rights are social constructs wherein individual rights to invest capital embody social interests as expressed through regulation.[101] In a sense, laws already reflect a societal consensus of a sort in restricting certain investments. For instance, corporations must abide by a multitude of social and environmental regulation, which constrain the investments of individuals who opt to invest in securities of such firms. SRI regulation takes this one step further to target investment decisions directly.

With these considerations in mind, the principal governance themes canvassed in this book are outlined below. They do not exhaust the potential

---

100 C.A. Williams and J.M. Conley, "Corporate Social Responsibility in the International Context: Is There an Emerging Fiduciary Duty to Consider Human Rights?" *University of Cincinnati Law Review* 74(Fall) (2005): 75.

101 R.H. Pildes, "Why Rights are Not Trumps: Social Meanings, Expressive Harms, and Constitutionalism," *Journal of Legal Studies* 27(2) (1998): 725.

legal analysis of SRI, but capture the most pressing governance concerns not sufficiently examined in the extant scholarship.

III. SRI Governance Themes

A. LEVERAGING CHANGE THROUGH MARKET-BASED REGULATION

The way financial institutions are governed has made the business case approach to SRI dominant. Pious calls for more ethical practices, on their own, won't motivate reform. To leverage change, we must link ethical values to other governance reforms. A key avenue of reform is fiduciary responsibilities. The fiduciary duties of institutional investors implicitly emphasize maximization of financial returns.[102] Relatedly, their internal governance does not empower democratic participation and reflection about investment goals. By these ways, investors are cast into a passive role, and traditional investment philosophies inappropriate for the challenges of sustainability go uncontested. Governance of corporations is similar; SRI-focused shareholders do not have an easy avenue to advocate change.[103] Further, the problem of bounded rationality among fiduciaries is exacerbated by corporate reporting norms that marginalize information about corporate environmental and social performance unless deemed financially material.[104]

Governments however have not entirely ignored SRI-related regulation. Their measures are classified into several groups. First, there are normative frameworks that provide substantive values as well as foundational principles and guidance on appropriate or desirable standards of performance. They occur in the legislative mandates of some national pension funds; but they are otherwise quite rare. Second, states have furnished process standards to enable assessment, verification, and communication of performance. Most SRI regulations are of this type: including corporate sustainability reporting standards,

---

102 R. Ellison, "The Golden Fleece? Ethical Investment and Fiduciary Law," *Trust Law International* 5(4) (1994): 157; P. Ali and K. Yano, *Eco-Finance: The Legal Design and Regulation of Market-Based Environmental Instruments* (Kluwer Law, 2004), 128–40.

103 J.M. Roe, "Political and Legal Restraints on Ownership and Control of Public Companies," *Journal of Financial Economics* 27 (1990): 7; Parkinson, note 60, 24.

104 KPMG, *International Survey of Corporate Responsibility Reporting* (KPMG Global Sustainability Services, 2005).

requirements to disclose proxy voting and SRI policies, and other transparency measures. Third, economic incentive mechanisms are used to correct market failures to tip the balance in favor of a business case for responsible investment. These range from taxation concessions for green investment to lender liability for pollution.

Recurring questions of policy instrument design arise from these and other instruments. Apart from questions of function and effectiveness of such policy mechanisms, there is a deeper, foundational issue of overall regulatory design. Should the state consign itself to light-touch instruments, such as incentive and informational policy instruments? Or, should it be more interventionist, such as by mandating SRI and negotiating international laws to govern financial markets? And what combination of policy instruments, both hard and soft, can best promote SRI?

Some regulatory theorists favor "reflexive" regulation, noting the apparent failures of bureaucratic, "command and control" style regulation.[105] Certainly, some command controls have suffered serious implementation failures.[106] Regulation sometimes may function best when it uses methods congruent with the codes and norms of the market; informational, incentive, and other procedural policy tools that facilitate rather than dictate behavioral changes are of this genre. Reflexive law also dovetails with arguments for flexible, collaborative mechanisms of governance, in which policy functions are shared with or devolved to private interests.[107] Many policy mechanisms applied to or proposed for financial markets resonates this style of reflexive regulation. Corporate environmental reporting has reflexive properties: facilitating investors' scrutiny of the environmental activities of firms. Similarly, economic instruments such as pollution taxes seek to factor the price of environmental neglect in the language of the market.[108] These forms of regulation support business-case SRI, as they respect the prevailing norms of financial markets, and seek to engineer change within those parameters. However, because of evidence regarding the limited impact of the current

---

105 G. Teubner, "Substantive and Reflexive Elements in Modern Law," *Law and Society Review* 17 (1983): 239; E.W. Orts, "Reflexive Environmental Law," *Northwestern University Law Review* 89(4) (1995): 1227.

106 C. Abbot, "Environmental Command Regulation," in *Environmental Law for Sustainability*, note 43, 61.

107 J.Q. Wilson, *The Politics of Regulation* (Basic Books, 1980); I. Ayres and J. Braithwaite, *Responsive Regulation* (Oxford University Press, 1992); P. Grabosky, "Using Non-Governmental Resources to Foster Regulatory Compliance," *Governance* 8(4) (1995); 527.

108 Orts, note 105.

menu of reforms, it is becoming doubtful whether the current tool-box of reflexive policy instruments alone will make a difference.

B. STRENGTHENING THE HAND OF THE STATE

An alternative path of more invasive, mandatory obligations to invest ethically and responsibly raises the dilemma of coherently defining SRI for governance purposes.[109] What should investors be mandated to do? The goal of safe-guarding ecological integrity to ensure sustainability must be articulated in more specific and concrete ways. The SRI movement presently lacks an articu-lated consensus on key terminology and concepts.[110] "Socially responsible investment" tends to be a self-awarded title; individual institutions set their own criteria. A study by the Natural Capital Institute found "the screening methodologies and exceptions employed by most SRI funds allow practically any publicly-held corporation to be considered as an SRI portfolio company."[111] Without some societal control over what qualifies as SRI for sustainability purposes, the sector risks degenerating into promiscuous marketing slogans that mask true corporate behavior.[112] Leaving this aspect of SRI governance to the market marginalizes some environmental and social perspectives from SRI discourses.[113] The dominance of business case SRI partly reflects how many participants believe only the financial materiality standard can unify SRI practices. One way to overcome this disheartening situation short of rigid bureaucratic prescriptions would be to redefine the fiduciary duties of investment decision-makers. Fiduciaries could be obliged to promote actions

---

109 See generally G. Frost, et al., "Bringing Ethical Investment to Account," *Australian Accounting Review* 14(3) (2004): 3; M.S. Schwartz, "The 'Ethics' of Ethical Investing," *Journal of Business Ethics* 43(3) (2003): 195.

110 See C. Cooper and B. Schlegelmilch, "Key Issues in Ethical Investment," *Business Ethics: A European Review* 2 (1993): 213; R. Sparkes, "Ethical Investment: Whose Ethics, Which Investment?" *Business Ethics: A European Review* 10 (2001): 194.

111 Hawken, note 79.

112 D.H. Schepers and S.P. Sethi, "Do Socially Responsible Funds Actually Deliver What they Promise? Bridging the Gap Between the Promise and Performance of Socially Responsible Funds," *Business and Society Review* 108(1) (2003): 11.

113 On the construction of environmental discourses, see M.A. Hajer, *The Politics of Environmental Discourse* (Clarendon Press, 1995); D. Salskov-Iversen, H.K. Hansen, and S. Bislev, "Governmentality, Globalization and Local Practice: Transformations of a Hegemonic Discourse," *Alternatives: Social Transformation and Humane Governance* 25 (2000): 183.

consistent with sustainable development, harnessing advances in social accounting and sustainability indicators to provide a reasonably objective basis for determining the social and ecological impacts of investment choices.

Another consideration is whether governments should become more involved in capital allocation, rather then merely telling others how to invest. Fashionable theories of financial market deregulation deride the economic inefficiencies that allegedly ensue from state intervention in the market.[114] Conversely, some scholarship highlights constructive roles of the state,[115] including partial socialization of the process of capital investment.[116] Harnessing the capital of state pension funds is a step in this direction. Already, legal reforms to national pension schemes in France, New Zealand, Norway, and Sweden mandate SRI, although with only limited statutory guidance on what this standard requires.[117] Another possibility for the state is to co-finance development with commercial entities, such as through export credit agencies,[118] creating leverage to impose sustainability conditions.

At the very least, governments must ensure more intergovernmental regulation of financial markets. Technological advances and capital market deregulation have expanded the mobility of capital able now to search globally for the most lucrative returns.[119] Globalization of banking, insurance,

---

114 See E.S. Shaw, *Financial Deepening in Economic Development* (Oxford University Press, 1975); G. Yago, "Financial Repression and the Capital Crunch Recession: Political and Regulatory Barriers to Growth Economics," in *Economic Policy, Financial Markets, and Economic Growth*, eds B.S. Zycher and C. Lewis (Westview Press 1993), 81.

115 E.g., J.K. Staniskis and Z. Stasiskiene, "Promotion of Cleaner Production Investments: International Experience," *Journal of Cleaner Production* 11(6) (2003): 619.

116 T. Ghilarducci, *Labour's Capital: The Economics and Politics of Private Pensions* (MIT Press, 1992); R. Unger, *Democracy Realised: The Progressive Alternative* (Verso Books, 1998); R. Blackburn, "The New Collectivism: Pension Reform, Grey Capitalism and Complex Socialism," *New Left Review* 233 (1999): 3.

117 See discussion and references in chapter 5.

118 In practice, though, export credit agencies have not tended to assist sustainable development: S. Stern, "International Project Finance: The Ilisu Dam Project in 2004 and the Development of Common Guidelines and Standards for Export Credit Agencies," *Journal of Structured and Project Finance* 10(1) (2004): 46.

119 A. Walter, *World Power and World Money* (Harvester Wheatsheaf, 1993), 202–4.

and investment services has hampered many individual states' ability to regulate cross-border financial activities.[120] Domestic regulatory shifts that threaten economic interests can prompt financial resources to migrate to jurisdictions offering a more benign regulatory milieu. As a corollary, if regulatory changes are within a significant capital market, it can dramatically affect international markets with economic ties. Therefore, international collaboration is necessary to protect proponents of SRI from competitive disadvantages in the global market. Hard international law weakly governs transnational financial activities, and is non-existent in relation to the social and environmental impacts of finance.[121] Most international governance has come from the non-state sector through voluntary codes of conduct.

C. GOVERNANCE BEYOND THE STATE

Examining the governance challenges of SRI must take a broad view of what "regulation" entails. Beyond the state, voluntary codes of conduct and other governance tools provided by the market and civil society increasingly shape the behavior of financiers.[122] In recent decades, market actors have substantially encroached on the traditional domain of state governance, often pursuant to government policies delegating decision-making to the private sector. Legal scholars emphasize that regulation functions ever more in a pluralistic setting, in which market governance involves an ensemble of multi-layered and often fragmented institutional networks.[123] Jody Freeman sees governance as a process of "negotiated relationships"

---

120 J. Braithwaite and P. Drahos, *Global Business Regulation* (Cambridge University Press, 2000), 7–8; and further S. Strange, *The Retreat of the State: The Diffusion of Power in the World Economy* (Cambridge University Press, 1996).

121 European Commission (EC), *Institutional Arrangements for the Regulation and Supervision of the Financial Sector* (EC Internal Market Directorate General, 2000); W. Dobson and P. Jacquet, *Financial Services Liberalization in the WTO* (Institute for International Economics, 1998).

122 E.g., B.J. Richardson, "The Equator Principles: The Voluntary Approach to Environmentally Sustainable Finance," *European Environmental Law Review* 14(11) (2005): 280.

123 See M. Rein, "The Social Structure of Institutions: Neither Public Nor Private," in *Privatization and the Welfare State*, eds S.B. Kamerman and A.J. Kahn (Princeton University Press, 1989); G. Stoker, "Governance as Theory," *International Social Sciences Journal* 155 (1998): 17.

between public and private actors,[124] while Leigh Hancher and Michael Moran theorize it as "shared regulatory spaces" inhabited by strategic governmental and private sector organizations.[125] Likewise, at a transnational level, Anne-Marie Slaughter describes "new governance networks" that have mobilized numerous categories of non-state entities, especially in the propagation of "soft law" standards.[126]

In this context, the last decade has witnessed a plethora of disparate standards, codes, and other non-state mechanisms designed to encourage responsible financing.[127] What have been the role, quality, and impact of these mechanisms?

As with state regulation, we find a mix of normative and process standards, as well as other governance techniques. Normative guidelines include the UNPRI and the work of the UNEPFI.[128] There are also many process standards. Corporate reporting and environmental assessment rules shape the quality and quantity of information available to social investors.[129] The Equator Principles (EPs)[130] and the Global Reporting Initiative (GRI)[131] are seminal examples. Additionally, management systems provide policy and procedural frameworks for organizations to continually manage their environmental and social activities. An example is the International Organization for Standardization (ISO) 14001 standard, to which some financiers have obtained certification.[132] Another technique of the non-state SRI sector is rating mechanisms, for evaluating and ranking corporate social and environmental performance for investment purposes. These include sustainability market

---

124 J. Freeman, "The Private Role in Public Governance," *New York University Law Review* 75 (2000): 543.

125 L. Hancher and M. Moran, "Organizing Regulatory Space," in *Capitalism, Culture and Economic Regulation*, eds L. Hancher and M. Moran (Clarendon Press, 1989), 271.

126 A.M. Slaughter, "Global Government Networks, Global Information Agencies and Disaggregated Democracy," *Michigan Journal of International Law* 24 (2003): 1041, 1057.

127 See D. Leipziger, *The Corporate Responsibility Code Book* (Greenleaf Publishing, 2003).

128 See http://www.unpri.org/principles.

129 KPMG, note 104, 51. See also J. Bebbington, et al., "Accountants' Attitudes and Environmentally-Sensitive Accounting," *Accounting and Business Research* 24(4) (1994): 109.

130 Http://www.equator-principles.com.

131 Http://www.globalreporting.org.

132 Http://www.iso.org.

indexes, notably the Dow Jones Sustainability Indexes.[133] From a legal standpoint, all of these mechanisms represent a form of private rule-making, which has flourished largely without state imprimatur.[134]

What has been the impact of this governance—both state and non-state—on the policies and practices of financiers, and ultimately, on the behavior of those they finance? A nagging criticism is that SRI governance, especially the voluntary kind, amounts to "greenwash"—a public facade of environmental regulation with an internal business-as-usual.[135] So far, policy changes span the adoption of responsible investment strategies, environmental risk assessment procedures, and sustainability reporting protocols. In turn, modifications in lending practices and inclusion of more SRI-conditioned finance in banks' and mutual funds' investment portfolios through SRI asset-selection screens are more prevalent. There is considerable research on whether SRI-driven finance influences capital costs of firms, or changes their policies through shareholder advocacy. While conventional finance theory doubts such effects,[136] some empirical evidence suggests SRI has some clout.[137] But, overall, the SRI market currently appears to be too small to induce profound market changes.

D. FINANCIERS' INSTITUTIONAL DIFFERENCES

Another seminal governance issue is how differences in the institutional characteristics of financiers influence their capacity or willingness to invest responsibly. Financial organizations are not homogeneous, and retain institutionally unique characteristics due to their specific legal form and market function.

---

133 See http://www.sustainability-indexes.com.

134 O. Perez, *The New Universe of Green Finance: From Self-Regulation to Multi-Polar Governance*, Working Paper No. 07-3 (Bar-Ilan University, Faculty of Law, 2007).

135 Ibid., 71. See further S. Wood, "Green Revolution or Greenwash? Voluntary Environmental Standards, Public Law and Private Authority in Canada," in *New Perspectives on the Public-Private Divide,* ed. Law Commission of Canada (University of British Columbia Press, 2002).

136 Outlined in M.S. Knoll, "Ethical Screening in Modern Financial Markets: The Conflicting Claims Underlying Socially Responsible Investment," *Business Lawyer* 57 (2002): 681.

137 P. Lanoie, B. Laplante, and M. Roy, "Can Capital Markets Create Incentives for Pollution Control?" *Ecological Economics* 26 (1998): 31; R. Heinkel, A. Kraus, and J. Zechner, "The Effect of Green Investment on Corporate Behavior," *Journal of Financial and Quantitative Analysis* 36(4) (2001): 431.

Two distinctive features of investment regulation that may produce divergent responses to SRI are the scope of fiduciary duties and internal governance. For example, the fiduciary duties of pension funds, life insurance companies, and mutual funds are not identical and may accommodate SRI considerations in different ways.[138] The internal governance of financial institutions also varies, with credit unions enabling more member involvement in decision-making than banks or mutual funds.[139] These and other institutional differences, in turn, may produce divergent responses to SRI. Some financiers' institutional characteristics plausibly create a preference for sustainable, long-term financing, particularly with better law reform. Knowing which institutions are best or worst placed to promote sustainable corporate financing can help policy-makers better target SRI reforms.

Consider occupational pension funds, for instance.[140] They have long-term financial liabilities that should extend their investment horizons. They do not directly compete for business (unlike retail mutual funds); they cater to ordinary workers; and are usually untainted by collateral business ties to their portfolio companies (unlike banks and insurance companies offering additional services to clients). Conversely, SRI may conflict with the fiduciary duties of pension plan trustees to achieve certain mandated thresholds of financial returns.[141] Further, pension funds often invest through intermediaries such as asset management companies, which tend to be compensated on much narrower and shorter-term investment perspectives. However, these latter constraints are not unique to pension funds.

Civil society investors, such as charities and churches, are sometimes better placed to invest ethically.[142] Their expectations of high financial returns are muted in order to defend their principles of faith. Financial cooperatives,

---

138 See especially Freshfields Bruckhaus Deringer, *A Legal Framework for the Integration of Environmental, Social and Governance Issues into Institutional Investment* (UNEPFI, 2005).

139 I. Carmichael, *Pension Power: Unions, Pension Funds, and Social Investment in Canada* (University of Toronto Press, 2005).

140 Ibid; J. Gifford, "Measuring the Social, Environmental and Ethical Performance of Pension Funds," *Journal of Australian Political Economy* 53 (2004): 139.

141 B.J. Richardson, "Do the Fiduciary Duties of Pension Funds Hinder Socially Responsible Investment?" *Banking and Finance Law Review* 22(1) (2006): 145.

142 Michael Jantzi Research Associates, *Investing in Change Mission-Based Investing for Foundations, Endowments and NGOs* (Canadian Council for International Cooperation, 2003); G.T. Gardner, *Inspiring Progress. Religions' Contributions to Sustainable Development* (W.W. Norton and Worldwatch Institute, 2006).

such as cooperative banks and credit unions, with ties to a particular community, also tend to be more committed to SRI than corporate-structured lenders. This suggests that if the SRI sector generally is to a have a strong ethical basis, it must deepen its ties to society. Purely market-based institutions seem less open to ethically-motivated SRI. Regulation of the financial sector may therefore need to find ways to strengthen these social ties, perhaps through more open and democratic governance within financial institutions including more "outside" stakeholder representation.

A final word of caution is that the centripetal forces of economic globalization dilute some of these institutional differences. Financial markets and services are becoming more integrated, evident by the emergence of financial conglomerates (supermarkets offering a panoply of financial services) and the integration of financial operations into global networks.[143] In this context, pension plans and mutual funds may increasingly share the same investment goals and practices. Yet, civil society based investors continue to retain their distinctive character and much stronger orientation to ethical investment.

E. SRI's SUBJECT-MATTER

A further governance theme of this book deals with the subject matter of SRI. To what extent and why does its subject matter, such as human rights, climate change, animal liberation, and an infinite host of other causes, elicit different responses from financiers and generate different governance solutions?

The SRI market embraces a plethora of issues, some of which garner significant interest while others do not.[144] SRI screened portfolios commonly exclude or limit businesses connected to tobacco, gambling, animal testing, armaments, and (in recent years) companies with climate change impacts. On the other hand, the SRI sector has been less interested in other issues, such as Indigenous land rights or fair trade, which may raise uncomfortable questions about control of economic resources. We should therefore be cautious about the range of issues we can expect the SRI sector to champion. More thought given to understanding what kind of governance mechanisms might

---

143 H.M. Kim, *Globalization of International Financial Markets: Causes and Consequences* (Ashgate Publishing, 1999).

144 C. Cowton, "The Development of Ethical Investment Products," in *Ethical Conflicts in Finance*, eds A. Prindl and B. Prodhan (Blackwell, 1994); Avanzi SRI Research, *Green, Social and Ethical Funds in Europe 2004* (SIRI Group, November 2004).

improve SRI's engagement with those under-serviced causes is important for sustainability.

One chapter of this book focuses on the response of SRI to two issues—climate change and Indigenous peoples—to provide a deeper, nuanced understanding of the goals, methods, and effectiveness of SRI and its governance. Whereas climate change has generated considerable interest from the financial sector, principally because of business case considerations, Indigenous peoples, who pose more explicit social justice issues, have garnered less attention in jurisdictions with Aboriginal denizens despite being a much more immediate, contemporary issue especially in the resource sector.

Managing global warming requires cooperation between governments and financiers, particularly for new investment in renewable energy and more energy efficient technologies.[145] States can make such financing more likely by creating or restructuring markets. The Kyoto Protocol[146] introduced economic mechanisms (e.g., emissions trading and the Clean Development Mechanism) for this purpose.[147] Policies to reduce fossil fuels and promote renewable energies create new market opportunities and roles for financiers, ranging from brokerage services in carbon allowance trading to climate change risk assessments for financing transactions. Institutional investors are responding to some extent to the threat of global warming.[148] In 2000, they established the Carbon Disclosure Project to encourage companies to report their carbon emissions and risk management policies.[149] In 2003 an Investor Network on Climate Risk was formed to improve understanding of the financial risks and investment opportunities at stake.[150]

Indigenous peoples, by contrast, have received limited attention even in countries with Indigenous populations and ongoing conflicts over land and

145 M. Grubb and R. Vigotti, *Renewable Energy Strategies for Europe: Vol. II: Electricity Systems and Primary Electricity Sources* (Royal Institute of Economic Affairs, 1997); J. Zarnikau, "Consumer Demand for 'Green Power' and Energy Efficiency," *Energy Policy* 31(15) (2003): 1661.

146 ILM 37 (1998): 22.

147 K. Halsnaes, "Market Potential for Kyoto Mechanisms. Estimation of Global Market Potential for Co-Operative Greenhouse Gas Emission Reduction Policies," *Energy Policy* 30 (2002): 13; J. Janssen, "Implementing the Kyoto Mechanisms: Potential Contributions by Banks and Insurance Companies," *Geneva Papers on Risk and Insurance* 25(4) (2000): 602.

148 A. Dlugolecki, *Climate Change and the Financial Services Industry* (UNEPFI Climate Change Working Group, 2002).

149 Http://www.cdproject.net.

150 Http://www.incr.com.

cultural rights. Indigenous land claims can seriously hinder mining, forestry, and other natural resource projects.[151] These are much more immediate threats than climate change, which is still just a forecast problem of uncertain although likely grave magnitude. Nevertheless, some ethical mutual funds do acknowledge the rights of Indigenous peoples.[152] The plight of such peoples is also increasingly highlighted at major international SRI conferences, such as at the 2007 UNEPFI Roundtable in Australia and the "SRI in the Rockies" conference in the US. The first SRI code to refer to Indigenous peoples is the 2003 Equator Principles for project financing,[153] although the World Bank has had policies on mitigating the impacts of development financing on Indigenous peoples since the 1980s.[154]

Why then are private financiers seemingly less aware of or less interested in Indigenous peoples in jurisdictions where they should be a more salient concern? Is it because Indigenous rights give rise to uncomfortable questions about access to land, control of environmental resources, and other social justice considerations that are incongruous with the prerogatives of private capital? Conversely, does the escalating interest in global warming have something to do with how climate risks can more readily factor into business case SRI? And, with both issues, to what extent is the response of the financial sector shaped by prevailing regulation?

IV. Plan of the Book

A. SCOPE

This book explores the possibilities and the limits of SRI for sustainability, and considers the adequacy of possible reforms to its governance. It takes a broad view of the SRI sector, considering not only investment institutions such as pension plans and mutual funds, but also banks and lending relationships. The banking sector has increasingly been scrutinized for its policies and impacts on sustainable development. Focusing on the goal of sustainable development, the book understandably concentrates on SRI's *environmental*

---

151 B.J. Richardson and D. Craig, "Indigenous Peoples, Law and the Environment," in *Environmental Law for Sustainability*, note 43, 195.

152 U. Trog, *SRI—Socially Responsible Investments* (Eco Design Foundation, 2001), 5–6.

153 Http://www.equator-principles.com.

154 G.A. Sarfaty, "The World Bank and the Internalization of Indigenous Rights Norms," *Yale Law Journal* 114(7) (2005): 1791.

aspects rather than its broader social agenda that encompasses a cocktail of issues including child labor, pornography, gambling, and other activities. Although, given that sustainability has significant social justice dimensions, particularly for Indigenous peoples, the social side of SRI is certainly not ignored.

This book concentrates on possible solutions achievable through financial markets and corporate financing in the exploration of SRI and its governance. It largely ignores other facets of financing for sustainability, such as charitable patronage to communities, foreign aid and debt relief, or World Bank development finance. Those issues entail some different legal and policy questions, and they enjoy a relative abundance of literature.[155] For the same reasons, the book does not examine the insurance industry and environmental risk management.[156]

This work is also necessarily selective in its jurisdictional coverage. It focuses on the major economies where the SRI market and concomitant legal reforms have principally arisen. These predominantly include developed nations: the UK, Germany, the Netherlands, and Scandinavian countries, among various Western European examples; as well as the US, Canada, Australia, and New Zealand. Prospects for reforming corporate finance appear most promising in these jurisdictions as they control most international capital resources, and may become examples for other jurisdictions on SRI governance. In 2007, a staggering 52 percent of global assets of investment companies were sourced in the US, and 35 percent in Europe, leaving only about 13 percent in the rest of the world.[157] The US and Western Europe similarly dominate other financial sectors, such as pension funds.[158]

---

155 E.g., K. Miles, "Innovative Financing: Filling the Gaps in the Road to Sustainable Environmental Funding," *Review of European Community and International Environmental Law* 14(3) (2005): 202; J.P. Resor, "Debt-for-Nature Swaps: A Decade of Experience and New Directions for the Future," *Unasylva* 48(1) (1997): 1; World Bank, *Mainstreaming the Environment: The World Bank Group and the Environment* (World Bank, 1995); S.A. Silard, "The Global Environment Facility: A New Development in International Law and Organization," *George Washington Journal of International Law and Economics* 28(3) (1995): 607.

156 See further my other work: B.J. Richardson, "Mandating Environmental Liability Insurance," *Duke Environmental Law and Policy Forum* 12(2) (2002): 293.

157 Investment Company Institute (ICI), *Worldwide Mutual Fund Assets and Flows Second Quarter 2007* (ICI, November, 2007).

158 Watson Wyatt, *2007 Global Pensions Asset Study* (Watson Wyatt, 2007), 6.

Corporate finance and SRI in emerging markets is however a growing topic which the book examines to a lesser extent. Their capital markets are less mature, and foreign aid and other forms of public development financing often play a pivotal role in promoting sustainable development there. Although one international study in 2003 described SRI as "a developed-country phenomenon having yet to make significant inroads into emerging markets,"[159] the latest indications show the SRI market in the latter regions is taking off.[160] Governance changes should also ensue. For instance, in July 2007 the People's Bank of China instructed banks to call in existing loans, and to restrict new credit, to projects deemed environmentally undesirable by the government.[161]

This book inclines towards an optimistic view that SRI can help control unseen polluters, but only with significant changes to its aims, methods, and regulation. While some commentators have trumpeted an SRI "revolution,"[162] they hardly acknowledge the enabling role of legal institutions. "Law" and "governance" are not confined to official regulation of course; disparate non-state mechanisms of governance and their interaction, from voluntary codes of conduct to market index providers, are considered highly pertinent to SRI. Financial markets take their cue from a variety of institutions, and their governance is a result of a fragmented mix of state, market, and civil society institutions.

Underlying the book's arguments is a rejection of the fetishist notions that capital markets have a natural institutional form, organized around the logic of a financial system divorced from social and environmental responsibilities. In place of that hubris, a more civilized governance of capital markets for socially just and ecological sustainable development, centered on new forms of governance and policy enhancing the SRI sector, is recommended. As a priority, we should redefine the overarching fiduciary duties of

159 M. de Sousa-Shields, ed., *Towards Sustainable and Responsible Investment in Emerging Markets: A Review and Inventory of the Social Investment Industry's Activities and Potential in Emerging Markets* (International Finance Corporation, 2003), 10.
160 See sessions on "Principles for Responsible Investment in Emerging Markets Asia-Pacific," and "Hidden Treasure: The Sustainable Upside to Emerging Markets" (UNEPFI Global Roundtable, Melbourne, Australia, October 24–25, 2007).
161 "China Banks Told to Cut Lending to Heavy Polluters," *Reuters*, July 8, 2007.
162 E.g., R. Sparkes, *Socially Responsible Investment: A Global Revolution* (John Wiley and Sons, 2002); J. Ambachtsheer, *Socially Responsible Investing—Moving into the Mainstream* (June 23, 2005), at http://www.merceric.com.

financial institutions. Further, we must improve the decision-making processes of financial organizations to ground SRI goals and practices in a more democratic and defensible discourse. Other challenges include enhancing the strategic role of national pension funds in sustainable finance; building new forms of international cooperation for transnational financial markets; and providing a better mix of economic incentives and informational resources for SRI.

B. RESEARCH METHODS

This study of SRI governance derives from an interdisciplinary theoretical framework and extensive empirical research of SRI "in practice." Researching the legal and institutional form of capital markets alone does not reveal enough about the realities of SRI, as a product of culture, economics, and politics.[163] The book draws on an eclectic framework of inquiry, taking inspiration from reflexive law and other regulatory theories, legal pluralism, finance theory, applied ethics, and ecological economics.

While it is certainly not a formal work of *comparative* law scholarship, it incorporates comparative perspectives in the inter-jurisdictional aspects of the subject matter. SRI practices and legal mechanisms of various countries are canvassed, and variations investigated. Globalization of financial markets has encouraged considerable convergence in SRI methods and governance, such as through the UNPRI.

An ambitious research program was undertaken with funding from Canada's Social Sciences and Humanities Research Council. It utilized a composite of interviews as well as archival, library, and electronic research. There is a vast volume of policy papers, regulations, and corporate documentation, some available electronically, and others accessible only by archival research. The SRI literature exploded during the course of the research, making it difficult to keep abreast of the plethora of reports and studies produced by SRI think-tanks, individual scholars, and financial institutions. A team of students from Osgoode Hall Law School assisted ably during this phase.

Subsequent research phases required extensive empirical research on actual practices of SRI institutions and their governance. This investigation included approximately sixty interviews of representatives from all the major constituencies (e.g., public authorities, financiers, public interest NGOs,

---

163 See J.T. Klein, *Interdisciplinarity: History, Theory and Practice* (Wayne State University Press, 1990).

and consultants).[164] The interviews were semi-structured face-to-face or telephone discussions, with questions formulated to elicit a range of experiences and perceptions relevant to SRI and its governance. To maintain the confidentiality of individuals consulted, sometimes only their institutional affiliation is identified or the generic organizational type is noted. It must be noted that arguments in this book do not necessarily reflect the views of the interviewees. Additional sources of empirical information were harvested to verify findings, including: surveys and case studies conducted by SRI associations, consultancy reports, graduate theses, and other data sources.

Despite the diverse and extensive research tools deployed, certain methodological problems inhere in this kind of study. Given the difficulty of isolating the impact of specific variables, sometimes only contingent and tentative conclusions about the role of SRI governance can be drawn. This problem inheres in most law in context research, and should not detract from the importance of this research to illuminate the strengths and weaknesses of SRI governance.

C. STRUCTURE

This book has eight chapters. The next chapter introduces finance capitalism and the SRI movement's attempts to bring some social and environmental accountability to it. It canvasses the various types of financial institutions, and explains the history, philosophies, and methods of SRI. Chapter 3 assesses the impact of SRI—its market size, financial performance, and influence on

---

164 Organizations consulted or interviewed include: Association for Responsible and Sustainable Investment in Asia, Association of Superannuation Funds of Australia, Responsible Investment Association (Australasia), Canadian Institute of Chartered Accountants, Ethical Funds Company (Canada), Export Development Canada, Jantzi Research (Canada), KAIROS— Canadian Ecumenical Justice Initiatives, Mercer Investment Consulting (Canada), Interpraxis (Canada), Royal Bank of Canada, Scotiabank (Canada), Social Investment Organization (Canada), United Church of Canada, Domini Social Investments (US), KLD Research and Analytics (US), Social Investment Forum (US), Dutch Sustainability Research (Netherlands), Council for Socially Responsible Investment (New Zealand), New Zealand Superannuation Fund, Rodger Spiller and Associates (New Zealand), Ekobanken (Sweden), Ethical Investment Research Service (UK), Fair Pensions (UK), Henderson Global Investors (UK), UK Social Investment Forum, Universities Superannuation Scheme (UK), and United Nations Environment Program Finance Initiative.

financiers and the corporations they service. Evaluation of the effectiveness of SRI helps to understand which forms of regulation can best facilitate it. Chapter 4 examines how the legal system has traditionally hindered SRI. It focuses on the governing fiduciary duties and decision-making procedures within financiers, as well as the international framework for financial markets regulation.

Chapters 5 and 6 delve into recent governance reforms intended to boost SRI, dealing with official regulation (chapter 5) and non-state contributions (chapter 6). In reality, there is no clear-cut division between state and non-state governance, as there are many intertwined initiatives in SRI. A proliferation of codes, standards, and other mechanisms now structure the SRI market. Among them are the UNEPFI, EPs, UNPRI, and many more. Within state law, transparency regulation has prevailed, reflected for instance by requirements for pension funds to disclose whether they invest ethically, and obligations on mutual funds to reveal how they vote as shareholders in their portfolio companies.

Of the remaining chapters, the seventh explores SRI in practice in more detail, unveiling how differences in the character of environmental and social issues influence financiers' responses. It contrasts the responses of the SRI sector to climate change and Indigenous peoples, providing case studies that illuminate the interplay between business and ethical motivations for responsible financing. The eighth and final chapter, "The Path to Ethical Investment for Sustainability," ponders the steps to take if SRI is to offer something more useful to the quest for safeguarding the environment. It emphasizes reform of the fiduciary duties of institutional investors as a means to promote ethical investment.

CHAPTER 2

Corporate Financiers and the SRI Movement

I. The Era of Finance Capitalism

A. THE MARKET CONTEXT OF SRI

SRI's potential to advance sustainable development is shaped by the system of finance capitalism. SRI seeks solutions to our social and environmental dilemmas within the framework of capitalism, rather than outside that system. Therefore, it is useful to begin with an overview of the operation of financial markets, its principal institutions, and the way corporations raise capital.[1] To understand SRI properly requires some knowledge of the financial system that it works within. The second half of this chapter considers the SRI movement itself, including its actors, instruments, and goals.

According to textbooks, an economy's financial system serves to mobilize and allocate capital, to organize the settlement of payments, and to manage risks associated with financing and exchange. In particular, the financial system enables the crucial distribution of capital from savers to borrowers, and thereby in theory facilitates the efficient allocation of resources among different economic sectors and across time.[2] This resource transfer occurs through the services of financial intermediaries, such as banks, and through

---

1 This chapter, like the book generally, does not consider in detail how financial institutions fund the household and consumer markets, such as real estate and personal loans.
2 E.g., from F.J. Fabozzi, et al., *Foundations of Financial Markets and Institutions* (Prentice Hall, 2001); M. Levinson, *Guide to Financial Markets* (Bloomberg

stock and bond markets. The finance sector serves to bridge disparities in the maturity preferences of savers and borrowers, so that short-term deposits are transformed into the means for longer-term lending. It also provides a framework whereby numerous daily financial transactions can be settled, ranging from retail purchases to foreign currency exchanges. Finally, among its principal functions, the financial sector helps to assess and manage financial risks. It enables risk to be allocated and compensated more widely across the economy.

The health and functioning of the financial system depends on government policies and controls.[3] States can be major borrowers in their own right to fund public expenditure, and they are often major savers in managing and financing public pensions of employees and for social security systems. Central banks play a prominent role in issuing of fiat money, in supporting the payments system, and in ensuring financial stability.[4] Further, specialist financial regulators supervise markets to ensure institutions' solvency, and provide investor protection, among various policy goals. Mechanisms of intergovernmental cooperation, such as the International Monetary Fund and the Basel Committee of Banking Supervision, may provide yet another layer of market discipline.[5]

This economic system, known as finance capitalism, is not a recent phenomenon. In the late nineteenth century as the Industrial Revolution powered the European and North American economies, many businesses fell into the hands of financiers. This period was the first to be described, by Marxist economists, as "finance capitalism."[6] It was characterized by subordination of the process of production to accumulation of money profits in a financial system.[7] It entailed the increasing ownership of industry by investors divorced from the production process, and the propagation of a complex system of banking services, securities markets, and other financial instruments.[8]

Press, 2006); F.S. Mishikin, *Economics of Money, Banking, and Financial Markets* (7th ed., Addison-Wesley, 2006).

3   J. Zysman, *Governments, Markets and Growth: Financial Systems and the Politics of Change* (Cornell University Press, 1983), 11–54.

4   C. Goodhart, *The Evolution of Central Banks* (MIT Press, 1988).

5   R.J. Herring and R.E. Litan, *Financial Regulation in the Global Economy* (Brookings Institution Press, 1995).

6   For an historical perspective, see L. Neal, *The Rise of Financial Capitalism: International Capital Markets in the Age of Reason* (Cambridge University Press, 1990).

7   R. Hilferding, *Finance Capital* (Routledge, Keagan, and Paul, 1910, reprinted 1981).

8   See G.W. Edwards, *The Evolution of Finance Capitalism* (Longmans, Green, and Company, 1938); W.G, Roy, *Socializing Capital: The Rise of the Large Industrial Corporation in America* (Princeton University Press, 1997).

A century later, finance capitalism has matured into a system of international scope, dominated by institutional investors.[9] The legal system has been critical in ordering power relationships, decision-making processes, and regulating the economic incentives of markets. Kevin Phillips, in his *Political History of the American Rich*, identifies the deregulation of financial markets as pivotal to the increasing "financialization" of the economy.[10] By this process, financial institutions manage large investment portfolios and through control of these assets have become economically commanding. Unsurprisingly, approximately forty of the one hundred largest companies in the world are financial firms.[11] Their influence is not just confined to the major developed economies, as investors are reaching into emerging and developing country economies to diversify their portfolios and to exploit new market niches.[12]

Another significant facet of global finance has been the entrance of institutional investors into the market.[13] Institutional investors, generally, are entities such as pension funds, life insurance businesses, and mutual fund management firms that collectively invest on behalf of many individuals or other institutions, in companies and other investment assets. The growth of institutional investment has been matched by the rise of asset management firms, providing portfolio management services for institutional investors. While retail investors, by contrast, can invest and directly own stocks and bonds, they also more commonly invest through institutional investors. Banks have historically stood at the apex of financial systems by intermediating capital in the form of deposits and savings into loans,[14] although in recent decades,

---

9 J. Froud, A. Leaver, and K. Williams, "New Actors in a Financialised Economy and the Remaking of Capitalism," *New Political Economy* 12(3) (2007): 339; D.K. Das, "Globalization in the World of Finance: An Analytical History," *Global Economy Journal* 6(1) (2006): article 1, at http://www.bepress.com/gej.

10 K. Phillips, *Political History of the American Rich* (Broadway Books, 2002).

11 M.V. Stichele, *Critical Issues in the Financial Industry: SOMO Financial Sector Report* (Stichting Onderzoek Multinationale Ondernemingen, 2005), 58. And one study in 2000 showed that, of the one hundred largest economies in the world, fifty-one are corporations and forty-nine are nations (based on a comparison of corporate revenue and country GDPs): S. Anderson and J. Cavanagh, *Top 200: The Rise of Corporate Global Power* (Institute for Policy Studies, 2000).

12 World Bank, *Global Development Finance: Harnessing Cyclical Gains for Development* (World Bank, 2004), 37–105.

13 H. Blommestein and N. Funke, eds, *Institutional Investors in the New Financial Landscape* (OECD, 1998).

14 F.R. Edwards, *The New Finance: Regulation and Financial Stability* (American Enterprise Institute Press, 1996), 4–9; T. Rybczynski, "A New Look at the

savers and borrowers have increasingly foregone or supplemented banks' mediating role to interact through the stock and bond markets.[15] Banks still remain critical to the financial economy, as evident by the growth of assets of the world's 1,000 largest banks from some US$23 trillion in 1990 to over US$74 trillion in 2006.[16] Banks have also taken advantage of market deregulation by foraying into other financial services.

Yet, it is the recent surge in institutional investment that makes the contemporary period of finance capitalism distinctive. Many factors have shaped this sector's exponential growth. On the supply side they include market deregulation and new technological developments and, on the demand side, demographic changes, greater household wealth, and strains on traditional social security systems.[17] Institutional investment managers provide better risk management and return on investment than is generally possible by individual investors. These economies of scale advantages also lower transactional costs.[18] Institutional investment assets now vastly exceed the financial resources that many governments control. Compared to the world's top dozen sovereign funds' wealth of about US$2.5 trillion,[19] including the giant Norwegian Pension Plan, institutional investors globally held nearly US$62 trillion in 2006,[20] of which the vast majority of assets were sourced in the major economies of the OECD.[21] Table 1 illustrates the astonishing growth of institutional assets in some major industrial economies since 1980 and Table 2 breaks down the recent asset holdings of the major institutional classes. Pension fund management is the largest institutional sector, while investment companies have grown the fastest during this period.

Evolution of the Financial System," in *The Recent Evolution of Financial Systems*, ed. J. Revell (Macmillan, 1997).

15 H. Rose, *The Changing World of Finance and Its Problems* (British-North American Committee, 1993), 6.

16 International Financial Services London (IFSL), "Worldwide Assets of the Banking Industry," from "International Statistics" at http://www.ifsl.org.uk/research.

17 Ibid., xxvi.

18 Ibid., 13.

19 "Sovereign Wealth Funds: The World's Most Expensive Club," *The Economist*, May 24, 2007, 94.

20 IFSL, "Global Funds under Management," from "International Statistics," at http://www.ifsl.org.uk/research.

21 Working Group established by the Committee on the Global Financial System, *Institutional Investors, Global Savings and Asset Allocation*, CGFS Papers No. 27 (Committee on the Global Financial System, February 2007), 5.

Table 1: Growth of assets of institutional investors as a percentage of GDP in various nations: 1980–2000[22]

Country	Total institutional investment		
	1980	1990	2000
Australia	n/a	47.2	129.6
Canada	34.9	57.7	113.7
Germany	17.5	32.8	79.8
Japan	n/a	82.3	97.7
UK	49.4	103.9	212.8
US*	69.9	113.2	198.7

* Figures for US start with 1981 rather than 1980.

Table 2: Total global funds (US$ trillion) under management: 1998–2006[23]

Year	Insurance sector	Pension funds	Investment companies	Total
1998	10.4	13.6	9.4	33.4
2000	10.1	15.7	11.9	37.7
2002	10.4	14.3	11.3	36.0
2004	13.9	18.9	16.2	49.0
2006	17.4	22.6	21.8	61.8

The surge in institutional investment has paralleled a decline in households' direct ownership of companies. Unlike the dominant but amorphous individual ownership that Adolph Berle and Gardiner Means depicted in 1932,[24] in the UK the proportion of shares held directly by individuals declined from 54 percent in 1963 to slightly below 13 percent in 2006.[25] Concurrently, UK institutions' ownership of corporate stock rose from approximately 35 percent of the market to about 84 percent.[26] In the US,

22 OECD, *Financial Assets of Institutional Investors as a Percentage of GDP* (OECD, 2005).
23 IFSL, note 20.
24 A. Bearle and G. Means, *The Modern Corporation and Private Property* (Commerce Clearing House, 1932).
25 Office for National Statistics (ONS), *Share Ownership: A Report on Ownership of UK Shares as at 31st December 2006* (ONS, 2007) (figures include foreign ownership of shares).
26 Ibid.

institutional investors' share of equity markets grew from slightly below 13 percent in 1960 to just over 61 percent in 2005.[27] Their stakes are even higher in the largest 1,000 corporations, holding nearly 68 percent of these firms' equity at the end of 2005.[28] In the international bond market, institutional investors are even more dominant, in recent years estimated to hold about 90 percent of corporate and government bonds and related securities.[29]

B. SOCIAL AND ENVIRONMENTAL IMPLICATIONS

Together, the globalization of finance and the concomitant ascendancy of institutional investors present the most salient features of modern financial capitalism. There are varying assessments as to their wider repercussions.

Global financial markets have been ubiquitously disparaged as worlds of irrational exuberance,[30] vectors of economic crisis in developing countries,[31] and instruments of environmental crisis.[32] Global finance, transacted through international banks, giant pension funds and other behemoths, operates at a scale and intensity that intuitively contradicts a vision of ecologically sustainable and socially just societies. It distances investors from the economic, social, and environmental consequences of their decisions. Thus, "money traverses national capital markets with dramatic speed and callous scrutiny, bringing with it both the ability to enhance local economic opportunities or break an economy at its very core."[33] Such effects can spawn much wider and more dangerous consequences. Ulrich Beck warns that the global financial

---

27 The Conference Board, *2007 Institutional Investment Report* (The Conference Board, 2007), 26.

28 Ibid., 27.

29 IFSL, *Securities Dealing* (IFSL, 2003), 17.

30 R.J. Shiller, *Irrational Exuberance* (Princeton University Press, 2000).

31 R. Glick, R. Moreno, and M. Spiegel, eds, *Financial Crisis in Emerging Markets* (Cambridge University Press, 2001) (such as the East Asian financial meltdown of 1997–98).

32 See D. Ehrenfeld, "The Environmental Limits to Globalization," *Conservation Biology* 19(2) (2005): 318; C. Serfati, "Globalised Finance-dominated Accumulation Regime and Sustainable Development," *International Journal of Sustainable Development* 3(1) (2000): 40; J. Agyeman, R.D. Bullard, and B. Evans, eds, *Just Sustainabilities: Development in an Unequal World* (MIT Press, 2003).

33 C.J. Mailander, "Financial Innovation, Domestic Regulation and the International Marketplace," *George Washington Journal of International Law and Economics* 31 (1997–98): 341, 378.

risks of this system cannot be "ke[pt] on one side, but flood and transform themselves into social and political risk."[34]

In its economic effects, commentators point to "heavy involvement of institutional investors in both buying and selling waves."[35] To some, institutional investors smack of opportunistic short-term trading and self-interest masquerading as commitment to long-term shareholder value.[36] They have incurred criticism for their acquiescence to the corporate world of "financial engineering and manufactured earnings," where the prices of stocks overshadow the building of "intrinsic corporate value."[37] They have been a powerful force behind many corporate "restructurings," commonly to the detriment of workers and other stakeholders. Institutional investors have also been complicit in promoting corporate governance standards and business models of questionable suitability to host countries, especially in developing countries.[38]

More restrained assessments concur that finance capitalism is remaking economies, but highlight some of the advantages. Gordon Clark and Dariusz Wójcik concede that global finance has reshaped the economic landscape of twenty-first century capitalism by facilitating efficient corporate restructurings, promoting technological innovation, and boosting economic growth.[39] Finance capitalism has spawned myriad ways to transform money into an instrument of economic development, shifting capital geographically, from areas or sectors with surplus savings to places lacking capital.[40] The financial sector can also efficiently transform money by time, from holders with short-term surplus funds to those with long-term investment needs. Economic historians have shown how measures of financial system sophistication, such as the system's liquidity, and stock and bond market capitalization,

34 U. Beck, *World Risk Society* (Polity, 1999), 7.

35 E.P. Davis and B. Steil, *Institutional Investors* (MIT Press, 2001), 268.

36 F. Jameson, "Culture and Finance Capitalism," *Critical Inquiry* 24 (1997): 246.

37 J.C. Brogle, *The Battle for the Soul of Capitalism* (Yale University Press, 2005), 103, 115.

38 S.M. Soederberg, "The 'New Conditionality' of Socially Responsible Investing Strategies: The Politics of Equity Financing in the Emerging Markets," *New Political Economy* 12(4) (2007): 477; A. Harmes, "Institutional Investors and the Reproduction of Neoliberalism," *Review of International Political Economy* 5(1) (1998): 92.

39 G.L. Clark and D. Wójcik, *The Geography of Finance: Corporate Governance in the Global Marketplace* (Oxford University Press, 2007), 22–23.

40 See generally R.G. Hubbard, *Money, The Financial System and the Economy* (Addison-Wesley, 1994); P.S. Rose, *Money and Capital Markets* (Irwin, 1994); R.G. Hubbard, *Money, the Financial System, and the Economy* (Pearson/Addison-Wesley, 2005).

positively correlate to economic growth.[41] Lawyers stress the essential role of regulation in "providing the underlying framework" for a sophisticated, modern financial system to facilitate such effects.[42]

We may also benignly view globalization as a means to disseminate standards for corporate social responsibility (CSR) and increase accountability. Some commentators herald global finance as a key driver for standard-setting in domains such as corporate governance.[43] Globalization appears to have facilitated the diffusion of CSR norms, the exchange of information and best practices, and the building of alliances such as the UNEPFI.[44] Transnational collaboration among social investors has been instrumental in forging new governance standards, such as the UNPRI.[45] Institutional investors' staggering size potentially gives them the leverage to engender positive change rarely made possible by other actors.[46]

Further, while investment institutions are concentrating formerly dispersed shareholders with ownership stakes unknown since the great industrialists of the nineteenth century, some critics do not necessarily believe that the general public has become disenfranchised from the financial market. Stephen Davis and his colleagues in *The New Capitalists* contend that because pension plans, mutual funds, and other financial institutions invest on behalf of millions of beneficiaries, to whom they owe fiduciary duties, they have surreptitiously democratized corporate ownership.[47] Yet, agency problems within the financial sector may result in enhancing the power of fund managers and investment executives.[48] Assigning portfolio

41 R. Levine and S. Zervos, "Stock Markets, Banks and Economic Growth," *American Economic Review* 88(3) (1998): 537; R.G. King and R. Levine, "Finance and Growth: Schumpeter Might Be Right," *Quarterly Journal of Economics* 108(3) (1993): 717; J. Hicks, *A Theory of Economic History* (Clarendon Press, 1969).

42 D.W. Arner, *Financial Stability, Economic Growth, and the Role of Law* (Cambridge University Press, 2007), 337.

43 Clark and Wójcik, note 39, 163–65.

44 Http://www.unepfi.org.

45 Http://www.unpri.org.

46 R. Sparkes and C.J. Cowton, "The Maturing of Socially Responsible Investment: A Review of the Developing Link with Corporate Social Responsibility," *Journal of Business Ethics* 52 (2004): 45, 49.

47 S. Davis, J. Lukomnik, and D. Pitt-Watson, *The New Capitalists. How Citizen Investors are Reshaping the Corporate Agenda* (Harvard Business School Press, 2006), 6–7.

48 A. Harmes, *Unseen Power: How Mutual Funds Threaten the Political and Economic Wealth of Nations* (Stoddard, 2001).

management to asset management firms further distances the original investor from the companies they ultimately fund. Certainly, as chapter 4 will show, the internal governance of financial institutions is generally not conducive to democratic decision-making.

Despite which view of financial markets is subscribed to, they undeniably have a major bearing on the prospects for sustainability. The dyadic character of finance capitalism both exacerbates unsustainable development practices while also engendering some remedial responses. By enlarging the pool of liquidity for production, consumption, and exchange, the financial system critically shapes economic patterns. It can mobilize capital for sustainable development, such as renewable energy projects and new clean technologies. Conversely, by fuelling economic growth, often of a socially disruptive kind that seems to contribute little to real productive activity,[49] the finance economy surely intensifies humanity's ecological footprint. Many financial institutions lack policies to manage such impacts. A recent report for the OECD concluded that "over 50 percent of the financial institutions" worldwide "had no environmental policy or their policy was of 'inadequate' quality," and "over 70% ... do not publish environmental reports or publish environmental reports of 'inadequate' quality."[50] Without remedial policies and rules, the financial sector will accelerate trends towards environmental degradation when capital is easily transferred to those companies that profit from exploitation of the environment.

Can a reformed SRI movement help to negate that looming threat? Before considering the potential of the SRI movement, we should digress briefly to examine the principal institutions of the financial sector, the means by which they mediate capital flows, and the ways companies raise funds for new investment and growth. A nuanced understanding of the workings of financial markets helps us to appreciate the methods and practices of those financiers who choose to invest responsibly. Readers already familiar with the workings of financial markets may wish to skip this section.

---

49 R. Brenner, "The World Economy at the Turn of the Millennium: Toward Boom or Crisis," *Review of International Political Economy* 8(1) (2001): 6.

50 Ethical Investment Research Service (EIRIS), *Corporate Responsibility Practices of Financial Institutions in OECD and Important Non-OECD Countries* (EIRIS and OECD, May 2007), 7, 9.

II. Corporate Financing

A. MECHANISMS OF FINANCING

1. The Capital Structure of Firms

At a very simplistic level, corporate finance involves firms making three types of interrelated decisions—investment, financing, and dividend distribution decisions, typically in order to achieve the lowest cost of capital.[51] Investment decisions serve to create revenues and profits (e.g., new product lines and entrance into new markets), as well as to save money (e.g., efficient technology). Dividend distributions deal with the proportion of surplus capital to return to the company's shareholders or reinvest into the business in the form of retained earnings. Financing decisions—of most relevance to this book—involve how companies raise capital to fund operations.[52]

Basically, businesses may draw on any surplus funds generated by cash flows and retained earnings, and/or raise capital through financial markets. Numerous choices exist within these general options.[53] "Internal equity" describes profits retained within a company for expenditure rather than distributed to shareholders as dividends.[54] External financing comes principally from bank loans and corporate bonds (debt financing) or from the proceeds of the issuance of new shares (equity financing). The composition of these sources of finance within a company makes up its capital structure.

---

51 This section draws on A. Damodaran, *Corporate Finance: Theory and Practice* (John Wiley and Sons, 1997); as well as S.A. Ross, R.W. Westerfield, and J.F. Jaffe, *Corporate Finance* (7th ed., McGraw-Hill Irwin, 2005); E. Ferran, *Company Law and Corporate Finance* (Oxford University Press, 1999).

52 A further aspect of the financing process is known as the "internal capital market" (ICM): R.H. Gertner, D.S. Scharfstein, and J.C. Stein, "Internal Versus External Capital Markets," *Quarterly Journal of Economics* 109 (1994): 1211. The ICM is the process by which companies allocate the capital available from both external and internal sources among competing investment possibilities within the corporation.

53 There are also hybrid securities, combining characteristics of equity and debt. For instance, a convertible bond is a bond that its holder can convert into a predetermined number of shares: Damodaran, note 51, 398–99.

54 Ibid., 406: Damodaran explains the rationale for calling it "internal equity" as follows: "[u]sing the reasonable presumption that the earnings of a firm belong to the stockholders, it can be argued that any portion of these earnings that is not paid out in dividends is still equity being reinvested back in the firm."

Two major theories explain how firms arrange their finance. The "pecking order" hypothesis of Stewart Myers and Nicholas Majluf[55] posits that companies finance according to a hierarchy of preferred sources. In theory, firms prefer internal equity, followed by debt, and then external equity.[56] These preferences are based primarily on cost effectiveness.[57] Further, "internal finance is attractive because it is the form of finance where management has the least bother explaining and justifying what it wants to do."[58] Assumptions of the pecking order theory are debatable as they suggest that the interests of managers and shareholder are closely aligned. The "trade-off" theory suggests a different approach to financing decisions.[59] When determining their capital structure, firms primarily balance the tax advantages of debt financing against risks of being highly leveraged. Financial options are also evaluated against further trade-offs such as corporate governance arrangements and other institutional factors.[60] Also, governments can discourage debt financing through regulation constraining companies' debt to specified ratios or by limiting the tax deductibility of borrowing interest.[61]

These are not the only influences on a firm's capital structure. Companies operating in different economic sectors often have varying capital needs. Further, their financial structure must be dynamic to respond to new investment plans, variable economic conditions, and an infinite host of other variables.[62]

---

55 S.C. Myers and N.S. Majluf, "Corporate Financing and Investment Decisions When Firms Have Information that Investors Do Not Have," *Journal of Financial Economics* 13 (1984): 187.

56 Damodaran, note 51, 466–67.

57 For determinants of capital structure, see further S. Titman and R. Wessels, "The Determinants of Capital Structure Choice," *Journal of Finance* 43 (1988): 1.

58 M. Hellwig, "Corporate Governance and the Financing of Investment for Structural Change," Bundesbank Spring Conference, *Investing Today for the World of Tomorrow* (Frankfurt, 2000), 7.

59 M.H. Miller, "Debt and Taxes," *The Journal of Finance* 32(2) (1977): 261.

60 R. La Porta, et al., "The Legal Determinants of External Finance," *Journal of Finance* 52(3) (1997): 1131.

61 Damodaran, note 51, 404–5.

62 See C. Chiarella, et al., "Determinants of Corporate Capital Structure: Australian Evidence," in *Pacific Basin Capital Markets Research*, Volume 3, eds S.G. Rhee and R.P. Chang (Elsevier, 1992); V. Murinde, J.A. Agung, and A.W. Mullineux, "Patterns of Corporate Financing and Convergence of Financial Systems in Europe," *Review of International Economics* 12(4) (2004): 693; B. Friedman, ed., *Corporate Capital Structures in the United States* (Chicago University Press, 1985).

2. Equity Finance

"Equity" denotes the ownership claim that shareholders acquire, usually expressed as a residual claim on the cash flows and assets of the company. Equity financing means raising capital by selling corporate shares to the public. Firms may issue different classes of shares, such as common stock or preferred stock, which carry different rights and benefits.[63] The conventional way for a publicly traded company to raise funds is to issue common stock, offered through a regulated stock exchange at current market prices. Preferred shares are similarly offered, but differ in that they carry a greater claim to the company's assets and earnings. A private company (sometimes labeled an "unlisted" company) does not offer its shares for sale on the open market; its shares are typically held by the directors. New (primary) issues of shares may be sold directly to investors by the issuing corporation or be underwritten and distributed through an intermediary such as an investment bank. Alternatively, a firm may choose private placement, whereby it sells its securities directly to one or few investors.[64]

Venture capital, by contrast, is a seminal source of finance for young, unlisted businesses.[65] Traditionally, small, private companies have fewer financing choices; they can issue shares to raise capital, but not on a public stock exchange.[66] Venture capitalists provide equity financing to small and often risky businesses in return for a commensurate share of ownership. If the business prospers and eventually goes public, venture capitalists may profitably dispose of their stake at the prevailing market price. These investments may provide very handsome returns, hence the incentive to assume greater risk. If additional capital is sought to grow the business, private firms must normally either "go public" by issuing shares on a regulated stock exchange or borrow.[67] The recent boom in private equity financing, and evidence that some public companies have even reverted to private

---

63 J. Walmsley, *New Financial Instruments* (John Wiley and Sons, 1998), 418–75.

64 Y.L. Wu, "The Choice between Public and Private Equity Offerings," *Journal of Financial Economics* 74 (2000): 93.

65 See A.N. Berger and G.F. Udell, "The Economics of Small Business Finance," *Journal of Banking and Finance* 22 (1988): 613; W.A. Sahlman, "Aspects of Financial Contracting in Venture Capital," *Journal of Applied Corporate Finance* 1 (1988): 23.

66 Damodaran, note 51, 391.

67 Ibid., 392.

status, suggest that the traditional limitations of private firms may become a relic of the past.[68]

3. Debt Finance

Debt represents a fixed claim on the cash flows and assets of the company. Debt finance means using capital that has to be repaid. The main choices are bank loans and bonds.

Historically, in many countries, bank loans were the primary source of corporate funds.[69] Loans are contractual arrangements between the lender and borrower, where finance is provided on a short-term (e.g., bills of exchange, line of credit) or long-term (e.g., term loan) basis.[70] Protective covenants, provision of loan security, and monitoring conditions are often introduced into the lending relationship to protect banks from borrower misconduct and risk of default. Borrowing costs are based on many factors, particularly the credit rating of the borrower and the lender's cost of raising capital.

A corporate bond is a long-term debt obligation by which the corporate borrower agrees to pay a set rate of interest until the bond matures, at which time it must repay the principal.[71] Like bank loans, corporate bonds do not confer ownership or voting rights on the holder.[72] Bonds are commonly sold by public sales and through a secondary market for previously issued bonds.[73] Firms issue them for a defined term, although the interest rate may be fixed or floating. Some bonds are secured while others are unsecured and therefore riskier investments.

Debt financing, whether by loans or bonds, enjoys two advantages over equity financing. First, in many jurisdictions, interest payments on corporate debt are tax deductible, whereas cash flows on equity are not. Second, having to make regular repayments of the debt imposes additional discipline on

---

68 T. Boulton, K. Lehn, and S. Segal, "The Rise of the U.S. Private Equity Market," in *New Financial Instruments and Institutions: Opportunities and Policy Challenges*, eds Y. Fuchita and R.E. Litan (Brookings Institution Press, 2007), 141.

69 M. Collins, *Banks and Industrial Finance in Britain, 1800–1939* (Cambridge University Press, 1995).

70 P. Boorke, *An Introduction to Bank Lending* (Addison-Wesley, 1991).

71 See D.S. Kidwell, R.L. Peterson, and D.W. Blackwell, *Financial Institutions, Markets and Money* (5th ed., Dryden Press, 1993), 211–27, 395.

72 M.W. McDaniel, "Bondholders and Corporate Governance," *Business Law* 41 (1986): 413.

73 Kidwell, Peterson, and Blackwell, note 71, 214.

corporate management.[74] Conversely, businesses without debt enjoy a large financial cushion that may dull management incentive to be efficient and vigilant operators.[75] The downside of borrowing however is the increased risk of insolvency.

Bank debt has some unique advantages. Companies can borrow relatively small or large amounts of money. Moreover, for companies not well known in the market, the loan agreement process enables lenders to gather information in evaluating the amount and cost of the loan. In contrast, corporate bond issues depend on economies of scale (i.e., larger issues incur lower marginal costs). The presence of numerous investors in bond issues makes assessing the risk of individual debtors impractical. Also, to issue bonds, companies normally arrange for a credit rating agency to rate them.

Bond issues are not without advantage. Bonds tend to provide more favorable financing terms than bank loans, primarily because a larger pool of investors shares the credit risk.[76] Bond issues can also include special features (e.g., bonds convertible into common stock) not readily incorporated into bank debt. Finally, compared to equity financing, it is usually less expensive for a firm to issue corporate bonds.[77]

B. WHY CORPORATE FINANCING MATTERS TO SRI

1. Points of Leverage

A basic tenet of corporate finance theory is that it costs businesses more to raise capital externally than to invest retained earnings. If companies can self-finance in this way, socially responsible investors may have difficulty influencing corporate behavior. Presumably, therefore, SRI has greater influence over companies requiring external capital to sustain operations. Yet, before canvassing the empirical research on corporate financing, we must note that a financially self-sufficient company is not entirely insulated from SRI pressures. Apart from shareholder advocacy to influence companies from within, the stock market creates several incentives for companies to be mindful of their behavior.

Stock prices matter to public companies for several reasons. Apart from where a company seeks to buy back its own shares, it takes no part in the

---

74 P. Marsh, "The Choice between Equity and Debt: An Empirical Study," *Journal of Finance* 37(1) (1982): 121.

75 Damodaran, note 51, 449.

76 Ibid., 395–96.

77 Ibid., 405.

trading of its shares as its share capital remains fixed. Fluctuations in share prices do not directly affect the firm.[78] Yet when a company issues new shares it is affected, as the price at which the company's shares currently trade influences the new issue price.[79]

Mature companies with little need for external financing also have reason to pay attention to market signals. The size of a firm's market capitalization is one of the bases for its inclusion in a listed stock exchange.[80] Market capitalization is the value of a corporation as determined by the market price of its stock. It is calculated by multiplying the number of shares outstanding by the current market price of a share. To express it another way, market capitalization equals the amount someone would have to pay to buy the firm. Each stock exchange has its own minimum market capitalization rules as a pre-condition for being listed. Firms may be demoted from lead indexes if the market sells off its stock, which in turn often triggers further costs.[81] In such circumstances, the firm may also become a target for a hostile takeover (a situation where one company attempts to acquire another firm against the wishes of the targeted management).

A further incentive to watch market signals is that corporate managers' remuneration often includes stock options.[82] A stock option is a guarantee by the company to sell an individual a share of stock at a fixed price at a specific time.[83] Stock options became prevalent in the 1980s to provide executives with strong incentive to maintain shareholder value.[84] By the mid-1990s the issuance of stock options to US corporate executives accounted for virtually the entire link between pay and performance (as opposed to salary raises and

---

78 I.G. MacNeil, *An Introduction to the Law on Financial Investment* (Hart Publishing, 2005) (discussing UK company law).

79 Ibid.

80 S. Saudagaran, "An Empirical Study of Selected Factors Influencing the Decision to List on Foreign Stock Exchanges," *Journal of International Business Studies* 19(1) (1988): 101.

81 J.R. Macey, M. O'Hara, and D. Pompilo, *Down and Out in the Stock Market: The Law and Finance of the Delisting Process* (Cornell University, 2005).

82 Symposium, "Management and Control of the Modern Business Corporation: Executive Compensation and Takeovers," *University of Chicago Law Review* 69 (2002): 847.

83 For example, a manager may be given the option to buy 10,000 shares at $10 per share. If the stock value rises to $20, the manager, by exercising the option, would pay $10 per share and reap a net profit of $10 per share.

84 M. Jensen and K. Murphy, "CEO Incentives—It's Not How Much You Pay, But How," *Harvard Business Review* 68(3) (1990): 138.

performance bonuses).[85] Today this link may have become too strong, contributing to an obsession with day-to-day share prices and even fraudulent behavior to inflate stock values.[86]

2. Corporate Financing Data

Empirical evidence suggests that corporations in OECD markets mostly raise finance by the pecking order thesis,[87] relying primarily on retained earnings, followed by debt and finally, new equity. In emerging markets, the pecking order hypothesis appears less applicable as firms tend to rely heavily on external finance, either from equity or debt. Many other variables influence financing preferences, including firm size, profitability, investment opportunity, collateral value of assets, and stock market development. These may be overly generalized conclusions as there are discrepancies among individual studies on this subject. For example, scholars disagree on whether to use aggregate company sector statistics or individual company accounts data. Further, some researchers rely on balance sheets while others look at cash flow trends to deduce corporate financing trends.

In mature markets, seminal studies by Colin Mayer,[88] and later Jenny Corbett and Tim Jenkinson,[89] conclude that retained earnings are the dominant mode of financing in all countries surveyed.[90] Corbett and Jenkinson

---

85 B. Hall and J. Liebman. "Are CEOs Really Paid Like Bureaucrats?" *Quarterly Journal of Economics* 113(3) (1998): 653. In the US, supposedly high marginal income tax rates have induced firms to shift some of their managerial compensation packages from fixed salaries to stock options: Shiller, note 30, 23.

86 M. Weber. "Sensitivity of Executive Wealth to Stock Price, Corporate Governance and Earnings Management," *Review of Accounting and Finance* 5(4) (2006): 321; J.C. Coffee, Jr, "What Caused Enron? A Capsule of Social and Economic History of the 1990s," in *Corporate Governance and Capital Flows in a Global Economy*, eds P.K. Cornelius and B. Kogut (Oxford University Press, 2003), 29, 31.

87 S.C. Myers and N.S. Majluf, "Corporate Financing and Investment Decisions When Firms Have Information that Investors Do Not Have," *Journal of Financial Economics* 13 (1984): 187.

88 C. Mayer, "New Issues in Corporate Finance," *European Economic Review* 12 (1988): 1167.

89 J. Corbett and T. Jenkinson. "The Financing of Industry, 1970–1989: An International Comparison," *Journal of the Japanese and International Economies* 10 (1996): 71.

90 Another study that favors this methodology is: A. Cobham, *Sources of Finance for European Investment*, Working Paper No. 04-41 (Finance and Trade Policy Research Centre, University of Oxford, 2004).

found that between 1970 and 1989, retained earnings provided an average of 91 percent of the gross financing of non-financial enterprises in the US, 97 percent in the UK, 69 percent in Japan and 61 percent in France.[91] Over time, in a period of financial liberalization, Corbett and Jenkinson suggest that firms all nations except Japan have become more internally, and less market, financed. Since the late 1990s, the corporate sector has tended to reduce its appetite for external financing owing to record profits from lower corporate taxes and historically cheap interest rates.[92]

Some other research suggests that external finance is more important. Eugene Fama and Kenneth French determined that retained earnings provided an average of 70 percent of the capital for investments in the non-financial corporate sector in the US from 1951 to 1996, with the remainder provided by debt (22 percent) and new equity (8 percent).[93] Other recent research since 2000, using different methodologies, by Andreas Hackethal and Reinhard Schmidt on US, Japanese, and German companies,[94] and Apostolos Serletis and Karl Pinno on Canadian firms,[95] reveals that external corporate finance is probably even more significant than previously estimated.

Researchers mostly agree that bank loans are the principal source of finance in the "bank-based" corporate governance systems of Germany and Japan, while the bond market is more significant in Anglo-American economies.[96] Federico Galiza and Thomas Steinberger establish that during the 1980s and 1990s, banks loans provided the largest share of corporate financing in the major EU economies, followed by shares, and bonds a distant third.[97] In recent years, though, even European companies have increasingly turned to capital markets (equity investment and bonds).[98]

---

91 Corbett and Jenkinson, note 89.

92 A. Tomas, *Recent Trends in Corporate Finance Some Evidence from the Canadian System of National Accounts*, Research Paper (Statistics Canada, March 2006).

93 E. Fama and K. French, "The Corporate Cost of Capital and the Return on Corporate Investment," *Journal of Finance* 54 (1999): 1939.

94 A. Hackethal and R.H. Schmidt. *Financing Patterns: Measurement Concepts and Empirical Results*, Working Paper (University of Frankfurt, 2003).

95 A. Serletis and K. Pinno, "Corporate Financing in Canada" (36th Meeting of the Canadian Economics Association, Calgary, June 2004).

96 Hackethal and Schmidt, note 94, 30; Corbett and Jenkinson, note 89.

97 F. Galiza and T. Steinberger, *The "Savings Gap" of European Corporations: A First Look at the Available Data* (European Investment Bank, 2001).

98 L. Assassi, A. Nesvetailova, and D. Wigan, "Global Finance in the New Century: Deregulation and Beyond," in *Global Finance in the New Century: Beyond Deregulation*, eds L. Assassi, A. Nesvetailova, and D. Wigan (Palgrave Macmillan, 2007), 1, 7.

In the emerging markets of East Asia and Latin America, companies typically rely more on external finance, although researchers are divided on the relative significance of debt and equity financing.[99] Family-run firms wishing to retain kinship control often prefer debt financing.[100] Jack Glen and Ajit Singh, surveying 8,000 listed companies in forty-four mostly developing countries for the period 1994–2000, concluded that debt financing accounted for approximately 49 percent and external equity 22 percent of total financing resources, while retained earnings represented only 29 percent.[101] An analysis of corporate financing in some 300 firms in various Latin American economies during 1990–1995 deduced that firms mostly prefer to finance investment with new equity.[102] Examining corporate financing in six East Asian economies from 1975 to 1996, John Wei and colleagues similarly found that companies choose new equity.[103]

These corporate financing patterns will not necessarily endure. The global deregulation of financial markets has spawned an array of funding sources. The growth of institutional investment has encroached on the banking sector.[104] In the major OECD economies, the securities market has blossomed, especially corporate bonds, while reliance on bank loans is declining.[105]

3. Sectoral and Temporal Issues in Corporate Financing

Generalizations about corporate financing must also accommodate how companies' financial needs differ across economic sectors and fluctuate over time.

---

99 See A. Singh and J. Hamid, "Internal Capital Markets and the Competition for Finance," *Journal of Finance* 52 (1997): 111; J. Glen and A. Singh, *Capital Structure, Rates of Return and Financing Corporate Growth: Comparing Developed and Emerging Markets, 1994–00,* Working Paper No. 265 (ESRC Centre for Business Research, University of Cambridge, 2003), 32.

100 J. Glen and A. Singh, *Corporate Governance, Competition and Finance: Re-Thinking Lessons from the Asian Crisis,* Working Paper No. 288 (ESRC Centre for Business Research, University of Cambridge, 2004), 13.

101 Glen and Singh, note 99, 17.

102 M.M. Fogarty, *Corporate Capital Structure and Equity Market Development in Latin America,* PhD dissertation (Georgetown University, 1998).

103 K.C.J. Wei, Z. Wei, and F. Xie, *Financing Capital Investments: Evidence from Emerging Markets in East Asia,* Working Paper (Southern Connecticut State University, 2003).

104 Davis and Steil, note 35, 243.

105 IFSL, note 29.

Small firms usually depend more heavily on external finance, than large, mature companies.[106] They often begin by relying on the capital of a founding entrepreneur before tapping into venture finance capital.[107] To ensure survival, private, unlisted companies may need more external finance if their retained earnings are insufficient to support expansion. Banks are often their first port of call.[108] Lenders have a comparative advantage among financiers in the monitoring and control of fledgling firms that lack a track record. Banks use contractual methods through loan agreements to acquire information not publicly available, to impose covenants and to take security from the borrower.

Another option in the evolution of a private company's financing is an initial public offering, converting it to a public corporation. An initial public offering may be necessary when a company is too highly leveraged through bank debt. Afterwards, mature firms can either offer another share issue or take advantage of the corporate bond market.[109] Bond markets were traditionally only an option for reputable companies. High credit quality is helpful because bondholders lack the influence and control over company management that shareholders or banks may exert. Credit rating agencies have helped to ease information deficits and compensate for the uncertain reputations of emergent businesses.

Apart from the size and age of a company, its economic activities also influence its financial needs.[110] Therefore, capital-intensive sectors are potentially more vulnerable to SRI or other market pressures. These typically include: oil and gas development, mining, chemical industry, telecommunications, energy utilities, forestry, real estate, and transport sectors such as shipping and airlines.[111] These industries are particularly sensitive to fluctuations in the cost of capital. Distinctions however cannot simply be made on the basis of economic sector. Capital requirements not only vary across different industries, but also diverge dramatically within a single industry, such as among various automobile manufacturers depending on the adopted business model.[112]

---

106 Galiza and Steinberger, note 97, 15–16.

107 See S. Myers, "The Capital Structure Puzzle," *Journal of Finance* 34 (1984): 575.

108 Davis and Steil, note 35, 26.

109 Ibid.

110 See R. Semenov, "Financial Systems, Financing Constraints and Investment: Empirical Analysis of OECD Countries," *Applied Economics* 38(17) (2006): 1963; S.C. Myers, "Capital Structure," *Journal of Economic Perspectives* 15(2) (2001): 81, 82.

111 Myers, ibid.

112 H. Elmasry, *Capital Intensity and Stock Returns* (Morgan Stanley Investment Management, 2004).

4. Conclusions

Making definite conclusions about corporate reliance on external financing is difficult. Studies are not congruent on the choice of methodologies for measuring corporate finance. Although Hackethal and Schmidt show flaws in older research underestimating the level of external financing, the debate has not settled.[113] Regardless, the capital markets can discipline public companies in other ways, as firms desire high share prices to maintain their stock market listing and to improve executive remuneration.

In the present low interest rate and low taxation environment, record corporate profits have made the business sector generally less dependent on external finance. Despite this trend, empirical evidence suggests that small firms or large firms undergoing expansion (e.g., for new physical investment), still depend external finance. Different economic sectors have different capital requirements, as some industries by nature are more capital-intensive. International firms in emerging economies are less self-sufficient for capital than those in developed country markets. Among developed nations, bank loans figure more prominently in Continental Europe and Japan, while bond and equity market financing is more prevalent in Anglo-American economies. Understanding such patterns should help social investors to appreciate the potential and limits to their influence over corporations.

By way of further setting the financial markets context to SRI, the next section briefly introduces the main financial institutions and actors. Readers knowledgeable about this topic should jump to the succeeding section which examines the SRI movement.

III. Types of Financial Institutions

A. INVESTMENT COMPANIES AND COLLECTIVE INVESTMENT SCHEMES

Generally, investment firms (structured as corporations, trusts, or other entities) pool capital from individuals or institutions to invest in a portfolio of assets.[114] The collective investment schemes (CISs) they offer are commonly

---

113 See the rebuttal of J. Corbett, et al., *A Response to 'Financing Patterns: Measurement Concepts and Empirical Results' by Andreas Hackethal and Reinhard Schmidt*, Working Paper (University of Oxford, 2004), 7.

114 For a general introduction, with a US focus, see A.J. Fredman and R. Wiler, *How Mutual Funds Work* (2nd ed., Prentice Hall Press, 1997).

known as mutual funds, unit trusts, or other descriptions, depending on the jurisdiction. Typically, an investment company manages a roster of funds, offering investors specialist investment options such as an SRI portfolio.

The mutual fund emerged as an investment vehicle in Western Europe in the late nineteenth century,[115] although the industry did not blossom until after the Second World War.[116] As of mid-2007, there were 63,200 mutual funds and other CISs worldwide.[117] For the same period, total assets for the CIS sector globally was over US$24 trillion, of which just over half was held by US funds and about one-third by European funds.[118] They cater to both retail and institutional investors. Retail CISs sell units (shares) to the general public, where each unit denotes a proportionate ownership of the underlying securities in the fund.[119] Each CIS issues a prospectus that outlines key investment objectives and other relevant information, forming the underlying contract between the fund and investor. CISs afford investors access to professional fund management and a diversified portfolio, which together potentially reduce financial risk. CISs also cater to institutional investors interested in the same benefits, such as pension plans.[120]

A special type of CIS is a hedge fund, which is essentially a private mutual fund open only to a limited group of wealthy entrepreneurs.[121] Hedge funds are relatively new to the financial sector. They have been seen as aggressive short-term investors, focusing on high-risk assets in exchange for the prospect of absolute, higher returns, although some recent empirical research depicts a more benign and responsible role in the market.[122] Hedge funds commonly take the organizational form of an offshore investment partnership or investment fund registered in a largely unregulated Caribbean tax haven.[123]

---

115 Pozen suggests the first CIS was established in the UK in 1868: R.C. Pozen, *The Mutual Fund Business* (MIT Press, 1998), 55.

116 International Investment Company, "The Origination of the Investment Company Concept," at http://www.ici.org/home/bro_etf.html#TopOfPage.

117 Investment Company Institute (ICI), *Worldwide Mutual Fund Assets and Flows Second Quarter 2007* (ICI, November, 2007).

118 Ibid.

119 Pozen, note 115, 17.

120 Investment Company Institute (ICI), *2007 Investment Company Fact Book* (ICI, 2005), 137 (detailing the size of institutional accounts in US mutual fund industry).

121 See B. Eichengreen and D. Mathieson, *Hedge Funds and Market Dynamics*, Occasional Paper No. 166 (International Monetary Fund, 1998).

122 T.W. Briggs, "Corporate Governance and the New Hedge Fund Activism: An Empirical Analysis," *Journal of Corporation Law* 32(4) (2007): 681.

123 Stichele, note 11, 34.

Another special type of investment product is the private equity fund.[124] It does not raise capital from public stock markets, but through direct intermediation between companies and investors. Individual entrepreneurs or institutional investors can invest in a private equity fund, which targets smaller, unlisted firms that offer greater potential returns. Private equity funds play a key role in the venture capital finance (VCF) market. The stereotypical view of a venture capitalist is a fabulously wealthy person chauffeured in a limousine from meeting to meeting, showering vast sums of money on entrepreneurs with inventions that promise to make millions. More accurately, VCF typically involves a professionally managed fund, organized as a private partnership or limited liability company, with finance from private and public pension funds, foundations, and wealthy individuals.[125] VCF funds in turn acquire stakes in private firms including directorship positions. Successful VCF generally yields high returns, compensating for the risk that some ventures will fail.[126] Some VCF networks, such as the Investors' Circle, also have an explicit mission to promote sustainable development, emphasizing "social returns" as much as private, financial returns.[127]

B. PENSION FUNDS

A pension fund is a retirement plan set up by a corporation, trade union, or government authority to invest income contributed by the founding sponsor and fund members to provide future retirement income for its members.[128] Pension plans were created in Europe in the seventeenth century, initially to help war veterans and retiring senior civil servants.[129] They have since grown to become one of the largest pools of capital in the world. At the close of 2006, pension plan assets in the world's eleven largest pension markets totaled about US$23 trillion in assets, of which 59 percent were held

124 F.W. Fenn, N. Liang, and S. Prowse, "The Private Equity Market: An Overview," *Financial Markets, Institutions and Instruments* 6(4) (1997): 1
125 Kidwell, Peterson, and Blackwell, note 71, 632.
126 See B. Zider, "How Venture Capital Works," *Harvard Business Review* 76(6) (1998): 131.
127 See http://www.investorscircle.net.
128 See E.P. Davis, *Pension Funds, Retirement-Income Security and Capital Markets— An International Perspective* (Oxford University Press, 1995).
129 R. Blackburn, *Banking on Death. Or, Investing in Life: the History and Future of Pensions* (Verso, 2002), 34–39.

by US pension funds, 13 percent by Japanese funds, and nearly 10 percent by UK funds.[130]

Four types of pension schemes exist: state-sponsored pension plans associated with national social security systems; public sector occupational pension plans for employees of government agencies, universities, and related institutions; private sector occupational pensions; and, fourthly, personal pension plans arranged privately. Occupational pension funds are pre-funded by employer and/or employee contributions, which trustees or their agents invest to produce a return sufficient to provide income for retirees. Systems of universal state pensions, typically funded from consolidated government revenue, have increasingly been supplemented or supplanted by occupational pension plans. Generous tax incentives for pension contributions have helped these schemes to flourish, especially in the UK, US, Australia, and Canada.[131] Individuals can also organize private pension plans, useful where employers do not offer a pension scheme or for self-employed workers. Life insurance companies commonly offer long-term savings vehicles to meet this demand.

In common law jurisdictions, occupational pension schemes are typically legal "trusts," whereby the employer (sponsor) vests the pension fund and its earnings in one or more trustees to act on behalf of the beneficiaries (employees and retirees). At times and particularly in the public sector, pension plans derive from collective bargaining deals. In such cases, the employer and trade union may jointly sponsor the pension plan. Typically, a plan administrator manages the scheme,[132] including formulating investment procedures, ensuring plan solvency, and calculating pay benefits to beneficiaries.

Plan administrators often lack adequate expertise to make complex investment decisions and therefore delegate this to an external asset manager. Plan administrators assume duties to oversee the performance of these hired agents. An asset manager in turn is usually subject to the same statutory standards of knowledge, skill, and diligence as apply to an administrator.[133] Asset managers may be retained by specialist investment companies, as in the US and UK, or life insurers and trust banks, more common in Japan.[134]

---

130 Watson Wyatt, *2007 Global Pensions Asset Study* (Watson Wyatt, 2007), 6.

131 See J.B. Forman, "The Tax Treatment of Public and Private Pension Plans around the World," *American Journal of Tax Policy* 14 (1997): 299.

132 See Z. Bodie and E.P. Davis, eds, *The Foundations of Pension Finance* (Edward Elgar Publishing, 2000).

133 A.N. Kaplan, *Pension Law* (Irwin Law, 2006), 354–55.

134 Davis and Steil, note 35, 178.

C. INSURANCE COMPANIES

Insurance companies have become giant institutional investors with assets rivaling pension funds.[135] The insurance sector principally comprises providers of life insurance, and property and casualty insurance. At the end of 2005, insurance companies held some US$16.6 trillion in funds under management, of which about 80 percent were held by life insurance companies and the remainder in the property and casualty risk sector.[136] Insurance companies generally take the form of either mutual or stock companies. Mutual companies are owned by the policyholders, while shareholders (who may or may not own policies) underpin insurance companies.[137] This traditional distinction is disappearing as market competition drives mutual insurers to demutualize to become public companies. Relatedly, due to deregulation of financial markets in many jurisdictions, numerous insurance firms have restructured to become full-service financial "supermarkets," offering mutual funds, personal pension plans, traditional insurance products, and ancillary financial advisory services.

Life insurers' staple business is selling insurance policies to cover risk of death. Increasingly they advertise related long-term saving vehicles such as whole-life policies (term policies with a savings component), annuities (providing a fixed or variable income for the remainder of the insured person's life), and other specialist savings vehicles such as guaranteed investment contracts.[138] As in the pension sector, in many countries governments allow investors to defer the tax on interest income on life insurance policies and annuities, thereby encouraging savings in this sector. Life insurance companies also sometimes act as external asset managers for pension plans, thereby widening their influence in financial markets.

The property and casualty insurance sector covers for all risks other than life. While it holds abundant assets, it does not constitute a form of household saving as in life insurance products or mutual funds.[139] As property and casualty insurance policies typically are subject to renewal annually,

---

135 See the OECD Statistics on Institutional Investors: http://www.oecd.org.
136 IFSL, *Fund Management: City Business Series* (ILSL, August 2006), 6.
137 J. Hansmann, "The Organization of Insurance Companies: Mutual Versus Stock," *Journal of Law, Economics, and Organization* 1(1) (1985): 1.
138 E.P. Davis, *Portfolio Regulation of Life Insurance Companies and Pension Funds* (OECD, 2001), 10.
139 D.F. Babbel and F.J. Fabozzi, *Investment Management for Insurers* (John Wiley and Sons, 1999), 77–88.

these insurance companies generally match their liabilities by investing in short-term or highly liquid investments such as bonds.

D. BANKS

Although banks have lost some share of the corporate financing market to institutional investors, the banking industry worldwide remains very impressive. Assets of the world's largest 1,000 banks grew from about US$23 trillion in 1990 to over US$74 trillion in 2006.[140]

The banking industry is traditionally split between investment and commercial banks.[141] Commercial banking provides credits for financing production and distribution of consumable goods. This includes temporary bridging loans for specific transactions, seasonal loans to manage cash flows, and long-term capital asset loans, such as for purchase of new equipment.[142] In these ways, commercial banks supply the mechanisms for the transmission of government monetary policy decisions (i.e., interest rate changes) to the rest of the economy. Other specific services include cash management, deposit services, and foreign exchange. By contrast, traditionally investment banks neither hold deposits from, nor issue loans to, individuals.[143] Investment banking deals with long-term capital financing, particularly through underwriting securities newly issued by companies or governments. Investment banks also commonly facilitate corporate mergers, acquisitions, and restructuring through advice and financing.

Notable international trends in banking include the emergence of universal banks and a convergence towards the Anglo-American model of arm's-length relationships in banking. First, market deregulation has enabled increased convergence between the activities of investment and commercial banks, particularly in Europe and North America, leading to universal banking service providers.[144] Market deregulation has allowed banks to enter the investment services industry, and many now manage mutual funds and offer insurance services through their subsidiaries.

---

140 IFSL, note 16.
141 By way of introduction, see Kidwell, Peterson, and Blackwell, note 71, chapters 13 and 21.
142 Ibid., 358.
143 R.C. Eccles and D.B. Crane, *Doing Deals: Investment Banks at Work* (Harvard Business School Press, 1988).
144 R.C. Smith and I. Walter, *Global Banking* (2nd ed., Oxford University Press, 1997), 191–98, 219–23.

Second, the globalization of the banking industry has contributed to some convergence in banking regimes towards the Anglo-American model.[145] The "relationship banking" model found in Continental European and Japan has correspondingly declined.[146] In Germany, France, and Japan, long-term relationships between banks and firms were common, with banks even holding seats on the governing boards of their clients. In the US and UK, such relationships are more arm's-length, with banks generally distancing themselves from corporate governance and operational matters.

Several traditional characteristics of banks differentiate this sector from institutional investors.[147] First, transaction costs force households and small businesses to rely on commercial banks for financing needs, while large companies have additional options in equity and bond markets. Second, through information obtained in the loan process, banks have a comparative advantage in screening and monitoring clients. Banks are also better able to influence borrower behavior before a loan matures, as they can seize assets in the case of default. Market-based capital finance by contrast has traditionally been available primarily to companies with well-established reputations, although the popularity of private equity funds is eroding that advantage.

E. CREDIT UNIONS

A credit union is a financial co-operative, owned and controlled by its members, who contribute personal savings into a common fund and in return may receive low interest loans and other financial services and benefits.[148] Credit unions originated in Germany in the nineteenth century, traditionally focusing on residential mortgage financing, small business loans, consumer credit, and deposit services to members.[149] They differ from commercial banks in many ways, notably that they are not structured as corporations.

---

145 A. Bartzolas, *Financial Markets and the European Economy: A Synthesis of Research Findings*, Working Paper No. 04-37 (Institute for New Technologies, United Nations University, 2004).

146 See A. Fakuda and S. Hirota, "Main Bank Relationships and Capital Structure in Japan," *Journal of Japanese and International Economics* 10 (1996): 250; D. Harhoff and T. Körting, "Lending Relationships in Germany— Empirical Evidence from Survey Data," *Journal of Banking and Finance* 22 (1998): 1317.

147 Davis and Steil, note 35, 304.

148 See C. Ferguson and D. McKillop, *The Strategic Development of Credit Unions* (John Wiley and Sons, 1997).

149 Kidwell, Peterson, and Blackwell, note 71, 564.

However, some banks are structured as cooperatives, including several that specialize in responsible lending, such as the Co-operative Bank (UK)[150] and Ekobanken (Sweden).[151]

Credit union legislation typically requires that members of the union have a common bond, such as by occupation or residence.[152] As each member becomes a shareholder and has one vote, regardless of financial contribution, in theory they provide a more democratic form of governance than offered by other financial organizations. Thus, each member has an equal vote for election of credit union directors, and may even stand for election.[153]

Credit unions fill niches overlooked by other lenders. They may offer credit to poorer people typically ignored by conventional banks. They also provide services that help ensure that credit is used effectively, such as financial literacy training and credit counseling to customers, and technical assistance to small businesses. Their more specialized knowledge of the communities they cater to and the closer relationships they often form with their customers facilitates individualized and specialized financial products that mainstream large banks may consider too time-consuming or costly. Although credit unions nominally have a greater commitment to their members, they also must compete in the market. Their capacity to continue to service their members in such ways is at risk, as in recent years credit unions have suffered from tough market competition and technology changes, being unable sometimes to keep pace by offering the full range of banking services that customers increasingly expect. In the US, this has caused many mergers and liquidations and the number of credit unions has declined.[154]

F. SPECIALIST INVESTMENT INTERMEDIARIES

1. Asset Managers and Financial Advisers

Institutional investors often delegate investment management to asset management firms. Asset management (also known as fund management) simply refers to the process of managing various investments.[155] It is the interface

---

150 Http://www.co-operativebank.co.uk.
151 Http://www.ekobanken.se.
152 See e.g., the membership rules detailed in s. 30(1)-(2) of Ontario's *Credit Unions and Caisses Populaires Act*, S.O. 1994.
153 Kidwell, Peterson, and Blackwell, note 71, 567–68.
154 Ibid., 580.
155 J. Franks, C. Mayer, and L.C. da Silva, *Asset Management and Investor Protection: An International Analysis* (Oxford University Press, 2003).

between investors, on the one hand, and financial markets and businesses, on the other.

Management of assets may be provided internally, within the pension fund or other investment institution, or by services hired externally, such as from a bank or insurance company with an asset management division or a specialist asset management firm.[156] The world's largest asset management providers include Barclays Global Investors, UBS, and State Street Global Advisors.[157] Usually only the largest institutional investors retain in-house asset managers.[158] In accordance with the guidelines or directions of the asset owners, asset managers commonly research companies, determine asset allocation, select securities, trade, provide financial accounting, and process transactions.[159] In the case of a dedicated SRI fund, the asset manager has additional responsibilities to ensure the investment portfolio meets the asset owner's specific social and environmental goals.

Asset management strategies range from active to passive.[160] Passive management assumes that capital markets are efficient and it seeks to maximize returns by tracking market benchmarks.[161] In 2000, 20 to 25 percent of institutional investment assets in the US and UK were estimated to be invested in market-tracking index funds.[162] Active management involves acquiring specific investments on the assumption that the market contains inefficiencies and that some securities may be wrongly valued. It also allows for shareholder advocacy and strategies to improve corporate governance and shareholder value.

While the client base of the asset management industry has been primarily institutional, the growth of the retail investment market coupled with technological improvements in information management has meant that

---

156 P.L. Davies, "Institutional Investors in the United Kingdom," in *Contemporary Issues in Corporate Governance*, eds D.D. Prentice and P.R.J. Holland (Clarendon Press, 1993), 69, 73; and see I. Walter, "The Global Asset Management Industry: Competitive Structure and Performance," *Financial Markets, Institutions and Instruments* 8(1) (1999): 1.

157 "P&I/Watson Wyatt World 500: The World's Largest Managers," *Pensions and Investments*, October 1, 2007.

158 Davis and Steil, note 35, 138, 154 (e.g., in 2000 about 80 percent of the portfolios of UK pension funds were externally managed).

159 Ibid., 114–15.

160 Ibid., 58.

161 See E. Fama, "Efficient Capital Markets II," *Journal of Finance* 45 (1991): 1575.

162 Davis and Steil, note 35, 134, 154.

asset managers can now more easily accommodate even small investors. Understandably, they particularly covet the lucrative "high net worth individuals" market segment.[163]

Traditionally, however, financial planners or advisers have been the main point of contact for retail investors and small businesses. They typically work for specialist financial planning or brokerage firms, or represent banks and life insurance companies. They assist with personal financial planning including retirement and investment planning, risk management and insurance planning, and even estate and tax planning. Financial planners are in effect gatekeepers to the financial market for this segment of investors, translating their vague investment goals into concrete investment strategies. As the following chapter will discuss, the retail market for SRI products depends heavily on financial planners' recommendations.[164]

2. Credit Rating Agencies

Credit rating agencies (CRAs) are informational intermediaries that appraise the creditworthiness of corporations and states issuing debt instruments.[165] Credit ratings reflect various risk factors including relative default probability, financial strength, and related concepts. Credit ratings provide financial market participants with a framework to compare how companies will make timely payments on their debts. Diverse information is condensed into a single rating symbol (typically from AAA as the highest creditworthiness to C or D as the lowest). Through research, expertise, and economies of scale in providing ratings, CRAs can enhance the efficiency of capital markets by mitigating some of the informational asymmetries present between debt issuers and investors. While credit ratings do not convey a CRA's view of the actual value of an issuer's securities and make no buy/sell recommendations, CRA decisions influence how companies access debt markets. Some investors deal only with bonds from companies and governmental institutions that have a high rating from a reputable CRA.[166] In some jurisdictions, regulations restrict pension funds to bonds rated at a certain investment grade (i.e., usually at least BBB).[167]

---

163 A. Rivkin, "How I Make the Rich Richer," *The Times*, December 12, 2006.

164 Some mutual fund companies sell directly to retail investors without an intermediary (e.g., Altamira).

165 For an introduction, see G. Majnoni and C.M. Reinhart, eds, *Ratings, Rating Agencies and the Global Financial System* (Kluwer, 2002).

166 Stichele, note 11, 41.

167 Ibid.

Despite the tremendous influence they wield over financial markets, CRAs are sparsely regulated and have become a source of private ordering and regulation in their own right.[168] Although there are some 130 CRAs worldwide,[169] the US triumvirate of S&P's, Moody's and Fitch dominates the industry. This concentration creates a risk of anticompetitive behavior, which could impair the legitimacy of the ratings provided.

The recent spate of corporate scandals has indeed raised questions about the reliability and integrity of credit ratings.[170] Rating agencies have sometimes proved unable to anticipate changes in the creditworthiness of borrowers. Stephen Davis and others question the impartiality of CRAs on the basis that corporations, not investors, pay for the ratings.[171] They cite for instance how both Moody's and S&P's gave Enron and Worldcom investment-grade ratings shortly before each imploded. A further source of a potential conflict of interest is the collateral consulting services offered by CRAs. Their rating decisions may be influenced by whether or not an issuer buys its additional services.[172] CRAs have also been accused of failing to adequately monitor the reliability of assigned ratings.[173] These and other concerns have fueled calls for greater transparency and regulatory supervision.[174]

---

168 See generally T.J. Sinclair, *The New Masters of Capital* (Cornell University Press, 2005); J. Flood, "Rating, Dating and the Informal Regulation and the Formal Ordering of Financial Transactions: Securitisations and Credit Rating Agencies," in *Privatising Development: Transnational Law, Infrastructure and Human Rights*, ed. M.B. Likosky (Martinus Nijhoff, 2006), 147.

169 Estimated in 2000 by the Basel Committee on Banking Supervision, as cited by the International Organization of Securities Commission (IOSCO), Technical Committee, *Report of the Activities of Credit Rating Agencies* (IOSCO, 2003), 4.

170 S. Rousseau, "Enhancing the Accountability of Credit Rating Agencies: The Case for a Disclosure-Based Approach," *McGill Law Journal* 51 (2006): 618; F. Partnoy, "The Siskel and Ebert of Financial Markets? Two Thumbs Down for the Credit Rating Agencies," *Washington University Law Quarterly* 77 (1999): 619.

171 Davis, Lukomnik, and Pitt-Watson, note 47, 142. Other studies doubt that such conflicts of interest have led to abuses: D.M. Covitz and P. Harrison, *Testing Conflicts of Interest at Bond Rating Agencies with Market Anticipation: Evidence that Reputation Incentives Dominate*, Working Paper No. 2003-68 (Federal Reserve Board, 2003).

172 Rousseau, note 170, 629.

173 Ibid., 632.

174 IOSCO, *Code of Conduct Fundamentals for Credit Rating Agencies* (IOSCO, 2004).

Having sketched the roles of the main financial institutions and how companies raise finance, to provide an elementary understanding of the broader market context of SRI, the following discussion outlines the rise of SRI and its principal actors and methods.

IV. The SRI Movement

A. ACTORS AND ISSUES

1. Historical Advances

Despite its more recent popularity, SRI has a long history that predates the ascendancy of global finance. Largely without official imprimatur, SRI has grown since the eighteenth century when the Quakers, joined later by other religious denominations, eschewed financial ties to "sin" businesses involved in slavery or production of intoxicants.[175] Some commentators trace the antecedents of SRI even earlier, to ancient Jewish law proscriptions against specific business transactions.[176] Allegorically, SRI was a prophetic voice largely outside the gates of the financial world. This has since changed, with SRI increasingly "mainstream," with investors viewing attention to environmental and social issues as prudent financial risk management.[177] Consequently, SRI is evolving into a dominant financial risk management strategy, integrating social and environmental issues where financially material, distinct from a smaller, values- or mission-based sector, stressing ethics and political change. Sometimes there is no clear division between these styles of investment,

175 See J.R. Soderlund, *Quakers and Slavery: A Divided Spirit* (Princeton University Press, 1985); for more recent examples, see R. Sparkes, *The Ethical Investor* (HarperCollins, 1995), 114–15, 130–48.

176 M.S. Schwartz, M. Tamari, and D. Schwab, "Ethical Investing from a Jewish Perspective," *Business and Society Review* 112(1) (2007): 137; D.B. Bressler, "Ethical Investment: The Responsibility of Ownership in Jewish Law," in *Jewish Business Ethics: The Firm and Its Stakeholders,* eds M. Pava and A. Levine (Jason Aronson, 1999), 303.

177 R. Sparkes, "A Historical Perspective on the Growth of Socially Responsible Investment," *in Responsible Investment*, eds R Sullivan and C Mackenzie (Greenleaf Publishing, 2006), 39; N. Kreander, D. Molyneaux, and K. McPhail, *An Immanent Critique of UK Church Ethical Investment*, Working Paper 2003/1 (Department of Accounting and Finance, University of Glasgow, 2003), 7.

or SRI generally and other forms of investment, as financiers commonly blend investment philosophies.

The modern era of SRI gained momentum in the late 1960s. In the US, civil rights activists appealed to institutional shareholders to use their voting power to improve corporate policy.[178] SRI began to gather wider appeal captivated by more diverse causes in the wake of opposition to the Vietnam War and South Africa's apartheid regime.[179] Churches were active in these anti-violence campaigns. In 1969, one of the first SRI shareholder resolutions was filed against Dow Chemicals concerning napalm production.[180] In 1977, the US General Board of the National Council of Churches recommended that members withdraw all funds from banks that invested in South Africa. Some universities and philanthropic foundations also emerged as ardent proponents of responsible finance.[181] University campuses became immersed in protracted conflicts over the investment policies of university pension plans and endowment funds, particularly in regard to investment in South Africa.[182]

In recent years mainstream institutional investors have become more receptive to SRI, largely to the extent that they perceive it as financially material. Pension funds have characteristics that should make them inclined to practice SRI.[183] According to a study by Canada's National Round Table on the Environment and the Economy (NRTEE), "pension plan profiles evince a natural fit with sustainability considerations. ... In fact, given the long-term nature of their liabilities, pension funds should be—and often

---

178 B.G. Markiel and R.E. Quandt, "Moral Issues in Investment Policy," *Harvard Business Review* March–April (1971): 38.

179 See W. Kaempfer, J. Lehmen, and A. Lowenberg, "The Economics of Anti-Apartheid Investment Sanctions," *Social Science Quarterly* 68(3) (1987): 528; M. Lashgari and D. Gant, "Social Investing: The Sullivan Principles," *Review of Social Economy* 47(1) (1989): 74.

180 T. Guay, J.P. Doh, and G. Sinclair, "Non-governmental Organizations, Shareholder Activism, and Socially Responsible Investments: Ethical, Strategic, and Governance Implications," *Journal of Business Ethics* 52(1) (2004): 125, 127.

181 S. Buzby and H. Falk, "Demand for Social Responsibility Information by University Investors," *Accounting Review* 54(1) (1979): 23.

182 P.M.C. Carroll, "Socially Responsible Investment of Public Pension Funds: The South Africa Issue and State Law," *Review of Law and Social Change* 10 (1980–81): 407, 412–13.

183 See A. Neale, "Pension Funds and Socially Responsible Investment," *Journal of Corporate Citizenship* 1(2) (2001): 43; J. Gifford, "Measuring the Social, Environmental and Ethical Performance of Pension Funds," *Journal of Australian Political Economy* 53 (2004): 139.

are—the long-term investors *par excellence*."[184] Occupational pension funds in the public sector and the trade union movement have emerged as the most vocal social investors.[185] Insurance companies have also to a lesser extent shown an interest in SRI. The US insurer AIG and the German insurer Allianz for instance are earmarking capital to projects and technologies that reduce carbon emissions.[186]

In the debt finance market, some banks and credit unions have targeted community financing and environmentally responsible lending. While many lenders increasingly incorporate environmental risk appraisal in their loan procedures, a few have gone beyond simple "defensive" banking to consciously finance sustainable development.[187] They move further to offer environmental products, services and incentives, including "green mortgages," NGO-affinity credit cards, and specialist environmental advisory services. Anneke Hoijtink's survey in 2005 of 29 commercial banks worldwide for their commitment to sustainable development found that European banks were generally pioneering best practices.[188] Deutsche Bank, Rabobank (Netherlands), ING Bank (Netherlands), National Westminster Bank (UK), and Westpac (Australia) are notable examples.[189]

Some lenders, particularly in the cooperative sector, entrench sustainable development as a core mission.[190] They include UmweltBank (Germany), Triodos Bank (the Netherlands), Banca Etica (Italy), and the Co-operative

184 NRTEE, *Capital Markets and Sustainability: Investing in a Sustainable Future. State of the Debate Report* (NRTEE, 2007), 20.

185 J. Quarter, et al., "Special Investment by Union-based Pension Funds and Labour-Sponsored Investment Funds in Canada," *Industrial Relations* 56(1) (2001): 92; UNEPFI Asset Management Working Group and UKSIF, *Responsible Investment in Focus: How Leading Public Pension Funds are Meeting the Challenge* (UNEPFI, 2007).

186 E. Mills, *From Risk to Opportunity: 2007. Insurer Responses to Climate Change* (CERES, 2007), 33.

187 See J.J. Bouma, M. Jeucken, and L. Klinkers, eds, *Sustainable Banking: The Greening of Finance* (Greenleaf Publishing, 2001).

188 A. Hoijtink, *The Sustainability Attitude of Commercial Banks*, Graduate thesis (Faculty of Economics and Business Administration, University of Tilburg, 2005), 41.

189 Ibid., 50–51; S. Labatt and R.R. White, *Environmental Finance: A Guide to Environmental Risk Assessment and Financial Products* (John Wiley and Sons, 2002), 76.

190 M.H.A. Jeucken and J.J. Bouma, "The Changing Environment of Banks," *Greener Management International* 27 (1999): 21, 30–31.

Bank (UK).[191] Common characteristics include: increasing accountability through regular and independently verified sustainability reporting; screening borrower operations for sound environmental management; financing local community development; implementing ethical policies; and improving access to banking services through social inclusion policies.[192] The Co-operative Bank, for instance, reduces interest rates for corporate borrowers who meet the Natural Step's criteria for sustainability.[193] Some banks also offer sustainable investment funds for clients, such as Triodos Bank's Wind Fund and Solar Investment Fund.[194] Climate Change Capital, a UK investment bank, specializes in commercial opportunities in energy efficiency, renewable energy, and carbon markets.[195] Environmental policies of these banks have taken cues from the public development finance sector. In the mid-1980s, multilateral development banks (MDBs) initiated procedures and standards to reduce and monitor the impacts of loan capital on local communities and their environments.[196] The European Bank of Reconstruction and Development has a specific mandate for sustainable development.[197] MDBs' environmental and social lending standards have provided benchmarks for private banks interested in sustainability.[198]

SRI has also acquired influence in the community financing and charity sectors. The credit union movement, particularly in North America, has supported SRI for some decades, well before many of its financial peers.

---

191 See also the members of the European Federation of Ethical and Alternative Banks: http://www.febea.org.

192 J. Guiseppe, "Assessing the 'Triple Bottom Line': Social and Environmental Practices in the European Banking Sector," in *Sustainable Banking*, note 187, 96, 100–1; European Association of Co-operative Banks (EACA), *Corporate Social Responsibility: The Performance of Cooperative Banks* (EACA, 2005).

193 A.B. Coulson and V. Monks, "Corporate Environmental Performance Considerations within Bank Lending Decisions," *Eco-Management and Auditing* 6 (1989): 1, 5.

194 Http://www.triodos.co.uk/uk/about_triodos/history/?lang=.

195 Http://www.climatechangecapital.com.

196 World Bank, *Mainstreaming the Environment: The World Bank Group and the Environment* (World Bank, 1995).

197 Article 21(vii) requires the Bank to "promote in the full range of its activities environmentally sound and sustainable development": *Agreement establishing the European Bank for Reconstruction and Development*, (1990) O.J. L. 372.

198 E.g., Bank of America, *1999 Environmental Progress Report* (Bank of America, 2000), 17; J. Barta and V. Éri, "Environmental Attitudes of Banks and Financial Institutions," in *Sustainable Banking*, note 187, 120, 123 (referring to Hungarian banks).

VanCity (Canada) and Mecu (in Australia) pioneered financial products with environmental pricing incentives. Credit unions have also provided financial services and loans targeted to the underprivileged and to charitable causes and sustainable development in local communities.[199] However, in some markets credit unions have lagged on advancing social financing.[200] While charitable foundations presumably are even closer to SRI, surprisingly some have faced complaints for failing to align their investments with their philanthropic missions.[201] No more than 15 percent of foundations in the US in 2002 used any SRI screen to manage their investments.[202] The behemoth Gates Foundation, with some US$65 billion in assets as of 2007, has incurred criticism for reaping profits from companies whose actions contradict its mission.[203] Its difficulties contrast with the exemplary Nathan Cummings Foundation, which has done much to coordinate its investments with its social and environmental aspirations.[204]

Since the 1990s, the SRI market for retail investors began to flourish.[205] It has attracted considerable media attention in newspapers' personal finance and business sections.[206] The world's first SRI mutual fund actually dates to 1928, with the establishment in the US of the Pioneer Fund that excluded

199 B. Balkenhol, ed., *Credit Unions and the Poverty Challenge: Outreach, Enhancing Sustainability* (International Labour Organization, 1999); D. Fuller, *Credit Unions and Sustainable Development—The Potential for Credit Unions to Make Progress Towards Sustainable Development* (University of Northumbria, 1998).

200 C. Valor, et al., "Socially Responsible Investments among Savings Banks and Credit Unions: Empirical Findings in the Spanish Context," *Annals of Public and Cooperative Economics* 78(2) (2007): 301.

201 R. Tieman, "Socially Responsible Investment: Practising What They Preach," *Financial Times (FT.Com)*, July 5, 2007.

202 J. Emerson, "Horse Manure and Grantmaking," *Foundation News and Commentary* 43(3) (2002), at http://www.foundationnews.org/CME/article.cfm?id=1950&issueID=1927.

203 C. Piller, "Money Clashes with Mission," *Los Angeles Times*, January 8, 2007.

204 Http://www.nathancummings.org.

205 C. Cowton, "The Development of Ethical Investment Products," in *Ethical Conflicts in Finance*, eds A. Prindl and B. Prodhan (Blackwell, 1994), 213; M. Statman, "Socially Responsible Mutual Funds," *Financial Analysts Journal* 56 (3) (2000): 30.

206 E.g., D. Berman, "Hot for Green Investing," *Financial Post*, February 19, 2007; R. Kerber, "From the Basement to the Mainstream: Boomers Bring their Brand of Social Activism to Retirement Investing," *Boston Globe*, April 1, 2007; T. Grant, "Investors Seek Eco-Disclosure," *Globe and Mail*, October 4, 2006, B14.

investments in alcohol and tobacco stocks.[207] The first SRI fund open generally to the public was the Pax World Fund, launched in 1971.[208] Specialist SRI funds are now available in many other markets, including Australia,[209] Canada,[210] and more recently Japan.[211] Mutual funds are adaptable to a wide variety of investment goals, including various forms of ethical finance. Some are dedicated to environmental issues, such as the Merlin Ecology Fund in the UK, and Green Century Funds in the US.[212] SRI-focused mutual funds' clientele is diverse, although it tends to be better educated, wealthier, mostly female, and to work in the public sector or caring professions.[213]

The venture finance market, a subset of the private equity market, has also forayed into SRI.[214] It can channel capital to emerging businesses pioneering new environmental technologies, products, and services. Venture funds invest in fledgling private enterprises, often unable to raise finance from more conventional sources.[215] New companies developing fuel cell technologies, wind turbines, and organic foods often lack the capital to expand their business.[216] Environmental venture finance is not only a business-financing model that considers environmental risks as material to business development, but also

---

207 R. Sparkes, *Socially Responsible Investment: A Global Revolution* (Wiley, 2002), 43.

208 Ibid; see http://www.paxworld.com/02_history.htm.

209 PriceWaterhouseCoopers, *The Role of Australia's Financial Sector in Sustainability* (PriceWaterhouseCoopers, 2001); NSW State Chamber of Commerce, *The Unseen Revolution: Ethical Investment in Australia* (NSW State Chamber of Commerce, 2001).

210 See generally E. Ellmen, *The 1998 Canadian Ethical Money Guide* (James Lorimer and Company, 1997); D. Skinner, *The Ethical Investor: A Guide to Socially Responsible Investing in Canada* (Stoddart Publishing, 2001).

211 See http://www.nikko-am.co.jp/fundinfo/252263.

212 C. Mackenzie, *Ethical Investment and the Challenge of Corporate Reform: A Critical Assessment of the Procedures and Purposes of UK Ethical Unit Trusts* (PhD, University of Bath, 1997), chapter 2, 12.

213 For UK evidence, see P. Shepherd, "A History of Ethical Investment" (UKSIF, May 2001), 1; J. Brown, *Going Green: How Financial Services are Failing Ethical Consumers* (New Economics Foundation, 2007), 13–15. From the US, see B.N. Rosen, D.M. Sandler, and D. Shani, "Social Issues and Socially Responsible Investment Behavior: A Preliminary Empirical Investigation," *Journal of Consumer Affairs* 25(2) (1991): 221.

214 See generally C. Bovaird, *Introduction to Venture Capital Finances* (Pitman, 1990).

215 See E.A. Zelinsky, "The Dilemma of the Local Social Investment," *Cardozo Law Review* 6 (1984): 111; S. Diefendorf, "The Venture Capital and Environmental Industry," *Corporate Environmental Strategy* 7 (2000): 388.

216 Diefendorf, ibid.

treats eco-innovations as the core of the business. Such venture financing is driven particularly by "high net-worth individuals" (HNWI) who donate to or invest in philanthropic causes.[217] They are generally free to invest without the regulatory and fiduciary obligations that constrain institutional investors. For most HNWIs, SRI generally remains a satellite asset class rather than a mainstream financial choice.[218]

Traversing all of these actors and issues is the emergence of an array of consultancy and research organizations to service the SRI community. For instance, Innovest and the Ethical Investment Research Service (EIRIS) help investors identify good corporate citizens and understand the linkages between corporate sustainability performance and overall investment returns. Mercer Investment Consulting specializes in institutional clients and has played a pivotal role in assisting UNEPFI.[219] Groupe Investissement Responsible in Quebec is one of many organizations specializing in assisting investors with shareholder advocacy and proxy voting.[220]

2. Drivers and Future Directions

Ideally, SRI will become the benchmark for all investors, thereby contributing to sustainable development. A dominant view in the SRI industry is that only business case considerations can drive this transformation, with the shift away from ethical investment viewed as a natural progression in the evolution and maturation of SRI. References to "ethics" are thus waning, being replaced by the ostensibly placid and less controversial concept of "responsible investment."[221]

While SRI is courting mainstream financial markets, it has not yet won them over. It still has its fierce critics who simplistically associate SRI with only "conservative religious principles and dated liberal social

---

217 R. Sullivan, "Rich Get Taste for Social Responsibility," *Financial Times*, July 2, 2007, 18.
218 See the session: "Unlocking Value in Private Banking" (UNEPFI Global Roundtable, Melbourne, Australia, October 24–25, 2007).
219 Http://www.mercer.com/ic.
220 Http://www.investissementresponsable.com.
221 J.F. Solomon and A. Solomon, "Private Social, Ethical, and Environmental Disclosure," *Accounting, Auditing and Accountability* 19 (2006): 564, 583 (providing quotations from investment professionals that "SRI" is more appropriate terminology than "ethical" investment).

notions,"[222] or consider it a nefarious excuse for private political interests to disregard long-term shareholder value.[223] Many SRI commentators however remain optimistic about the sector's prospects. Jason Hollands, of F&C Asset Management, explains that: "this is the growing area. This is becoming mainstream. It is not just because investors want it—for pension trustees, regulation and policy is moving in a direction which demands it."[224] Leo McCann and others suggest: "SRI in its current form is very different from earlier modes of ethical investment. SRI. . . is being adopted increasingly by the majority of pension funds and large institutional investors."[225] Thus, an international survey of 157 investment management firms published by Mercer Investment Consulting in 2006 found that "the proportion of managers expecting increased client demand for the integration of ESG analysis into mainstream investment processes is 13 percent in [2006], rising to 38 percent over the next three years."[226] Of factors they thought "will become or remain material in five years," fund managers rated globalization (55 percent) and corporate governance (55 percent) highest.[227]

With its traditions of stakeholder capitalism and relatively high awareness of environmental challenges, Europe will likely lead such changes in SRI. One study in 2005 found that 75 percent of European institutional investors surveyed held environmental sustainability to be a core investment concern, compared to 20 percent of US respondents.[228] Another indicator of the surging European interest in SRI is that in 2006 European financial institutions comprised 55 percent of the UNEPFI signatories, compared to just

222 J. Entine, "The Myth of Social Investing: A Critique of Its Practices and Consequences for Corporate Social Performance Research," *Organization and Environment* 16(3) (2003): 352, 365.

223 C.E. Rounds, Jr., "Why Social Investing Threatens Public Pension Funds, Charitable Trusts, and the Social Security Trust Fund," *Pension Fund Politics: The Dangers of Social Investing*, ed. J. Entine (American Enterprise Institute, 2005): 56.

224 Quoted in M. Grimond, "Now All of Us are Turning Ethical," *The Times*, July 30, 2005, M1.

225 L. McCann, A. Solomon, and J.F. Solomon, "Explaining the Growth in U.K. Socially Responsible Investment," *Journal of General Management* 28(4) (2003): 15, 19.

226 Mercer Investment Consulting (MIC), *2006 Fearless Forecast Survey: What Do Investment Managers Think About Responsible Investment?* (MIC, 2006), 3.

227 Ibid., 6.

228 Davis, et al., note 47, 154.

11 percent from North America.[229] However, the SRI market within Europe is heterogeneous, and it is lagging in some countries.[230] The position in North America is likewise diverse. Encouragingly, for example, a 2007 survey of defined contribution (DC) retirement plans in the US pension sector concluded that 19 percent of DC plans already offer an SRI option and that a 41 percent of all DC plan sponsors not currently offering SRI options expect to do so by 2010.[231] Among other OECD markets such as Japan, SRI is generally much weaker.[232]

SRI is gaining traction in emerging and rapidly industrializing economies. Microcredit institutions for community development and poverty reduction are the strongest element of SRI in the developing world, epitomized by the successful Grameen Bank in Bangladesh.[233] In South Africa, the Johannesburg Securities Exchange launched an SRI Index in 2004 to cater to anticipated market demand.[234] India's first SRI fund, the Amro Sustainable Development Fund, was launched in early 2007.[235] In Asia, the Association for Sustainable and Responsible Investment (ASrIA) was formed to exchange information and coordinate action, pointing to continued SRI growth in this economic powerhouse region.[236]

No single factor explains the recent rise of SRI.[237] Its growth is partly attributed to the precedent effect of reforms to public finance, especially in international development financing and state pension funds. Oren Perez argues that that "the trigger to the evolvement of green finance can be traced back to the environmental campaign against the World Bank and the GATT

---

229 UNEPFI, *2006 Overview* (UNEPFI, 2006).

230 E.g., in Spain: see J.M. Lazano, L. Albareda, and M.R. Balaguer, "Socially Responsible Investment in the Spanish Financial Market," *Journal of Business Ethics* 69(3) (2006): 305.

231 Mercer Investment Consulting (MIC), *Defined Contribution Plans and Socially Responsible Investing in the United States: A Survey of Plan Sponsors, Administrators and Consultants* (MIC, June 2007).

232 H.H. Jin, O.S. Mitchell, and J. Piggott, "Socially Responsible Investment in Japanese Pensions," *Pacific-Basin Finance Journal* 14 (2006): 427.

233 J. Santiso, "Markets in Virtue: The Promise of Ethical Funds and Microcredit," *International Social Science Journal* 57(185) (2005): 493, 501–5.

234 S. de Cleene and D. Sonnenberg, *Socially Responsible Investment in South Africa* (2nd ed., AICC Centre for Sustainability Investing, 2004), 30–31.

235 M. Raja, "Ethical Investing Comes to India," *Asia Times Online*, April 5, 2007, at http://www.atimes.com/atimes/South_Asia/ID05Df01.html.

236 See http://www.asria.org.

237 See McCann, Solomon, and Solomon, note 225.

in the 1980s ..."[238] MDBs incorporated social and environmental impact assessment into their project financing well before most private lenders.[239] Today, some in the SRI community look to public finance to set an example, such as how in New Zealand and Sweden responsible investment has been legislated for their national pension funds since 2000.

Reforms to MDB and public financing may reflect deeper value shifts in society. Society's expectations of businesses and investors have become more demanding in recent decades, in line with increased concerns for environmental protection and social justice. During 2006 and 2007 public concern about environmental problems grew substantially, attaining levels not experienced since the spike in the late 1980s.[240] NGOs increasingly mobilize resources to target financiers and companies, exposing their failings, as well as cooperating with investors in order to address common social and environmental issues. Notably, animal liberationists' vociferous campaign against the drug testing firm Huntington Life Sciences precipitated its severe business woes during 2000–2001.[241] BankTrack has been vigilant in scrutinizing banks' compliance with the Equator Principles, while the World Wide Fund for Nature (WWF) has begun a dialogue with investors to address climate change risks.

Yet, the hegemony of business case rationales in SRI points to other, more influential factors, shaping SRI. The insurance industry was one of the first sectors in the financial sector to draw connections between environmental risks and their potential costs.[242] The growth of SRI mutual funds has become substantially tied to competitive returns.[243] Many investors are lured by the prospect of greater prosperity, believing that investment in CSR-driven

---

238 O. Perez, *The New Universe of Green Finance: From Self-Regulation to Multi-Polar Governance*, Working Paper No. 07-3 (Bar-Ilan University, Faculty of Law, 2007).

239 D.L. Nielson and M.J. Tierney, "Delegation to International Organisations: Agency Theory and World Bank Environmental Reform," *International Organizations* 57 (2003): 241, 253–71.

240 E.g., James Hoggan and Associates, *What Canadians Think About Sustainability—The Word, the Concept, the Values* (James Hoggan and Associates, 2006).

241 I. McKerron and D. Harrison, "Animal Testing Lab Faces Ruin as Bank Cancels Overdraft," *Sunday Telegraph*, June 19, 2001.

242 M.A. White, "Environmental Finance: Value and Risk in an Age of Ecology," *Business Strategy and the Environment* 5 (1996): 198.

243 F. Déjean, "L'émergence de l'investissement socialement responsable: Le rôle des sociétés de gestion," *Revue de l'Organisation Responsable* 1(1) (2006): 18.

companies yield higher profits.[244] A substantial research industry devoted to underlining the "nexus" between corporate sustainability and financial performance has accompanied the growth of SRI. In other words, in a competitive market-place, for some investors SRI represents another investment model to gain an advantage.

Not all SRI is so crudely self-serving, and a resilient though much smaller ethically-driven strand persists.[245] Traditionally affiliated with faith-based investors, ethical investment is increasingly tied to the activities of environmental NGOs. Groups such as Friends of the Earth and WWF ever more scrutinize financiers in the same manner that they have long campaigned against regular companies.[246] Shareholder activism and direct protesting against banks and other financial providers is akin to older economic pressure tactics like consumer boycotts.[247] Sometimes an institution's adoption of an SRI policy stems directly from such pressure, such as the campaign by People and Planet to reform the UK's Universities Superannuation Scheme (USS).[248] SRI networks such as UKSIF crucially help to forge dialogue between NGOs and market actors, providing a way to amplify influence through peer pressure. Ruth Aguilera and others explain that "[e]ven if institutional investors are motivated primarily by instrumental factors, relational motives to conform with emerging industry norms are also in evidence."[249] Investors participating in networks face pressures to be attentive to issues and conform to norms raised by other groups.

Investor responsibly is thus gradually becoming a requirement for the "social license" of financial institutions. This license is particularly acute for

244 R. Lowry, *Good Money: A Guide to Profitable Social Investing in the 90s* (W.W. Norton, 1991); D.J. Stanley and C.R. Herb, "The Moral and Financial Conflict of Socially Responsible Investing," *Graziadio Business Report* 10(1) (2007), at http://gbr.pepperdine.edu/071/sri.html.

245 P.H. Dembinski, et al., "The Ethical Foundations of Responsible Investment," *Journal of Business Ethics* 48 (2003): 203.

246 E.g., WWF and BankTrack, *Shaping the Future of Sustainable Finance: Moving from Paper Promises to Performance* (WWF, 2006); C. Berger, *False Profits: How Australia's Finance Sector Undervalues the Environment and What We Can Do About It* (Australian Conservation Foundation, 2006).

247 M. Winston, "NGO Strategies for Promoting Corporate Social Responsibility," *Ethics and International Affairs* 16(2) (2002): 71, 80–82.

248 S. Waygood, *Capital Market Campaigning. The Impact of NGOs on Companies, Shareholder Value and Reputational Risk* (Risk Books, 2006), 89–106.

249 R.V. Aguilera, et al., "Corporate Governance and Social Responsibility: A Comparative Analysis of the UK and the US," *Corporate Governance and Social Responsibility* 14(3) (2006): 147, 154.

institutions perceived as intimately involved in development decisions, such as project financing banks. Yet, as with the CSR movement, financiers' uptake of SRI can serve merely to deflect demand for more rigorous oversight.[250] As will be explored in the following chapter, a recurrent concern is that SRI merely tinkers with the market, largely perpetuating the problems of finance capitalism rather than transforming it. While SRI is not a protégé of neo-liberalism, the latter has certainly been one catalyst for its growth. Business case SRI helps to project a humane face to market transactions, to counter the avarice and hubris typically associated with unadulterated free market doctrines. Governments, in turn, encourage SRI because it helps to lessen the need for their responsibility to regulate the market.

B. PHILOSOPHIES AND METHODS OF SRI

1. Ethical and Financial Motivations

SRI incorporates disparate financial, social, and environmental objectives.[251] Traditionally, SRI's primary concern was "sin stocks": tobacco, armaments, gambling, alcohol, and pornography. While the collapse of South Africa's apartheid regime removed the SRI sector's most visible grievance, lately oppressive regimes in Burma and Sudan have become fresh targets for ethical divestment campaigns.[252] Other recent SRI causes or concerns include climate change, Indigenous peoples, animal liberation, fair trade, and even junk food. It has thus become a crowded smorgasbord of issues vying for investors' attention. The methods of SRI are as diverse as its causes, ranging from exclusionary screens to shareholder engagement.[253]

While conceivably all forms of investment may be viewed as "ethical," in the sense that any investment choice reflects some underlying values such as a belief that the accumulation of private wealth is socially beneficial, ethical investment refers to financing predicated on particular values beyond private economic gain. The ethically motivated strand of investment historically was closely associated with religious or charitable investors, comprising invest-ments chosen primarily on fundamental morality, rather than only on financial

---

250 M. Haigh and J. Hazelton, "Financial Markets: A Tool for Social Responsibility?" *Journal of Business Ethics* 52(1) (2004): 59, 66–67.

251 See P. Kinder, S. Lydenberg, and A. Domini, *The Social Investment Almanac* (Henry Holt, 1992).

252 See the Sudan Divestment Task Force, at http://www.sudandivestment.org.

253 C. Strandberg, *The Future of Socially Responsible Investment: Thought Leader Study* (Vancity Credit Union, 2005), 15.

considerations. While ethical investments differ from philanthropy, some entail below-market returns.[254] Although such investments were heavily based on deontological ethics (focusing on the rightness or wrongness of an act), they also now commonly derive from teleological ethics (focusing on the *consequences* of a particular action).[255]

Deontological ethics prescribe certain duties regardless of the consequences. Epitomized by Immanuel Kant's categorical imperatives, characterized by absolutism and normative universalizability, this ethos focuses on the principles that guide human conduct.[256] From such an ethical perspective, investors seek "peace of mind," without attempting to have an impact on corporate behavior. The deontological ethical investor thus wishes to avoid profiting from activities considered intrinsically immoral. This position is most closely associated with faith-based investors, shunning financial ties to pornography, gambling, and intoxicants.

Teleological ethics, by contrast, defines the morality of an action according to its consequences. Teleological ethics is associated with Jeremy Bentham's and John Stuart Mill's philosophy of utilitarianism.[257] The ultimate criterion of morality is some independent value that results from acts. William Irvine argues that "what makes certain investments morally objectionable is the fact that by making such investments, investors enable others to do wrong."[258] With its consequentialist orientation, this type of ethics treats SRI as a means to change the allocation of capital to promote sustainable development, for instance. Thus, Neil Carter and Meg Huby conceptualize SRI as a form of "ecological citizenship," whereby individuals assume

---

254 For example, the "One Percent Campaign" is a partnership launched in 2001 between the SIF and Co-op America, aiming to get responsible investors to dedicate at least 1 percent of their assets to community investments with a charitable aim: see http://www.communityinvest.org.

255 N. Carter and M. Huby, "Ecological Citizenship and Ethical Investment," *Environmental Politics* 14(2) (2005): 255 (exploring the different rationales of ethical investment for individual investors); and P.H. Dembinski, et al., "The Ethical Foundations of Responsible Investment," *Journal of Business Ethics* 48(2) (2003): 203.

256 H.J. Paton, *The Categorical Imperative; A Study in Kant's Moral Philosophy* (University of Pennsylvannia Press, 1971).

257 J. Bentham, *An Introduction to the Principles of Morals and Legislation* (first printed in 1780; Oxford University Press, 1996); J.S. Mill, *Utilitarianism* (first printed in 1863; Hackett Publishing, 2002).

258 W. Irvine, "The Ethics of Investing," *Journal of Business Ethics* 6 (1987): 233, 233.

non-contractual ethical responsibilities to reduce their ecological footprint by taking responsibility for companies they invest in.[259]

The interrelationship between these ethical approaches is complex. Some sustainable development issues of concern to teleological ethicists may also involve intrinsic values, such as the belief of some environmentalists in the inherent value of all life forms.[260] Conversely, a stance motivated by deontological ethics can hurt some forms of SRI. For instance, a moral taboo against financing gambling businesses may distress Indigenous communities who rely on casinos located on their reservations for revenue to finance their economic development and tribal governance.[261] Of course, while teleological or deontological-driven investors will not invest in activities contrary to their beliefs, and are prepared to suffer some financial sacrifice, ultimately they remain investors, not charities.[262]

In relation to the environmental dimensions and impacts of financial markets, a mature body of ethical principles concerning our relationship to the environment is available to inform ethical approaches to SRI.[263] Its impetus is to promote certain modes of moral reasoning and prescriptions for human conduct in relation to nature. Although "sustainability" is a contested discourse, an irrefutable unifying principle is the need to ensure ecological integrity by accepting fundamental restraints to use of the biosphere.[264] The field of ecological ethics provides a normative framework for responsible investors to implement the challenges of promoting sustainable development.[265]

However, the motivation to invest responsibly is commonly based on the prospect of financial advantage. While many social investors of course wish

---

259 Carter and Huby, note 255.

260 B. Devall and G. Sessions, *Deep Ecology—Living as if Nature Mattered* (Gibbs Smith, 2001).

261 See E. Darian-Smith, *New Capitalists: Law, Politics, and Identity Surrounding Casino Gaming on Native American Land* (Thomson Wadsworth, 2004).

262 A. Lewis, *Morals, Markets and Money* (Prentice Hall, 2002), 60–75. Although, inconsistently, some research indicates that investors may hold mixed portfolios of both SRI funds and conventional funds: A. Lewis and C. Mackenzie, "Morals, Money, Ethical Investing and Economic Psychology," *Human Relations* 53(2) (2000): 179.

263 A. Light and H. Rolston III, *Environmental Ethics: An Anthology* (Blackwell, 2002).

264 E.g., H. Henderson, "Beyond Economism: Toward Earth Ethics," in *The Earth Charter in Action: Toward a Sustainable World*, eds P. Corcoran, M. Vilela, and A. Roerink (KIT Publishers, 2005), 17.

265 See M.C. Cordonier Segger and A. Khalfan, *Sustainable Development Law: Principles, Practices, and Prospects* (Oxford University Press, 2004).

to render the market environmentally benign, their primary motivation is to be prosperous, not virtuous. Their assimilation of ESG issues into investment decisions can be financially rewarding, minimizing financial risks or yielding superior returns.[266] In 1987, in a prescient book that attempted to lay the conceptual foundations of modern SRI, Severyn Bruyn contended: "[s]ocial and economic values can be maximised together, and this creative synergism is the practical direction taken by social investors today."[267] The business case takes this amoral approach to SRI, whereby corporate social and environmental behavior is analyzed through the lens of financial materiality, risks, and returns.[268] The danger insufficiently appreciated by Bruyn is that social values may struggle to find a voice in such metrics, which tend to shift investors' focus from ends (such as making the world more humane and ecologically sustainable) to means (financial returns).

One of many possible examples of this outlook is the support institutional investors gave to the UK-initiated Extractive Industry Transparency Initiative,[269] to encourage oil, gas, and mining companies to disclose royalties and other payments to host countries for rights to exploit resources. Investors support the Initiative as a way to reduce the potential for corruption among host countries and thereby improve political and social stability, which presumably lessens financial risks of their portfolio companies.[270] These collateral social and political benefits matter to investors because their absence may affect their bottom line.

"Socially responsible investment" or just "responsible investment" is thus displacing "ethical investment" as the dominant parlance.[271] The change in

---

266 R. Chami, T.F. Cosimano, and C. Fullenkamp, "Managing Ethical Risk: How Investing in Ethics Adds Value," *Journal of Banking Finance* 26 (2002): 1697.

267 S.T. Bruyn, *The Field of Social Investment* (Cambridge University Press, 1987), 12.

268 M.R. Jayne and G. Skerratt, "Socially Responsible Investment in the UK—Criteria That Are Used to Evaluate Suitability," Corporate *Social Responsibility and Environmental Management* 10 (2003): 1.

269 See http://www.eitransparency.org.

270 "Investors' Statement on Transparency in the Extractives Sector," at http://www.eitransparency.org/UserFiles/File/investorsstatementoctober06.pdf; see further C. Williams, "Civil Society Initiatives and 'Soft Law' in the Oil and Gas Industry," *New York University Journal of International Law and Politics* 36 (2004): 457.

271 Sparkes and Cowton, note 46, 46.

language more readily accommodates the business case imperative.[272] A recent Canadian study predicted:

> SRI as an investment style will move away from exclusionary screening and best of class selection of stocks towards an integrated assessment of both financial and non-financial considerations. Rather than SRI functioning as a pre-investment decision, investment will consider financial and non-financial issues concurrently.[273]

This style of investor is also increasingly being described as the "universal investor," who looks at corporate social and environmental behavior in terms of its impact on the economy as a whole, in which the investor has ubiquitous stakes.[274]

While this trend to a more integrated and holistic investment analysis implies consigning ethical investment to a boutique niche, some financial institutions draw on both approaches. Mission-based investors and mainstream financiers interested in SRI sometimes work in tandem. Some religious investors sponsor shareholder resolutions that garner support from mainstream investors motivated primarily by financial considerations. For instance, the Missionary Oblates of Mary Immaculate and the Ethical Funds Company cooperated in 2006 to file a resolution against Alcan, the Canadian mining behemoth, calling on it to establish an independent advisory committee to develop recommendations to improve community relations and impact assessment for an Indian mining project.[275] In April 2007, the major Dutch pension funds, PGGM and ABP, divested their holdings in manufacturers of cluster bombs.[276]

---

272 A few commentators reject that this type of SRI is in fact "SRI" at all. Knoll contends, "SRI should also be distinguished from the practice of examining socially and politically charged factors that might impact on financial soundness, such as labor-relation practices and the history of compliance with environmental regulations." Knoll wrongly equates SRI with merely traditional ethical investment practices reliant on exclusionary screens: M.S. Knoll, "Ethical Screening in Modern Financial Markets: The Conflicting Claims Underlying Socially Responsible Investment," *Business Lawyer* 57 (2002): 681, 692.

273 Strandberg, note 253, 6.

274 S. Lydenberg, "Universal Investors and Socially Responsible Investors: A Tale of Emerging Affinities," *Corporate Governance: An International Review* 15(3) (2007): 467.

275 Ethical Funds Company, *Shareholder Action Program: 2006 Status Report* (Ethical Funds Company, 2007), 23.

276 "Dutch ABP, PGGM Say Sold Shares in Weapons Producers," *Reuters*, April 6, 2007.

This was largely a values-based decision reflecting changes in Dutch public opinion following widespread media outrage.

The business case philosophy may incorporate ethical imperatives indirectly through the lens of "reputational risks" and "enhanced" investment analysis to price those risks. "When an investor systematically integrates all relevant variables into their decision making there is no such thing as an extra-financial factor: just enhanced analytics," claims Hendrik du Toit of Investec Asset Management.[277] However, the rationale is to address risks to corporate value, not to uphold exogenous environmental or social values because they intrinsically warrant protection. Even with "enhanced analysis," some values may be overlooked either because they have no material financial relevance or countervailing economic considerations override.

The differences between business and ethical approaches to SRI can be illustrated by the following examples of banking lending, which require considering both the environmental effects of the activities financed and the terms of the loan. Suppose an ethically-minded bank provides a loan for construction of a wind farm, with the interest rate discounted by 0.25 percent to reward the environmental benefits of the project. The bank supports the project because it is truly committed to sustainable development despite a lower profit margin. Alternatively another bank may finance a solar energy facility at a higher market interest rate due to perceived additional market risks linked to this emerging technology. While both loans finance environmentally positive activities, only the first rewards the investment and ethical foresight. Although the second loan does generate environmental benefits despite the lender, finance on inferior market terms is hardly laudable. Similarly, where a bank undertakes an environmental risk assessment and charges higher interest to compensate for the liability hazards, this is not necessarily environmentally proactive. It may be simply protecting itself against the costs of future liabilities. An ethical bank may have rejected the prospective borrower's project altogether.

The following discussion canvasses specific methods used by responsible investors, whether motivated ethically or financially.

2. Screens

In SRI parlance, portfolios are commonly subject to both positive and negative social screens.[278] All portfolios, whether based on SRI or conventional

277 Quoted in B. Baue, "Applying an Ant Colony Mentality to Extra-Financial Factors and Enhanced Analytics," *Social Funds Sustainability Investment News*, May 30, 2006.

278 P. Kinder, "Social Screening: Paradigms Old and New," *The Journal of Investing* 6(Winter) (1997): 12.

investment strategies, use screens to choose securities. For SRI, a negative screen excludes companies involved in activities identified by the financial institution as inappropriate. Thus, for instance, the Parnassus Fund in the US promises not to invest in companies that manufacture alcohol, tobacco, or weapons, or companies involved in gambling or nuclear power generation.[279] Conversely, a positive screen favors firms perceived as particularly desirable. Domini Social Equity, to illustrate, seeks companies engaged in innovative and generous charitable giving programs, companies with women and minorities in management positions, good employee relations, and exemplary respect for the environment.[280] Another screening method is norms-based screens, which look for compliance with international standards on social and environmental issues. Screens are also used to construct SRI market indexes (discussed later), on which funds may base their portfolio selections.

Reflective of the primacy of financial imperatives, some SRI funds apply their screens only after they have prescreened companies using conventional financial criteria. Meritas Mutual Funds, for instance, claims to select firms "displaying strong financial fundamentals," in addition to ESG criteria.[281] The result is that some firms' sustainability performance while exemplary may still be excluded from a fund's investment universe because of suspect financial performance. On the other hand, some SRI market index providers, such as KLD Research and Analytics, purport to construct their index criteria solely with regard to ESG factors; any evaluation of financial performance is made retrospectively.[282]

When asset managers hold wide discretionary powers and are measured on short-term financial performance, they may fail to implement satisfactorily vague screening criteria. Many funds do not provide a clear framework to apply screens. For instance, at what point is a firm's participation in a prescribed activity sufficient to justify screening? SRI methods may also have difficultly taking into account indirect and secondary effects. Would an SRI fund that excludes investment in munitions manufacture also exclude investment in a mining company that supplies materials to armaments producers? Or would an SRI screen against pornography capture hotel chains that distribute in-room, cable TV adult movies? Screens may discount business activities conducted through franchises, subsidiaries, contractors and other

---

279 Http://www.parnassus.com.
280 Http://www.domini.com/domini-funds/Domini-Social-Equity-Fund.
281 Http://www.meritas.ca/invest.shtml.
282 See, e.g., the methodology for its Global Sustainability Index, at http://www.kld.com/indexes/gsindex/methodology.html.

types of partnerships. The activities of the parent firm may be acceptable, but not its affiliates from which it profits.

3. Best-of-Sector

The "best-of-sector" or "best-in-class" method offers seemingly even more flexibility than screens. Instead of a one-dimensional view of corporate behavior, investors choose firms that perform best in their economic sector according to various performance indicators.[283] This approach builds on the assumption that corporate environmental and social behavior should be judged relative to an industry sector's average performance because only firms operating in the same sector face comparable sustainability challenges. Thus, whereas an ethical screen might exclude the entire oil industry because of climate change concerns, the best-of-sector method would condone the oil company that had done the most to diversify its energy portfolio to include renewable energies. Or, in relation to alcoholic beverages, this method would favor firms that had best promoted responsible product advertising and responsible drinking, and contributed most to their local economy such as by using resident suppliers.[284] One example is the HESTA "Eco Pool" in Australia, which explains its methodology as follows:

> Companies are classified according to industry sectors—such as insurance, telecommunications and building materials. They are then evaluated and rated for environmental management/sustainability practices within their sector. In conjunction with being assessed for healthy financial performance, investments are made in the best-rated companies in each sector based on environmental/sustainability performance. ...[285]

Others methods to determine the best performers are available. For example, Canada's Ethical Funds Company rates firms on a scorecard of 120 performance

---

283 T.W.M. Van den Brink and F. Van der Woerd, "Industry Specific Sustainability Benchmarks: An ECSF Pilot Bridging Corporate Sustainability with Social Responsible Investments," *Journal of Business Ethics* 55 (2004): 187.

284 See session on "Next Generation Sin Screens: What to do with Alcohol, Gambling, and Tobacco in SRI Investment Portfolios" (18th Annual SRI in the Rockies Conference, Santa Ana Pueblo, New Mexico, November 3–6, 2007).

285 HESTA Super Fund, "Socially Responsible Investing," at http://www.hesta.com.au/content.asp?document_id=159.

indicators based on international standards such as the GRI, investing only in firms meeting minimum scores.[286]

The best-in-class method may be more onerous to implement than simple ethical screens, as investors must scrutinize corporate performance in detail, and how a firm compares to its peers. Such information is often not readily available or easy to obtain. Yet this method may offer companies stronger incentives to improve their behavior. In comparison, screens may lead to whole sectors being ostracized from investment portfolios without regard to material differences in firms' efforts to improve their social or environmental performance.[287]

4. Financial Risk Management

This method of SRI is closest to the business case ethos. It purports to consider ESG issues only when financially "material" to the investor, if they pose risks and liabilities, or may boost financial returns.[288] While it can be an SRI technique in its own right, financial risk management also can serve as an adjunct methodology to other techniques, such as helping to pick "best-in-class" companies.

The traditional approach to assessing materiality in corporate or project valuation regards information as material if its omission or misstatement could influence investment decisions. SRI incorporates ESG factors into this framework where a polluting firm poses liability or reputational risks.[289] Conversely, a firm designing new environmental technologies and products to meet market demand may appeal to investors on financial grounds alone. Risk affects the cost of capital. In equity financing, investors will expect higher returns (dividends and appreciating stock prices) to offset increased risk that may arise from regulatory sanctions or reputational harm to business goodwill. In project financing, bank lenders take into account risks associated with a firm generally and specific projects it wishes to fund. Firms with abnormally high risks associated with poor environmental management could pay a higher cost of capital.

---

286 Ethical Funds Company, *A Guidebook to Sustainable Investing* (Ethical Funds Company, 2005), 12–13.

287 Personal communication, Michael Jantzi, President, Jantzi Research (Toronto, November 15, 2007).

288 Brokerage House Analysts, *The Materiality of Social Environmental and Corporate Governance Issues to Equity Pricing* (UNEPFI, 2004).

289 R. Crowe, *Risk, Returns and Responsibility* (Association of British Insurers and Innovest, 2004).

Substantial research now validates the value of this form of risk management, as detailed further in chapter 3. A 2004 study commissioned by the UK Environment Agency reviewed the literature on the relationship between corporate environmental management and financial performance.[290] It concluded that: "[i]n 85% of the total number of studies assessed, we found a positive correlation between environmental governance and/or events, and financial performance."[291] These indicators of financial performance commonly include shareholder value, share price, operating costs, and reputational risks.[292]

Investors do not necessarily measure financially materiality in the same way.[293] As universal investors with stakes throughout the economy, to large pension plans, what is financially "material" can be very broad. The pension fund sector has a relatively low risk tolerance, because it tends to carry a large exposure over long investment periods. By contrast, venture capital funds with a different business model bear much higher risk. Environmental risks tend to be more financially material to long-term institutional investors and of lesser significance to investors driven by a short-term considerations.

Yet, for all investors, John Ganzi and Anne DeVries predict that where the general financial risk to an investment is high, environmental or social risks *per se* will likely be considered relatively immaterial to the transaction.[294] Often environmental issues are perceived as immaterial, as investors cannot readily quantify the nature and extent of their potential financial significance.[295] While the financial sector is increasingly aware of climate change risks, for instance, investors often struggle to find ways to measure and quantify that risk.

The banking industry has gone the furthest in due diligence scrutiny of ESG risks.[296] Lenders seek to protect themselves from direct environmental

---

290 Innovest and Environment Agency, *Corporate Environmental Governance* (UK Environment Agency, 2004).

291 Ibid., 1.

292 Ibid., 7.

293 Ernst and Young, *The Materiality of Environmental Risk to Australia's Finance Sector* (Commonwealth of Australia, 2003), 17–18.

294 J. Ganzi and A. DeVries, *Corporate Environmental Performance as a Factor in Financial Industry Decisions* (US Environmental Protection Agency, 1998).

295 See B. Gentry and L. Fernandez, *Valuing the Environment: How Fortune 500 CFOs and Analysts Measure Corporate Performance* (UNDP Office of Development Studies, 1997).

296 A. Hoijtink, *The Sustainability Attitude of Commercial Banks* (University of Tilburg, 2005); G. McKenzie and S. Wolfe, "The Impact of Environmental

liabilities as well as to protect their borrowers from insolvency.[297] In some jurisdictions lenders face liability risks if they fail to undertake due diligence checks, become too immersed in their borrower's business, or take possession of loan security.[298] Further, they face reputational risks if associated with "funding" controversial projects. Barclays Bank was thus targeted by NGOs because of its funding of Asia Pulp and Paper's controversial logging activities.[299] Lenders, sometimes locked into long-term relationships with borrowers, cannot as easily divest as equity investors. Thus, banks increasingly assess prospective borrowers against their environmental track-records and the specific risks posed by the loan application.[300] They may also incorporate environmental protection covenants into the loan agreement.[301] Ideally, the cost of credit will reflect any residual environmental risks.

5. SRI Index Tracking

A market index is a basket of securities selected to represent and reflect a particular market. SRI indexes are distinctive by listing only firms that meet social and environmental criteria set by the index provider. The first SRI indexes were developed by Good Money in 1976 as alternatives to the Dow Jones Industrial and Utility Averages.[302] The SRI-based index can serve as a template for the investor's own portfolio. For example, the Meritas Jantzi Social Index Fund is passively managed according to the composition of Canada's Jantzi Social Index.[303] Some SRI mutual families maintain their own SRI index, which serves to shape the investment portfolios of funds in

Risk on the UK Banking Sector," *Applied Financial Economics* 14 (2004): 1005; T. McDermott, A. Stainer, and L. Stainer, "Contaminated Land: Bank Credit Risk for Small and Medium Size UK Enterprises," *International Journal of Environmental Technology and Management* 5 (2005): 1.

297 B.J. Richardson, "Environmental Liability and Banks: Recent European Developments," *Journal of International Banking Law* 17 (2000): 289, 290.
298 See discussion on lender liability in chapter 5.
299 Friends of the Earth (FoE), *Paper Tiger, Hidden Dragons* (FoE, May 2001).
300 E.g., Deutsche Bank, *Lending Policy—Or, How We Integrate Environmentally Relevant Aspects into Our Credit Decisions*, at http://www.umwelt.deutsche-bank.de/en/8_145.htm.
301 See T. Zimmerman, "An Approach to Writing Loan Agreements Covenants," in *Classics in Commercial Bank Lending*, ed. W.W. Sihler (Robert Morris Associates, 1981), 213.
302 J.A. Brill and A. Reder, *Investing From the Heart: The Guide to Socially Responsible Investments and Money Management* (Crown Publishers, 1993), 388–89.
303 Meritas, *Simplified Prospectus* (Meritas, January 2007), 12–13.

the family, such as the Calvert Social Index Fund.[304] Other SRI indexes are provided by third parties and sometimes associated with major international stock exchanges, such as the Dow Jones Sustainability Indexes[305] and the Financial Times Stock Exchange (FTSE) 4Good series.[306] Emerging markets are also establishing SRI indexes, such as the OWW Consulting Responsibility Malaysia SRI Index.[307] The workings of these SRI indexes are canvassed in chapter 6.

SRI indexes commonly use a mix of screens and best-in-class methods. The index provider appoints a committee that determines selection criteria and hires a research provider to assess companies' sustainability performance against those criteria. The committee may add or remove firms from an index, based on changes in SRI criteria or variations in a company's sustainability performance. Passive index-based SRI strategies work for equity markets, but some other asset classes such as real estate and venture finance are not easily indexed.

6. Advocacy and Engagement

Investors sometimes prefer to influence corporate behavior from "within" through the exercise of shareholder rights, dialogue, and informal engagement with management.[308] Engagement and activism has become a preferred strategy for many large institutional investors because it is considered more in line with fiduciary duties than exclusionary screens.[309] Engagement however tends to be ad hoc in comparison to screening unless undertaken pursuant to specific corporate codes of conduct. Shareholder advocacy has gained prominence after passive investment styles made investors complicit in corporate scandals and resultant losses. Shareholder activism for SRI arose in the US, beginning at Eastman Kodak in 1966,[310] where it remains more common

304 Http://www.calvert.com.
305 Http://www.sustainability-index.com.
306 Http://www.ftse4good.com.
307 See http://www.oww-consulting.com.
308 A.K. Prevost and R.P. Rao, "Of What Value are Shareholder Proposals Sponsored by Public Pension Funds?" *Journal of Business* 73(2) (2000): 177.
309 For instance, the Canada Pension Plan professes to rely mainly on engagement and activism: remarks by B. Barnett, Manager, Responsible Investing, CPP Investment Board (2007 Canadian Responsible Investment Conference, Montreal, May 27–29, 2007).
310 D. Vogel, *Lobbying the Corporation* (Basic Books, 1978), 31–35.

than other jurisdictions.[311] Institutional investors increasingly revere share-holder rights such as proxy voting as an asset to utilize and protect.

Methods of advocacy include voting in shareholder meetings, submitting proposals for the agenda of such meetings,[312] proposing nominees for or elect-ing the board of directors, expressing specific concerns to the board and making public statements, and media communications.[313] Informal engage-ment and dialogue alone can sometimes achieve desired changes without the necessity to intimidate management by lodging a shareholder resolution. Consider the following policy statement of the Calvert family of SRI funds, which outlines some of these methods:

> **Dialogue with company executives and managers**. We regularly initiate conversations with management as part of our social research process. After we've become a shareholder, we continue our dialogue with management through phone calls, letters, and meetings. Through our interactions, we learn about management's successes and challeng-es and try to press for improvement in specific areas of concern.
>
> **Proxy voting**. As company shareholders, Calvert votes on issues of corporate governance and social responsibility at annual stockholder meetings. We take our responsibility seriously and vote each proxy in a manner consistent with the financial and social objectives of our Funds, in support of most social shareholder resolutions. ...
>
> **Shareholder resolutions**.... In 1986, Calvert Social Investment Fund (CSIF) became the first mutual fund to file a shareholder resolution—with the Angelica Corporation on labor/management issues.

---

311 See the Institutional Shareholder's surveys on shareholder activism for SRI at: http://www.ishareowner.com.

312 A shareholder proposal, whereby eligible shareholders can request company boards to undertake specified actions, can be published in the company's annual proxy statement, and all the company's shareholders vote to endorse or reject the proposal: R. Monks, et al., "Shareholder Activism on Environmental Issues: A Study of Proposals at Large U.S. Corporations (2000–2003)," *Natural Resources Forum* 28 (2004): 317, 317–19.

313 R. Sullivan and C. Mackenzie, "Shareholder Activism on Social, Ethical and Environmental Issues: An Introduction," in *Responsible Investment*, note 177, 150, 153; and W.F. Mahoney. *The Active Shareholder: Exercising Your Rights, Increasing Your Profits, and Minimizing Your Risks* (John Wiley and Sons, 1993).

Today, Calvert funds continue to propose shareholder resolutions on a variety of issues that concern us. We generally file shareholder resolutions when our dialogue with corporate managers is unsuccessful in persuading a company to take action. In most cases, our efforts have led to negotiated settlements with mutually beneficial results for shareholders and companies.[314]

Sometimes NGO activists buy shares in firms solely as a means to apply pressure for corporate change.[315] For instance, Friends of the Earth purchased £30,000 of Balfour Beatty stock to lobby the UK construction company against its involvement in a controversial Turkish dam.[316] Likewise, Amnesty International's Business Group in 2004 brought shares in Swedish companies as a means of engaging with them to improve their stance on human rights.[317] Terrence Guay and others observe that "[b]ecause of their public profile and stakeholder status, NGOs may influence corporate governance to a degree disproportionate to the shares owned."[318] This activism complements moves by some NGOs, such as the Sierra Club, to launch their own SRI funds.[319]

To enhance their leverage, shareholders also collaborate both within individual firms and across economic sectors. Collaborative networks include the Institutional Investors' Group on Climate Change, the Pharmaceutical Shareowner Group, and the Interfaith Center on Corporate Responsibility. These cooperative mechanisms enable investors to impart a unified position on SRI issues, "thereby ensuring that companies are not facing competing and contradictory priorities from different investors."[320]

Such activism is also driven by the potential benefits of investing in companies with robust corporate governance. In a review of the activism conducted by the California Public Employees' Retirement System (CalPERS), Michael Smith found: "the evidence indicates that shareholder activism is

---

314 Calvert, *Shareholder Advocacy*, http://www.calvert.com/sri_648.html.

315 Guay, Doh, and Sinclair, note 180.

316 A. Hay, "Ethical Activists Buy Stocks to Force Change," *Planet Ark Daily News,* February 27, 2002.

317 E. Sjöström, "The Financial Market as a Vehicle for Protecting Human Rights: On Shareholder Activism" (paper presented at the 12th International Sustainable Development Research Conference (Hong Kong, April 6–8, 2006), 6–8.

318 Guay, Doh, and Sinclair, note 180, 134.

319 W. Baue, "Sierra Club Launches SRI Mutual Funds," *Social Funds Sustainability Investment News,* January 15 2003.

320 Sullivan and Mackenzie, note 313, 155.

largely successful in changing governance structure, and, when successful, results in a statistically significant increase in shareholder wealth."[321] Improving corporate governance to align the decisions of management with shareholders, such as having more independent directors on boards and more impartial auditing, can help to reduce costly agency problems.

Activism and engagement may also occur among debt financiers. Unlike shareholders, banks and bondholders do not have the right to vote or file resolutions. But banks may engage with borrowers to help manage environmental risks and impacts; this engagement might range from friendly advice to imposition of conditions in a loan agreement. The bond market has recently become a more active domain for SRI.[322] Bondholders may also ventilate concerns informally with corporate managers through meetings and correspondence. Insight Investment, a UK asset management firm geared to SRI, engages with companies in which it holds or proposes to purchase bonds, seeing engagement as necessary as ESG "issues can be material to the likelihood of default by a company on the bonds it has issued."[323]

7. Economically Targeted Investment (ETI)

ETI provides collateral benefits to assist regional economies and local communities.[324] Through investment commonly in small private companies, ETI seeks to stimulate local economies through job creation, development, and savings. It also assists business creation, increases in the stock of affordable housing, and improvement of local infrastructure. A range of financial institutions may practice ETI, including cooperative banks and credit unions, special community development loan funds, and community-focused venture capital funds.[325] One example in Canada is the network

---

321 M. Smith, "Shareholder Activism by Institutional Investors: Evidence from CalPERS," *Journal of Finance* 51 (1996): 227, 251.

322 S. Grene, "Bond Investors Enter World of SRI," *Financial Times (FT.Com)*, September 12, 2007.

323 K. ten Kate and A. Evans, "Integrating Governance, Social, Ethical and Environmental Issues into the Corporate Bond Investment Process," in *Responsible Investment*, note 177, 92, 102.

324 See A. Sauchik, "Beyond Economically Targeted Investments: Redefining the Legal Framework of Pension Fund Investments in Low-to-Moderate Income Residential Real Estate," *Fordham Urban Law Journal* 28(6) (2001): 1923.

325 P. Camejo, *The SRI Advantage: Why Socially Responsible Investing has Outperformed Financially* (New Society Publishers, 2002), 217–18.

of "labour-sponsored investment funds" (LSIF), created under provincial legislation.[326]

A special kind of ETI is known as microfinance. It arose from a philanthropic rather than a commercial model. Generally, microfinance describes the practice of providing financial services including microcredit, insurance, savings facilities, and financial literacy education for empowering poor people.[327] It often involves small loans made to low-income individuals (particularly women) and communities to sustain self-employment or to begin small businesses. Microfinance serves to help people excluded from the financial sector, thus breaking the perpetuation of poverty and social exclusion.[328] Increasingly, civil society groups harness microfinance as a tool for a wider agenda, to promote grass-roots sustainable development. The microfinance movement has grown rapidly since the 1970s, and 2005 was designated by the UN as the "International Year of Microcredit."[329] A 2005 study conducted by the Wharton Business School counted more than 500 microfinance institutions worldwide, having loaned US$7 billion to some thirty million small business people—indicative of the size but not necessarily the impact of the sector.[330]

Traditionally, the microfinance institutional sector has comprised not-for-profit organizations, which have relied mainly on grants and soft loans from international donors. Credit unions are also significant providers of microfinance services.[331] Lately the sector has become more commercialized, with some banks designing microfinance portfolios, such as Deutsche Bank,[332] and the National Australia Bank (NAB),[333] and several institutions such as

326 J. Quarter, et al., "Social Investment by Union-Based Pension Funds and Labour-Sponsored Investment Funds in Canada," *Industrial Relations* 56(1) (2001): 92.
327 For an overview, see J.L. Fernando, ed., *Microfinance: Perils and Prospects* (Routledge, 2006); and see articles in the *Journal of Microfinance*.
328 C. Cuevas, "Sustainable Banking for the Poor," *Journal of International Development* 8(2) (1996): 145.
329 Http://www.yearofmicrocredit.org.
330 Wharton Business School, *Microcredit is Becoming Profitable, Which Means New Players and New Problems* (April 20, 2005), http://knowledge.wharton.upenn.edu. See also M. Robinson, *The Microfinance Revolution: Sustainable Finance for the Poor* (World Bank, 2005).
331 See the work for the World Council of Credit Unions: http://www.woccu.org.
332 K. Tully, "Charity that Offers Fair Profit," *Financial Times (FT.Com)*, July 29, 2007.
333 NAB, *Establishing a Microenterprise Development and Loans Program in Australia* (NAB, 2006).

Citigroup and ABN AMRO have packaged microfinance facilities for developing country clients.[334] The leading microfinance provider is undoubtedly the Grameen Bank, whose efforts to create economic and social development in rural Bangladesh were recognized by a Nobel Peace prize in 2005.[335] The Grameen Bank was established in 1976 and, as of January 2008, served approximately 7.5 million borrowers (overwhelmingly women) in some 80,000 villages in Bangladesh.[336] Through the Grameen Foundation, the Bank has partnered with an international network of microfinance institutions to disseminate the Grameen philosophy.[337]

Current microfinancing mechanisms generally fail to meet the enormous demand.[338] Numerous market, institutional, and regulatory barriers hinder mainstream financiers' involvement in microfinancing. These include: lack of fit with traditional investment strategies; regulatory restrictions to financing in what is perceived as a more risky sector offering mediocre returns; greater transactional costs administering numerous miniscule loans; and the problem that shares in microfinance institutions are not typically tradable, impacting liquidity.[339] The growing commercialization of the sector suggests these barriers are diminishing, but with the risk that heightened profitability imperatives may taint the original charitable mission.

8. SRI Products and Services

SRI can also include specific eco-friendly retail products and services for individuals and businesses. Green car loans, eco-savings deposits, energy efficiency mortgages, and charity-affinity credit cards are among the various offerings. Commonly provided by banks and credit unions, they allow consumers to reduce their individual environmental footprint.[340]

Some lenders sell "green mortgages" to meet consumer demand for eco-friendly, energy-efficient houses. These lending schemes, which vary in

334 Stichele, note 11, 107.
335 M.K. Hassan and L. Renteria-Guerrero, "The Experience of the Grameen Bank of Bangladesh in Community Development," *International Journal of Social Economics* 24(12) (1997): 1488. The Bank's founder, Professor Muhammad Yunus, also won the award.
336 Http://www.grameen-info.org.
337 Http://www.grameenfoundation.org.
338 J. Meehan, *Tapping Financial Markets for Microfinance* (Grameen Foundation USA, 2005), 1.
339 Ibid., 13–14.
340 UNEPFI, North American Taskforce, *Green Financial Products and Services* (UNEPFI, 2007), 15.

criteria and benefits, generally offer borrowers higher credit ratios and, some-times, lower interest rates.[341] The ING Bank for instance allows buyers of sustainably designed houses to negotiate a mortgage at 1 or 2 percent below market rates.[342] This principle has been extended to car loans. Australia's Mecu credit union offers a goGreen car loan that differentiates the applicable interest rate on the approximate environmental impact of the vehicle.[343] VanCity in Canada also offers differential interest rates for financing energy efficient houses and cars.[344] Bendigo Bank, in Australia, markets differential interest rates to encourage purchases of high-efficiency appliances and a range of home renovation services to improve environmental performance.[345]

For savers, some banks provide linked deposit products that can mobilize capital for SRI. The concept is that banks will only invest funds deposited in such an account for specified social and environmental purposes. These schemes have been most successful in the Netherlands, fueled by specific government tax incentives for SRI. In the US, Chittenden Bank offers deposit accounts that support green lending programs.[346] Westpac, an Australian lender, runs a Landcare Term Deposit, where the bank lends support to farmers for sustainable agriculture practices equivalent to every dollar deposited.[347]

Some banks also incorporate environmental and social fringe benefits into credit card services.[348] The UK's Co-operative Bank issues credit affinity cards with Oxfam, Greenpeace, and other charitable or civic institutions. These partnered NGOs receive donations from income generated by the credit card users.[349] The Scandinavian Swedbank developed a World Nature Card in collaboration with the WWF, where 0.5 percent of the total card payment transactions fund the NGO's projects in Scandinavia.[350] Dutch bank Rabobank offers a Climate Credit Card that earmarks money innovatively to the WWF. The size of the donation depends on the energy-intensity of the service or product bought with the card.[351]

---

341 See, e.g., S. Brady, "Fannie Mae/NAHB Launch Effort to Develop 'Green' Mortgages," *Professional Builder* 6 (1999): 1.
342 Http://www.ing.com; Labatt and White, note 189, 72.
343 Http://www.mecu.com.au/index_general.asp?menuid=020.090.010.
344 Http://www.vancity.com.
345 Http://www.bendigobank.com.au.
346 Http://www.chittenden.com.
347 Http://www.westpac.com.au.
348 UNEPFI, note 340, 17.
349 Http://www.co-operativebank.co.uk.
350 Http://www.swedbank.com.
351 UNEPFI, note 340, 17.

C. CONCLUSIONS

Ostensibly, SRI has become a vibrant movement indulged in by an array of institutions. Social investors deploy a miscellany of techniques to exert leverage, including screening, targeted investment, and shareholder advocacy. Crucial to SRI's broader acceptance has been its transformation from faith-based, ethical investment to a business case model. By appealing to the bottom line, SRI has garnered many more adherents. While SRI is not a mainstream feature of finance capitalism, it is no longer commonly viewed derogatively as an eccentric backwater.

Strategically accommodating rather than renouncing finance capitalism, SRI has also courted danger. While engaging with banks, mutual funds, and other financiers is necessary to advance sustainable development, the nature of this cooperation may have eviscerated SRI's raison d'être. The increasingly rare use of the term "ethical investment" testifies to its changing purpose and methods. As the next chapter explores, despite some positive benefits, business case SRI is no assurance for ending the unsustainable market practices. The following discussion examines the impact of SRI, exploring the size of the market and its capacity to leverage change through divestment, shareholder advocacy, and other means.

CHAPTER 3

SRI's Challenges and Impact

I. Business-as-Usual or a Shift to Sustainability?

A. INTRODUCTION

Does SRI tangibly impact social and environmental issues or is it merely given a platform within the "status quo," with financial institutions continuing to sponsor and profit from unsustainable practices? This chapter assesses the SRI market to determine whether it is mere parlance or actually effects transformation towards sustainability. While the analysis focuses on SRI in the developed country economies, which presently dominate the responsible investment market, much of the argument is equally applicable to SRI in emerging markets.[1] In a global economy, business case imperatives have shaped SRI worldwide.[2]

---

1 See sessions on "Principles for Responsible Investment in Emerging Markets Asia-Pacific," and "Hidden Treasure: The Sustainable Upside to Emerging Markets" (UNEPFI Global Roundtable, Melbourne, Australia, October 24–25, 2007).

2 See International Finance Corporation (IFC) and SustainAbility, *Developing Value: The Business Case for Sustainability in Emerging Markets* (IFC, 2002).

If SRI is to provide a path to sustainability, incremental changes to financial markets will likely be insufficient. The financial sector hinders sustainable development in many ways, including a bias to short-term investment, externalization of many social and environmental costs of investment, and limited valuation and promotion of ethical behavior. Imaginative and determined reform is likely necessary to overcome ingrained habits and entrenched self-interest. Nick Robins of Henderson Global Investors believes: "[a]chieving sustainable development is set to involve profound changes in the structure and dynamics or the global economy, a shift that is likely to be as disruptive as any the investment world has faced."[3]

Most SRI seeks to influence change rather than to refute that economic system altogether. Contemporary SRI does not generally challenge the hallowed institutions of private property, corporations, and global markets, or other pillars of finance capitalism. Ceding control over investment decisions to the holders of capital appears to foreclose other means of directing finance for sustainability, such as greater state or societal control. Yet the gravity of our ecological problems is such that the present system of finance capitalism may ultimately not have any place in our future if we are to have one. Thus, it is necessary to first outline some of the principal ways the prevailing economic system creates environmental problems before reviewing how successfully SRI has responded to these challenges.

B. CAPITALISM AND NATURE

We live in an age of seemingly great economic bounty and material abundance. Industrialization, the rise of consumerism, and the ascendancy of the global marketplace have fueled exponential increases in production, trade, and lifted millions out of poverty. Yet, parallel to these immense strides, capitalism and markets have engendered some deeply troubling social and ecological problems that suggest some fundamental constraints to our use of nature.

Humanity often acts brazenly as though the Earth's resources are infinitely abundant and free.[4] We derive innumerable economic and life-support

3 N. Robins, "Shaping the Market: Investor Engagement in Public Policy," in *Responsible Investment*, eds R. Sullivan and C. Mackenzie (Greenleaf Publishing, 2006), 312, 313.
4 Its economic value is undoubtedly staggering, and was quantified by one notorious study in 1997 at somewhere between US$16–54 trillion annually, dwarfing a then annual global gross economic product of about

benefits from natural ecosystems, for which there appear to be no substitutes.[5] In economists' jargon, "critical natural capital" denotes these superlative natural resources that perform vital and irreplaceable functions for humanity.[6] Ecological economists have tremendously deepened our understanding of the economic value of the environment, pricing both marginal changes in the flow of services of environmental assets,[7] to valuing the entire stock of natural capital.[8] Yet the market can behave in short-sighted ways that disregard such critical values.

Many economists also laud the market as crucial to human welfare.[9] On the one hand, markets may help mitigate environmental problems through competitive pressures for pioneering innovative green technologies, allocating capital for environmental protection, and pricing pollution risks. Financial markets should be intrinsically relevant to the sustainability goal of maintaining natural and human capital for future generations, as they mobilize capital through loans and investments with the aim that it should grow and derive a certain return.[10] Mark White concludes, "[t]here is nothing inherent in the structure of the financial system which necessarily leads to environmental destruction."[11] From this benign perspective, financial capital is simply a fungible entity. In other words, it is a store of wealth supposedly reflecting the value derived from other forms of capital whose use depends on variables external to the financial system.

US$18 trillion: R. Costanza, et al., "The Value of the World's Ecosystem Services and National Capital," *Nature* 389 (1997): 253.

5 See G.C. Daily, *Nature's Services: Societal Dependence on Natural Ecosystems* (Island Press, 1997); Y. Baskin and P.R. Ehrlich, *The Work of Nature: How the Diversity of Life Sustains Us* (Island Press, 1998); T. Prugh, et al., *Natural Capital and Human Economic Survival* (2nd ed., CRC Press, 1999).

6 See J.F. Noel and M. O'Connor, "Strong Sustainability and Critical Natural Capital," in *Valuation for Sustainable Development: Methods and Policy Indicators*, eds S. Faucheux and M. O'Connor (Edward Elgar Publishing, 1998), 75.

7 K.G. Willis, K. Button, and P. Nijkamp, eds, *Environmental Valuation* (Edward Elgar Publishing, 1999).

8 D. Azqueta and D. Sotelsek, "Valuing Nature: From Environmental Impacts to Natural Capital," *Ecological Economics* 63(1) (2007): 22.

9 See generally K. Midgley and R. Burns, *The Capital Market: Its Nature and Significance* (Macmillan, 1977).

10 See R.W. England, "Natural Capital and the Theory of Economic Growth," *Ecological Economics* 34(3) (2000): 425 (discussing the analytical relationship between capital accumulation, economic growth and the natural world).

11 M.A. White, "Environmental Finance: Value and Risk in an Age of Ecology," *Business Strategy and the Environment* 5 (1996): 198, 200.

In practice, financial markets intensify exploitation and transform natural capital into social and manufactured capital for human consumption. Ease of access to capital through financial markets removes corporate financial constraints that may otherwise prevent firms from exploiting nature in profoundly unsustainable ways. Thus, while financial institutions' portfolios have recorded stunning growth in recent decades, that growth has coincided with massive depletion of natural capital. The ozone layer has thinned, the atmosphere has warmed, and wildlife has become less abundant.[12] And, on the social side, the divide between the rich and the poor, both within and across nations, has widened. The mountain of goods and services funded by financial markets cannot adequately substitute for such losses to nature's life-sustaining properties.[13] Even the role of financial markets in creating social and manufactured capital is not beyond reproach. The financial system is too often associated with speculative, ephemeral, and short-term activities appearing to contribute little to social and economic infrastructure requiring a longer term focus.[14] Robert Shiller's vituperative *Irrational Exuberance* is among the most sensational dissections of the market, revealing how investors' greed, ignorance, and herd-like behavior have fuelled economically harmful speculative bubbles.[15]

While humanity's hubris towards nature has much deeper cultural and biological explanations than can be blamed on financial markets,[16] they are linked to our worst environmental problems. The relentless degradation of nature nearly wherever touched by capitalism has left a legacy that suggests that we have not reached Francis Fukuyama's arrogant proclamation of the "End of History."[17] A likely more accurate outlook is John McMurtry's *The Cancer Stage of Capitalism*, metaphorically suggesting that the economy's looting of

---

12 Worldwatch Institute, *Vital Signs 2006–2007* (Worldwatch Institute, 2006).

13 J. O'Neill, *Ecology, Policy and Politics: Human Well-Being and the Natural World* (Routledge, 1993), 107–10.

14 F. Jameson, "Culture and Finance Capitalism," *Critical Inquiry* 24(1) (1997): 246, 247; A. Harmes, *Unseen Power: How Mutual Funds Threaten the Political and Economic Wealth of Nations* (Stoddard, 2001), 76.

15 R.J. Shiller, *Irrational Exuberance* (Princeton University Press, 2000).

16 Leading works include: S. Boyden, *Western Civilization in Biological Perspective: Patterns in Biohistory* (Oxford University Press, 1987); J. Diamond, *Collapse: How Societies Choose to Fail or Succeed* (Penguin Books, 2004).

17 F. Fukuyama, *The End of History and the Last Man* (Penguin Books, 1992) (arguing that the triumphant global success of capitalist liberal democracy is the final stage in human history).

nature exhibits all the signs characteristic of a carcinogenic invasion.[18] Ecological economists explain the interface between nature and economic activity, highlighting ingrained market weaknesses to respect environmental constraints. These weaknesses have been conceptualized in various ways, including the fugitive "externalities" of private development,[19] degradation of public goods such as the atmosphere,[20] undervaluation of ecological amenities and characteristics such as biodiversity,[21] myopic decision-making ignoring impacts on posterity[22] and, above all, an addiction to economic growth.[23] Underlying all such weaknesses is that the market has separated from environmental restraints by making the foundations of capitalism individual self-interest, competition, and autonomy.

Economists and policy-makers have advanced various theories and methods for reversing these trends.[24] Contrary to Ernst Schumacher and others who favor radically alternate economic systems,[25] Geoffrey Heal optimistically contends, "this poor [environmental] record is not intrinsic to markets. They can be reoriented in a positive direction, in which case their potential for good is immense."[26] Similarly, through dematerialization, new technologies, better management systems, and investment in a knowledge-based economy, Paul Hawken and colleagues champion a benevolent "natural capitalism"

18 J. McMurtry, *The Cancer Stage of Capitalism* (Pluto Press, 1998).

19 A.A. John and R.A. Pecchenino, "International and Intergenerational Environmental Externalities," *Scandinavian Journal of Economics* 99(3) (1997): 371.

20 T. Cowen, *Public Goods and Market Failures: A Critical Examination* (Transaction Publishers, 1991).

21 M. Common, *Environmental and Resource Economics: An Introduction* (2nd ed., Longman, 1996), 330–35.

22 Ibid.

23 D.H. Meadows, D.L. Meadows, and J. Randers, *Beyond the Limits to Growth* (Universe Books, 1989).

24 See, e.g., M. Common and C. Perrings, "Towards an Ecological Economics of Sustainability," *Ecological Economics* 6 (1991): 1; A.M. Jansson, et al., eds, *Investing in Natural Capital: The Ecological Economics Approach to Sustainability* (Island Press, 1994); R. Costanza, "What is Ecological Economics?" *Ecological Economics* 1 (1989): 1.

25 E.F. Schumacher, *Small is Beautiful: Economics as if People Really Mattered* (Abacus Books, 1973); A. Etzioni, *The Moral Dimension: Toward a New Economics* (Free Press, 1988).

26 G. Heal, "Markets and Sustainability, in *Environmental Law, the Economy and Sustainable Development*, eds R.L. Revesz, P. Sands, and R.B. Stewart (Cambridge University Press, 2000), 410, 427.

that respects the critical interdependency between the economy and nature.[27] These more optimistic sentiments have informed the corporate social responsibility and ecological modernization movements as means of reforming business behavior.[28]

C. RECONCILIATION THROUGH CORPORATE SOCIAL RESPONSIBILITY (CSR)

One of SRI's antecedents is the movement for CSR, which shares the same tension between accommodating financial and ethical imperatives. CSR has a long history in the context of industrial capitalism, dating back to the nineteenth century in the first movement for improved labor conditions.[29] Its influence has generally been episodic and fleeting. It has more recently regained prominence as modernist economic virtues such as efficiency, profits, and maximum growth have waned in an increasingly cynical world plagued by social and environmental problems.[30]

Yet CSR seeks to show that business can operate under responsible environmental management while remaining profitable. Rejecting the unbridled free market doctrines of previous years,[31] the World Business Council for Sustainable Development (WBCSD) explains: "corporate social responsibility is the continuing commitment by business to behave ethically and contribute to economic development while improving the quality of life of the workforce and their families as well as of the local community and society at large."[32]

---

27 P. Hawken, L.H. Lovins, and A. Lovins, *Natural Capitalism: Creating the Next Industrial Revolution* (Earthscan, 2000).

28 Among the voluminous literature, see, e.g., M.S. Andersen and I. Massa, "Ecological Modernisation—Origins, Dilemmas and Future Directions," *Journal of Environmental Policy and Planning* 2 (2000): 337; S.C. Young, *The Emergence of Ecological Modernisation: Integrating the Environment and the Economy?* (Routledge, 2000); R.E. Freeman, J. Pierce, and R.H. Dodd, *Environmentalism and the New Logic of Business* (Oxford University Press, 2000).

29 J.J. Asongu, "The History of Corporate Social Responsibility," *Journal of Business and Public Policy* 1(2) (2007): 1.

30 E. Garriga and D. Mele, "Corporate Social Responsibility Theories: Mapping the Territory," *Journal of Business Ethics* 53 (2004): 51. D. Birch, "Corporate Social Responsibility: Some Key Theoretical Issues and Concepts for New Ways of Doing Business," *Journal of New Business Ideas and Trends* 1(1) (2003): 1.

31 On financial and corporate management attitudes in the 1980s, see A. Smith, *The Roaring '80s* (Viking Press, 1988).

32 WBCSD, *Corporate Social Responsibility: Meeting Changing Expectations* (WBCSD, 1999), 3. Among general CSR literature in recent years,

Thus, companies' social license is validated by good corporate citizenship concerned for all stakeholders.[33] From one perspective, CSR prescribes a company's success measured by the "triple bottom line"—not only the financial bottom line, but also its social and environmental performance.[34]

Business self-regulation and voluntary measures have provided CSR's toolbox.[35] Numerous domestic and international corporate codes of conduct have arisen in the past two decades, constituting a source of governance norms that either rival or supplement official regulation.[36] Other CSR tools include corporate environmental management systems, environmental performance auditing and reporting, negotiated performance agreements with government agencies, and investments in new environmental products and services.

Mirroring the changes in the SRI sector, the CSR movement's evolution has splintered into various philosophical strands, and a gulf exists between business case and ethical case approaches. While the latter does not ignore financial considerations, it seeks to redefine the business enterprise from a purely economic entity to a socially responsible institution considerate of a wide range of stakeholders.[37] Corporations should act on social and environmental issues as a fundamental and integral part of their operations. Whether at the corporate or investment level, such stances take their cues

see D. Crowther and L. Rayman-Bacchus, eds, *Perspectives on Corporate Social Responsibility* (Ashgate Publishing, 2004); D. Vogel, *The Market for Virtue: The Potential and Limits of Corporate Social Responsibility* (Brookings Institution Press, 2005).

33 D. Logan, I. Regelbrugge, and D. Roy, *Global Corporate Citizenship: Rationale and Strategies* (The Hitachi Foundation, 1997).

34 J. Elkington, *Cannibals with Forks: The Triple Bottom Line of 21st Century Business* (New Society Publishers, 1998).

35 See OECD, *Meeting on Alternatives to Traditional Regulation* (OECD, 1994); W. Cragg, ed., *Ethics Codes, Corporations and the Challenge of Globalization* (Edward Elgar Publishing, 2005); S. Zadek, "The Path to Corporate Responsibility," *Harvard Business Review* 82 (2004): 125.

36 OECD, *Codes of Corporate Conduct: Expanded Review of their Contents* (OECD, 2001).

37 See, e.g., A.B. Carroll, "Corporate Social Responsibility: Evolution of a Definitional Construct," *Business and Society* 28 (1999): 268; P. Shrivastava, "Industrial/Environmental Crises and Corporate Social Responsibility," *Journal of Socio-Economics* 24(1) (1995): 211; R.F. O'Neil, "Corporate Social Responsibility and Business Ethics: A European Perspective," *International Journal of Social Economics* 13(10) (1986): 64; R. Welford, Environmental Strategy and *Sustainable Development, The Corporate Challenge for the Twenty-First Century* (Routledge, 1995).

from various ethical theories that situate business enterprise within a larger cultural framework of relationships and responsibilities.[38]

Alternatively, the dominant business case for CSR retains the assumption of private, self-interested corporations. Yet, it finds that because environmental issues create financial risks and opportunities, it is in companies' economic self-interest to improve sustainability performance.[39] Efficient environmental management can often be a bellwether for more general operational competence. Companies that manage their environmental profile can presumably gain market advantages through cost reductions, quality improvements, and profitability.[40] However, without a tangible business case, this form of CSR may unravel. For example, in a PricewaterhouseCoopers' survey of companies in 2002, the primary reason respondents gave for not introducing sustainable development practices was the "lack of a solid business case."[41] Thus, whether CSR can make capitalism socially just and ecologically sustainable is hugely contentious.

Not surprisingly, SRI itself is subject to the same increasing emphasis on business opportunity and wealth. This trend is evident for instance in how the SRI market indexes define corporate sustainability[42] and the SRI industry's marketing around promises of prosperity.[43] Naturally, some critics

38 B. Devall and G. Sessions, *Deep Ecology—Living as if Nature Mattered* (Gibbs Smith, 2001); A. Naess, A. Drengson, and B. Devall, eds, *The Ecology of Wisdom: Writings by Arne Naess* (Counterpoint, 2008).

39 E.g., C. Holliday, S. Schmidheiny, and P. Watts, *Walking the Talk: The Business Case for Sustainable Development* (Greenleaf Publishing, 2002); B. Willard, *The Sustainability Advantage: Seven Business Case Benefits of a Triple Bottom Line* (New Society Publishers, 2002); M.C. Epstein and M.J. Roy, "Making the Business Case for Sustainability: Linking Social and Environmental Actions to Financial Performance," *Journal of Corporate Citizenship* 9(Spring) (2003): 79; D. Levy and P. Newell, eds, *The Business of Global Environmental Governance* (MIT Press, 2005).

40 M.E. Porter and C. van der Linde, "Green and Competitive: Ending the Stalemate," *Harvard Business Review* 73(5) (1995): 120; R. Earle, *The Emerging Relationship between Environmental Performance and Shareholder Wealth* (Assabet Group, 2000).

41 PricewaterhouseCoopers, *2002 Sustainability Survey Report* (Pricewaterhouse-Coopers, 2002), 2.

42 It explains it as: "a business approach to create long-term shareholder value by embracing opportunities and managing risks deriving from economic, environmental and social developments": Dow Jones Sustainability Indexes, "Corporate Sustainability," at http://www.sustainability-index.com/htmle/ sustainability/corpsustainability.html.

43 See R. Lowry, *Good Money: A Guide to Profitable Social Investing in the 90s* (W.W. Norton and Co., 1991); P. Kinder, A.I. Domini, and S. Lydenberg, *Investing*

therefore view CSR and SRI as greenwash,[44] or capitalism's newest "Maginot Line,"[45] intended to appease environmental constituents while deflecting attention from meaningful reform.[46] If this is the case, it begs what kind of reforms could make a real difference.

In searching for alternatives to the business case, one starting point is to investigate more closely the policies and practices of those institutions most closely associated with ethical motivations—namely, churches and other religious organizations that have pioneered an ethical approach to SRI. The following section examines faith-based investment to learn more about the practice of ethical investment as an alternative means of reconciling the tensions between capitalism and the values of ecological protection and social justice.

D. RECONCILIATION THROUGH ETHICAL PRINCIPLES: THE EXAMPLE OF FAITH-BASED INVESTMENT

1. Putting Your Money Where Your Faith Is

In contrast to SRI or CSR motivated primarily by financial advantage, a much older tradition of faith-based investment exists. Today, religious investors participate in the financial sector while seeking to invest without compromising their tenets of faith. Perhaps more than any other financial player, religious investors emphasize an ethical-approach to SRI.[47] They may tolerate lower financial returns in order to defend their principles of faith.[48]

for Good: Making Money While Being Socially Responsible (HarperCollins, 1993).

44 See J. Greer and K. Bruno, Greenwash: The Reality Behind Corporate Environmentalism (Apex Press, 1996).

45 H. Glasbeek, "The Social Responsibility Movement: The Latest in Maginot Lines to Save Capitalism," Dalhousie Law Journal 11 (1988): 363.

46 T. Miwa, "Corporate Social Responsibility: Dangerous and Harmful, Though Maybe Not Irrelevant," Cornell Law Review 84(July) (1999): 1227; Christian Aid, Behind the Mask: The Real Face of Corporate Social Responsibility (Christian Aid, 2004); K. Bruno and J. Karliner, Earthsummit.biz: The Corporate Takeover of Sustainable Development (Food First Books, 2002).

47 C. Jacob, "A Christian on the Stock Exchange," in Ethics in the World of Finance, ed. R. Hopps (Chester House Publications, 1979).

48 Personal communication, Joy Kennedy, Ecological Justice Program Coordinator, United Church of Canada (Toronto, September 29, 2007).

The only sector that rivals faith-based investors in this respect is charitable investors. Charities and foundations sometimes practice mission-based investment (MBI), integrating philanthropic goals into their investment policies. MBI not only aligns charities' actions with their purposes, it can also enable them to better leverage their assets in support of their mission, not just the portion they grant.[49] Thousands of mission-based investors exist worldwide; prominent examples interested in sustainable development financing include: the National Wildlife Federation (US), Amnesty International, and the Joseph Rowntree Charitable Trust (UK).[50]

Faith-based investors have a long history. The Quakers, who have advocated social justice and pacifism since their foundation in England in the seventeenth century, pioneered SRI.[51] They refused financial ties to businesses that transported slaves. More recently they contributed to the founding of the UK's Ethical Investment Research Service (in 1983) and established the Friends Provident's Ethical Funds (in 1984).[52] Another historical innovation of faith-based investors has been their willingness to collaborate to forge change. For instance, a century ago, in 1908, the US Federal Council of Churches adopted *The Social Creed of the Churches*, a set of social standards applying to corporations, which enunciated an agenda of social justice that remains just as relevant today.

Faith-based investment is often wrongly dismissed as of limited scope, focusing on a sparse miscellany of moral issues, such as admonitions against pornography and gambling. Religious investors have demonstrated a much wider compass of concerns, ranging from human rights to environmental protection. All major religions have developed doctrine around such questions.[53] Critics have also sometimes wrongly equated their methods with

---

49 Trillium Asset Management (TAM), *Mission-Related Investing for Foundations and Non-Profit Organizations: Practical Tools for Mission/Investment Integration* (TAM, 2007), 2.

50 Michael Jantzi Research Associates, *Investing in Change Mission-Based Investing for Foundations, Endowments and NGOs* (Canadian Council for International Cooperation, 2003), 8.

51 For an introduction, see W.A. Cooper, *A Living Faith: An Historical and Comparative Study of Quaker Beliefs* (2nd ed., Friends United Press, 2006); see also the Quakers website at http://www.quaker.org.uk, and the Quaker UN Office, at http://www.quno.org.

52 T. Jepson, *The Ethical Investment Research Service: Origins, Development, Prospects* (EIRIS, 1995).

53 P. Triolo, M. Palmer, and S. Waygood, *A Capital Solution: Faith, Finance and Concern for a Living Planet* (Pilkington Press, 2000), 26–53.

inflexible ethical screens; in fact, faith-based investors pioneered shareholder advocacy and engagement as means of influence.

Leveraging political change is reflected in churches that pioneered the divestment movement against apartheid South Africa. Initiated in the 1970s, the divestment campaign involved shareholder activism encouraging firms to cease operations there. If they did not, social investors pressured remaining companies to at least end racial discriminatory practices in their businesses.[54] This campaign gave birth to the Sullivan Principles, a voluntary code of conduct for corporations remaining in South Africa, developed by Reverend Leon Sullivan.[55] The effectiveness of this campaign is debated, but appears to have contributed to a decline in foreign investment in South Africa during the 1980s.[56] And, of the 275 US companies remaining in South Africa in the late 1980s, the vast majority was signatories of the Sullivan Principles.[57]

The depth of the churches' involvement in the South Africa divestment crusade was illustrated when in 1971 the US Episcopal Church filed a shareholder resolution at General Motors' annual general meeting condemning its investments there.[58] Also, in 1973 the Interfaith Center on Corporate Responsibility (ICCR) was established to coordinate SRI among US religious investors, quickly taking up the cudgel against apartheid. Further, in 1985 it coordinated a coalition of fifty-four religious congregations targeting twelve companies most tied to the apartheid regime.[59]

Canadian churches were particularly active on the South African issue. In 1973 the Young Women's Christian Association (YWCA) published a landmark report detailing links between economic investment and maintenance

54 D. Beaty and O. Harari, "Divestment and Disinvestment from South Africa—A Reappraisal," *California Management Review* 29(4) (1987): 31; C. Coons, "Divestment Steamroller Seeks to Bury Apartheid," *Business and Society Review* 57 (1986): 90.

55 R.D. Weedon, Jr., "The Evolution of Sullivan Principle Compliance," *Business and Society Review* 57 (1986): 56. The Principles stressed non-segregation of the races. They were re-visited in 1999 in conjunction with the UN and re-released as the Global Sullivan Principles.

56 R. Sparkes, *Socially Responsible Investment: A Global Revolution* (John Wiley and Sons, 2002), 52–58.

57 Ibid.

58 Ibid., 44.

59 ICCR, "US Churches Pledge Intensive Opposition to US Corporate investment in Apartheid—Part One," *The Corporate Examiner* 14(4) (1985): 1. The twelve firms were IBM, Control Data, Burroughs, Citicorp, Mobil, Texaco, Chevron, Fluor, General Electric, Ford, General Motors, and Newmont Mining.

of apartheid.[60] Its recommendations were justified on mainly moral grounds, as to invest in South Africa was "demeaning and destructive to the fundamental values of Canadian society."[61] In 1975, the Taskforce on the Churches and Corporate Responsibility (TCCR) was created in Canada to stop investment in South Africa, Rhodesia, and other countries with human rights abuses.[62] The TCCR's advice helped religious and other ethical investors "to steer clear of controversial stocks."[63] Although the TCCR was unsuccessful in persuading the Canadian government to revise its banking legislation to require more transparency on foreign bank loans, the major Canadian banks eventually agreed to cease further loans to South Africa.[64] The TCCR also coordinated shareholder resolutions against companies such as Alcan with ties to South Africa,[65] despite rules in Canadian corporate law that restricted shareholder resolutions filed merely for grand-standing political or social causes.[66] After South Africa, in 2001 the Canadian churches reorganized their efforts under a coalition called KAIROS (Canadian Ecumenical Justice Initiatives), which continued to participate in shareholder campaigns on new issues such as climate change and Indigenous rights, as well as public policy advocacy.[67] The churches contributed to a successful lobbying campaign which called upon the federal government to liberalize the *Canada Business Corporation Act*'s provisions on filing shareholder resolutions.[68]

Faith-based investors were also responsible for pioneering many of the techniques of SRI, including screening and shareholder activism. In 1928 in the US, financier Philip Carret founded the Pioneer Fund to service church investors, with a policy of screening investments on ethical grounds.[69] Shareholder advocacy

---

60 World Relationships Committee, *Investment in Oppression: Report on Canadian Economic Links with South Africa* (YWCA, 1973).

61 Ibid., 40.

62 R. Pratt, *In Good Faith: Canadian Churches against Apartheid* (Wilfred Laurier University Press, 1997).

63 A. Ross, "Towards the Pure Portfolio: The Search for Ethical Investments in a Wicked, Wicked World," *Canadian Business* 59(5) (1986): 139.

64 Pratt, note 62, 33–34.

65 "Canadian Churches Press Alcan Aluminium Ltd to Sell South African Investments," *The Corporate Examiner* 14(10) (1985): 1.

66 *Varity Corporation v. Jesuit Fathers of Upper Canada*, (1987) 59 O.R. (2d) 459 (court ruling against the Jesuits filing a resolution on divestment from South Africa). Varity however eventually withdrew from South Africa in 1991.

67 Http://www.kairoscanada.org.

68 Personal communication, Nancy Palardy, Jantzi Research (Toronto, October 12, 2007). Palardy previously worked for KAIROS.

69 J. Harrington, *Investing with Your Conscience* (John Wiley and Sons, 1992), 6.

was forged in the campaign against South Africa. Faith-based investors also pioneered investor networks and by collaboration amplified their voice. The ICCR is the most significant such network. Founded in 2005, the International Interfaith Investment Group (known as "3iG") is the most recent addition to assist with spreading religious values through capital markets.[70]

Despite their noteworthy track record, the churches' traditionally hierarchical decision-making structures do not innately dovetail with the participatory deliberation associated with ethical decision-making. The church is a theocracy, not a democracy, where investment policy is presumed to flow from scriptural teachings. A trust or corporate structure is commonly used to manage church funds. Thus, a board of trustees or directors oversees investment policy, although often delegating substantial responsibilities to specialist asset managers within key investment parameters. This structure can further hinder ethical deliberation. In 1992, the Church of England's investment policy was unsuccessfully challenged in court by a bishop who argued that the Church Commissioners should give ethical factors more weight, in accordance with Christian doctrine.[71] The Church of England later appointed, like some other denominations, an ethical investment advisory committee to provide a forum for wider participation and critical reflection on SRI. Individual religious orders do not always impose a consistent investment policy owing to the decentralized structure of many churches. Individual fellowships of each denomination may retain their own investment strategies.

2. SRI in Some Major Faiths

Churches and other faiths continue to participate in the SRI market, and while in absolute terms their investments remain large, their market share has shrunk.[72] As recently as 1997, religious institutions in the UK reportedly held about 50 percent of the SRI market,[73] but this plummeted

---

70 Http://www.3ignet.org.

71 *Harries and others v. Church Commissioners for England*, [1992] 1 W.L.R. 1241; [1993] 2 All E.R. 300 (the bishop had argued for more forceful screens against investments in South Africa).

72 E.g., C. Valor and M. de la Cuesta, "An Empirical Analysis of the Demand of Spanish Religious Groups and Charities for Socially Responsible Investments," *Business Ethics* 16(2) (2007): 175.

73 G.T. Gardner, *Inspiring Progress. Religions' Contributions to Sustainable Development* (W.W. Norton and Co., and Worldwatch Institute, 2006), 133.

to a mere 5 percent in 2001 as secular SRI exploded.[74] In an era where business-case SRI is displacing ethical investment, Stephen Davis and others contend:

> religious investors may form the core of the coalition, but they lack the muscle of less "values-driven" investors, such as pension funds, mutual fund companies, and other institutional investors. Faith funds often work in conjunction with such "bottom-line" oriented investors, so the issues need to have business rationales, lest their partners rebel.[75]

While faith-based investors willingly take a moral stand on some issues, their overall investment strategy often has the same desire for returns as other financial institutions given that religious bodies have financial obligations such to cover pension plan liabilities. An ethical approach does not preclude such financial goals, but they are no longer the sole investment criteria, and investments that conflict with religious doctrine are eschewed.[76] Religious investors' emphasis thus may be on reasonable, not maximal returns.

Consider the Church of England, one of the largest religious investors in the world. The Church's investment policy aims primarily to "to obtain the best possible long term return from a diversified investment portfolio."[77] Its SRI policy was developed collaboratively through the Church's Ethical Investment Advisory Group, established in 1994. The Church Commissioners' current policy excludes investments associated with alcohol, tobacco, pornography, and some military equipment. Conversely, it favors companies that "demonstrate responsible employment and best corporate governance practices, [and] are conscientious with regard to environmental performance and human rights ..."[78] The Church recently demonstrated its willingness to leverage its weighty financial resources to protect its values. In November 2006

---

74 Ibid., 134.

75 S. Davis, J. Lukomnik, and D. Pitt-Watson, *The New Capitalists. How Citizen Investors are Reshaping the Corporate Agenda* (Harvard Business School Press, 2006), 181.

76 T. Takala and Kääriäinen, "Ethical Investment Policy of the Evangelical Lutheran Church of Finland," *Business Ethics: A European Review* 12(3) (2003): 258, 262.

77 Church Commissioners for England, *Church Commissioners' Annual Report 2005* (Church of England, 2006), 1. See further N. Kreander, K. McPhail, and D. Molyneaux, "God's Fund Managers: A Critical Study of Stock Market Investment Practices of the Church of England and UK Methodists," *Accounting, Auditing and Accountability Journal* 17(3) (2004): 408; C. Cowton, "Where Their Treasure Is: Anglican Religious Communities and Ethical Investment," *Crucible* 8(2) (1990): 51.

78 Ibid., 53.

the Church was able to persuade British Airways to back down on a proposed uniform policy, which would have banned staff from wearing the Christian cross on a necklace, after threatening to divest its some £10.25 million worth of shares in the high-profile airline.[79]

The Methodist Church has a longer history of involvement in SRI, dating from the early twentieth century.[80] In the retail market, the US Methodists launched the Pax World Fund in 1971, a pioneering retail SRI fund that initially screened against munitions, alcohol, and gambling. For their own funds, the Church established a Joint Advisory Committee on the Ethics of Investment in 1983. The Methodist Central Finance Board's latest ethical investment policy, adopted in 2004, requires that any investments that involve the following matters be assessed and screened if necessary: alcohol and tobacco; armaments; corporate governance and business ethics; environment; fair trade and debt relief; gambling; human rights; media ethics (including pornography); and medical and food safety issues.[81]

Among other major Christian denominations, the Catholic Church similarly eschews investments in the usual vices such as intoxicants and gambling.[82] It professes to exclude businesses or countries with major human rights violations and unremediated environmental damage.[83] Lutherans have been active in SRI in Scandinavia and North America.[84] In Sweden it opened an ethical fund based on Lutheran principles.[85] In 2000, the church synod decreed that the Church of Sweden invest its assets "in an ethical and accessible way in keeping with the fundamental values of the church."[86]

---

79 J. Hooper and J. Treanor, "How the Archbishop Took on the World's Favourite Airline—and Won," *Guardian*, November 25, 2006.

80 N. Kreander, D. Molyneaux, and K. McPhail, *An Immanent Critique of UK Church Ethical Investment*, Working Paper 2003/1 (Department of Accounting and Finance, University of Glasgow, 2003), 4.

81 Methodist Church, "Ethical Investing," at http://www.methodist.org.uk/index.cfm?fuseaction=information.content&cmid=923.

82 CCI Investment Management, *Catholic Values Trust Investment Policies* (CCI Investment Management, September 2001), 6–7.

83 Ibid., 7. See further G.R. Beabout, "Socially Responsible Investing: An Application of Catholic Social Thought," *Logos: A Journal of Catholic Thought and Culture* 6(1) (2003): 63.

84 K. Inskeep, "Views on Social Responsibility: The Investment of Pension Funds in the Evangelical Lutheran Church in America," *Review of Religious Research* 33(3) (1992): 270; Takala and Kääriäinen, note 76.

85 Kreander, McPhail, and Molyneaux, note 77, 5.

86 Cited by R. Sparkes, *Socially Responsible Investment: A Global Revolution* (John Wiley and Sons, 2002), 275.

Among other faiths, Islamic policy on financing shares some principles of the Christian churches and also contains some unique ones. Shari'ah (Islamic law) forbids investments related to alcohol, tobacco, certain entertainments, financial services, and certain foods (e.g., pork).[87] Islamic law specifically prohibits usury, and therefore excludes interest-bearing securities such as bonds, mortgages, and debentures.[88] Yet generally under Islamic law profit may be taken to the extent that the normal course of the market will allow.[89] The Dow Jones, which offers several SRI portfolio indexes, has established an Islamic Market Sustainability Index comprising companies that are compatible with Islamic investment guidelines and concomitantly rank high on the Dow Jones' sustainability criteria.[90] Islamic mutual funds, such as the Azad funds, allow individual Muslims to invest in accordance with their faith.[91]

Not all religious investment focuses on social and environmental issues connected to sustainable development. In the retail market, some faith-based mutual funds have emerged that promote values controversial for other ethical investors.[92] Among such evangelical funds in the US, the Timothy Plan family of Christian funds declares it "is steadfastly committed to maintaining portfolios that do not contain the securities of any company that is actively contributing to the moral decline of our society."[93] It associates "moral decline" with businesses connected to vulgar entertainment, which support non-traditional married lifestyles, and health care industries providing elective abortions and contraception. The Timothy Plan sits within "a religious right financial movement that uses fundamentalist values to push conservative evangelism into corporate suites."[94]

While churches retain individual SRI policies, they often collaborate on shared concerns. In the UK, the Ecumenical Council of Corporate Responsibility and the Church Investors Group, established in 1989 and

---

87 R. Wilson, "Islamic Finance and Ethical Investment," *International Journal of Social Economics* 24(11) (1997): 1325.

88 S. Chiu and R. Newberger, "Islamic Finance: Meeting Financial Needs with Faith Based Products," *Profitwise News and Views* February (2006): 8, 12.

89 D. Jackson, "Muslim Investors Tread Carefully: Islamic Values and Capitalism Find Common Ground Despite Restrictions," *Globe and Mail*, July 14, 2006, B9.

90 See http://www.sustainability-index.com.

91 Http://www.azzadfund.com.

92 A. Day, "Put Your Money Where Your Faith Is," *Australian Financial Review*, February 4, 2004, 44.

93 Http://www.timothyplan.com/Funds/frame-OurFunds-factsheets.htm.

94 C.L. Cooper, "Religious Right Discovers Investment Activism Bible Thumpers Boycott 'Cultural Polluters'," *CorpWatch*, August 3, 2005.

2005 respectively, promote cooperation among British and Irish Churches on SRI and CSR policies.[95] In Australia, the Christian Centre for SRI coordinates advocacy among Australian Christian groups.[96] The US-based ICCR is described by Davis and others as "the single most potent source of investor activism over two decades in the United States."[97] Established in 1971, the ICCR now comprises an international coalition of over 275 faith-based institutional investors.[98] It facilitates exchange of research and provides a channel for cooperation on shareholder resolutions.[99] Such peak bodies do not dictate how individual churches invest, but help them to coordinate action for shared concerns.

Faith-based investors not only collaborate among themselves but also reach out to other civil society networks. ICCR itself has an associate membership class that includes NGOs such as Amnesty International. Religious groups have worked with the Earth Charter network to promote education among religious constituencies in ecological values.[100] The Alliance of Religions and Conservation is another inter-faith network that collaborates with environmental organizations.[101] In Canada, KAIROS has cooperated with environmental groups such as the Climate Action Network. Churches also work with non-religious investors in shareholder advocacy and corporate engagement; for example, the United Methodist Church in the UK has signed the Carbon Disclosure Project (CDP).

Contrary to stereotypes, faith-based investors demonstrate the ability to address contemporary social and environmental concerns through invest- ment, and can work collaboratively and democratically, across traditional religious groups and with secular organizations. Through coalitions, they have scored some major successes in shaming polluting companies.[102] Perhaps the key to understanding their willingness to prioritize ethics over financial returns is that churches are civil society institutions, shaped by a wider universe of values than provided by the market. This suggests that if the

---

95 "British and Irish Churches Trustee Bodies Unite for Ethical Investment," *Christian Today*, April 16, 2005.

96 Http://www.ccsri.org.

97 Davis, et al., note 75, 179.

98 Http://www.iccr.org/about.

99 See ICCR, *The Proxy Resolutions Book* (ICCR, January 2007) (detailing 277 resolutions its members filed on various issues recently).

100 E.g., "ECI Religion Strategy Launched," at http://www.earthcharter.org.

101 Http://www.arcworld.org.

102 E.g., "Religious Shareholders Force GE to Disclose Millions Spent to Delay PCB Cleanups," *FinancialWire*, January 11, 2006, 1.

SRI sector generally is to a have sturdy ethical basis, it must deepen its ties to society. Purely market-based institutions, immersed in a normative universe that stresses monetary exchange, financial risks, and profitability, would seem much less open to ethically-motivated SRI.

The remainder of this chapter reviews the extent and impact of SRI in the market generally, and draws conclusions about its capacity to promote sustainable development. While faith-based investors provide one enlightening example of how SRI can respond to the challenges of achieving sustainability and social justice, the rest of the SRI market dominated more heavily by business case motivations offers different lessons.

II. What Has Modern SRI Achieved?

A. EXTENT OF SRI

1. SRI Market Surveys

The SRI literature is increasingly effusive about the prospects for responsible investment. It tells us that "a tipping point has been reached in the growth of SRI,"[103] and that it marks one of the market's great "megatrends."[104] Similarly, the business pages of the popular press report on "soaring" SRI.[105]

How credible are such assertions? Worryingly, for instance, recent research by the environmental research organization Trucost, which graded the UK's largest 185 investment funds on the carbon footprint of their portfolios, found that one-quarter of the ostensible SRI funds were more polluting than the industry benchmark.[106] Despairingly, Jason Zweig found so many inconsistencies in the screening processes of SRI funds that he advised ethical investors simply to choose funds that will likely yield the optimal financial returns and donate part of the proceeds to causes of their choice.[107] Let's now peer behind

103 H. Henderson, *Ethical Markets: Growing the Green Economy* (Chelsea Green Publishing, 2006), 220.
104 P. Aburdene, *Megatrends 2010: The Rise of Conscious Capitalism* (Hampton Roads Publishing, 2005), 140.
105 E.g., T. Grant, "Social Investment Assets Soar," *Globe and Mail*, March 22, 2007, B17.
106 Discussed in H. Williams, "News: Carbon Footprint Casts Doubt on SRI Products," *PensionsWeek*, July 23, 2007, 1; and see Trucost, *Carbon Counts 2007: The Carbon Footprint Ranking of UK Investment* (Trucost, July 2007).
107 J. Zweig, "Why 'Socially Responsible' Investing Isn't Quite as Heavenly as It Might Sound," *Money* 25(June) (1996): 64.

the conflicting claims about SRI to assess more comprehensively its extent, quality, and impact.

An obvious starting point is to consider the size of the SRI market. A plethora of studies, as canvassed below, suggest a flood of loans and investments for responsible choices. Concomitantly, various opinion polls show a public increasingly mindful of investing ethically.[108] However, because of problematic research methods, much of this data strains credibility. Evaluations of the size of the SRI market use inconsistent methodologies. The disparate methods for quantifying SRI also reflect the underlying lack of an objective basis to defining SRI. Loose, generic definitions of SRI that underpin this research deflect attention from critical questions about what should qualify as ecologically sound and socially just investment. Thus, given the proliferation of broad and vague concepts of SRI, the research has likely significantly exaggerated the size of the SRI market. One recent positive trend in the market research is moves by some of the peak SRI associations to align their surveying around the approach of the European Social Investment Forum, which distinguishes between "core" and "broad" SRI, implying that not all SRI is of the same quality. Even so, none of the studies assesses whether firms targeted by SRI changed their behavior or simply arranged finance from alternative, less scrupulous sources.

The following data suggests that neither commercial nor ethical compulsions have so far proved adequate to make SRI dominant in the market. The ethical approach is too controversial for most investment institutions, which fear financial losses or unresolvable disputes over the correct ethical course. The business case, while potentially more appealing, cannot work widely because many social and environmental issues defy easy measurement in financial terms or simply because there remains a compelling countervailing business case for continued pillage of the environment.

Beginning with the US market, the Social Investment Forum (SIF) reported in 2007 that US$2.71 trillion (up from US$2.29 trillion in 2005) or "roughly 11 percent of assets under professional management . . . are now involved in socially responsible investing."[109] This market share is comparable to that recorded in the SIF's survey in the mid-1990s.[110] Moreover, while 11 percent

---

108 Vogel, note 32, 60.

109 SIF, *2007 Report on Socially Responsible Investing Trends in the United States* (SIF, 2008), ii; see also S. Schueth, "Socially Responsible Investing in the United States," *Journal of Business Ethics* 43(3) (2003): 189.

110 SIF, *After South Africa: The State of Socially Responsible Investing in the United States* (SIF, 1995), 1.

of the market may sound impressive, the SIF relies on very broad and ambiguous standards for measuring what constitutes SRI. It counts funds that screen merely against tobacco, alcohol, or gambling. Indeed, twenty-five percent of nominal SRI funds in SIF's 2005 survey screened only on the basis of *one* of these activities.[111] Conversely, while tobacco was a screening criterion in funds with assets worth US$159 billion, the environment (potentially encompassing a much wider basket of issues) was a screening factor in funds with assets of only US$31 billion.[112] The SIF's most recent study also attempts to quantify shareholder advocacy, noting that shareholder resolutions on ESG issues rose to record high of 367 in 2006, up marginally from 360 such resolutions in 2005.[113] While the 2006 resolutions also garnered generally more votes compared to recent years, their average level of support of 15.4 percent suggests continuing resistance to ESG issues.

The European Social Investment Forum (Eurosif) has traced SRI trends in Europe.[114] Its 2006 report covers pension funds and insurance companies, but excludes retail funds and community microfinancing.[115] Eurosif quantified SRI in Europe as worth between €105 billion (based on core SRI screens and best-in-class methods) and €1,033 trillion (incorporating, in addition, the value of shareholder activism and engagement, and other types of broad SRI screens).[116] The latter, larger figure is the equivalent of between 10 to 15 percent of managed assets in all European funds at the time.[117] These figures suggest substantial growth in the European SRI market since Eursosif's 2003 study, although owing to changes in the survey methodology direct comparisons are not straightforward.[118] The European figures would be significantly larger if they included Scandinavia, as the ethically-driven Norwegian pension fund alone has assets of some €175 billion. In contrast to the US market, armaments production is the most commonly excluded sector by European funds while tobacco is relatively unimportant to them.[119] The UK and the Netherlands have by far the largest SRI markets in

---

111 SIF, *2005 Report on Socially Responsible Investing Trends in the United States: A 10-Year Review* (SIF, 2005), 9.

112 Ibid., 8.

113 SIF, note 109, iv.

114 The Eurosif study did not include Scandinavia or Eastern Europe.

115 Eurosif, *European SRI Study 2006* (Eurosif, 2006).

116 Ibid., 4–5.

117 Ibid., 13.

118 Eurosif, *Socially Responsible Investment among European Institutional Investors* (Eurosif, 2003).

119 Eurosif, note 115, 7.

their region.[120] In the retail market another study suggests there were 437 SRI funds in Western European markets as of June 30, 2007, up from 159 such funds in 1999.[121] Most were UK-based, although with rapid growth in the French fund industry. Their assets amounted to €49 billion under management, compared to less than €12 billion in 1999. Despite such expansion, as a proportion of total assets managed by retail funds in Europe, the SRI sector stood at just 0.75 percent in 2007, up from 0.62 percent in 2006.[122]

Among other markets, SRI is likewise apparently surging but overall remains relatively small. According to the 2007 report of the Responsible Investment Association Australasia (RIAA, formerly known as the Ethical Investment Association), "core" assets of retail and institutional SRI in Australia grew by 43 percent in the twelve months to June 30, 2007, totaling AU$19.39 billion.[123] Taking into account the value of corporate engagement and ESG integration strategies, the "broad" SRI market was estimated at AU$52.8 billion.[124] This pool of SRI included managed portfolios, community investment, environmental responsible loans, and the ethical portfolios of charities and clients of financial advisers. Large superannuation funds adopting SRI policies for their portfolios spearheaded much of this progress. By market share, SRI managed portfolios in Australia (the primary component of "core" SRI) comprised 1.87 percent of the market, and retail funds amounted to just 1 percent of total retail funds under management.[125] The market share for "broad" SRI is at least double these numbers.

A survey of the Canadian SRI sector, conducted in 2006 by the Social Investment Organization (SIO) comprehensively covered retail and

120 Ibid., 35–36.
121 Avanzi SRI Research—Vigeo Italia, *Green, Social and Ethical Funds in Europe, 2007 Review* (Vigeo Italia, October, 2007), 5, 8 (apart from Poland, the report excludes Eastern Europe); for comparisons to earlier years, see also Avanzi SRI Research, *Green, Social and Ethical Funds in Europe 2006* (SIRI Group, September 2006), 6–7.
122 Ibid., 6.
123 Corporate Monitor, *Responsible Investment: A Benchmark Report on Australia and New Zealand by the Responsible Investment Association Australasia* (RIAA, October 2007), 3 (the study defined SRI as "an umbrella term to describe an investment process which takes environmental, social, ethical or governance considerations into account," at 5). See also the earlier study of Total Environment Centre, *Socially Responsible Investment: Assessing the Non-Financial Performance of Companies* (Environmental Resources Management, 2002) (survey of SRI funds in Australia).
124 Ibid., 18.
125 Ibid., 14.

institutional investment, as well as the value of shareholder advocacy and ethically responsible bank lending. As of June 30, 2006, it found Canadian SRI worth C$503.61 billion, amounting to a hefty 19.6 percent of the market.[126] Astonishingly, according to the SIO, the value of SRI assets jumped from a mere C$65.46 billion in 2004, when it represented just 3.6 percent of the market.[127] The SIO attributes this change largely to the "recent adoption of socially responsible investment practices by several major pension funds" such as the Canada Pension Plan (CPP).[128]

However, like other SRI surveys, it is hard to verify the quality of the investment practices behind such numbers. Simply because a pension fund declares that it follows certain engagement and proxy voting practices pursuant to an SRI policy does not prove that it invests responsibly across its entire portfolio. In fact, the CPP engages with only up to fifteen companies per year, of the nearly 2,000 in its portfolio.[129] Consider for instance the mining giant Goldcorp, in which the CPP holds significant shares—some C$181 million of investment as of March 2007.[130] Yet, at that time the *Globe and Mail* awarded Goldcorp a grade of D+ in its survey of corporate social responsibility,[131] and other research on Goldcorp's operations in Central America reveals a dubious record of environmental mismanagement and disrespect of local communities.[132] Perhaps a more credible statistic in the SIO's survey is the much lower figure of C$57.38 billion of "core SRI" including ethical screens and socially responsible lending, which represented only 2.2 percent of the market.[133]

In emerging markets, with little hard data on SRI trends available, the market appears to be miniscule. SRI in all emerging markets was estimated at US$2.7 billion in 2003, representing about 0.1 percent of worldwide

---

126 SIO, *Canadian Social Investment Review 2006* (SIO, March 2007), 5–6.

127 Ibid., and SIO, *Canadian Social Investment Review 2004* (SIO, April 2005).

128 Ibid., 5.

129 D.M. Raymond, CPP Investment Board, "Mainstreaming Responsible Investment: Our Approach" (presentation at Globe 2006, Vancouver, March 30, 2006).

130 CPP Investment Board, "Canadian Equity Holdings: As of March 31, 2007," http://www.cppib.ca/files/PDF/CDN_Equity_Holdings_March31_2007_-_ENG.pdf.

131 S. Brearton, et al., "Beyond the Bottom Line," *Globe and Mail: Report on Business Magazine*, February 23, 2007, 51.

132 S. Imai, L. Mehranvar, and J. Sander, "Breaching Indigenous Law: Canadian Mining in Guatemala," *Indigenous Law Journal* 6(1) (2007): 101.

133 SIO, note 126, 6.

responsible investment.[134] Most of this SRI is in East Asia. According to the Association for Sustainable and Responsible Investment in Asia (ASrIA), in July 2007 there were 159 SRI funds in its region (excluding Oceania).[135] Malaysia had the most funds of any country (67, comprising mainly faith-based funds) followed by Japan (35 funds). China had only one SRI fund and India three SRI funds. South Africa boasts the most mature SRI market in Africa, evident for example in the launching in 2004 of an SRI market index on the Johannesburg Stock Exchange.[136] Growth of responsible investment in Latin America has been sluggish, with the largest SRI pool in Brazil.[137]

Much of the SRI data in both developed and emerging markets excludes the banking sector. At best, it counts explicit "green loans" but not the harder-to-quantify ESG analyses in debt financing generally. Other research suggests shortfalls in the quality and implementation of lenders' environmental policies. Earlier studies in the 1990s found that environmental due diligence was ostensibly practiced by 50 percent[138] to 80 percent[139] of lenders sampled. Commentators interpreted such data as indicating that environmental risk was becoming in some markets "an integral part of the credit appraisal process."[140] More recently, a 2002 study of European banks found "much room for improvement,"[141] largely due to weak implementation rather than an absence of environmental risk protocols.[142] In 2002, Marcel Jeucken reported that one-third of US banks did not conduct environmental

---

134 M. de Sousa-Shields, ed., *Towards Sustainable and Responsible Investment in Emerging Markets: A Review and Inventory of the Social Investment Industry's Activities and Potential in Emerging Markets* (IFC, 2003), 6.

135 ASrIA SRI Funds Portal: http://www.asria.org/portal/SRI_Fund/srifund.

136 UNEPFI and Centre for Corporate Citizenship, *The State of Responsible Investment in South Africa* (UNEPFI, 2007).

137 E. Peinado-Vara, *Corporate Social Responsibility in Latin America and the Caribbean* (Inter-American Development Bank, 2004); de Sousa-Shields, note 134, 38–39.

138 J. Ganzi and A. DeVries, *Corporate Environmental Performance as a Factor in Financial Industry Decisions* (Office of Cooperative Environmental Management, US Environmental Protection Agency, 1998).

139 UNEP, *Greening Financial Markets* (UNEP, 1994).

140 See J. Rowan-Robinson, C. Theron, and A. Ross, "Policing the Environment: Private Regulation and the Role of Lenders," *Environmental Liability* 4(6) (1994): 114, 116–17 (survey of UK banks).

141 ISIS Asset Management, *A Benchmarking Study: Environmental Credit-Risk Factors in the Pan-European Banking Sector* (ISIS Asset Management, 2002), 1.

142 Ibid., 12.

risk assessments.[143] Encouragingly, in emerging markets, a comprehensive survey conducted in 2005 by the International Finance Corporation (IFC) of 120 banks and related financiers in forty-three jurisdictions found that 98 percent of lenders "consider social and environmental issues, either by managing risks, developing business opportunities, or both."[144] Protecting business reputation was the principal reason cited by the banks (68 percent of respondents) for integrating environmental considerations into their management practices.

Other research has examined banks' overall commitment to sustainable development, not just defensive environmental risk assessment. A 2006 survey by WWF and BankTrack of thirty-nine international banks for their compliance with the EPs and other global codes found that "with few exceptions bank policies are lagging significantly behind relevant international standards and best practices."[145] Banks with the highest overall average score in the evaluations were ABN AMRO and the HSBC Group. A subsequent study in 2007 by BankTrack evaluated the credit policies of forty-five international banks for the content, transparency, and implementation of their policies on sustainable development. It rated the overall quality of the credit policies as "fairly poor," their transparency and accountability practices as "well behind best international standards," and it documented thirty so-called "dodgy deals" involving the surveyed banks.[146] BankTrack identified HSBC and Rabobank as among the few lenders to have made substantial progress. In retail banking, SRI-related products such as green mortgages have not yet gained significant market share, owing in part to lack of consumer awareness caused by insufficient marketing, and lack of consumer confidence in projected savings of energy efficiency measures.[147] Recent UNEPFI research on North American banking paints a more optimistic assessment.[148]

---

143 M. Jeucken, "Behind the Green Door," *Financial World* August (2002): 41.

144 IFC, *Banking on Sustainability: Financing Environmental and Social Opportunities in Emerging Markets* (IFC, 2007), 12.

145 WWF and BankTrack, *Shaping the Future of Sustainable Finance: Moving from Paper Promises to Performance* (WWF, 2006), 4.

146 BankTrack, *Mind the Gap: Benchmarking Credit Policies of International Banks* (BankTrack, December 2007), xi, xii, 116–37.

147 S. Roberts, C. Chambers, and B. Kaur, *Making Mortgages Energy Efficient?* (Centre for Sustainable Energy, 2005).

148 UNEPFI, North American Taskforce, *Green Financial Products and Services* (UNEPFI, 2007),

The environmental venture financing sector provides another snapshot of SRI trends. In absolute terms it has grown exponentially in the last five years, yet remains somewhat of a fringe sector by market size.[149] One study estimated that €1.25 billion was raised for such financing in Europe in 2006, compared to venture capital financing totaling €76 billion.[150] While this amounts to less than 2 percent of European venture capital, it represents a relatively hefty increase from 2000, when venture financing for sustainability in Europe was worth approximately €100 million.[151] In North America, the sector has also ballooned, worth almost US$2.6 billion in 2007.[152] The majority of venture financing comes from institutional investors.[153]

2. Other Indicators of the SRI Market

Apart from market surveys, an indication of the extent of SRI can be gleaned from the number of financiers voluntarily adhering to SRI codes and standards. For instance, the nearly sixty signatories to the EPs cover about 85 percent of the global project finance market.[154] As of late 2007, the UNPRI boasted over 250 signatories managing approximately US$10 trillion.[155] This impressive statistic compares to nearly US$62 trillion in funds under management worldwide at the end of 2006.[156] Presently, UNPRI investors' assets are worth about 15 percent of all global capital under management.[157] What these 250 signatories have done to implement the UNPRI is

---

149 Henderson, note 103, 216–20.
150 Eurosif, *Venture Capital for Sustainability 2007* (Eurosif, 2007), 5.
151 J. Randjelovic, A. O'Rourke, and R.J. Orsato, "The Emergence of Green Venture Capital," *Business Strategy and the Environment* 12 (2003): 240, 244. Like venture finance generally, SRI-focused venture financing faces hurdles such as undeveloped business plans and convincing financial supporters that the technology or product is commercially viable. New businesses based merely on proposed innovations lack a track-record or established management systems on which to evaluate investments (at 243).
152 A. Das, "Cleantech Sector Rising, May Overvalue Sector: VCs," *Reuters,* January 8, 2008.
153 Eurosif, note 150, 12.
154 See http://www.equator-principles.com.
155 UNEPFI, *PRI: Report on Progress 2007* (UNEPFI, 2007), 6.
156 IFSL, "Global Funds Under Management," from "International Statistics" at http://www.ifsl.org.uk/research.
157 Remarks, N. Purcell, Group General Manager, Westpac (UNEPFI Global Roundtable, Melbourne, Australia, October 24–25, 2007).

altogether another matter, for significant discrepancies can arise between what is promised and practiced with voluntary standards lacking credible enforcement machinery.

Finally, public opinion and investor surveys provide another snapshot of the SRI market. They typically conclude that most people favor SRI, especially to address environmental and human rights issues. For instance, a Canadian survey in 2007 by the Investors Group reported that 56 percent of Canadians believe environmental considerations are important when choosing invest-ments.[158] Some Australian research suggests that a majority of those surveyed would consider SRI as a portion of their portfolio.[159] Seventy percent of respondents felt similarly about human rights issues. A poll in the UK conducted in late 2006 found similar environmental values, with 48 percent of respondents expressing a desire to invest ethically, and of this group about one-third indicating they would do so even if this entailed a financial sacrifice.[160] However, such attitudes do not appear to have yet translated into actual investment decisions, given other data on the SRI retail market.

One can reasonably conclude that the SRI market remains small in nearly all jurisdictions, averaging just a few percentage points of all investment assets. The market is effectively even smaller given that some funds are one-off ethical investors, taking a stand in a specific instance but otherwise investing conventionally. To illustrate, the Harvard Corporation, guardian of the university's sizeable endowment fund and historically indisposed to SRI, in 2005 announced that it would divest Harvard's stake in PetroChina solely because of that company's alleged ties to the atrocities in Sudan's Darfur region.[161] Overall, what can be learned about the impact of the SRI market from such statistics and surveys is limited, given the lack of "apples to apples" research methodologies and an underlying failure among surveyors to

---

158 "Canadians Weigh Social and Environmental Factors in Investment Decisions, Investors Group Research Finds," *Canada Business Online*, November 6, 2007, at www.canadianbusiness.com.

159 M. Watmore and L. Bradley, *The Rothschild Report—Ethical Investing, A Study into Current Perceptions* (Rothschild Australia, 2001).

160 F&C Asset Management, *Research Commissioned by F&C Asset Management into the Ethical Investment Concerns of the UK Public* (F&C Asset Management, 2006).

161 "Harvard Announces Decision to Divest from PetroChina Stock," *Harvard University Gazette*, April 4, 2005. For its earlier stance on SRI, see the opinions of its former University President Derek Bok, in "Reflections on the Ethical Responsibilities of the University in Society," *Harvard University Gazette*, March 9, 1979.

critically reflect on what should qualify as SRI. Such studies also generally fail to judge SRI's ultimate impact on corporate behavior.

Another way to assess SRI is to canvass how social investors address specific market and institutional barriers to sustainability. In recent years numerous government and private sector studies have measured the impact of financial markets on sustainable development. Their findings are remarkably homogenous. For example, commonly identified barriers to sustainability include short-term investment horizons, difficulties analyzing the financial significance of environmental issues, and problems in coordinating action.[162] The following sections examine these and other obstacles, and how the SRI community has addressed them, beginning with the problem of fungible criteria for determining ethical or responsible investment.

B. FUNGIBLE STANDARDS

SRI is a protean concept. Difficulties in gauging the size of the SRI market partly result from financiers setting their own criteria for what is ethical or socially responsible. Much of the SRI industry's parlance is vague, broad, and indiscriminate.[163] Commonly used terminology such as "innovator" or "best-in-class" may confuse rather than enlighten investors. Without some common standards over SRI's nomenclature and terminology, it risks degenerating into shallow marketing and greenwash.[164] Not knowing which financiers are leaders or laggards determined by such standards hampers effective policy measures to stimulate SRI in a more accountable direction.

The peak SRI associations set their own definitions, detailed in the table below. These typically boilerplate statements, which leave unclear as to by whom, why, how, or when ESG factors are considered, could rationalize much market behavior.

---

162 NRTEE, *Capital Markets and Sustainability: Investing in a Sustainable Future. State of the Debate Report* (NRTEE, 2007), 22.

163 G. Frost, et al., "Bringing Ethical Investment to Account," *Australian Accounting Review* 14(3) (2004): 3.

164 D.H. Schepers and S.P. Sethi, "Do Socially Responsible Funds Actually Deliver What they Promise? Bridging the Gap Between the Promise and Performance of Socially Responsible Funds," *Business and Society Review* 108(1) (2003): 11.

Table 3: Various definitions of SRI

Association for Sustainable and Responsible Investment in Asia	"Investment which allows investors to take into account wider concerns, such as social justice, economic development, peace or a healthy environment, as well as conventional financial considerations."
Canadian Social Investment Organization	"The integration of environmental, social and governance (ESG) factors in the selection and management of investments."
European Social Investment Forum	"SRI combines investors' financial objectives with their concerns about social, environmental, ethical (SEE) and corporate governance issues. ... SRI is based on a growing awareness among investors, companies and governments about the impact that these risks may have on long-term issues ranging from sustainable development to long-term corporate performance."
Responsible Investment Association Australasia	"Responsible investment is an umbrella term to describe an investment process which takes environmental, social, ethical or governance considerations into account. This process stands in addition to (or is incorporated into) the usual fundamental investment selection and management process."
UK Social Investment Forum	"UKSIF promotes responsible investment and other forms of finance that support sustainable economic development, enhance quality of life and safeguard the environment."
US Social Investment Forum	"An investment process that considers the social and environmental consequences of investments, both positive and negative, within the context of rigorous financial analysis"

Source: SRI associations' websites.

These definitions mask one characteristic common to much SRI, namely the emphasis on a business case. To the extent that business objectives pervade the SRI industry, socially-conscious investors may have a false sense of hope that they are making a real difference.

In the retail sector, SRI standards are at their most fungible, where salesmanship and marketing prevail.[165] Investors face innumerable choices, spanning a bewildering array of philosophies, from conservative evangelical Christian ethics to deep ecology. This SRI market offers a retail ethics, where consumers can shop for a better world. This retail market tends to consider ethical investment as only personal values determined by each individual. This impoverishes the nature of ethical principles, "render[ing] ethics into a subjective realm incapable of any thoughtful discussion or analysis."[166]

In this supermarket of funds, the novice investor may be unable to decipher the logic and criteria behind the offerings.[167] Many investors "do not have access to the methodology, the screening, the ranking criteria, or any other data that would inform them about how or why a particular company is included in a portfolio."[168] A 2007 study of the French SRI market was critical of the diversity of criteria used by funds for taking into account ESG criteria and their failure "to measure the environmental footprint of the investments they pursue."[169] Many SRI funds worldwide typically offer a pre-determined investment prospectus, where statements of investment philosophy or objectives are disclosed in general terms. To illustrate, the Ariel Fund explains in its 2006 prospectus that:

> We do not invest in corporations whose primary source of revenue is derived from the production or sale of tobacco products, the generation of nuclear energy or the manufacture of handguns. We believe these industries are more likely to face shrinking growth prospects, draining litigation costs and legal liability that cannot be quantified.[170]

---

165 J.C. Brogle, *The Battle for the Soul of Capitalism* (Yale University Press, 2005), 164.

166 M.S. Schwartz, "The 'Ethics' of Ethical Investing," *Journal of Business Ethics* 43(3) (2003): 195, 208.

167 C.J. Cowton, "Playing by the Rules: Ethical Criteria at an Ethical Investment Fund," *Business Ethics* 8(1) (1999): 60.

168 P. Hawken, *Socially Responsible Investing* (Natural Capital Institute, 2004), 22.

169 Novethic études, *The New Frontier of SRI: The Green Investments Claiming to be SRI* (Novethic études, 2007), 27.

170 Ariel Mutual Funds, *Prospectus* (Ariel Mutual Funds, 2006), 9.

There are exceptions, however. The Calvert Social Index Fund provides quite useful statements of policy on Indigenous peoples, international operations and human rights, product safety, and corporate governance, among other SRI goals.[171] So too does Domini Social Investments, which published a comprehensive fifty-page guide to its policies.[172]

In other funds, an objective basis for screening methods is often hard to discern. For example, when is a company's involvement in a screened activity sufficient to trigger exclusion? Would an SRI fund that excludes investment in nuclear energy also exclude investment in a steel or electronics manufacturer that supplies materials to nuclear power plants? Or what of a paper company that supplies cigarette paper to a tobacco business or a bank that raises money for a weapons manufacturer? Simplistic screens do not account for firms operating through franchises, subsidiaries, and contractors that undertake questionable activities one step removed from parent companies.

Another unreliable trait of screens is their use of seemingly arbitrary standards that may confuse investors. Many SRI funds set thresholds that determine whether to exclude a company. For example, the Desjardins Ethical Canadian Balanced Fund explains that it does "not invest in companies that generate a significant proportion of their income from tobacco products."[173] What does "significant" mean, and why was that threshold chosen? Even an insignificant amount of such activity can be substantial for a large company in absolute terms.[174] Therefore, whatever the practicalities of such thresholds, it does pose a dilemma in principle by partially condoning undesirable activities in an investment portfolio.

The lack of principle behind some SRI criteria is at times demonstrated. For example, in 2005 Australia's BT Financial Group reversed its decision not to invest in the uranium industry.[175] This occurred after BHP Billiton bought WMC Resources, a uranium miner. This mining behemoth constitutes about 10 percent of the Australian stock market, so few funds could afford to exclude BHP from their portfolio. Ethical investors in Canada face a similar dilemma where resource and energy stocks comprise a major part of the market. According to Michael Jantzi, a leading figure in the

---

171 Http://www.calvert.com.

172 Domini Social Investments (DSI), *Global Investment Standards* (DSI, 2006).

173 See http://www.fondsdesjardins.com/en/gamme_fonds/35_ethical_can_balanced. pdf.

174 Schepers and Sethi, note 164, 17.

175 J. Collett, "Nuclear Warning for Ethical Funds," *Sydney Morning Herald*, July 20, 2005; and see http://www.bt.com.au/investors.

Canadian SRI community, "[e]liminating all resource stocks is unrealistic, because it wipes out about 40 percent of the Toronto market and causes an investor to lose diversity."[176]

Thus, differences between the portfolio of a fund marketed as SRI and other funds may be illusory. An international study by the Natural Capital Institute in 2004 found "the screening methodologies and exceptions employed by most SRI funds allow practically any publicly-held corporation to be considered as an SRI portfolio company."[177] For example, over 90 percent of the Fortune 500 market index is included in the SRI mutual funds portfolios reviewed by the Institute.[178] In 2003 Wal-Mart featured in the portfolio of thirty-three SRI funds, Coca-cola in fifty-six SRI funds, and McDonald's in forty-one of such funds.[179] The growth in best-in-class and corporate engagement methods of SRI, at the expense of exclusionary screens, signals a further blurring of the distinction between SRI and non-SRI portfolios.[180] One example is the recent decision of Pax World Funds to repeal a long-standing ban on alcohol and gambling-related investments.[181] While some SRI funds may justify a "mainstream" portfolio on the basis of their reliance on shareholder activism to leverage change, most funds are not activists.

C. ECONOMY-WIDE INVESTORS

1. Universal Owners

In contrast to these problems that plague the retail market, some commentators contend that institutional investors investing broadly across the economy are directing financial markets towards responsible, sustainable development.[182] Two factors apparently underpin this orientation.

---

176 S. Won, "Ethical Summa Above Average," *The Globe and Mail*, November 29, 1995, B17.

177 Hawken, note 168, 16.

178 Ibid., 3.

179 Ibid., 18 (of approximately 600 SRI funds sampled).

180 G.J. MacDonald, "A Rethink of Shunning Sin," *Christian Science Monitor*, October 23, 2006.

181 Pax World Funds, "Pax World Modernizes Social Investing Criteria" (October 26, 2006), at http://www.paxworld.com.

182 J.P. Hawley and A.T. Williams, *The Rise of Fiduciary Capitalism: How Institutional Investors Can Make Corporate America More Democratic* (University of Pennsylvania Press, 2000); F. Amalric, *Pension Funds, Corporate Responsibility and Sustainability*, Centre for Corporate Responsibility and Sustainability Working Paper 01/04 (University of Zurich, 2004); S. Lyndenberg,

First, because of the size of their asset base, diverse portfolios, and longer-term investment horizons, institutional investors (or "universal owners," as Robert Monks and Neil Minow first described them) should be better placed than other types of investors to promote sustainable development.[183] Large banks also commonly hold substantial and diverse lending portfolios. Because of their economy-wide investments, universal investors supposedly "have no interest in abetting behavior by any one company that yields a short-term boost while threatening harm to the economic system as a whole."[184] Acting as a universal investor implies that what is an "externality" at the level of an individual company can result in an "internality," or a material factor for an investor's global portfolio. As James Gifford explains further:

> Therefore, if one company causes environmental damage, another company will often suffer, and that company will also be in the fund's portfolio so it is a zero sum game for the fund. Similarly, if the environmental cost is externalised onto the taxpayer (i.e. to clean up a toxic waste site), those taxpayers will most likely also be members of the fund.[185]

The universal owner status, boast James Hawley and Andrew Williams, also gives such investors a stake in public policy issues beyond traditional macro-economic concerns, such as environmental policy, public health, and other policies that help build natural and social capital.[186] Climate change is one such policy concern.[187]

By contrast, single or limited asset financiers presumably view investments in isolation. They may support companies at the expense of the economic welfare of society as a whole. Any environmental damage caused by "profitable" companies becomes a hidden cost, with others bearing the burden. Therefore, from a societal perspective, this self-interested investment model hinders sustainable development.

"Universal Investors and Socially Responsible Investors: A Tale of Emerging Affinities," *Corporate Governance* 15(3) (2007): 467.

183 R.A.G. Monks and N. Minow, *Corporate Governance* (Basil Blackwell, 1995), 132.

184 Davis, et al., note 75, 18.

185 J. Gifford, "Measuring the Social, Environmental and Ethical Performance of Pension Funds," *Journal of Australian Political Economy* 53 (2004): 139, 140–41.

186 Hawley and Williams, note 182, 170.

187 Mercer Investment Consulting, *Universal Ownership: Exploring Opportunities and Challenges.* Conference report, April 10–11, 2006, Saint Mary's College of California (Mercer Investment Consulting, 2006), 16–17.

Expressed differently, the universal owner thesis suggests a way to resolve in the context of financial markets the generic collective action problems mapped by Garrett Hardin[188] and Mancur Olson,[189] where seemingly rational choices for individuals are irrational for society collectively. In other words, in contrast to individual investors with incentives to exploit market failures for their personal gain, which ultimately leaves all worse off as the externalities accumulate, universal owners have motivations to act in the interests of all for the long-term.

A second feature of this thesis is the presumption that institutional investors invest responsibly because they are accountable to a broader constituency of investors. They represent multiple investors, as against a lone shareowner. Given the breadth of institutions' membership, to whom their portfolio managers and trustees owe fiduciary duties, in theory the interests of fund members should dovetail with those of society as a whole. Thus, Stephen Davis and others believe universal investors are forging a new style of public engagement in capital markets, helping to create a "civil economy."[190]

Nonetheless, the universal owner thesis has some drawbacks. One is that financiers commonly focus on credit risks of individual borrowers or financial risks of a specific security. While investors design diversified portfolios to minimize overall financial risks, they tend to evaluate assets on a case-by-case basis. Some investment analysis is based on an industry sector or is applied macro-economically, but hard valuations are made principally in regard to specific assets or borrowers. Evaluating a country's entire economy does not factor the social and environmental costs of that market, because GDP or other macro indicators do not normally account for depletions of natural capital.[191] Disparate and cumulative environmental impacts associated with numerous financial decisions defy easy measurement. Thus, constraints arise when institutions have characteristics of universal owners but rely on one-off or narrowly framed analytical techniques in evaluating financial transactions.

Second, while an economy-wide investor may scrutinize the externalities of individual companies, the economy as a whole does not internalize all of its environmental and social costs. A principal weakness of markets is the absence of an internal mechanism to keep the economy's total resource use within

---

188 G. Hardin, "The Tragedy of the Commons," *Science* 162 (1968): 1243.

189 M. Olson, *The Logic of Collective Action: Public Goods and the Theory of Groups* (Harvard University Press, 1965).

190 Davis, et al., note 75, 5–8.

191 G. Arnold, *Handbook of Corporate Finance* (Prentice-Hall, 2005), 324–25.

biosphere limits.[192] This is the problem of "scale." Many environmental values are also too remote for market actors to recognize. A recent report by the IUCN concludes that the financial sector generally has a poor understanding of the diffuse risks posed by biodiversity loss.[193] Thus, we cannot assume that the current health of the economy as a whole is an adequate proxy for the long-term health of the biosphere.

A third weakness of the universal owner thesis derives from the management of investment portfolios. The portfolio of large institutional investors is sometimes dispersed over several asset management companies, possibly resulting in each portfolio being narrower than the original "universal" portfolio.[194] Further, their portfolios in the stock market can be highly fluid, as liquidity is highly prized by investors. Short-term traders may vote on issues in a company they may not own tomorrow. The growth of "fund of funds," whereby institutions invest in a fund that holds a portfolio of other investment funds rather than invest directly in shares or other securities, is another market characteristic that distances universal owners from the companies they ultimately finance.[195]

Fourth, although not a shortcoming of the universal owner thesis per se, we should note that it is inapplicable to other financial contexts with social and environmental impacts. One example is consumer and residential financing. Home loans are collectively associated with major land use changes, for the availability of credit contributes to the structure, density, and quality of residential development. This has resulting implications for transport, waste management, climate change, and urban sprawl. Similarly, easily-accessible personal loans to finance cars fuel widespread environmental problems of a car-dependent consumer society. A similar lacuna in the universal owner thesis arises with financing of small, private companies. They are not typically within the portfolio of large institutional investors, except to some extent through private equity funds.[196] Through their sheer numbers, small companies can devastate the environment just as much as large public ones. While some

---

192 H. Daly, "Allocation, Distribution and Scale: Towards an Economics that is Efficient, Just and Sustainable" *Ecological Economics* 6 (1992): 185.

193 I. Mulder, *Biodiversity, the Next Challenge for Financial Institutions?* (IUCN, 2007).

194 C. Mackenzie, "The Scope for Investor Action on Corporate Social and Environmental Impacts," *Responsible Investment*, note 3, 22.

195 H. Avery, "The Funds of Hedge Funds that are Too Hot to Handle," *Euromoney Magazine* (November 2006).

196 D. Cumming and S. Johan, "Socially Responsible Investment in Private Equity," *Journal of Business Ethics* 75(4) (2007): 395.

private equity funds are infusing SRI into the venture financing market, the emphasis on high returns to compensate for high risks makes this model problematic for ethical investment.

Finally, the argument that universal owners invest responsibly because they are accountable to a broad investment base is questionable. Institutional investors are not a proxy for the interests of all stakeholders in society.[197] Some costs affect the poor, marginalized, and dispossessed, without a stake in the economy. Environmental problems, such as bioaccumulation of toxic chemicals in contaminated wildlife harvested by Indigenous people of the Arctic, or filthy sweatshops in China at the bottom of the supply chain, may be too remote, limiting their relevance to financial decision making. These people have little or no voice in investment policy-making. And neither do the direct beneficiaries of pension plans or other funds. As the following chapter explains, financial institutions such as mutual funds and pension plans are not run democratically. Fund managers to whom asset management is commonly delegated may enjoy substantial discretion and power, provided they meet investment objectives and performance targets. Giant financial conglomerates manage many mutual funds and pension plans, concentrating power in the hands of few money managers at the expense of fund beneficiaries.[198]

2. Signs of Responsible Investment

Despite such limitations, some universal owners strive to invest responsibly. Public sector pension funds most closely epitomize the universal owner.[199] In Canada, the Ontario Municipal Employees Retirement System[200] and the Ontario Public Services Employees Union[201] are among various public sector

197 M. Patry and M. Poitevin, "Why Institutional Investors are Not Better Shareholders," in *Corporate Decision-Making in Canada*, eds R.J. Daniels and R. Morck (University of Calgary Press, 1995), 341.

198 Brogle, note 165, 81.

199 UNEPFI Asset Management Working Group and UKSIF, *Responsible Investment in Focus: How Leading Public Pension Funds are Meeting the Challenge* (UNEPFI, 2007).

200 Ontario Municipal Employees Retirement System (OMERS), "Statement of Investment Policies and Procedures for the Ontario Municipal Employees Retirement System" (January 2003), http://www.omers.com/investments/statementofinvpol.html#social. OMERS, "Proxy Voting Guidelines" (January 2002), http://www.omers.com/investments/proxyvoting_guidelines/E-intro.htm.

201 Ontario Public Services Employees Union's (OPSEU), "OPSEU Policy Statement with respect to Union Appointed Trustees and Sponsors for Jointly Trusteed Pension Plans" (undated), http://www.opseu.org/benefit/policystatement.htm.

funds that have adopted SRI policies and publicly report on how they vote on proxy contests. In the US, CalPERS,[202] the New York State Teachers Retirement System,[203] and the Connecticut Retirement Plans and Trust Funds[204] are among the leaders in responsible fiduciary activism. In Europe, the USS in Britain[205] and the Dutch ABP fund[206] are equivalent examples.

The USS was one of the first UK pension funds to adopt a comprehensive SRI policy. Its current policy provides that its fund managers will:

> pay appropriate regard to relevant extra-financial factors including corporate governance, social, ethical and environmental considerations in the selection, retention and realisation of all fund investments.
> ... [And] ... undertake appropriate monitoring of the policies and practices on material corporate governance and social, ethical and environmental issues of current and potential investee companies so that these extra-financial factors can, where material, be taken into account when making investment decisions.[207]

As recently as the late 1990s, the USS shunned SRI activism. Since then it has been a catalyst for collaborative projects impossible for individual investment institutions to achieve alone. In cooperation with investors and other stakeholders, the USS has focused on engagement and dialogue with the pharmaceutical industry on access to medicines, and campaigned in other economic sectors for more attention to climate change issues.

It was instrumental in setting up the Institutional Investors Group on Climate Change (IIGCC).[208] The IIGCC aims to promote a better understanding of the implications of climate change among investors, and to encourage companies and markets in which its members invest to address any material risks and opportunities of global warming. As of January 2008 it had approximately forty members including religious, corporate, and municipal investment institutions. Its mandate includes: educating the property investment industry about global warming, and policy advocacy such as on carbon emissions trading. In 2005, IIGCC extended its influence by forming a strategic partnership with the Climate Group, a collection of

---

202 Http://www.calpers.ca.gov.
203 Http://www.nystrs.org.
204 Http://www.state.ct.us.
205 Http://www.usshq.co.uk.
206 Http://www.abp.nl.
207 USS, *Statement of Investment Principles* (USS, 2006).
208 Http://www.iigcc.org.

companies, investors, governments and other stakeholders working to shift to a lower carbon economy.[209]

Investors also collaborate with non-financial actors. In Canada, the Ethical Funds Company joined the Boreal Leadership Council of the Canadian Boreal Initiative. This is a multi-stakeholder coalition whose aim is to protect Canada's 1.4 billion acre boreal forests region.[210] The coalition comprises oil and gas firms, forest products companies, Indigenous First Nations, environmental organizations, and investors. Its participation commits Ethical Funds to use its financial leverage with companies (e.g., forestry and mining companies) to encourage them to protect the ecological integrity of the entire region and to commit to more sustainable use resources in the boreal forests.[211]

Further signs of responsible ownership come from investors' policy advocacy to effect change where voluntary action has failed.[212] Some lobbying targets regulatory reform, such as measures facilitating shareholder activism and corporate disclosure. For instance, in 1999 the SRI community in the UK advocated changes to pension fund regulation requiring trustees to disclose policies on responsible financing. In recent years, pension funds have petitioned the US Securities and Exchange Commission to require stronger disclosure of climate change risks.[213] These examples are all the more notable given that traditionally most mainstream investors have been astonishingly silent about corporate governance failures.[214]

D. INVESTMENT HORIZONS

1. Thinking Long-term

A universal financier should presumably not only hold a broad portfolio invested in the whole economy, but also favor companies with long-term contributions to sustainable development. Extended financial liabilities maturing over several decades should cause pension funds and life insurance

---

209 Http://www.theclimategroup.org.

210 Http://www.borealcanada.ca.

211 Personal communication, Robert Walker, Vice-President of Sustainability, Ethical Funds (by telephone, November 2, 2006).

212 Robins, note 3, 317.

213 CERES, "Thirteen Pension Leaders Call on SEC Chairman to Require Global Warming Risks in Corporate Disclosure," Press release, April 15, 2007.

214 Brogle, note 165, 90.

companies in particular to have long-term horizons.[215] Likewise, banks disbursing loans amortizing over several decades should be attentive to the broader sustainability of their borrowers' activities. By contrast, household and retail investors tend to have less patience and tolerance for underperforming investments.[216] They hold relatively more liquid and short-term investments than institutional investors, partly because institutions "have a comparative advantage in compensating for the increased risk of long-maturity assets by pooling."[217]

Sustainable development depends on institutions investing for the long term. Because ecological systems function over indefinite time horizons, valuing the future is essential. A World Economic Forum report commented:

> Responsible investment requires an orientation towards strategies that optimize long-term returns, both because this delivers better financial returns over the time profile that interests intended beneficiaries, and because over these periods social and environmental issues become more material and so can be better considered.[218]

Planning over several decades or lifetimes however defies the normal range of most economic or political decision-making.[219]

One financial group dedicated to this task is the UK-based Marathon Club.[220] It was formed in 2004 by a cohort of large pension funds concerned about the paucity of practical guidance for trustees on long-term investment management. With eighteen members as of early 2008, the Marathon Club's recommendations include: prepare a clear investment mandate for long-term investment philosophy; restructure fund managers' performance fees; provide longer term mandates for fund managers; have fund managers invest some of

---

215 P.L. Davies, "Institutional Investors in the United Kingdom," in *Contemporary Issues in Corporate Governance*, eds D.D. Prentice and P.R.J. Holland (Oxford University Press, 1993), 69, 79. However, life insurers also need some short-term liquidity to meet early surrender of insurance policies.

216 Personal communication, David Simpson, Interpraxis (Toronto, November 3, 2006).

217 E.P. Davis and B. Steil, *Institutional Investors* (MIT Press, 2001), 293.

218 World Economic Forum (WEF), *Mainstreaming Responsible Investment* (WEF and AccountAbility, 2005), 10.

219 Difficulties in valuing the future are not unique to markets. Governments may discount the interests of posterity as electoral prospects tend to be enhanced by policies that maximise services for current constituencies and defer costs to future taxpayers.

220 Http://www.marathonclub.co.uk.

their money in the fund; undertake less frequent but more in-depth reviews of investment management; and assess long-term social and environmental risk factors.[221] If widely implemented, such recommendations could remove one of the biggest obstacles to SRI.

2. Barriers to Long-term Investment

In practice, many investors behave myopically, preferring short-term trading to patient, long-term investment.[222] In one survey of UK fund managers, one-third of respondents considered less than two years "long term," while 13 percent stated a ten-year time horizon and just 4 percent twenty years.[223] What causes such truncated perspectives?

Investment institutions commonly delegate portfolio management to specialist fund or asset managers, hired externally or employed in-house.[224] To reduce agency problems, they are commonly given a short mandate, typically for three years, with regular performance reviews.[225] This arrangement motivates asset managers to seek the highest returns or at least outperform their peers within their contractual term.[226] This inhibits long-term investing. A 2004 survey in the UK by the National Association of Pension Funds (NAPF) and the Investment Management Association found that fund managers were normally appointed on a three-year term (in 69 percent of cases surveyed), while 16 percent were given a term of less than three years, and none longer than five years.[227] Research for the UK's Myners report on institutional investment found similar evidence; 29 percent of investment

221 Marathon Club, *Guidance Note for Long-term Investing* (Marathon Club, 2007).

222 R.A.G. Monks and N. Minow, *Power and Accountability* (HarperCollins, 1991), 201–2; see also A. Sykes, *Capitalism for Tomorrow: Reuniting Ownership and Control* (John Wiley and Sons, 2000); T. Odean, "Do Investors Trade Too Much?" *American Economic Review* 89(5) (1999): 1279 (discussing investors with discount brokerage accounts, who may lower their returns by frequent trading).

223 Cited in British Telecommunications (BT), *Just Values: Beyond the Business Case for Sustainability* (BT, 2003), 10.

224 Davies, note 215, 72.

225 Davis and Steil, note 217, 136.

226 Innovation Advisory Board, *Innovation: City Attitudes and Practices* (UK Department of Trade and Industry, 1990).

227 National Association of Pension Funds (NAPF) and the Investment Management Association (IMA), *Short-termism Study Report* (NAPF and IMA, 2004), 3.

schemes gave fund managers contracts of twelve months or less.[228] By contrast, fund managers of state-sponsored pension plans have much longer tenure, up to ten years.[229] From her survey of sixty-four UK fund managers, Mae Baker found that the "performance benchmarking and monitoring system in use for pension fund managers provides a perceived pressure to adopt more short-termist attitudes and shorter holding periods than would otherwise be the case."[230]

Compensation arrangements for fund managers exacerbate this short-term focus. They are based primarily on size of assets under management and performance relative to benchmarks or peers. CSR objectives normally do not form part of compensation packages. Fund managers commonly receive a substantial portion of their remuneration in the form of bonuses, based on quarterly or yearly relative return performance.[231] Consequently, they may trade frantically to seek any perceived immediate market advantage.[232] According to Tony Golding's fascinating account of investors in the City of London:

> External pension fund managers, unit trust and unit-linked managers are under constant and intense pressure to maximize current performance. The current quarter is what matters, perhaps the next quarter, certainly not next year's equivalent quarter. Confronted with the prospect of an uplift in the value of his portfolio from a bid, or a decline in performance as a company reports a short-term blip in an upward trend, the gut reaction of a professional fund manager will be to go for whatever enhances or protects his current performance figures.[233]

Such myopic behavior may contrast sharply with the underlying long-term financial liabilities of their institutional principals.

---

228 UK Department of Work and Pensions (DWP), *The Myners Principles and Occupational Pension Schemes*, Volume 2 (DWP, 2004), 114.

229 K. Kjaer, "The Norwegian Petroleum Fund," in *Public Pension Fund Management*, eds A.R. Musalem and R.J. Palacios (World Bank, 2004), 241, 244 (referring to the Irish National Pension Reserve Fund).

230 M. Baker, "Fund Managers' Attitudes to Risk and Time Horizons: The Effect of Performance Benchmarking," *European Journal of Finance* 4 (1998): 257, 272.

231 K.D. Krawiec, "Accounting for Greed: Unravelling the Rogue Trader Mystery," *Oregon Law Review* 79 (2001): 301.

232 Davis and Steil, note 217, 136. Performance measurements however are uncommon in Continental Europe and Japan (170–71, 178).

233 T. Golding, *The City: Inside the Great Expectation Machine* (Financial Times and Prentice Hall, 2002).

Financial accounting norms and practices further inhibit a long-term outlook. Driven largely by the demands of market investors to know companies' financial performance on a frequent basis, accountants track assets and liabilities to provide a picture of the financial health of companies. Pension planners attempt to manage their long-term pension plan liabilities and alleviate problems from economic downturns by using "asset smoothing" techniques. Smoothing basically spreads out unusual losses or gains over a period of years (typically five years), as opposed to recognizing them in a single year period.[234]

Prompted by a painful bear market in the early 2000s, numerous businesses began to regard their pension plans as expenses in their financial statements. Concomitantly, the accounting profession, faced with demands for transparency, began to abandon asset smoothing on the basis that it masked the severity of actual losses. The shift to mark-to-market approach is favored in many European accounting standards boards, and is spreading to North America.[235] In the US, the federal *Pension Protection Act* of 2006[236] and new rules issued by the Financial Accounting Standards Board reduced the scope for asset smoothing.[237] This change in accounting policy may exacerbate short-termism. To reduce the volatility of pension plan expenses and liabilities in companies' financial statements, fund managers seek portfolios that lessen the disparity between liabilities and assets on an *annual* basis. One study predicts this will entail "moving away from assets that could provide a more sustainable performance on a long-term basis."[238]

There is a close parallel to this short-term perspective on the corporate management side, as public companies must report earnings to the market on a quarterly or semi-annual basis, and the structure of executive compensation often encourages a preoccupation with short-term performance.[239] Management thus has strong incentives to engage in practices to boost near-term returns

---

234 W.B. Fornia, "Public Sector Retirement Systems: What Does the Future Hold?" *Employee Benefits Journal* 28(2) (2003): 13.

235 W.P. Schuetze, *Mark to Market Accounting: "True North" in Financial Reporting* (Routledge, 2004) (mark-to-market accounting involves basing financial reports on up-to-date prices—current selling prices for assets and current prices for liabilities).

236 Pub. L. No. 109-280, 120 Stat. 780.

237 K.A. Stockton, *Pension Reform: A Shifting Landscape for Plan Sponsors* (Vanguard Investment Counseling and Research, 2006), 4–5.

238 NRTEE, note 162, 34.

239 Privately-held firms, by contrast, are not subject to the same reporting requirements and thus capital market pressures. Therefore, they may have

while postponing costs for future owners and managers.[240] This reporting cycle may also cause the market to undervalue firms with good earnings prospects in the long term but low current profitability.[241] Thus, the SRI community has called for regulatory changes allowing for less frequent corporate earnings reporting.[242]

Abundant evidence testifies to a market bias to short-term performance.[243] In a 2004 survey of 400 American CEOs, over 78 percent of respondents said they would sacrifice some of their company's economic value in exchange for reporting better quarterly earnings "to avoid the severe market reaction for under-delivering."[244] They would delay new investment, maintenance, or other important expenditures. Other evidence comes from a study commissioned by NAPF and the Investment Management Association.[245] In a 2004 survey, 66 percent of NAPF members said they checked fund manager performance quarterly,[246] and 57 percent had terminated between one to three fund managers' contracts within the last five years primarily on the basis of investment performance.[247]

Asset turnover also points to the market's short-term partiality. Phillips and Drew estimated in 1990 that over the preceding ten year period the

---

more leeway to indulge in socially responsible measures for the long-term: Vogel, note 32, 71–72.

240 Centre for Financial Market Integrity (CFAI) and the Business Roundtable Institute for Corporate Ethics (BRICE), *Breaking the Short-term Cycle* (CFAI and BRICE, 2006), 3.

241 However, the market does not entirely ignore long-term prospects, as evident by the high stock market ratings of drug companies (with large research and development (R&D) expenditures) and emerging Internet companies (with possible strong future earnings). Announcement of new capital expenditure or R&D typically strengthens share prices: J.J. McConnell and C.J. Muscarella, "Corporate Capital Expenditure Decisions and the Market Value of the Firm," *Journal of Financial Economics* 14 (1985): 399.

242 CFAI and BRICE, note 240.

243 D. Miles, "Testing for Short Termism in the UK Stock Market," *Economic Journal* 103 (1993): 1379; J.M. Poterba and L.H. Summers, *Time Horizons of American Firms: New Evidence from a Survey of CEOs* (Harvard Business School, 1992).

244 J.R. Graham, C.R. Harvey, and S. Rajgopal, *The Economic Implications of Corporate Financial Reporting* (National Bureau of Economic Research, June 2004), 2.

245 NAPF, *Short-termism Study Report* (NAPF and IMA, September 2004).

246 Ibid., 6.

247 Ibid., 5.

average holding period for UK equity fell from ten years to less than four years.[248] Philip Davis reports that in 1982 UK pension funds held foreign stocks for an average of two years, declining to an average six-month holding period by 1994.[249] Mutual funds are also fickle stock owners. In the US, stock was held for an average of seven years in the 1950s, declining to a short ten-month average in 2003.[250] Stock ownership is even more transitory in some emerging economy markets.[251] The average holding period for SRI-focused funds may be longer however.[252] In the US, Christopher Geczy and others have documented that "non-SRI funds turn over their investments twice as frequently as their SRI counterparts on average."[253]

Other aspects of the market may produce different investment horizons. Tying investment portfolios to market index tracking funds has not necessarily altered short-term thinking; rather, it may simply make institutions "perpetual investors," constantly turning over stocks as they track the index.[254] But in markets with limited liquidity dominated by a few large companies, as in New Zealand, investors are more constrained to the long term as they cannot afford to omit such large firms from their portfolios. Corporate bonds typically have maturities ranging from just one to over ten years, while government bonds span longer terms, up to thirty years. Corporate bonds can be sold at any time prior to maturity in the active secondary trading market, reducing the average holding period.[255]

248 Phillips and Drew, *Pension Fund Indicators* (Phillips and Drew Fund Management, 1990).

249 E.P. Davis, "The Role of Institutional Investors in the Evolution of Financial Structure and Behaviour," in *The Future of the Financial System*, ed. M. Edey (Reserve Bank of Australia, 1996), 49, 76.

250 World Economic Forum, note 218, 19; and J. Bogle, "The Mutual Fund Industry 60 Years Later: For Better or Worse?" *Financial Analysts Journal* 61(1) (2005): 15.

251 N.K. Kjaer, *The Chinese Stock Market: Possibilities and Pitfalls* (Trade Council of Denmark–China, 2006), 26 (reporting an average holding period of only two months in the Chinese stock market).

252 J.C. Coffee, Jr, "Liquidity Versus Control: The Institutional Investor as Corporate Monitor," *Columbia Law Review* 91(6) (1991): 1277 (discussing CalPERs).

253 G.C. Geczy, R.F. Stambaugh, and D. Levin, *Investing in Socially Responsible Mutual Funds* Working Paper (Wharton Business School, University of Pennsylvania, 2003), 13.

254 World Economic Forum, note 218, 19.

255 See generally R.S. Wilson and F.J. Fabozzi, *Corporate Bonds; Structure and Analysis* (Wiley, 1995).

Some institutional and market trends may continue to intensify short-term investment practices in the future. One trend is the advent of hedge funds, targeted at investors with an appetite for higher risk by exploiting short-term market movements. Another trend in the pension and life insurance sector is the shift from defined benefit to defined contribution plans. This allows individuals to determine their own portfolios, and may consequently weaken any institutional bias to long-term investments in these sectors.[256] The growing preoccupation in the SRI retail market with financial performance can also exacerbate short-termism. Indicative of this mindset is a new online service allowing investors to track the day-to-day performance of over one hundred sustainability funds.[257]

The SRI community is certainly aware of these barriers to long-term investment, and devotes considerable resources to analyzing such problems and prescribing remedies. As chapter 6 will show, these issues are acknowledged in many of its codes of conduct, such as the UNPRI, and the work of bodies such as UNEPFI. The long-term financial liabilities of some investment institutions, coupled with growing understanding how ESG factors can influence returns over the long term, have provided their main arguments for change. Financial markets as a whole, however, have yet to change.

E. FINANCIAL ANALYSIS OF SUSTAINABILITY ISSUES

1. Traditional Methodologies

Financiers do not generally evaluate the possible environmental or social impacts of investments. A Canadian study observed that "[m]ost institutional fund managers in Canada have yet to develop sufficient analytical capabilities to document, analyze, and thereby integrate ESG factors into their financial analysis for investments."[258] In 2005, research by Innovest and others of the extent of integration of environmental issues into company valuations by the financial community in North America found that "environmental issues are not yet on the radar screen in any significant way among investment professionals."[259]

256 Davis and Steil, note 217, 293.
257 See http://www.sustainable-investment.org.
258 NRTEE, note 162, 31.
259 S. McGeachie, M. Kiernan, and E. Kirzner, *Finance and the Environment in North America: The State of Play of the Integration of Environmental Issues into Financial Research* (Environment Canada, 2005), 2.

Many factors inhibit comprehensive analysis, as identified by the US Environmental Protection Agency's (EPA) Capital Markets Committee, including the absence of universal benchmarks to measure corporate sustainability performance and investors' inability to understand how environmental issues affect the bottom line.[260] Corporate financial reporting has traditionally not addressed these challenges. Partly owing to inadequate regulation, the scope and quality of corporate disclosures on social and environmental performance has been poor and uninformative, thereby hindering SRI.[261]

Financial analysts have traditionally acknowledged environmental issues only defensively, once a potential risk materializes into a likely, substantial, and immediate liability. *Positive* social and environmental conduct by companies is undervalued. Further, they typically consider environmental risks only for specific transactions, such as development on contaminated land, rather than systemically across entire investment portfolios. Commercial lenders' environmental credit risk analysis focuses on the likelihood of default or diminishment of loan security.[262] Investment banks typically do not consider ESG criteria when underwriting new securities or in the prospectuses they issue.[263] Even in the insurance sector, insurers typically only seek to identify and quantify environmental risks to underwriting exposures, rather than across their investment portfolios. As to recognition of positive performance, if at all, it transpires mainly through valuation of brand equity, goodwill, or reputation.[264]

---

260 W. Howes, et al., *Green Dividends?* (EPA, 2000).

261 Australia, Parliamentary Joint Committee on Corporations and Financial Services, *Corporate Responsibility: Managing Risk and Creating Value* (Commonwealth of Australia, 2006), 72.

262 Lenders use several risk identification and appraisal methods, depending on the perceived magnitude and gravity of risk. They range from desktop reviews through internal research to the hiring of external expertise for more complex risks. Concurrently, prospective borrowers may complete specialized questionnaires to identify environmental issues that need managing and to record the company's regulatory compliance history. Any identified environmental risk is then usually incorporated into the bank's system for rating a borrower's overall credit risk: S. Labatt and R.R. White, *Environmental Finance: A Guide to Environmental Risk Assessment and Financial Products* (John Wiley and Sons, 2002), 67–68.

263 M.V. Stichele, *Critical Issues in the Financial Industry: SOMO Financial Sector Report* (Stichting Onderzoek Multinationale Ondernemingen, 2005), 115.

264 L. Nicholson and S. Dalgarno, "The Tangible Headache of Intangible Assets in a Global Accounting Environment," *Keeping Good Companies* 5 (2005): 266.

Yet this recognition tends to be realized retrospectively, on disposition or takeover of a company.

Credit rating agencies (CRAs) do not generally include information about a company's environmental and social behavior in their rating schemes. Some rating agencies seek to take such conduct into account, such as the Sustainable Investment Research International Group.[265] Yet they do not combine this with an assessment of a rated firm's capacity to repay its debts. Thus, such evaluations do not have the established credibility of CRAs that assess creditworthiness.

2. The Response of the SRI Sector

The challenge for social investors therefore has been to devise ways by which financiers can transition environmental risk analysis and disclosure from a transactional, ad hoc applications to an ongoing, portfolio-wide approach, disclosing upside and downside performance. Encouragingly, the SRI community is devoting significant effort to address this challenge, building on the pioneering work of ecological economists to design new environmental and social valuation tools.[266]

SRI-focused banks are advancing more sophisticated and comprehensive financial assessments of environmental issues. The Dutch bank ABN AMRO for instance created a Sustainable Risk Advisory unit, adopted sector specific assessment policies (e.g., for mining, oil, and gas), and applies a routine environmental, social, and ethical risk filter to all lending transactions, which may trigger additional probing by the unit.[267] Further, ABN AMRO's policy includes a "Social and Ethical Country Risk Framework," allowing it to identify countries where poor governance necessitates further evaluations to ensure respect for environmental and social considerations. The Sustainable Risk Advisory department appears to have influence; of the 358 industry-based transactions worldwide that the unit reviewed in 2006, it vetoed thirty-three, required mitigating measures in a further eighty-three, and supported 242 transactions unconditionally.[268]

---

265 See http://www.siricompany.com/services.shtml.

266 J. Rietbergen-McCracken and H. Abaza, eds, *Environmental Valuation: A Worldwide Compendium of Case Studies* (Earthscan, 2000); K.G. Willis, K. Button, and P. Nijkamp, eds, *Environmental Valuation. Volume 1. Methods and Anomalies* (Edward Elgar Publishing, 1999).

267 ABN AMRO, *Sustainability Report 2006* (ABN AMRO, 2007), 24.

268 Ibid., 27.

Another innovation is JPMorgan Chase's policy to assess and report on the total impacts of at least one aspect of its corporate lending portfolio. Thus, the financier has committed itself to "annually report the aggregate greenhouse gas emissions from [its] power sector projects beginning in 2006."[269] A practical obstacle to this approach is that JPMorgan Chase like other financiers has not collected historical data about the environmental aspects of its transactions as they occurred. Credit Suisse/First Boston and UBS among others have also advanced sophisticated financial models to assess climate risk for the power sector, taking into account for instance the projected price of carbon emission allowances.[270]

Interest in CSR and SRI has fuelled a large research industry that investigates and reports on companies' environmental and social behavior.[271] Contrary to the static, retrospective summary of corporate performance provided by old methods of financial analysis, SRI research providers such as Innovest (US),[272] Jantzi (Canada),[273] and Sustainable Investment Research International (Germany)[274] are pioneering a more dynamic, progressive picture of companies' actual risk exposure and competitive prospects with regard to their social and environmental performance. On the corporate governance side, research providers such as GovernanceMetrics International[275] and Institutional Shareholder Services[276] are also forging new metrics that evaluate companies' governance, and thereby alert shareholders to comparative risks. Social investors will pay for this information. Members of the Enhanced Analytics Initiative,[277] a consortium of institutional investors, each allocate a minimum of 5 percent of their respective brokerage commission budgets to research bodies in order to gain improved investment analysis.

---

269 JPMorgan Chase, *Environmental Policy* (2006), at http://www.jpmorganchase. com/cm/cs?pagename=Chase/Href&urlname=jpmc/community/env/policy/clim.

270 David Gardiner and Associates, LLC, *Best Practices in Climate Change Risk Analysis for the Electric Power Sector: The Results of the Ceres Electric Power/ Investor Dialogue* (CERES, 2006), 20.

271 J. O'Loughlin and R. Thamotheram, *How the Investment Industry Can Use Extra-financial Factors in Investing* (USS, May 2006); B. Heemskerk, P. Pistorio, and M. Scicluna, *Sustainable Development Reporting: Striking a Balance* (WBCSD, 2002).

272 Http://www.innovestgroup.com.

273 Http://www.jantziresearch.com.

274 Http://www.scoris.de.

275 Http://www.gmiratings.com.

276 Http://www.issproxy.com.

277 Http://www.enhancedanalytics.com.

Much of the work of this SRI research industry is directed to unsolicited ratings, involving the assessment and ranking of firms according to specific ESG criteria.[278] These ratings assist investors to apply portfolio screens and to pick "best-in-class" performers. Prominent CSR rating agencies include EIRIS, Ethibel, Sustainable Asset Management, Sustainable Investment Research Institute, as well as ratings connected to SRI stock market indexes, such as the FTSE4Good index. Their research has also spawned new sustainability reporting techniques, to incorporate ESG factors into traditional financial reports for securities regulators, as well as stand-alone sustainability reports for the broader public. These trends in sustainability reporting, and their regulation, are examined further in chapter 5.

However, this flurry of often uncoordinated initiatives has contributed to a "huge divergence in SRI research standards,"[279] which will require more effort to ensure the independence, standardization, and transparency of SRI research and ratings. Further, under a business case agenda, the new analyses often rely on economically-oriented concepts (i.e., criteria such as eco-efficiency that likely correlate with an economic effect on the evaluated company), rather than normative or ethical evaluation criteria that represent values in themselves.[280]

F. COLLECTIVE ACTION PROBLEMS

1. Barriers to SRI Cooperation

Another hindrance to SRI derives from the "public goods" nature of social and environmental amenities. Investors, and companies themselves, have economic incentives to avoid taking costly actions that improve social and environmental well-being ("positive externalities") unless they can exclusively capture that value financially. SRI actions take time and resources, while the benefits generated from those activities may accrue to many investors and society as a whole, not just the one taking the initiative. Presumably, the individual financier bears all the costs and only, at best, a small portion of the benefits. Consequently, there tends to be reduced investment than otherwise in the collective interests of financiers and their beneficiaries. Because the

---

278 H. Schäfer, et al., *Who is Who in Corporate Social Responsibility Rating? A Survey of Internationally Established Rating Systems that Measure Corporate Responsibility* (Bertelsmann Foundation, 2006).

279 H. Peeters, "Sustainable Development and the Role of the Financial World," *Environment, Development and Sustainability* 5 (2003): 197, 218.

280 Schäfer, et al., note 278, 2.

market fails to capture such externalities, government regulation has become the standard policy prescription.

If SRI is to prosper, it must provide ways by which ethical financiers can cooperate and thereby share rewards from actions that enhance social and environmental capital. The universal owner thesis, discussed earlier, implies that large institutional owners are sufficiently diversified in the economy to address such externalities. However, as explained, the thesis is generally overstated, and institutional investors working alone normally do not have sufficient motivation and means to take account of long-term social and environmental problems.

Competitive financial markets significantly inhibit such cooperation. The mutual fund industry is fiercely competitive, as funds vie to attract investors on the basis of top returns. Deeply ingrained market practices dissuade individual mutual funds from taking measures that would increase corporate value that benefit all shareholders, and thereby rival funds.[281] Similarly, insurance companies compete both with each other and with savings products offered by other financial companies. Ostensibly, pension funds are not competitive as they usually are monopoly providers of retirement benefits to employees within a given organization. They focus on generating returns adequate to meet anticipated liabilities, not necessarily to attract new members. Nonetheless, competitive pressures in this sector may arise surreptitiously at the asset manager level, as funds out-source investment management.

Fund managers are typically judged on relative rather than absolute performance, such as by reference to the performance of their peers or a specific market index.[282] This emphasis on relative over absolute returns diminishes a fund manager's willingness to promote good corporate governance or environmental behavior, even if it would boost her returns, unless she can exclusively capture the financial reward for such actions.[283]

SRI-driven financiers who raise the environmental standard bar too high risk losing opportunities to less scrupulous competitors. A lender who

---

281 E. Becker and P. McVeigh, "Social Funds in the United States: Their History, Financial Performance, and Social Impacts," in *Working Capital: The Power of Labor's Pensions*, eds A. Fung, T. Hebb, and J. Rogers (Cornell University Press, 2001), 44, 64 (referring to pitiful levels of shareholder resolutions sponsored by US ethical mutual funds).

282 Mackenzie, note 194, 33; M. Baker, "Fund Managers' Attitudes to Risk and Time Horizons: The Effect of Performance Benchmarking," *The European Journal of Finance* 4(3) (1998): 257.

283 McGeachie, Kiernan, and Kirzner, note 259, 70–71.

charges a higher interest rate for environmentally harmful loans or refuses to finance altogether may lose high-impact borrowers to lenders offering cheaper credit or credit with fewer restrictions.[284] Thus, although many financial institutions shunned China's Three Gorges Dam project and Peru's Camisea natural gas project, some opportunistic lenders stepped in to provide the necessary loans.[285] However, it would be misleading to imply a crass race-to-the bottom in financing. Other research, on World Bank financing, suggests that such arbitrage is not pervasive, as borrowers and co-financiers sometimes want the Bank's imprimatur on a project because it brings additional credibility.[286]

Clearly, no individual financier or coalition of investors could ever come near to monopolizing all sources of development finance. But if a sufficient number dominate the market, they may alter the cost of capital for polluters and thereby, in effect, create something analogous to a Pigouvian tax.[287] If responsible financiers can differentiate the cost of capital on the basis of environmental risks, they could impose a powerful fillip for companies to improve their behavior. Later in this chapter the theoretical arguments and empirical evidence for such influence is examined closely.

Collective action dilemmas also inhere in corporate governance. Through shareholder resolutions, selling shares, and informal dialogue and pressure, in theory investors can coax management to make policy changes.[288] In practice, various factors keep shareholders, especially when small, numerous, and dispersed, from exerting control. Individual investors lack the requisite resources, information, and mechanisms to monitor and control management.[289] Unless they can work in concert, and share any resulting benefits, individual shareholders are

---

284 ISIS Asset Management, note 141, 24.

285 C. Wright and A. Rwabizambuga, "Institutional Pressures, Corporate Reputation, and Voluntary Codes of Conduct: An Examination of the Equator Principles," *Business and society Review* 111(1) (2006): 89.

286 B. Kingsbury, "Operational Policies of International Institutions as Part of the Law Making Process: The World Bank and Indigenous Peoples," in *The Reality of International Law: Essays in Honor of Ian Brownlie*, eds G. Goodwin-Gill and S. Talmon (Oxford University Press, 1999): 323.

287 A. Pigou, *The Economics of Welfare* (Macmillan, 1932).

288 Banks and other debt financiers do not have this same kind of power, though they can exert influence through loan covenants and monitoring of borrowers. Cooperation among lenders can arise through syndicate loans involving a consortium of lenders.

289 V. Brudney, "Corporate Governance, Agency Costs, and the Rhetoric of Contract," *Columbia Law Review* 85 (1985): 1403, 1405–8.

unlikely to meaningfully engage with management. By contrast, institutional investors' combination of large shareholdings and economies of scale reduces such barriers to collective action.[290] In reality they too have traditionally been passive and uncooperative.[291] Institutional investors tend to maintain liquid, diverse portfolios, thereby leaving them with small equity stakes and often insufficient motivation to take action against management.[292] There are exceptions though, as the following section illustrates.

2. New Forms of SRI Collaboration

Some investors are collaborating to pool their expertise and leveraging on collectivism to achieve change. They are designing common standards, coordinating pressure on wayward companies, exchanging information, and promoting dialogue. Through such partnerships, driven by altruistic or commercial motives, the SRI community helps to ameliorate the collective action problems that traditionally plague financial markets. This collaboration occurs at two levels: at a company level, involving shareholder activism within individual firms; and collaboration at a sector level, such as targeting whole industry groups or environmental issues involving many firms.

The work of the USS in Britain is an exemplary case. The pharmaceutical industry was one of the first sectors it targeted. To encourage a more responsible pharmaceutical industry required a sector-wide approach to ensure no company would suffer a competitive disadvantage. USS engaged with the sector by challenging its business model based on heavy investment in a few super drugs protected by patents. Through the Pharmaceutical Shareowners Group[293] and the Pharma Futures project,[294] USS led a campaign of engagement concerning drug companies' business model to address the risks associated with the public health crisis in developing countries. USS posited that this public health crisis threatens their business model, as hard-pressed governments in developing countries might allow generic versions of

---

290 B.S. Black, "Shareholder Passivity Reexamined," *Michigan Law Review* 89 (1990): 520, 575–91; B.S. Black, "Agents Watching Agents: The Promise of Institutional Investor Voice," *UCLA Law Review* 39 (1992): 811, 873–88.

291 P. Myners, *Institutional Investment in the United Kingdom: A Review* (H.M. Treasury, 2001); B.S. Black, "Shareholder Activism and Corporate Governance in the United States," in *The New Palgrave Dictionary of Economics and the Law*, ed. P. Newman (Palgrave, 1998).

292 J.G. MacIntosh, "Institutional Shareholders and Corporate Governance in Canada," *Canadian Business Law Journal* 26 (1996): 145, 158–71.

293 Http://www.pharmashareownersgroup.org.

294 Http://www.pharmafutures.org.

patented drugs to be sold cheaply in their markets. Consequently, USS teamed up with other investors to promote a more socially responsible business model in the pharmaceutical industry that gave better access to medicines in developing countries, health provision, while aligning intellectual property protection to these imperatives, ensuring the firms' research and development expenditures remain worthwhile.[295]

Another noteworthy initiative, in Australia, is Governance Research and Engagement (Regnan).[296] Established by a consortium of financial institutions including the BT Financial Group, it undertakes research and analysis to identify ESG trends and risks facing the market, and using that analysis it provides an engagement service on behalf of institutional investors. Participating investors pay a fee to Regnan, which then conducts engagement for all of its clients on major ESG issues. The service does not target issues specific to an individual investor or company, but rather tackles issues of broad concern to most clients. Regnan has conducted research into and supported action on environmental risk management disclosure, human rights, and supply chain issues, for instance.

Among religious investors, the ICCR and the 3iG help coordinate religious investment and campaigns for policy reforms for environmental justice, global warming, access to water, and food quality.[297] For example, resolutions filed in 2005 and 2006 with the aid of the ICCR network included asking 3M Company to look into China's labor and human rights practices, and requesting Alliant Energy Corporation to respond to global warming issues arising from its the new coal-fired plants.[298]

Further collaboration is arising through SRI institutional networks that mushroomed in recent years. One example is UNEPFI, discussed in more detail in chapter 6.[299] UNEPFI is not an investor or an agent of investors, but rather facilitates networking, institutional collaboration, dialogue, and development of best practice standards. Also significant is the CDP, established in 2000 to provide an international secretariat for the world's major institutional

295 P. Casson and D. Russell, "Universities Superannuation Scheme: Implementing Responsible Investment," in *Responsible Investment*, note 3, 158, 164–65.
296 Http://www.regnan.com.au.
297 Personal communication, staff, ICCR (New York, October 19, 2006).
298 ICCR, "Resolutions Filed During the 2005–2006 Season," at http://www.iccr.org/shareholder/proxy_book06/06statuschart.php. See further ICCR's annual *Proxy Resolutions Book* for the complete texts of all SRI shareholder resolutions filed.
299 Http://www.unepfi.org.

investors to collaborate on the business implications of climate change.[300] Also, an Investor Network on Climate Risk (INCR) was formed to promote better understanding of financial risks and investment opportunities posed by climate change.[301] Other collaborative mechanisms include the Eurosif,[302] the Council of Institutional Investors,[303] and the International Corporate Governance Network.[304]

The shortcoming of these collaborative forums is that they cater mainly to investors with similar values. They lack commensurate influence over the behavior of funds with different priorities or goals. Thus, for instance, while the ICCR has extensive support from among mainstream and socially liberal religious denominations, it has virtually no members from the evangelical and conservative Christian sects.

G. AGENCY PROBLEMS WITHIN FINANCIAL INSTITUTIONS

Internal governance of financial organizations, as in corporations generally, affects SRI. The financial world is not an exemplar of democratic rule. Contributors to pension funds or mutual funds typically have scant opportunity to participate in or be consulted about investment decisions. While the SRI industry is increasingly opposed to undemocratic corporate governance, which hinders their shareholder advocacy, ironically, financiers have not reflected closely on their own governance.

Elitist modes of decision-making in financial institutions reflect both assumptions about ways to achieve efficient asset management and a lack of formal rights and legal procedure for investors to participate in investment policy-making. This regime of decision-making concentrates power in the hands of a cadre of experts. Legal barriers to participatory governance in the financial sector are canvassed in the next chapter, but some comments about the culture of investment decision-making should be made here.

Investment institutions commonly delegate asset management to specialist fund managers, such as asset management companies, further distancing beneficiaries from those who administer their money.[305] Fund managers may

---

300 Http://www.cdproject.net.
301 Http://www.incr.com.
302 Http://www.eurosif.org.
303 Http://www.cii.org.
304 Http://www.icgn.org.
305 Harmes, note 14, 32–33.

usurp or implement perfunctorily any SRI mandates because their short-term contracts induce them to focus on quarterly financial performance or they are simply too busy with other priorities.[306] They may also surreptitiously collude with corporate management to protect any collateral business opportunities.[307] As one illustration, the giant Fidelity fund group in the US apparently made over half of its US$9.8 billion operating revenues in 2001 from collateral services to companies at which it voted proxies on behalf of fund investors.[308] A 2006 study of nearly 1,000 individual Canadian mutual funds concluded that the funds strongly support the status quo, on average following management's line about two-thirds of the time when voting on shareholder resolutions.[309] In recent years the mutual fund industry generally has come under scrutiny for various financial scandals and unethical conduct associated with fund managers.[310]

Governing boards of trustees or directors are a poor surrogate voice for investors. Directors commonly sit on several mutual fund boards, within a single investment company, leaving them with little time and energy to devote to better governance within individual funds. The Teachers Insurance and Annuity Association, College Retirement Equities Fund (TIAA-CREF) is one of the few funds in the US whose members routinely vote on board candidates.[311] Public sector plans, particularly in the US and UK, often combine elected and appointed trustees to represent members. However, in most corporate sector plans members do not choose trustees, who sometimes lack the time and qualifications to be attentive to their mandates.[312] Significant amendments to the UK's *Pensions Act* in 2004 for example were designed to address both problems, with provisions for members to nominate such

---

306 D. Wheeler and J. Thomson, *Comparative Study of U.K. and Canadian Pension Fund Transparency Practices* (NRTEE, 2004), 20.

307 Harmes, note 14, 187–88.

308 C.A. Williams and J.M. Conley, *An Emerging Third Way? The Erosion of the Anglo-American Shareholder Value Construct*, Research Paper No. 04-09 (University of North Carolina Legal Studies, 2005), 34.

309 SIO, *A Survey of Canadian Mutual Funds on Proxy Voting* (SIO, 2007).

310 E.g., J.L. Davis, G.T. Payne, and G.C, McMahan, "A Few Bad Apples? Scandalous Behavior of Mutual Fund Managers," *Journal of Business Ethics* 76(2–3) (2007): 319.

311 Http://www.tiaa-cref.org.

312 See N. Kakabadse and A. Kakabadse, "Pension Funds Governance: An Overview of the Role of Trustees," *International Journal of Business Governance and Ethics* 1(1): 3 (discussing UK pension funds).

trustees and requirements for trustees to have sufficient knowledge to run their schemes properly.

In the retail market, financial advisers and planners comprise another set of intermediaries who can hinder SRI. They are professionals who advise people on financial planning, investing, and budgeting. Financial advisers, often affiliated with banks or specialist financial planning firms, are gate-keepers to investment product sales. They have not necessarily been diligent in advising clients of SRI products.[313] Research on German retail banks offering SRI mutual fund products observed that "no advisor demonstrated the initiative to inform customers proactively about ethical funds and some bank employees even falsely denied their existence."[314] A recent Canadian survey by GlobeScan, a public opinion agency, found that merely 8 percent of financial advisers broach the option of SRI with their clients.[315] In private banking servicing HNWI clients, financial advisers also tend to lack competency in and awareness of SRI issues.[316] While public polls frequently show strong support for SRI, the small size of the SRI retail market suggests that buyers and sellers are not adequately connected.[317] Most financial planners are not well informed of SRI issues, or view it disparagingly as too risky or a fringe product. Mindful of their reputation among clients, financial planners tend not to wish to sell investment products they perceive as more likely to perform poorly. Only a few financial planning firms specialize in SRI.[318]

Some commentators see hopeful signs of change. Stephen Davis and others believe that the rise of institutional investment is "mandating a new focus on accountability" that "is quietly laying foundations of an accountable capitalism capable of winning public trust."[319] A variety of bodies seek to align the

---

313 Schueth, note 109, 192; also remarks by D. Foley, Vice-President, Strategic Analysis, Inhance Investment Management (2007 Canadian Responsible Investment Conference, Montreal, May 27–29, 2007).

314 U Schrader, "Ignorant Advice—Customer Advisory Service for Ethical Investment Funds," *Business Strategy and the Environment* 15 (2006): 2000, 2000.

315 Cited in L. MacKenzie, "Putting Your Money Where Your Heart Is," *Canadian Living* November (2007): 279.

316 See discussion in the session "Unlocking Value in Private Banking" (UNEPFI Global Roundtable, Melbourne, Australia, October 24–25, 2007).

317 Calvert Group, *Attitudes Toward Socially Responsible Investing* (Calvert, 2006); Resnik Communications and KPMG Consulting, *Money Where Your Mouth Is* (KPMG, 2000).

318 E.g., Investing Ethically, http://www.investing-ethically.co.uk.

319 Davis, et al., note 75, 15, 26.

behavior of financial institutions with their investors. These accountability mechanisms include Morningstar's Stewardship Grade for Funds, which scrutinizes and grades mutual funds on their governance with regard to board independence, whether manager remuneration aligns with fund performance, and corporate culture.[320] In 2005, Mercer launched a service rating fund managers on share voting records, corporate engagement practices, and incorporation of ESG factors in portfolio selection.[321] On the corporate governance side, many advisory services assist institutional investors to vote their shares. They include the Institutional Shareholders Service (US), Corporate Governance International and ISS Proxy (Australia); Proxinvest (France); IVIS and Manifest (UK); and the Korea Corporate Governance Service (South Korea).[322]

The SRI community also targets financial planners; for instance, UKSIF and the Caisse d'économie solidaire in Quebec have designed toolkits and training seminars for this group.[323] Likewise, the RIAA has pioneered a useful certification system for Australian financial planners to verify their competence in advising on SRI issues.[324] Recent evidence suggests that financial firms have started hiring more SRI advisers to meet escalating market demand, although the shortage of suitable expertise may hinder the market for some time.[325]

H. CONCLUSIONS

The financial sector poses an array of significant barriers to sustainable development, and therefore to the aspirations of the SRI movement. The foregoing discussion is not an exhaustive account of these market and institutional barriers, but canvasses the most pervasive ones.

Commendably, the SRI community recognizes many of these challenges and has devoted considerable resources to address them. A flourishing research industry is helping to enhance valuation of corporate sustainability and governance performance. Institutional investors have also collaborated to improve corporate governance standards, exerting pressure for more informative environmental disclosures, and taking other means that bring them closer to

---

320 Http://www.morningstar.com.
321 Mercer, "What Gets Rated Gets Reviewed," at http://www.mercer.com/ESGresearch.
322 Davis, et al., note 75, 135–36.
323 Http://www.uksif.org; http://www.cecosol.coop.
324 Http://www.eia.org.au.
325 J. Mincer, "Investor Demand Brings More 'Green' Financial Advisers to Street," *Wall Street Journal*, December 5, 2007.

fulfilling the promise of the universal owner. Various problems remain, however, including short-sighted investment horizons, undemocratic governance within financial institutions and, above all, a prevailing business case approach to SRI that suppresses ethical considerations.

Quite a few of these constraints hinge on the legal structure of investment institutions and their regulation. The impact of the legal system on the growth of SRI is explored in ensuing chapters. For now, the following sections discuss a further, critical aspect of SRI. To what extent has it been able to influence the cost of capital and thereby improve firms' behavior? The ultimate measure of SRI is not its market share or number of signatories to codes of conduct, but rather its ability to change the social and environmental conduct of economic actors.

III. Doing Good While Doing Well?

A. DETERMINANTS OF SUCCESS

Advocates of SRI assert that it changes corporate social and environmental behavior (doing good) while making investors wealthier (doing well).[326] Traditionally, as Neil Carter and Meg Huby explain, SRI "implies that individuals may be prepared to place ethical concerns, such as a desire to protect the planet from pollution, above financial returns in their personal investment choices."[327] Likewise, Russell Sparkes and Chris Cowton proclaim that the "shift in SRI from margin to mainstream could play a crucial role in obliging or influencing quoted companies to address CSR issues."[328] However, for many investors today, the lure of SRI is that they can also attain prosperity. Thus, Peter Camejo trumpets that "SRI has financially outperformed conventional investment strategies. ... The empirical evidence for SRI's out-performance is overwhelming."[329] The success of the SRI movement is thus framed in terms of its ability to build both natural and financial capital.

---

326 See H. Brill, J.A. Brill, and C. Feingenbaum, *Investing with Your Values: Making Money and Making a Difference* (Bloomberg Press, 1999); J. Hancock, *The Ethical Investor: Making Gains with Values* (Financial Times Management, 1998).

327 N. Carter and M. Huby, "Ecological Citizenship and Ecological Investment," *Environmental Politics* 14(2) (2005): 255, 256.

328 R. Sparkes and C.J. Cowton, "The Maturing of Socially Responsible Investment: A Review of the Developing Link with Corporate Social Responsibility," *Journal of Business Ethics* 52 (2004): 45, 45.

329 P. Camejo, *The SRI Advantage: Why Socially Responsible Investing Has Outperformed Financially* (New Society Publishers, 2002).

In these perspectives, SRI can do good by influencing targeted firms' cost of capital. In theory, when SRI favors a company, the reduced cost of capital provides the financial resources required for socially beneficial projects. Conversely, by shunning or divesting from less compliant companies, SRI's influence can raise their cost of finance. Presumably, affected firms would then be motivated to reform their policies, making them more attractive to SRI-driven financiers. The heart of the purpose of SRI for the purely ethically-driven investors is often to improve corporate behavior.

Apart from redeeming corporations, many SRI investors also personally hope to do well.[330] The extent to which they are prepared to trade virtue for prosperity is unresolved. Some empirical studies suggest that while investors may willingly trade some financial performance to meet SRI goals, their tolerance for losses is limited.[331] Self-styled ethical investors also commonly hold investments in conventional funds, confirming the inclination for financial returns.[332] Other empirical research points to a "clear link between perceptions of financial performance of SRI and the amount invested in SRI profiled mutual funds," with SRI mutual funds perceived as offering higher returns attracting more investment.[333] Conversely, some other surveys conclude that SRI is probably driven more by investor attitudes toward the social aims of firms and the feeling of good, rather than by financial returns.[334]

---

330 S. Foerster and P. Asmundson, "Socially Responsible Investing: Better for Your Soul or Your Bottom Line?" *Canadian Investment Review* 14(4) (2001): 26; D. Edwards, *The Link Between Company Environmental and Financial Performance* (Earthscan, 1998); R.P. Lowry, *Good Money: A Guide to Profitable Social Investing in the '90s* (W.W. Norton, 1991).

331 B.N. Rosen, D.M. Sandler, and D. Shani, "Social Issues and Socially Responsible Investment Behavior: A Preliminary Empirical Investigation," *Journal of Consumer Affairs* 25(2) (1991): 221. J. McLachlan and J. Gardner, "A Comparison of Socially Responsible and Conventional Investors," *Journal of Business Ethics* 52 (2004): 11, 20–21; A. Lewis and P. Webley, "Social and Ethical Investing: Beliefs, Preferences and the Willingness to Sacrifice Financial Return," in *Ethics and Economic Affairs*, eds A. Lewis and K.E. Wärneryd (Routledge, 1994), 171.

332 A. Lewis and C. Mackenzie, "Morals, Money, Ethical Investing and Economic Psychology," *Human Relations* 53(2) (2000): 179.

333 J. Nilsson, "Investment with a Conscience: Examining the Impact of Pro-Social Attitudes and Perceived Financial Performance on Socially Responsible Investment Behavior," *Journal of Business Ethics* (2008): forthcoming.

334 G. Williams, "Some Determinants of the Socially Responsible Investment Decision: A Cross-Country Study," *Journal of Behavioral Finance* 8(1) (2007): 43; D.J. Beal, M. Goyen, and P. Phillips, "Why Do We Invest Ethically?" *Journal of Investing* 14(3) (2005): 66.

Given economists' models of the corporation and capital markets that assume that shareholders are interested only in wealth and risk avoidance, some scholars doubt that investors can *both* do good and do well. David Henderson sees CSR as costly to shareholders because it requires the diversion of resources that firms could dedicate to maximizing profits.[335] Roberta Romano has denounced SRI-driven shareholder proposals as anathema to the "objective of U.S. corporate law," i.e., the maximization of corporate wealth.[336] Along similar lines, Daniel Fischel explains:

> let us assume a corporation decides to modify its behavior—say, discontinuing investment in South Africa or ceasing manufacture of war munitions—in direct response to a defeated [shareholder] proposal. While reformers would no doubt be ecstatic about this result, shareholders as a class have little to be excited about. What has occurred is that a tiny minority, subsidized by the vast majority of shareholders, has caused the corporation to abandon a wealth-maximizing strategy favored by the very majority of shareholders who are forced to provide the subsidy. A less "democratic" result or one more inconsistent with the goal of maximizing shareholders' welfare is hard to find.[337]

Regardless of such views, Donald Schepers and Prakash Sethi caution that "SRI funds have very little, if any, bargaining leverage to influence corporate behavior based on its equity holdings."[338] Similarly, Matthew Haigh and James Hazelton view SRI as ineffective in altering company behavior because the "underlying economic opportunities remain."[339]

Yet, if there is a clear business case for SRI, there should be no trade-off between being prosperous and virtuous. Corporations that operate sustainably should enhance shareholder value, by anticipating tightening government

---

335 D. Henderson, *Misguided Virtue: False Notions of Corporate Social Responsibility* (Institute of Economic Affairs, 2002).

336 R. Romano, "Less is More: Making Institutional Investor Activism a Valuable Mechanism of Corporate Governance," *Yale Journal on Regulation* 18 (2001): 174.

337 D.R. Fischel, "The Corporate Governance Movement," *Vanderbilt Law Review* 35 (1982): 1259, 1279.

338 D.H. Schepers and S.P. Sethi, "Do Socially Responsible Funds Actually Deliver What They Promise? Bridging the Gap Between the Promise and Performance of Socially Responsible Funds," *Business and Society Review* 108(1) (2003): 11, 26.

339 M. Haigh and J. Hazelton, "Financial Markets: A Tool for Social Responsibility?" *Journal of Business Ethics* 52(1) (2004): 59, 59.

regulation, using natural resources frugally, and appealing to the flourishing green consumer market. Conversely, polluters should face regulatory challenges, marred reputations, and other hard and soft costs. As noted earlier, this perspective dovetails with the vast literature in business and environmental policy exploring how markets provide firms with carrots and sticks to act environmentally responsibly. It is when SRI seeks to force change for which the market does not recognize a business case that problems arise from the perspective of economic theory.

In assessing the impact of SRI more systematically, the following discussion examines a variety of theoretical and empirical literature. Modern corporate finance theory doubts that SRI can change corporate conduct while benefiting investors financially, at least in the short term.[340] However, much of this theoretical criticism conceptualizes SRI narrowly, based on strict exclusionary screens and restricted ethical criteria. Empirical literature sheds insight into the influences of SRI. These include the financial performance of SRI funds as well as of companies with good sustainability records, and the impact of shareholder advocacy. Most of the theoretical and empirical research canvasses SRI in equity markets. We know much less about SRI's impact in the context of the debt financing, such as bonds and bank loans.[341]

B. SRI AND FINANCE THEORY

1. Does SRI Entail a Financial Sacrifice?

Finance theory generally suggests a tradeoff between social and financial investment goals. Modern portfolio theory holds that a diversified investment universe is more likely to produce optimal risk-adjusted returns than a narrowly constructed portfolio.[342] Put simply, your investment portfolio will yield better returns if you own shares in both mining and transportation sectors, rather than holding only mining stocks. The gains of diversification

---

340 J.H. Langbein and R.A. Posner, "Social Investing and the Law of Trusts," *Michigan Law Review* 79 (1980): 72; M.S. Knoll, "Ethical Screening in Modern Financial Markets: The Conflicting Claims Underlying Socially Responsible Investment," *Business Lawyer* 57 (2002): 681.

341 One study of European banks found that because it was hard to isolate the impact of specific variables, it could offer no concrete evidence of a link between good environmental credit risk procedures and improved shareholder value for the banks: ISIS, note 141, 44–45.

342 H. Markowitz, "Portfolio Selection," *Journal of Finance* 7(1) (1952): 77. Returns for instance include dividends paid by firms as well as appreciation of the firms' stock prices.

flow from the fact that the profitability of all companies does not move in tandem. From the assumption of a perfect capital market, "it assumes that every investment's return compensates for its risk and the only way to reduce risk without sacrificing return is to diversify well."[343] The only risk an investor cannot eliminate is economy-wide or market risk. Therefore, meta-phorically, rather than place all your eggs in one basket (e.g., the mining sector), an investor should hold a portfolio of various assets of dissimilar risk characteristics. From this perspective, exclusionary SRI screens constrain diversification and may increase the non-market risks of the investment portfolio and thereby ultimately hurt returns.[344]

However, the axioms underlying these financial theories have been subject to a barrage of empirical tests, which challenge the validity of some of their assumptions.[345] Therefore, critics extrapolate that markets are not as efficient as modern portfolio theory assumes and that SRI may thus avoid a financial sacrifice.

The efficient market theory posits that, "the prices of goods sold in that market fully reflect all available information about those goods."[346] Therefore, no one can "beat the market" as, to do so, the investor would need information that is not yet generally known. In an inefficient market, a social investor could pick under-priced stocks, with their "hidden value" associated with being a good corporate citizen. This could enable that discerning investor to eventu-ally outperform the market which only belatedly appreciates this additional value. This epitomizes the rationale of business-case SRI, which is not about placing seemingly esoteric ethical considerations ahead of financial impera-tives, but rather applying a more sophisticated assessment of corporate value. Herbert Blank and Michael Carty for instance found that during 1997–2000

---

343 R. Barber and T. Ghilarducci, "Pension Funds, Capital Markets, and the Economic Future," in *Transforming the U.S. Financial System: Equity and Efficiency for the 21ˢᵗ Century*, eds G.A. Dymski, G. Epstein, and R. Pollin (M.E. Sharpe, 1993), 287, 304.

344 A. Rudd, "Social Responsibility and Portfolio Performance," *California Management Review* 23(4) (1981): 55.

345 B.G. Malkiel, "The Efficient Market Hypothesis and Its Critics," *Journal of Economic Perspectives* 17(1) (2002): 59; R. Ball, "The Theory of Stock Market Efficiency: Accomplishments and Limitations," *Journal of Applied Corporate Finance* 30(2–3) (1995): 4; C.H. Coombs, "Portfolio Theory and the Measurement of Risk," in *Human Judgment and Decision Process*, eds M. Kaplan and S. Schwartz (Academic Press, 1975), 63.

346 E. Fama, "Capital Markets: A Review of Theory and Empirical Work," *Journal of Finance* 25(2) (1970): 383.

the companies rated highest by Innovest for social responsibility outperformed the market.[347] Similarly, Sarah and Peter Stanwick observed a significant correlation between firms with the lowest pollution emissions under the US Toxics Release Inventory (TRI) and their financial success and ranking in Fortune magazine's Corporate Reputation Index for the period 1987–92.[348] Maria O'Brien Hylton adds that in an inefficient "noisy" market, where herd-like investors are caught up in the commotion of a speculative bubble or bust, patient SRI investors who look to fundamentals can profitably anticipate investor trends before others.[349]

Conversely, even if the market is inefficient, Michael Knoll believes that SRI will continue to under-perform because social investors will still allow ethical motivations to overlook financially promising firms.[350] In other words, an inefficient market may under- or over-rate both ethical or unethical businesses, leaving social investors with no special advantage. Further, any underlying financial advantage for SRI may be offset by the costs of constructing such a specialized portfolio. It may carry "higher transaction costs and management fees due to the relatively small size of funds and need to collect specialised information data concerning the ethical practices of firms."[351] Christopher Geczy and others find evidence of this in their sample of US mutual funds, with regular funds having an annual average management fee of 1.10 percent compared to 1.33 percent for SRI funds.[352] The SRI industry however believes these research costs reward investors through quality assurance that minimizes environmental liabilities, corporate governance failures, and reputational risks.[353]

---

347 H.D. Blank and C.M. Carty, *The Eco-Efficiency Anomaly* (QED International, June 2002).

348 P.A. Stanwick and S.D. Stanwick, "The Relationship between Corporate Social Performance and Size, Financial and Environmental Performance," *Journal of Business Ethics* 17(2) (1998): 195.

349 M. O'Brien Hylton, "'Socially Responsible' Investing: Doing Good Versus Doing Well in an Inefficient Market," *American University Law Review* 42 (1992): 1, 23–27.

350 Knoll, note 340, 706.

351 G. Michelson, et al., "Ethical Investment Processes and Outcomes," *Journal of Business Ethics* 52 (2004): 1, 5.

352 C.C. Geczy, R.F. Stambaugh, and D. Levin, *Investing in Socially Responsible Mutual Funds*, Working Paper (Wharton Business School, University of Pennsylvania, 2003). 32.

353 Personal communication, David Simpson, Interpraxis (Toronto, October 31, 2006).

As discussed later in this chapter, empirical studies suggest that risk-adjusted returns for SRI portfolios do not generally under-perform the market. While we know that historical returns are not indicative of the future, claims of an SRI financial penalty increasingly sound hollow. Given the plethora of stocks available, the cost of a slightly less diversified portfolio is often inconsequential.[354] Moreover, many SRI funds do not, as critics such as Knoll assume, rely on exclusionary screens. Rather, they retain diversified portfolios but use best-of-sector methods for asset selection and rely on the influence of shareholder activism. In an era of business case SRI, where the very purpose of much responsible finance has become to seek alpha, the criticisms of SRI's indifference to financial fundamentals seem rather dated.

2. Can SRI Improve Corporate Behavior?

A. EQUITY FINANCING

Finance theory also implies criticisms of SRI's influence over corporate environmental and social behavior. Proponents of SRI contend that it financially rewards ethical firms by additional investment and punishes unethical firms by divestment, presumably raising capital costs.[355] Finance theory however suggests otherwise, namely that social investors are price takers, not price makers.

In what circumstances and how may SRI affect the behavior of firms? As noted in the previous chapter, one factor to consider is the extent to which companies depend on external financing. One theorist predicts that "SRI is more likely to be relevant whenever companies are heavily dependent on the stock market as a financing instrument. For example companies are crucially dependent on the stock market in the phase of the initial public offering."[356] Even divestments, which nominally produce only a transfer of ownership of stock, may also have wider effects. Public companies desire high stock prices for many reasons. It improves corporate market capitalization, which has benefits for raising capital, and it improves management remuneration often tied to stock options which increase in value with rising share prices.

---

354 A.H. Munnell and A. Sundén, "Social Investing: Pension Plans Should Just Say 'No'" (paper presented at conference on Costs and Benefits: "Socially Responsible," Investing and Pension Funds, American Enterprise Institute, Washington, D.C., June 7, 2004), 15.

355 H. Hong and M. Kacperczyk, *The Price of Sin: The Effects of Social Norms on Markets*, Working Paper (Princeton University, 2006).

356 A. Beltratti, *Socially Responsible Investment in General Equilibrium* (Fondazione Eni Enrico Mattei, 2003), 21.

If companies must pay more for capital, it undermines their ability to undertake new projects relative to other firms. High stock prices also enable firms to raise more capital when they issue new equity.[357]

Thus, in this perspective, the ability of SRI to change corporate behavior is not by moral suasion as much as by affecting the bottom line. The hypothesis is that fewer buyers for a stock due to an SRI boycott could hurt the targeted company because it would have to offer investors higher returns to hold its stock. The effect is supposedly reversed with positive ethical screening, as the preferred firms' stock prices rise and their cost of capital declines. Yet, apart from affecting firms' cost of capital, some researchers believe SRI may achieve influence by having an educative effect on targeted firms. Having to respond to SRI institutions' correspondence for instance may "provoke firms to rethink their environmental performance."[358] Feedback from SRI funds and rating agencies may influence firms to evaluate more closely and improve their environmental performance.[359]

Such effects are not predicted by conventional finance theory. Major finance concepts, including the capital asset pricing model and the efficient markets hypothesis, assume that demand curves for individual equities are horizontal (as against downward sloping curves).[360] Under this hypothesis, investors can trade any quantity of a firm's shares without affecting its price. This is because, in an efficient equity market where demand for a company's stock is almost perfectly elastic,[361] the price of a stock simply reflects the

---

357 However, one advantage of a low stock price is that it enables firms to buy back their shares cheaply: A. Mahajan and S. Tartaroglu, "Market to Book Ratios, Equity Market-timing and Capital Structure: International Evidence," 2006 *Financial Management Association Annual Meeting* (October 12, 2006), 1.

358 O. Weber, "Investment and Environmental Management: The Interaction between Environmentally Responsible Investment and Environmental Management Practices," *International Journal of Sustainable Development* 9(4) (2006): 336, 337.

359 Ibid.

360 P. Krugman and R. Wells, *Microeconomics* (Worth Publishers, 2005), chapter 7; A. Shleifer, "Do Demand Curves for Stocks Slope Down?" *Journal of Finance* 41(3) (1986): 579; H.J. Cha and B.S. Lee, "The Market Demand Curve for Common Stocks: Evidence from Equity Mutual Fund Flows," *Journal of Financial and Quantitative Analysis* 36(2) (2001): 195.

361 C. Loderer, et al., "The Price Elasticity of Demand for Common Stock," *Journal of Finance* 46 (1991): 621. In contrast, for an asset that is relatively unique and has few close substitutes, the demand curve should be steep and less elastic.

expected future cash flows, and all informed investors value the company's stock at the same price.[362] As shareholder divestment does not per se change the expected cash flow from the firm's activities, therefore its stock prices should not yield.[363] Only if potential traders believed the sale or purchase of stock reflected a downward or upward view of the company's financial prospects would the stock price vary significantly. Business case SRI that educates the market to the financial consequences of firms' environmental behavior may have such an effect.

Consequently, substantial defections of shareholders because of ethical concerns divorced from the bottom line should have a negligible effect on a firm's stock price. Many social investors by selling may momentarily depress its share price, yet other investors would buy thus soon returning the stock price to its former level. As Meir Statman concludes: "[s]ocially responsible investors can raise the cost of capital ... only in the absence of numerous conventional investors who stand by ready to provide substitute capital at the same cost."[364] Conversely, social investors could put upward pressure on a favored stock, but the market would likely consider it overvalued and sell out, thus returning the firm's value to its previous, "normal" level.

Because of the centrality of this assumption to finance theory, researchers have tested the hypothesis in various studies.[365] Some suggest that the demand curve for stock may not be perfectly horizontal and that shifts in demand could affect price. In the context of SRI, the most comprehensively studied action is the South African boycott. Some research suggests that the divestment movement had virtually no effect on the economic performance of targeted companies.[366] Siew Teoh and others examined how the share prices of seventeen US firms with extensive ties to South Africa were affected by

362 Arnold, note 191, 314, 330.
363 W.N. Davidson, D.L. Worell, and A. El-Jelly, "Influencing Managers to Change Unpopular Corporate Behavior Through Boycotts and Divestitures," *Business and Society* 34(2) (1995): 171.
364 M. Statman, "Socially Responsible Mutual Funds," *Financial Analysts Journal* 56(3) (2000): 30, 36.
365 E.g., M. Scholes, "The Market for Securities: Substitution Versus Price Pressure and the Effects of Information on Share Prices," *Journal of Business* 45 (1972): 179; L.S. Bagwell, "Dutch Auction Repurchases: An Analysis of Shareholder Heterogeneity," *Journal of Finance* 47 (1992): 71; A. Shleifer, "Do Demand Curves for Stocks Slope Down?" *Journal of Finance* 41 (1986): 579.
366 S.H. Teoh, I. Welch, and C.P. Wazzan, "The Effect of Socially Activist Investment Policies on the Financial Markets: Evidence from the South African Boycott," *Journal of Business* 72 (1999): 35.

announcements by nine pensions funds (on different dates) that they would divest from those companies. Their results show that, apart from the first divestment announcement, share prices did not drop significantly in response to subsequent notices of divestment. However, when apartheid ended, and Nelson Mandela called for an immediate end to the sanctions, the equity prices of various multinational companies with existing ties to South Africa abruptly rose. Raman Kumar and colleagues suggest that this points to the influence of the SRI divestment campaign.[367] Regardless, most SRI funds do not exhibit this level of coordination.

The significant divestment from sin stocks such as the tobacco industry, by large funds such as CalPERS, provides another case study. It appears to have had no impact on stock prices in this sector and has possibly negatively affected the funds that forewent the value of appreciating tobacco stock prices.[368] Likewise, the performance of other objectionable stocks commonly excluded by social investors, such as alcohol and weapons manufacturers, has not suffered.[369] In the US, a "Vice Fund" dedicated to investment in sin stocks such as tobacco and munitions was established in 2002, and claims to have out-performed the market since its inception.[370]

Other theoretical research that takes a more granular perspective of capital markets predicts that SRI can influence the cost of capital when the stock is risky, the stock is unique, or the stock trades in small, restrictive markets.[371] Assuming that all investors are not fully diversified across a large market, Robert Merton believes that investors will expect higher returns to compensate for greater risk.[372] The reduced diversification of investor portfolios should cause them to pay more attention to company-specific risks and therefore share prices should be more responsive to changes in the number

367 R. Kumar, W.B. Lamb, and R.E. Wokutch, "The End of South African Sanctions, Institutional Ownership, and the Stock Price of Boycotted Firms," *Business and Society* 41(2) (2002): 133.

368 P.G. Pan and J.K. Mardfin, *Socially Responsible Investing*, Report No. 6 (Hawaii Legislative Reference Bureau, 2001), 99.

369 Vogel, note 32, 63; see, e.g., T. Burroughes, "Ethical Investors Losing Out as Tobacco Stocks Burn Up Britain's Equity Markets," *The Business*, February 24, 2007.

370 Http://www.vicefund.com.

371 P. Rivoli, "Making a Difference or Making a Statement? Finance Research and Socially Responsible Investment," *Business Ethics Quarterly* 13(3) (2003): 271.

372 See R.C. Merton, "A Simple Model of Capital Market Equilibrium with Incomplete Information," *Journal of Finance* 42(3) (1987): 483.

of investors. A similar effect is predicted by Pekka Hietala's model where investment regulations restrict investors' security choices.[373] To maintain their pool of investors, firms therefore should have an incentive to behave responsibly to avoid exclusion from SRI portfolios.[374]

For example, an expanded investor base from a firm's stock exchange listing may positively correlate with an improved share price after allowing for changes in liquidity.[375] Andrei Shleifer found that inclusion of a company in the S&P 500 had that effect on share prices.[376] Inclusion in the main SRI indexes such as the Dow Jones Sustainability Indexes and the FTSE4Good Indexes may do likewise. Some research however queries whether such a financial boost is sustained for the long term.[377]

Using data from the respected KLD Research and Analytics, Jeroen Derwall sought to disentangle the significance of specific CSR variables on firms' cost of capital. He found that "leaders along the dimensions of environmental performance, product quality, and governance enjoy a lower cost of equity capital, than do laggards."[378] However, he concluded that financial markets tend to penalize a firm's investment in social practices (e.g., employment diversity policies, human rights, and community involvement), perhaps because they are more costly to implement and their value harder to quantify.[379] Like the authors of other studies, Derwall believed that the change in the investor base might explain changes in firms' cost of equity capital.

373　P.T. Hietala, "Asset Pricing in Partially Segmented Markets: Evidence from the Finnish Market," *Journal of Finance* 44(3) (1989): 697.

374　However, such screening may not, per se, induce good firms to behave better. Under this model, good firms are already screened in to the SRI portfolio and have nothing further to gain by costly expenditures to improve their sustainability performance.

375　E.g., G.B. Kadlec and J.J. McConnell, "The Effect of Market Segmentation and Illiquidity on Asset Prices: Evidence from Exchange Listings," *Journal of Finance* 49(2) (1994): 611.

376　A. Shleifer, "Do Demand Curves for Stocks Slope Down?" *Journal of Finance* 41(3) (1986): 579.

377　Harris and Gurel found that while inclusion in the S&P 500 immediately boosted the firm's stock price, the increase was short-lived and nearly fully reversed within two weeks: L. Harris and E. Gurel, "Price and Volume Effects Associated with Changes in the S&P 500 List; New Evidence for the Existence of Price Pressures," *Journal of Finance* 41 (1986): 815.

378　J. Derwall, *The Economic Virtues of SRI and CSR* (PhD dissertation, Erasmus School of Economics, Erasmus University Rotterdam, 2007), 204.

379　Ibid., 208.

Pietra Rivoli theorizes other conditions that may make firms more susceptible to SRI pressures. She posits that "riskier" firms should be more responsive to SRI.[380] In other words, where there is relatively high uncertainty in the market about a firm's future and therefore its share value, the price elasticity of demand for that firm's shares should be lower and, concomitantly, investors will expect greater returns to compensate for greater risk. Rivoli further predicts that relatively "unique" firms should be more responsive to SRI pressure.[381] If investors believe that a security has few substitutes, the price elasticity of demand should decline. Thus, firms in sectors with many comparable firms, such as motor vehicle manufacturers, should be less responsive to SRI than boutique firms, such as firms specializing in innovative technologies, with more unique characteristics that make them sensitive to market impulses. Larry Wall argues that SRI should focus on small firms. He contends that SRI is most likely to have influence where it bids up the price of small companies that follow socially desirable policies.[382] He believes that social investors are more likely to succeed by bidding up the price of desirable stocks for extended periods of time than in attempting to force down the price of undesirable firms.

If we accept such arguments, how much SRI must there be in the market to exert this kind of influence? Given the SRI sector's current small size, it would seem improbable that it could significantly affect companies financially.[383] Rivoli and James Angel caution that "unless a substantial fraction of the capital market boycotts a firm, the increase in the cost of equity as a result of a boycott by ethical investors is likely to be quite small."[384] Under general market conditions, they estimated that 75 percent of investors would have to boycott a stock in order for the targeted firm's cost of equity to increase by even 1 percent. Robert Heinkel and others developed a theoretical model of corporate environmental responsibility, which predicted that SRI investors

---

380 Rivoli, note 371.

381 Ibid.

382 L.D. Wall, "Some Lessons from Basic Finance for Effective Socially Responsible Investing," *Economic Review of the Federal Reserve Bank of Atlanta* 80(1) (1995): 1.

383 R. Heinkel, A. Kraus, and J. Zechner, "The Effect of Green Investment on Corporate Behavior," *Journal of Financial and Quantitative Analysis* 36(4) (2001): 431; I. Aslaksen and T. Synnestvedt, "Ethical Investment and the Incentives for Corporate Environmental Protection and Social Responsibility," *Corporate Social Responsibility and Environmental Management* 10 (2003): 212.

384 J. Angel and P. Rivoli, "Does Ethical Investing Impose a Cost Upon the Firm? A Theoretical Perspective," *Journal of Investing* 6(4) (1997): 57.

would need to hold at least 20 percent of the market in order to lower the cost of capital sufficiently to induce a business to invest in environmental improvements.[385] These numbers greatly exceed the present size of the SRI market even under the most liberal interpretation of SRI. The impact is further reduced because SRI funds have different notions of what is "ethical" or "responsible," and often do not work in concert. Of course, if SRI is driven primarily by pragmatic business considerations, which the wider market comes to appreciate, then SRI will wield greater influence.

B. DEBT FINANCING

By comparison, banks appear to have more influence over borrowers, especially small enterprises that have fewer financing options than large public companies.[386] Academic literature identifies bank financing as a potentially useful avenue to promote CSR.[387] Environmentally sensitive firms have showed abnormally high stock valuations immediately following announcement of receiving a major bank loan.[388] While some authors envision a benevolent role for banks as social gatekeepers, the majority find that self-interested risk mitigation principally motivates lenders to promote CSR among borrowers.[389] Risk management serves to protect the value of loan security against risks such as regulatory directions to cleanup contaminated land.

---

385 R. Heinkel, A. Kraus, and J. Zechner, "The Effect of Green Investment on Corporate Behavior," *Journal of Financial and Quantitative Analysis* 36(4) (2001): 431.

386 T. McDermott, A. Stainer, and L. Sainer, "Contaminated Land: Bank Credit Risk for Small and Medium Size UK Enterprises," *International Journal of Environmental Technology and Management* 5(1) (2005): 1.

387 B. Scholtens, "Finance as a Driver for Corporate Social Responsibility," *Journal of Business Ethics* 68 (2006); 19.

388 S. Aintablian, P.A. McGraw, and G.S. Roberts, "Bank Monitoring and Environmental Risk," *Journal of Business Finance and Accounting* 34(1–2) (2007): 389.

389 M. Jeuken, *Sustainable Finance and Banking: The Financial Sector and the Future of the Planet* (Earthscan, 2001). Jeuken suggests concepts such as "[n]on-risk-related premium differentiation" in bank lending, where firms with better sustainability practices, but an equivalent risk profile, would be given preferential rates on loans (at 70). On environmental risk management, see P. Thompson, "Bank Lending and the Environment: Policies and Opportunities," *International Journal of Bank Marketing* 16(6) (1998): 243; R.S. Frye, "The Role of Private Banks in Promoting Sustainable Development, from Outside Counsel's Perspective," *Law and Policy in International Business* 29(4) (1998): 481.

One study of lender influence examined a microlending scheme run by the Royal Bank of Canada (RBC) in collaboration with an NGO, Calmeadow. It found that the lender was able to use its dominant position to induce borrowers to more closely abide by government regulations.[390] Yet, while banks have considerably more leverage in microfinancing compared to an SRI fund buying shares, because many commercial banks perceive microlending to carry high transaction costs and low returns, they may go elsewhere for business.

In project financing of major infrastructure, banks may exploit contractual techniques to obtain information about a borrower's environmental activities and to insist on adoption of specific environmental or health and safety protocols as a condition of financing. For example, in financing a liquid natural gas facility in the Middle East, a syndicate of lenders including RBC required the project sponsor, a US-based company, to apply US standards of best practice to manage environmental risks.[391] While in theory a company could look elsewhere for financing, its options may be limited; rival banks increasingly apply similar environmental standards (to some extent due to the harmonizing effect of the EPs).[392] Lenders do not commonly adjust the cost of a loan to reflect environmental risks. Instead, when confronted with a project or firm associated with problematic environmental characteristics, lenders may decline financing altogether, require the borrower to adopt specific environmental safeguards, or demand more valuable security relative to the value of the loan.[393]

The bond market is also not necessarily a convenient option for polluters, as creditors in this market are also becoming attentive to the environmental reputation of a borrower, and bond market financing can be administratively unfeasible except for large firms. One Australian report suggested that companies' sustainability performance was becoming a factor in the "cost equation" for corporate bonds.[394]

---

390 R. Hudson and R. Wehrell, "Socially Responsible Investors and the Microentrepreneur: A Canadian Case," *Journal of Business Ethics* 60 (2005): 281.

391 Personal communication, James Evans, Senior Manager, Corporate Environmental Affairs, RBC (Toronto, September 20, 2007).

392 Ibid.

393 Ibid.

394 S. Mays, *Corporate Sustainability—An Investor Perspective: The Mays Report* (Department of the Environment and Heritage, 2003), 14.

C. RELATIONSHIP BETWEEN SUSTAINABILITY AND FINANCIAL PERFORMANCE

1. SRI's Financial Performance

Ideally, to assess whether SRI can lessen the market's environmental footprint requires an empirical investigation, with regressing reliable measures of corporate sustainability performance on the amount of capital invested in firms, while controlling all other material variables. However, most research focuses on the financial performance of SRI funds, and the companies they finance, which may serve as proxies for such analysis.

Despite occasional bad press regarding SRI's apparent financial downside,[395] most academic research suggests that SRI does not materially lower returns. The reliability of the data for comparative purposes is reproachable because investigators use diverse methodologies and criteria, including use of small samples and short performance periods, as well as inadequate controls for industry, country, and other factor biases. In particular, the research lacks a standardized measure of corporate social responsibility for determining what qualifies as "SRI." Moreover, many SRI funds' screening methods are proprietary and kept confidential. Even if SRI under-performs the market, this should not imply a lower contribution to social welfare. The market may not factor SRI's wider social benefits, such as mitigating climate change or protecting biodiversity. Conversely, the superlative returns of a traditional investment may mask subsidization of polluting companies; how well would fossil fuel stocks perform if this industry were required to pay for its full contribution to global warming through carbon taxes?[396]

Despite this disadvantage, numerous studies confirm that SRI accrues a financial advantage. Sandra Waddock and others contend: "[s]ignificant evidence ... suggests at a minimum a neutral, and quite likely a positive, relationship between responsible corporate practices and corporate financial performance."[397] Research by Gottsman and Kessler,[398] Orlitzky and

---

395 E.g., T. Burroughes, "Lower Returns is the Price Investors have to Pay for Taking the Ethical Path," *The Business,* June 23, 2007, 1.

396 N. Lansbury, *Socially Responsible Climate Change? Fossil Fuel Investments of the Socially Responsible Investment Industry in Australia* (Mineral Policy Institute, 2002), 27–28.

397 S.A. Waddock, C. Bodwell, and S.B. Graves, "Responsibility: The New Business Imperative," *Academy of Management Executive* 16(2) (2002): 132.

398 L. Gottsman and J. Kessler, "Smart Screened Investments: Environmentally-screened Equity Funds that Perform," *Journal of Investing* 7(3) (1998): 15.

colleagues,[399] Guenster and others,[400] Garz and others,[401] and Barber[402] among others claim that SRI outperforms the market. A 2007 mega-survey by UNEPFI of academic and broker studies of responsible investment performance at the level of individual corporate stock and whole investment portfolios concluded that SRI does not generally under-perform the market.[403] Much of the SRI advantage apparently accrues from active risk management. Among specific studies, for example, Darren Lee concluded from his investigation of firms in the Dow Jones Sustainability Index (DJSI) that "the DJSI does not underperform the market portfolio, suffer from higher levels of risk, or result in increased diversification costs."[404] In relation to banking, Gary Simpson and Theodor Kohers examined the financial performance of US banks rated under the *Community Reinvestment Act* (CRA) of 1977 for their commitment to servicing disadvantaged local communities, and other indicators of social performance. Their survey of 385 banks for the period 1993–94 showed that banks' financial success appears to correlate positively with having a high rating under the CRA.[405]

Other research is equivocal,[406] concluding no material difference between SRI and non-SRI returns or a statistically significant cost associated

---

399 M. Orlitzky, F.L. Schmidt, and S.L. Rynes, "Corporate Social and Financial Performance: A Meta-Analysis," *Organization Studies* 24 (2003): 403.

400 N. Guenster, et al., *The Economic Value of Corporate Eco-Efficiency*, Working Paper (Erasmus University, July 2005).

401 H. Garz, C. Volk, and M. Gilles, *More Gain than Pain. SRI: Sustainability Pays Off* (WestLB Panmure, 2002).

402 B.M. Barber, *Monitoring the Monitor: Evaluating CalPERS' Shareholder Activism*, Working Paper (Graduate School of Management, University of California at Davis, March 2006).

403 UNEPFI Asset Management Working Group and Mercer, *Demystifying Responsible Investment Performance: A Review of Key Academic and Broker Research on ESG Factors* (UNEPFI, October 2007).

404 D. Lee, *An Analysis of the Sustainability Investment Strategy Employing the Dow Jones World Sustainability Index*, PhD thesis (Monash University, 2006). vii.

405 W.G. Simpson and T. Kohers, "The Link between Corporate Social and Financial Performance: Evidence from the Banking Industry'," *Journal of Business Ethics* 35(2) (2002): 97 (however, this study did not attempt to explain precisely why there is an association between CSR and financial performance among the banks).

406 See, e.g., M.V. Russo and P.A. Fouts, "A Resource-Based Perspective on Corporate Environmental Performance and Profitability," *Academy of Management Journal* 40(3) (1997): 534; C.A. Mallin, B. Saadouni, and R.J. Briston, "The Financial Performance of Ethical Investment Funds," *Journal of Business Finance and Accounting* 22(4) (1995): 483; G.A. Mill,

with SRI. While surveys by Hamilton and others,[407] Reyes and Grieb,[408] Abramson and Chun,[409] Kreander and others,[410] and Bauer and colleagues[411] suggest no SRI advantage, they at least imply no financial penalty. Another stream of research reaches negative conclusions about SRI.[412] Eric Girard and colleagues find SRI mutual fund managers in the US perform poorly compared to various benchmark indexes.[413] Other research indicates that any SRI advantage may be attributed to extraneous factors, such as a preference for small cap firms which did well during the period of evaluation, rather than evidence of an enduring "sustainability" premium.[414] Meir Statman found that SRI indexes outperformed the S&P 500 during the bull market of the late 1990s but lagged it during the bust of the early 2000s.[415]

"The Financial Performance of a Socially Responsible Investment Over Time and a Possible Link with Corporate Social Responsibility," *Journal of Business Ethics* 63(2) (2006): 131.

407 S. Hamilton, H. Jo, and M. Statman, "Doing Well While Doing Good? The Investment Performance of Socially Responsible Mutual Funds," *Financial Analysts Journal* 49(6) (1993): 62.

408 M.G. Reyes and T. Grieb, "The External Performance of Socially-Responsible Mutual Funds," *American Business Review* 16 (1998): 1.

409 L. Abramson and D. Chung, "Socially Responsible Investing: Viable for Value Investors," *Journal of Investing* 9(3) (2000): 73.

410 N. Kreander, et al., "Evaluating the Performance of Ethical and Non-ethical Funds: A Matched Pair Analysis," *Journal of Business Finance and Accounting* 32(7–8) (2005): 1465.

411 R. Bauer, R. Otten, and A. Tourani-Rad, "Ethical Investing in Australia: Is there a Financial Penalty?" *Pacific-Basin Finance Journal* 14(1) (2006): 33.

412 See J.B. Guerard, Jr., "Is There a Cost to Being Socially Responsible in Investing," *Journal of Investing* 6(2) (1997): 11; J.J. Griffin and J.F. Mahon, "The Corporate Social Performance and Corporate Financial Performance Debate: Twenty-Five Years of Incomparable Research," *Business and Society* 36(1) (1997): 5; D.A. Sauer, "The Impact of Social-Responsibility Screens on Investment Performance: Evidence from the Domini 400 Social Index and Domini Equity Mutual Fund," *Review of Financial Economics* 6(2) (1997): 137; P.U. Ali and M. Gold, "Investing for Good— The Cost of Ethical Investment," *Company and Securities Law Journal* 20 (2002): 307.

413 E. Girard, H. Rahman, and B. Stone, "Socially Responsible Investments: Goody-Two-Shoes or Bad to the Bone?" *Journal of Investing* 16(1) (2007): 96.

414 A. Gregory, J. Matatko, and R. Luther, "Ethical Unit Trust Financial Performance: Small Company Size Effects and Fund Size Effects," *Journal of Business Finance and Accounting* 24(5) (1997): 705.

415 M. Statman, "Socially Responsible Indexes: Composition, Performance, and Tracking Errors," *Journal of Portfolio Management* 32(Spring) (2006): 100.

Overall, the fact that most research suggests SRI does as well as conventional investments may have a very simple, unrelated explanation. As Matthew Haigh and James Hazelton explain: "[t]he reason for correlations between the performance of conventional and SRI funds may be that the portfolios of SRI funds are not markedly different to those of conventional mutual funds."[416] A survey of more than 600 SRI funds, by the Natural Capital Institute, found evidence of this situation.[417] Likewise, in a study of the financial performance of Canadian ethical mutual funds, Rob Bauer and others speculate that one reason the funds did not under-perform is that they do not have significantly different investment portfolios to the market generally.[418] In other words, SRI is likely too inclusive.[419]

2. Financial Implications of Corporate Sustainability Performance

Researchers have also examined how markets value CSR, which presumably should be reflected in SRI fund returns. Efficient market theory predicts that, as for all financially material events, the market will factor in companies' environmental activities that generate known costs or savings for the firm.[420] Research on the financial side of CSR has certain drawbacks. First, as with the studies of SRI performance, there is no theoretically defensible concept of CSR.[421] Scholars use different data sources with many different accounting measures and methodologies.[422] Second, it is difficult to determine causation.

---

416 Haigh and Hazelton, note 339, 65.

417 Hawken, note 168.

418 R. Bauer, J. Derwall, and R. Otten, "The Ethical Mutual Fund Performance Debate: New Evidence from Canada," *Journal of Business Ethics* 70(2) (2007): 111, 122.

419 Although, Derwall found that SRI's financial record is "reasonably insensitive to the choice of social screening criteria and methodology. Neither the least stringent social screeners nor their most stringent counterparts underperform conventional mutual funds" (note 378, at 213). However, Derwall differentiates funds on the SRI criteria applied by the US SIF which, as explained earlier in this chapter, are not rigorous (at 33–35).

420 B.G. Malkiel, "Efficient Market Hypothesis," in *The New Palgrave: A Dictionary of Ecnomics,* Volume 2, eds J. Eatwell, M. Milgate, and P. Newman (Palgrave, 1987), 120–23.

421 A. Bassen, et al., *The Influence of Corporate Responsibility on the Cost of Capital: An Empirical Analysis* (University of Hamburg, and Schlange and Company, 2006), 13.

422 J. Margolis and J. Walsh, *People and Profits? The Search for a Link Between a Company's Social and Financial Performance* (Laurence Erlbaum Associates, 2001) (reviewing the findings and methodologies of other studies).

Perhaps the more profitable firms could afford to devote more resources to CSR, rather than that these firms are more profitable because they have adopted better sustainability practices. David Vogel also suggests "it is possible that some more responsible firms might be even more profitable if they were less responsible."[423]

Various "mega-studies" have attempted to collate disparate findings of many specific studies to arrive at an overall picture. Academics from the Universities of Sydney and Iowa have undertaken such a study.[424] Canvassing data from fifty-two surveys since the early 1970s, they found a statistically significant, "highly to modestly positive" association between CSR and financial performance. Also, Joshua Margolis and James Walsh reviewed ninety-five reports from 1971 to 2001. They concluded a positive correlation between CSR and profitability in fifty-five studies, a negative one in seven, and inconclusive results in those remaining.[425]

Some research specifically investigates changes to the cost of capital. A lower cost of capital for companies committed to CSR builds the business case for sustainability. It also reflects some change in investors' perception of the company's past and future financial performance. Steven Garber and James Hammitt estimated that liabilities associated with contaminated land cleanup orders issued under the US's Superfund legislation caused an average increase in financing costs for large chemical companies of 0.25–0.4 percent per year over 1988–92.[426] Stanley Feldman and colleagues applied a conceptual model which, when applied to a sample of 330 major US companies from 1980–94, predicted that adoption of specific environmental management systems that go beyond strict regulatory compliance would lead to a reduction in perceived financial risk with an accompanying increase in stock price of about 5 percent.[427] German researchers' analysis of CSR among power utilities however discerned no clear and quantifiable relationship between CSR and

423 Vogel, note 32, 33.
424 Orlitzky, Schmidt, and Rynes, note 399.
425 J. Margolis and J. Walsh, *Misery Loves Companies: Whither Social Initiatives by Business?* Social Enterprise Series No. 19 (Harvard Business School, 2003).
426 S. Garber and J.K. Hammit, "Risk Premiums for Environmental Liability: Does Superfund Increase the Cost of Capital?" *Journal of Environmental Economics and Management* 36 (1998): 267.
427 S.J. Feldman, P.A. Soyka, and P.G. Ameer, "Does Improving a Firm's Environmental Management System and Environmental Performance Result in a Higher Stock Price?" *Journal of Investing* 6(4) (1997): 87.

the cost of capital.[428] Miwaka Yamashita and others examining the relation-ship between environmentally conscientious corporate rankings and stock returns found that the US capital markets have only weakly rewarded environmentally exemplary firms.[429] Researchers evaluating the stock value of Greek businesses that apply environmental management systems discerned that improved environmental management and performance reduced the volatility of the firms' share prices.[430]

Another avenue of enquiry examines the financial impact of specific events. These event studies investigate whether disclosure of new information about a company's environmental or social performance impacts its share price. Specifically, they isolate the abnormal market returns (i.e., the difference between actual and expected returns) in the immediate aftermath of a major environmental disaster, such as a pollution leak, for instance.

James Hamilton checked whether US pollution data released by the EPA's TRI in 1989 were "news" to the media and investors.[431] Shareholders in polluting manufacturing companies listed in the TRI suffered abnormal returns of between 0.2 and 0.3 percent upon initial disclosures. These returns translated into an average loss of US$4.1 million in stock value for each firm on the day the TRI figures were released. Other US studies corroborate such market reactions to regulatory action against polluters.[432] In Canada, Paul Lanoie and colleagues found that companies perceived by investors to be environmental laggards experienced abnormal losses (based on lists published by the British Columbia Ministry of Environment during 1990–93 identifying firms in breach or potential breach of its regulations).[433] Nathan Lorraine and others reached similar conclusions in a 2004 paper by examining whether publicity (adverse or positive) regarding environmental performance affects

428 Bassen, et al., note 421, 5, 44.

429 M. Yamashita, S. Sen, and M.C. Roberts, "The Rewards for Environmental Conscientiousness in the U.S. Capital Markets," *Journal of Financial and Strategic Decisions* 12 (1999): 73.

430 G. Halkos and A. Sepetis, "Can Capital Markets Respond to Environmental Policy of Firms? Evidence from Greece," *Ecological Economics* 63(2–3) (2007): 578.

431 J.T. Hamilton, "Pollution as News: Media and Stock Market Reactions to the Toxics Release Inventory Data," *Journal of Environmental Economics and Management* 28(1) (1995): 98.

432 E.g., J.C. Bosch, et al., "Environmental Regulation and Stockholder Wealth," *Managerial and Decision Economics* 19 (1998): 167.

433 P. Lanoie, B. Laplante, and M. Roy, "Can Capital Markets Create Incentives for Pollution Control?" *Ecological Economics* 26 (1998): 31.

UK companies' stock prices.[434] They observed that the stock market reaction to such news (e.g., pollution fines or commendations for environmental achievements) typically lasts up to one week after release of the information.

In one of the few developing country studies, Susmita Dasgupta and others examined forty-eight mostly Latin American public companies in correlation to environmental events over 1990–94.[435] The firms' market value (stock price) declined on average from 4 to 15 percent when involved in pollution which attracted public complaints and protests. In an interesting indication of the value of business reputation, a study of Korean firms covering the period 1990–2000 concluded that "the publication of environmental news in printed media (newspapers) *along with* the firm's awareness of this news publication is the key predictor of environmental performance, irrespective of the reaction of stock markets."[436]

One lacuna of the cost of capital and event studies is that they generally do not track long-term market reactions. The rare longitudinal research that exists has drawn inconclusive findings.[437] Further, event studies do not resolve whether such a decline in market value reflects actual losses incurred (e.g., connected to regulatory sanctions) or whether an additional market penalty occurs (e.g., costing risk of future increased attention from regulators,

434 N. Lorraine, J. Collison, and D. Power, "An Analysis of the Stock Market Impact of Environmental Performance Information," *Accounting Forum* 28 (2004): 7–26.

435 S. Dasgupta, B. Laplante, and N. Mamingi, *Capital Market Responses to Environmental Performance in Developing Countries* (World Bank Development Research Group, 1998).

436 N. Mamingi, B. Laplante, and S. Dasgupta, *Firms' Environmental Performance: Does News Matter?* Policy Research Working Paper 3888 (World Bank, April 2006), 4.

437 D. Cormier, M. Magnan, and B. Morard, "The Impact of Corporate Pollution on Market Valuation: Some Empirical Evidence," *Ecological Economics* 8 (1993): 135 (finding weak evidence of a market impact in a study of twenty-six Canadian companies from the forestry, energy, mining, chemical, and metals sectors over the period 1986–88); G. Dowell, S. Hart, and B. Yeung, "Do Corporate Global Environmental Standards Create or Destroy Value?" *Management Science* 46(8) (2000): 1,059 (a sample of eighty-nine US-based transnational firms during 1994–97, finding that adherents to global environmental standards had higher market values than firms merely applying host country standards or US government standards); M.A. White, *Investor Response to the Exxon Valdez Oil Spill*, Working Paper (University of Virginia, 1995) (finding an adverse investor response over a 120-day post incident period).

possible public pressure, and smeared corporate brand-name).[438] Mark Cohen suggests that Enron incurred an additional market penalty beyond cleanup and litigation costs connected to the Exxon Valdez disaster.[439] Conversely, Jonathan Karpoff and others found no additional market penalty in their US study of 283 cases of public companies subjected to environmental regulatory sanctions during 1980–91.[440]

In conclusion, some of this research implies that the more robust the environmental regulatory system, the more likely financiers will differentiate companies on sustainability performance. The market reaction is not wholly divorced from firms' regulatory context. A regulatory system, with bark and bite, will facilitate the business case for sustainability; the latter inescapably relies on the legal system and can hardly replace it. The only other major lever for change thus is reputational risk, connected to firms' social license. Reputational damage may ensue where companies comply with local regulations but stakeholders, such as consumers, local communities and investors, expect them to exceed those minimal standards and this affects their cost of capital.

D. CHANGING COMPANIES FROM WITHIN: SHAREHOLDER ADVOCACY

Research on shareholder advocacy provides another way to map the impact of SRI. Social investors sometimes choose to influence laggards by dialogue and applying pressure from within rather than by divestment. According to CalPERS, "[s]hareowners collectively have the power to direct the course of corporations. The potential impact of this power is staggering."[441] Larry Ribstein believes that where social investors hold sufficient shares to file

438 Lanoie, et al., note 433.
439 M.A. Cohen, "Monitoring and Enforcement of Environmental Policy," in *International Yearbook of Environmental and Resource Economics*, Volume III, eds T. Tietenberg and H. Folmer (Edward Elgar Publishing, 1999), 44. Among other studies finding an additional market penalty, see M.E. Barth and M.F. McNichols, "Estimation and Market Valuation of Environmental Liabilities Relating to Superfund Sites," *Journal of Accounting Research* 32 (1994): 177.
440 J.M. Karpoff, J.R. Lott, and G. Rankine, *Environmental Violations, Legal Penalties, and Reputation Costs,* John M. Olin Law and Economics Working Paper No. 71 (University of Chicago, 1998).
441 CalPERS, "Shareowner Action," at http://www.calpers-governance.org/alert/default.asp.

proposals, ask questions, and exert their presence in other ways, they can both "educate managers on society's needs and prod them on particular issues," as well as create "clienteles of shareholders with nonprofit-oriented goals" who can encourage managers to "depart to some extent from strict profit maximization."[442] However, the effectiveness of shareholder advocacy is hard to measure for several reasons.[443] First, investors' dialogue with firms is often done informally and in private, away from shareholder meetings. Firms may therefore be disinclined to concede that pressure from investors caused their behavior to change. Second, a causal relationship between a particular shareholder demand and the change in a firm's policies or practices is not easily proven.[444]

Traditionally, shareholder advocacy was uncommon, whether motivated by SRI or other business concerns. Institutional shareholders have generally been passive investors, lacking knowledge and incentives to monitor and supervise companies because of the costs involved and difficulties of coordinating action.[445] The portfolio of a large institutional investor may comprise tiny stakes in thousands of companies, thereby giving asset managers little time or motivation to pay attention to corporate social or environmental activities not immediately relevant to the bottom line.[446] The legal system has also discouraged activism, imposing barriers to shareholders working in concert and filing resolutions, and restrictions on institutional investors acquiring a controlling interest in order to protect the integrity of the market.[447] Retail investors have also generally been inactive. The nature of retail investment products creates a complex link between the ultimate investor and the

---

442 L.E. Ribstein, "Accountability and Responsibility in Corporate Governance," *Notre Dame Law Review* 81 (2006): 1431, 1448–49.

443 Gifford, note 185, 154–55.

444 S.L. Gillan and L.T. Starks, "Corporate Governance, Corporate Ownership and the Role of Institutional Investors: A Global Perspective," *Journal of Applied Finance* 13(2) (2003): 4.

445 J.E. Parkinson, *Corporate Power and Responsibility: Issues in the Theory of Company Law* (Clarendon Press, 1995), 168–69.

446 For example, the CPP holds shares in some 2,000 companies worldwide: J.A. MacNaughton, "The Canadian Experience on Governance, Accountability and Investment," in *Public Pension Fund Management*, eds A.R. Musalem and R.J. Palacios (World Bank, 2004), 107, 119.

447 E.g., in Canada, *National Instrument 81–102 Mutual Funds* (Canadian Securities Administrators, 2000), cl. 2.2(1), restricts mutual funds to holding securities representing no more than 10 percent of the voting rights of issued shares, or purchasing a security for the purpose of exercising control over management of the issuer of the security.

company, thereby moderating intermediaries such as mutual funds from assuming an activist role.[448] In the banking sector, if the borrower apparently complies with relevant environmental laws and does not cause environmental harm to the secured asset, banks rarely bother to monitor and influence the ongoing operations of the client's business.[449]

Recent trends indicate more SRI-driven advocacy and engagement.[450] Hazel Henderson claims "[s]hareholder activism played a part ... in phasing out polystyrene containers at McDonalds, in increasing the amount of recycled and alternative fiber in the paper sold at Staples, and in persuading Home Depot to carry sustainably-harvested wood."[451] Much of the advocacy is directed by institutional investors interested in improving corporate governance.[452] Some have abandoned strict exclusionary screens in favor of engagement strategies ranging from informal dialogue to exertion of formal rights such as proxy voting.[453] Investor coalitions, sometimes working with NGOs, increase their leverage. Investors holding the market for the long term through market indexing strategies need alternatives to divestment also contribute to this trend.

Most pronounced in the US and UK, these trends are fueled by large pension funds such as CalPERS and the USS, and coalitions of religious investors. SRI-driven shareholder advocacy in other jurisdictions, such as Australia[454] and Japan,[455] remains less common. Most shareholder activism still focuses on corporate governance issues rather than traditional SRI

---

448 See J. Gray, "Personal Finance and Corporate Governance: The Missing Link," *Journal of Corporate Law Studies* 4(1) (2004): 187.

449 Ernst and Young, *The Materiality of Environmental Risk to Australia's Finance Sector* (Environment Australia, 2003), 14.

450 Davis, et al., note 75, 15–16; Henderson, note 103, 143–54.

451 Ibid., 145.

452 S. Wahal, "Public Pension Fund Activism and Firm Performance," *Journal of Financial and Quantitative Analysis* 31 (1996): 1; D. Del Guercio and J. Hawkins, "The Motivation and Impact of Pension Fund Activism," *Journal of Financial Economics* 52 (1999): 293.

453 D. McLaren, "Global Stakeholders: Corporate Accountability and Investor Engagement," *Corporate Governance: An International Review* 12 (2004): 191.

454 Corporate Monitor, note 123, 21 (noting that for the financial year ending in June 30, 2007, "there were no specific shareholder resolutions that related to an issue of environmental or social responsibility").

455 M. Suto, *New Development in the Japanese Corporate Governance in the 1990s—The Role of Corporate Pension Funds,* Working Paper 100 (Hamburg Institute of International Economics, 2000), 28–30.

concerns.[456] According to the SIF's analysis of the US market, "shareholder resolutions on social and environmental issues increased more than sixteen percent from 299 proposals in 2003 to 348 in 2005. Social resolutions reaching a vote rose more than 22 percent, from 145 in 2003 to 177 in 2005."[457] And 2006 was the most active year ever for shareholder resolutions advancing ESG concerns, with 367 resolutions filed.[458] Institutional investors are also asking more questions of corporate management, such as the extent of their greenhouse gas emissions (e.g., via the CDP). The number of shareholder resolutions filed in US companies concerning climate change issues rose from two in 1994 to thirty-two in 2005.[459]

Does shareholder activism change corporate policies? We cannot judge its effect by voting records alone. Typically, well received SRI resolutions garner about 10 percent of votes cast.[460] Yet, even defeated shareholder resolutions may induce management to work cooperatively with investors.[461] And defeated resolutions may be resubmitted to maintain pressure on management; under US securities law, the resubmission thresholds presently stand at 3 percent to re-file resolutions after the first year, 6 percent after the second year and 10 percent thereafter.[462] Many extraneous factors limit the votes that shareholder proposals muster, and therefore corporate managers may interpret even modest tallies of votes as reflective of broader unease about company policies and decisions.[463]

Progressive environmental management appears to be often associated with good corporate governance. Jonathan Naimon and others evaluated various corporate governance characteristics and related human resource and auditing policies of S&P 500 companies, concluding that certain measures

---

456 E.g., P.E. Wallace, "The Globalization of Corporate Governance: Shareholder Protection, Hostile Takeovers and the Evolving Corporate Environment in France," *Connecticut Journal of International Law* 18 (2002): 1.

457 SIF, note 111, v.

458 SIF, note 109, iv; B.B. Burr, "Social, Green Proposals Feel the Love," *Pensions and Investments*, October 16, 2006, 8.

459 D.G. Cogan, *Corporate Governance and Climate Change: Making the Connection* (CERES, 2006), 16.

460 Davis, et al., note 75, 16.

461 Sparkes and Cowton, note 328, 51.

462 P. Tkac, "One Proxy at a Time: Pursuing Social Change through Shareholder Proposals," *Economic Review of the Federal Reserve Bank of Atlanta* 3 (2006): 1, 4.

463 Davis, et al., note 75, 18.

were highly relevant to good environmental performance.[464] Among their findings, firms with strong, internally developed policies exhibited better environmental performance than those merely signing to corporate codes of conduct.

Good corporate governance, facilitated by shareholder advocacy, also appears to financially benefit investors.[465] Surveys of CalPERS, one of the most activist investors, imply such financial rewards.[466] Another study by GovernanceMetrics International revealed that over a one, three, and five-year sampled period, companies rated in the top 10 percent of its global database for exemplary corporate governance achieved a higher return on equity, assets, and capital than the average for all companies rated by GovernanceMetrics International.[467] Other studies are less sanguine.[468] Such advocacy costs time and resources, which may outweigh any financial premium and not necessarily improve corporate environmental behavior. Typically, SRI-focused shareholder actions have prompted companies either to study and then report on their environmental impacts, rather than commit to action.

Large public sector pension funds have tended to be the most energetic shareholders,[469] and mutual funds the least.[470] Often preoccupied with short-term trading, mutual funds may not hold shares long enough to be eligible to file shareholder resolutions, let alone to have an incentive to advocate for

---

464 J.S. Naimon, K. Shastri, and M. Sten, "Do Environmental Management Programs Improve Environmental Performance Trends?" *Environmental Quality Management* 7(1) (1997): 81.

465 See, e.g., G. Morgenson, "Shares of Corporate Nice Guys Can Finish First," *New York Times*, April 27, 2003, s. 3, 1; P.A. Gompers, J.L. Ishii, and A. Metrick, *Corporate Governance and Equity Prices* (National Bureau of Economic Research, 2001).

466 S. Nesbitt, *The CalPERS Effect* (Wilshire Associates, July 1995); S. Nesbitt, *The "CalPERS Effect" on Targeted Company Share Prices* (Wilshire Associates, January 2001); R. Hewsenian and J. Noh, *The "CalPERS Effect" on Targeted Company Share Prices* (Wilshire Associates, July 2004).

467 See http://www.gmiratings.com.

468 S.L. Gillan and L.T. Starks, *Relationship Investing and Shareholder Activism by Institutional Investors*, Working Paper (University of Texas, 1995); M.P. Smith, "Shareholder Activism by Institutional Investors: Evidence from CalPERS," *Journal of Finance* 51 (1996): 227; S.L. Gillan and L.T. Starks, "A Survey of Shareholder Activism: Motivation and Empirical Evidence," *Contemporary Finance Digest* Autumn (1998): 2.

469 Davis and Steil, note 217, 313–14.

470 R.C. Pozen, *The Mutual Fund Business* (MIT Press, 1998).

improved corporate governance. Private sector pension funds are little better, with an abysmal record of filing dissident shareowner resolutions.[471] Public sector pension plans, with trade union influence and more member-nominated trustees, tend to be the most active shareholders.[472] Growth in shareholder advocacy has contributed to some public companies returning to closely-held, private firms, which are better insulated against public pressure.[473] The concomitant growth of private equity financing funds may in turn however provide a new channel for advocacy and influence.

E. CONCLUSIONS

SRI has generally yet to transform financial markets and the companies they finance. Certainly, more capital now flows into self-proclaimed SRI funds than has occurred historically. Some investors are becoming more active share-holders, and markets increasingly heed corporate environmental performance when it is perceived as financially salient. But there is no SRI revolution so far. Overall, SRI remains an expanding but still niche sector, insufficient to absolve the financial sector of its responsibility for funding unsustainable development.

Moreover, apart from among faith- and mission-based investors, SRI is largely tethered to a business case. The latter relies heavily on environmental regulation to alter the financial advantages between polluters and socially responsible firms. SRI has generally not yet had the strength of a surrogate regulator, able to impose on companies a separate market license to operate. Much of the hype and salesmanship that accompanies some SRI suggests that it is a means by which investment institutions seek to differentiate themselves in the market to further their own financial success. Vogel believes the SRI industry will likely only significantly change corporate behavior only "if it were more willing to also invest in companies that earned less because they had chosen to act more responsibly. Such a policy might of course also require investors to accept lower returns."[474] Most investors appear unprepared to do so.

Current evidence shows that while SRI has returns comparable to regular investment, it has not radically improved corporate behavior from the perspective of sustainable development. Having captured only a small market,

---

471 Davis, et al., note 75, 77.

472 T. Hebb, *No Small Change: Pension Funds and Corporate Engagement* (Cornell University Press, 2008).

473 B. Mongoven, *Private Equity Firms and Public Policy* (Public Policy Intelligence Report, March 8, 2007).

474 Vogel, note 32, 166.

often comprising portfolios not materially different from mainstream invest-ment, this result is not surprising. It is clear however that the market takes notice of corporate environmental misbehavior that affects the bottom line. There is nothing controversial about this for standard finance theory; information about corporate environmental activities simply becomes part of the market evaluation of corporate securities, as would anything perceived to affect future profitability. Thus, to the extent business case SRI dovetails with market sentiments regarding corporate sustainability behavior, it will fortify the logic of the market. It is when SRI views unethical behavior differently from the market as a whole that it may not affect economic fundamentals and thus corporate behavior.

If financial markets are to leverage change towards sustainability, the market alone is unlikely to engender enough change without additional regulation. The changes required are much more systemic. The more rigorous the environmental regulatory system, with more sweeping financial penalties for non-compliance, the more likely financiers will differentiate firms on their sustainability performance. Matthew Haigh and James Hazelton suggest that the SRI industry can amplify its influence by lobbying governments for policy changes to ensure negative externalities are priced and other market failures corrected.[475] Better regulation in controlling SRI itself should also help reduce the fungible and superficial standards in its own industry. Legal standards for CSR and SRI should mitigate the problem of much corporate communication being cheap talk.

This chapter has identified numerous institutional and market obstacles to responsible financing. They include short-term investment horizons, difficulties coordinating action among enlightened investors, insufficient institutional capacity to analyze corporate sustainability performance, and agency problems that may augment the power of fund managers at the expense of social investors. SRI faces even greater hurdles in emerging markets, commonly associated with additional problems including a paucity of corporate disclosures, lack of skilled SRI advisors, illiquid equity markets, and greater market volatility. Certainly, the SRI industry literature demon-strates widespread awareness of these and other problems, and networks such as UNEPFI and national SRI champions such as UKSIF are working to attenuate these obstacles. But we face ingrained habits and entrenched self-interest that likely require more systematic reform through regulation and public policy. The following chapters explore the impact of the legal system on the growth of SRI and options for legal reform.

---

475 Haigh and Hazelton, note 339, 68.

CHAPTER 4

Obstacles to SRI: Investment Regulation

I. Introduction

Previous chapters examined how market factors affect and impede SRI. But how does the legal system influence SRI? Before canvassing the various SRI-related reforms pioneered by governments and non-state actors, we must first analyze the constraints posed by traditional financial regulation.

While the financial sector as a whole has the general role of distributing and investing capital, its various institutions also have individually distinct functions and objectives. Despite the frenzy of market deregulation and relentless integration and mixing of financial services, some institutionally salient differences remain. Some of these differences derive from financiers' legal forms, functions, and responsibilities. Insurance companies, pension plans, banks, and other institutions are governed by distinct legal frameworks that affect their capacity and motivation to invest responsibly. Even within a particular institutional category, such as pension plans, legal differences can arise across jurisdictions as states may adopt different regulatory standards and policy tools.

This chapter focuses on three critical aspects of financiers' governance to help understand how financial law affects SRI: international regulation of financial markets, the fiduciary duties of investment decision-makers, and the legal framework governing investors' voices within financial organizations. In each case, extensive barriers to SRI persist. Promoting ethical investment will likely require democratizing governance of financiers, aligning their fiduciary duties to sustainable development imperatives, and strengthening international governance of cross-border financial flows. These are not the only governance issues relevant to SRI, but they are among the gravest.

While *individual* investors who invest on their own account may freely express their ethical values through their choice of investments, *institutional* investors investing on behalf of others incur special constraints. Legal rules in many countries establish fiduciary relationships between investors and the financial institutions that control their assets. The fiduciary responsibility is particularly entrenched in pension funds, required to invest prudently and impartially in the interests of their beneficiaries (who generally do not have the option, like retail investors in mutual funds, of shopping elsewhere). While commentators increasingly view fiduciary duties as capable of accommodating SRI, only business case SRI appears permissible in the absence of an express mandate to give priority to ethical standards.

The second institutional attribute examined in this chapter is member participation in the internal governance of financial organizations. Investors in mutual funds, pension plans, and other institutions typically sit at the bottom of the financial market food chain. They have little say in fund governance, and this may dampen the prospects for SRI policy-making. The value of participation has been overlooked in most SRI literature, which dwells on how the governance of non-financial corporations affects shareholder advocacy rather than the impact of financiers' own governance on the capacity of social investors to advocate change. Recent reforms in some countries giving beneficiaries more representation on pension boards and committees is a rare step forward.

Thirdly, we are confronted with the problem of under-regulation in global financial markets. International law has lagged behind the boom in transnational financial activity, resulting in a dearth of official norms to address social and environmental pressures and a paucity of rules to control even the "conventional" financial issues. Market liberalization policies among nations in the OECD and the efforts of international financial organizations extending those policies to "the South" (the so-called developing countries) have made finance capitalism as significant as international trade for the prospects of sustainability. A miscellany of soft law codes of conduct and standards has partially filled the void in hard international regulation.

II. Financial Markets Regulation

A. METHODS AND TRENDS

Historically, environmental and social policy has had virtually no place in the regulation of financial markets. Financial regulations aim for efficient allocation of capital, promotion of market competition, and improved market stability.[1] They serve to create the optimal conditions for capital markets to support economic growth. This system attributes the environmental costs of funding damaging activities to the front-line companies, for regulation at an operational level through separate environmental laws.

Consequently, SRI governance has no logical wellspring within the traditions of financial sector law. Unless those traditions are overhauled, that sector will limit promotion of SRI to light-touch controls that dovetail with existing regulatory techniques such as information disclosure, investor protection, and risk management. Within this regulatory oeuvre, it is hard to conceive how financial supervisory authorities' mandates could include requirements to further social justice or protect natural capital. Thus, when UKSIF made a novel proposal to include environmental standards in the mandate of the regulator of Britain's *Financial Services and Market Act* of 2000, the Financial Services Authority, it was virtually a foregone conclusion that it would be swiftly rejected by parliamentarians.[2]

At the epicenter of contemporary financial regulation sit the specialist financial market regulators.[3] One model, the super regulator—assigned responsibility for the entire financial sector—is found in the Scandinavian countries, the UK, Germany, and Japan. Other nations (e.g., as in Switzerland, Australia, and Canada) favor a semi-integrated model in which only some sectors fall under the auspices of a single authority. Alternatively, some (e.g., the US) opt for specialist regulators for designated divisions in the financial sector. Supervisory authorities also display different operational structures.[4] The "sector model" organizes supervision around each financial institution, rather than by reference to financial services or products (e.g., there is a regulator of the pension fund sector, but pension products provided by insurers are supervised by a regulator of the insurance sector). The "functional model," by contrast, focuses on the financial products or

1 C. Goodhart, et al., *Financial Regulation. Why, How and Where Now?* (Routledge, 1998); P.D. Spencer, *The Structure and Regulation of Financial Markets* (Oxford University Press, 2002).
2 UKSIF, "UK Social Investment Forum Tells MPs of Need to Include Environment in Framework for Financial Services Regulator," Press release, April 19, 1999.
3 OECD, *Insurance Solvency Supervision: OECD Country Profiles* (OECD, 2002), 43; also D. Masciandaro, "Unification in Financial Sector Supervision: The Trade-off between Central Bank and Single Authority," *Journal of Financial Regulation and Compliance* 12 (2004): 151.
4 Ibid., 43–44.

services rather than the institutional form of the provider. Combinations of these supervisory approaches also occur.

The intensity of financial regulation has fluctuated. Additional regulation has been triggered by periodic bouts of market instability and crisis.[5] Yet, over time, most countries have generally sought to lighten the regulatory burden on financiers. This trend has gained momentum in recent decades under the guidance of neoliberal economic policies; but other sorts of public controls have also emerged to ensure capital adequacy, protection of retail investors, and improved information disclosure and transparency. In addition to official rules, a miscellany of informal and quasi-private norms also punctuates governance of financial markets.[6]

Traditionally in most jurisdictions, regulation has segmented financial service providers.[7] Parceled into discrete branches (e.g., banking or insurance) with separate legal regimes, each sector was restricted to providing specific products or services. The former Glass-Steagall Act in the US barring commercial banks from engaging in investment banking and other business illustrates this approach.[8] Its rationale was to minimize contagion risks and to curb any concentration of power. If a bank had a large stake in an insurance business, it would be exposed to additional, non-banking sector risks, potential losses of which it might not have sufficient capital to absorb. Thus, most OECD countries once maintained regulatory firewalls between financial sectors.[9] Market deregulation policies to improve competition have greatly broken down demarcation lines between financial services and activities.

Presently, investment regulation aims primarily to control financial risks and thereby ensure that institutional investors meet their financial liabilities to their beneficiaries: insurance policyholders, pensioned retirees, or others as applicable.

---

5 The US's previously fledgling mutual fund sector collapsed in the wake of the Great Depression and was only revived after the *Investment Company Act* of 1940, Pub. L. No. 768, 54 Stat. 789, introduced rigorous standards to restore market confidence.

6 See J. Black, *Rules and Regulators* (Clarendon Press, 1997), 214–50 (discussing UK financial regulation).

7 I.G. MacNeil, *An Introduction to the Law on Financial Investment* (Hart Publishing, 2005), 31.

8 *Banking Act* 1933, ch. 89, 48 Stat. 162; see further J.R. Brown, Jr., "The 'Great Fall': The Consequences of Repealing the Glass-Steagall Act," *Stanford Journal of Law, Business and Finance* 2 (1995): 129.

9 OECD, note 3, 36, 39.

There are two common regulatory approaches for this purpose.[10] The first, known as quantitative regulation (or portfolio regulation), limits the type and the extent of investments.[11] It may involve limits by asset classes (e.g., real estate, bonds, equities), by the issuer (e.g., proportion of a single company's shares), and by jurisdiction (e.g., the country where the investment is located). Alternatively, prudential investment standards mainly prescribe the *way* investments and loans are managed.[12] Prudent investment standards imply adequate portfolio diversification, liquidity, and due diligence in asset selection and management.[13] While this approach offers asset managers the flexibility for adapting to dynamic market conditions, the discretion also calls for additional supervision in order to protect investors. Rules addressing specific technical and managerial risks augment these two core methods of regulation. For example, licensing rules typically require fund managers and trustees to be "fit and proper" persons possessed of appropriate skill and knowledge for their responsibilities.[14]

Both portfolio restrictions and prudential standards have consequences for SRI. Ostensibly, quantitative restrictions do not affect SRI. Investors can select companies or assets based on social and environmental performance criteria so long as each selection falls within the allowable portfolio limit. However, given that social investors sometimes target certain asset classes, such as venture capital, quantitative restrictions may hinder SRI. Further, restrictions on a fund's holdings in a single company can blunt SRI leverage via shareholder advocacy. Conversely, prudent investment standards offer freedom to choose any investment so long as it is chosen wisely in the interests of the beneficiaries. However, legal problems may arise where SRI exclusionary screens or other tactics trade profit for amorphous ethical or political goals.

---

10 OECD, *Survey of Investment Regulations of Pension Funds* (OECD, 2006); J. Carmichael and M. Pomerleano, *The Development and Regulation of Non-Bank Financial Institutions* (World Bank, 2002).

11 E.P. Davis, *Portfolio Regulation of Life Insurance Companies and Pension Funds* (OECD, 2001).

12 B. Longstreth, *Modern Investment Management and the Prudent Man Rule* (Oxford University Press, 1986).

13 For example, Canada's *Bank Act,* S.C. 1991, provides: "[t]he directors of a bank... shall adhere to investment and lending policies, standards and procedures that a reasonable and prudent person would apply in respect of a portfolio of investments and loans to avoid undue risk of loss and obtain a reasonable return" (s. 465).

14 OECD, *Guidelines for Pension Fund Governance* (OECD, July 2002).

No country relies on any single regulatory approach, although all rely increasingly on prudential standards. Under the aegis of neoliberal philosophy, many states have embraced the mantra of economic deregulation to improve the efficiency and competitiveness of their financial markets.[15] They dismantled institutional firewalls, thereby opening competition for financial products and services.[16] Quantitative and prescriptive regulations were mostly jettisoned in favor of solvency and liquidity standards and other prudential investment principles. To illustrate, Japan's *Foreign Exchange and Foreign Trade Control Act* of 1998 boosted the Japanese mutual fund market by enabling banks and insurance companies to sell mutual funds.[17] Portfolio restrictions on Japanese pension funds were concurrently removed.[18] Likewise, India liberalized its capital markets in 1992 through the *Securities and Exchange Board of India Act*.[19] Concomitant worldwide regulatory trends include the abolishing of interest-rate controls, floating currencies, and deregulating financial services fees. These trends have spawned the growth of conglomerate banks and insurance companies offering one-stop shopping of loans, investments, and other financial services. In the US, where this trend has become pronounced, the *Financial Modernization Act* of 1999[20] authorized the creation of a new form of institution: the "financial holding company," capable of offering myriad financial services within a single entity.[21]

In the wake of market abuses, some countervailing re-regulation emerged to protect investors. In the US, massive corporate scandals at Worldcom and Enron helped to return financial regulation and corporate governance to a central policy concern, spurring responses such as the 2002 Sarbanes-Oxley legislation.[22] It is thus somewhat of a paradox that the evolution of financial

---

15 World Bank, *Financial Deregulation: Changing the Rules of the Game* (World Bank, 1992); G. Dufey, "The Changing Role of Financial Intermediation in Europe," *International Journal of Business* 3(1) (1998): 49.

16 See E. Kintner, "Politics and Deregulation in the Canadian Banking Industry," *American Review of Canadian Studies* 23 (1993): 231.

17 E.P. Davis and B. Steil, *Institutional Investors* (MIT Press, 2001), 181.

18 Ibid., 180.

19 R.N. Agarwal, *Financial liberalization in India* (B.R. Publishing, 1996).

20 Pub. L. No. 106-102, 113 Stat. 1338.

21 See further C.M. Horn, "The Gramm-Leach-Bliley Financial Modernization Act: A New Course in US Financial Services," *International Journal of Insurance Law* 2 (2000): 109.

22 *Public Company Accounting Reform and Investor Protection Act*, 2002, Pub. L. No. 107-204, 116 Stat. 745.

markets, commonly linked to the "diminution of state power and authority," has sometimes been followed by an *"expansion* of law and prescriptive regulation governing the structure and the conduct of parties within these markets ..." [23]

The overall effect of these regulatory trends has been to massively expand financial markets, thereby increasing their economic influence and, ultimately, their environmental footprint. In a deregulated economy, a flood of financing options is available for developers. It is unclear whether countervailing SRI standards can be surgically grafted into the existing matrix of regulation. So far, virtually all governments continue to treat environmental and social policy as largely distinct spheres of concern, regulated by separate authorities and laws. As financial markets increasingly operate transnationally, the challenges of impregnating SRI values into the web of financial regulation grow.

B. FINANCIAL REGULATION IN A GLOBAL CONTEXT

1. *Globalization of Finance and Implications for SRI*

"Globalization" in relation to financial markets refers to the dynamic, pervasive, and intense interconnectedness of investment and other financial activities across national borders and individual communities.[24] Particularly since the 1980s, technological advances coupled with implementation of market deregulation policies have greatly accelerated the mobility and liquidity of capital.[25] Market liberalization has gone the furthest among OECD nations, while the neoliberal policies of international financial

---

23 J.W. Cioffi, "Expansive Retrenchment: The Regulatory Politics of Corporate Governance Reform and the Foundations of Finance Capitalism" (presentation at workshop, The State after Statism: New State Activities in the Age of Globalization and Liberalization, University of California Berkeley, November 13–14, 2003), 2.

24 C.A. Williams, "Corporate Social Responsibility in an Era of Economic Globalization," *University of California Davis Law Review* 35 (2002): 705, 731 (defining "globalization" as "the process of denationalization of markets, laws and politics in the sense of interlacing peoples and individuals for the sake of the common good").

25 See A. Walter, *World Power and World Money* (Harvester Wheatsheaf, 1993), 202–4 (discussing causes of financial globalization); G. Caprio, P. Honohan, and J.E. Stiglitz, eds, *Financial Liberalization. How Far, How Fast?* (Cambridge University Press, 2001); M. Schaberg, *Globalization and the Erosion of the National Financial Systems* (Edward Elgar Publishing, 1999).

institutions have extended their ambit to emerging markets.[26] Broadly, these liberalization measures have lifted restrictions on foreign exchange, the allocation of credit, and access to markets. Largely missing from these policy prescriptions are mechanisms ensuring that transnational corporations (TNCs) and institutional investors benefiting from the liberal economic framework adhere to a high standard of corporate governance and social responsibility.

Global finance has created market conditions that may hinder SRI. Some observers correlate it with an upsurge in market volatility, such as the Mexican peso crisis of 1994–95 and the East Asian financial meltdown in 1997— conditions not intuitively conducive to sustainable development.[27] By eroding the distinction between domestic and international markets, globalization requires investors to pay greater attention to a wider context. Yet, this new scale may simply further distance financiers from the social and environmental ramifications of the companies they finance. Investors may have difficulty assessing the environmental performance of foreign companies in jurisdictions with rudimentary or difficult-to-comprehend environmental reporting standards. The massive scale and number of financial transactions hinder incorporation of sustainability considerations into loans and investments on a case-by-case basis.

The globalization of financial markets also has implications for the conceptual and practical foundations of governance and law. We can no longer treat "government" and "governance" as synonymous, as though governing is simply what governments do. Concomitantly, we cannot consider "law" as just official regulation. Rather, the norms and processes that steer markets increasingly emanate from a diversity of institutions beyond the state, such as TNCs, NGOs, and international organizations, as well as from other informal and unofficial rules, such as business codes of conduct and industry accreditation standards. These can be just as influential as official regulation in shaping behavior.[28] The "new governance" regimes blur the traditional boundaries between the public and private, and the state and market. It also

---

26 J.E. Stiglitz, *Globalization and its Discontents* (W.W. Norton and Company, 2002).

27 R. Glick, R. Moreno, and M. Spiegel, eds, *Financial Crisis in Emerging Markets* (Cambridge University Press, 2001).

28 J. Braithwaite and P. Drahos, *Global Business Regulation* (Cambridge University Press, 2000); J. Freeman, "Private Parties, Public Functions and the New Administrative Law," *Administrative Law Review* 52 (2000): 813, 831–35.

entails new categories of actors and decision-making processes in governance, epitomized by such initiatives as the UN Global Compact.[29]

However, such a potpourri of actors and norms raises doubts about whether globalization can really be governed at all.[30] Commentators suggest that, "reforms at the domestic level will be inadequate if not accompanied by major institutional and legal reforms at the international level."[31] States, individually, typically lack the capacity to control mega-sized banks and other financial behemoths engaged in complex cross-border deals.[32] Consolidation of financial services into a few super firms has been one of the most prominent consequences of market globalization.[33] Governmental regulations are resisted when they set environmental financing standards that create competitive disadvantages for local financiers. Conversely, global finance widens the sources of capital, thereby enabling polluting companies to find alternatives to socially conscious local financiers.

More fundamentally, globalization not only erodes the power of traditional sources of regulation, it also diminishes the very relevance of state sovereignty.[34] With globalization, states can no longer count on complete and exclusive authority over a discrete territory. Some TNCs and international financiers rival the powers of individual nations in international affairs. How can such economic forces be properly governed by states individually or collectively?

One theory predicts that international competition for economic investment fuels a "race to the bottom" or a "regulatory chill" in the quality, extent,

---

29 A.M. Slaughter, "Global Government Networks, Global Information Agencies and Disaggregated Democracy," *Michigan Journal of International Law* 24 (2003): 1041, 1057.

30 S. Sassen, *Losing Control? Sovereignty in the Age of Globalization* (Columbia University Press, 1996); R. Falk, *Predatory Globalization: A Critique* (Polity, 1999); M. Wolf, "Will the Nation-State Survive Globalization?" *Foreign Affairs* 80(1) (2001): 178.

31 K. Alexander, R. Dhumale, and J. Eatwell, *Global Governance of Financial Systems* (Oxford University Press, 2006), 3.

32 To compete in a global market can require new economies of scale among financiers: D.F. Channon, *Global Banking Strategy* (John Wiley and Sons, 1988), 4 (discussing internationalization of US banking operations).

33 M.V. Stichele, *Critical Issues in the Financial Industry: SOMO Financial Sector Report* (Stichting Onderzoek Multinationale Ondernemingen, 2005), 64, 73.

34 A. Chayes and A.H. Chayes, *The New Sovereignty* (Harvard University Press, 1995).

and enforcement of regulation.[35] Theorists postulate that competition for investment capital stymies regulatory behavior in such areas as environmental and labor policy. Stringent environmental rules in one jurisdiction for example may induce businesses to seek capital from institutions or governments with less costly standards.[36] Chinese banks for instance have been accused of predatory lending in developing countries without performing the environmental due diligence checks, now increasingly applied by multilateral and commercial banks.[37] Under these conditions, states may compete downwards to lower their environmental regulation standards in order to entice investment. Even if that were not true, competitive concerns may affect environmental decision-making by causing a regulatory "chill."[38] Authorities may refrain from stricter environmental controls that might deter new investors.[39]

Conversely, a benign view of globalization associates it with dissemination and universalization of new standards and norms relevant to SRI and CSR.[40] Under this view, global financial markets may spur a race to the top. The international proliferation of codes of conduct for SRI, such as the UNPRI and the EPs, perhaps illustrates this effect.[41] Some commentators even laud the supposed economic "efficiencies" that ensue from regulatory

35 For an overview of these debates, see H. Nordstrom and S. Vaughan, *Trade and Environment* (WTO, 1999).
36 R. Kozul-Wright and R. Rowthorn, "Spoilt for Choice? Multinational Corporations and the Geography of International Production," *Oxford Review of Economic Policy* 14(2) (1998): 74.
37 "EIB Warns Africa May Suffer as Chinese Banks Move in," *Environmental Finance* (March 2007), at http://www.environmental-finance.com/2007/0703mar/news.htm#on2.
38 D.C. Esty and D. Geradin, "Environmental Protection and International Competitiveness," *Journal of World Trade* 32 (1998): 5; H.J. Leonard, "Confronting Industrial Pollution in Rapidly Industrializing Countries: Myths, Pitfalls, and Opportunities," *Ecology Law Quarterly* 12 (1985): 779.
39 See Nordstrom and Vaughan, note 35.
40 See H.J. Leonard and C.J. Duerksen, "Environmental Regulation and the Location of Industry: An International Perspective," *Columbia Journal of World Business* 15 (1980): 52; J.D. Wilson, "Capital Mobility and Environmental Standards: Is there a Theoretical Basis for a Race to the Bottom?" in *Fair Trade and Harmonization: Economic Analysis*, Volume 1, eds J. Bhagwati and R.E. Hudec (MIT Press, 1996), 393.
41 See further chapter 6 of this book.

standards competition.[42] There would be no race to the bottom where stringently governed markets can attract financial institutions seeking the reputational advantages of association with such high standards.[43] Globalization has also brought some benefits to civil society institutions, whose transnational collaboration was critical to the groundswell of opposition and eventual defeat of the OECD's proposed Multilateral Agreement on Investment in 1998.[44]

2. Governing Global Financial Markets

Global-level governance of financial markets is limited and deeply fragmented, ranging from formal intergovernmental agreements to informal "gentlemen's agreements." Having evolved haphazardly, they serve primarily to facilitate cooperation among national regulators and to promote capital mobility.[45] The universe of this governance includes the constitution and working procedures of intergovernmental financial institutions; general rules concerning the behavior of private institutions, such as data-disclosure principles and capital adequacy rules; and transactional rules that govern aspects of international financial intercourse, such as lending and investment criteria.

The institutions of the Bretton Woods Agreement (notably the International Monetary Fund and World Bank), the OECD and its subgroup of leading economies (the "Group of 10" (G10) or subsets thereof), and the World Trade Organization (WTO) are the principal organs of global economic cooperation and market liberalization.[46] The optimistic view applauds their contributions to facilitating trade, opening new markets, and stabilizing global markets. The contrary perspective rebukes them for perpetuating

---

42 See especially R.L. Revesz, "Federalism and Environmental Regulation: An Overview," in *Environmental Law, the Economy, and Sustainable Development*, eds R.L. Revesz, P. Sands, and R.B. Stewart (Cambridge University Press, 2000), 37.

43 Braithwaite and Drahos contend that financiers can win competitive advantages when they base themselves in those jurisdictions with the most scrupulous regulatory standards: Braithwaite and Drahos, note 28, 131, 167 (discussing the example of listing on the New York Stock Exchange).

44 R. O'Brien, et al., *Contesting Global Governance: Multilateral Economic Institutions and Global Social Movements* (Cambridge University Press, 2000).

45 M. Carlberg, *International Economic Policy Coordination* (Springer, 2005).

46 See generally P.B. Kenen, *Managing the World Economy: Fifty Years After Bretton Woods* (Institute for International Economics, 1994); J. Trebilcock, *The Regulation of International Trade* (Routledge, 2005); Alexander, Dhumale, and Eatwell, note 31.

unequal economic relations that favor the North and for disseminating environmentally unsustainable and socially unjust models of development.[47]

Within international trade governance, the General Agreement on Trade in Services[48] (GATS) extends the WTO free trade principles to financial services.[49] Liberalization of financial services is also furthered by various regional and bilateral trade agreements, such as the North American Free Trade Agreement (NAFTA).[50] While the WTO regime and its specific trade agreements have been subject to extensive denigration for advancing free trade with insufficient regard for environmental considerations,[51] this debate has hardly extended to the financial sector agreement. Commentators have hailed the 1997 GATS Annex on Financial Services[52] as a landmark achievement for market liberalization.[53] It aims to eliminate discriminatory and market access-impairing measures so that insurers, banks, and other institutions

---

47 See F. Farina and E. Savaglio, *Inequality and Economic Integration* (Routledge, 2006).

48 GATS and Annexes, WTO Agreement, ILM 33 (1994): 1167.

49 Y. Wang, "Most-Favoured Nation Treatment under the General Agreement on Trade in Services: and its Application in Financial Services," *Journal of World Trade* 30 (1996): 91.

50 ILM 32 (1993): 289.

51 The literature on this topic is immense: see, e.g., M. Meier, "GATT, WTO, and the Environment," *Colorado Journal of International Environmental Law and Policy* 8 (1997): 241; T.J. Schoenbaum, "International Trade and Protection of the Environment: The Continuing Search for Reconciliation," *American Journal of International Law* 91 (1997): 268; E. Antal, "Lessons From NAFTA: The Role of the North American Commission for Environmental Cooperation in Conciliating Trade and Environment," *Michigan State Journal of International Law* 14 (2006): 167.

52 V. Presti, "Barings Bar None: The Financial Service Agreement of the GATS and its Potential Impact on Derivatives Trading," *Maryland Journal of International Law and Trade* 21 (1997): 145. The legal text of the GATS, including the Annex on Financial Services and the Understanding on Commitments in Financial Services are part of the Final Act Embodying the Results of the Uruguay Round of Multilateral Trade Negotiations: see http://www.wto.org/english/docs_e/legal_e/ final_e.htm.

53 See W. Dobson and P. Jacquet, *Financial Services Liberalization in the WTO* (Institute for International Economics, 1998); M. Taylor, "The WTO's Financial Services Agreement and the Imperative of Further Liberalization of Trade in Insurance and Reinsurance," *Geneva Papers on Risk and Insurance: Issues and Practice* 25(4) (2000): 473.

have access to financial service markets of all member countries.[54] Under it, regulations that discriminate against foreign lenders or investors or otherwise constitute a disguised trade restriction may be rendered unlawful. Also, GATS's "national treatment" principle may restrict governments from legislating to require preferential investment policies for impoverished and distressed communities.[55]

The GATS assumes that many barriers to financial services stem from government regulation, rather than market forces such as the increased concentration of financial services in the hands of a few large players.[56] Financial firms of developing countries face difficulties competing in those concentrated sectors at an international level. Also, GATS should not be seen as simply intergovernmental policy. The financial industry was an active force in the GATS negotiations.[57]

The GATS tolerates domestic measures to address "prudential concerns" (e.g., depositor protection and economic stability) so long as they do not constitute a means of surreptitiously avoiding the Agreement's commitments.[58] Perhaps unhelpfully, though, it does not delineate the precise scope of permissible prudential market supervision. This indeterminacy could allow for SRI-directed regulation to pass the GATS test.[59] On the other hand, such vagueness may expose SRI measures to challenges from WTO members in adjudication proceedings of the GATS, which may not be sympathetic to social- or environmental-policy motivated market controls. The NAFTA also includes a prudential supervisory exemption and, as in the GATS Annex, it provides a non-exhaustive list of considerations that it deems as "prudential."[60] Apart from the WTO and its dispute resolution panels, GATS does not provide any organizational machinery to supervise financial markets. That function is left to a medley of other institutions,[61] resulting in

---

54 The agreement was brought into force on March 1, 1999. See further A. Mattoo, *Financial Services and the WTO: Liberalization in the Developing and Transition Economies* (WTO, 1998).

55 Stichele, note 33, 163.

56 Ibid., 174.

57 Ibid., 196.

58 Art 2(a), Annex on Financial Services, note 48.

59 L.E. Panourgias, *Banking Regulation and World Trade Law: GATS, EU and "Prudential" Institution Building* (Hart Publishing, 2006), 2.

60 North American Free Trade Agreement, U.S.–Canada–Mexico, art. 1410(1), ILM 32 (1993): 289.

61 See M. Giovanoli, "A New Architecture for the Global Financial Market: An Outline of Legal Issues," in *International Monetary Law: Issues for the New Millennium*, ed. M. Giovanoli (Oxford University Press, 2000).

a fragmented and incomplete ensemble of market controls, described by Sol Picciotto as "a spaghetti bowl or spider's web of intertwined organizations and arrangements."[62] Representatives of the G10 countries typically dominate these institutions, which further diminishes their wider international legitimacy.[63]

Among these disparate entities, the Bank for International Settlements (BIS) is essentially the bank of the central banks.[64] Its diverse functions include monitoring cross-border capital flows, facilitating emergency finance to nations in trouble, and promoting cooperation among central banks.[65] Affiliated to the BIS are several specialist committees, among which the most important is the Basel Committee of Banking Supervision. Founded in 1974, it compiles recommendations on principles and standards for banking oversight.[66] The Basel Committee has formulated standards for capital adequacy and supervision of market risks for adoption by national authorities.[67] The Committee itself does not act as a market regulator.[68] Its major achievements are the Basel Capital Accords I and II, adopted in 1998 and 2004 respectively.[69] A further committee that works with the BIS is the Committee on the Global Financial System, composed of the central banks of thirteen nations. It was established by the G10 to monitor financial markets and formulate policy recommendations to promote market stability.[70]

---

62 S. Picciotto, "Introduction: What Rules for the World Economy?" in *Regulating International Business: Beyond Liberalization*, eds S. Picciotto and R. Mayne (Macmillan, 1999), 1, 9.

63 Alexander, Dhumale, and Eatwell, note 31, 44–45.

64 See L. de Rosa, ed., *International Banking and Financial Systems, Evolution and Stability* (Ashgate Publishing, 2003).

65 Http://www.bis.org. See further K. Howell, "The Role of the Bank for International Settlements in Central Bank Cooperation," *Journal of European Economic History* 22 (1993): 367.

66 Http://www.bis.org/bcbs/index.htm.

67 See J.J. Norton, "Trends in International Bank Supervision and the Basle Committee on Banking Supervision," *Consumer Finance Law Quarterly* 48 (1994): 415.

68 D. Zaring, "International Law by Other Means: The Twilight of International Financial Regulatory Organizations," *Texas International Law Journal* 33 (1998): 281, 289.

69 Http://www.bis.org/publ/bcbsca.htm. See Basel Committee on Banking Supervision (BCBS), *Basel II: International Convergence of Capital Measurement and Capital Standards: A Revised Framework* (BCBS, June 2004).

70 Http://www.bis.org/cgfs/index.htm.

Another notable institution is the International Organization of Securities Commissions (IOSCO),[71] which has helped some 170 national regulators, since 1982, to develop collaborative standards to regulate the securities and futures markets. It also formulates standards for surveillance of global securities markets. The IOSCO provides mutual assistance to implement the standards and promote rigorous enforcement against offences. Though the IOSCO has no compliance machinery of its own, experts describe its standards as "a powerful benchmark of how domestic regulators are expected to govern."[72]

Other international regimes for cooperation in the financial industry include the International Network of Pension Regulators and Supervisors,[73] the Committee on Payment and Settlement Systems,[74] and the International Association of Deposit Insurers.[75] International standards for accounting and auditing are set at the International Accounting Standards Board[76] and the International Auditing and Assurance Standards Board.[77] Overall, these examples are not the only transnational coordination mechanisms, but they are among the more indispensable for financial markets.

Like most national legal systems, there is a legislative void at the international level when it comes to articulating standards of social and environmental behavior for financial institutions and TNCs generally.[78] At most, through their prudential investment and lending standards, current international regimes may facilitate some business case motivations for responsible financing. For example, while the new Basel Capital Accord II does not set specific procedures for dealing with the environmental aspects of project finance, it may compel banks to disclose and assess their management of environmental risks, and to set aside more capital for contingencies. The Basel Committee's consultative document on the Accord II specifies that "the bank must appropriately monitor the risk of environmental liability arising

---

71 Http://www.iosco.org/iosco.html. See further F. Oditah, ed., *The Future of the Global Securities Market* (Clarendon Press, 1996).

72 M. Condon and L. Philipps, "Transnational Market Governance and Economic Citizenship: New Frontiers for Feminist Legal Theory," *Thomas Jefferson Law Review* 28(2) (2005): 105, 134.

73 Http://www.pensions-research.org.

74 Http://www.bis.org/cpss.

75 Http://www.iadi.org.

76 Http://www.iasc.org.uk.

77 Http://www.ifac.org/IAASB.

78 J.A. Zerk, *Multinationals and Corporate Social Responsibility Limitations and Opportunities in International Law* (Cambridge University Press, 2006), 243–98.

in respect of the collateral, such as the presence of toxic material on a property."[79]

Perhaps more relevant to the quest for responsible financing are the multilateral development banks (MDBs), such as the World Bank, that support economic projects in developing countries and emerging economies. They have drafted policies to manage the potential impacts of their loans and policies on the environment and local communities.[80] The European Bank for Reconstruction and Development (EBRD) even has a specific mandate in its charter to promote sustainable development.[81] Their policies and procedures have provided precedents for private financiers.[82] They may also exert direct leverage over the private sector through co-financing and loan guarantee arrangements. The World Bank has taken a lead role among MDBs to establish trust funds for co-financing climate change mitigation projects.[83] The EBRD has become involved in concessional and co-financing arrangements for sustainable energy investments in Eastern Europe.[84] While MDBs have made extensive improvements to their environmental policies in response to the furious criticism they endured in the 1980s, their influence on financial markets outside of project financing is somewhat limited.[85]

---

79 Basel Committee on Banking Supervision (BCBS), *Basel II: The New Basel Capital Accord—Third Consultative Paper* (BCBS, April 2003), 87.

80 See generally A. Gray, "Development Policy, Development Protest: The World Bank, Indigenous Peoples and NGOs," in *The Struggle for Accountability: The World Bank, NGOs, and Grassroots Movements,* eds J.A. Fox and L.D. Brown (MIT Press, 1998), 267.

81 Art. 2.1(vii) requires the EBRD to "promote in the full range of its activities environmentally sound and sustainable development": Agreement Establishing the European Bank for Reconstruction and Development, 1990, O.J. L. 372.

82 B.J. Richardson, "The Equator Principles: The Voluntary Approach to Environmentally Sustainable Finance," *European Environmental Law Review* 14(11) (2005): 280.

83 See http://www.CarbonFinance.org.

84 C. Wold and D. Zaelke, "Promoting Sustainable Development and Democracy in Central and Eastern Europe: The Role of the European Bank for Reconstruction and Development," *American University Journal of International Law and Policy* 7 (1992): 559.

85 I.A. Bowles and C.F. Kormos, "The American Campaign for Environmental Reforms at the World Bank," *Fletcher Forum of World Affairs* 23 (1999): 211; P. Aufderheide and B. Rich, "Environmental Reform and the Multilateral Banks," *World Policy Journal* 5(2) (1988): 301.

Even Western government donors have at times failed to meet the standards set by the MDBs, which they politically control. Their export credit agencies (ECAs) have come under mounting scrutiny for lax environmental practices.[86] ECAs provide publicly subsidized loans and government-backed guarantees for commercial bank loans in mainly poor countries to buyers of goods and services of businesses of Western countries. Criticized as geared to enriching these businesses rather than the host countries, ECAs have been denigrated as "rogue agencies that make the World Bank" seem like a "model of benevolence and accountability."[87] Their involvement in China's Three Gorges Dam, which the World Bank did not finance, illustrates this concern. Belatedly, the OECD has promulgated some guidance to improve environmental standards in ECA financing,[88] and some individual states have tightened environmental standards for their ECAs.[89]

Some voluntary codes and standards for CSR and SRI have emerged under the auspices of the UN, OECD, World Bank, and other international bodies.[90] These include the UNEPFI, the UNPRI, and the EPs.[91] However, they are poorly integrated with the mainstream supervisory institutions for financial markets, and their voluntary nature undermines compliance and enforcement. Chapter 6 of this book scrutinizes their role and impact.

3. Regional Initiatives in the European Union (EU)

At a regional level, the most substantial regulatory regime for financial markets has emerged in the EU.[92] Over several decades, their law-makers have built a single market for financial services, originally based on the principle

---

86 NGOs have established a special campaign forum to address ECAs: http://www.eca-watch.org.

87 B. Rich, "Exporting Destruction," *The Environmental Forum* 17(5) (2000): 32.

88 OECD, *Recommendation on Common Approaches on Environment and Officially Supported Export Credits* (OECD, 2003).

89 J. Clapp and P. Dauvergne, *Paths to a Green World: The Political Economy of the Global Environment* (MIT Press, 2005), 210–14.

90 J. Dine, *The Governance of Corporate Groups* (Cambridge University Press, 2000), 151–75.

91 See discussion and references in chapter 6 of this book.

92 By way of introduction, see EC, *Institutional Arrangements for the Regulation and Supervision of the Financial Sector* (EC Internal Market Directorate General, January 2000); M. van Empel, *Financial Services and EC Law: Materials and Cases* (Kluwer Law, looseleaf service, since 1991).

of mutual recognition rather than harmonization of regulatory standards. Thus, under the Second Banking Directive of 1989, banks of any EU Member State may offer the full panoply of services in any other Member.[93] Market harmonization however has not extended to creation of specialist EU-wide market regulators, which remains in the province of individual EU Member States.

In the wake of the Lisbon Strategy of 2000, the EU embarked on unprecedented reform to further integrate and improve the efficiency of European capital markets, among other economic and social goals to transform Europe.[94] Through the Financial Services Action Plan, providing a framework to implement the Lisbon Strategy's goals for this sector, the EU has adopted over twenty new directives.[95] Concomitant reforms were made to corporate governance and securities law in many EU states.[96] Much of this recent tranche of EU legislation departs from the principle of minimum harmonization by creating self-standing regulatory regimes in several areas, most notably in the regulation of market abuse and of licensed financial exchanges.[97] Recent reforms include the Market Abuse Directive,[98] Disclosure Directive,[99] Occupational Pensions Fund Directive,[100] Prospectuses Directive,[101] and the Transparency Directive.[102]

---

93 Directive 89/646/EEC of 15 December 1989, OJ L 386/1. While a bank must comply with the market rules of the country in which it does business, the home country retains responsibility for regulating that institution.

94 "Presidency Conclusions, Lisbon European Council, March 23–24, 2000," *European Union Bulletin* 3 (2000): 7.

95 EC, *Financial Services: Implementing the Framework for Financial Markets: Action Plan* COM(1999) 232 (May 11, 1999).

96 The EC defined the scope of its corporate governance activities in the Financial Services Action Plan of May 11, 1999, COM(1999)232, and the Corporate Law Action Plan of May 21, 2003.

97 For analysis, see E Avgouleas, "A Critical Evaluation of the New EC Financial-Market Regulation: Peaks, Troughs, and the Road Ahead," *The Transnational Lawyer* 18 (2005): 179; J.F. Mogg, "Regulating Financial Services in Europe: A New Approach," *Fordham International Law Journal* 26 (2002): 58.

98 Directive 2003/6/EC of 28 January 2003. O.J. L. 96/16.

99 Directive 2003/124/EC of 22 December 2003. O.J. L. 339/70.

100 Directive 2003/41/EC of 3 June 2003, O.J. L. 235/10.

101 Directive 2003/71/EC of 4 November 2003, O.J. L. 345/64.

102 Directive 2004/109/EC of 15 December 2004, O.J. L. 390/38. The Transparency Directive is particularly significant, establishing standards for shareholder information, and shareholder proxy voting. For other EU financial market directives, see Panourgias, note 59, 40–43.

The original Lisbon Strategy did not consider the social and environmental dimensions of financial markets, although the Strategy was subsequently amended at a meeting of the European Council to add an environmental dimension to the initial political and economic commitments.[103] The Amsterdam amendments of 1997 to the EU Treaty sought to strengthen the principle of integration of environmental standards across all EU policy sectors.[104] So far, integration of environmental matters into the single market has applied mainly to cross-border trade in goods, rather than to capital and investment flows.[105] In its mid-term assessment of the Lisbon strategy, the Kok Report called for reinforcing the integration of environmental considerations, and making it a "source of competitive advantage for Europe."[106] Some of the legal changes that emerged in the wake of the Lisbon Strategy may facilitate a pan-European market for SRI mutual funds in the retail sector by removing market barriers. But otherwise, they do not address the numerous institutional and market obstacles to SRI. Ultimately, EU financial law, like international financial regulation generally, contains pervasive lacunae regarding the social and environmental dimensions of the financial sector.

III. Fiduciary Duties of Institutional Investors

A. THE FIDUCIARY RELATIONSHIP

1. Fiduciaries and Beneficiaries

Financial institutions do not have unfettered authority to deal in funds they manage on behalf of their investors. The legal system imposes responsibilities on financial decision-makers to make investments carefully in the interests of investors and in accordance with the purpose of the particular fund. The shift to prudential standards, in place of portfolio restrictions and

---

103 See Communication from the Commission to the Gothenburg European Council, *A Sustainable Europe for a Better World: A European Union Strategy for Sustainable Development*, COM (2001) 262 final (May 15, 2001).

104 Consolidated version of the Treaty establishing the European Community, art. 6, O.J. C 340/3 (1997); ILM 37 (1998): 79.

105 See EC, *Single Market and the Environment* (EC Communication, June 10, 1999) (discussing integration of single market and environmental policies).

106 W. Kok, *Facing the Challenge. The Lisbon Strategy for Growth and Employment* (EC, 2004), 35.

detailed investment prescriptions, has resulted in elevating the importance of the fiduciary norms that inform such standards.

The evolution of fiduciary standards far predates the SRI movement, and their current impact on SRI is a source of much debate and confusion. The narrow focus on the interests of investors and their financial welfare may hinder the breadth of perspective necessary for SRI. A study on capital markets undertaken for Canada's NRTEE concluded: "current interpretations of the fiduciary duties of pension fund managers may unnecessarily constrain their ability to address the full range of relevant corporate responsibility considerations related to prospective investments."[107] Conversely, a 2005 report commissioned by UNEPFI suggests that SRI is not precluded or overly hampered by such fiduciary duties.[108]

The following doctrinal exegesis of investment standards similarly argues that SRI does not normally or necessarily conflict with financial institutions' fiduciary duties (or functionally equivalent standards in non-common law jurisdictions). Indeed, consistent with business case SRI, prudent investment should require careful attention to the social and environmental performance of corporations that may affect the bottom line. However, the prevailing discourse on fiduciary duties is arguably inadequate as a basis for a deeper, ethical approach to investing for sustainability.

In simple terms shorn of context-specific labels, a fiduciary relationship is a bond of responsibility and dependency.[109] It typically arises where the exercise of some discretionary power in the interests of another person gives rise to a relationship of trust and confidence. The fiduciary is the entity that acts on behalf of another party, the beneficiary.[110] The latter, as the dependant party, relies upon the fiduciary to manage some aspect of personal or economic affairs over which the fiduciary has been assigned control and has accepted responsibility. Two features of this relationship stand out. First, considerable discretion is vested in the fiduciary, to exercise within broad parameters of care and loyalty. Second, the beneficiary is typically precluded

---

107 Stratos, *Corporate Disclosure and Capital Markets* (NRTEE, 2004), 12.

108 Freshfields Bruckhaus Deringer, *A Legal Framework for the Integration of Environmental, Social and Governance Issues into Institutional Investment* (UNEPFI, October 2005).

109 See generally R. Flannigan, "The Boundaries of Fiduciary Accountability," *Canadian Bar Review* 83 (2004): 35; J.C. Shepherd, "Towards a Unified Concept of Fiduciary Relationships," *Law Quarterly Review* 97 (1981): 51.

110 D.G. Smith, "The Critical Resource Theory of Fiduciary Duty," *Vanderbilt Law Review* 55 (2002): 1399, 1483.

from exercising any control over that area. These principal elements of the fiduciary relationship inform specific legal duties.

Consequential to the powers provided, fiduciaries must act in the dependant's interests, and not their own. Thus, the fiduciary's foremost duty is one of loyalty to the beneficiary—to act in their sole or best interests.[111] This principle underpins the prohibitions on engaging in conflict-of-interest transactions adverse to the interests of investors in a pension plan or mutual fund.[112] Further, the fiduciary has a duty of competence or care, requiring skill and diligence. In the context of investment management, the duty of competence is usually expressed as the "prudent person rule" or the "prudent investor rule."[113] Depending on the jurisdiction, the sources of these legal duties come from the common law, legislation, and specific instruments governing each investment entity (e.g., a pension plan's trust agreement or a contract).

Fiduciary responsibilities can arise in various ways. In common law jurisdictions, they occur in relationships that are presumptively fiduciary, such as in the trustee-beneficiary relationship. Fiduciaries can be boards of trustees governing a pension plan, as well as investment managers, advisers, and directors of corporations. The "trust" is a concept of English law by which specific assets are constituted and managed by the trustee for the benefit of the beneficiary.[114] A trust can also serve to advance specific purposes, as in the case of charitable trusts. The entity (e.g., an individual or a corporation) that creates the trust is the settlor. The equitable notion of a fiduciary relationship arose because the beneficiary had no rights recognized in traditional common law. The English courts of equity began to acknowledge the beneficiary's interest and imposed a responsibility upon the fiduciary to protect that interest. Today, trusts are widely used as a means of corporate financing, in both

---

111 J.D. Hutchinson and C.G. Cole, "Legal Standards Governing Investment of Pension Assets for Social and Political Goals," *University of Pennsylvania Law Review* 128(4) (1980): 1340, 1367; J. Langbein, "Questioning the Trust Law Duty of Loyalty: Sole Interest or Best Interest?" *Yale Law Journal* 114 (2005): 929.

112 A. Hudson, *The Law on Investment Entities* (Sweet and Maxwell, 2000), 85–86.

113 See generally Longstreth, note 12.

114 See D.J. Hayton, "The Irreducible Core Content of Trusteeship," in *Trends in Contemporary Trust Law*, ed. A.J. Oakley (Clarendon Press, 1996), 47; A. Hudson, *Principles of Equity and Trusts* (Cavendish, 1999); D. Hayton, "English Fiduciary Standards and Trust Law," *Vanderbilt Journal of Transnational Law* 32 (1999): 555.

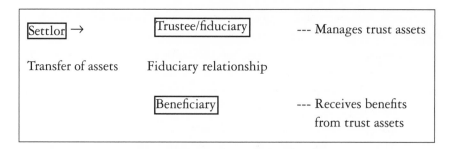

Figure 1: Basic Structure of a Trust Arrangement

pension plans and mutual funds.[115] The trust differs from other fiduciary relationships because of the presence of trust property. Not all fiduciary relationships involve property. Directors and officers of corporations are also fiduciaries by virtue of their offices. Factual circumstances of a relationship can also engender fiduciary obligations, such as in the relationship between an investment advisor and her client.[116]

Fiduciary responsibilities materialize in different ways across the financial sector. Broad fiduciary obligations to invest prudently and loyally in the interests of beneficiaries apply to pension trusts. Banks do not normally owe their depositors a fiduciary duty and therefore may use deposited money as they see fit within the parameters of banking regulation. Although fiduciary principles arise in mutual funds, the legal system tends to defer to contractual techniques and disclosure-based regulation for aligning investment decisions with the interests of fund members.

2. Duty of Care: Prudent Investor Rule

In its simplest terms, the duty of care requires fiduciaries to exercise the care that a person in a like position should exercise under similar circumstances. Early versions of this rule in the context of investment management focused on avoiding risk and preserving capital, rather than on promoting asset growth. In 1720 the South Sea Company spectacularly collapsed; trust assets were invested in it and suffered great loss. Subsequently, British authorities legislated to restrict trustees to a limited list of allowable investments.[117] The fiduciary obligation became framed around the need to preserve the beneficiaries' capital.

115 P. O'Hagan, "The Use of Trusts in Finance Structures," *Journal of International Trust and Corporate Planning* 8(2) (2000): 85.

116 G.A. Clarke, *Liability and Damages in Unsuitable Investment Advice Cases* (Fasken Martineau DuMoulin LLP, 2005).

117 J. Carswell, *The South Sea Bubble* (Cresset Press, 1960).

In time, market forces lengthened the allowable list, but the notion that certain types of asset classes (e.g., investment in equities) might be inherently imprudent persisted for centuries afterwards. Importantly, fiduciaries were also expected to evaluate the risk-adjusted returns of presumptively allowable investments on an investment-by-investment basis rather than by evaluating the overall portfolio.[118]

The traditional formulation of the prudent investor standard effectively precluded any SRI that posed an unusual risk, as a fiduciary had to assess and justify each investment individually.[119] A fiduciary could not dilute or offset that specific risk by evaluating it in the context of the entire investment portfolio. Under the influence of modern portfolio theory (MPT), this traditional understanding of prudent investment has given way to the view that optimal returns derive from a large, diversified portfolio where risk-adjusted returns are assessed by reference to the entire portfolio rather than assessed on individual investments in isolation.[120] Thus, while an individual ethical investment in a new environmental technology business might seem, in isolation, too risky, it may in combination with other investments constitute a prudent choice. The MPT has reformulated the prudent investor rule through statutory reforms and judicial activism.[121] It requires an investment strategy that incorporates sound risk and return objectives over the entire portfolio.[122] Concomitantly, legislation has commonly freed trustees from the restrictions of the laundry list of permissible investments.

The trustees, as fiduciaries, normally must possess adequate skills in investing, which may require obtaining expert advice.[123] The integrity of the fiduciary's conduct is judged with regard to when the investment decision was made, and not the performance of the investment with "the prescience of hindsight."[124]

---

118 *King v. Talbot*, (1869) 40 N.Y. 76. See also the US case of *Harvard College v. Amory*, 26 Mass. 454 (1830) and the British case of *Re Whiteley*, (1886) 33 Ch. D. 347.

119 P. Ali and K. Yano, *Eco-Finance* (Kluwer Law, 2004), 131.

120 P.G. Haskell, "The Prudent Person Rule for Trustee Investment and Modern Portfolio Theory," *North Carolina Law Review* 69 (1990): 87.

121 See e.g., the US's *Employee Retirement Income Security Act*, 1974, Pub. L. No. 93-406, 88 Stat. 829, s. 404; and Australia's *Superannuation Industry (Supervision) Act*, 1993 (Cth), s. 52(2)(f)(ii).

122 See further W.F. Sharpe, *Portfolio Theory and Capital Markets* (McGraw-Hill, 1970), 20–24; R.A. Brealey and S.C. Myers, *Principles of Corporate Finance* (McGraw-Hill, 1988), 136–39.

123 Hayton, note 114, 562–63.

124 *Fales v. Canada Permanent Trust Company*, [1977] 2 S.C.R. 302, 317.

3. Duty of Loyalty

In addition to a duty to invest prudently, fiduciaries owe beneficiaries a duty of loyalty. It is a long-standing and most fundamental duty in the fiduciary relationship. Traditionally, this duty has been interpreted as requiring fiduciaries to act exclusively for the beneficiaries, as opposed to acting for their own interest or any third party interests. In the US, authorities expressed this duty of "undivided loyalty"[125] as requiring a trustee "to administer the trust solely in the interest of beneficiaries."[126] Courts and legislatures have articulated prophylactic rules to ensure that fiduciaries act loyally: to avoid conflict of interests (the "conflict" rule); not to profit personally from their office (the "profit" rule); not to delegate responsibilities (the "personal performance" rule); and to act impartially towards beneficiaries (the "even hand" rule).[127]

The duty of loyalty has often been interpreted as requiring fiduciaries to demonstrate that only the *financial* interests of the beneficiary motivate their decisions. This particularly applies where the explicit purpose of the trust is to provide financial benefits to beneficiaries, such as a pension fund providing retirement income. However, even where an institution has financial objectives, some experts believe fiduciaries may consider non-financial criteria. As early as 1979, Austin Scott's *The Law of Trusts*, a leading scholarly authority in the US, explained that trustees may properly consider the social performance of a corporation as a factor in investment decisions:

> [t]hey may decline to invest in, or to retain, the securities of corporations whose activities, or some of them, are contrary to fundamental and generally accepted ethical principles. They may consider such matters as pollution, race discrimination, fair employment and consumer responsibility.[128]

Perhaps, therefore, a "benefit" need not necessarily be limited to a financial benefit. If beneficiaries share a moral objection to a particular form of investment, they may benefit if their trust avoided that investment, possibly even at the cost of a lower financial return.[129] In one US case, the court stressed the

---

125 *Meinhard v. Salmon*, (1928) 164 N.E. 545 (N.Y.).

126 S.P. Serota and F.A. Brodie, *ERISA Fiduciary Law* (BNA Books, 1995), 25.

127 A.B. Laby, "Resolving Conflicts of Duty in Fiduciary Relationships," *American University Law Review* 54 (2004): 75, 99–108.

128 A.W. Scott, *The Law of Trusts* (3rd ed., Little Brown and Company, 1967 and Supplement 1979), s. 227.17.

129 P. Palmer, et al., *Socially Responsible Investment: A Guide for Pension Schemes and Charities* (Haven Publications, 2005), 97.

importance of the trustees safeguarding "unique scenic, paleontological, and archaeological values that would have little economic value on the open market."[130] Even where the purpose of the trust is construed to provide financial benefits, some courts have interpreted the duty of loyalty as only to seek a reasonable rate of return rather than to *maximize* financial returns. A judge in one UK case stated: "I cannot conceive that trustees have an unqualified duty ... simply to invest trust funds in the most profitable investment available."[131] Where an entity is established as a trust to advance a particular purpose, such as a charitable trust, the fiduciary trustee's "loyalty" is to the *purposes* of the trust. A charitable trust is an example where the purpose may require furtherance of social or ethical aims rather than financial goals. Also relevant is the legislative trend in a few jurisdictions to defer the duty of loyalty to the duty of care. One example is the Canadian province of Manitoba, which takes this approach in its pension benefits and trustee statutes. They provide that unless the pension plan or trust instrument dictates otherwise, an investment decision partially motivated by non-financial criteria is permissible so long as trustees follow the duty of care.[132]

In all jurisdictions, fiduciaries are potentially liable to beneficiaries for investments that breach duties of loyalty and prudence.[133] A fiduciary could be held liable for the consequences of improper disposal of investments, including the losses with respect to the value of the stock and transaction costs, offset by the value and earnings of the replacement assets.[134] Criminal sanctions could apply for more serious and flagrant derelictions of fiduciary duties. In a charitable trust lacking a discrete class of beneficiaries, and without the goal strictly defined to enhance financial returns, the measurement of damages is more difficult. Oren Perez cites one option, as developed by the Israeli Supreme Court in another context, involving the creation of a new tortious remedy that focuses "on the grievance to the individual's integrity or autonomy, manifested in the deliberate disregard of his moral

---

130 *National Parks and Conservation Authority v. Board of State Lands*, (1993) 869 P.2d 909, 921 (S.C. Utah).

131 *Martin v. Edinburgh (City) District Council*, [1988] S.L.T. 329, 334 (per Lord Murray).

132 *Trustee Act*, S.M. 1995, s. 79.1; *Pension Benefits Amendment Act*, S.M. 2005, s. 28.1(2.2).

133 L. Ho, "Attributing Losses to a Breach of Fiduciary Duty," *Trust Law International* 12 (1998): 66.

134 On the problems of proving loss and causation generally, see G. Watt and M. Stauch, "Is there Liability for Imprudent Trustee Investment?" *Conveyancer* 62 (1998): 352.

beliefs and preferences."[135] Even though a charitable trust may have no specific beneficiaries, the fiduciary's obligations may be enforceable by the Attorney-General and possibly by any persons materially interested in the work of the charity.[136]

B. IMPLICATIONS OF FIDUCIARY STANDARDS FOR SRI

1. Accommodating Non-financial Benefits

While some commentators maintain that the duties of prudent investment and loyalty significantly constrain SRI,[137] this view is waning.[138] Current formulations of fiduciary responsibilities for investment institutions may not generally allow them to disregard financial returns, yet there is ample scope for some forms of SRI within the fiduciary framework. Although ethically driven SRI is problematic, business case SRI can dovetail with the current fiduciary paradigm. Before looking at fiduciary duties specifically within pension funds and other financial institutions, some general observations about the implications of fiduciary standards for SRI can be drawn.

Firstly, fiduciaries have an overarching responsibility to promote the interests of their beneficiaries. In the context of modern financial markets, this standard usually is understood as to require optimizing financial returns. To illustrate, the Ontario Teachers' Pension Plan defines its fiduciary duty as "to obtain the highest return for the plan commensurate with acceptable levels of risk. Consequently, non-financial considerations cannot take precedence over risk and return considerations in the management of the pension fund."[139] The Ontario Teachers' Pension Plan concedes a role for SRI, but

135 O. Perez, *The New Universe of Green Finance: From Self-Regulation to Multi-Polar Governance*, Working Paper No. 07-3 (Bar-Ilan University, Faculty of Law, 2007) citing *Daaka v. Carmel Hospital—Haifa*, (1993) Supreme Court Case 2781/93 and *Tnuva v. Ravi Tufic*, (1997) Supreme Court Case 1338/97.
136 A.J. Oakley, *Parker and Mellows: The Modern Law of Trusts* (Sweet and Maxwell, 1998), 440.
137 Ali and Yano, note 119, 128–39; J.H. Langbein and R.A. Posner, "Social Investing and the Law of Trusts," *Michigan Law Review* 79 (1980): 72; A.H. Munnell, *Should Public Pension Plans Engage in Social Investing?* (Centre for Retirement Research, 2007).
138 Freshfields, note 108; G.R. Gray and J.A. Klaassen, "Retirement Investment, Fiduciary Obligations, and Socially Responsible Investing," *Journal of Deferred Compensation* 10(4) (2005): 34.
139 Ontario Teachers' Pension Plan, "Social Responsibility," at http://www.otpp.com/web/website.nsf/web/Guidelines_SocialResponsibility.

only "as a means of maximizing long-term shareholder value" rather than as an ethical imperative.[140]

A doctrinal emphasis on financial returns implies a "homo economicus" view of individuals' interests. In this narrative, the human agent is depicted as an unboundedly rational utility maximizer with a restricted and predictable range of predominantly *economic* desires.[141] Outside of the specific confines of charitable or mission-based investment, this perspective ignores the array of psychological benefits and costs that an individual may also experience, such as ecological values (e.g., a concern for the plight of endangered species) or altruistic concerns (e.g., interest in social emancipation). Such concerns, reflected in SRI, are marginalized by fiduciary doctrine that assumes a homo economicus who is a self-interested, materialistic creature preoccupied with enlarging her financial gains regardless of the interests of others.

It is doctrinally possible however that the "interests" of beneficiaries may accommodate a wider field of concerns, depending on whether we see the fiduciary duty as an obligation to act in beneficiaries' "best" interests or in their "sole" interests. The traditional sole interest standard was designed to prevent conflicts of interest and a fiduciary gaining personally at the expense of beneficiaries. Presumably, a sole interest test could also prohibit a fiduciary from considering whether an investment may provide collateral benefits to others (e.g., a local community or enhanced environmental protection). However, even the US's *Employee Retirement Income Security Act* (ERISA) of 1974,[142] which posits a "sole interests" standard, has been interpreted by the US Department of Labor as "not preclud[ing] consideration of collateral benefits, such as those offered by a 'socially-responsible' fund. ..."[143] Thus, in the US case of *Donovan v. Walton* (1985), the court ruled that the interests of the beneficiaries are paramount, but not necessarily exclusive:

> ERISA ... simply does not prohibit a party other than a plan's participants and beneficiaries from benefiting in some measure from a prudent

---

140 Ibid.

141 The behavioral validity of this concept has been questioned extensively: H. Gintis, "Beyond *Homo Economicus*: Evidence from Experimental Economics," *Ecological Economics* 35 (2000): 311; J. Henrich, et al., "In Search of Homo Economicus: Experiments in 15 Small-Scale Societies," *American Economic Review* 91 (2001): 73.

142 Pub. L. No. 93-406, 88 Stat. 829, s. 404(a)(1).

143 R.J. Doyle, Pension and Welfare Benefits Administration, Office of Regulations and Interpretations, Advisory Opinion (May 28, 1998), at http://www.calvert.com/pdf/sri_DOL_Letter.pdf.

transaction with the plan. Furthermore, by adopting the "exclusive purpose" standard, Congress did not intend to make illegal the fact of life that most often a transaction benefits both parties involved.[144]

Legal commentators in the US have since argued that pension fund trustees should have the authority to make community-beneficial investments, analogous to how a director of a corporation may distribute reasonable charitable donations.[145] US jurisprudence has come a long way since the classic case of *Dodge v. Ford Motor Company*,[146] when the Michigan Supreme Court disallowed the directors of Ford from withholding dividends to shareholders in order to fund reduced prices of their cars in the interests of consumers and to provide more jobs for Ford's workers. US courts have since modified the fiduciary duty doctrine so that shareholders' interests may be weighed to some extent against the interests of other social groups, thereby permitting corporate philanthropy in the long-term interests of the company.[147]

Where the law enunciates a "best interest" formula, the fiduciary relationship should be able to accommodate collateral benefits even more easily, so long as conflicts of interest do not arise. Pension plan management often involves the best-interest standard. The EU's Occupational Pensions Directive provides in its investment rules that "the assets shall be invested in the best interests of the members and beneficiaries."[148] Also, the UK's *Occupational Pension Schemes (Investment) Regulations* of 2005 characterize trustee's chief duty to beneficiaries as acting in their "best interests," except "in the case of a potential conflict of interest, [where they must act] in the sole interest of members and beneficiaries."[149]

Whether acting loyally in the best or sole interests of beneficiaries allows fiduciaries to accommodate third-party benefits, of course depends also on how we define the "interests" of beneficiaries. The Canadian case of *Re Irving*[150]

---

144 (1985) 609 F. Supp. 1221, 1245 (D.C. Fla.).
145 E. Adams and K.D. Knutsen, "A Charitable Corporate Giving Justification for the Socially Responsible Investment of Pension Funds: A Populist Argument for the Public Use of Private Wealth," *Iowa Law Review* 80 (1995): 211.
146 (1919) 204 Mich. 459, 170 N.W. 668.
147 E.g., *A.P. Smith Manufacturing Co. v. Barlow*, (1953) 13 N.J. 145, 98 A. 2d. 581; 346 U.S. 861; *Union Pacific Railroad Co. v. Trustees*, (1958) 8 Utah 2d. 101, 329 P. 2d. 398.
148 Directive 2003/41/EC of 3 June 2003, O.J. L. 235/10, art. 18.
149 Clause 4(2).
150 (1975) 66 D.L.R. (3d) 387; 11 O.R. (2d) 443 (case involving variation of a trust, ostensibly contrary to the original intention of the settlor). The Ontario

stated that in relation to trusts, the word "benefit" should be interpreted liberally and not confined to financial benefit. If the settlor establishes a trust for financial benefits, the interests of beneficiaries will normally be construed as financial. But "benefit" need not carry only financial connotations. If the trust is established to further some ethical, social, or charitable goal, then fiduciaries would need to promote those benefits.

Regardless of whether we can conceptualize the "interests" of beneficiaries as extending to the concerns of other stakeholders, there remains the pragmatic question of whether third parties have a right to enforce their interests against the fiduciary. In the Canadian case of *Peoples Department Stores v. Wise*,[151] the federal Supreme Court conceded that the *Canada Business Corporations Act*'s[152] duty on directors to promote the "best interests of the corporation" required directors to consider factors beyond the maximization of the value of the company, such as "consumers, governments and the environment."[153] However, the Court stressed the difference between considering the interests of other parties and *owing the duty* to those parties. The duty of loyalty that a director owes remains exclusively to the corporation itself.[154] While the Supreme Court clarified directors' duty of care regarding other constituencies, this was hardly a gain as the "business judgment rule" protects directors who take reasonable steps with regard to the interests of the corporation itself (e.g., the directors are justified in determining that a potential harm to the corporation outweighs the potential harm to an outside party).[155] Thus, while this Canadian decision weakens the position of shareholder primacy, precluding the shareholders from asserting that directors who favor other constituencies over value maximization derogate their duties, it does not allow much recourse for those other constituencies. The recognition of other stakeholders' interests verges on the functionally unenforceable.

A second observation concerning a trust providing financial benefits is that courts should not find a fiduciary acting imprudently for considering non-financial objectives that were not predicted to sacrifice financial returns

---

High Court stressed that the benefit must be one that a prudent adult, motivated by rational self-interest, would recognize as a good bargain.

151 [2004] 3 S.C.R. 461.

152 R.S.C. 1985.

153 Note 151, para. 42.

154 Ibid., para. 43

155 Ibid., para. 57.

and where they constitute a subordinate objective of the trust.[156] Given the evidence discussed earlier that SRI funds do not generally under-perform the market (albeit with not materially different investment portfolios), socially responsible companies can arguably constitute a prudent choice on financial criteria.[157] Social and environmental risks often affect shareholder value.[158]

Indeed, fiduciary investors who utterly ignore financially material environmental and social considerations may contravene their fiduciary obligations. Some ecological and human rights issues have become so pervasive and serious that few investors can ignore their impact. Climate change is an example. Some investment advisors and commentators suggest that institutions have an emerging fiduciary duty to specifically consider the financial risks of climate change.[159] The UK-based Institutional Investors Group on Climate Change (IIGCC) was formed precisely for this reason, to promote better understanding of the financial risks and investment opportunities posed by climate change for the purposes of fiduciary investors.[160] It commissioned a guide to climate risk for investment trustees, which advises trustees to "investigate the linkages between climate change and their fiduciary duties with respect to providing pension funds over the long term."[161]

International human rights law is another domain for emerging fiduciary standards. Cynthia Williams and John Conley argue that "risks to companies' reputations and therefore to the value of their brands from highly-publicized problems with stakeholders or human rights issues may" give rise to fiduciary duties to "consider the rights and interests of stakeholder groups."[162]

---

156 E.g., *Harries and others v. Church Commissioners for England*, [1992] 1 W.L.R. 1241.

157 See S. Labatt and R.R. White, *Environmental Finance: A Guide to Environmental Risk Assessment and Financial Products* (John Wiley and Sons, 2002), 151–55.

158 E.g., S.A. Waddock and S.M. Graves, "The Corporate Social Performance Financial Performance Link," *Strategic Management Journal* 18(4) (1997): 303; D. Edwards, *The Link Between Environmental and Financial Performance* (Earthscan, 1998).

159 Mercer Investment Consulting, *A Climate for Change—A Trustee's Guide to Understanding and Addressing Climate Risk* (Mercer Investment Consulting, 2005).

160 Http://www.iigcc.org.

161 Mercer Investment Consulting, note 159, 15.

162 C.A. Williams and J.M. Conley, "Corporate Social Responsibility in the International Context: Is There an Emerging Fiduciary Duty to Consider Human Rights?" *University of Cincinnati Law Review* 74(Fall) (2005): 75, 76–77.

They cite companies' risks of litigation under the US's *Alien Tort Claims Act* of 1789,[163] which has helped to engender the notion that "fiduciary duties now include a duty to be aware of human rights risks and potential violations within a company's global operations and to develop policies and management procedures to reduce the risks of such violations."[164]

Both of these examples perhaps illustrate the evolving fiduciary duties of "universal owners." The breadth of institutional investors' assets across the economy conceivably creates fiduciary-like responsibilities to respect the wider social and environmental ramifications of their investments.[165] The universal owner thesis posits that it is a zero-sum game for investors to favor a profitable yet polluting business if it creates risks and costs for other sectors in which the investor has a stake.

2. Fiduciary Obligations in the Context of SRI Policies

Apart from these foregoing arguments about how social and environmental considerations might dovetail with the fiduciary duties owed to beneficiaries, we must also look at the specific methods and practices of SRI. While the modern imperative to hold a diversified portfolio has resolved the traditional problem related to narrow evaluation of investments on a case-by-case basis, the new standard may also still hinder SRI. For example, extensive SRI exclusionary screens can clearly hamper diversification.[166] Yet, in some situations the duty to diversify can actually favor SRI choices; for example, in the energy sector, this should entail expanding from the fossil fuel sector to investing in clean, renewable energy suppliers. In other situations, diversified portfolios may lead to smaller holdings in each of the investments, thereby reducing the fiduciary investor's influence in individual companies. This may obstruct shareholder activist methods of SRI.[167]

---

163 U.S.C. 28 (2000): 1350.

164 Williams and Conley, note 162, 87.

165 See J.P. Hawley and A.T. Williams, *The Rise of Fiduciary Capitalism: How Institutional Investors Can Make Corporate America More Democratic* (University of Pennsylvania Press, 2000); R.A.G. Monks, *The New Global Investors: How Shareowners Can Unlock Sustainable Prosperity Worldwide* (Capstone Press, 2001).

166 P. Luxton, "Ethical Investment by Charities: A Slippery Slope?" *New Law Journal* 142 (1992): 16; R. Ellison, "The Golden Fleece? Ethical Investment and Fiduciary Law," *Trust Law International* 5(4) (1991): 157.

167 J.E. Parkinson, *Corporate Power and Responsibility: Issues in the Theory of Company Law* (Clarendon Press, 1995), 168–69.

A second aspect of SRI policies is that where fiduciaries seek to account for the social, ethical, and environmental considerations to provide non-financial benefits, they should consult with the beneficiaries. While the beneficiaries may not all share the same values, they may at least agree on matters of process and procedure regarding the methods by which SRI factors should be evaluated, such as by reference to an SRI market index. While mutual fund investors are free to shop around, pension plan beneficiaries generally have no such choice, and therefore have a greater entitlement to be heard in the making of investment policies.

Where fiduciaries factor in ethical preferences into their investment policy, they should ensure that these preferences are those of their beneficiaries.[168] Fiduciaries should ascertain the views of the beneficiaries, and keep them informed about implementation of an SRI policy. A further pragmatic reason to consult with beneficiaries is that they probably cannot hold the trustee liable for a breach of trust after having been properly informed and given consent to the choices.[169] Enforcing the beneficiary's consent in this way is directly responsive to the policy of the loyalty rule—to maximize the best interests of the beneficiary.

A third aspect of the methods of SRI is that while inflexible exclusionary screens may breach fiduciary duties, courts may accept other SRI strategies. Best-of-sector methods that allow for retention of a diverse portfolio should meet fiduciary standards. Likewise, such standards should accommodate a financier tracking a broadly-based SRI market index. Further, shareholder advocacy, where investors seek to influence companies from within, should contribute to the fulfillment of fiduciary responsibilities.

Indeed, fiduciaries have a duty to monitor their investments and to protect those investments actively through proxy voting, dialogue, and other strategies.[170] Commentators increasingly concur that "active" investing

---

168 See *Re Clore's Settlement Trusts,* [1966] 2 All E.R. 272, 275.

169 Langbein, note 111, 964–65; and US *Uniform Trust Code,* (2004) 7C U.L.A. 229 (Supp.), s. 802(b)(4).

170 B. Goodman, *The Environmental Fiduciary: The Case for Incorporating Environmental Factors into Investment Management Policies* (Rose Foundation for Communities and the Environment, 2004), 32; E. Tasch and S. Viederman, "New Concepts of Fiduciary Responsibility," in *Steering Business Toward Sustainability,* eds F. Capra and G. Pauli (UN University Press, 1995), 125; R.H. Koppes and M.L. Reilly, "An Ounce of Prevention: Meeting the Fiduciary Duty to Monitor an Index Fund Through Relationship Investing," *Iowa Journal of Corporation Law* 20 (1995): 414.

is crucial to fiduciary investment,[171] and that improved corporate governance enhances financial returns.[172] The UK's Myners report on institutional investment considered that where shareholder activism was in the best financial interests of the beneficiaries, it was "arguably already a legal duty of both pension fund trustees and their fund managers to pursue such strategies."[173] Likewise, the US Department of Labor has issued rulings (legal guidance) that suggest occupational pension plans have a fiduciary duty to invest actively. In the first of such rulings, in 1988, it stipulated that shareholding votes at the annual meeting are important assets of institutional investors.[174] In its second ruling, an Interpretation Bulletin issued in 1994, the Department stated that shareholder activism itself is consistent with a fiduciary's obligations where "there is a reasonable expectation that such monitoring or communication with management . . . is likely to enhance the value of the plan's investment in the corporation, after taking into account the costs involved."[175] Lamentably, many pension funds according to recent surveys still do not see shareholder activism as a fiduciary duty.[176]

Finally, we must always remember that the applicable trust instrument is the foremost authority in governing a trustee's duties and investment

171 Hawley and Williams, note 165; G. Yaron, *Acting Like Owners: Proxy Voting, Corporate Engagement and the Fiduciary Responsibilities of Pension Trustees* (Shareholder Association for Research and Education, 2005).

172 See S. Wahal, "Pension Fund Activism and Firm Performance," *Journal of Financial and Quantitative Analysis* 31(1) (1996): 1; C.E. Crutchley, C.D. Hudson, and M. Jensen, "The Shareholder Wealth Effects of CalPERS' Activism," *Financial Services Review* 7(3) (1998): 1; J.E. Bethel and S.L. Gillan, *The Impact of the Institutional and Regulatory Environment on Shareholder Voting,* Working Paper 1-100100 (TIAA-CREF Institute, 2002).

173 P. Myners, *Institutional Investment in the United Kingdom: A Review* (H.M. Treasury, 2001), 92.

174 Letter from Deputy Assistant Secretary of Labor Alan Lebowitz to Helmuth Fandl, Avon Products Inc., reprinted in *Pensions Reporter* (BNA) 15 (February 29, 1988): 391; see also E. Stone, "Must We Teach Abstinence? Pensions' Relationship Investments and the Lessons of Fiduciary Duty," *Columbia Law Review* 94(7) (1994): 2222.

175 US Department of Labor, *Interpretative Bulletin Relating to Statements of Investment Policy, Including Proxy Voting Policy or Guidelines), Code of Federal Regulations,* 29 Ch. XXV, 2509, 94–2 (1994).

176 K. Peach, "Shareholder Activism 'Not a Fiduciary Responsibility'," *Global Pensions*, September 8, 2006, http://globalpensions.com/?id=me/17/news/39/39092/0.

decisions.[177] This reflects another aspect of the duty of loyalty. If the trust deed expressly requires investment to further a specified mission, such as local community economic regeneration, then the trustee must fulfill those criteria.[178] However, pension legislation may prohibit pension plans from altering statutorily prescribed investment principles.[179] Charitable trusts and other eleemosynary-based institutions are typically organized under a trust mandate that expressly directs how the institution will invest for its particular philanthropic purposes. The UK Charity Commission, which supervises British charities under the *Charities Act* of 1993, has issued guidance stressing that charities can make investments that do not seek the best financial returns, if they advance the organization's charitable goals.[180] But where an instrument charges trustees with managing a charity's assets for investment purposes, courts will imply an obligation to maximize financial returns subject to avoiding a conflict with the charity's mission.[181]

In conclusion, SRI policies can meld with fiduciary responsibilities. But, they normally cannot substantially sacrifice financial returns unless the governing trust instrument gives primacy to non-financial goals. In any event, many methods of SRI, such as shareholder activism, actually enhance fulfillment of fiduciary responsibilities. Further, fiduciaries must not ignore significant environmental risks that may impact financial performance. However, because of the arbitrary and subjective nature of some SRI policies compared to the seeming clarity of traditional fund management objectives for optimizing financial returns, some explicit regulatory guidance on SRI would help. The question of how to more thoroughly reformulate fiduciary duties to support ethically-driven SRI is canvassed in this book's final chapter.

---

177 See *McCreight v. 146919 Canada Ltd*, [1991] O.J. No. 136.

178 Although, discriminatory provisions in a trust may be voided by courts on the basis of being against public policy or statutory human rights provisions: see, e.g., *Canada Trust Company v. Ontario Human Rights Commission*, (1990) 74 O.R. (2d) 481.

179 E.g., in the US, see ERISA, s. 404(a)(1)(D).

180 UK Charity Commission, "Guidance on Programme-Related Investment" (Charity Commission, May 2001).

181 A.J. Oakley, *Parker and Mellows: The Modern Law of Trusts* (Sweet and Maxwell, 1998), 543.

IV. Fiduciary Duties of Pension Funds

A. BASIC PRINCIPLES

An occupational pension fund is a financial institution established by employers and workers to pay benefits upon retirement of the fund members. In common law jurisdictions, they are usually established under a trust arrangement.[182] Typically, the employer, as settlor, vests the pension fund and its earnings in one or more pension trustees on behalf of the employee beneficiaries. The trustees have legal title to the fund's assets (the beneficiaries hold an equitable interest) and control the investment and management of those assets. Thus, they incur fiduciary duties to exercise those powers in the interests of their beneficiaries.[183] The trustees of pension funds commonly enjoy a plenary power to invest anywhere subject to restrictions posed by the trust deed, in addition to applicable common law rules and government regulation such as portfolio investment standards.[184]

Trustees of pension plans often delegate aspects of investment decision-making to professional asset managers.[185] Contrary to the common law prohibition on such delegations, pension legislation typically authorizes delegation of responsibility for implementing decisions, so long as the fiduciary retains control over policy decisions, is satisfied of the agent's suitability to perform the requisite tasks, and carefully supervises the agent. An investment management agreement typically governs the relationship between trustees and their fund managers. Fiduciary duties may also apply directly to fund managers, depending on the nature of the specific principal-agent relationship.[186] Legislation typically makes fund

---

182 E.g., E. Gillese, "Pension Plans and the Law of Trusts," *Canadian Bar Review* 75 (1996): 221; L. Millett, "Pension Schemes and the Law of Trusts: The Tail Wagging The Dog?" *Trust Law International* 14(2) (2000): 27.

183 OECD, *Guidelines on Pension Fund Asset Management* (OECD, 2006), clause 2.2.

184 OECD, *Survey of Investment Regulations of Pension Funds* (OECD, 2006). A standard trust deed contains details of the rights, powers, and remuneration of the trustee(s), details of benefits of members, winding up provisions, disclosure, record keeping and actuarial review. See e.g., *Trustee Act*, 2000 (UK), ss 3(1) and 6(1)(b); *Pensions Act*, 1995 (UK) s. 34(1).

185 K.P. Ambachtsteer and D. Ezra, *Pension Fund Excellence: Creating Value for Stockholders* (John Wiley and Sons, 1998), 67–71.

186 See generally S. Willey, "Investment Management and Fiduciary Duties," in *Law and Regulation of Investment Management,* ed. D. Frase (Sweet and Maxwell, 2004), 237.

managers effectively subject to the same prudential obligations as their principals.[187]

While pension trustees have traditionally shunned SRI in the belief that it contravenes fiduciary duties,[188] little case law supports this assumption. The following sections canvass developments in the UK, the US, and Canada; these countries have had the most litigation or legislative interest in SRI issues. Some consideration is given to other states, including Australia and some civil law jurisdictions. In the emerging economies of East Asia, also with some significant pension fund systems, their legal systems have generally not yet addressed the legal status of SRI.[189] Recent legislation adopted by some countries to require pension funds to disclose their SRI policies is canvassed in the next chapter.

B. PENSIONS REGULATION

1. Common Law Jurisdictions

In the common law jurisdictions, pension fund regulation generally clarifies rather than radically alters the fiduciary standards found in the common law.

In the UK, the *Pensions Act* of 1995[190] and its subordinate regulations[191] insist that trustees exercise their powers of investment "in a manner calculated to ensure the security, quality, liquidity and profitability of the portfolio as a whole."[192] Also, the legislation requires trustees to invest assets "in the best interests of members and beneficiaries,"[193] and to ensure portfolio diversification.[194] Further, the trustees must obtain proper advice when preparing their statement of investment principles,[195] and act in accordance with

---

187 E.g., UK's *Pensions Act*, 1995, s. 36 (duties to assess the suitability of each investment and have regard to the need for diversification); see further J. Franks and C.P. Mayer, *Risk, Regulation and Investor Protection: The Case of Investment Management* (Oxford University Press, 1989).

188 See A. Emid, "The Ethical Choice: It Takes a Steady Hand to Balance Fiduciary Responsibility with Ethical Goals," *Benefits Canada* 21(4) (1997): 89; Hayton, note 114.

189 ASrIA, *SRI and Pensions in Asia* (ASrIA, 2002), 7.

190 See ss 33–36.

191 *Occupational Pension Schemes (Investment) Regulations*, 2005 (UK).

192 Ibid., cl. 4.

193 Ibid., cl. 4(2)(a).

194 Ibid., cl. 4(7).

195 Ibid., cl. 2(2)(a)).

those principles as far as practicable.[196] UK pension regulation is also shaped by EU regulations, such as the Occupational Pensions Fund Directive.[197] This Directive includes the modern prudent investment standards already familiar to UK law.[198]

Pension fund law in the US contains similar investment rules. ERISA outlines the applicable norms for private occupational pension plans. It principally requires plan trustees and their fund managers to exercise their responsibilities "solely" in the interests of plan beneficiaries, for the "exclusive purpose of providing benefits," according to a prudent person standard, and by diversifying investments managed in accordance with pension plan documents.[199] Public pension funds are regulated by the state governments, which impose similar fiduciary duties. However, some states have enacted legislation that mandates divestment or responsible financing on a limited set of issues, such as countries associated with terrorism or genocide.[200] Conversely, in a few cases, states have legislated to tighten fiduciary duties to prevent any drift towards SRI. For example, in Nebraska, the law on the duties of the Investment Council states that: "[n]o assets of the retirement systems… shall be invested or reinvested if the sole or primary investment objective is for economic development or social purposes or objectives."[201]

Although ERISA does not explicitly refer to the possibility of SRI, the Department of Labor has issued relevant non-binding Interpretative Bulletins contemplating the issue. In 1980, the chief administrator of the Department of Labor's pension division presented an influential paper arguing that SRI exclusionary screens conflicted with ERISA's prudence and loyalty standards.[202] While the Department later cautioned fiduciaries not to subordinate the interests of participants and beneficiaries "to unrelated objectives," it also advised that proxy voting and shareholder activism is "consistent with a fiduciary's obligations under ERISA."[203] Also, in 1998, the Department of Labor

---

196 *Pensions Act*, 1995 (UK), s. 36(5).
197 Directive 2003/41/EC of 3 June 2003, O.J. L. 235/10.
198 Ibid., Article 18 (the Directive is most relevant to the civil law EU jurisdictions which have historically favoured quantitative investment rules rather than prudent investment standards).
199 Pub. L. No. 93-406, 88 Stat. 829, s. 404(a).
200 L.J. Dhooge, "Condemning Khartoum: The Illinois Divestment Act and Foreign Relations," *American Business Law Journal* 43(2) (2006): 245.
201 Nebraska Revised Statutes, (2007), s. 72-1239.01.
202 I. Lanoff, "The Social Investment of Private Pension Fund Assets: May it be Done Lawfully under ERISA?" *Labor Law Journal* 31(7) (1980): 387.
203 US Department of Labor, note 175.

224 SOCIALLY RESPONSIBLE INVESTMENT LAW

issued an official Advisory Opinion to the Calvert mutual funds group regarding the offering of SRI options in certain pension plans.[204] It regarded an SRI-focused mutual fund as acceptable, so long as the pension plan's trustees determined that the SRI fund's expected returns would match other investments of similar risks.

In Canada, legal guidance on SRI is scarce, although legislation and case law have unequivocally affirmed that trust law precepts govern pension funds.[205] So it is unusual that the provinces of Manitoba and Ontario have legislated partial exemptions. In 1993 the Manitoba Law Reform Commission recommended that the province allow trustees to consider non-financial criteria in their investment policies.[206] Based on this recommendation, in 1995 Manitoba's *Trustee Act* was amended to provide:

> Subject to any express provision in the instrument creating the trust, a trustee who uses a non-financial criterion to formulate an investment policy or to make an investment decision does not commit a breach of trust if, in relation to the investment policy or investment decision, the trustee exercises the judgment and care that a person of prudence, discretion and intelligence would exercise in administering the property of others.[207]

In 2005, a similar provision was embedded in Manitoba's pension legislation.[208]

Ontarian authorities have clarified the legality of SRI. In 1992 the province's Financial Services Commission issued a bulletin in which it stated that it is not necessarily imprudent for a pension fund to make ethical investments, so long as the fund's statement of investment policies states this position, sets out the criteria for investments, and notifies plan members.[209] Earlier, in 1988, Ontario enacted the *South African Trust Investments Act* to discourage Ontarian companies from investing in an apartheid system.[210] Where a majority of beneficiaries supported the move, the Act permitted trustees to divest or to reject investments in profitable companies conducting business in

204 Doyle, note 143.
205 See e.g., *Bathgate v. National Hockey League Pension Society*, (1994) 16 O.R. (3d) 761, 776 (CA); *Boe v. Alexander*, (1987) 41 D.L.R. (4th) 520, 526–27.
206 Manitoba Law Reform Commission (MLRC), *Ethical Investment by Trustees* (MLRC, 1993), 32.
207 *Trustee Act*, S.M. 1995, s. 79.1.
208 *Pension Benefits Amendment Act*, S.M. 2005, s. 28.1(2.2).
209 Financial Services Commission of Ontario, "Ethical Investments" *Bulletin* 2/4 (February 1992).
210 R.S.O. 1990, (repealed in 1997).

South Africa without infringing their duty as trustees. The latter reform is significant because it sanctioned divestments even with the possibility of an *adverse* effect on investment returns. Yet, like the Manitoban reform, Ontario did not actually mandate SRI, leaving it as a discretionary consideration for trustees.

These two exceptional legislative pronouncements have significance in the context of comprehending the nature of fiduciary investment standards. The fact that the Manitoban and Ontarian legislatures felt compelled to explicitly allow trustees to consider non-financial criteria may imply that those considerations do not otherwise meet prudential investment norms. Conversely, the provisions can be seen simply as measures to clarify and provide trustees with greater certainty regarding the common law position.

Australian occupational pension plans (known as "superannuation funds") are governed primarily by the *Superannuation Industry (Supervision) Act* of 1993, which incorporates fiduciary investment standards similar to other common law jurisdictions.[211] Australian courts have not yet considered the legality of SRI by superannuation funds, although the topic has generated some scholarly debate.[212] The former Insurance and Superannuation Commission viewed the legislation's "sole purpose" test for the objectives of funds as excluding non-financial investment criteria not material to financial risk.[213] Recently, a 2006 federal parliamentary report concluded that "consideration of social and environmental responsibility is in fact so far bound up in long term financial success that a superannuation trustee would be closer to breaching the sole purpose test by ignoring corporate responsibility."[214]

Today, SRI appears to have become accepted in the Australian pension sector as a legitimate investment strategy. The federal *Superannuation Legislation Amendment (Choice of Superannuation Funds) Act* of 2005 allows employees to choose where their contributions to superannuation funds

---

211 E.g., ss 7, 52(2) and 62.

212 A. Leigh, "'Caveat Investor': The Ethical Investment of Superannuation in Australia," *Australian Business Law Review* 25 (1997): 341; J. Donnan, "Regulating Ethical Investment: Disclosure under the Financial Services Reform Act," *Journal of Banking and Finance Law and Practice* 13(3) (2002): 155.

213 Insurance and Superannuation Commission (ISC), *Superannuation Circular III.A.4. The Sole Purpose Test and Ancillary Purposes* (ISC, 1995).

214 Australia, Parliamentary Joint Committee on Corporations and Financial Services, *Corporate Responsibility: Managing Risk and Creating Value* (Commonwealth of Australia, 2006), 74.

are invested. Thus, it enables employees to elect funds offering SRI.[215] An advisory statement of the Association of Superannuation Funds of Australia indicates that SRI is acceptable so long as funds adhere to prudential investment standards, they implement their investments without costly administrative overheads, and the investment policy has wide acceptance among fund members.[216]

2. Civil Law Jurisdictions

In continental Europe and East Asia, pension funds are not structured as a trust—a legal concept not generally relevant to the civil-law systems.[217] However, pension fund managers generally incur duties similar to common law standards: to invest prudently in the interests of fund members. There appears to be no case law on the legality of pension fund SRI in these jurisdictions although, as in Australia and the UK, several nations have adopted regulations mandating that pension funds disclose whether they invest ethically and responsibly, as explained in the next chapter.

In Germany, company pension schemes can take various institutional forms governed by a miscellany of legislation.[218] In general, the employer enters into a service agreement with the pension fund undertaking to manage the investments for its employees. By law, the fund's custodians must seek the highest possible profitability and security for the fund, ensure diversification and liquidity of the portfolio, and manage investments professionally. Legislation also imposes some investment portfolio restrictions. SRI is neither explicitly prohibited nor mandated under German law, although if a pension fund decides to invest ethically, it must inform its members.

German pension fund law, as in other EU states, must also comply with the EU's Occupational Pensions Directive.[219] It requires Member States to ensure that pension plans formulate and review, at least every three years,

---

215 E.g., the fund offerings of the Health Employees Superannuation Trust of Australia: http://www.hesta.com.au.

216 Association of Superannuation Funds of Australia (ASFA), *Development of ASFA Policy on "Ethical Investment"* (ASFA, October 2000), 8.

217 Although the concept of trusts exists in Japanese business law, it differs from the common law trust: see J. Pitts, S. Toyohara and G. Raftery, "Trusts and Trust Banking," *International Financial Law Review* (2004), January supplement: 74.

218 The most important laws are the *Insurance Supervision Act, 1978* (Versicherungsaufsichtsgesetz); *Company Pension Act, 1974* (Betriebsrentengesetz); *Pension Reform Act, 1999* (Rentenreformgesetz).

219 Directive 2003/41/EC of 3 June 2003, O.J. L. 235/10.

a statement of investment policy principles.[220] The Directive posits several investment rules that dovetail with the common law fiduciary standards. These include obligations to act in the "best interests" of beneficiaries and to ensure the security, diversification, liquidity, and profitability of the investment portfolio. None of these rules, however, mentions environmental or social considerations. During negotiation of the Directive, the EU Parliamentary Committee on Economic and Monetary Affairs proposed an amendment to require each fund to include a statement of its "ethical and socially responsible investment principles."[221] The European Parliament did not support the amendment.

Similar regulatory norms for pension funds exist in Japan, which has a large state pension system, supplementary pension schemes offered by private companies, as well as personal pension options. The *Employees' Pension Insurance Law* of 1954 includes Anglo-American style fiduciary duties governing investment of plan assets.[222] More recently, the *Defined Benefit Corporate Pension Law* and the *Defined Contribution Pension Law* of 2001 allow Japanese companies to adopt defined personal pension plans similar to the "401(k) plans" in the US under ERISA. These statutes also outline the fiduciary responsibilities of the employer, trustee, and plan administrator, essentially requiring them to act solely in the interests of the beneficiaries and with a high level of professional expertise.[223] Other fiduciary investment standards are enshrined in the comprehensive *Financial Instruments and Exchange Law* of 2007.[224] However, no legal rules or official guidance prescribe or encourage SRI in the Japanese pension sector. Japan's Pension Fund Association announced its voluntary standards on shareholder activism in February 2003.[225] They stipulate that pension funds should encourage companies to fulfil their

220 Ibid., Article 12.
221 European Parliament, Committee on Economic and Monetary Affairs, *Draft Report on the Proposal for a European Parliament and Council Directive on the Activities of Institutions for Occupational Retirement Provision*, PE 295.986/ AM/48–134 (May 8, 2001), 52.
222 Art. 120–2; and see G. Tonami, *Considerations for Fiduciary Duty in the Corporate Pension Law- Specialization of Fund Functions and the Litigation Rights of Participants*, Paper No. 149 (NLI Research Institute, 2001), 30–32.
223 E.g., *Defined Benefit Corporate Pension Law*, arts 69–72.
224 When giving investment advice, managing investments, or administering securities, trustees have duties of care and loyalty (arts 41–43); see further K. Kodacjhi, "About the Financial Instruments and Exchange Law," *Nomura Capital Market Review* 9(2) (2006): 21.
225 Cited by Freshfields, note 108, 72–73.

social responsibilities, by improving their relationships with customers, employees, and the wider community, and by reducing their environmental impact. The Association's standards however do not refer specifically to SRI screening. The first occupational pension fund in Japan to explicitly adopt an SRI policy was the Teachers Aid Association for Tokyo Metropolitan Teachers and Officials in 2003.[226]

C. CASE LAW ON SRI

The case law has not been particularly instructive for SRI. Relevant case law is sparse, although the existing rulings have influenced the behavior of fiduciaries in the pension industry.

In the UK, the country with the richest case law, the fiduciary responsibilities of trustees and the capacity for ethical investment was considered in *Cowan v. Scargill*,[227] *Martin v. City of Edinburgh District Council*,[228] and *Harries and others v. Church Commissioners for England*.[229]

The earliest of these cases, *Cowan v. Scargill*, has attracted considerable attention in the financial industry.[230] Trustees appointed jointly by the National Coal Board and the National Union of Mine Workers governed the pension plan in question. Union trustees disapproved of the proposed investment plan unless it prohibited any increase in foreign investment and, in particular, any investment in energy industries in competition with coal. The Coal Board trustees commenced legal proceedings against the union trustees claiming that they were in breach of fiduciary duties by insisting on the proposed restrictions.

The judge, Vice-Chancellor Robert Megarry, agreed with the National Coal Board trustees. Starting from the proposition that trustees must treat the interests of the beneficiaries as paramount, where the trust purpose is to provide financial benefits for the beneficiaries, he reasoned, the best interests of the beneficiaries normally mean their *financial* interests.[231] If the actual or

---

226 A. Solomon, J. Solomon, and M. Suto, "Can the UK Experience Provide Lessons for the Evolution of SRI in Japan?" *Corporate Governance* 12(4) (2003): 552.

227 [1985] 1 Ch. 270.

228 [1988] S.L.T. 329.

229 [1992] 1 W.L.R. 1241; [1993] 2 All E.R. 300.

230 E.g., P. Docking and I. Pittaway, "Social Investment by English Pension Funds: Can it be Done?" *Trust Law and Practice* February (1990): 25.

231 [1985] 1 Ch. 270.

potential beneficiaries of a trust were only those individuals with strict views on moral or social matters, Megarry conceded that it would be understandable that it may not be for their "benefit" to invest in certain problematic activities just to maximize financial return. Finally, Megarry emphasized the applicable statutory duty to diversify the investment portfolio. Trustees could consider non-financial criteria in constructing such a portfolio, provided such alternate investments were equally financially beneficial to the beneficiaries as the available conventional investments.

Despite the attention it received, *Cowan* is technically not a significant precedent and has at times been misread.[232] Megarry was a sole judge sitting in the Chancery Division of the High Court, the lowest tier of the higher English civil law courts. Also, the possibility of improved investment returns from taking into account social, environmental, and ethical considerations never arose in the case. What the Megarry judgment does prohibit are SRI decisions based on the "personal interests and views" of the trustees, which can "not be justified on broad economic grounds."[233] Unusually, Megarry reflected on his decision in an academic article in 1989.[234] He explains that his judgment in *Cowan* did not mean profit maximization alone was consistent with the fiduciary duties of a pension fund trustee. Moreover, he writes that if the trustees in *Cowan* had framed their investment policy as a preference rather than an absolute prohibition, then it would have been difficult to admonish.

In the next British case, the Bishop of Oxford and some fellow clergy sought a declaration that the Church of England Commissioners should not invest in a manner incompatible with the Christian faith, even if there was a risk of significant financial detriment.[235] The Court found that the Commissioners were in the same position as trustees, and that although the Commissioners had an ethical investment policy, at the time it applied only to the extent that such considerations would not be financially injurious. In declining to approve the more activist approach sought by the Bishop of Oxford,[236] Vice-Chancellor Donald Nicholls considered that where charitable

---

232 For criticisms of Mcgarry's judgment, see J.H. Farrar and J.K. Maxton, "Social Investment and Pension Scheme Trusts," *Law Quarterly Review* 102 (1986): 32.

233 [1985] 1 Ch. 270, 296.

234 R. Megarry, "Investing Pension Funds: The Mineworkers Case," in *Equity. Fiduciaries and Trusts*, ed. T.G. Youdan (Carswell, 1989), 149.

235 [1992] 1 W.L.R. 1241; [1993] 2 All E.R. 300.

236 The Church Commissioners' investment policy already excluded investment in 13 percent (by value) of publicly-listed UK companies, while the Bishop of Oxford proposed further ethical exclusions which would have increased

trustees held assets as investments, as considered in this case, the discharge of their duty of furthering the purpose of the trust normally required them to seek the maximum return which was consistent with commercial prudence. Nicholls agreed that there were at least two exceptions to the duty to maximize financial returns. Namely, where the aims of the charity and the objects of investment would conflict, and, where particular investments would detract from the charity's work, the trustees must balance the extent of financial loss from offended supporters and the financial risks of exclusion.[237] Thus, in his reasoning, trustees choosing between two investments of equal suitability according to conventional principles of prudent investment may account for the ethical considerations as the deciding factor ("the tie-breaker principle"). In this case, Nicholls thought the Church Commissioners' existing ethical investment policy was proper, but it would be improper for them to adopt a more restrictive policy that carried significant financial risks. However, whether such principles would apply to all investment trusts such as pension plans is unclear. Nicholls cautioned that this case involved charities whose "purposes are multifarious," unlike other trusts whose purposes are for the "provision of financial benefits for individuals."[238]

In the Scottish case of *Martin v. City of Edinburgh District Council,* a majority of the Edinburgh District Council trustees decided to divest from South African-based assets owing to concerns on apartheid.[239] The policy was successfully challenged. The court concluded that the trustees of the municipality's fund breached the trust by implementing a policy of divestment without expressly considering the best interests of the beneficiaries and without obtaining professional advice. However, the court did not consider whether such an investment policy on South Africa was contrary to trust principles per se. It addressed only the issue of how the above omissions constituted a breach of the trustee's duties. Significantly, Lord Murray added:

> I cannot conceive that trustees have an unqualified duty simply to invest trust funds in the most profitable investment available. To accept that without qualification would, in my view, involve substituting the discretion of financial advisers for the discretion of trustees.[240]

---

the level of exclusion to 37 percent of the total market: G. Watt, *Trusts and Equity* (2nd ed., Oxford University Press, 2006), 436.

237 [1993] 2 All E.R. 300, 304.
238 Ibid.
239 [1988] S.L.T. 329.
240 Ibid., 334.

Further circumventing the *Cowan* ruling, Lord Murray also rejected the notion that trustees must rid themselves of all personal preferences: "[w]hat he must do... is to recognize that he has those preferences, commitments or principles but nonetheless do his best to exercise fair and impartial judgment on the merits of the issue before him."[241]

The first SRI-related lawsuit in the US was brought in 1978 by the Associated Students of the University of Oregon against the State Attorney-General. They challenged his legal opinion on the legality of divestment policies in connection to South Africa, which viewed divestment as a likely violation of Oregon's prudent investment rule.[242] The legal manoeuvres continued until 1986 when a final ruling was made in *Associated Students of the University of Oregon v. Oregon Investment Council*.[243] University student organizations brought action against the Investment Council and State Board of Higher Education seeking a declaration that the Council could not invest higher education endowment funds in corporations doing business in South Africa, Zimbabwe, and Namibia. However, the substantive legal issues were never addressed in court. In denying the students standing, the Court of Appeals of Oregon noted "they do not allege any legally recognized injury, and neither agreement with plaintiffs' opposition to apartheid nor the desirability of encouraging students to become concerned with social and moral wrongs and to seek to right them can turn the alleged 'injuries' into legally recognized ones."[244]

The most noteworthy US case on the legality of SRI was the *Board of Trustees of Employee Retirement System of the City of Baltimore v. City of Baltimore*.[245] It dealt with a public sector pension plan, governed by fiduciary duties analogous to ERISA standards. The Maryland Court of Appeal examined the City's ordinances requiring its four municipal pension funds to divest from companies engaged in business in South Africa. The trustees argued that the ordinances unlawfully altered their common law duties of prudence by substantially reducing the universe of eligible investments.

While the court in *City of Baltimore* agreed that SRI policies adopted pursuant to the ordinances excluded a "not insignificant segment of the investment universe,"[246] it accepted the evidence that the reduction in the rate of

241 Ibid.
242 Pre-trial Order, *Associated Students v. Hunt*, (1978) No. 78-329 (Or. Ct. App.).
243 (1987) 82 Or. App. 145, 728 P.2d 30.
244 Ibid., 150.
245 (1989) 317 Md. 72; 562 A.2d 720.
246 Ibid., 103.

return expected from the divestiture in South Africa would only amount to about ten basis points per year,[247] and that the measured way the divestments were to occur meant that the divesture program did not alter the trustees' prudential duties. The court explained: "[t]hus, if... social investment yields economically competitive returns at a comparable level of risk, the investment should not be deemed imprudent."[248] The trustees also argued that the ordinances altered the common law duty of loyalty, as the investment choices were no longer governed exclusively for providing benefits to members. Again, the judges found the ordinances acceptable on this point so long as the cost of investing according to social responsibility precepts was *de minimis*, as was considered here. The court explained that a trustee's duty is not to maximize return on investments, but to secure a "just" and "reasonable" return, while avoiding undue risk.[249]

Although not strictly an SRI case, the decision in *Withers v. Teachers Retirement System*[250] also suggests US courts' willingness to condone pension trustees taking collateral issues into account. Here, the trustees of a teachers' pension fund invested US$860 million in bonds issued by the City of New York, without a guarantee of a return, as the bond issue was an attempt to prevent the looming bankruptcy of New York. The City was also the major employer of the teachers, and as a substantial contributor to their fund, it was in effect the ultimate guarantor of the liabilities of the fund. After much research, the trustees were satisfied that the City could not obtain financing from other sources. In those circumstances, the court held that the trustees' seemingly overly risky investment was acceptable because of the strong connection between the fund and the City.

While some critics distinguish the *Withers* case based on its exceptional facts[251] (where the pension plan's survival depended on the solvency of the City in which it invested), the recent spate of corporate insolvencies and under-funded pension plans suggest that the *Withers* situation is not unique. The latitude conceded to the trustees in *Withers* was also influenced by the perceived weaker conflicts of interest. In contrast, conflicts of interest were determinative in *Blankenship v. Boyle*.[252] There, the union pension plan trustees

---

247 Basis points are the smallest measure used to calculate interest rates or yields on investments. For example, ten basis points equal 0.1 percent.
248 Ibid., 107.
249 Ibid.
250 (1978) 447 F. Supp. 148 (SDNT).
251 Hutchinson and Cole, note 111, 1363; Langbein and Posner, note 137, 1.
252 (1979) 329 F. Supp. 1089, 1112.

were condemned for holding assets in a union-owned bank for the benefit of the bank.

D. CONCLUSIONS

Clearly, no jurisdiction formally prohibits pension funds from socially responsible investing. Nor does the extant case law support the view of the minority of investment advisors and legal commentators that the governing legal principles (in trust law or regulation) preclude or severely restrict SRI. However, further clarification of the law is desirable, rather than leaving the matter to ad hoc judicial rulings or academic commentary. A government inquiry in Canada recently recommended new guidelines or regulations "to clarify that the fiduciary obligation of the trustee includes the consideration of ESG issues that are financially material to investment decisions."[253]

A simple solution, of course, would be for pension funds seeking to invest ethically to have an explicit mandate in their governing plan. Trustees exercising fiduciary investment powers must exercise those powers for the purpose granted. However, pension funds are also subject to regulation, which channels their function into providing retirement income for beneficiaries. Presently, there may not be much statutory freedom to manage pension trusts for other than financial benefits, although trustees probably could lawfully consider environmental and social factors that may hurt long-term returns.

Absent an SRI mandate, a pension fund could invest with regard to social and environmental criteria and satisfy fiduciary obligations so long as the portfolio is reasonably diversified, trustees have taken proper investment advice and consulted with their fund membership, and the investment policy can be implemented without burdensome and costly administrative procedures. SRI will surely become a safe bet if it can continue to match or exceed the returns of conventional investment portfolios.[254] Alternatively, a pension fund could follow a standard investment process and seek SRI aims through

---

253 NRTEE, *Capital Markets and Sustainability: Investing in a Sustainable Future. State of the Debate Report* (NRTEE, 2007), 10.

254 See e.g., M.V. Russo and P.A. Fouts, "A Resource-Based Perspective on Corporate Environmental Performance and Profitability," *Academy of Management Journal* 40(3) (1997): 534; J. James, "The Calculus of Conscience: Socially-responsible Investing can be Both Profitable and Ethical," *Times International* 156(6) (2000): 33; R.M. Roman, S. Hayibor, and R.A. Bradley, "The Relationship Between Social and Financial Performance: Repainting a Portrait," *Business and Society* 38(1) (1999): 109.

234 | SOCIALLY RESPONSIBLE INVESTMENT LAW

the less problematic option of shareholder engagement rather than through exclusionary screening.

Crucially, while the dominant business case discourse of SRI may fit with fiduciary investment standards, whether that discourse is appropriate for achieving sustainability is another matter. So long as pension funds are construed simply as a means for building retirement income, it will be difficult to advance an alternate fiduciary standard capable of accommodating ethically-driven investment strategies. Fiduciary duties should convey the imperative that protection of the biosphere is equally essential to the welfare of retirees. Retiring into an environmentally degraded world inevitably would cost pensioners in other ways. As the following discussion shows, the investment duties of other financial organizations similarly do not advance us much closer to a sustainability-based fiduciary standard.

V. Investment Duties of Other Financiers

A. FIDUCIARY DUTIES IN CORPORATE GOVERNANCE

Several types of financial organizations take the form of a corporation. These include banks, as well as some insurance and mutual fund businesses. Thus, it is useful to comment on fiduciary duties in the context of corporate governance, before considering them within financial corporations.

The cardinal principle of Anglo-American systems of corporate governance is the implicit contractual term between the shareholders and the corporation which requires the managers and directors to act in the best interests of the corporation, often understood as simply the interests of its shareholders.[255] These principles materialize as the fiduciary duties of care and loyalty.[256] They serve to provide the unspecified terms in the web of contracts that lawyers assume corporations embody. The broader debate about the purpose of corporate governance is framed around the issue of to whom the fiduciary duties is owed.

---

255 R. Grantham and C. Rickett, eds, *Corporate Personality in the 20th Century* (Hart Publishing, 1998). In most public corporations, of course, senior management makes decisions, which are usually rubber-stamped by the board of directors.

256 L.P.Q. Johnson and D. Millon, "Recalling Why Corporate Officers are Fiduciaries," *William and Mary Law Review* 46 (2005): 1597.

A long-standing question concerns whether corporations should be governed exclusively to protect the interests of shareholders, or whether corporate governance should also accommodate the needs of other constituencies, labeled as "stakeholders."[257] The conventional legal view holds that directors owe fiduciary duties exclusively to the company or the company and its shareholders, depending on the jurisdiction.[258] Bondholders and other creditors such as banks are not generally seen as owed a fiduciary duty, except perhaps when a firm is in a financially parlous state or more certainly when it is insolvent.[259] The standard objection to extending fiduciary duties to other interests is that it would unduly complicate corporate governance. Specifically, if directors must serve other constituencies, the decision-making process might become an arbitrary balancing act between many interests that could merely cloak self-interested decisions by directors emboldened by greater discretionary power.

Corporate law in the Anglo-American systems, however, does not entirely exclude non-shareholder constituencies. Directors' fiduciary responsibilities are increasingly understood as requiring attention to other interests, such as employees, consumers, creditors, and other parties with whom the corporation

---

257 S. Worthington, "Reforming Directors' Duties," *Modern Law Review* 64 (2001): 439; C. Francis, "*Peoples Department Stores Inc. v. Wise:* The Expanded Scope of Directors' and Officers' Fiduciary Duties and Duties of Care," *Canadian Business Law Journal* 41 (2005): 175; R.E. Freeman, "The Politics of Stakeholder Theory: Some Future Directions," *Business Ethics Quarterly* 4 (1994): 409.

258 Canadian law for example provides that directors owe a fiduciary duty to the corporation (*Peoples Department Stores v. Wise*, [2004] 3 S.C.R. 461, 2004 S.C.C. 68), while US law courts define the duty as owed to the corporation and its shareholders. Those interests are often not discussed separately, because they often do not conflict. The interests of shareholders and the company may conflict when a company's board adopts defences to takeovers: see especially *Unocal Corp. v Mesa Petroleum Company*, (1985) 493 A. 2d 946 (Del.) and *Kahn v. Sullivan*, (1992) 594 A.2d 48 (Del.). The US law also provides that controlling shareholders owe a duty of fairness, basically to treat all shareholders equally: *Weinberger v. UOP*, (1983) 457 A.2d 701 (Del.).

259 The standard reason given is that creditors have no ownership interest in a debtor-corporation's assets while the corporation is solvent. Instead, they have contractual rights: T.R. Hurst and L.J. McGuiness, "The Corporation, the Bondholder and Fiduciary Duties," *Journal of Law and Commerce* 10 (1991): 187; A.D. Shaffer, "Corporate Fiduciary—Insolvent: The Fiduciary Relationship Your Corporate Law Professor (Should Have) Warned You About," *American Bankruptcy Institute Law Review* 8(Winter) (2000): 479.

has contractual and other legal relationships that may affect its financial success. In Canada, where directors owe a duty directly to the corporation, rather than its shareholders, the Supreme Court in *Peoples Department Stores v. Wise* held that directors may therefore properly consider the interests of parties the company interacts with in furthering its interests.[260] This position also appears explicitly in the UK *Companies Act* of 2006, where directors' fiduciary duties were reformulated to include consideration of community and environmental impacts as integral components to the "success" of the company.[261] Cynthia Williams and John Conley salute it as "close to a stakeholder model of director's duties."[262] The US has enacted so-called "constituency statutes," which allow (but only rarely obligate) directors to consider the effects of their decisions on specific categories of stakeholders, such as employees, suppliers, customers, and local communities.[263] But as the stakeholders cannot directly enforce these provisions, constituency statutes have had limited impact. In addition, in most jurisdictions the business judgment rule gives boards and managers ample latitude to make decisions that benefit other stakeholders, possibly even at the expense of shareholders.[264] Courts have ruled in favor of corporate philanthropy on the assumption that collateral

---

260 [2004] 3 S.C.R. 461, 2004 S.C.C. 68.

261 Section 172(1).

262 C.A. Williams and J.M. Conley, "Triumph or Tragedy: The Curious Path of Corporate Disclosure Reform in the UK," *William and Mary Environmental Law and Policy Review* 31(2) (2007): 317, 354.

263 S.M. Bainbridge, "Interpreting Nonshareholder Constituency Statutes," *Pepperdine Law Review* 19 (1992): 991.

264 K. Davis, "Discretion of Corporate Management to Do Good at the Expense of Shareholder Gain: A Survey of, and Commentary on, the U.S. Corporate Law," *Canada–United States Law Journal* 13 (1988): 7. It creates a strong presumption in favor of the legality of their actions. Courts tend to resist imposing their own notion of what is a sound business judgment if it appears "the directors of a corporation acted on an informed basis, in good faith and in the honest belief that the action taken was in the best interests of the company": *Sinclair Oil Corp. v. Levien*, (1971) 280 A.2d 717, 720 (Del.). See also *Shlensky v. Wrigely*, (1968) 237 N.E. 2d 776 (Ill. App. Ct.) (the court refused to direct the corporate owner of a sports ground to install lights so the Chicago Cubs could play games at night, notwithstanding that the reason the Cubs' owners would not upgrade the lighting to allow night games was because of their view of the harm to the adjacent community). See further P.A. McCoy, "Political Economy of the Business Judgment Rule in Banking: Implications for Corporate Law," *Case Western Law Review* 47(1) (1996): 1.

benefits, such as an enhanced reputation, may accrue to the corporation and its shareholders.[265]

Significantly, the fact that in a corporate context fiduciary duties are not necessarily owed exclusively to shareholders means we cannot treat the latter as analogous to the beneficiaries of a pension fund. Corporations are embedded in a much more complex array of relationships than a pension fund, as they have a workforce, customers, creditors, and other parties to contend with. Unlike the trustees of a pension fund, who simply serve the interests of investors in the fund, directors of a company must be cognizant of many more interests.

A stronger stakeholder approach to corporate governance has long been a prominent feature of the corporate systems found in Continental Europe and Japan. They tend to treat companies as "industrial partnerships" in which the management must accommodate a network of interests, including creditors and workers, with an emphasis on consensus and long-term economic results.[266] For example, the German system of labor "co-determination," incorporating employees into the firm's governing bodies, has in theory led companies to be mindful of interests beyond shareholders.[267] Fiduciary responsibilities in German corporate law also once unequivocally prescribed a "duty on management to be socially responsible," but now only imply such an obligation.[268]

In the context of financial corporations, often having more economic significance than non-financial firms, a more expansive view of the interests being protected by fiduciary duties is warranted. A failure of a financial institution can ripple through the economy like a tsunami, decimating the life savings that people have entrusted to their bank or investment company. Financial corporations also face greater risks, being highly leveraged and

---

265 M.A. Blair, "A Contractarian Defense of Corporate Philanthropy," *Stetson Law Review* 28 (1998): 27, 42–49. Some governments have also legislated to put beyond doubt the legality of corporate charitable giving.

266 M. Gerlach, *Alliance Capitalism: The Social Organization of Japanese Business* (University of California Press, 1992); J. Edwards, et al., "Corporate Governance in Germany: The Role of Banks and Ownership Concentration," *Economic Policy* 15(31) (2000): 237.

267 K.J. Hopt and P.C. Leyens, *Board Models in Europe. Recent Developments of Internal Corporate Governance Structures in Germany, the United Kingdom, France, and Italy* (European Corporate Governance Institute, 2004), 7.

268 G. Teubner, "Corporate Fiduciary Duties and their Beneficiaries," in *Corporate Governance and Directors' Liabilities*, eds K.J. Hopt and G. Teubner (Walter de Gruyter, 1985), 149, 154.

holding illiquid assets, which amplifies their vulnerability to unexpected adverse events. Traditionally, these considerations have tended to be addressed through additional prudential regulation, rather than by redefining core fiduciary duties. Furthermore, the capacity of corporate financiers to fund and enable other economic actors to undertake socially and environmentally injurious development is grounds for widening their fiduciary responsibilities beyond that governing a typical non-financial company.

B. FIDUCIARY DUTIES AND REGULATION OF FINANCIAL CORPORATIONS

1. Banks

Banks have fiduciary duties similar to those applied in non-financial corporations. The directors of banks owe a fiduciary duty to act in the best interests of the bank and its shareholders. In relation to their customers, banks owe a fiduciary duty in certain transactions, such as when bank managers provide financial advice.[269] Yet, in the performance of core banking business, such as disbursing loans, in most jurisdictions the bank is not considered a trustee of the customer.[270] Therefore, concerning customers acting as mere depositors, the law has traditionally seen their relationship with banks as a contractual one of creditor and debtor. Once money is credited to a bank account it simply becomes a debt due by the bank to the account holder. In the classic 1848 English case of *Foley v. Hill*, the House of Lords explained:

> the money placed in the custody of a banker is, to all intents and purposes, the money of the banker, to do with it as he pleases; he is guilty of no breach of trust in employing it; he is not answerable to the principal if he puts it in jeopardy, [or] if he engages in hazardous speculation.[271]

In the subsequent 1931 case of *Royal Bank of Scotland v. Skinner* it was ruled:

> it is now well settled that the relationship of customer and banker is neither a relation of principal and agent nor a relation of a fiduciary nature, trust, or the like, but a simple relation. . . of creditor-debtor.

---

269 See J. Glover, "Banks and Fiduciary Relationships," *Bond Law Review* 7(1) (1995): 50.

270 R. Plato-Shinar, "The Bank's Fiduciary Duty: An Israeli-Canadian Comparison," *Banking and Finance Law Review* 22 (2006): 1 (explains how Israeli law imposes a general fiduciary duty on banks with regard to their customers).

271 2 H.L. Cas. 28.

The banker is not, in the general case, the custodian of money. When money is paid in, despite the popular belief, it is simply consumed by the banker, who gives an obligation of equivalent amount.[272]

While the business of modern banking has considerably enlarged since these cases, giving rise to fiduciary duties in certain dealings, they do not extend to situations relevant to SRI. Thus, for instance, a mere depositor could not legally challenge a bank that makes loans to companies engaged in questionable environmental practices. A bank has no fiduciary obligation to take into account any ethical concerns of the depositor. It would not matter if she felt that such loans were financially risky and could jeopardize the bank's ability to repay the deposit. However, if a bank makes public representations that it is a socially responsible lender, and makes loans contrary to its stated policy, one US commentator speculates that "a customer who did business with the bank in reliance on that policy might assert a claim against the bank for fraud, false advertising, or on some other grounds."[273]

Conversely, when banks lend money, courts would not find that banks owe borrowers a fiduciary duty to advise them of any myriad social and environmental risks; however, they may incur liability for inappropriate financial advice that a client relies upon.[274] Any financial risks involving lenders are typically a matter governed by separate regulation, such as capital adequacy standards, not a matter of fiduciary duties. Nor do banks owe a fiduciary duty to any other interest groups in society. Therefore, subject to the constraints of banking regulation and other laws, lenders are free to provide finance without regard to any social or environmental costs imposed on third parties.

Yet, given banks' special place in the economy, are such circumscribed fiduciary duties appropriate?[275] First, bank business is very opaque and complex, which could create more opportunities for bank insiders to pursue their own interests at the expense of others. Second, the unusual structure of bank balance sheets, including high leverage, significant illiquid assets, and reliance

---

272 S.L.T. 382, 384.
273 J.A. Snyder and A.B. Muir, "Green Wave or Greenwash?" *The Secured Lender* 61(6) (2005): 32, 35.
274 Glover, note 269, 57–61.
275 D. Heremans, *Corporate Governance Issues for Banks. A Financial Stability Perspective* (Department of Economics, K.U. Leuven, 2006); J.R. Macey and M. O'Hara, "The Corporate Governance of Banks," *Economic Policy Review* 9(1) (2003): 91; G. Caprio Jr. and R. Levine, *Corporate Governance of Banks: Concepts and International Observations*, Working Paper (Global Corporate Governance Forum, 2002).

on customers' confidence, makes banks vulnerable to market shocks. Third, banks' stability has wider significance, as the 2008 subprime mortgage lending crisis in the US showed. The banking sector contains propagation mechanisms that can amplify initial, small shocks throughout the economy; insolvency of a bank usually has far greater ramifications for the economy than the collapse of a non-financial company. Failure of a bank may erode public confidence in the banking system generally, leading to a credit crunch and concomitant impacts on the real economy.

Given such special characteristics, governments commonly subject banks to additional prudential regulation.[276] It addresses both the financial conditions of individual banks and the stability of the banking sector generally. These regulations accommodate investor-protection and consumer service standards through capital adequacy and liquidity requirements, risk management systems, deposit guarantee systems, and payment systems controls.[277] Governments can also use banks as a means to further specific policy objectives, such as money-laundering controls. While prudential regulation serves to accommodate other economic interests and policy goals in governing banks, it does not directly seek to advance sustainability policy.

A rare example of a stakeholder approach in banking legislation is the US's *Community Reinvestment Act* (CRA) of 1977.[278] It obliges banks to help meet the financial needs of the local communities in which they are chartered. The premise of the legislation is that public access to banking services is crucial to avoid poverty, social exclusion, and social injustice. The CRA aims to improve the credit services of low-income and minority communities, and to ensure the availability of low-cost banking services for low-income households and small businesses.[279] Banks' record on such matters is periodically reviewed and taken into account in considering a lender's application for deposit facilities and institutional mergers. Unsurprisingly, banks have generally been unenthusiastic about the CRA, seeing it as an unjustified

---

276 R. Lastra, *Central Banking and Banking Regulation* (London School of Economics, 1996).

277 R. Lastra, *Central Banking and Banking Regulation* (Financial Markets Group, 1996); J.J. Norton, et al., eds, *International Banking Regulation and Supervision: Change and Transformation in the 1990s* (Graham and Trotman, and Martinus Nijhoff, 1994); J.R. Macey, et al., *Banking Law and Regulation* (Aspen Publishers, 2001).

278 Pub. L. No. 95-128, 91 Stat. 1147.

279 J.T. Campen, "Banks, Communities and Public Policy," *Transforming the U.S. Financial System: Equity and Efficiency for the 21st Century*, eds G.A. Dymski, et al. (M.E. Sharpe, 1993), 221.

regulatory burden and offering little financial reward for investing in seemingly risky low-income communities.[280]

2. Insurance Firms

Insurance policies and savings plans are contracts between the insurance company and its policyholders. Insurance regulation serves to protect purchasers of insurance contracts, mainly by solvency standards and rules governing the conduct of selling financial products and administering claims.[281] Investment management by life insurance companies is usually more closely regulated than property and casualty insurance business, because non-life insurance contracts are usually short-term and therefore less exposed to investment risk.[282]

A mix of contract law and public regulation governs the investment activities of insurers.[283] Regulatory standards draw on both quantitative portfolio regulation and prudent investment standards. Typically, insurance companies must quarantine sufficient reserves to cover the aggregate of their liabilities and maintain a specified solvency margin. They must also disclose obligations to policyholders and comply with any restrictions on investments in specific asset classes.[284] In the US, state laws tightly regulate the investment choices of insurance companies (a laundry list of allowable, safe investments), overlain by general regulations to protect the insurer's loss reserves and to maintain liquidity.[285] German insurers have statutory duties to ensure diversification and to seek the highest possible security and profitability.[286] Likewise, Japanese insurance firms must abide by the standards of profitability, safety, liquidity and diversification specified by the *Insurance Business Law* of 1995.

---

280 Ibid., 223.
281 OECD, note 3.
282 Ibid., 29.
283 See generally, OECD, *Policy Issues in Insurance—Investment, Taxation and Insolvency* (OECD, 1996); G.M. Dickinson, "Issues in the Effective Regulation of the Asset Allocation of Life Insurance Companies," in *Institutional Investors in the New Financial Landscape*, eds H. Blommestein and N. Funke (OECD, 1998), 422.
284 E.g., Australia's *Life Insurance Act*, 1995 (Cth).
285 S. Randall, "Insurance Regulation in the United States," *Florida State University Law Review* 26 (1999): 625.
286 *Insurance Supervision Act* (Versicherungsaufsichtsgesetz), s. 54(1); *Investment Decree Law* (Anlageverordnung), s. 6.

Insurance companies in common law jurisdictions incur specific fiduciary duties, although they function somewhat differently to fiduciary duties in pension trusts. First, with life insurers, the beneficiary of the fiduciary duties is determined depending on whether the business is organized as a mutual company or a stock company. A mutual life insurance company is owned by, and managed for the benefit of, its policyholders. Thus, directors have fiduciary duties to those policyholder-owners, just as the board of directors of a stock company has fiduciary duties to its stockholders. For an insurer organized as a stock company, typically governments have not imposed a fiduciary obligation to their insured policyholders; fiduciary duties arise only on the part of directors and officers to shareholders.[287] Thus, in the *Fidelity and Casualty* case in the US, the court stated that "the policyholder acquires certain specified proprietary interests [in the company] but, apart from these, the relationship is not of a fiduciary nature and is essentially ... measured by the contractual terms of the policy."[288] Thus, in stock companies directors have no express fiduciary duty to policyholders except via specific regulatory requirements.

Courts nevertheless have recognized that some functions of insurance businesses are trustee-like and have imposed fiduciary obligations on the insurance company's management in situations such as where insurers offer pension plans and savings products. In the US case of *John Hancock Mutual Life Insurance Co. v. Harris Trust and Savings Bank*,[289] the Supreme Court held that general account assets of a guaranteed annuity contract are "plan assets" and must therefore be managed according to ERISA's fiduciary standards. Thus, like pension fund trustees, a life insurance company is required under ERISA to manage its general account assets "solely in the interest of participants and beneficiaries" of such annuity contracts and "for the exclusive purpose of providing benefits to such participants and beneficiaries."[290]

---

287 T. Allegaert, "Derivative Actions by Policyholders on Behalf of Mutual Insurance Companies," *University of Chicago Law Review* 63 (1996): 1063, 1071–72.

288 *Fidelity and Casualty Co. of New York v. Metropolitan Life Insurance Company,* (1963) 42 Misc. 2d 616; 248 N.Y.S.2d 559, 623.

289 (1993) No. 92-1074, 510 U.S. 86.

290 Section 404(a); see further W.T. Barker, et al., "Is an Insurer a Fiduciary to Its Insureds?" *Tort and Insurance Law Journal* 25 (1989): 1. Some commentators however dispute this application of ERISA fiduciary standards. Carucci contends that "because an insurer's general account is its operating account and is not segregated in any way, the general account cannot be managed for the 'exclusive benefit' of anyone": C.J. Carucci, "John Hancock v. Harris

Therefore, similar questions about the legality of SRI arise in this context. In particular, arguably insurers need to pay attention to climate risks. Climate change and the risk of greater weather-related losses pose enormous financial threats to insurance companies, which they will have to increasingly address in their investment portfolios and insurance underwriting policies.

C. COLLECTIVE INVESTMENT SCHEMES

Collective investment schemes (CISs), such as mutual funds, commonly take the form a corporation, a business trust, or a purely contractual relationship. Each is subject to extensive investment legislation,[291] and the investment management responsibilities differ depending on the organizational form.[292] Separate legal arrangements sometimes apply to special types of pooled investment vehicles, ranging from minimal regulation (for hedge funds)[293] to complex statutory regimes (for venture capital finance).[294]

Whether structured as trusts or as corporations—the principal models— the controllers owe fiduciary responsibilities to their unit-holders or share-holders to pursue stated investment objectives in a loyal and competent manner.[295] These duties fall on custodial trustees or corporate directors, as well as on the fund managers to whom they delegate routine operation of the fund. Financial planners and advisers who control the selling of mutual fund and other financial products also have fiduciary obligations towards clients, and they are regulated separately.[296] Investment management in CISs also commonly gives rise to concurrent contractual relationships between scheme members and the fund provider.[297]

Trust: Should Insurers' General Accounts be Subject to ERISA?" *St. John's Law Review* 68 (1994): 557, 568.

291 J.K. Thompson and S.M. Choi, *Governance Systems for Collective Investment Schemes in OECD Countries* (OECD, 2001).

292 Freshfields, note 108, 16.

293 H.B. Shadab, "The Challenge of Hedge Fund Regulation," *Securities and Investment* 30(1) (2007): 36.

294 E.g., South Korea's *Special Law to Promote Venture Capital Companies*, 1997.

295 R.C. Pozen, *The Mutual Fund Business* (MIT Press, 1998), 22.

296 G. McMeel and J. Virgo, *Financial Advice and Financial Products: Law and Liability* (Oxford University Press, 2002).

297 C.Z. Qum, "Australia's Managed Investment Schemes: The Nature of Relationships among Scheme Participants," *Asia Pacific Law Review* 12(1) (2004): 69, 84–85.

Thus, where the CIS is a trust, as often used in Canada, New Zealand, and the UK, common law fiduciary duties to invest prudently and loyally apply.[298] Investors in the trust hold "units" that represent a proportionate beneficial interest of the trust's assets. Conversely, directors of US mutual fund businesses have duties under the *Investment Company Act* of 1940, supervised by the SEC, to act in the interests of the fund's shareholders with the care and diligence that an ordinary prudent person would exercise under similar circumstances.[299] A different approach occurs under the German *Investment Modernization Act* of 2003, which stipulates that the fund must act not only "in the sole interest of its investors" but also for "the integrity of the market."[300] The specific content of fiduciary obligations to investors is also informed by the contractual terms of the fund's relationship with investors, as reflected in the fund's prospectus.[301]

Unlike occupational pension funds, which do not sell investment products, CISs allow investors to shop for the fund that best meets their goals. Thus, a mutual fund that advertises an SRI policy has a fiduciary and contractual obligation to investors accepted into the fund on that basis to follow that policy.[302] George Djurasovic discusses a US case where an investor who had contributed to a self-styled environmental fund filed a complaint with the SEC upon discovering that the fund had invested in firms subject to pollution regulation violations.[303] The *Investment Company Act* prevents an investment company from changing its stated investment policy without a majority vote of its outstanding voting securities.[304]

CISs have been a popular vehicle for SRI in the retail market, as fund providers can readily tailor them to meet diverse market demands. The articles of incorporation or the trust instrument as the case may be establish the basic constitution of the CIS, including a statement of investment objectives. These need not be exclusively financial objectives. For example, the Australian *Corporations Act* of 2001 does not require an investment fund scheme to act in

---

298 See especially K.F. Sin, *The Legal Nature of the Unit Trust* (Clarendon Press, 1998); J. Thompson, *Corporate Governance and Collective Investment Schemes* (OECD, 2001), 24–30.

299 See *Galfand v. Chestnutt Corporation*, (1976) 545 F.2d 807.

300 *Investment Modernization Act* (Investmentmodernisierungsgesetz), 2003, s. 9(2).

301 Ibid., ss 43(1), 43(4).

302 G. Djurasovic, "The Regulation of Socially Responsible Mutual Funds," *Journal of Corporation Law* 22 (1997): 257, 259.

303 Ibid., 276.

304 Section 13.

the best *financial* interests of its members.[305] Instead, "the members are left to determine for themselves, through their [fund's] constitution, what the best interests of the fund are to be."[306] However, in Australia and other jurisdictions, an SRI fund like other retail funds remains encumbered with duties to manage its investments prudently with care and diligence.[307]

While SRI-driven funds are not subject to unique fiduciary standards, authorities increasingly subject them to transparency regulation, likewise with other funds, to ensure they fully disclose their policies to investors. To illustrate, the *Investment Company Act* in the US contains registration and filing requirements for investment companies and establishes a "corporate-like oversight structure to minimize the opportunities for abuses in the investment company industry."[308] The legislation requires investment companies to disclose their financial condition, service fees, and investment policies when stock is initially sold and also, subsequently, on a regular basis.

D. CONCLUSIONS

Globally, financial institutions ranging from insurance companies to pension trusts must adhere to investment standards stipulated by contracts, regulations, or common law. These standards commonly emphasize optimal financial returns, portfolio diversification, restricted investment in certain asset classes, and require maintenance of adequate reserves to meet liabilities and buffer against risks. The precise enunciation of these standards varies somewhat from institution to institution.

The key governance mechanism is the fiduciary duties that dictate how investment decision-makers should act and for whose benefit. Regardless of the institution, these fiduciary duties perform a similar function: they serve to enhance the private wealth of investors, whether they are workers in an occupational pension fund, purchasers of life insurance savings products, or shareholders of a bank. Formally, SRI for the general collective good has had virtually no place in this model.

---

305 Section 601FC(1)(c).

306 Parliamentary Joint Committee on Corporations and Financial Services, note 214, 73.

307 Section 601FC(1)(b); see also P. Ali, "Investing in the Environment: Some Thoughts on the New Breed of Green Hedge Funds," *Derivates Use, Trading and Regulation* 12(4) (2007): 351 (arguing for the importance for prudential investment duties).

308 W.J. Baumol, et al, *The Economics of Mutual Fund Markets: Competition versus Regulation* (Kluwer Academic, 1990), 52.

Yet the SRI sector has grown in recent years in all of these financial sectors. Banks increasingly take into account the social and environmental impacts of corporate project financing, mutual funds sell SRI products to eager mum and dad investors, and "universal" pension funds have become more mindful of the long-term risks to their portfolios. Can we then sanguinely conclude that fiduciary duties are of little consequence to SRI?

SRI has prospered because it hardly challenges the economic values that underpin fiduciary norms. Despite earlier legal skirmishes, the current SRI market sits quite comfortably with the dominant fiduciary norms because it does not entail a radically different type of financing. The composition of many mutual funds' SRI portfolios is remarkably similar to regular portfolios. Their investment goals make similar promises of prosperity. For pension funds and banks, SRI is mainly a means to manage another type of business risk. Ethical imperatives get downplayed unless they fit within a business case rationale.

But, if there was a cultural shift in the financial sector, could the current formulations of fiduciary duties accommodate a different style of *ethical* investment? With difficulty. The trust governing a pension fund could be drafted to define beneficiaries' "interests" as inclusive of non-financial goals. However, intermediary prudential regulation tends to frame those interests as being of a financial character. Mutual funds have more flexibility to meet diverse investment goals including ethical objectives. A few SRI funds apply strict exclusionary screens, narrowing their investment universe and possibly hurting financial returns. Because investors can shop for funds that meet their ethical or financial needs, the primary way the legal system seeks to protect their interests is through disclosure regulations, rather than with fiduciary standards. The interests of retail investors and fund managers are mainly aligned by ensuring that funds disclose the nature of their investment products. Regardless, however, current fiduciary investment standards do not *require* explicit consideration of social and environmental matters. They remain discretionary concerns, to be weighted by the very market forces that have traditionally ostracized social and environmental issues.

VI. Participation in Investment Management

A. THE DEMOCRATIC IMPERATIVE FOR SRI

The SRI community has not commented a great deal about the internal governance of financial organizations. Members of the SRI industry cajole financiers to be more active owners in their portfolio companies, yet have spoken only fleetingly on the internal governance of financial institutions since Severyn Bruyn's prescient call for democratizing capital through credit unions and other economic cooperatives.[309] Recently, Gordon Clark has noted emerging social pressures for institutions such as pensions finds to be more representative of their members, perhaps as a response to larger weaknesses of accountability and legitimacy in capitalist democracies.[310] Yet the SRI sector mostly dwells on accountability and openness in the firms it finances. Consider the SIF's statement in 2002 for a "new wave" of corporate governance reform, advocating audit reforms, democratic elections of boards of directors, and so on. Yet, apart from proxy voting disclosures, SIF made no mention of the inner workings of financial institutions.[311] Surely, at the very least, financiers must give the same commitment to transparency and participation. Without a democratic basis, SRI's social legitimacy may wane as it becomes seen as an elite realm dominated by consultants, fund managers, and rich entrepreneurs.

Financial institutions are not exemplars of democratic decision-making. Finance capitalism reduces investors to suppliers of capital. Members of pension plans typically have less power with respect to their investments than do shareholders of an ordinary company. Many pension funds operate with no representation from the very members they are obliged to benefit.[312]

Financial regulators can be equally opaque, with some exceptions. The UK's *Financial Services and Markets Act* of 2000 imposes a general duty on the financial regulator to "make and maintain effective arrangements for consulting practitioners and consumers" regarding its policies and practices.[313] In relation to SRI itself, the public inquiry undertaken by Canada's NRTEE into capital markets and sustainability provided for generous public participation and dialogue.[314]

---

309 S.T. Bruyn, *The Field of Social Investment* (Cambridge University Press, 1987); since then, see Stichele, note 33, 165; World Economic Forum (WEF), *Mainstreaming Responsible Investment* (WEF, 2005), 48.

310 G.L. Clark, "Expertise and Representation in Financial Institutions: UK Legislation on Pension Fund Governance and US Regulation of the Mutual Fund Industry," *Twenty-First Century Society* 2(1) (2007): 1.

311 SIF, *Statement on Corporate Scandals and Proposals for Reform the Perspective of Socially Responsible Investors and Proposals for Reform* (SIF, 2002).

312 S. Davis, J. Lukomnik, and D. Pitt-Watson, *The New Capitalists. How Citizen Investors are Reshaping the Corporate Agenda* (Harvard Business School Press, 2006), 75.

313 Section 8.

314 NRTEE, note 253.

Participation in other contexts is much reduced. The accounting rules that underpin corporate financial disclosures are prepared by specialist accounting standards boards, dominated by the accountancy profession with very restricted membership.[315] In international financial regulation, one recent book stated "the setting and administration of financial governance arrangements [is] characterized by narrow participation mainly consisting of experts from national administrations, independent regulatory agencies and industry representatives."[316] IOSCO, which coordinates international standard-setting among national securities regulators, has been described as operating "under a significant veil of secrecy" and "very low standards of 'public' accountability."[317] Likewise, the BIS and the Basel Committee have been criticized for their closed and clandestine decision-making.[318]

By contrast, in environmental regulation and policy-making, public participation is extensive and widely applauded.[319] Democratic decision-making has been rationalized from both process and substantive perspectives. The latter reflects arguments that public participation improves the substantive quality of decision-making. The former is based on claims that it bolsters the public legitimacy of those decisions. Specifically, public participation may assist decision-makers to understand and identify public interest concerns.[320] Further, it may enhance the accountability, and thus acceptability,

315 T. Lee, "Accounting from the Inside: Legitimizing the Accounting Academic Elite," *Critical Perspectives on Accounting* 10(6) (1999): 867.

316 P. Mooslechner, H. Schuberth, and B. Weber, "Financial Market Regulation and the Dynamics of Inclusion and Exclusion," in *The Political Economy of Financial Market Regulation: The Dynamics of Inclusion and Exclusion*, eds P. Mooslechner, H Schuberth, and B. Weber (Edward Elgar Publishing, 2006), xii, xx.

317 Condon and Philipps, note 72, 134–35. The IOSCO adopted a new consultation policy recently to deflect some of these criticisms: Executive Committee of IOSCO, *IOSCO Consultation Policy and Procedure* (IOSCO, April, 2005).

318 Alexander, Dhumale, and Eatwell, note 31, 44.

319 See D.L. Van Nijnatten, "Participation and Environmental Policy in Canada and the United States: Trends over Time," *Policy Studies Journal* 27(2) (1999): 267. B.J. Richardson and J. Razzaque, "Public Participation in Environmental Decision-making," in *Environmental Law for Sustainability*, eds B.J. Richardson and S. Wood (Hart Publishing, 2006), 165.

320 E. Petkova, et al., *Closing the Gap: Information, Participation, and Justice in Decision-making for the Environment* (World Resources Institute, 2002), 66–67.

of decisions.[321] The sustainable development principles of inter- and intra-generational equity reflect the belief in the centrality of public involvement and social justice as means of safeguarding the planet.[322]

Financial institutions and their regulators should also be opened to the participation of investors and other stakeholders affected by the financial economy Among its virtues, participation can help to control agency problems that lead fund managers to diverge from agreed investment policies. A 2002 survey of SRI practices in UK pension funds concluded that "[m]ost pension funds' reluctance or inability to monitor the activities of their investment managers in assessing social, environmental and ethical investment issues is one of the most disturbing findings of this report."[323] Broader member participation in funds can increase the number of eyes and ears to keep errant fund managers in check.

A second value of participation is in that SRI should be grounded in a process of ethical deliberation. SRI proceeding from ethical deliberation assumes that investors have a role in the governance of their fund. Decision-making processes within a mutual fund or pension trust should provide a space for investors to debate and reflect on the social and environmental goals and ramifications of the fund policies.[324] The democratic basis would lead to an answer to the criticism of "whose ethics?" in SRI, and it would also bolster the social legitimacy and the authority of SRI as a means of market governance.

Of course, conceding fund members more voice may be insufficient to change the policies of financial institutions. If SRI is to be a vehicle for fundamental social change, promoting consideration of the interests affected by investment, it must be more inclusive. SRI must give a voice even to those without the means to invest. For instance, there is unequal access to occupational pension plans; non-unionized workers and self-employed and unemployed individuals usually have no pension fund and are left to devise,

---

321 N.P. Spyke, "Public Participation in Environmental Decision-making at the New Millennium: Structuring New Spheres of Public Influence," *Boston College Environmental Affairs Law Review* 26 (1999): 263, 269–70.

322 I. Voinovic, "Intergenerational and Intragenerational Equity Requirements for Sustainability," *Environmental Conservation* 22(3) (1995): 223.

323 D. Coles and D. Green, *Do UK Pension Funds Invest Responsibly? A Survey of Current Practice of Socially Responsible Investment* (JustPensions, UKSIF, 2002), 1.

324 In the traditions of deliberative democracy, see M. Arias-Maldonado, "An Imaginary Solution? The Green Defence of Deliberative Democracy," *Environmental Values* 16(2) (2007): 233.

resources permitting, their own personal pension plans.[325] SRI policy-making must also hear from those who may be materially affected by investment decisions. Indigenous peoples, who are the subject of some SRI causes, often do not to have the financial resources to invest. As such, they rely on others to champion their interests. Therefore, an enduring and credible SRI movement must find ways to include marginalized voices in investment decision-making. If they cannot participate in financial institutions directly, they should at least have an opportunity to participate in fashioning the codes of conduct and other SRI standards to protect their interests.

Finally, we must recognize that "participation" is a term of many meanings. Some forms of participation may not be meaningful. Sherry Arnstein's famous "Ladder of Citizen Participation" illustrated how participation may span a spectrum of actions, ranging from manipulating, to informing and consulting, and even higher up the ladder to negotiating and delegating power.[326] So far, participation rights in the financial sector have been confined to the low end of the spectrum, mostly to public entitlements to information as a corollary of disclosure and transparency rules. Occasionally investors have rights to nominate representatives on governing boards, as in some pension funds, and to file resolutions and ask questions, as for shareholders in investment companies. But such rights do not extend to non-investor constituencies. At most, they may have rights to be consulted about financial deals, such as provisions in the EPs requiring parties in project finance transactions to consult with affected local communities. The level of participation appropriate for SRI depends on many factors, including the nature of the financial institution, the type of investments, and their social and environmental ramifications. At the very least, SRI should be supported by opportunities for investors to debate and be consulted about proposed investment policies, to be fully informed about the social and environmental issues their investments may give rise to, and about arrangements to hear from and take into account outside interests acutely distressed by those investments.

B. BARRIERS TO PARTICIPATION

Despite the appealing rhetoric of democracy, modern financial markets pose numerous obstacles to mass or structured participation. Legal rules are not

---

325 UK Pensions Commission, *Implementing an Integrated Package of Pension Reforms: The Final Report* (Pensions Commission, 2006), 13 (discussing UK workers' declining rates of participation in pension plans).

326 S. Arnstein, "Ladder of Citizen Participation," *Journal of the American Institute of Planners* 35(4) (1969): 219.

the only barrier. Institutional investors commonly delegate decision-making to external asset managers and invest through other intermediaries, such as "funds of funds," thereby further distancing beneficiaries from ultimate investment decisions.[327] To seasoned fund managers, who typically view investors as apathetic and uninformed, public participation in the world of finance would seem preposterous. If investors wish to control their own investments more closely, there is a corollary belief that they can always invest directly in the market on their own account. Otherwise, a tension may arise between increasing representation of uninformed investors in decision-making and ensuring competent and efficacious decision-making.[328] However, not all criticisms of participation have merit and the legal obstacles are not insurmountable.

Fiduciary standards foster the democratic deficit in investment decision-making by projecting a passive role for beneficiaries. Rather than treating beneficiaries in pension plans as self-governing and responsible owners, fiduciary norms reduce them to a passive and voiceless status, merely entitling them to be "informed" about how fiduciaries deal with trust assets. Trustees, unlike agents who are subject to control of their principal, need not consult with beneficiaries. They only need to act in their "best interests," though they need not inquire what those best interests are. The beneficiaries' powers reside only in their equitable remedies for breaches of trust, requiring resort to the courts.

The legal principle of beneficial ownership separates those who contribute capital from those who manage capital. The fiduciary's legal ownership of the fund property entitles the trustee to make all decisions in regard to the administration of the fund. The fragmentation of ownership under the "bundle of rights" structure in property law severs the tie between ownership and responsibility in an investment context.[329] The ideals of an active and participatory investment community that integrates civil society and the market are displaced by an impoverished "retail ethics," where social investors supply the capital and retain little further role other than to receive the returns. The absence of mass investor participation means that SRI, unable to serve as a forum for ethical deliberation and civic education, becomes heavily

327 A. Harmes, *Unseen Power: How Mutual Funds Threaten the Political and Economic Wealth of Nations* (Stoddard, 2001), 32–33.

328 Clark, note 310 (suggesting however that that tension is resolvable).

329 K. Gray and S.F. Gray, "The Idea of Property in Land," in *Land Law: Themes and Perspectives*, eds S. Bright and J. Dewar (Oxford University Press, 1998), 15.

driven by a discourse of risk assessment and financial materiality dominated by investment analysts and asset managers.

The burgeoning number of middle-class investors has contributed to more transparent regulation of fund management to improve disclosure and enable more informed decisions.[330] Yet in most cases, such regulation has not extended to actual participation. Certainly, engaging fund beneficiaries in investment policy-making would require the beneficiaries to be well-informed, able to interpret relevant information, and with the means to act on that information. Transparency regulation is thus a necessary precursor to participation. But transparency should not be the end of the matter.

The legal silencing of investors might operate on the assumption that investment management is a complex, specialist activity that few fund members could competently undertake. It would require considerable input of time and resources, which presumably few would wish to devote. Mutual funds for example are designed precisely to appeal to individuals who would prefer to leave investment to full-time professionals. Existing transparency measures do not address the issues of technical complexities; they are mainly directed to making funds disclose their fees and commissions, and to explain their investment policies in plain language.

A related justification for silencing investors is that they are rationally apathetic.[331] Traditional economic theory posits "homo economicus" as a rational, self-interested actor who, in regard to financial matters, has a limited and predictable range of desires. In this worldview, it is rational to be apathetic about how corporate or investment entities are run, because the individual does not have a big enough stake for active involvement in governance to make any difference. It is also rational to free-ride on the knowledge and expertise of institutional investors who have greater capacity to monitor corporate entities. These assumptions about investors' ignorance and apathy— which are not necessarily empirically demonstrated[332]—hardly justify denying

---

330 For instance, in 2004, 55 percent of adult Australians owned shares directly or indirectly, as did 49 percent of Canadians: Australian Securities Exchange, *Australia's Shareowners: An ASX Study of Share Investors in 2004* (ASX, 2004), 41.

331 B.S. Black, "Shareholder Passivity Reexamined," *Michigan Law Review* 89 (1990): 520, 526–29.

332 The "rational apathy" theory has been subject to considerable critique by behavioral economists as empirically inaccurate: S.J. Stabile, "The Behaviour of Defined Contribution Plan Participants," *New York University Law Review* 77 (2002): 71; H. Simon, *Reason in Human Affairs* (Stanford University Press, 1983); S. Amartya, "Rational Fools: A Critique of the Behavioral Foundations of Economic Theory," *Philosophy and Public Affairs* 6 (1977): 317.

investors the right to participate if they choose to inform themselves and devote the necessary time. We don't remove democratic rights in the political sphere simply because some citizens could not be bothered to vote in elections. On the contrary, when citizens have more meaningful, rather than token, opportunities to participate, active participation may increase—as seen in some forms of environmental decision-making such as impact assessment studies and land use planning.[333] Similarly, we need to look at how we can "boost democratic participation in the governance of economic affairs."[334]

While institutional investors, with many small and dispersed holdings in their portfolio, may decline to devote their resources to active shareholding, a similar argument cannot be so easily made about individual investors in a pension plan for instance. Their "rational" incentives to participate are presumably stronger. Unlike a shareholder, a typical pension member's stake usually is not small relative to her whole investment portfolio. A fund member usually has interests in only one pension fund, while a shareholder usually owns shares in many firms. The pension stake often represents the individual's biggest asset after the family home. Moreover, it is much easier for plan participants to monitor their trustees than it is for shareholders to monitor the plethora of firms they invest in. Individual investors in life insurance policies and mutual funds may be in a similar position to pension plan members in this regard.

If we can overcome the legal hindrances to participation, the major concern from the SRI perspective is whether more democratic governance will actually inform ethical investment decisions. Investment funds may be too disparate in their interests and values to constitute a meaningful community for ethical deliberation. Divergent interests may simply lead to relentless squabbling and paralysis. Such divergent interests presumably are greater in mutual funds as they lack the commonality of employment or residence that traditionally characterizes the membership of pension funds and credit unions. Some models of deliberative democracy tend to assume a community with shared or reasonably congruent values. This assumption is rarely reflected in modern life. Disagreement is rife, especially with issues of environmental policy.[335] The normative-generating capacity of society has also eroded in our

---

333 Richardson and Razzaque, note 319.
334 Condon and Philipps, note 72, 131.
335 M.E. Zimmerman, *Contesting Earth's Future: Radical Ecology and Postmodernity* (University of California Press, 1994).

postmodern world of more information, but with less meaning.[336] Yet, while postmodern theories suggest that we should abandon the notion of a singular public interest in favor of recognizing a pastiche of interests,[337] they also advocate participation processes to embrace the cultural and economic differences of society.[338]

For now, the following sections canvass the details of the specific legal constraints against participation that inhere in different types of financial institutions.

C. PARTICIPATION IN A CORPORATE SETTING

1. Corporate Governance Issues for SRI

As shareholders, investors acquire a voice in corporate affairs, which they can assert to influence corporate behavior. This voice is relevant to SRI, both for governing financial institutions structured as corporations, such as banks and investment companies, and for these financiers' participation in the affairs of the companies they fund. Social investors may use shareholder rights to vote, file resolutions, and take other actions to sway corporate policy.

Two core problems with governance of public corporations stand out. First, money talks. Those who hold a majority of the (voting or proxy) stock in a shareholders, meeting have little need either to speak or to listen to their colleagues. Voice is not on the basis of "one member, one vote," but derives from the aggregate size of one's shareholding. This voting regime that systematically allows the proprietary interest to crush the authority of reasoned discussion would be discouraging for social investors with relatively small holdings. Those who do not own any shares have even less voice. Corporate governance rarely creates space for non-shareholder interests such as consumers or local communities affected by corporate decisions.[339]

---

336 J. Baudrillard, "The Hyper-realism of Simulation," in *Art in Theory 1900–1990: An Anthology of Changing Ideas*, eds C. Harrison and P. Wood (Blackwell, 1990), 1049.

337 M.J. Dear, "Postmodernism and Planning," *Environment and Planning D* 4 (1986): 367.

338 L. Sandercock, "Voices from the Borderlands: A Meditation on a Metaphor," *Journal of Planning Education and Research* 15 (1995): 77.

339 S. Letza, X. Sun, and J. Kirkbirde, "Shareholding versus Stakeholding: A Critical Review of Corporate Governance," *Corporate Governance: An International Review* 12(3) (2004): 242; P. Ireland, "Corporate Governance, Stakeholding and the Company: Towards a Less Degenerate Capitalism?" *Journal of Law and Society* 23 (1996): 287.

The second problem is that with the separation of ownership and control in the modern public corporation, shareholders cannot easily control managers and prevent them from making self-interested decisions. This is the agency problem.[340] For instance, management may cut allocations to long-term investment areas, such as research and development, to drive up short-term profits and secure their positions.[341] Management may choose to ignore pollution problems created by the company because they are too costly to remedy and would hurt current corporate earnings. They may postpone such costs to be accounted in the future by other managers, shareholders, or outsiders. The efficacy of mechanisms of corporate control has been severely questioned in the wake of corporate scandals in the US (e.g., Worldcom, Enron, Tyco), Europe (e.g., Parmalat, Vivendi, Ahold, etc), and other places such as Australia (e.g., One.Tel). The scandals highlighted the need for greater regulation and supervision of corporate managers and their associates.[342]

The ways these problems transpire and are addressed vary from country to country depending on its model of corporate governance.[343] Broadly, two main models persist: the Anglo-American systems of the UK, US, Canada, and Australia among others, and the corporate systems of Continental Europe and Japan. Some nuanced differences remain within each model, such as between the regimes in Germany, France, and Scandinavian countries.[344] Corporate governance in developing countries draws on both systems.[345] Worldwide, there is also some convergence in corporate governance towards

340 E. Fama, "Agency Problems and the Theory of the Firm," *Journal of Political Economy* 88 (1980): 288.

341 J.S. Harrison and J.O. Fiet, "New CEOs Pursue their Own Self-Interests by Sacrificing Stakeholder Value," *Journal of Business Ethics* 19(3) (1999): 301.

342 See M.M. Jennings, "A Primer on Enron: Lessons from a Perfect Storm of Financial Reporting, Corporate Governance and Ethical Culture Failures," *California Western Law Review* 39 (2003): 163; J. Armour and J. McCahery, eds, *After Enron. Improving Corporate Law and Modernising Securities Regulation in Europe and the US* (Hart Publishing, 2006).

343 R. Dore, W. Lazonick, and M. O'Sullivan, "Varieties of Capitalism in the Twentieth Century," *Oxford Review of Economic Policy* 15 (1999): 102; J. Weimer and J.C. Pape, "A Taxonomy of Systems of Corporate Governance," *Corporate Governance* 7 (1999): 152.

344 Explained in R. La Porta, et al., "Law and Finance," *Journal of Political Economy* 106 (1998): 1113.

345 D. Reed, "Corporate Governance Reforms in Developing Countries," *Journal of Business Ethics* 37(3) (2002): 223.

the Anglo-American model.[346] Global finance markets, particularly institutional investors, increasingly drive changes in corporate governance, with these trends currently most pronounced in Continental Europe.[347]

2. Market-based and Stakeholder Models of Corporate Control

The Anglo-American system relies heavily on market controls to keep management in check.[348] It is epitomized by arm's-length relations between sources of finance and firms and the supremacy of shareholder interests.[349] If a firm follows policies that hurt shareholders, others may oust management in a takeover. The market for corporate control functions through proxy contests, friendly mergers, and hostile takeovers.[350] In practice, managerial power is often entrenched. Takeovers are very costly, and triggered only by major performance failures.[351]

Company law has also sought to protect shareholders through the right to vote on seminal corporate matters such as the election of the board of directors.[352] However, various factors keep shareholders from effectively exerting control over the corporation, especially when they are small, numerous, and dispersed. Shareholders can elect the directors and approve "organic" changes, but typically that is the extent of their power. Strategic corporate decisions (e.g., investment and environmental policies) are largely beyond their influence. Legislation also commonly restricts the form and content of shareholder resolutions. It also restricts beneficial shareholders (e.g., members

---

346 H. Hansmann and R.H. Kraakman, "The End of History for Corporate Law," *Georgetown Law Journal* 89 (2001): 439; J. McCahery, et al., *Corporate Governance Regimes: Convergence and Diversity* (Oxford University Press, 2002).

347 G.L. Clark and D. Wójcik, *The Geography of Finance: Corporate Governance in the Global Marketplace* (Oxford University Press, 2007), 18–21.

348 Although both private and public companies have the same legal form, private companies are not traded on public markets. Private company shareholders closely connected to the company thus somewhat resemble traditional nineteenth-century industrial capitalists: J. McCahery, T. Raaijmakers, and E.P.M. Vermeulen, eds, *The Governance of Close Corporations and Partnerships: US and European Perspectives* (Oxford University Press, 2004).

349 A. Rappaport, *Creating Shareholder Value: The New Standard for Business Performance* (Free Press, 1998).

350 H. Manne, "Mergers and the Market for Corporate Control," *Journal of Political Economy* 73 (1965): 110.

351 M. Jensen, "Takeovers: Their Causes and Consequences," *Journal of Economic Perspectives* 2 (1988): 21.

352 R.C. Nolan, "The Continuing Evolution of Shareholder Governance," *Cambridge Law Journal* 65 (2006): 92.

of pension funds) from even filing a proposal. Management typically retains control of the proxy voting process and may refuse to circulate the proposal to shareholders for any number of reasons. Often, shareholder resolutions lack legal significance even when they are passed. Instead they serve merely as a statement of principle regarding the shareholders' wishes.[353] Many public companies also maintain dual class share structures, allowing a small number of shareholders to wield control though they only own a small percentage of stock.

In addition to the frustration of shareholder powers, other interests affected by corporate decisions such as customers, employees, and local communities are rendered mostly voiceless in corporate affairs. In banks, depositors have no rights to participate in the banks' governance.[354] In insurance companies, shifting from mutual companies to public stock companies has reduced policyholders' role in governance.[355]

Corporations' boards of directors have tended to act as lapdogs rather than watchdogs for shareholders.[356] Boards are eviscerated for several reasons. The nominees are commonly selected by the incumbent board and the CEO influences the choice of new candidates and the election process.[357] Corporate elections have been caricatured as "procedurally much more akin to the elections held by the Communist party of North Korea" than genuine democratic elections as "they normally provide only one slate of candidates."[358]

Some commentators hail concentrated ownership through institutional investors as an answer to the agency problems of corporate governance. Stephen Davis and colleagues contend that the rise of mass public investing through pension plans and other institutions is surreptitiously democratizing

---

353 J. Sarra, "The Corporation as Symphony: Are Shareholders First Violin or Second Fiddle?" *University of British Columbia Law Review* 36 (2003): 403, 413.

354 R. Levine, *The Corporate Governance of Banks: A Concise Discussion of Concepts and Evidence*, Policy Research Working Paper No. 3404 (World Bank, September 2004).

355 K.S. Viswanathan and J.D. Cummins, "Ownership Structure Changes in the Insurance Industry: An Analysis of Demutualization," *Journal of Risk and Insurance* 70(3) (2003): 401.

356 L. Eaton, "Corporate Couch Potatoes: The Awful Truth about Boards of Directors," *Barron's*, December 24, 1991, 22.

357 M. Weisbach, "Outside Directors and CEO Turnover," *Journal of Financial Economics* 20 (1988): 431: M. Jensen, "The Eclipse of the Public Corporation," *Harvard Business Review* 67 (1989): 60.

358 E.J. Epstein, *Who Owns the Corporation? Management vs. Shareholders* (Priority Press, 1986), 13.

corporate ownership.[359] Bernard Black argues that institutional investors' combination of large shareholdings and economies of scale allows them to overcome the traditional problems of shareholder passivity and thus effect changes in corporate policy.[360] Until recently, institutional shareholders had not fulfilled these expectations.[361] The 2001 Myners Review found a culture of passive investing among UK institutions.[362] Institutional investor activism in North America has historically been stronger, although not to the extent of taming corporations.[363]

Recently, particularly in Europe, there are signs of more active styles of investment coinciding with the growth of institutional investment. Gordon Clark and Dariusz Wójcik depict a rising interest among global portfolio managers in transparent and accountable modes of corporate governance.[364] Through their demands for more transparency, Clark and Teresa Hebb see institutional investors as helping all stakeholders obtain better information to evaluate corporate behavior and to apply pressure for change.[365] Investor coalitions, some of which appreciate SRI, have been crucial for enhancing institutions' leverage. These include financial sector associations, such as the Australian Council of Super Investors, as well as issue-based associations, such as the Institutional Investors Group on Climate Change. Pension funds, particularly public sector funds, increasingly use their voice to engage companies.[366] Public sector pension funds have tended to be the most active, partly because they are not constrained by the collateral business ties that

359 Davis, et al., note 312, 6–7.
360 B.S. Black, "Agents Watching Agents: The Promise of Institutional Investor Voice," *UCLA Law Review* 39 (1992): 811, 873–88. The average small stockholder lacks the requisite information and resources to monitor and control management: V. Brudney, "Corporate Governance, Agency Costs, and the Rhetoric of Contract," *Columbia Law Review* 85 (1985): 1403, 1405–8.
361 See e.g., A. Dolin, "Boosting Shareholder Participation—How Well Do you Know your Investors?" *Keeping Good Companies* July (2002): 334 (discussing Australian corporate governance).
362 Myners, note 173, 89–92.
363 S.L. Gillan and L.T. Starks, "The Evolution of Shareholder Activism in the United States," *Journal of Applied Corporate Finance* 19(1) (2007): 55.
364 Clark and Wójcik, note 347.
365 G.L. Clark and T. Hebb, "Why Should They Care? The Role of Institutional Investors in the Market for Corporate Global Responsibility," *Environment and Planning A* 37(11) (2005): 2015.
366 G.L. Clark and T. Hebb, "Pension Fund Corporate Engagement: The Fifth Stage of Capitalism," *Industrial Relations* 59(1) (2004): 142.

mutual funds and other investment institutions sometimes have in their portfolio.[367]

Enlightened institutional investors have also helped to advance new international, voluntary codes of conduct, such as the OECD Principles of Corporate Governance[368] and the Statement on Global Corporate Governance Principles issued by the International Corporate Governance Network.[369] Major stock exchanges are also pioneering corporate governance standards, for listed firms on a "comply with or explain otherwise" basis.[370] Further, large institutional players, such as CalPERS, have pushed their own corporate governance benchmarks for portfolio companies.[371]

At a national level, the UK has gone the furthest among its peers in corporate law reform. Through the *Companies Act* of 2006, Britain has shifted to what some describe as the "enlightened shareholder value" model of corporate governance.[372] The reformulation of directors' fiduciary duties to be considerate of other stakeholders constitutes one such measure introduced to "enlighten" companies. Australia and Canada have also advanced some reforms, strengthening the rights of minority shareholders to file resolutions[373] and removing restrictions on resolutions of political and social issues.[374] Reform has lagged in the US; in 2007 the SEC was considering rule changes to allow companies to restrict shareholders' rights to file advisory resolutions, which accounted for the vast majority of shareholder resolutions

367 G.F. Davis and E.H. Kim, "Would Mutual Funds Bite the Hand that Feeds Them? Business Ties and Proxy Voting," *Conference on Agency Problems and Conflicts of Interest in Financial Markets* (November 2004), 5.

368 OECD, *Principles of Corporate Governance* (OECD, 2004).

369 See http://www.icgn.org.

370 E.g., Australian Securities Exchange (ASE), *Principles of Good Corporate Governance and Best Practice Recommendations* (ASE, March 2003).

371 P. Enardiog, "Emerging Markets: Time to Shape Up: CalPERS Sets Tough New Governance Standards," *Business Week*, March 11, 2002.

372 R.V. Aguilera, et al., "Corporate Governance and Social Responsibility: A Comparative Analysis of the UK and the US," *Corporate Governance and Social Responsibility* 14(3) (2006): 147.

373 Amendment to Australia's *Corporations Act* in 1998, s. 249D (to enable either a minimum of one hundred shareholders or 5 percent of all shareholders to put a resolution to an extraordinary general meeting).

374 Amendments in 2001 to the *Canada Business Corporations Act*, R.S.C. 1985, s. 137(5). A court had allowed a corporation to refuse to circulate a proposal on disinvestments in South Africa: *Varity Corporation v. Jesuit Fathers of Upper Canada*, (1987) 60 O.R. (2d) 640, 41 D.L.R. 284 (C.A.).

over recent decades.[375] The SEC had also flagged the possibilities of allowing companies to pass bylaws to opt out of the resolution process, insulating the most recalcitrant companies from their shareholders' concerns, as well as replacing advisory resolutions with electronic forums, so that a shareholder proposal would no longer materialize on a firm's proxy statement.[376] While the SEC announced in November 2007 that it would not pursue some of its controversial proposals,[377] the current Republican-leaning SEC continues to reinterpret some long-standing rules in a way that bolsters the position of corporate management.[378]

Corporate governance in Continental Europe and to a lesser extent in Japan has embodied a concept of stakeholder capitalism. It conceives companies as industrial partnerships where management must equally respect a network of interests including creditors and workers, with an emphasis on consensus and long-term economic results.[379] Capital markets play a relatively weaker role in disciplining companies.[380] The most direct method of ensuring that corporate management adequately represents all of its constituencies is to grant seats on the board of directors.[381]

In Germany, specialized two-tier supervisory and management boards for the public corporations combined with the so-called "Universalbankensystem,"

375 Shareholder Association for Research and Education, "Shareholder Proposal Rights at Risk in US" (E-News, June 2007).
376 J. Burns, "SEC Draws Criticism for Competing Proxy-Access Plans," *Dow Jones News Service*, July 26, 2007.
377 SIF, "Socially Responsible Investors Applaud SEC Decision Not to Curtail Shareholder Resolutions, But Strongly Oppose Curbs on Director Nomination Process," Press release, November 28, 2007.
378 See session on "The Changing Face of the Securities and Exchange Commission, and What it Means for Socially Conscious Investors" (18th Annual SRI in the Rockies Conference, Santa Ana Pueblo, New Mexico, November 3–6, 2007).
379 M. Gerlach, *Alliance Capitalism: The Social Organization of Japanese Business* (University of California Press, 1992); J. Edwards, et al., "Corporate Governance in Germany: The Role of Banks and Ownership Concentration," *Economic Policy* 15(31) (2000): 237.
380 J. Frank and C. Mayer, "Capital Markets and Corporate Control: A Study of France, Germany and the UK," *Economic Policy* 10 (1990): 189.
381 See J.B. Bonanno, "Employee Co-Determination: Origins in Germany, Present Practice in Europe, and Applicability to the United States," *Harvard Journal on Legislation* 14 (1977): 947.

in which a bank is both an investor and creditor simultaneously.[382] This interaction led to corporate financing by "house banks," where a lead bank is both a shareholder in the company and also the organizer of all financial services for that company.[383] Another German peculiarity is its strong labor "co-determination" regime, involving the incorporation of employee representatives on the firm's supervisory board.[384] The system of co-determination, however, has never been a serious threat to the power of large shareholders and managers.[385] Its status has become more precarious in recent years with substantial reforms to German corporate and securities laws, such as the *Control and Transparency in Business Act* of 1998 and the soft law German *Corporate Governance Code*,[386] incorporating elements of the Anglo-American system that strengthen the capital market and shareholders' rights.[387]

Corporate governance in Japan is structured around the keiretsu system; it involves groups of companies having cross-shareholdings, cross-appointments on boards of directors, and other business ties such as using one another's suppliers and purchasers.[388] The Japanese system gives little influence to "outside" shareholders in corporate affairs.[389] Historically, each keiretsu would center on one bank, which would commonly hold shares in each firm.[390] In the Japanese economic recession of the 1990s, many banks failed

382 J. Edwards and K. Fischer, *Banks, Finance and Investment in Germany* (Cambridge University Press, 1994).

383 S. Prigge, "A Survey of German Corporate Governance," in *Comparative Corporate Governance,* eds K.J. Hopt, et al. (Clarendon Press, 1998), 943.

384 Hopt and Leyens, note 267, 7.

385 W. Streeck, "German Capitalism: Does It Exist? Can It Survive?" *New Political Economy* 2(2) (1997): 23.

386 Although the code is soft law, the *Stock Corporation Act* (s. 161) requires German companies to disclose whether and how they have complied with the Code's "best principles."

387 U. Noack and D. Zetzsche, *Corporate Governance Reform in Germany: The Second Decade* (Center for Business and Corporate Law, Heinrich-Heine University, 2005).

388 H.N. Higgins, "Corporate Governance in Japan: Role of Banks, Keiretsus and Japanese Traditions," in *The Governance of East Asian Corporations: Post Asian Financial Crisis,* ed. F.A. Gul and S.I. Tsui (Palgrave Macmillan, 2004), 96.

389 C.L. Heftel, "Corporate Governance in Japan: The Position of Shareholders in Publicly Held Corporations," *University of Hawaii Law Review* 5 (1983): 135, 165.

390 M. Aoki and H. Patrick, *The Japanese Main Bank System* (Clarendon Press, 1994).

and this led to companies turning to the capital markets. As in Germany, reforms to Japan's *Commercial Code* and the *Corporations Law* in recent years making it easier for companies to raise capital from the stock markets have introduced elements of Anglo-American corporate structures into their governance systems.

Thus, regulatory reforms to corporate governance and securities markets in these jurisdictions increasingly accommodate the Anglo-American model of channeling capital flows to corporations through investment funds, pension plans, and insurance companies.[391] Nearly all the European states including Germany and France have adopted new codes of corporate governance in recent years, addressing the role of the board of directors, financial reporting, auditors, and shareholder rights.[392] There have also been some EU-wide reforms, although corporate governance remains substantially in the realm of national law.[393]

While some significant national differences are likely to endure,[394] the overall result is an enhancement of the power of institutional investors and their capacity to be a means of corporate control. To the extent institutional investors take an interest in SRI, as "universal owners," this promises even within the confines of business case SRI to be a significant improvement on traditional, passive investment practices.

D. PENSION FUND GOVERNANCE

1. *Voiceless and Passive Beneficiaries*

Because occupational pension funds invest the savings of ordinary workers, some commentators see them as a vehicle to democratize economic decision-making and social investment. From the employment relationship perspective, participation of employees in workplace decisions should extend to their pension funds.[395] Another perspective in the literature looks at worker

---

391 Hopt and Leyens, note 267, 24.

392 K. Lannoo and A. Khachaturyan, "Reform of Corporate Governance in the EU," *European Business Organization Law Review* 5 (2004): 37.

393 Ibid., 44; and see High Level Group of Company Law Experts, *Report of the High Level Group of Company Law Experts on a Modern Regulatory Framework for Company Law in Europe* (EC, 2002).

394 C.J. Milhaupt and M.D. West, *Economic Organizations and Corporate Governance in Japan: The Impact of Formal and Informal Rules* (Oxford University Press, 2004).

395 J. Gates, *The Ownership Solution: Toward a Shared Capitalism for the 21st Century* (Addison-Wesley Publishing, 1998).

control in the context of pension fund investment decisions, as a means to enable employees to influence corporate governance and economic development for their benefit.[396] Those who oppose democratization of pension fund governance typically contend that it harms investment strategy and that it results in unwieldy and divisive boards.[397]

Perhaps the most effusive contribution to this literature is Peter Drucker's claims in *Unseen Revolution: How Pension Fund Socialism Came to America*[398] that the US was becoming the world's first socialist country because its workers, through their pension plans, were acquiring a controlling stake in American businesses. Through that voice, Drucker believed, there would be a shift from short-term profit goals to long-term investment of real benefit to workers and their communities. Drucker downplayed several problems in pension fund governance. Corporate management typically appoints the trustees to private pension plans.[399] Furthermore, their administration has become highly concentrated in the hands of investment banks and insurance companies, to whom plans commonly delegate fund management responsibilities.[400] Nevertheless, Drucker's cudgel has been taken up by another generation of scholars hopeful of the transformative potential of labor-controlled pension funds.[401]

A related claim is that not only may democratization of pension plans empower their membership; it may also enhance the welfare of society as a whole. James Gifford reasons: "[g]iven the ubiquity of pension fund membership, especially in the developed world, it can also be argued that the interests of members of funds are broadly consistent with those of the society

---

396 A. Fung, T. Hebb, and J. Rogers, eds, *Working Capital: The Power of Labor's Pensions* (Cornell University Press, 2001).

397 R. Hannah, "The Control of Pensions: A Brief History and Possibilities for the Future," *Management Decision* 40(10) (2002): 938, 943.

398 P. Drucker, *Unseen Revolution: How Pension Fund Socialism Came to America* (Heinemann, 1976).

399 J. Rifkin and R. Barber, *The North will Rise Again: Pensions, Politics and Power in the 1980s* (Beacon Press, 1978), 104–9.

400 See R. Minns, "The Social Ownership of Capital," *New Left Review* 21 (1996): 42, 48; R. Blackburn, "The New Collectivism: Pension Reform, Grey Capitalism and Complex Socialism," *New Left Review* 233 (1999): 3, 5.

401 E.g., G.L. Clark, "Pension Fund Governance: Expertise and Organizational Form," *Journal of Pension Economics and Finance* 3(2) (2004): 233, 238; T. Ghilarducci, *Labor's Capital: The Economics and Politics of Private Pensions* (MIT Press, 1992); T. Hebb, *No Small Change: Pension Funds and Corporate Engagement* (Cornell University Press, 2008).

in which the members live."[402] It is however questionable to assume that pension plan members always provide a proxy for the interests of society at large. Unfortunately, many people do not have access to an occupational pension scheme: particularly the unemployed, part-time, and self-employed workers. Pension funds may broadly reflect the middle-class professions, but not all of society. Only national pension schemes, such as the Canada Pension Plan or Sweden's AP-Funds, could possibly approximate such a broad public interest.

Regardless of how we view their representativeness, the voices of pension fund members in practice often carry little weight in the administration of their plans.[403] A 2005 survey of UK occupational pension fund trustees revealed that 53 percent of respondents attached "no significance" and only 13 percent attached "great significance" to the views of their members when considering social, ethical, and environmental issues in their investment policies.[404] Conversely, 39 percent attached "great significance" to the views of their investment consultants. The most democratically run pension plans tend to be among public pension schemes[405] and those plans managed jointly by trade union and employer representatives.[406] Some large US funds noted for their SRI practices have beneficiary-elected trustees, including CalPERS and TIAA-CREF.

Greater member participation in pension plans should be a matter of public policy. Most fundamentally, if we expect pension funds like other financial institutions to be more accountable for the social and environmental consequences of their investments, then the ultimate owners of pension capital must have more voice in the determination of those investments. Even now, it would be dubious to treat the occupational pension system as just a private matter between a company and its workers. The schemes often benefit from state tax concessions, and serve as mechanisms for implementing government policy on retirement income. More voice is essential if you have

---

402 J. Gifford, "Measuring The Social, Environmental and Ethical Performance of Pension Funds," *Journal of Australian Political Economy* 53 (2004): 139, 141.

403 G.S. Alexander, "Pensions and Passivity," *Law and Contemporary Problems* 56(1) (1993): 111, 113.

404 C. Gribben and M. Gitsham, *Will UK Pension Funds Become More Responsible: A Survey of Trustees* (JustPensions, UKSIF, 2006), 14.

405 S. Waygood, *Capital Market Campaigning: The Impact of NGOs on Companies, Shareholder Value and Reputational Risk* (Risk Books, 2005) (discussing the case of the USS in Britain).

406 M. O'Connor, "Labor's Role in the Shareholder Revolution," in *Working Capital,* note 396, 67, 69.

limited ability to take your savings elsewhere. Unlike members of mutual funds, members of occupational pension plans do not normally have the exit option. Unless legislation gives them the right to direct their contributions to another fund, workers cannot switch investments unless they change jobs. Evidence of the benefits of greater participation of pension fund members including promotion of SRI is discussed later in this chapter.

2. Fiduciary Law and Member Passivity

The usually passive and voiceless position of pension fund beneficiaries is not a result of unpredicted behavior. It derives substantially from the legal structure of a pension plan. In common law jurisdictions, fiduciaries hold pension assets in trust. The governing fiduciary law principles stifle members' participation.[407] Pension governance in civil law systems effectively achieves the same result via legislative arrangements that separate investors from fund administrators. Trust law generally assumes that the beneficiaries of the trust are passive. Historically, trusts were designed primarily to protect family wealth and to provide for the wife and children, who were socially constructed as passive and dependent.[408] Modern pension law transplants the trust law assumption of passive beneficiary to a different and somewhat inappropriate context. The deprivation of plan members' opportunities to participate in investment decisions means they cannot, even if they wish to, direct the trustees or fund managers to invest ethically. This gives plan members less voice than corporate shareholders who, in principle, elect the board of directors. As discussed later, pension legislation in some jurisdictions allows for limited member-nominated trustees, although this is not the norm.

Pension legislation may further distance the members from decision-making by allowing pension trustees to delegate (as they mostly do) the investment function to external asset managers.[409] In this respect, pension legislation deviates from the fiduciary principle of non-delegation,[410] and does so in a way that aggravates rather than ameliorates the problem of disempowered members. Pension trustees favor delegation, not only because it absolves them of the need to commit the necessary time and resources to invest prudently, but also because they may be relieved of liability for the

---

407 Alexander, note 403, 124.

408 On the roots of trusts, see A. Hudson, *Principles of Equity and Trusts* (Cavendish Publishing, 1999).

409 ERISA, s.402(c)(3).

410 E.g., ERISA s. 402(c)(3); and for the common law position, see *Marshall v. Frazier*, (1938) 81 P.2d 132 (Or.).

decisions of their delegates, as occurs in the US under ERISA.[411] However, trustees who delegate typically retain "responsibility to monitor the selection and performance of co-fiduciaries and financial intermediaries."[412] In practice, trustee boards are notoriously ineffective in supervising fund managers, leaving fund managers too much leeway to interpret what is in the plan members' "best interests."[413] The result is a "system of absentee ownership with management exercising powers."[414]

Another legal factor that contributes to passivity is the equitable nature of members' rights in their investment portfolio. A share comprises two legal interests—a registered interest and a beneficial interest.[415] The registered shareholder is the person named on the share or on the company's register, such as the appointed fund manager. Unless provided by special legislation, pension members' beneficial ownership interest does not allow them to exercise voting rights or other entitlements attendant to the shares.[416] Instead, the trustee or fund member exercises those rights as the registered owners. While voting proxies is a fiduciary act, which trustees must perform for the exclusive benefit of plan participants, fiduciary law does not require them to consult with the beneficiaries. Thus, in one Canadian case in 1996, *Verdun v. Toronto Dominion Bank*, the court disallowed a beneficial shareowner to file ten proposals for inclusion in the annual shareholders' meeting information circular. The court agreed with the bank's refusal "on the basis that the appellant was not a registered shareholder.... "[417] The effect of this case was subsequently nullified by a legislative amendment to allow beneficial owners of shares to advance proposals or requisition meetings, but subject to certain restrictions.[418] Some other jurisdictions have not advanced similar legal reforms.

---

411 ERISA absolves trustees of liability for mismanagement of plan assets assigned to fund managers: s. 405(d)(1).

412 R.H. Koppes and M.L. Reilly, "An Ounce of Prevention: Meeting the Fiduciary Duty to Monitor an Index Fund through Relationship Investing," *Journal of Corporation Law* 20 (1995): 414, 431.

413 US Government Accountability Office (GAO), *Pension Plans: Additional Transparency and Other Actions Needed in Connection with Proxy Voting*, GAO-04-749 (GAO, 2004).

414 Davis, et al., note 312, 78.

415 G. Barton, "The Legal Nature of a Share," in *Interests in Goods*, eds N. Palmer and E. McKendrick (Lloyds of London Press, 1998).

416 Alexander, note 403, 127.

417 [1996] 3 S.C.R. 550.

418 *Canada Business Corporations Act*, R.S.C. 1985, s. 137(1). However, shareholders must own either own 1 percent of total outstanding shares or have shares with a market value of at least C$2,000: A.A. Dhir, "Realigning the

The shift from defined-benefit to defined-contribution pension plans further necessitates giving members' more voice.[419] In the wake of fluctuating stock market returns and market uncertainty, which make it difficult to guarantee returns, many companies in recent years have sought to convert their pension plans to defined-contribution schemes. They therefore shift investment risk to contributors, but often without a corresponding increase in their right to be heard in investment decisions.[420] Recent OECD guidelines on occupational pension regulation recommend that beneficiaries in defined-contribution plans should be able to choose their investment options.[421]

Of course, with more voice one should also accept more responsibility. Enhancing the influence of beneficiaries in the administration of a pension trust could make them liable for torts or other causes of action committed in the conduct of the trust's business. Austin explains the law: "the beneficiaries are not personally liable if the trustees are merely trustees. But where the beneficiaries have power to control the conduct of the trustees to such an extent that the trustees are their agents, the beneficiaries are personally liable as principals. . . . "[422] Such a scenario is presently far-fetched.

3. Legislative Reforms for Participation

The dominant legislative response has been information transparency reforms, advanced as a means of accountability. A few jurisdictions, such as Australia, Canada, and the UK, have gone further to legislate for worker representation

Corporate Building Blocks: Shareholder Proposals as a Vehicle for Achieving Corporate Social and Human Rights Accountability," *American Business Law Journal* 43(2) (2006): 365, 387.

419 On this shift, see A. Byrne, "Investment Decision Making in Defined Contribution Plans," *Pensions: An International Journal* 10(1) (2004): 37. As at the end of 2006, in the world's eleven major pension fund markets, defined-benefit plans represented 58 percent of total assets, compared to 42 percent for defined-contribution plan assets. However, the average growth of contribution plan assets since 1997 was 9.8 percent per annum compared with 5.5 percent per annum for benefit plans: Watson Wyatt, *2007 Global Pensions Asset Study* (Watson Wyatt, 2007), 3.

420 R.A.G. Monks and N. Minow, *Power and Accountability* (HarperCollins, 1991), 223.

421 OECD, *Recommendation on Core Principles of Occupational Pension Regulation* (OECD, July 21, 2004), 5.16, 5.24 and 5.27.

422 R.P. Austin, "The Role and Responsibilities of Trustees in Pension Plan Trusts: Some Problems of Trusts Law," in *Equity Fiduciaries and Trusts*, ed. T. Youdan (Carswell, 1989), 111.

in governing pension boards. Their capacity to put the interests of the nominating fund members such as their trade union ahead of the interests of all beneficiaries is not unlimited. A member-appointed trustee could be construed as in a position analogous to a corporate director nominated by a major shareholder. Corporate law may allow such a nominee to act in a manner that concurrently benefits the nominating shareholder; the Canadian Supreme Court ruled that this was permissible where the interests of the company and the nominating shareholder innocently and genuinely coincide.[423]

In Britain, employers traditionally reigned over pension plans, but after the Maxwell scandal of the early 1990s, power was put in the hands of pension trustees. Improved accountability introduced by the *Pensions Act* of 1995, however, did not extend significantly to ordinary plan members,[424] though statutory amendments since 2004 have begun correcting this anomaly. The *Pensions Act* of 2004 prescribed that "at least one-third" of the trustees must be "member-nominated."[425] The Act also allows the government to enact regulations to change the member-nominated trustee provisions to require one-half of trustees to be member-nominated.[426]

Australia's *Superannuation Industry (Supervision) (SIS) Act* of 1993 mandates 50 percent member representation on trustee boards of funds with at least five members, giving members of all funds regular investment information, and allowing members to bring civil and criminal action against trustees and investment managers who err in their duties.[427] In addition, members have access to a comprehensive mechanism for dispute resolution including, in certain situations, the Superannuation Complaints Tribunal.[428] Most recently, pursuant to the *Superannuation Legislation Amendment (Choice of Superannuation Funds) Act* of 2005, most employees acquired the ability to choose the specific fund into which their employer's compulsory superannuation contributions are paid. This could include an SRI-directed fund.

Canadian governments have also established a range of mechanisms for member participation in pension plan governance. At a federal level, the *Pension Benefits Standards Act* requires that the pension committee include a member-nominated representative if a majority of the pension plan's members

---

423 *Peoples Department Stores v. Wise*, [2004] 3 S.C.R. 461, at paras. 39–41.
424 J. Coates, "Change in the Balance of Power for UK Pensions," *Pensions* 10 (2005): 308, 309.
425 Section 241(1)(a).
426 Section 243(1).
427 Sections 52, 58, 89, 101, 107.
428 Established by the *Superannuation (Resolution of Complaints) Act*, 1993 (Cth).

so request.[429] Quebec law requires establishment of an elected pension committee, separate from the employer-administered plan unit, with some decision-
making authority.[430] Another legislative model is the joint trusteeship of
public sector pension schemes, such as in British Columbia's *Public Sector
Pension Plan Act*[431] and Ontario's *Public Service Employees' Union Pension Act*.[432]
A further forum for employee involvement in several provinces is advisory
committees.[433] Beneficiaries may also acquire by contractual negotiations
additional rights.[434] Ontario's *Pension Benefits Act* does not normally allow for
employees' representation in plan administration, but will give effect to such
provisions in collective bargaining deals.[435] Interestingly, in one of the few
legislative mandates for SRI, Ontario's former *South African Trust Investments
Act* of 1988 provided that, regarding pension funds with over one hundred
beneficiaries, trustees had to make inquiries and have reasonable grounds for
believing that most of the beneficiaries would consent and that they held
a majority of the beneficial interests in the pension fund's assets, before
refusing to acquire or disposing of a South African investment.

Moves toward employee representation or joint-trusteeship have also
occurred in some other jurisdictions. South African law mandates at least
50 percent member representation on trustee boards.[436] Brazilian legislation,
since 2001, stipulates mandatory employee representatives to make up
between one-third and one-half of the governing organs of public and private
pension funds.[437] In Denmark, trade unions largely control the governance of
pension plans as a matter of law and practice.[438] Representation of employees
in the governing boards of pension funds occurs in several other European
countries, including Italy, Switzerland, and the Netherlands, among examples.
In the US, while many public sector funds, especially state and municipal

---

429 R.S.C. 1985.
430 *Supplemental Pension Plans Act*, S.Q. 2001, s. 147.
431 S.B.C. 1999.
432 S.O. 1994.
433 E.g., British Columbia's *Pension Benefits Standards Act*, R.S.B.C. 1996, s. 69;
    Ontario's *Pension Benefits Act*, R.S.O. 1990, s. 24.
434 A.N. Kaplan, *Pension Law* (Irwin Law, 2006), 13, 17.
435 R.S.O. 1990, ss 1(2), 8(1)(b)–(c).
436 *Pension Funds Act*, 1956, as amended, s. 7A.
437 Lei Complementar No. 109 (2001), Capítulo III, art. 31; Lei Complementar
    No. 108 (2001), Capítulo III, art. 9.
438 E. Overbye, "The Politics of Voluntary and Mandatory Pensions in Nordic
    Countries," *Review of Labour Economics and Industrial Relations* 12(1) (1998):
    169, 185.

government plans, have various provisions for member representation in governing boards and other functions, corporate sector plans under ERISA do not provide equivalent rights.[439] Except however the trustees of multi-employer plans (Taft-Hartley funds) must be appointed jointly by participating employers and employee organizations.[440]

Does boosting member participation in investment policy-making enhance the prospects for SRI? Do pension fund members advocate more responsible investment if given more voice? While employees have traditionally preferred to bargain for defined-benefit plans and income security, rather than to seek more voice,[441] more democratically governed funds often seem to be at the forefront of SRI. A pioneering research program on US public pension plans and urban revitalization coordinated by Harvard and Oxford Universities has documented a wealth of case studies of investors partnering with community development associations and local financial intermediaries to promote urban renewal and community economic development.[442] Such partnerships give institutional investors access to intermediaries with the financial engineering expertise to achieve scale and minimize risk, as well as access to grass-roots organizations to ensure that real estate and infrastructure projects reflect community needs and achieve the social returns. Such financial intermediaries include the Urban Strategy America Fund (specializing in real estate renewal) and Cherokee Investment Partners (specializing in the cleanup and sustainable redevelopment of contaminated properties).[443]

Among other evidence, Tessa Hebb's landmark new study on pension fund engagement in North America found that public sector funds such as CalPERS were more committed than private pension funds to engage with companies on SRI issues, partly because of the greater presence of member-nominated trustees and trade union-influence in pension plan governance.[444]

---

439 Hannah, note 397, 943.

440 *Labor Management Relations Act*, 1947, Pub. L. No. 80-101, 61 Stat. 136, s. 302(c).

441 W.H. Simon, "The Prospects of Pension Fund Socialism," *Berkeley Journal of Employment and Labor Law* 14 (1993): 251, 255.

442 See http://urban.ouce.ox.ac.uk/research.php. See, in particular, G.L. Clark, T. Hebb, and L.A. Hagerman, *U.S. Public Sector Pension Funds and Urban Revitalization: An Overview of Policy and Programs* (School of Geography and the Environment, University of Oxford, 2004).

443 L.A. Hagerman, G.L. Clark, and T. Hebb, *Investment Intermediaries in Economic Development: Linking Pension Funds to Urban Revitalization* (Labor and Worklife Program, Harvard Law School, 2007), 34–35.

444 Hebb, note 401.

David Hess however is less enthusiastic about US funds' commitment to SRI, although his main point of comparison was the higher levels of interest in SRI among European and Australasian financiers.[445] An older Canadian study on the impact of union representation in 189 pension funds found "some evidence that union involvement is facilitative of social investment." But the correlation was not significant.[446]

More participation alone may not engender meaningful change without giving elected fiduciaries training, technical assistance, and teamwork skills. Some research on US public sector funds expresses the criticism that more voice tends to "politicize" investment decision-making, creating conflict rather than consensus.[447] Canadian researchers have observed that "[l]abor trustees . . . face many challenges acquiring the skills, knowledge and networks to assist them in becoming active and integrated participants on the pension board."[448] They therefore tend to defer to the advice of fund advisers.[449] Employee representatives may also be intimidated by their fiduciary responsibilities and thus adhere to conservative investment paths.[450] The following statement of an SRI advisory committee of the Ontario Teachers' Pension Plan Board reflects several of these various difficulties:

> The committee does not recommend any attempt to put definitive screens, either positive or negative, in place. We feel that any attempt

---

445 D. Hess, *Public Pensions and the Promise of Shareholder Activism for the Next Frontier of Corporate Governance: Sustainable Economic Development*, Working Paper No. 1080 (Ross School of Business, University of Michigan, March 2007), 23–24.

446 J. Quarter, et al., "Special Investment by Union-based Pension Funds and Labour-Sponsored Investment Funds in Canada," *Industrial Relations* 56(1) (2001): 92, 108.

447 D. Hess, "Protecting and Politicizing Public Pension Fund Assets: Empirical Evidence on the Effects of Governance Structures and Practices," *University of California-Davis Law Review* 39(1) (2005): 187, 199; S.S. Taylor, *Public Employee Retirement Systems: The Structure and Politics of Teacher Pensions* (Cornell University Press, 1986).

448 J. Weststar and A. Verma, "What Makes for Effective Labor Representation on Pension Boards?" *Labor Studies Journal* 32(4) (2007): 382.

449 R.L. Deaton, *The Political Economy of Pensions: Power, Politics and Social Change in Canada, Britain and the United States* (University of British Columbia Press, 1989).

450 T. Schuller and J. Hyman, "Forms of Ownership and Control: Decision-making within a Financial Institution," *Sociology* 18(1) (1984): 51; Weststar and Verma, note 448.

to satisfy some particular part of the membership by being definitive about the kinds of investments to be prohibited would simply lead some other part of the membership to feel disadvantaged, or worse, disenfranchised in the decision making process. At worst, screens could lead to litigation on the part of those who feel that the risk accepted or returns realized had negatively affected their pension promise.[451]

Such dilemmas of course are not reasons to abandon democratic imperatives in pension fund governance; they could exist regardless of how trustees were appointed. But these difficulties should remind us of the need to shore up the skills and training of fiduciaries to enable ethical investment.

E. PARTICIPATION IN CISs

Mutual funds and other types of CISs operate on the assumption that most investors are not interested in getting involved in investment decisions,[452] on the basis that they are too busy or unqualified. Investors are considered as customers buying financial products, rather than as active owners of investment assets.[453] Mutual funds emerged to cater to people who do not wish to invest in the stock market themselves, but prefer to delegate responsibility to fund managers who can offer portfolio diversification, economies of scale, and other risk-management strategies seemingly unintelligible to most individual investors. Reflective of the rational apathy view of investors, the Investment Funds Institute of Canada (a lobby group for the mutual fund industry) explains:

> [m]utual fund investors, by conscious choice, pay to have management issues competently addressed on their behalf. They will thus be ill-motivated and disinclined to become involved in precisely the types of matters that they have already paid to have dealt with and resolved for them.[454]

---

451 *Report of the Ad Hoc Committee on Socially Responsible Investment* (Ontario Teachers' Pension Plan Board, June 2005), 18.

452 Personal communication, Glorianne Stromberg, former Commissioner of the Ontario Securities Commission (Toronto, November 20, 2006).

453 D.T. Llewellyn, "Issues in the Governance of Mutuals in the Financial Sector," Paper commissioned for the Myners enquiry into *Governance of Life Mutuals* (December 4, 2004), 10.

454 Investment Funds Institute of Canada (IFIC), *IFIC Response to CSA Mutual Fund Governance Concept Proposal 81-402* (IFIC, June 4, 2002), 3.

Most docile investors appear to give little attention to their fund's investment prospectus or annual report. At best, they simply wish to know about bottom-line financial performance, as reflected in the quarterly performance statements. If dissatisfied, they can simply exercise their right to withdraw their funds.

Unlike many pension plan beneficiaries, investors in mutual funds typically have some rights, on paper, regarding major changes to their fund. In the US, the *Investment Company Act* requires that major decisions concerning the investment company—such as to close a mutual fund to new investors, to change its investment strategy, to modify restrictions on investments, or to terminate funds—must be submitted to the board of directors and, in some cases, submitted to the shareholders.[455] Normally, the investment company can deviate from its official investment policy only by a majority vote of its outstanding voting securities.[456] The independent directors (who comprise at least 40 percent of the board) can play a pivotal role in the fund governance, to select service providers and to monitor the adequacy of internal controls and compliance programs.[457] Similar member rights in fund governance also exist in some other jurisdictions, such as in Australia under the *Managed Investments Act* of 1998. However, these control mechanisms of independent directors and member voting rights are largely absent in the Continental European funds, which rely on mechanisms such as an independent depository and independent auditors to ensure accountable governance.[458]

In practice, the notion of "mutual" has been taken out of the mutual fund business. Most funds are effectively controlled by large financial conglomerates rather than investing shareholders. The investment company that organized the mutual fund and formulated its investment policy, controls the fund's promotion and administration, and appointed the specialist asset manager, is the driving force behind the fund.[459] As mutual fund companies are

455 Pozen, note 295, 22.
456 Section 80(a)-3.
457 Section 80(a)-16.
458 J. Thompson, *Corporate Governance and Collective Investment Instruments* (OECD, 2001) (noting at 13 that "[t]he investor has no particular rights in selecting the management of the company or in changing the investment policy of the CIS").
459 M. Sargent, "Mutual Fund Regulation in the Next Millennium Symposium Panels: I. Fund Governance," *New York Law School Law Review* 44 (2001): 431, 433–36.

increasingly drawn under goliath financial conglomerates, the reigns of control are pulled further away from individual shareholders.[460]

Crucially, investment companies and the fund managers also control the powers to vote the portfolio shares and to file resolutions. The investors typically hold only the beneficial ownership interest in those securities, which does not afford them the right to assert control over how their interest is exercised. The fund managers effectively enjoy a free reign, which one prominent commentator on the US mutual fund industry describes as the "triumph of salesmanship over stewardship."[461] Collusion with corporate management, trading scandals, and inflated commissions, all to the cost of investors, contributed to the SEC's 2003 regulation requiring mutual funds to publicly disclose how they vote proxies (discussed in detail in the next chapter).[462]

Canadian securities regulators adopted a similar disclosure requirement in 2005.[463] They also introduced a new governance institution, the "independent review committee," to deal with the potential for conflict of interest in investment transactions.[464] Unfortunately, the opportunity to use this institution as a means to provide some voice for investors in mutual fund governance was not availed. The committee must have some members "independent" of the fund, although they are not appointed from among the unit-holders. The responsibilities of the independent review committee are also very limited and do not extend to reviewing the appropriateness of investment policies. However, the committee may have a collateral benefit: the Ontario Securities Commission advises that the situations where the committee could issue a standing instruction to the fund manager include the "manager's ongoing voting of proxies on securities held by the investment fund when the manager has a business relationship with the issuer of the securities ..."[465]

---

460 J.C. Brogle, *The Battle for the Soul of Capitalism* (Yale University Press, 2005), 178–79.

461 Ibid., 141.

462 SEC, *Disclosure of Proxy Voting Policies and Proxy Voting Records by Registered Management Investment Companies* (January 31, 2003), 17 CFR Parts 239, 249, 270, and 274.

463 Canadian Securities Administrators (CSA), *National Instrument 81–106 Investment Fund Continuous Disclosure and Companion Policy 81-106CP* (CSA, 2005).

464 Canadian Securities Administrators (CSA), *National Instrument 81-107. Independent Review Committee for Investment Funds* (CSA, 2005).

465 Ontario Securities Commission (OSC), *National Instrument 81-107 Independent Review Committee for Investment Funds—Supplement to the OSC Bulletin* (OSC, July 28, 2006), 132.

Among dedicated SRI funds, generally no special emphasis is placed on members' participation. One might think that the democratic and ethical objectives of such funds would extend to their own internal governance. A few funds however take positive steps to consult formally and informally with investors. Ethical Funds Company, for example, uses annual member surveys to gauge investors' views on social, ethical, and environmental issues. It also maintains systems for dealing with correspondence from members.[466] Domini Social Investments has similar arrangements to liaise with its members, and it operates an internet blog to allow clients to voice opinions and shares views.[467] Generally, however, SRI funds provide only an informal space for additional information gathering, but no actual "participation."[468] The SRI fund providers' justification for excluding members from policy-making, on issues such as what investments should be screened on ethical grounds, is that it is nearly impossible to find unanimity among fund members.[469] The SRI fund industry places more weight on transparency, disclosing to prospective investors the portfolio selection criteria and engagement practices.

Admittedly, compared to pension funds, the democratic imperative is less compelling for mutual funds. Investors can shop for funds offering portfolios that meet their ethical and financial goals. They can exit funds that betray their values. By contrast, pension plan beneficiaries are normally tied to the fund provided by their employer, and they may not have the option of switching to another pension plan even if they are dissatisfied. An exception is a pioneering Australian legislation in 2005 that gave superannuation scheme contributors the right to choose their preferred fund.[470] The lack of participation in mutual funds still remains a concern to the extent that it denies investors the opportunity to engage in ethical debates about investment policy. While a market that offers a choice of funds may seem an unalloyed benefit,

---

466 Personal communication, Robert Walker, Vice-President, Ethical Funds Company (November 2, 2006); and see the explanation on the Ethical Funds website, at: http://www.ethicalfunds.com/do_the_right_thing/sri/ethical_principles_criteria.

467 Personal communication, Adam Kanzer, Managing Director and General Counsel, Domini Social Investments (November 5, 2007); and see http://blog.kld.com.

468 C.J. Cowton, "Playing by the Rules: Ethical Criteria at an Ethical Investment Fund," *Business Ethics* 8(1) (1999): 60, 64.

469 Personal communication, anonymous, Canadian fund manager (Toronto, December 5, 2006).

470 *Superannuation Legislation Amendment (Choice of Superannuation Funds) Act,* 2005 (Cth).

if it is a benefit, then it is one that comes at the price of an SRI market driven by salesmanship and retail ethics. Though retail investors may make their ethical deliberations and choices *before* they select a mutual fund, such deliberations may be limited to private reflections, devoid of the interactive experience provided by collective, ethical deliberations.

F. CREDIT UNIONS

Credit unions are relatively small players in the financial markets; in theory, they are the most democratically governed.[471] As a cooperative, they are "owned by those who use them, not by investors or partners whose interest is to make a profit from them."[472] The credit union model arose precisely to assist and involve people, often sharing common bonds such as occupation or residence, who had experienced struggles obtaining credit and other financial services.[473] The ethos of the contemporary credit union movement is reflected in the International Cooperative Alliance's cooperatives principles of 1995, which include "voluntary and open membership," "democratic member control," and "member economic participation."[474] Thus, credit unions should be able to involve members in investment policy and sustainable development financing—more readily than any other financiers, in theory.

The co-operative status of credit unions gives them a different organizational structure than the stockholder-owned commercial banks and insurance companies. Internationally, credit union legislation commonly contains several key democratic features. Members hold shares in their credit union. Unlike a corporation, credit union elections are based on a one-member, one-vote structure. This rule gives members formally an equal voice in the management of the credit union. Members are not only the shareholders, but typically, they are also the consumers of credit union services (loans), the suppliers of capital to credit unions (deposits), and frequently, the managers of credit union operations (serving voluntarily on the governing board or

471 See K. Arness and B. Howcroft, "Corporate Governance Structures and the Comparative Advantage of Credit Unions," *Corporate Governance: An International Review* 9(1) (2001): 59.

472 B. Fairbairn, *The Meaning of Rochdale: The Rochdale Pioneers and the Cooperative Principles*, Occasional Paper Series (Centre for the Study of Co-operatives, University of Saskatchewan, 1994).

473 A. McArthur, A. McGregor, and R. Stewart, "Credit Unions and Low-income Communities," *Urban Studies* 30(2) (1993): 399.

474 Http://www.ica.coop.

advisory committees). These features may attenuate the agency problems that arise in corporate or pension fund governance.

Technically, the members own their credit unions. Traditionally, credit union memberships have been restricted to those persons with a common bond, for instance by residence or employment.[475] Common bond requirements have been relaxed by the law in many countries (e.g., in Australia and the US), although they may remain as part of a credit union's constitution. In the US, the *Credit Union Membership Access Act* of 1998 allows for single credit unions to represent a variety of members from different occupational or associational backgrounds.[476] While the common bond has been diluted, credit union legislation still consistently insists on membership status to access credit union services and to participate in union governance.[477] Only members can borrow or deposit funds at a credit union; and only members can serve as directors.

Voting and other participation rights are integral to the credit union democratic ideal. The concepts that only individuals shall be members of a credit union, that one member shall have one vote, and that there will be no proxy voting, are core legislative standards. As one example, the US *Federal Credit Union Act* of 1934 provides that "[n]o member shall be entitled to vote by proxy, but a member . . . may vote through an agent designated for the purpose. Irrespective of the number of shares held, no member shall have more than one vote."[478] Similar provisions are found in other jurisdictions.[479] Canada's *Cooperative Credit Associations Act* of 1991 illustrates the extent of members' rights to participate in decision-making at an annual meeting of a credit union: "any member may . . . submit to the association notice of any matter that the member proposes to raise at the meeting . . . and . . . discuss at the meeting any matter in respect of which the member would have been entitled to submit a proposal."[480]

While credit unions have the appearance of a bastion of grass-roots, democratic financial management, the reality is somewhat different, and has been for some time. Writing in 1981, Christopher Axworthy commented on

475 See World Council of Credit Unions (WCCU), *Guide to International Credit Union Legislation* (WCCU, 2005).
476 Pub. L. No. 105-219, 112 Stat. 913, s 2.
477 Hudson, note 112, 276–94.
478 Pub. L. No. 73-467, c. 750, 48 Stat. 1216, s. 1760.
479 E.g., UK's *Credit Unions Act*, 1979, s. 5(9); New Zealand's *Friendly Societies and Credit Unions Act*, 1982, s. 106(8).
480 Section 152(1).

Canadian credit unions: "[f]rom a practical point of view, co-operatives often appear to function in a similar way to traditional businesses . . . credit unions have been economically successful, but in the process they have moved away from their two main assets—their members and their community roots . . ."[481] Credit unions in many OECD countries face challenges surviving in a deregulated market with brutal competition from much larger, commercial banks. Many credit unions have merged to survive. The resulting fewer but larger unions are increasingly losing their original constitution as local, community-based institutions.[482] Mergers have strengthened the solvency of credit unions and improved their services, but possibly diminished their community ties and democratic moorings.[483] Conversely, in developing countries, a thriving microfinance movement involving credit unions remains a beacon of hope that this sector can continue to demonstrate grass-roots financing for sustainable development.[484]

VII. Conclusions

While the legal system does not explicitly ban SRI, it certainly blunts it. This chapter has examined three areas where financial sector regulation has created obstacles to SRI. The next chapter will canvass some legal reforms to facilitate SRI.

One problem from an SRI perspective is the normative lacunae at the international level. Quite simply, there is no international legal framework that squarely addresses the social and environmental impacts of transnational finance. Even with regard to "traditional" regulatory subjects, only a patchwork of partial controls and standards exists at the international level. Thus, the acquisitive demands of global capital face few official legal barriers. This regulatory void has been left to civil society and market institutions

---

481 C.S. Axworthy, "Credit Unions in Canada: The Dilemma of Success," *University of Toronto Law Journal* 31(1) (1981): 72.

482 J.A. Goddard and D.C. McKillop, *The Growth of US Credit Unions* (Credit Union Research, 2001); M. Klinedinst and H. Sato, "The Japanese Cooperative Sector," *Journal of Economic Issues* 28(2) (1994): 509.

483 See S.K. Kaushik and R.H. Lopez, "The Structure and Growth of the Credit Union Industry in the United States: Meeting Challenges of the Market," *American Journal of Economics and Sociology* 53(2) (1994): 219.

484 M. Robinson, *The Microfinance Revolution: Sustainable Finance for the Poor* (World Bank, 2005).

themselves to fill, through voluntary codes of conduct and other soft law instruments, which chapter 6 examines.

At a national level, two legal barriers to SRI are the fiduciary duties of institutional investors and their undemocratic governance. These factors tend to reinforce each other. Fiduciary duties are commonly premised on the "best interests" of the beneficiaries defined in narrow financial terms and the beneficiary investors concomitantly cast in largely passive and voiceless roles. Although we might interpret fiduciary duties to require consideration of wider societal concerns that may affect the best interests of beneficiaries, there is presently no concrete basis upon which other stakeholders, owed no duty by the fiduciary, could assert their interests. Even beneficiaries face obstacles to having a voice in investment decisions. Stakeholder pressure has leveraged some regulatory concessions, such as greater informational rights and mostly token representation on pension plans' governing committees and boards. But no serious challenge has been mounted against the dominion of fund managers and other investment cadres.

In mutual funds, catering to retail investors, the market provides a surrogate means of "choice" and "participation." Mutual funds have more flexibility to address diverse social and environmental goals than pension plans and other financiers. Fiduciary duties do not substantially hinder such goals. They allow mom and dad investors to shop for policies that meet their ethical or financial needs, and to exit funds that do not. What could be fairer? Yet, lacking a forum where investors can debate and meaningfully consider investment policies, what the SRI mutual funds offer is a retail ethics, on a take-it-or-leave-it basis. Transparency reforms to improve disclosures to investors target dubious selling practices and dodgy investment customs that have contributed to a greedy and short-sighted fund management culture. Regulation has not yet taken the next step to allow investors and other stakeholders to partake in fund governance.

Credit unions, at the fringes of the financial sector, promise democratic governance and community-based investment. They probably come closest among financiers to the sustainable development ideals. Yet, in deregulated, global financial markets, credit unions often just wilt away. Competing against much bigger players, many have either died or merged, thus becoming less community-like to survive.

Finally, while the legal system critically shapes financial markets and SRI, it is certainly not omnipresent. Although markets do not exist in a state of nature, without a legal framework, neither do they necessarily yield easily to legal intervention and control. Non-state actors can sometimes be more effective than governments at wielding influence in the market. For instance, although before 2001 Canadian company legislation created significant hurdles to shareholder resolutions on SRI issues, in some cases investors were able to informally engage firms or generate media publicity to provide leverage for change.[485] Yet, just as the legal system does not always hinder SRI for determined social investors, despite contrary appearances, legal measures to promote SRI do not necessarily work in practice, as the following chapter explains.

---

485 E. Ellmen, "Socially Conscious Investors Hobbled by Old Legislation: Clause that Allows Corporations to Exclude Proposals Needs Reform," *Globe and Mail*, March 9, 2000, B15.

CHAPTER 5

SRI Regulation

I. The Impetus to SRI Governance

A. MAKING FINANCIERS ACCOUNTABLE

Some four decades of environmental law-making in the modern era has mitigated but hardly ended humanity's abuse of nature.[1] The economy's unsustainable path is linked to environmental policy-makers' disavowal of the financial sector. Environmental regulation has historically governed companies and organizations that most visibly consume or pollute the environment. They have been obliged, with varying degrees of success, to observe certain requirements such as obtaining licenses for exploiting resources or adopting pollution control technologies. However, regulations have not traditionally included the financial sector that capitalizes companies and projects that may harm the environment. Thus, in this context, we can consider financiers as the unseen polluters.

It is fair to ask, what can policy measures to target financiers accomplish that current "front-line" company-directed regulation cannot? If for instance authorities regulate a mining company's environmental impacts, how could regulating its financial sponsors be advantageous? There are several reasons why environmental law should address financial markets.

First, perfect regulation of front-line companies is a rarity. Poorly designed and inadequately enforced environmental laws handicap efforts to

---

1 See B.J. Richardson and S. Wood, eds, *Environmental Law for Sustainability* (Hart Publishing, 2006); D. Bodansky, J. Brunnée, and E. Hey, *The Oxford Handbook of International Environmental Law* (Oxford University Press, 2007).

promote sustainability. Even countries with relatively advanced environmental law systems are challenged by cross-border investments in jurisdictions with less rigorous environmental standards. Global finance enables investors to sponsor projects and firms in foreign jurisdictions lacking in equivalent or acceptable environmental standards. This of course begs the valid question that if environmental laws are often poorly designed, why would regulation of financial companies by the same environmental law-makers improve results? Targeting financial institutions will often require different kinds of regulation; rather than requiring banks to obtain pollution permits, as manufacturing firms do, for instance, SRI governance needs different policy instruments that motivate or compel financiers to consider the social and environmental ramifications of their decisions. If effective, targeting financiers to fill present regulatory lacunae may help decrease initiation of polluting developments. Ideally, such developments would never receive finance, or would have to be redesigned to meet sustainable development standards in order to secure affordable financing.

Thus, by requiring financiers to consider the social and environmental sequelae of the projects and organizations they finance, governments can work with the financial sector as surrogate regulators. Because of their diverse asset portfolios, institutional investors unlike individual companies are potentially in a position to take a broad perspective of the health of the economy including multifarious and long-term environmental threats. While chapter 3 highlighted obstacles to "universal investing," through better regulation these financiers could be harnessed as a means to propagate more environmentally enlightened economic activity. In recent years, regulatory systems in many countries have shifted towards more cooperative and flexible networks of governance, whereby states involve the market and civil societal institutions in defining and achieving public policy objectives. Through tax incentives, informational policy instruments, and sometimes regulatory "sticks," authorities can engage banks, pension funds, and other financiers to provide a means of amplifying primary regulatory standards throughout the economy. To illustrate, a government that provides tax concessions for investors of renewable energy projects will encourage more capital investments into such worthwhile schemes. Or, authorities may compel lenders to disclose how they seek to minimize the environmental impacts of their borrowers' projects. The insurance sector already undertakes to some extent such a surrogate regulatory role for pollution liability risks.[2] Money laundering controls,

---

2 B.J. Richardson, "Mandating Environmental Liability Insurance," *Duke Environmental Law and Policy Forum* 12(2) (2000): 293.

which require banks to report suspicious transactions, also illustrate the government's ability to harness financiers as surrogate regulators.[3]

However, treating financiers only as surrogate regulators may wrongly imply that they have only a positive role, by helping governments to regulate the "real" polluters —such as the Enrons and the ExxonMobils of the world. Direct regulation of financiers fixing direct culpability could illuminate this misconception. Thus, a third, and ultimately the most fundamental reason for targeting financiers is that in deriving profits from lending to companies responsible for environmentally degrading and socially harmful activities, they can also be considered accountable. Capital financing is instrumental to development choices; that those who enable, and benefit from, those choices through financial investment must also share in the responsibility is an argument with important practical implications. For example, imposing joint liability for reckless financing would potentially provide a larger pool of capital to compensate for environmental damage and deter lenders from financing future damage. Alternatively, regulators could impose obligations on institutional investors to promote sustainable development with prophylactic rules such as to assess the potential environmental impacts of their portfolios and to modify problematic investments.

Financial institutions were set up precisely to mobilize capital and to facilitate financial returns for investors. Anyone who has ever inquired at a bank about a personal loan, credit card, or mortgage, will understand that financial institutions do not want their capital idly sitting around. To quote a well-known aphorism, "money does not grow on trees." Rather, money has to be actively managed and be reinvested to generate profit. This pervasive drive to put capital to use, to make more capital, invariably creates an economic process that generates social and environmental changes as financial capital harnesses natural capital in creating new "wealth." Therefore, one solution in ensuring sustainable development is targeting regulation to financiers.

B. A TURNING POINT?

Encouragingly, in the last decade or so, some jurisdictions have begun to canvass a new style of environmental governance on financial institutions. A lattice of laws promoting SRI and research into new policy instruments is growing. Canada's National Roundtable on the Environment and Economy (NRTEE) indicates such a trend. It published a pioneering report in 2007,

---

3 A. Brown, "Money Laundering: A European and U.K. Perspective," *Journal of International Banking Law* 12(8) (1997): 307.

recommending ways for governments to steer and support capital markets to promote sustainability.⁴ Similar steps are being taken in the UK, Australia, and other countries.

However, these fledgling initiatives do not subject financiers to the same level of regulatory controls imposed on developers such as mining and manufacturing firms. The regulatory agenda, for now, is generally much less intrusive. SRI regulation has marginally touched investment activity, without imposing burdensome regulatory costs on financial markets. Thus, authorities have shown a preference for non-invasive mechanisms such as informational and incentive-based policy instruments. In the words of Canada's NRTEE: "we do not see the need for increased regulation, increased taxation, or increased interference in the normal value-creating activities of Canadian businesses."⁵ Authorities generally assume that financial institutions should not be considered "responsible" for environmental harm. Rather, the financial sector is depicted as being environmentally neutral, able to contribute positively to sustainable development if equipped with better information and incentives.

SRI reforms can be classified into several groups. First, some governments have established normative frameworks providing foundational principles and guidance for "best practices" to improve performance. Normative guidelines occur in SRI mandates given to national pension funds, but otherwise are rare. Second, another governance technique is process standards enabling assessment, verification, and communication of performance. Informational policy instruments such as sustainability reporting standards, proxy voting disclosures, pension funds' publication of SRI policies, and other transparency measures are commonly used. Another kind of process standard reform has targeted corporate governance to facilitate shareholder advocacy. Third, economic incentive mechanisms serve to correct market failures and tilt the balance in favor of a business case for responsible investment. Such mechanisms range from taxation incentives for SRI to lender liability for pollution.

Several interwoven factors have shaped these regulatory predispositions, among which is neoliberalism. This ideology has influenced many nations, in varying degrees, guiding policy prescriptions ranging from privatization of state assets, governance of financial markets, and market-based environmental controls. "Financialization" of the economy has been a core part of the

---

4 NRTEE, *Capital Markets and Sustainability: Investing in a Sustainable Future. State of the Debate Report* (NRTEE, 2007).
5 Ibid., 3.

neoliberal agenda.[6] Its impact has spread extensively throughout developing countries, under the aegis of World Bank and International Monetary Fund policies.[7] Neoliberalism posits that the state and the market should reinforce the motivation of individual self-interest, and that markets provide the most efficient means of allocating resources and maximizing social wealth.[8] At the center of this discourse is the notion of inevitability: that "economic forces cannot be resisted."[9] Thus, neoliberal policy prescriptions usually de-emphasize onerous command-and-control regulation in favor of leveraging on market forces through voluntary codes, economic incentives, and cooperative partnerships between the state and the business sector.

However, countervailing pressures for more assertive market governance persist from the anti-globalization movement, environmental NGOs, church groups, and growing public anxiety about climate change and other environmental threats.[10] These have moderated the neoliberal agenda. SRI has deep historical roots and certainly is not a protégé of neoliberalism. Yet, the recent shift from ethical to business case SRI is intertwined with the wider reconfiguration of the relationship between the state and the market. Therefore, while emerging SRI governance has elements of the deregulatory agenda, it contains disparate techniques and objectives reflective of its often turbulent political context.

Gently incorporating the financial sector into environmental policy development also partly reflects a new characterization of environmental problems. Traditionally, regulation was based on an underlying premise that environmental problems are best addressed where they physically occur and where impacts lie, associated with images of fuming smokestacks, leaking pipelines, and the like. Yet, many of today's most urgent environmental problems have emerged slowly and surreptitiously, through cumulative

---

6 L. Assassi, A. Nesvetailova, and D. Wigan, "Global Finance in the New Century: Deregulation and Beyond," in *Global Finance in the New Century: Beyond Deregulation*, eds L. Assassi, A. Nesvetailova, and D. Wigan (Palgrave Macmillan, 2007), 1, 3.

7 S. Soederberg, *The Politics of the New International Financial Architecture: Reimposing Neoliberal Domination in the Global South* (Zed Books, 2004).

8 A. Saad-Filho and D. Johnston, eds, *Neoliberalism: A Critical Reader* (Pluto Press, 2005); D. Harvey, *A Brief History of Neoliberalism* (Oxford University Press, 2005).

9 P. Bourdieu, *Acts of Resistance: Against Tyranny of the Market* (New Press, 1998), 31.

10 C. Rootes, "Globalisation, Environmentalism and the Global Justice Movement," *Environmental Politics* 14(5) (2005): 692.

activities from numerous and highly dispersed sources, not effectively targeted by existing point-source regulation.[11] These include climate change, persistent organic pollutants in the food chain, and erosion of biodiversity. Greenhouse gases and ozone-depleting chemicals are invisible, for instance. Causal connection is difficult as these insidious environmental problems are often widely disconnected by time and space.

Therefore, environmental policy instruments must do more than target mere end-of-pipe sources. They must also address the underlying processes in the economy that fuel unsustainable practices. As Paul Thompson explains, "the number of industries under fire from environmentalists has grown very rapidly from a few 'smokestack' industries to include all constituents of the supply chain, with banking now very much in the firing line."[12] Yet, state regulation of this vast domain of economic activity poses levels of coerciveness that are impracticable and unacceptable to most policymakers and the business sector. Thus, authorities have turned to market-based instruments promising more flexible and cooperative ways to address environmental threats.[13]

Other models of regulation have also been advanced to address these environmental challenges. One approach, found in SRI regulation, is described as "reflexive law." Rejecting the social-democrat dreams of harnessing the state as a means of social and economic reform, guided by scientific-rational planning and social-engineering through the means of law, reflexive regulation modestly confines itself to controlling the internal organization of corporations in the hope of encouraging more socially responsible behavior.[14] Reflexive law aims to promote self-regulation within companies by restructuring their internal decision-making to facilitate more consideration of the interests of other stakeholders and social norms.[15]

Another governance model informing SRI and other environmental regulation is ecological modernization. Essentially, it treats environmental

---

11 B. Adam, *Timescapes of Modernity: The Environment and Invisible Hazards* (Routledge, 1998).

12 P. Thompson, "Bank Lending and the Environment: Policies and Opportunities," *International Journal of Bank Marketing* 16 (1998): 243, 243.

13 T.L. Anderson and D.R. Leal, *Free Market Environmentalism* (Pacific Research Institute for Public Policy, 1991), 24–35; R. Stroup, R.E. Meiners, and W.K. Viscusi, eds, *Cutting Green Tape: Toxic Pollutants, Environmental Regulation and the Law* (Transaction Publishers, 2000).

14 E.A. Christodoulidis, *Law and Reflexive Politics* (Kluwer Law, 2002).

15 S.E. Gaines and C. Kimber, "Redirecting Self-Regulation," *Journal of Environmental Law* 13(2001): 157.

risks as challenges arising from inefficient use of natural resources: that economic development can be made sustainable through technological innovation, managerial know-how, and the entrepreneurial spirit.[16] Ecological modernization has optimistic visions of various scenarios where what is good for the environment is also good for business, based on the notion that cutting waste improves market competitiveness and profitability.[17]

This chapter further delves into the regulatory and political issues outlined above, setting the context of SRI governance. Several sections then examine the various regulatory and policy measures promoting SRI. Included among these are informational policy instruments such as mandatory environmental reporting and SRI policy disclosure rules; economic instruments such as taxation concessions for SRI; the less common "harder" measures such as liability of financiers for social and environmental impacts; and direct regulations, including responsible investing requirements for public sector and state-sponsored pension funds.

II. Regulatory Design for Sustainability Challenges in Financial Markets

A. FROM THE REGULATORY STATE TO REGULATORY GOVERNANCE

The widespread failure of states to stem environmental degradation is often attributed to their methods of regulation. The regulatory state, associated with the norms and institutions of the welfare state, relies on instruments of public ownership, hierarchical and coercive "command-and-control" regulation, and state provision of services and benefits.[18] While these techniques have

---

16 S. Young, *The Emergence of Ecological Modernisation: Integrating the Environment and the Economy?* (Routledge, 2001).

17 E. Cohen-Rosenthal and J. Musnikow, eds, *Eco-Industrial Strategies: Unleashing Synergy between Economic Development and the Environment* (Greenleaf Publishing, 2003).

18 C.R. Sunstein, "Paradoxes of the Regulatory State," *University of Chicago Law Review* 57 (1990): 407; M. Loughlin and C. Scott. "The Regulatory State," in *Developments in British Politics*, eds P. Dunleavy, et al. (Macmillan, 1997), 5; M. Moran, "Understanding the Regulatory State," *British Journal of Political Science* 32 (2002): 391.

undoubtedly helped to tackle many social and economic ills, their suitability for controlling complex environmental issues is questionable on various grounds.[19]

One of these grounds is the operational complexity resulting from the sheer volume and breadth of regulatory controls. The enormous extension and intensification of environmental standards and rules worldwide since the 1970s display signs of "hyper-regulation"[20] or "juridification."[21] The dense maze of legal controls often appears to have reached the point of diminishing marginal returns: the effectiveness of further regulation outweighed by the administrative costs and poor compliance, resulting in escalation of unresolved social conflicts. Thus, modern environmental law is often strained by its "fragmentation, gaps, overlaps and inconsistencies."[22]

Gunther Teubner and his proponents contend that the cognitive limits of such regulation are linked to the "differentiation" of modern society into various semi-autonomous subsystems.[23] According to Niklas Luhmann's theory of autopoiesis (meaning self-production), the economy, civil society and other such subsystems function self-referentially.[24] Having developed its own operational codes, protocols, and means of communication, a subsystem can respond only to problems defined by its own terms. Thus, the legal subsystem, emphasizing rights, duties, and rules, cannot readily shape the market built around norms of money, exchange, competition, and profit. The legal system functions as just one of many social subsystems in a milieu lacking a single dominant mechanism to direct and coordinate action. Consequently, believe Teubner and Luhmann, policy-makers must limit themselves to using less ambitious, market-compatible tools to influence

19 See, e.g., P.C. Yeager, *The Limits of Law: The Public Regulation of Private Pollution* (Cambridge University Press, 1991); Stroup, Meiners, and Viscusi, note 13.

20 R. Susskind, *The Future of Law: Facing the Challenges of Information Technology* (Clarendon Press, 1996).

21 G. Teubner, "Juridification: Concepts, Aspects, Limits, Solutions," in *A Reader on Regulation*, eds R. Baldwin, C. Scott, and C. Hood (Oxford University Press, 1998), 389, 398.

22 R.B. Stewart, "A New Generation of Environmental Regulation?" *Capital University Law Review* 29 (2001): 21, 30–31.

23 G. Teubner, *Law as an Autopoietic System* (Blackwell, 1994); A.J. Jacobson, "Autopoietic Law: The New *Science* of Niklas Luhmann," *Michigan Law Review* 87 (1989): 1647.

24 N. Luhmann, *Ecological Communication* (Polity Press, 1986); N. Luhmann, *The Differentiation of Society* (Columbia University Press, 1982); see also Teubner's later contributions: "How the Law Thinks: Toward a Constructivist Epistemology of Law," *Law and Society Review* 23 (1989): 727.

the behavior of economic actors rather than to attempt to engineer grand change through interventionist, prescriptive controls. As Teubner suggests, "the corporate world will not observe legal norms as precise normative commands requiring obedience. Rather, this world perceives legal norms highly selectively and reconstructs them in a wholly different meaning context."[25]

While empirical evidence may not entirely support such theories, certainly many nations have experienced substantial legal innovations lately. Recent state-market realignments have shifted the regulatory state towards regulatory governance, creating greater roles for markets and, to a lesser extent, civil society institutions. These changes have been particularly pronounced in environmental governance.[26] Commentators have advanced the notions of "mutual regulation,"[27] "self-organization,"[28] "responsive regulation,"[29] "reflexive adaptation"[30] "smart regulation,"[31] and "post-regulatory governance,"[32] both descriptively and prescriptively. Paradoxically, however, there has also been some countervailing expansion of states' legal capacity to correct market abuses and unresolved impacts, particularly following more recent corporate scandals.[33]

---

25 G. Teubner, "The Invisible *Cupola*: From Causal to Collective Attribution in Ecological Liability," *Cardozo Law Review* 16(2) (1994): 429, 451.

26 E.g., B.C. Karkkainen, "Default Rules in Private and Public Law: Extending Default Rules Beyond Purely Economic Relationships: Information-Forcing Environmental Regulation," *Florida State University Law Review* 33 (2006): 861, 861–63.

27 See P. Simmons and B. Wynne, *State, Market and Mutual Regulation? SocioEconomic Dimensions of the Environmental Regulation of Business* (Lancaster University, 1994).

28 G. Teubner, L. Farmer, and D. Murphy, eds, *Environmental Law and Ecological Responsibility: The Concept and Practice of Ecological Self-Organisation* (John Wiley and Sons, 1994).

29 I. Ayres and J. Braithwaite, *Responsive Regulation: Transcending the Deregulation Debate* (Oxford University Press, 1992).

30 E.J. Kane, "Reflexive Adaptation of Business to Regulation and Regulation to Business," *Law and Policy* 15(3) (1993): 179.

31 N. Gunningham and P. Grabosky, *Smart Regulation: Designing Environmental Policy* (Oxford University Press, 1998).

32 C. Scott, "Regulation in the Age of Governance: The Rise of the Post Regulatory State," in *The Politics of Regulation: Institutions and Regulatory Reforms for the Age of Governance*, eds J. Jordana and D. Levi-Faur (Edward Elgar Publishing, 2004), 145.

33 J.W. Ciofii, *Corporate Governance Reform, Regulatory Politics, and the Foundations of Finance Capitalism in the United States and Germany*, CLPE Research Paper 1/2005 (Comparative Research in Law and Political Economy, York University, 2005), 1–2.

These regulatory changes are not confined to the juridical space within individual states, but transcend national boundaries. Eliminating barriers against trade and other economic activities has curtailed individual states' ability to perform unilateral actions that protect local economies, while at the same time the elimination of these barriers has enhanced corporate power.[34] Scholars depict a progressive diffusion of regulatory power among global networks of state and non-state actors.[35] These transnational networks have been particularly influential for SRI, such as the various initiatives under the auspices of the UN including the UNEPFI and the UNPRI.

Among the common elements of these so-called "decentered" forms of regulation are the preference for legal systems that are "less heavy-handed, and more responsive to the demands and possibilities of their context"[36] and also, the enlistment of non-state actors in regulatory governance. Teubner describes reflexive law as one of these approaches —a system of regulation that does not seek coercive policy direction but confines itself to the "regulation of organization, procedures and the redistribution of competences."[37] With the vision that governance should occur through the internal reconfiguration of decision-making within corporations, detailed regulatory prescription is thus replaced by mechanisms encouraging internal reflection, learning, and behavioral changes. Thus, the function of law is recast from direct control to "procedural" control.[38] For environmental policy,

---

34 R. Boyer and D. Drache, *States against Markets: The Limits of Globalization* (Routledge, 1996).

35 A.M. Slaughter, "Global Government Networks, Global Information Agencies, and Disaggregated Democracy," *Michigan Journal of International Law* 24 (2003): 1041, 1059.

36 J. Steele and T. Jewell, "Law in Environmental Decision-Making," in *Law in Environmental Decision-Making. National, European and International Perspectives*, eds T. Jewell and J. Steele (Clarendon Press, 1998), 1, 14; see further D. Osborne and T. Gaebler, *Reinventing Government: How the Entrepreneurial Spirit is Transforming the Public Sector* (Addison-Wesley Publishing, 1992); J. Black, "Decentring Regulation: Understanding the Role of Regulation and Self-Regulation in a 'Post-Regulatory World'," *Current Legal Problems* 54 (2001): 103.

37 G. Teubner, "Social Order from Legislative Noise? Autopoietic Closure as a Problem for Legal Regulation," in *State, Law, Economy as Autopoietic Systems: Regulation and Autonomy in a New Perspective*, ed. G. Teubner (Giuffrè, 1992); G. Teubner, "After Legal Instrumentalism?" in *Dilemmas of Law in the Welfare State*, ed. G. Teubner (Walter De Gruyter, 1986), 222.

38 J. Black, "Proceduralising Regulation: Part I," *Oxford Journal of Legal Studies* 20 (2000): 597.

Eric Orts describes reflexive law as seeking "to encourage internal self-critical reflection within institutions about their environmental performance. The primary regulatory method ... aims to set up processes that encourage institutional self-reflective thinking and learning about environmental effects."[39]

This trend towards decentered and market-modulated regulation dovetails with the Foucauldian notion of governance, which discounts the sovereign state (and state law) as the source of social norms or the paramount site of power. Like theories of political pluralism, governmental powers and governance norms are viewed by Foucault-influenced legal theorists as diffused and fragmented in a web of societal institutions.[40]

Thus, many jurisdictions increasingly rely on informational policy instruments, norms of self-governance, economic incentives, and contractual agreements to govern markets.[41] These regulatory changes are particularly important in SRI governance, and as the following chapter explains, they are becoming more associated with the "soft" end of the regulatory continuum. However, harder measures, such as outright bans on investments in certain nefarious activities, also remain possible, as the "responsive regulation" theory stresses a residual role for coercive law at the apex of regulatory control and an enforcement pyramid.[42]

B. THE POLITICAL ECONOMY OF ENVIRONMENTAL GOVERNANCE

The fragility of environmental law stems not only from operational constraints inhering in its chosen policy instruments. It also reflects the power of businesses. That power limits the scope for SRI regulation, as in

39 E.W. Orts, "Reflexive Environmental Law," *Northwestern University Law Review* 89(4) (1995): 1227, 1254; see further Teubner, Farmer, and Murphy, note 28.

40 A. Hunt, *Explorations in Law and Society: Towards a Constitutive Theory of Law* (Routledge, 1993).

41 See D.A. Farber, "Taking Slippage Seriously: Noncompliance and Creative Compliance in Environmental Law," *Harvard Environmental Law Review* 23 (1999): 297; A. Iles, "Adaptive Management: Making Environmental Law and Policy More Dynamic, Experimentalist and Learning," *Environmental and Planning Law Journal* 13 (1996): 288; E.W. Orts and K. Deketelaere, eds, *Environmental Contracts: Comparative Approaches to Regulatory Innovation in the United States and Europe* (Kluwer Law, 2000).

42 Ayres and Braithwaite, note 29.

other forms of regulation, which potentially undermine the position of holders of capital.

While the state exerts significant economic influence through its monetary policies and other mechanisms, it remains largely outside the realm of direct economic production and therefore "must either react *a posteriori* to events it cannot directly control and/or engage in ineffective *a priori* planning."[43] The state faces the ongoing dilemma between the need to restrict capital accumulation to minimize the environmental impacts that risk social turmoil, and the need to allow capital free reign to generate material wealth.[44] Environmental regulation is acutely problematic because it tends to increase economic actors' costs.[45] Since the 1970s major political disputes over forestry, nuclear power, and mining that pitch corporate power against civil groups have rocked Australia, the US, and other countries.[46] Environmentalists have lost many of these conflicts.

In capitalist societies, those who organize the economic process (i.e., primarily businesses) enjoy great strategic leverage in policy-making.[47] Business prosperity is crucial for preservation of political power. Governments at a time of reduced investment, unemployment, and other economic negatives,

---

43 B. Jessop, *State Theory: Putting Capitalist Societies in Their Place* (Pennsylvania State University Press, 1990), 356.

44 See K.J. Walker, "The State in Environmental Management: The Ecological Dimension," *Political Studies* 37(1) (1989): 25; C.E. Lindblom, "The Market as Prison," *Journal of Politics* 44(2) (1979): 324.

45 See D. Press, *Democratic Dilemmas in the Age of Ecology: Trees and Toxics in the American West* (Duke University Press, 1994).

46 E.g., B.J. Richardson, "A Study of Australian Practice Pursuant to the World Heritage Convention," *Environmental Policy and Law* 20(4–5) (1990): 146; I. Watson, *Fighting Over the Forests* (Allen and Unwin, 1990); D.S. Meyer, "Protest Cycles and Political Process: American Peace Movements in the Nuclear Age," *Political Research Quarterly* 46 (1993): 451.

47 See especially C.E. Lindblom, *Politics and Markets: The World's Political-Economic Systems* (Basic Books, 1977). The interests of particular businesses and industries are not however the same as the interests of capital as a whole. Businesses oppose each other through competition in the market. Companies in different economic sectors can have divergent interests. Climate change, for instance, is of concern to the insurance industry and fossil fuel industries for very different reasons, with the former supportive of government action and the latter mostly favoring inaction: P. Newell and M. Paterson, "A Climate for Business: Global Warming, the State and Capital," *Review of International Political Economy* 5(4) (1998): 679, 696.

typically suffer an abridged political agenda through electoral defeat.[48] Since the capitalist state's governance cannot rely on any substantive moral consensus, its political success is measured by its more neutral economic performance. Hannah Arendt describes the modern state as the *parens patriae* of a gigantic national household that it must feed, clothe, and shelter.[49] Politics are driven by the imperatives of national housekeeping, as sustained by economic growth.

The power of business, coupled with declining societal confidence in effective governance by the state, has contributed to more decision-making shifting to market institutions, including the financial sector.[50] Faced with systemic crises in public economic management including chronic budget deficits, during the 1980s governments began privatizing state services and assets and liberalizing market controls in the hope of increased cost efficiency and reduced regulatory burden on industry.[51] As a result, Britain, New Zealand, and the US have undertaken some of the most radical types of free market reforms. In these countries whole economic sectors such as energy supply, railways, airlines, and telecommunications have come under much greater market auspices. The *instruments* of public governance have also been revamped,[52] with more emphasis on market-friendly policy instruments, including information provision, financial incentives and contractual relationships, and delegation of responsibilities to private institutions.[53]

48 The evidence for this is legion: see W.P. Nordhaus, "The Political Business Cycle," *Review of Economic Studies* 42 (1975): 169; S. Brittan, "The Economic Contradictions of Democracy," *British Journal of Political Science* 5(1) (1975): 129.

49 H. *Arendt, The Human Condition* (University of Chicago Press, 1957).

50 C. James, C. Jones, and A. Norton, eds, *A Defence of Economic Rationalism* (Allen and Unwin, 1993); D. Boaz and E.H. Crane, eds, *Market Liberalism: A Paradigm for the 21st Century* (Cato Institute, 1993).

51 The literature is massive; see e.g., O. Letwin, *Privatizing the World: A Study of International Privatisation in Theory and Practice* (Cassell, 1988); B. Bortolotti and D. Siniscalco, *The Challenges of Privatization: An International Analysis* (Oxford University Press, 2004).

52 See D.J. Fiorino, "Towards a New System of Environmental Regulation: The Case for an Industry Sector Approach," *Environmental Law* 26(2) (1996): 457; A. Moran, "Tools of Environmental Policy: Market Instruments versus Command and Control," in *Markets, the State and the Environment: Towards Integration*, ed. R. Eckersley (Macmillan, 1995), 73.

53 C. Donnelly, *Delegation of Governmental Power to Private Parties: A Comparative Perspective* (Oxford University Press, 2007).

These trends may seem at odds with autopoietic theory, which implies that no single societal element can dominate.[54] Luhmann conceded that subsystems differ in their degree of organization, and that the one achieving the greatest organizational complexity and flexibility will tend to be more dominate. He suggested that in modern societies, the economic sector likely wields the most influence.[55] The power of capital, however, is not absolute. Companies depend on the state to create regulations that are clear and effective, yet not stifling to investment growth. They also depend on state policies for stemming social protest and removing the worst instances of ecological damage, possibly threatening the legitimacy of industry.[56] The pluralist perspective of political power suggests that government policy can factor all of the variable influence of a smorgasbord of interests, including social movements, community groups, trade unions, and others participating in democratic politics.[57] It posits that while business may exert considerable influence, that influence is conditional, rather than immutable.

Also, the state itself should be recognized as an object of regulation as much as an agent of regulation.[58] Bob Jessop chastises theorists who treat the state "as a mere epiphenomenon of an economic base and den[y] it any empirical influence on that base."[59] The organs of the state are not mere jostling arenas for rivaling social and economic concerns, but are to be reckoned with as powerful interests themselves.[60] Furthermore, the state is not a homogeneous "internally coherent, organizationally pure" system, but rather, involves a complex and somewhat contradictory amalgam of institutions, authorities, and procedures.[61] Thus, its environmental laws can be subject to deliberate legislative and agency sabotage by rival interests within the state. This interference

---

54 Luhmann, note 24.
55 Discussed in Jessop, note 43, 333.
56 J.S. Dryzek, "Ecology and Discursive Democracy: Beyond Liberal Capitalism and the Administrative State," in *Is Capitalism Sustainable? Political Economy and the Politics of Ecology*, ed. J. O'Connor (Guilford Press, 1994), 176, 179.
57 D. Held and J. Krieger, "Theories of the State: Some Competing Claims," in *The State in Capitalist Europe*, eds S. Bornstein, D. Held, and J. Krieger (Allen and Unwin, 1984), 1.
58 See T. Skocpol, R.E. Evans, and D. Rueschemeyer, *Bringing the State Back In* (Cambridge University Press, 1985).
59 Jessop, note 43, 37.
60 See especially the work of M. Foucault, *Discipline and Punish* (Tavistock, 1969); S. Hall, *Drifting into a Law and Order Society* (Cobden Trust, 1980) (discussing authoritarian statism).
61 Jessop, note 43, 316.

can arise at the legislative formation stages, as well as at the bureaucratic levels. Officials may seek to weaken regulatory standards and use delay tactics to hinder implementation. The territorial, turf-protecting culture of government bureaucracy fosters insular decision-making, such as the separation of financial regulation from other policy sector regulation. Finance ministries and environmental departments in states typically have different agendas and constituencies to serve, which undermines coordinated governmental regulation including policies for SRI.

C. SUSTAINABLE DEVELOPMENT AND ECOLOGICAL MODERNIZATION

Also shaping SRI regulation is the concept of "sustainability," which emerged in the late twentieth century as the dominant concept in environmental policy and discourse. In its most prevalent formulation, "sustainable development," it has been widely endorsed as a goal of states, international bodies, businesses, and NGOs. For example, sustainability has been enshrined in the EU's Treaty as a fundamental objective,[62] and it features in many international environmental treaties, multilateral development policies, national environmental strategies and legislation, and as we shall see, in SRI regulation.[63]

The sustainable development ideal seeks a responsible balance between the otherwise incongruous imperatives of unfettered economic exploitation of resources and the dependence of all life on healthy ecosystems. Most fundamentally, sustainability has been interpreted as implying consumption of renewable resources at their regeneration rate, and limiting waste and pollution to the assimilative capacity of the biosphere, thereby maintaining critical ecological processes and the biodiversity of the planet.[64] It is supported by the "polluter pays" principle requiring polluters to bear the expenses of pollution prevention and remediation (although rarely treating providers

62 Article 2, Consolidated version of the Treaty establishing the European Community, O.J. C. 340, (November 10, 1997).

63 M.C. Cordonier Segger and A. Khalfan, *Sustainable Development Law: Principles, Practices, and Prospects* (Oxford University Press, 2005); Richardson and Wood, note 1; S.A. Atapattu, *Emerging Principles of International Environmental Law* (Transnational Publishers, 2006); R.L. Revesz, P. Sands, and R.B. Stewart, *Environmental Law, the Economy and Sustainable Development: The United States, the European Union and the International Community* (Cambridge University Press, 2000).

64 H.E. Daly, "Toward Some Operational Principles of Sustainable Development," *Ecological Economics* 2 (1990): 1.

of capital as co-polluters). The precautionary principle of sustainability addresses situations of uncertainty regarding the environmental risks of development choices.[65] Sustainability also adheres to principles of social justice by requiring fair distribution of the benefits and burdens of environmental policy, as reflected in the cognate principles of inter- and intragenerational equity.[66] In the context of financial markets, sustainability has been packaged into the concept of "sustainable finance," where capital should be allocated with regard to environmental constraints.[67]

Sustainability concepts have directly informed vast swathes of environmental governance reform including SRI regulation. These involve both substantive environmental goals as well as the means of making environmental policy. These reforms include strategic environmental plans, framework laws and reconfigured regulatory agencies, policy tools such as pollution taxation and environmental liability, as well as democratic reforms widening participation in environmental decision-making.[68] Considerable effort has been expended into devising "sustainability indicators" to measure progress.[69] Overall, the sustainability discourse supports a more principled and strategic approach to environmental policy in contrast to earlier somewhat fragmented efforts.

Part of sustainability's appeal is its ambiguity and open-endedness, enabling numerous actors with divergent objectives to commonly embrace it.[70] The success of sustainability also derives from how its broad possible implications

65 N. de Sadeleer, ed., *Implementing the Precautionary Principles: Approaches from the Nordic Countries, the EU and USA* (Earthscan, 2007).

66 I. Voinovic, "Intergenerational and Intragenerational Equity Requirements for Sustainability," *Environmental Conservation* 22(3) (1995): 223; J.E. Roemer, *Intergenerational Equity and Sustainability* (Palgrave Macmillan, 2007).

67 M. Jeucken, *Sustainable Finance and Banking: The Financial Sector and the Future of the Planet* (Earthscan, 2001).

68 J.C. Dembach, "Sustainable Development as a Framework for National Governance," *Case Western Reserve Law Review* 49(1) (1998): 1; K. Ginther, et al., eds, *Sustainable Development and Good Governance* (Graham and Trotman, and Martinus Nijhoff, 1995); G.C. Bryner, "Policy Devolution and Environmental Law: Exploring the Transition to Sustainable Development," *Environs: Environmental Law and Policy Journal* 26(Fall) (2002): 1.

69 S. Bell and S. Morse, *Sustainability Indicators: Measuring the Immeasurable* (Earthscan, 1999).

70 A.D. Basiago, "Methods of Defining Sustainability," *Sustainable Development* 3 (1995): 109; K. Pezzoli, "Sustainable Development: A Transdisciplinary Overview of the Literature," *Journal of Environmental Planning and Management* 40(5) (1997): 549.

have been channeled and neutralized in ways expedient to economic and political elites.

The strength of the sustainability mantra has been muted through the rhetoric that environmental protection and economic growth can mutually reinforce each other.[71] It is presented as supporting a means to gain competitive advantages, to build new markets, and to improve production efficiency, rather than as defending absolute ecological limits on business activity.[72] This ideology also implies soft business advantages, such as improved relations with employees and local communities, and therefore fewer costly disputes.[73] And, crucially, it suggests that it can lead to a lower cost of capital for firms. Hence, this underpinning philosophy of "ecological modernization" has become one of the most influential paradigms of environmental policy.[74]

Ecological modernization accepts environmental degradation as a systematic result of the modern industrial "risk" society,[75] but believes that this degradation can be resolved through rational and technocratic methods. Ecological modernization does not renounce capitalism. Rather, it promises more efficient and careful use of environmental resources, implemented through a framework of industrial modernity, harnessing innovative technologies, business acumen, and managerial techniques.[76] Thus, pollution

---

71 On the potential symbiosis of environmental and economic concerns, see M.E. Porter and V. der Linde, "Green and Competitive: Ending the Stalemate," *Harvard Business Review* 73(5) (1995): 120.

72 E.g., WBCSD and UNEP, *Cleaner Production and Eco-Efficiency, Complementary Approaches to Sustainable Development* (WBCSD, 1998).

73 M. Grieg-Gran, *Financial Incentives for Improved Sustainability Performance: The Business Case and the Sustainability Dividend* (Institute for the Environment and Development, WBCSD, 2002), 5–6.

74 For a discussion of the central tenets of ecological modernization, see M.S. Andersen and I. Massa, "Ecological Modernisation —Origins, Dilemmas and Future Directions," *Journal of Environmental Policy and Planning* 2 (2000): 337; A. Gouldson and J. Murphy, "Ecological Modernization and the European Union," *Geoforum* 27(1) (1996): 11, 13–14; M. Hajer, *The Politics of Environmental Discourse: Ecological Modernisation and the Policy Process* (Oxford University Press, 1995); S. Young, ed., *The Emergence of Ecological Modernisation: Integrating the Environment and the Economy?* (Routledge, 2000).

75 U. Beck, *Ecological Politics in an Age of Risk*, trans. A. Weisz (Polity Press, 1995).

76 See especially J. Huber, *Die verlorene Unshuld der Okologie* (Fischer Verlag, 1982); M. Jänicke, *Staatsversagen. Die Ohnmacht der Politik in der Industriegesellschaft* (Piper, 1986).

prevention and sustainable practices can yield competitive advantages.[77] This outlook also informs the business case model of SRI, which sees environmental constraints as opportunities for better investment returns through improved environmental performance. Therefore, it deftly reframes the ethical and political dilemmas of industrialization as mere technical and managerial challenges.[78]

Ecological modernization also supports the movement for "smart regulation"[79] This policy oeuvre asserts that detailed prescriptive regulation is no longer sufficiently able to address many contemporary environmental threats. While the smart regulation discourse is not a protégé of neoliberalism, it accepts that market and civil societal actors already undertake much governance. Smart regulation proposes ways for the state to govern through these surrogate regulators, including negotiated agreements, economic instruments, auditing, reporting, and management systems. Ecological modernization underlies "smart" environmental law reforms in various countries.[80]

This incremental and reformist approach to sustainable development has not gone uncontested. The anti-globalization movement represents the most visible form of resistance.[81] Diverse campaigns from civil society advocacy networks have exposed the environmental and social impacts of firms and investors, keeping their influence on the sustainable development discourse somewhat in check.[82] Growing international alarms about climate change loom menacingly, and over coming decades will likely severely test

---

77 See further J. Elkington, "Towards the Sustainable Corporation: Win-Win-Win Business Strategies for Sustainable Development," *California Management Review* 36(2) (1994): 90.

78 S. Baker, "The Evolution of European Union Environmental Policy," in *The Politics of Sustainable Development: Theory, Policy and Practice within the European Union*, eds S. Baker, et al. (Routledge, 1997), 91, 96.

79 Gunningham and Grabosky, note 31; J. Elias and R. Lee, "Ecological Modernisation and Environmental Regulation: Corporate Compliance and Accountability," in *Global Governance and the Quest for Justice. Volume 2: Corporate Governance*, ed. S. MacLeod (Hart Publishing, 2006), 163.

80 E.g., H. Nishimura, "The Greening of Japanese Industry," in *Business and the Environment*, ed. M.D. Rogers (Macmillan, 1995), 21; P. Christensen, ed., *Governing the Environment: Politics, Policy and Organization in the Nordic Countries* (Nordic Council, 1996).

81 N. Klein, *No Logo: Taking Aim at the Brand Bullies* (Vintage Canada, 2000).

82 D. Szablowski, *Transnational Law and Local Struggles: Mining, Communities and the World Bank* (Hart Publishing, 2007), 64–73.

the regulatory status quo with calls for far-reaching policy prescriptions.[83] The postmodern fabric of contemporary culture, associated with the erosion of legitimacy of the modernist "meta-narratives" of capitalism and liberalism,[84] has both undermined the conditions for developing universal norms for environmental action and opened possibilities for subversive perspectives.[85] In particular, there is considerable public skepticism of the risks associated with science and technology.[86] As the SRI movement itself is not homogenous, microcredit providers, public sector pension funds, religious investors, and NGO activism have also challenged a business-as-usual approach to responsible financing.

D. SRI REGULATION AND THE FINANCIAL SECTOR

Policy reforms promoting SRI mirror these governance trends and struggles. These reforms have shaped both official regulation (considered in this chapter) and the plethora of private sector codes of conduct and voluntary standards (considered in the next chapter). That the financial sector is being regulated at all for its social and environmental effects is notable. While authorities have often closely supervised financial organizations in relation to economic policy objectives,[87] environmental law has rarely affected them. We may be witnessing a paradigm shift in environmental law, away from a discrete system of environmental regulation administered by specific branches of government to a diaspora of controls diffused throughout the economy and society.

83 See already W. Douma, L. Massai, and M. Montini, eds, *The Kyoto Protocol and Beyond: Legal and Policy Challenges of Climate Change* (Asser Press, 2007); C. Redgwell, et al., eds, *Beyond the Carbon Economy* (Oxford University Press, 2008).

84 D. Harvey, *The Condition of Postmodernity: An Enquiry into the Origins of Cultural Change* (Blackwell, 1990); S. Lash, *Sociology of Postmodernism* (Routledge, 1990).

85 D. Shelton, "Environmental Justice in the Postmodern World," in *Environmental Justice and Market Mechanisms*, eds K. Bosselmann and B.J. Richardson (Kluwer Law, 1999), 21.

86 See, e.g., J. Rifkin, *Biosphere Politics: New Consciousness for a New Century* (HarperCollins, 1992).

87 C. Ford and J. Kay, "Why Regulate Financial Services?" in *The Future for the Global Securities Market: Legal and Regulatory Aspects*, ed. F. Oditah (Oxford University Press, 1996), 145.

These changes in governance pertaining to SRI involve new types of norms, instruments, and controllers. The regulatory norms of the state share governance space with an increasing presence of market and civil societal institutions. For instance, SRI reporting standards prescribed by the state have left considerable room for non-state actors to provide governing principles. These alternative norms may become mainstreamed without being formalized into law, via private, voluntary codes of conduct, or contracts between lenders and borrowers.

Another key characteristic of recent reforms is changes in the instruments of governance. As environmental law charts new territory so do the instruments in its arsenal. Tim Jewell and Jenny Steele believe that "distinctive imperatives may emerge both from economic logic and from commercial concerns [which] will have an impact on the nature and extent of legal interventions themselves."[88] The variety of instruments used for SRI regulation include transparency regulation, such as corporate disclosure requirements, economic incentives, and industry self-regulation; as well as the occasional use of more heavy-handed instruments redolent of command-and-control regulation, such as lender liability for environmental pollution.

The entities of control are also changing, whereby state regulatory bodies hold a less dominant place. Financial institutions such as insurance companies and CRAs have long played a surrogate regulatory role over companies, with minimal state oversight. In the context of SRI, other types of financial sector entities are assuming control functions over environmental-risk related behavior. These entities include SRI industry associations, market index providers, accreditation bodies, and large institutional investors. Such changes however carry risks. As Neil Gunningham and Peter Grabosky warn, harnessing third parties to assist as surrogate regulators "is a process with many pitfalls and, unless skillfully done, can result in negative rather than positive policy outcomes."[89]

In this dynamic and fluid system of governance, SRI law seems mostly confined to interjecting environmental and social messages into the financial markets to encourage, but not oblige, more responsible financing. Legal norms target those economic variables —costs, technologies, and investor confidence — that the right mix of signals and incentives can influence. To promote more reasoned decision-making within financial institutions, environmental and ethical concerns are re-characterized into investor formats and languages.

---

88 Steele and Jewell, note 36, 22.
89 Gunningham and Grabosky, note 31, 94.

Climate change, for instance, is not an environmental or ethical concern as much as a financially material risk to the bottom line. Echoing the philosophy behind reflexive law, Robert Repetto and Duncan Austin suggest this outlook is not necessarily a bad thing:

> unless environmental issues are dealt with inside the corporation in ways similar to those used to manage other business risks and opportunities, environmental control in such industries will remain an internal regulatory function superimposed on the company's core business concerns rather than part of the process of maximizing shareholder value.[90]

Information and disclosure-based legal strategies, such as environmental auditing and reporting, have strong reflexive law properties in the way they aim to imbue the business culture by intersecting financial decision-making with environmental issues.[91] Auditing and reporting have become part of the phenomenon that Michael Power describes as the "audit society."[92] He views the dissemination of methods for "checking and verification" as a shift in regulatory style that "straddles" the public-private divide by "connect[ing] internal organizational arrangements to public ideals."[93]

As the previous chapter noted, corporate governance reforms facilitating shareholder advocacy also enable SRI. With the growth of corporate power and the separation of ownership from management, shareholders rights in the governance of the corporation needed clearer enunciation. Filing resolutions and communicating among themselves have become necessary to balance shareholder interests with those of management. In Canada, for instance, a rule prohibiting shareholders from filing resolutions directed to "promoting general economic, political, racial, religious, social or similar causes" was overturned in 2001.[94]

90 R. Repetto and D. Austin, *Pure Profit: The Financial Implications of Environmental Performance* (World Resources Institute, 2000), 1.

91 K.H. Ladeur, "Coping with Uncertainty: Ecological Risks and the Proceduralization of Environmental Law," in *Environmental Law and Ecological Responsibility*, note 28, 299, 322–23.

92 M. Power, *The Audit Society: Rituals of Verification* (Oxford University Press, 1997).

93 Ibid., 10.

94 Amendments in 2001 to the *Canada Business Corporations Act*, R.S.C. 1985, s. 137(5).

Economic instruments can also facilitate SRI.[95] Left alone, the market often fails to consider the long-term costs of resource depletion and pollution.[96] Economic incentive mechanisms, such as pollution taxes and tradable emission allowances, offer one solution to this omission.[97] Economic instruments can reveal costs and benefits of environmental activities, highlighting the economic advantages of resource conservation and technological innovation, in line with ecological modernization precepts.[98]

More importantly, SRI law may serve to change more than the behavior of financial institutions. By regulating financiers, SRI regulation should also provoke changes to the environmental behavior of financed companies. Financial organizations hold strategic, intermediate positions between the state and the market. This intermediary position allows financiers to channel environmental norms to the wider economy. In the spirit of reflexive law, banks, institutional investors, and other financiers can become vehicles for "legal" communication, transmitting information about correct corporate environmental behavior. If the cost of finance reflects environmental risks, presumably borrowers would have incentives to alter their behavior to lower that cost. While acting as surrogate environmental regulators, financiers can help mitigate the problem of coordinating different subsystems predicted by reflexive law theory.[99]

---

95 Regarding the importance and uptake of economic instrument approaches, see T. Panayotou, *Instruments of Change: Motivating and Financing Sustainable Development* (Earthscan, 1998); J. Rietbergen-McCraken and H. Abaza, *Economic Instruments for Environmental Management: A Worldwide Compendium of Case Studies* (Earthscan, 2000).

96 See, e.g., G. Heal, *Valuing the Future: Economic Theory and Sustainability* (Columbia University Press, 1998); M. Common and S. Stagl, eds, *Ecological Economics: An Introduction* (Cambridge University Press, 2005).

97 See generally OECD, *Economic Instruments: A Classification* (OECD, 1989); *Managing the Environment: The Role of Economic Instruments* (OECD, 1994).

98 For arguments about the advantages of economic instruments, see OECD, *Environmental Policy: How to Apply Economic Instruments* (OECD, 1991); A. Ogus, "Nudging and Rectifying: The Use of Fiscal Instruments for Regulatory Purposes," *Legal Studies* 19(2) (1999): 245; N. Chalifour, et al., eds, *Critical Issues in Environmental Taxation* (Oxford University Press, 2008).

99 Jessop, note 43, 329.

III. Informational Mechanisms

A. TRANSPARENCY REGULATION

1. SRI Policy Disclosure

A. LEGISLATIVE STANDARDS

SRI governance relies heavily on transparency-based rules, which require that subject organizations regularly disclose factual information in standardized formats. Such mechanisms impose obligations on financiers to publicly disclose investment policies for SRI, to report proxy voting policies and voting records, and to adhere to general corporate sustainability reporting standards.

At first glance, transparency regulation may resemble a preference for soft-touch, business-as-usual arrangements.[100] Yet, in the spirit of reflexive law, transparency regulation may encourage investment institutions to consider SRI issues in composing their investment portfolios and by asking pertinent questions of the firms they invest in.[101] It may inchoately mark a stakeholder approach to investment management, as public access to information should increase stakeholder pressure on organizations to minimize environmental and social risks.

The general rationale for disclosure measures is to redress information asymmetry, and thereby enable a more efficient market. Specifically, they should help investors make informed decisions about the risks and benefits at stake. Incomplete or asymmetric access to material information can cause the over- or undervaluation of securities. While disclosure rules can also create a market incentive for prudent environmental management in the wider public interest, this has not been the primary aim of such rules: their focus has been the interests of investors. While there has been some industry resistance to SRI disclosure regulations, based on cost and lack of potential utility, there has generally been a marked increase in corporate disclosure of performance on ESG issues. Some firms are even disclosing information beyond regulatory reporting requirements.[102]

---

100 J. Braithwaite and P. Drahos, *Global Business Regulation* (Cambridge University Press, 2000), 57–65.

101 See D. Hess, "Social Reporting: A Reflexive Law Approach to Corporate Social Responsiveness," *Journal of Corporation Law* 25 (1999): 41.

102 Presentation by D. Sisti, Vice-President, ISS Canada (2007 Canadian Responsible Investment Conference, Montreal, May 27–29, 2007).

Rules for disclosure of SRI policies in the pension fund sector were pioneered in the UK, and later adopted in several other European countries and Australia.[103] In July 1999, the UK government issued a regulation under the *Pensions Act* of 1995 requiring trustees of occupational pension funds to amend their statement of investment principles to declare "[t]he extent (if at all) to which social, environmental or ethical considerations are taken into account in the selection, retention, and realization of investments."[104] Further, they must declare their "policy (if any) directing the exercise of the rights (including voting rights) attaching to investments."[105] A similar requirement was imposed on local government-sector pension funds.[106]

The main purpose of the UK reform was to counter misguided perceptions among pension fund trustees that SRI breaches their fiduciary obligations.[107] The court ruling in *Cowan v. Scargill*[108] had been wrongly interpreted by some investment professionals and legal commentators as implying that SRI is inherently illegal in a fiduciary context. The other purpose of the 1999 regulation was to improve transparency in the sector as a possible driver for change in investment practices. The regulation however does not in itself alter underlying fiduciary and other prudential investment standards.[109]

Several EU states followed the UK example.[110] In 2001 Germany introduced several specific SRI disclosure regulations. Pursuant to amendments to the *Insurance Supervision Act*, private pension funds and providers of life insurance products must disclose annually whether and how they consider ethical,

---

103 See B.J. Richardson, "Pensions Law Reform and Environmental Policy: A New Role for Institutional Investors?" *Journal of International Financial Markets: Law and Regulation* 3(5) (2002): 159.

104 *Occupational Pension Schemes (Investment, and Assignment, Forfeiture, Bankruptcy etc.), Amendment Regulations*, 1999, cl. 2(4). Now contained in the *Occupational Pension Schemes (Investment) Regulations*, 2005: cl. 2(3)(b)(vi)–(3)(c).

105 Ibid.

106 *Local Government Pension Scheme (Management and Investment of Funds) (Amendment) Regulations*, 1999.

107 Personal communication, Penny Shepherd, UKSIF (London, February 27, 2007).

108 [1985] 1 Ch. 270.

109 J. Donnan, "Regulating Ethical Investment: Disclosure under the Financial Services Reform Act," *Journal of Banking and Finance Law and Practice* 13(3) (2002): 155, 170 (discussing the equivalent provision in Australian legislation).

110 See Eurosif, *European Legal Briefing: A Current View of SRI and CSR Issues Relating to Recent European Laws* (Eurosif, March 2007).

social, and ecological criteria in their investment strategies.[111] A similar provision in the *Act on the Certification of Retirement Arrangement Contracts* applies the SRI disclosure provisions to specific government subsidized private pension schemes. Belgium's legislation of 2003 requires pension fund managers to disclose in their annual reports to what extent they take into account ethical, social, and environmental criteria in their investment policies.[112] Austria adopted similar regulations in its pension fund legislation in early 2005.[113] Likewise, Italy enacted its legislation in 2005 for SRI policy disclosure in the pension sector taking effect in January 2008.[114] Curiously, despite the spate of reform in individual EU states, no equivalent provision was included in the EU Occupational Pensions Directive of 2003 despite the matter being raised during its drafting.[115]

France adopted some of the most comprehensive disclosure rules. Its 2001 legislation requires each company's "employee savings plans" to explain how the plan addresses social, ethical, and environmental issues.[116] These rules surpass the UK reform in their expectation for considering such matters. A Committee for Employees' Savings (Comité intersyndical de l'épargne salariale) was set up in January 2002 by four trade unions to control investments of employee savings plans and to guide fund managers towards SRI options. In a seminal advance following the UK's legislative precedent, capital investment funds for employees must also explain how they implement any social and environmental considerations they report as following.[117]

111 *Versicherungsaufsichtsgesetz*, s. 10a Abs. 1, Appendix D, Chapter III, 2(cc); *Altersvorsorgevertraege-Zertifizierungsgesetz*, s. 7 Abs. 4; *Gesetzesentwurf Altersein-kuenftegesetz*, art. 5.
112 *Loi pensions complémentaires*—LPC, (April 28, 2003), art. 42(3), Moniteur Belge (2d ed.), (May 15, 2003), 26,407.
113 Eurosif, note 110, 3.
114 *Decreto Legislativo* (December 5 2005), n. 252. Specifically, the legislation states: "[p]ension funds are requested to show in their yearly reports, as well as in their periodical communications to all scheme's members, whether and to what extent any social, ethical and environmental investing aspects have been considered in their asset and resource management" (art. 6(14)). Discussed in Eurosif, *European SRI Study 2006* (Eurosif, 2006), 26.
115 Directive 2003/41/EC of 3 June 2003, O.J. L. 235/10; European Parliament, Committee on Economic and Monetary Affairs, *Draft Report on the Proposal for a European Parliament and Council Directive on the Activities of Institutions for Occupational Retirement Provision*, PE 295.986/AM/48–134 (May 8, 2001), 52.
116 *Projet de loi sur l'épargne salariale* (February 7, 2001). No. 2001-152, art. 21, 23; *Code monétaire et financier*, art. L. 214-39.
117 Ibid.

In 2001, Australia legislated for an SRI disclosure obligation for pension funds, mutual funds, and investment life insurance providers under the *Financial Services Reform Act* of 2001.[118] The disclosure legislation was adopted to foster a market for SRI products by providing investors with a form of quality assurance.[119] The regulation requires funds to provide a "product disclosure statement" (PDS) explaining "the extent to which labor standards or environmental, social or ethical considerations are taken into account in the selection, retention or realization of the investment."[120] The legislation imposes penalties for issuing a misleading PDS.[121] This has become more significant in light of other legislation in 2005 that gave superannuation scheme contributors the right to choose where their funds are invested.[122] The accompanying regulations to the 2001 reform require the product issuer to explain *which* labor standards or environmental, social, or ethical considerations it takes into account, and how far it takes them into account in selecting, retaining or realizing an investment.[123]

This reform is complemented by the Australian Securities and Investments Commission (ASIC) regulatory "guidelines."[124] The ASIC has the power to develop guidelines that investment institutions must comply with where their PDS claims that labor standards or environmental, social, or ethical considerations are taken into account. The guidelines do not define what constitutes such considerations, but they aim to facilitate the "quantity, format

---

118 The legislative changes were incorporated into the *Corporations Act*, 2001 (Cth).

119 G. Frost, et al., "Bringing Ethical Investment to Account," *Australian Accounting Review* 14(3) (2004): 3, 7.

120 *Corporations Act*, 2001 (Cth), s. 1013D(1)(l); see further B.J. Richardson, "Ethical Investment and the Commonwealth's Financial Services Reform Act 2001," *National Environmental Law Review* 2 (2002): 47.

121 Sections 1021D, 1021E and 1021F.

122 *Superannuation Legislation Amendment (Choice of Superannuation Funds) Act*, 2005 (Cth). A similar measured was proposed in 2004 in the US for federal government pension plans; the *Federal Employees Responsible Investment Bill* went further than the Australian legislation, as it would compel government pension plans to offer an SRI index fund option in the Thrift Savings Plan for all federal employees, administered under the *Employees' Retirement System Act*, 1986: H.R. 4140, at http://thomas.loc.gov/cgi-bin/query/z?c108: H.R.4140.IH.

123 *Corporations Regulations*, 2001 (Cth), reg. 7.9.14C.

124 ASIC, *Section 1013DA Disclosure Guidelines* (ASIC, December 2003) and *Policy Statement 168: Product Disclosure Statements* (ASIC, May 2005).

and accuracy of SRI disclosure."[125] If a fund claims to invest responsibly, the ASIC expects the fund's PDS to provide an explanation of the criteria for measuring investment standards or considerations, a general description of whether adherence to the methodology is monitored, and an explanation of actions taken when an investment no longer adheres to the stated investment policy. The ASIC's guidance is remarkably detailed and attentive to the problems of misleading SRI claims. For instance, in its Disclosure Guidelines ASIC states:

> if a claim is made that no investment is made in companies associated with product X, the disclosure should clarify what associations this negative screen captures. For example, is the negative screen limited to companies that are directly associated with product X (e.g., they manufacture, mine or grow it) or does it extend to companies that have indirect associations with it (e.g., they transport or retail it)?[126]

The ASIC has also reissued its Best Practice Guidelines for financial planners serving retail investors. These 2005 Guidelines state that: "as a matter of good practice (irrespective of any current legal requirement) providing entities should seek to ascertain whether environmental, social or ethical considerations are important to the client, and, if they are, conduct reasonable enquiries about them."[127] Thus, retail investors in Australia can now read about funds' SRI policies, and their financial advisers should educate them.

SRI disclosure obligations have been proposed in other jurisdictions, without success. In Canada in 2002, an opposition Private Member's Bill modeled on the UK law failed to pass.[128] In 2007 a similar proposal was recommended by the Advisory Group to the National Roundtables on CSR and the Canadian Extractive Industry.[129] So far Canadian lawmakers have only enacted a regulation mandating public accountability statements (PASs) for various lending institutions. It was imposed in the context of a wave of mergers in the banking industry that raised concerns about an unhealthy

---

125 A. George, N. Edgerton, and T. Berry, "Mainstreaming Socially Responsible Investment (SRI): A Role for Government —Policy Recommendations from the Investment Community" (Institute for Sustainable Futures, University of Technology, 2005).

126 ASIC, note 124, 11.

127 ASIC, *Policy Statement 175.110* (ASIC, 2005).

128 Bill C-394, *An Act to amend the Pension Benefits Standards Act*, 1985.

129 Advisory Group, *National Roundtables on Corporate Social Responsibility (CSR) and the Canadian Extractive Industry in Developing Countries* (Government of Canada, March 2007), x.

concentration of power among few large lenders.[130] Since 2002, all Canadian banks, insurance companies, and trust and loan companies with equity of at least C$1 billion must provide an annual PAS which describes their contribution to the Canadian economy and society.[131] The PAS must disclose the institution's charitable donations, involvement in community development projects, microcredit programs, and measures for improved access to financial services by disadvantaged people. The only reference to the environment in the PAS regulation is in the definition of "community development," which means "the social, cultural, economic or environmental enrichment of a community."[132]

SRI policy disclosure measures adopted in Europe, and to a much lesser extent Australia, have several weaknesses. For one, they focus on disclosure of investment *policies* rather than investment *practices*. Investors in SRI funds or beneficiaries of pension funds are not usually told the methodology or research behind SRI-based portfolio selections. Rarely must financiers report their implementation of disclosed SRI policies. Requiring investment institution to report on the steps they actually take to invest responsibly and to have their reports independently audited with sanctions for misleading statements would help reduce the temptation to make perfunctory SRI policy disclosures. Indeed, a 2007 Canadian government inquiry recommended adoption of an SRI disclosure law that would go so far as insisting on disclosure of how ESG considerations inform investment practices.[133]

The second deficiency in the policy disclosure measures is that the regulations do not define what constitutes "socially responsible investment." Thus, funds may freely determine their own notions of SRI. While this may not be an unreasonable arrangement given that investment institutions are not legally obliged to engage in SRI, the funds should, at the very least, justify *why* they view their investment policies as ethically, socially, and environmentally responsible. In order for transparency regulation to serve as a pedagogic tool, it should require fund providers to explain their methodology behind SRI policies. Only the Australian regime reasonably attempts to correct this problem through

130 M. Cooke, *Banking on Mergers: Financial Power Versus the Public Interest* (Centre for Social Justice, 2005), 36–37.
131 *Public Accountability Statements (Banks, Insurance Companies, Trust and Loan Companies) Regulations*, SOR/2002-133, March 21, 2002; *Bank Act*, S.C. 1991, s. 459.3(1); *Insurance Companies Act*, S.C. 1991, s. 489.1(4); *Trust and Loans Companies Act*, S.C. 1991, s. 444.2(4).
132 Ibid., cl. 1.
133 NRTEE, *Capital Markets and Sustainability: Investing in a Sustainable Future. State of the Debate Report* (NRTEE, 2007), 9.

regulatory directions.[134] The ASIC's rules specify that if an investment PDS claims to take social or environmental considerations into account, it must provide a general description of the methodology (or a statement that there is no set methodology), a timeframe for monitoring investments, and an explanation of the consequences where an investment does not satisfy the specified criteria.

B. IMPLEMENTATION

One would assume that the underlying aim of the disclosure reforms is to induce the subject investment institutions to consider ESG issues when making investment decisions and to actively manage the investments within their portfolios. In their study, Andrew Friedman and Samantha Miles predicted a "marked increase in the size and power of the SRI sector"[135] from Britain's SRI disclosure regulation. In 2004, Russell Sparkes and Chris Cowton suggested the UK's regulation was "a significant driver in the growth of SRI."[136]

The reality, however, appears to have been less dramatic. In reviewing the impact of the UK's regulation in its first year, Eugenie Mathieu found that 59 percent of 171 pension funds sampled had formally incorporated SRI into their investment strategies either by engagement or by specific request to the fund manager.[137] Another study by EIRIS in 2003 determined that 90 percent of UK pension funds sampled had SRI policies.[138] However, these surveys shed little light on how these policies were implemented. A later survey in 2004 by UKSIF's JustPensions project suggested "a gap has emerged between policy and practice."[139] Similarly, research by the UK Department of Work and Pensions found that pension funds' policies on SRI had not changed substantially, except in the case of very large funds.[140] A 2005 survey by

134 ASIC, note 124.
135 A. Friedman and S. Miles, "Socially Responsible Investment and Corporate Social and Environmental Reporting in the UK: An Exploratory Study," *British Accounting Review* 33(4) (2001): 523, 523.
136 R. Sparkes and C.J. Cowton, "The Maturing of Socially Responsible Investment: A Review of the Developing Link with Corporate Social Responsibility," *Journal of Business Ethics* 52 (2004): 45, 49.
137 E. Mathieu, *Response of UK Pension Funds to the SRI Disclosure Regulation* (UKSIF, 2000), 2.
138 EIRIS, *How Responsible is Your Pension?* (EIRIS, 2003).
139 C. Gribben and A. Faruk, *Will UK Pension Funds Become More Responsible? A Survey of Trustees—2004* (JustPensions, UKSIF, 2004), 4.
140 S. Horack, J. Leston, and M. Watmough, *The Myners Principles and Occupation Pension Schemes Volume 2 of 2: Findings from Quantitative Research,* Research Report No. 213 (Department for Work and Pensions, July 2004), 129–30.

JustPensions concluded that the use of exclusionary SRI screens increased from a mere 2 percent of respondents in 2003 to 11 percent in 2005, and engagement with portfolio companies grew from 26 percent of respondents in 2003 to 40 percent in 2005.[141] A 2006 Fair Pensions study of the UK's twenty largest pension funds concluded: "[o]nly a handful of pension schemes show evidence of serious attempts to develop and disclose robust policies to tackle specific environmental, human rights, or governance problems within their investments."[142]

One problem identified in several of these studies is the lack of active monitoring by fund trustees ensuring compliance with their SRI policies. They commonly delegate investment decisions to fund managers, leaving them with the broad discretion to take SRI issues "into account" where appropriate. Most trustees have not provided fund managers with adequate incentives to incorporate ESG issues into investment decisions, leaving largely unabated the short-term profitability culture.[143] A 2004 study found that "[m]ost [UK] pension funds seem reluctant or not equipped to monitor the activities of their fund managers on these issues. Therefore, it is common to see a lack of reporting from fund managers on how they integrate SEE issues into the investments.... "[144]

Many pension funds' SRI policies tend to be uninformative, boilerplate statements, conservatively couched with reference to fiduciary duties understood as demanding the best financial returns. For instance, the South Yorkshire Pensions Authority 2006 statement tersely provides: "[t]he Authority has considered how social, environmental, and ethical factors should be taken into account when managing investment portfolios that are run to obtain returns that are in the best interests of both contributors and beneficiaries of the Fund."[145] The Authority hardly explains what these "factors" are and how they are "taken into account." At most, we learn that the Authority favors corporate engagement rather than ethical screens, as the Authority "wishes to promote improved company performance amongst all the companies in which it

---

141 C. Gribben and M. Gitsham, *Will UK Pension Funds Become More Responsible: A Survey of Trustees* (JustPensions, UKSIF, 2006), 3.

142 Fair Pensions, *UK Pension Scheme Transparency on Social, Environmental and Ethical Issues* (Fair Pensions, November 2006), i.

143 Personal communication, staff, Fair Pensions (London, February 23, 2007).

144 D. Wheeler and J. Thomson, *Comparative Study of U.K. and Canadian Pension Fund Transparency Practices* (NRTEE, 2004), 20.

145 South Yorkshire Pensions Authority (SYPA), *Statement of Investment Principles as at 1 July 2006* (SYPA, 2006), cl. 7.

invests and, therefore, will not actively disinvest from companies solely or largely for social or ethical or environmental reasons."[146]

Another example of a vacuous statement of investment policy that leaves too much discretion to fund managers comes from the British Broadcasting Corporation. It merely discloses that:

> The Trustees have delegated responsibility to their active equity managers to take account of the social, environmental and ethical considerations in the selection, retention and realisation of Scheme investments so far as such considerations will affect the prospects or performance of the companies in which they invest for the Scheme.[147]

The USS, on the other hand, has one of the most informative policy statements. It explains how it applies SRI considerations and also outlines the role of its investment management committee for monitoring fund managers. In the context of its overall objective to "maximise the long-term investment return on the assets,"[148] the USS "requires its fund managers to pay appropriate regard to relevant extra-financial factors... in the selection, retention and realization of all fund investments."[149] Further, the USS's "management committee has instructed its [fund] managers to use influence as major institutional investors to promote good practice by investee companies" and "to undertake appropriate monitoring of the policies... so that these extra-financial factors can, where material, be taken into account when making investment decisions."[150] The USS has also published a separate policy guide on responsible investment.[151]

The foregoing evidence generally suggests that the UK's disclosure regulation has not had a significant effect. Yet it appears to have caused a shift among pension funds from not doing anything —believing that their fiduciary duties constrain them —to acknowledging that ESG issues can be taken into account.[152] The debate in the pension sector has thus shifted from "whether" to "how." For instance, the UK National Association of Pension Funds, which

146 Ibid.
147 British Broadcasting Corporation (BBC), *Statement of Investment Principles: BBC Pension Scheme* (BBC, 2006), cl. 6.2.
148 USS, *Statement of Investment Principles* (USS, 2006), 2.
149 Ibid., 7.
150 Ibid.
151 USS, "USS and Socially Responsible and Sustainable Investment: An Overview" (USS, undated).
152 Personal communication, Penny Shepherd, UK Social Investment Forum (London, February 27, 2007).

previously queried the regulatory changes, has declared that SRI "should be seen as an integral part of the normal investment management process."[153]

Less is known about the implementation of the SRI disclosure regulations in other jurisdictions. In Australia, a surge in retail SRI in recent years has been reported according to surveys commissioned by the RIAA.[154] Yet the quality of the funds' disclosures and underlying SRI policies appears less encouraging despite the more onerous requirements of the Australian regulations. In 2004, a survey by the Australian Conservation Foundation concluded that "many mainstream investment managers still do not appreciate the relationship between ethical corporate behavior and long-term financial performance."[155] For instance, Colonial First State's Managed Investment Fund's PDS of 2004 stated:

[w]e do not specifically take into account environmental, social or ethical considerations when making an investment decision for the fund, as unitholders have differing views about such issues. As the responsible entity for the fund, we therefore cannot take into account individual unitholders' particular interests if doing so may have a financial impact on the returns for other investors.[156]

While funds dedicated to SRI understandably have provided the most helpful and progressive disclosure statements on social investment,[157] a 2007 survey by the Australian Council of Superannuation Investors cautioned that "[m]any funds felt that they did not yet have enough skills or resources to consider ESG issues in their investment decision-making."[158] Further, because many funds held their investments in pooled trusts managed externally, they

153 National Association of Pension Funds, "The NAPF and CSR/SRI," para. 10, at http://www.napf.co.uk/policy/recentreports.cfm.
154 Corporate Monitor, *Responsible Investment: A Benchmark Report on Australia and New Zealand by the Responsible Investment Association Australasia* (RIAA, October 2007).
155 C. Berger, *Disclosure of Ethical Considerations in Investment Product Disclosure Statements: A Review of Current Practice in Australia* (Australian Conservation Foundation, August 2004), 1.
156 Cited in ibid., 2.
157 E.g., AMP Capital Investors, *Sustainable Future International Share Fund: Product Disclosure Statement* (AMP, 2004).
158 Australian Council of Superannuation Investors (ACSI), *The ESG Survey Report* (ACSI, June 2007), 1.

felt unable to dictate to those fund managers how they should incorporate ESG considerations.[159]

Canadian banks are legally required to release an annual PAS, and they usually incorporate their PAS into a general CSR report. The Bank of Montreal's recent PAS details its implementation of an environmental management system, its activities pursuant to the EPs, and its use of the GRI indicators.[160] The Royal Bank of Canada's PAS explains its "sustainable procurement" policy, environmental risk management procedures, and its commitment to relevant international codes such as the EPs.[161] Overall, Canadian banks' PASs provide reasonably informative descriptions of current policies and activities, exceeding the modest requirements of the PAS regulation.

Generally, disclosure regulations have succeeded to the extent that many financiers now publish statements regarding their consideration of ESG issues. The disclosure trend has expanded internationally, taking root even in countries without regulatory obligations. Major Dutch pension funds, for instance, announced in 2007 that they would fully disclose their investment policies, portfolios, and proxy voting records.[162] Still, existence of SRI policy does not equate to responsible investment. While SRI data suggest the amount of money labeled as SRI has increased exponentially, much of this self-styled SRI is attributable to pension funds embracing corporate engagement to exert change, rather than actually holding that change to account by applying exclusionary screens and other more aggressive methods.[163] The lag in practical SRI reflects issues with changing a long-standing investment culture resistant to public accountability. To the extent that this culture is altering, NGOs' activities to pressure and educate pension fund trustees and managers have been important. In Britain, Fair Pensions and the UKSIF have played seminal roles by providing various means to foster change: releasing toolkits, holding workshops, engaging in dialogue, and publishing various reports.

159 Ibid., 2.
160 Bank of Montreal (BMO), *BMO Financial Group 2006 Corporate Responsibility Report and Public Accountability Statement* (BMO, 2006).
161 Royal Bank of Canada (RBC), *Towards Sustainability. Where Our Values Lead Us. 2006 Corporate Responsibility Report and Public Accountability Statement* (RBC, 2006).
162 "Major Dutch Funds Charge Towards Full Disclosure," *European Pensions and Investment News,* March 26, 2007.
163 R. Rubinstein, "Really Responsible or Just Band Wagon Jumping?" *European Pensions and Investment News*, November 6, 2006.

2. Proxy Voting Disclosure

A. REGULATORY REFORM

Another transparency reform introduced by authorities that may help SRI obliges financiers to publicly disclose their proxy voting guidelines and voting records. To the extent that proxy voting involves delegating voting rights without guidance it is problematic from an ethical investment perspective. Ideally, ethical investors should take responsibility for their shareholding rights and vote personally. However, with clear guidance and instruction to fund managers, the proxy voting process can help shareholders monitor corporate managers and allow activist investors to advocate changes in corporate policies. Disclosure of proxy voting policies and practices can illuminate fund managers' passive collusion with corporate management, or perhaps, active representation of beneficiary shareholder rights. Potentially, the obligation to disclose such information will impel funds to become more responsible participants in corporate governance.

A properly executed proxy voting process, commonly used in Anglo-American corporate legal systems, can involve some advanced interactions. Before a shareholder meeting, management provides each registered shareholder entitled to vote at the meeting with notice of the meeting, a proxy circular enumerating matters for consideration, and a proxy form with which to vote. The registered shareholder then forwards the documents to the beneficial shareholder for consideration and instruction, unless this responsibility has been formally delegated. As authority is commonly delegated to a fund manager, the pension plan trustees or other parties do not see this documentation, let alone provide direction on how to vote. Commonly, proxy circulars indicate that management will act as the proxy holder if the shareholder fails to make an election. Thereby, the vote will be treated as a vote "for" management's recommendation. In any event, fund managers typically vote in accordance with the recommendations of corporate management unless their principals give other specific instructions.[164]

Proxy voting records in Canada show that mutual funds traditionally vote with management about 90 percent of the time.[165] They also generally vote against SRI-directed proposals. In the US, the Investor Responsibility Research Center (IRRC) reported in 2004 that "a majority of the nation's one

---

164 J.G. MacIntosh, "Institutional Shareholders and Corporate Governance in Canada," *Canadian Business Law Journal* 26 (1996): 145, 160.

165 K. Damsell, "Fund Industry Divided Over Proxy Voting," Globefund.Com, October 31, 2006.

hundred largest mutual funds opposed all social issue shareholder resolutions";
another 15 percent voted against virtually all such proposals; and some
30 percent cast abstentions.[166] SRI proposals tend to receive no case-by-case
assessment on grounds that their financial impact is too difficult to gauge or
that they pose operational issues best left to management.[167] Fund managers'
voting may also be inappropriately influenced by collateral business interests,
such as administrative work for the company's pension plan.[168]

To combat such attitudes and practices, the US and Canada introduced
proxy voting disclosure requirements for mutual fund sectors in 2003 and
2005, respectively.[169] Reforms were generally opposed by the mutual fund
industry citing administrative costs and anticipated politicization of the
proxy process.[170] Previous arrangements to encourage proxy disclosures on a
voluntary basis in the 1980s and 1990s had achieved little.[171]

In January 2003, the SEC adopted a rule under the *Investment Company Act*
to require investment funds to disclose how they vote proxies relating to
their portfolio securities.[172] The SEC also requires investment companies to
file annual reports with the Commission and to reveal the specific proxy
votes that they cast in shareholder meetings. Proxy voting policies and
voting records must be posted on the SEC's website and made available on
each fund's website, by open posting or on request. A similar rule was
adopted under the *Investment Advisers Act* governing proxy voting by

166 IRRC, "Most Mutual Funds Opposed All Social Proposals," Press release,
September 15, 2004, at http://www.irrc.com/company/Mutual_Funds_
0904.html.
167 D.G. Cogan, *Unexamined Risk: How Mutual Funds Vote on Climate Change
Resolutions* (CERES, 2006), 16.
168 The lack of confidential proxy voting allows company management to see
where fund managers are placing their support: R. Romano, "Does
Confidential Proxy Voting Matter?" *Journal of Legal Studies* 32 (2003): 465.
169 R. Teitelbaum, "For Funds, Disclosure Is Hardly in Fashion," *New York
Times*, January 5, 2003: s. 3, 28.
170 Davis and others explain that the US mutual fund industry fought the proposed proxy voting disclosure regulations "tooth and nail": S. Davis,
J. Lukomnik, and D. Pitt-Watson, *The New Capitalists. How Citizen Investors
are Reshaping the Corporate Agenda* (Harvard Business School Press, 2006), 73.
171 A.R. Palmiter, "Mutual Fund Voting of Portfolio Shares: Why Disclose?"
Cardozo Law Review 23 (2002): 1419, 1457–62.
172 SEC, "Disclosure of Proxy Voting Policies and Proxy Voting Records by
Registered Management Investment Companies" (January 31, 2003), 17
CFR Parts 239, 249, 270, and 274.

investment advisers.[173] The SEC acknowledged that proxy voting guidelines on "social and corporate responsibility issues" was one of several types of proposals that would be "appropriate" for disclosure.[174]

Comparable regulation was adopted by the Canadian Securities Administrators and took effect on June 1, 2005, governing Canadian mutual funds.[175] It requires the proxy voting policy to be placed on the investment company's website, so the information is available to investors without their having to request it. Each investment fund must establish policies and procedures for fund managers to follow when exercising voting rights. It must also prepare a proxy voting record on an annual basis.

While many European states have enacted rules mandating disclosure of SRI policies, most have not introduced similar transparency measures on proxy voting.[176] This stance may reflect different styles of corporate governance. In North America, there is a tendency among social investors for a more confrontational approach in direct shareholder activism. In Europe, shareholder engagement on ESG issues is traditionally conducted through quiet dialogue and subtle pressure. Perhaps indicative of some change, in 2004 Eurosif released its Transparency Guidelines for retail SRI funds,[177] and later issued draft guidelines for institutional investors.[178]

The UK, being the closest among EU states to the North American styles of corporate governance and financial regulation, has included reserve powers over disclosure of shareholder voting in the *Companies Act* of 2006. The government could require specified institutions such as unit trusts and pension schemes to publicize "the exercise or non-exercise of voting rights by the institution or any person acting on its behalf," and "any instructions" given "as to the exercise or non-exercise of voting rights."[179] This new power was

---

173 SEC, "Proxy Voting by Investment Advisors" (January 31, 2003), 17 CFR Part 275.

174 D.G. Cogan, *Unexamined Risk: How Mutual Funds Vote on Climate Change Shareholder Risk* (CERES, 2006), 14.

175 Canadian Securities Administrators (CSA), *National Instrument 81-106 Investment Fund Continuous Disclosure and Companion Policy 81-106CP* (CSA, 2005).

176 France has introduced similar reforms: see S. Davis, "Votes Rules," *Global Proxy Watch* 7(26) (2003): 1.

177 Eurosif, *Eurosif Transparency Guidelines for the Retail SRI Fund Sector* (Eurosif, November 2004).

178 Eurosif, *Transparency Guidelines for Addressing ESG Issues within Institutional Investment—1st Draft for External Piloting* (Eurosif, September 2005).

179 Sections 1277–80.

predictably opposed by the Confederation of British Industry and some investment institutions.[180]

B. IMPLEMENTATION

By requiring the transparent exercise of voting power, these regulations allow investors to monitor their funds' involvement in the corporate governance process. They may also help moderate agency problems arising from fund managers' conflicts of interest. Reforms may further enable SRI activists and non-shareholder constituencies to pressure management more effectively. At the corporate level, if the reform can encourage more voting of proxies on SRI issues, it should stimulate better disclosure by companies of their practices. A resolution on the ballot forces management to respond to questions, for example by having to explain how its policies meet or satisfy the issues tabled. Management can be liable for dishonest responses to a resolution, as demonstrated by the US case of the *United Paperworkers International Union*.[181]

Unfortunately, the current reforms do not require investment institutions to register their share votes. This could have spurred institutions to formulate and express a view on all the issues put to vote at shareholder meetings. Also, funds are not required to actively distribute their guideline information, thus burdening investors with having to search for them. One survey concluded that, "the voting data are difficult to find, access is cumbersome and voting details sparse."[182] Moreover, current disclosure requirements apply only to mutual funds, leaving out of their purview numerous other financial institutions.

Recent empirical research casts doubt on whether the proxy voting disclosure reforms have materially changed mutual funds' voting practices. Martijn Cremers and Roberta Romano of Yale University compared the changes in voting on both management and shareholder proposals before and after the adoption of the US disclosure requirement. They found "no evidence that the rule decreased mutual funds' voting in support of management. Indeed... mutual funds' support for management increased after the rule's adoption,

---

180 K. Litvack, "Calling Time on the Secret Ballot," *European Pensions and Investment News*, March 13, 2006.

181 *United Paperworkers International Union v. International Paper Company*, (1993) 985 F. 2d 1190 (2d Cir.) (a company's misrepresentation about its environmental regulatory offences).

182 K. Damsell, "Fund Industry Divided Over Proxy Voting," *Globefund.Com*, October 31, 2006.

particularly for executive equity incentive compensation plan proposals."[183] Similar findings apply to voting of shareholder resolutions of social and environmental issues. Surveys conducted by the Corporate Library found that funds are only slowly inching toward more responsible voting on SRI issues.[184] Overall support for SRI-related resolutions had fallen from 15.7 percent in 2004 to 14.8 in 2005, before rising to 21.0 percent in 2006. Among mainstream financiers as against dedicated SRI funds, support for such resolutions fell slightly from 2004 (7.8 percent) to 2005 (7.7 percent) before rising to 13.4 percent in 2006.[185]

Further evidence comes from a 2006 study of proxy voting patterns among almost 1,000 Canadian mutual funds, of which fifty-five were defined as SRI funds.[186] The SIO's survey of fifty-seven shareholder resolutions on social, environmental, and corporate governance issues found that the funds overwhelmingly support corporations' positions, noting that "in each issue area, conventional funds, *en masse*, voted with management and against investor resolutions the majority of the time."[187] The SRI funds were more likely than non-SRI funds to support shareholder resolutions opposed by management.[188]

While many mutual funds undoubtedly drag their feet, some dedicated SRI funds were voluntarily disclosing their proxy voting policies and record before the law changed.[189] Ethical Funds was the first Canadian investment company to voluntarily disclose its proxy voting guidelines and actual voting activity, beginning in 2000 and 2001 respectively, several years before it became mandatory. Its 2007 guidelines is a sizeable forty-two page document, containing specific entries on topics such as treatment of animals, the precautionary principle, and labor rights.[190]

---

183 M. Cremers and R. Romano, *Institutional Investors and Proxy Voting: The Impact of the 2003 Mutual Fund Voting Disclosure Regulation*, ECGI-Law Working paper No. 083/2007 (Social Science Research Network, April 24, 2007), 2–3.

184 J. Cook, *Analysis of Fund Voting Results for 2004–2005: Focus on Shareholder-sponsored Resolutions* (The Corporate Library, 2006); B. Baue, "Mutual Funds Inch Toward More Conscientious Proxy Voting on Social and Environmental Resolutions," *Institutional Shareholder News Online*, March 14, 2007, at http://www.ishareowner.com/news.

185 Ibid.

186 SIO, *A Survey of Canadian Mutual Funds on Proxy Voting* (SIO, 2007).

187 Ibid., 9.

188 Ibid.

189 S. Heinrich, "Ethical Funds Comes Clean on Voting Policies," *Financial Post*, July 6, 2000: D4.

190 Ethical Funds Company, *Proxy Voting Guidelines 2007* (8th edn., Ethical Funds Company, 2007).

B. CORPORATE SUSTAINABILITY REPORTING

1. Rationale and Effectiveness of Reporting

The rules and practices of financial reporting and accounting are critical to the economy. They affect how economic systems select and interpret information. Reporting and accounting standards guide which facts or circumstances become recognized as financially material. Further, they translate those material facts into reasonably estimated numerical indicators of a company's financial position. Through these functions, reporting norms influence both capital allocation in the market and economic decisions within companies. Issues not deemed to be "material" in this model risk exclusion from investment decision-making. Thus, according to the influential International Accounting Standards Board (IASB): "[i]nformation is material if its omission or misstatement could influence the *economic decisions* of users taken on the basis of the financial report."[191] It is because of their profound influence over economic activity that commentators contend that financial reporting and accounting "is more than a neutral technical practice... it shapes preferences, organizational routines, and the forms of visibility, which support and give meaning to decision making."[192] Thus, some legal commentators such as Cynthia Williams have championed mandatory CSR disclosures by public corporations.[193]

Reporting and accounting norms affect SRI principally in two ways. First, they influence how non-financial companies disclose their environmental and social (sustainability) performance to the market. Ethical investors depend on such information in screening companies.[194] In theory, with accurate information, market forces can incorporate environmental costs and performance into the price and the terms of finance. Second, reporting and accounting systems affect how financiers report their own sustainability performance, which is important for society and regulators in assessing the eco-footprint of the financial sector.

---

191 IASB, *Framework for the Preparation and Presentation of Financial Statements* (IASB, 2004), para. 30 (my emphasis),

192 M.K. Power, "Auditing and the Production of Legitimacy," *Accounting, Organizations and Society* 28 (2003): 379, 379.

193 C.A. Williams, "The Securities and Exchange Commission and Corporate Social Transparency," *Harvard Law Review* 112 (1999): 1197.

194 See G. Harte, L. Lewis, and D. Owen, "Ethical Investment and the Corporate Reporting Function," *Critical Perspectives on Accounting* 12(3) (1991): 227.

Financial institutions do not all have equal ability to gather information about corporate sustainability performance. Banks have the advantage of referring to contractual mechanisms to demand additional environmental information from their borrowers when required. Equity investors by contrast rely mostly on publicly reported information. Information about environmental activities of private, unlisted firms, with less exacting reporting standards, can be a problem for financiers.

Traditionally, and even now in many ways, corporate sustainability reporting has not fully disclosed companies' environmental performances. Here, a combination of demand and supply side factors is at work.[195]

On the supply side, numerous studies have documented extensive under-reporting of environmental activities and "material" environmental risks in corporate financial reports.[196] Published in 2006, a survey of UK pension fund trustees found that "[o]nly about one in ten trustees believe that companies are providing sufficient information to enable social and environmental impacts and risks to be assessed effectively."[197] More encouraging are large public companies shifting from purely environmental reporting to integrated sustainability (social, environmental, and economic) reporting. They increasingly issue stand-alone sustainability reports, in addition to environmental disclosures within their financial statements.[198] Still, the scope and quality of corporate disclosure has been uneven and sometimes unreliable.[199] Too often, glossy covers featuring enchanting images of happy

---

195 Numerous studies have canvassed these issues: see, e.g., Stratos, *Corporate Disclosure and Capital Markets: Demand and Supply of Financially Relevant Corporate Responsibility Information* (NRTEE, 2004); Ernst and Young, *The Materiality of Environmental Risk to Australia's Finance Sector* (Commonwealth of Australia, 2003).

196 E.g., D. Austin and A. Sauer, *Changing Oil: Emerging Environmental Risks and Shareholder Value in the Oil and Gas Industry* (World Resources Institute, 2002); R. Repetto, *Silence is Golden, Leaden, and Copper: Disclosure of Material Environmental Information in the Hard Rock Mining Industry*, Report No. 1 (Yale School of Forestry and Environmental Studies, 2004); R. Krut and A. Moratz, "The State of Global Environmental Reporting: Lessons from the Global 100," *Corporate Environmental Strategy* 7(1) (2000): 85; SEC, *Summary by the Division of Corporate Finance of Significant Issues Addressed in the Review of the Periodic Reports of the Fortune 500 Companies* (SEC, 2003).

197 Gribben and Gitsham, note 141, 2.

198 KPMG, *International Survey of Corporate Responsibility Reporting 2005* (KPMG, 2005), 4–5.

199 See D. Cormier, M. Magnan, and B. Van Velthoven, "Environmental Disclosure Quality in Large German Companies: Economic Incentives,

children playing in a verdant landscape serve to "greenwash." Given the voluntary nature of much reporting, firms select information reported, allowing them to cast themselves in the best light possible. The growing length of some sustainability reports, some of nearly one hundred pages, is what SustainAbility calls "carpet-bombing," where reports saturate readers with information that overwhelms rather than clarifies.[200] Lately, the paucity of disclosure of climate change risks and potential liabilities has become increasingly debated.[201] Further, the lack of consistent and financially relevant sustainability metrics to interpret disclosures generally limits the value of environmental performance information to investors.

On the demand side, the SRI community is emerging as a vocal constituency for enhanced disclosures. In the US, thirteen major pension fund leaders wrote to the SEC in 2004 requesting greater enforcement of disclosure standards on climate risks,[202] with calls on this issue continuing since.[203] The SRI community is also implementing its own disclosure standards. For instance, through the CDP, a voluntary reporting initiative, institutional investors have collaborated to demand reporting of the financial risks connected to climate change and greenhouse gas (GHG) emissions data from the world's largest firms.[204]

On the other hand, the financial sector's capacity to analyze and interpret these data is, although improving, often still insufficient. One Australian study commented: "[t]he level of understanding of how to deal with environmental risks and the [financial] sector's perceptions of what represents quality information might be more sophisticated if the sector was able to readily access relevant expertise and more robust and independently verified

Public Pressures or Institutional Conditions?" *European Accounting Review* 14(1) (2005): 3; J. Guthrie and L.D. Parker, "Corporate Social Disclosure Practice: A Comparative International Analysis," *Advances in Public Interest Accounting* 3 (1990): 159.

200 J. Kuszewski, *Issue Brief: Materiality* (SustainAbility, undated): http://www.sustainability.com/insight/issue-brief.asp?id=65.

201 E.E. Hancock, "Red Dawn, Blue Thunder, Purple Rain: Corporate Risk of Liability for Global Climate Change and the SEC Disclosure Dilemma," *Georgetown International Environmental Law Review* 17 (2005): 233.

202 CERES, "Thirteen Pension Leaders Call on SEC Chairman to Require Global Warming Risks in Corporate Disclosure," Press release, April 15, 2007.

203 "Pension Fund Urges More Climate Risk Disclosure," *Reuters*, October 31, 2007.

204 See http://www.cdproject.net.

environmental data."[205] Moreover, financiers consider "information on environmental risk... highly subjective when compared to mainstream financial risks (e.g., tax, regulatory, credit, and operational risks)."[206] The financial sector has a skewed interest in corporate sustainability reporting. According to a Canadian study: "[e]nvironmental or social issues of corporate performance are important only in terms of risk to the company's financial health, and therefore to capital market financial decision-making."[207] Further, "[w]here the markets do pay attention to [sustainability] issues, a premium for good environmental or social performance is not paid."[208]

In addition to better disclosures to advance SRI, sustainability reporting by financial institutions themselves must not be overlooked.[209] Such reporting should encompass not only financiers' direct ecological impacts (e.g., energy use and waste from their offices and day-to-day operations), but also their indirect effects through the companies they sponsor, at least in the firms in which they hold significant stakes. Surveys suggest a marked increase in sustainability reporting by financiers, particularly voluntary reporting.[210] While financial corporations such as banks and investment companies are typically subject to similar environmental reporting standards as other types of companies, unfortunately these disclosure systems do not capture the more significant, diffuse, and indirect impacts of lending and investment relationships. They may remain, therefore, unseen polluters.

Overall, while the trend is more extensive corporate sustainability reporting, its quality and value lag considerably. Large transnational companies and Western European firms typically demonstrate the best practices, while sustainability reporting among African and Latin American firms is much weaker.[211]

2. Reporting Regulations

Companies incur obligations to report on their environmental and social behavior in a variety of contexts: pursuant to environmental legislation, and

205 Ernst and Young, note 195, 3.
206 Ibid., 10.
207 Stratos, note 195, iv–v.
208 Ibid., v.
209 K. Tarna, "Reporting on the Environment: Current Practice in the Financial Services Sector," in *Sustainable Banking: The Greening of Finance*, eds J.J. Bouma, M. Jeucken, and L. Klinkers (Greenleaf Publishing, 2001), 149.
210 KPMG, note 198, 12.
211 Association of Chartered Certified Accounts (ACCA), *Towards Transparency: Progress on Global Sustainability Reporting 2004* (ACCA, 2004); KPMG, note 198.

under securities regulation rules. Reporting requirements in environmental law principally range from disclosing quantitative information about past conduct, such as pollution data, to environmental impact evaluations associated with proposed future projects. Securities regulations require companies to prepare and file financial statements, formulated in accordance with established accounting principles, which may include financial quantification of any environmental liabilities and risks to the corporation. Companies may also furnish narrative reporting, such as in the management discussion and analysis sections of their annual reports. Environmental disclosures in the latter context have had limited impact, as securities regulators tend to see their role conservatively as protecting investors rather than acting as "an instrument of corporate change."[212]

In Europe, legislative standards for corporate environmental reporting have mushroomed since the early 1990s.[213] The EU's Accounts Modernization Directive of 2003 requires companies to produce a "fair review of the business of the company" which includes a discussion of "environmental matters" using key performance indicators "to the extent necessary for an understanding of the development, performance or position of the business of the company."[214] Giving effect to this standard, the UK's *Companies Act* requires directors, in their annual business review, to report "to the extent necessary for an understanding of the development, performance, or position of the company's business … information about environmental matters (including the impact of the company's business on the environment;)" and "social and community issues, including information about any policies of the company regarding these matters and the effectiveness of the policies."[215] The overall purpose of the business review is to help shareholders assess how

---

212 R.H. Feller, "Environmental Disclosure and the Securities Laws," *Boston College Environmental Affairs Law Review* 22 (1995): 225, 248.

213 EC, *Communication from the Commission concerning Corporate Social Responsibility: A Business Contribution to Sustainable Development*, COM(2002) 347 final (July 2002), 14–15.

214 Directive 2003/51/EC of 18 June 2003, O.J. L. 178/16 (2003), art. 14 (providing for the amendment of Directive 78/660/EEC on annual accounts); However, the Directive allows EU Member States to exempt small and medium enterprises from the disclosure obligations if they wish (art. 14(b)).

215 Section 417(5). The UK Government however abandoned plans to require companies to disclose more comprehensive information about their social and environmental impacts and risks: see *Draft Companies Act 1985 (Operating and Financial Review and Directors' Report) Regulations,* 2004.

well directors have dispatched their duty to promote the success of the firm under section 172 of the *Companies Act*.

Scandinavian and Benelux countries were among the first in Europe to pioneer environmental reporting standards —they were, however, usually limited to targeting just the largest public companies.[216] These measures were included in Denmark's *Environmental Protection Act* of 1996,[217] the Netherlands' *Environmental Management Act* of 1997,[218] and Sweden's *Law of Accounts* of 1999.[219] Later, France[220] and Germany[221] enacted statutes requiring companies to report on certain environmental information. France's reporting law reform, one of the most comprehensive in scope and detail, partially based on the GRI indicators, was directly influenced by pressure from the French SRI community.[222] A 2006 study of the impact of the French legislation noted a marked improvement in the reporting of social and environmental issues in general, although some statutory reporting categories were often omitted from corporate filings.[223]

The US has some of the oldest and most elaborate environmental disclosure laws. Federal and state environmental legislation addressing pollution control and natural resource management contain disclosure requirements that are predominantly used for regulatory enforcement. The Toxics Release

216 KPMG, note 198; Global Reporting Initiative, *Government Initiatives to Promote Corporate Sustainability Reporting Roundtable* (UNEP, 2001).
217 *Environmental Protection Act*, s. 35; see further P. Rikhardsson, "Developments in Danish Environmental Reporting," *Business Strategy and the Environment* 5(4) (1996): 269.
218 T. Emtairah, *Corporate Environmental Reporting: Review of Policy Action in Europe* (International Institute for Industrial Environmental Economics, 2002), 28–29.
219 Chapter 6.1: see further ibid., 32–33.
220 *Nouvelles régulations economiques*, Law No. 2001-420 of May 15, 2001, J.O., May 16, 2001, art. 116.
221 *Accounting Law Reform Act*, 2004 (*Bilanzrechtsreformgesetz*).
222 C.A. Williams and J.M. Conley, *An Emerging Third Way? The Erosion of the Anglo-American Shareholder Value Construct*, Legal Studies Research Paper No. 04-09 (University of North Carolina, 2004), 12; L.J. Dhooge, "Beyond Voluntarism: Social Disclosure and France's Nouvelles Regulations Economiques," *Arizona Journal of International and Comparative Law* 21(2) (2004): 441, 447. However, Dhooge is critical of some omissions in the French reporting rules, such as concerning the activities of foreign subsidiaries (at 476).
223 Centre français d'information sur les entreprises (CFIE), *Application de la loi NRE dans les rapports annuels: une comparaison de la qualité des informations sociales, sociétales et environnementales* (CFIE, 2006).

Inventory (developed under the *Emergency Planning and Community Right to Know Act* of 1986)[224] is an example. The SEC reporting standards contain further reporting requirements designed for market participants. The SEC rules are hugely significant, as the SEC oversees the world's two biggest stock exchanges (the NYSE and the NASDAQ), also influencing various foreign companies cross-listed in these exchanges.

Under rules dating from the early 1970s, the SEC requires disclosure of corporate environmental liabilities and other environmental matters material to the financial condition of the company.[225] For instance, Item 101 of Regulation S-K requires registrants to disclose "the material effects that compliance" with government environmental regulations "may have upon the capital expenditures, earnings, and competitive position of the registrant and its subsidiaries."[226] With time, SEC requirements have become both "more particular and more insistent about the need for disclosure of environmental liabilities and obligations" by registered companies.[227]

In the wake of various corporate scandals, the Sarbanes-Oxley legislation of 2002 introduced further requirements for companies to maintain a system of controls facilitating more accurate reporting of material business risks.[228] This law did not change the fundamentals regarding disclosure of environmental risks and liabilities as much as it changed the process by which they are made.[229] In this way, it makes public companies better understand the seriousness of their disclosure obligations, thereby devoting the necessary expertise to properly process, analyze, and evaluate environmental information.

In practice, corporate environmental reporting to the SEC has often not been of high standard. Certainly, the volume of such reporting has

224 1986, Pub. L. No. 99-499, 100 Stat. 1729.
225 For more detail, see T. Pfund, "Corporate Environmental Accountability: Expanding SEC Disclosures to Promote Market-Based Environmentalism," *Missouri Environmental Law and Policy Review* 11 (2004): 118; M.M. Crough, "SEC Reporting Requirements: Environmental Issues," *Environmental Claims Journal* 7(2) (1994/95): 41.
226 Regulation S-K, 17 C.F.R., s. 229.101(c)(xii).
227 P.W. Wallace, "Disclosure of Environmental Liabilities under Securities Laws: The Potential of Securities-Market-Based Incentives for Pollution Control," *Washington and Lee Law Review* 50 (1995): 1093, 1098.
228 *Public Company Accounting Reform and Investor Protection Act, 2002,* Pub. L. No. 107-204, 116 Stat. 745.
229 N. Schwartz, "The Cost of Sarbanes-Oxley," *Information Management Journal* 37 (2003): 5, 8; C.G. Rose, *Financial Reporting of Environmental Liabilities and Risks after Sarbanes-Oxley* (John Wiley and Sons, 2005).

mushroomed in recent years, driven by the business-case dogma that it contributes to better corporate governance resulting in enhanced shareholder value.[230] According to Sanford Lewis and Tim Little, companies may obfuscate bad news by assigning it to notes to their financial statements, using questionable time horizons masking potential future costs, avoiding informative discussion of liabilities that cannot yet be accurately quantified, and making piecemeal analysis of the materiality of issues, thereby muting their cumulative or total impact.[231] For instance, Exxon Corporation's 1990 10-K report to the SEC noted the massive cleanup and litigation expenses from the Alaskan oil spills with estimated cost at US$1.68 billion as not material to the company's operations.[232]

The World Resources Institute's surveys of reporting practices under Item 101 found reporting to be mostly uninformative.[233] Companies, wary of creating a competitive disadvantage among other reasons, typically underestimate the financial materiality of environmental management to their operations. A 1998 study by the EPA found that 74 percent of companies failed to adequately report cases where environmentally related legal proceedings could result in monetary sanctions over US$100,000.[234] Only 26 percent of civil and administrative proceedings involving penalties were correctly disclosed, and only 16 percent of proceedings involving court-ordered supplemental environmental projects were disclosed. As recently as 2004, research published by the US Government Accountability Office suggests that firms continue to circumvent the SEC environmental disclosure standards.[235]

---

230 B. Heemskerk, P. Pistorio, and M. Scicluna, *Sustainable Development Reporting: Striking a Balance* (WBCSD, 2002), 20.

231 S. Lewis and T. Little, *Fooling Investors and Fooling Themselves* (Rose Foundation for Communities and the Environment, 2003), 3.

232 Exxon Valdez, *1990 Form 10-K, Notes to Consolidated Financial Statements* (1991) cited in Feller, note 212, 240.

233 World Resources Institute (WRI), *Coming Clean: Corporate Disclosure of Financially Significant Environmental Risks* (WRI, 2000); WRI, *Changing Oil: Emerging Environmental Risks and Shareholder Value in the Oil and Gas Industry* (WRI, 2003).

234 EPA Office of Enforcement and Compliance Assurance, *Guidance on Distributing the Notice of SEC Registrants' Duty to Disclose Environmental Legal Proceedings in EPA Enforcement Actions* (EPA, 1998).

235 Government Accountability Office (GAO), *Environmental Disclosure: SEC Should Explore Ways to Improve Tracking and Transparency of Information* (GAO, July 2004).

Studies by NGOs make similar findings, such as a report by Friends of the Earth on slack disclosure of climate related-risks.[236]

A similar gradual intensification of reporting rules in other jurisdictions is occurring, though coupled with various degrees of non-compliance. South Africa's innovative right-to-know law, the *Promotion of Access to Information Act* of 2000, allows any citizen access to certain information not only from state regulators, but also directly from private sector companies and financial institutions. Individuals can appeal to courts against companies that refuse to divulge information. In Canada, the Canadian Securities Administrators in 2004 issued a National Instrument to provide that material information not reflected in corporate financial statements must be discussed in the "Management Discussion and Analysis" section and the Annual Information Form.[237] The National Instrument directs corporations to disclose material environmental and social matters and policies in such reporting. Under the *Corporations Act* of 2001, companies operating in Australia must disclose performances related to any "particular and significant" environmental regulation, as a part of their annual directors' report.[238] This provision has been criticized for its narrow focus, and commentators disagree about the extent to which environmental reporting by Australian corporations has improved.[239] Australian corporate directors, as in other jurisdictions, must account for financially material environmental activities in their annual financial statements.[240] Further tightening of environmental reporting obligations in Australia is occurring in other contexts, such as under the *Energy Efficiency Opportunities Act* of 2006[241] and plans announced in 2007 for a new disclosure

---

236 M. Chan-Fishel, *Second Survey of Climate Change Disclosure in SEC Filings of Automobile, Insurance, Oil and Gas, Petrochemical, and Utilities Companies* (Friends of the Earth, 2003).

237 Canadian Securities Administrators (CSA), *National Instrument 51-102: Continuous Disclosure Obligations; Form 51-102 F1—MD&A Disclosure; Form 51-102F2—Annual Information Form* (CSA, 2004).

238 Section 299(1)(f).

239 Compare G.R. Frost, "An Investigation of Mandatory Environmental Reporting in Australia" (paper presented to the Third Asia Pacific Interdisciplinary Research in Accounting Conference, Adelaide, July 15–17, 2001) and K. Bubna-Litic, L. de Leeuw, and I. Williamson, "Walking the Thin Green Line: The Australian Experience of Corporate Environmental Reporting," *Environmental and Planning Law Journal* 18(3) (2001): 339.

240 Section 295.

241 It requires large private and public sector corporations to assess their energy use and report publicly on outcomes and their business responses.

regime concerning GHG emissions.[242] These reporting trends however are not uniform, and some jurisdictions such as Japan continue to rely heavily on voluntary environmental reporting guidelines.[243]

As in the US, corporate compliance with reporting standards is highly varied. A minority of Australian companies regularly issues separate sustainability reports that exceed the requirements of regulatory standards.[244] On the other hand, surveys of environmental reporting by UK companies indicate ongoing problems. In 2006, an Environment Agency survey of major firms found that "the level of quantified disclosures was still woefully low. Hard facts and figures were still too few and far between."[245] The Canadian Performance Reporting Board has discovered that Canadian companies with significant risk exposures related to climate change "are not always providing adequate disclosures in their regulatory filings and reporting to capital markets."[246]

3. Accounting Rules

Accounting principles that guide reporting in standard financial statements also contribute to deficiencies in reporting regimes from the perspective of reflecting the full impact of corporate social and environmental behavior. Rigorous accounting is essential to efficient markets, and lapses, such as in the case of Enron, can cause massive corporate governance failures.[247] Financial regulators require companies, as well as investment institutions such as pension funds, to file financial statements prepared in accordance with "generally accepted accounting principles" (GAAP) established by the

---

242 "Companies to Report Greenhouse Emissions," *Sydney Morning Herald*, July 9, 2007.

243 Japan, Ministry of the Environment, *Environmental Reporting Guidelines* (Ministry of the Environment, 2001), *Environmental Accounting Guidelines* (Ministry of the Environment, 2005), accessible at: http://www.env.go.jp/en.

244 Australia, Department of the Environment and Heritage (DEH), *The State of Sustainability Reporting in Australia 2005* (DEH, 2006) (commenting that 24 percent of 486 companies sampled regularly produce a sustainability report).

245 UK, Environment Agency (EA), *Environmental Disclosures* (EA, November 2006), 3.

246 Canadian Institute of Chartered Accountants (CICA), *MD&A Disclosure about the Financial Impact of Climate Change and Other Environmental Issues*. Discussion Brief (CICA, 2005), 3.

247 S. Siegel, "Global Accounting Dimensions of Corporate Governance," in *Corporate Governance Post-Enron: Comparative and International Perspectives*, eds J.J. Norton, J. Rickford, and J. Kleineman (British Institute for International and Comparative Law, 2006), 49.

accountancy profession and standard-setting bodies.[248] Since 1973, the IASB has promoted improvement and convergence of accounting principles through its International Financial Reporting Standards (IFRS).[249] These standards are not official law; they are norms of best practice. Still, national securities authorities and stock market exchanges commonly refer to the IASB standards or the US's version of GAPP as their benchmark.[250]

Accounting standards for the preparation of financial statements are limited by their design to capture financially material information concerning specific, past transactions. These principally comprise the expenses, liabilities, assets, and earnings associated with a company's operations. This system does not reflect the diffuse social and environmental externalities of corporate behavior, except if the financial consequences of those actions are captured in a specific transaction, such as the cost to a firm of purchasing pollution abatement technology to meet a new regulatory standard.[251] Moreover, because of the retrospective focus of accounting, summarizing a firm's financial position at the end of a reporting period (year or quarter, as the case may be), it largely ignores any future costs to the environment over the long term. An accounting standard may require firms to make contingent liabilities for anticipated environmental liabilities, but so long as the liabilities are both probable and capable of reasonable estimation.

A further limitation of accounting standards is their treatment of corporate goodwill, brand-name, and related intangibles.[252] As somewhere between 50 to 70 percent of the market value of major companies is tied up in intangible factors, many in the SRI community see corporate reputation as a key point of leverage for disciplining firms.[253] The social license for firms is

---

248 B.J. Epstein, R. Nach, and S.M. Bragg, *Wiley GAAP: Interpretation and Application of Generally Accepted Accounting Principles* (John Wiley and Sons, 2006).

249 Originally known as the International Accounting Standards Committee, and was restructured in 2001; see http://www.iasc.org.

250 A. Tarca, "International Convergence of Accounting Practices: Choosing between IAS and US GAAP," *Journal of International Financial Management and Accounting* 15(1) (2004): 60.

251 S. Schaltegger and R. Burritt, *Contemporary Environmental Accounting: Issues, Concepts and Practice* (Greenleaf Publishing, 2000), 76–86.

252 L. Nicholson, T. Playford, and S. Dalgamo, "The Tangible Headache of Intangible Assets in a Global Accounting Environment," *Keeping Good Companies* 5 (2005): 266.

253 Remarks, N. Purcell, Group General Manager, Westpac (UNEPFI Global Roundtable, Melbourne, Australia, October 24–25 2007); D.C. Courts, M.G. Leiter, and M.A. Loch, "Brand Leverage," *The McKinsey Quarterly* 2 (1999): 100.

increasingly shaped by public perception of their social and environmental behavior, regardless of the letter of the law. However, conventional accounting standards generally do not recognize the value of such intangibles except on disposition or takeover of a company.[254] For instance, the IFRS require any goodwill and intangible assets to be accounted for in a business acquisition.[255] While the IASB is striving for international consistency in accounting for intangibles,[256] it has not revolutionized accounting standards to capture a broader picture of corporate brand names or reputations related to social and environmental performance.

While financial quantification is commonly viewed as the safest and most objective measure of corporate performance, by emphasizing a numerical value of the corporation, accounting rules and practices constrain the incorporation of the full social and environmental effects of corporate behavior.[257] As Oren Perez explains, "the sensitivity of this form of environmental reporting to ecological concerns remains *bounded* by the need to re-present environmental data in monetary (cost) values and by the image of the investor as *homo investicus*."[258] Much environmental harm traceable to business will not create specific liabilities or costs, and thus does not need to be reported. In the context of inadequate or poorly enforced environmental regulation, long-term social and environmental impacts of corporations, decades from now, are virtually never considered "financially material." Even in relation to more concrete, immediate environmental problems, firms can potentially minimize the magnitude of possible liabilities in various ways:[259] treating environmental

254 Personal communications Julie Desjardins and Alan Willis, Advisors to the Canadian Institute of Chartered Accountants (Toronto, November 28, 2007).

255 See S. Powell, "Accounting for Intangible Assets: Current Requirements, Key Players and Future Directions," *European Accounting Review* 12(4) (2003): 797.

256 L. Quilligan, "Intangible Assets: Identification and Valuation Under IFRS 2," *Accountancy Ireland* 38(3) (2006): 10.

257 K.T. Maunders and R. Burritt, "Accounting and Ecological Crisis," *Accounting, Auditing and Accountability Journal* 4(3) (1991): 9.

258 O. Perez, "Facing the Global Hydra: Ecological Transformation at the Global Financial Frontier: The Ambitious Case of the Global Reporting Initiative," in *Constitutionalism, Multilevel Trade Governance and Social Regulation*, eds C. Joerges and E.U. Petersmann (Hart Publishing, 2006), 459, 471.

259 S.B. Goodman and T. Little, *The Gap in GAAP: An Examination of Environmental Accounting Loopholes* (Rose Foundation for Communities and the Environment, 2003), 4.

liabilities in a piecemeal way and thereby understating their total exposure;[260] simplifying the financial significance of complex environmental issues;[261] and assessing improper valuations to environmental services and functions.[262]

For several decades academics and the accountancy profession have considered new models of "social accounting" to correct these anomalies, but generally without success in altering the chief accounting rules in GAAP and IFRS.[263] The transaction-based nature of financial accounting is such that it is very difficult to recognize, measure, and report in financial statements widespread and long-term social and environmental impacts.[264] To the extent that there are taxes, fines, or other financial consequences attached to these impacts, then financial statements can recognize, measure, and report such transactions. Social accounting has best contributed to the propagation of satellite or supplementary mechanisms for measuring and reporting on corporate sustainability performance. These include voluntary CSR reporting regimes such as the GRI as well as inclusion of narrative disclosures in corporate filings to securities regulators. However, their effect on financial markets generally appears to be somewhat muted. A recent report on the North American finance sector noted, "many [investment analysts] stated firmly that they do not read companies' sustainability reports because the reports mean nothing to them. Analysts generally do not have the technical background to understand the data… [and it] is not in a form that resonates with analysts' thinking."[265] Investors attach much more weight to traditional forms of reporting, as they are more bottom line, short-term oriented

---

260 Ibid.

261 C. Cooper, "The Non and Nom of Accounting for (M)other Nature," *Accounting, Auditing and Accountability Journal* 5(3) (1992): 16, 36.

262 R. Gray, "Accounting and Environmentalism: An Exploration of the Challenge of Gently Accounting for Accountability, Transparency and Sustainability," *Accounting, Organizations and Society* 17(5) (1992): 399, 416.

263 E.g., Canadian Institute of Chartered Accountants (CICA), *Full Cost Accounting from an Environmental Perspective* (CICA, 1997); D. Owen, et al., "Struggling with the Praxis of Social Accounting: Stakeholders, Accountability, Audits and Procedures," *Accounting, Auditing and Accountability Journal* 10(3) (1997): 325; M.R. Mathews, *Socially Responsible Accounting* (Chapman and Hall, 1993).

264 Personal communications Julie Desjardins and Alan Willis, Advisors to the Canadian Institute of Chartered Accountants (Toronto, November 28, 2007).

265 S. McGeachie, M. Kiernan, and E. Kirzner, *Finance and the Environment in North America: The State of Play of the Integration of Environmental Issues into Financial Research* (Environment Canada, 2005), 68.

without necessarily wanting to understand the implications of poor corporate sustainability performance over the long term.[266] Contrary to the expectations of reflexive law, disclosure practices and their regulation has yet to provide the means to transform financial markets.[267]

IV. Financial Incentive Mechanisms

A. ECONOMIC INSTRUMENTS AS A MEANS OF SRI

Defined broadly, economic instruments (EIs) seek to alter the "costs and benefits of alternative actions open to economic agents, with the effect of influencing behaviour in a way favorable to the environment."[268] EIs implement the sustainable development principle of "internalization of environmental costs,"[269] also known colloquially as the "polluter pays" or "user pays" principle.[270] Particularly as a means of climate policy, use of EIs such as pollution charges and tradable emission allowances is spreading in many countries.[271] Capturing environmental costs and benefits of development is also a way for EIs to help promote SRI. EIs directly dissuade polluting behavior, as they provide concrete incentives for financiers to shun polluting companies. Given that SRI is primarily driven by financial imperatives, reflexive policy instruments that amplify the financial significance of corporate environmental behavior could considerably boost this SRI market.

---

266 L. Descano and B.S. Gentry, "Communicating Environmental Performance to the Capital Markets," *Corporate Environmental Strategy* 5(5) (1998): 31.

267 Wallace, note *227*, 1127.

268 OECD, *Environmental Policy: How to Apply Economic Instruments* (OECD, 1991), 10; see further OECD, *Managing the Environment: The Role of Economic Instruments* (OECD, 1994).

269 M. Massarrat, "Sustainability through Cost Internalisation," *Ecological Economics* 22(1) (1997): 29.

270 OECD, *The Polluter Pays Principle: Definition, Analysis, Implementation* (OECD, 1975).

271 For recent practice, see J. Snape and J. De Souza, *Environmental Taxation Law: Policy, Contexts and Practice* (Ashgate Publishing, 2006); T. H. Tietenberg, *Emissions Trading: Principles and Practice* (Resources for the Future, 2006); D. Stowell, *Climate Trading: Development of Greenhouse Gas Markets* (Palgrave Macmillan, 2005).

The main types of EIs are price-based measures (such as pollution taxes and resource use levies)[272] and marketable allowances (such as tradable rights to exploit specific resources or to emit pollutants within certain parameters).[273] Related categories of EIs include subsidies, such as financial grants supporting beneficial behavior,[274] and green procurement policies for stimulating the supply of environmentally friendly goods and services.[275] Environmental liability rules in tort or legislation that make polluters pay also constitute a type of EI. Beyond ad hoc EIs, some economists have proposed a more formal EI system of ecological tax or fiscal reform, comprising the redesign of the entire public financial system in support of sustainability.[276]

EIs as a means of environmental policy gained currency during the 1990s, as governments supplemented command-and-control regulation with market-incentive instruments.[277] However, although "market-oriented," EIs are generally not an unadulterated expression of neoliberal doctrine. Rather, they address the environmental impacts of unrestrained free markets, and therefore more accurately epitomize the ecological modernization oeuvre. EIs strive to provide cost-effective environmental policies at lower costs than other forms of governance, to achieve the same environmental result. Cost-saving opportunities are achievable as EIs generally allow firms to design their own means of reducing pollution, provided they pay.[278] Nevertheless, environmental regulation is rarely a blunt choice between command and market instruments. All types of EIs depend on some legal regulation for their successful operation, and many policy instruments blend the proverbial stick and carrot.

---

272 S. Beder, "Charging the Earth: The Promotion of Price-based Measures for Pollution Control," *Ecological Economics* 16(2) (1996): 51.

273 Tietenberg, note 271.

274 See F. Cairncross, "Natural Resource Management and Subsidies," in *Green Inc. A Guide to Business and the Environment,* ed., F. Cairncross (Earthscan, 1995), 74.

275 L. Mastny, *Purchasing Power: Harnessing Institutional Procurement for People and the Plant* (Worldwatch Institute, 2003).

276 E.U. von Weizsäcker and J. Jesinghaus, *Ecological Tax Reform* (Zed Books, 1992); K. Schlegelmilch, ed., *Green Budget Reform in Europe: Countries at the Forefront* (Springer, 1999).

277 Panayotou, note 95.

278 See R.B. Stewart, "Economic Incentives for Environmental Protection: Opportunities and Obstacles," in *Environmental Law, the Economy and Sustainable Development*, note 63, 171.

EIs have been applied to address a diverse range of environmental issues.[279] The EU has the most extensive eco-taxes imposed on energy use, consumer products, solid waste, and pollution emissions,[280] and in March 2007 the EC adopted a policy paper that recommends even greater use of EIs as a means of environmental policy.[281] Generally, Germany has gone the furthest in ecological tax reform, although not specifically with regard to SRI.[282] The UK pioneered several EIs, such as the climate change levy and the GHG emission trading scheme.[283] Elsewhere, Australia, New Zealand, and the US have embraced some EIs, particularly the tradable allowance schemes for water, fisheries, and air pollutants.[284] While US authorities have traditionally been averse to imposing pollution taxes, they do provide deductions for environmental improvements through taxation policy. Many US states offer tax incentives for the development of renewable and clean energy technologies.[285] Japan and its East Asian industrializing neighbors have also employed taxation policy for similar purposes.[286]

279 Rietbergen-McCracken and Abaza, note 95.

280 J. Vehmas, et al., "Environmental Taxes on Fuels and Electricity—Some Experiences from the Nordic Countries," Energy Policy 27 (1998): 343; K. Deketelaere, et al., Critical Issues in Environmental Taxation Volume II: International Comparative Perspectives (Oxford University Press, 2004); Chalifour, et al., note 98.

281 EC, Green Paper on Market-Based Instruments for Environment and Related Policy Purposes, COM(2007) 140 final.

282 P.J. Welfens, Energy Policies in the European Union: Germany's Ecological Tax Reform (Springer, 2001); C. Beuermann and T. Santarius, "Ecological Tax Reform in Germany: Handling Two Hot Potatoes at the Same Time," Energy Policy 34(8) (2006): 917.

283 B.J. Richardson, "Economic Instruments in EU Environmental Law Reform: Is the UK Government 'Sending the Right Signals'," European Journal of Law Reform 3(4) (2002): 427.

284 B.J. Richardson, "Economic Instruments and Sustainable Management in New Zealand," Journal of Environmental Law 10(1) (1998): 21; B.J. Richardson, "Economic Instruments in Australian Pollution Control Law," in Pollution Law in Australia, eds G. Bates and Z. Lipman (Butterworths, 2002), 51; D. O'Connor, "Applying Economic Instruments in Developing Countries: From Theory to Implementation," Environment and Development Economics 4 (1999): 91; R. Stavins, Lessons from the American Experiment with Market-based Environmental Policies (Resources for the Future, 2001).

285 The federal government offers tax credits under the Energy Policy Act, 2005, Pub. L. No. 109-58, 119 Stat. 594. See the database on all incentive schemes in the US at: http://www.dsireusa.org/index.cfm?EE=1&RE=1.

286 B.F. Barrett, ed., Ecological Modernization and Japan (Routledge, 2005);

B. IMPLICATIONS FOR THE FINANCIAL SECTOR

How can EIs support SRI and what is their relationship to corporate financing? Primarily, EIs assist financiers by factoring the costs and the benefits of environmental behavior into the overall financial health of a corporation. A major barrier to business case SRI has been insufficient information about such behavior and its financial quantification and its impacts to the bottom line. Unless equity and debt prices truly reflect environmental performances and risks, pragmatic financial managers may relegate SRI to a fringe, long-term afterthought. For instance, climate change becomes much more financially salient for investors, if a price tag is attached to carbon emissions to prevent pollution in the present, rather than to cure problems in the future, when costs could be far more exorbitant.

Ironically, if all polluting behaviors were priced and penalized in this way, much SRI would become unnecessary as presumably the most cost-effective market position would be socially responsible. Capital markets would possess all necessary information to price environmental risks and harms, as reflected in financing costs. At a very simplistic level, earnings of polluting companies incurring punitive taxes would decline and, as a matter of course, their stock prices. Their cost of raising capital would increase, and SRI's required role in the market would diminish. It would lapse into its former niche of church-based ethical investments: campaigns against gambling, pornography, and similar depravities.[287]

Yet, there are enormous political, economic, and technical obstacles to such a comprehensive system of EIs. Gaps arise even in countries with relatively advanced laws as they deal with cross-border investments involving jurisdictions without rigorous environmental standards. This may also mean the movement of employment and capital to jurisdictions with less stringent laws —today's borderless communications and globalization making this transition relatively easy. EIs tend to engender more resistance, compared with traditional regulation.[288] EIs can ignite vociferous opposition by simply attempting to expose the costs of environmental protection measures.[289]

A.P.J. Mol and J.C.L. Van Buuren, eds, *Greening Industrialization in Asian Transitional Economies: China and Vietnam* (Lexington Books, 2003).

287 There would although remain some further role for SRI in combating agency problems in corporate governance.

288 C. Larrue, "The Political (Un)feasibility of Environmental Economic Instruments," in *Environmental Policy in Search of New Instruments*, ed., B. Dente (Kluwer Law, 1995), 37, 45–49.

289 Ibid., 37.

For example, during the 1990s the fossil fuel industries successfully stalled a proposed carbon tax in the EU.[290] Civil society groups have also campaigned against EIs, driven by concern for the socially regressive impacts of user pay regimes for consumption of water, energy, and other basic necessities.[291]

Indisputable methodological difficulties also remain in implementing certain types of EIs, such as taxes to factor in all ecological costs.[292] Just as companies find it difficult to calculate the cost of complex environmental impacts in their financial statement disclosures, environmental policy-makers also face challenges quantifying environmental behavior and impacts into objective financial metrics. The accurate calculation of pollution or resource charges can be overwhelmingly complex, as they require identification of the users and the precise levels of their environmental effect. The complex, varied, and inter-connected nature of eco-systems make their valuation difficult.[293] For example, how can one quantify the value of fresh water aquifer, without first understanding the value of that aquifer to overall watershed management? Thus, some environmental costs and impacts will also have to be valued outside of market mechanisms, based on ethical judgments for instance.[294]

The financial sector itself however should not have strong resistance against current types of EIs. With their modest direct resource use and relatively low emissions, financial institutions do not face the same magnitude of costs as manufacturing and other intensive industries.[295] Moreover, emissions trading schemes create new market opportunities for financial intermediaries. Nonetheless, financiers would likely resist EIs if policy-makers recognize financial institutions as the "unseen polluters" and seek to target them directly. While financiers would welcome taxation incentives like subsidies

---

290 J. Sebenius, "Towards a Winning Climate Coalition," in *Negotiating Climate Change*, eds L. Mintzer and J. Leonard (Cambridge University Press, 1994), 227, 294.

291 G. Rowe, "Environmental Justice as an Ethical, Economic and Legal Principle," in *Environmental Justice and Market Mechanisms*, note 85, 70–71.

292 See generally OECD, *Implementation Strategies for Environmental Taxes* (OECD, 1996).

293 B. Gustafsson, "Scope and Limits of the Market Mechanism in Environmental Management," *Ecological Economics* 24 (1998): 259, 265–66.

294 R.S. de Groot, *Functions of Nature. Evaluation of Nature in Environment, Planning and Decision Making* (Wolters-Noordhoff, 1992).

295 On the direct environmental impacts of financiers, see, e.g., P. Street and P.E. Monaghan, "Assessing the Sustainability of Bank Service Channels," in *Sustainable Banking,* note 209, 72.

for green investment, they would disfavor mechanisms that sought to internalize anticipated environmental and social costs in financing transactions.

A business-case driven SRI movement should welcome EIs. Through their pedagogic articulation of the financial consequences of environmental harm, EIs can strengthen the underlying conditions for SRI. In the spirit of reflexive law, EIs should encourage internal learning by corporations about their environmental risks and costs, presumably leading to behavioral changes.[296] In turn, financiers could incorporate such information into their loans or investment decisions. Therefore, through EIs, SRI morphs from an ethical irrelevance to a financially material consideration.

C. ECONOMIC INSTRUMENTS FOR SRI

1. Tax Concessions for SRI

Beyond encouraging behavioral changes in companies, EIs can also stimulate SRI by targeting the financial sector with incentives to make investors and lenders more willing to fund sustainable development. As a means to correct an imperfect market that undervalues natural capital, EIs can alter the competitive advantage in favor of SRI. For instance, tax concessions for investing in renewable energy generation and clean technologies can boost financing of these beneficial ventures. Financial subsidies can also be applied directly to SRI funds.

The Netherlands has gone the furthest in using taxation law to stimulate SRI. Its 1995 *Green Project Directive* was initiated to provide concessions to approved environmental finance.[297] Originally restricted to Dutch projects, the scheme now also enables Dutch investors to fund certain sustainability projects in developing countries. Essentially, the directive exempts taxes on interest and dividend income from qualifying funds established by banks and other financial intermediaries. To qualify, a fund must invest at least 70 percent of its assets in environmentally useful projects, as designated by Dutch authorities.[298] Project proponents must also obtain a "green certificate" from the government to verify compliance with the official sustainable development criteria. These include projects predicted to be of high environmental

---

296 Orts, note 39, 1271.

297 The scheme was revamped and extended in 2002 and 2005: *Regeling groenprojecten buitenland, Staatscourant* 1 (January 2, 2002): 31; *Regeling groenprojecten, Staatscourant* 131 (July 11, 2005): 13.

298 Jeucken, note 67, 94.

benefit but low economic return.[299] Projects eligible for green certificates typically include woodland and landscape protection, organic agriculture, renewable energy, and sustainable housing construction and renovation. The scheme is designed to finance projects that could not generate sufficient return on investment without the tax advantage. In 2004 the Dutch government also introduced the *Regulation on Social and Ethical Projects*, a further measure for tax exemption on income from approved microcredit funds and a tax reduction on income from authorized social and ethical funds.[300] Like the *Green Project Directive*, eligible funds must invest at least 70 percent of their capital in approved projects.

The schemes have attracted participation from various financiers including Triodos Groenfonds, ABN AMRO Groen Fonds, and Postbank Groen. They have established green funds or bonds that offer depositors an environmental tax credit worth about an extra 2.5 percent return on their investments. The interest rate paid by the bank is typically lower than the market rate, which allows the bank to invest the funds in green projects at a lower interest rate. However, the preferential tax regime is sufficient to attract investors, and motivates lenders to shepherd more funds to sustainability projects. And it has the overarching benefit of encouraging innovative environmental projects that financiers might otherwise view as less profitable and too risky.[301]

What of their impact? The Dutch Association of Investors for Sustainable Development (Vereniging van Beleggers voor Duurzame Ontwikkeling) attributed about 50 percent of the growth in Dutch SRI from 1996 to 2004 to the *Green Project Directive*.[302] A 2002 KPMG study found that since 1996 the Directive had delivered €2.8 billion of investment from 140,000 individual investors in over 2,100 projects.[303] In 2001 alone, the scheme provided at least €50 million of environmental benefits (in addition to other conventional business returns and many unquantifiable technological

299 T. van Bellegem, "The Green and Social Funds System in the Netherlands," in *Solidarity-based Choices in the Market-place: A Vital Contribution to Social Cohesion* (Council of Europe, 2005), 157, 161.

300 *Regeling sociaal-ethische projecten, Staatscourant*, 44 (March 4 2004), 10.

301 Jeucken, note 67, 95.

302 Vereniging van Beleggers voor Duurzame Ontwikkeling (VBDO), *Socially Responsible Savings and Investments in the Netherlands: Developments in Volume and Growth of Socially-responsible Savings and Investments in Retail Funds* (VBDO, 2005), 11.

303 KPMG, *Sustainable Profit. An Overview of the Environmental Benefits Generated by the Green Funds Scheme* (KPMG, 2002), 6.

and social benefits).[304] KPMG found that the scheme "ensured a faster market introduction of new products and techniques such as wind energy" as well as an intensification of other developments such as organic agriculture.[305] The largest distribution of project capital pursuant to the scheme went to renewable energy (30 percent) and green label greenhouses (20 percent).[306] One academic study suggested the Directive's environmental effects were mixed, on the basis that some projects would have been undertaken anyhow and the policy instrument neglects environmental problems in some sectors including consumer households and transport.[307] Finally, according to the Dutch government, the scheme is a winner, having delivered by 2005 some €4 billion in additional environmental investments at a cost of €125 million in foregone tax revenue.[308]

No other jurisdiction provides a comparable scheme, but several offer ad hoc tax breaks for investments in specific environmental projects, such as wind farms or solar energy development. Several countries also furnish tax incentives for economically targeted investment (ETI), particularly in deprived communities.

The Belgium government created a fund[309] worth €75 million to disburse soft loans and to provide financial guarantees for long-term investments. A requirement for access to this fund is that 70 percent of the capital must be assigned to projects of benefit to the "social economy," and the remaining 30 percent to SRI projects that meet standards set by Ethibel, one of Belgium's leading SRI institutions.[310] Also, investors in the fund must retain their holdings for at least five years to reap the 5 percent tax relief. Unlike the Dutch system, where private financiers can create eligible funds without limit on the amount of capital, in the Belgian model only government-controlled funds can offer the tax breaks. Thus, this government scheme competes with private SRI funds and may stunt their growth as they are unable to offer comparable incentives.

---

304 Ibid.
305 Ibid., 5.
306 Ibid., 11.
307 B. Scholtens, "Borrowing Green: Economic and Environmental Effects of Green Fiscal Policy in The Netherlands," *Ecological Economics* 39(3) (2001): 425.
308 The Netherlands, Ministry of Finance, *The Green Funds Scheme: A Success Story in the Making* (Ministry of Finance, 2006), 5.
309 Set up by "la Société fédérale d'investissement," as authorized by La loi-programme (April 8, 2003).
310 See http://www.ethibel.org.

France has several instruments promoting SRI in the retail sector.[311] One mechanism offers tax breaks to investors in certain legally prescribed social enterprises.[312] These unlisted enterprises must meet various social welfare criteria (e.g., at least one-third of staff must comprise handicapped persons or the chronically unemployed) or be run as a cooperative. Apart from generous tax concessions offered to investors in these enterprises, these firms qualify as "solidarity fund" investments, which pension funds are obligated to offer as an option in their employee savings plans.[313] Such an investment plan must put between 5 and 10 percent of its funds in the socially responsible enterprises. Not surprisingly, the volume of social investment in France exploded after 2002 as employees flocked to take advantage of the new regime.[314] Another French innovation, introduced in 2007, is the Livret de développement durable, or sustainable development savings accounts, offered by financial institutions.[315] This initiative, which replaced the Codevi (accounts for industrial development) allows residents to deposit up to €6,000 in such an account, on which the interest is exempt from tax. The resultant pool of capital is used to finance projects promoting energy efficiency and other environmental benefits.

The UK and the US offer some tax incentive schemes. The British Community Investment Tax Relief Scheme assists communities marginalized by mainstream financial investment.[316] Enacted in 2003, it encourages investment in disadvantaged neighborhoods in Britain by providing substantial tax credits to long-term investors (minimum of five years) in businesses in the deprived localities. Community Development Finance Institutions administer the investments, channeling loans to enterprises in

---

311 See A.B. Antal and A. Sobczak, "Corporate Social Responsibility in France: A Mix of National Traditions and International Influences," *Business Society* 46(1) (2007): 9.

312 *Loi relative au mécénat, aux associations et aux foundations* (August 1, 2003), Loi No. 2003-709; *Les mesures d'accompagnement social des projets de la loi no, 2003-721 (August 1, 2003), pour l'initiative économique.*

313 Loi No. 2001-152, note 116.

314 J.M. Lecuyer, "Adapted Fiscal Rules for the Development of Initiatives of the Socially Responsible Economy: The Fabius Act on Employee Savings Schemes (February 2001)," in *Solidarity-based Choices in the Market-place: A Vital Contribution to Social Cohesion* (Council of Europe, 2005), 143, 150–51.

315 *Décret No. 2007-161 relatif au livret de développement durable* (February 6, 2007).

316 *Community Investment Tax Relief Accreditation of Community Development Finance Institutions) Regulations*, 2003.

the designated areas.[317] In the US, the *Community Development Banking and Financial Institutions Act* of 1994 created a fund for economic revitalization and community development by assisting community-based financial institutions through equity investments, grants, loans, and technical assistance.[318] Another Clinton administration initiative, the *Community Renewal Tax Relief Act* of 2000,[319] promotes community rejuvenation by channeling similar assistance to businesses operating in economically depressed communities. Federal tax credits have been instrumental in leveraging institutional investment into urban renewal projects such as the construction of affordable housing and community infrastructure.[320]

In Canada, labour-sponsored investment funds (LSIFs) emerged in the early 1980s, when the trade union movement in Quebec sought to develop new financing models to overcome the paucity of investment in small and medium enterprises and the attendant employment losses.[321] In 1983, the province created the Fonds de solidarité des travailleurs du Québec, which has since become the model for LSIFs across the country. LSIFs are a form of venture finance, in which trade union representatives control the funds' investment policies, and they are obligated to invest in certain small, community-based enterprises. LSIFs attract investments from workers via a government-provided tax credit that can be used with their retirement savings plan. However, the mediocre financial performance of LSIFs confirms in the minds of some critics the risks of government schemes "meddling" with the market. With poor financial returns, including the wind-up of Manitoba's Crocus LSIF in 2005, the LSIF sector has stagnated lately.[322] Still, such criticisms may overlook the value of any positive externalities of LSIFs' community-based investments not directly reflected in the funds' returns.

---

317 For evaluation, see P.A. Jones, "Giving Credit Where It's Due: Promoting Financial Inclusion Through Quality Credit Unions," *Local Economy* 21(1) (2006): 36.

318 Pub. L. No. 103-325, 108 Stat. 2163.

319 Pub. L. No. 106-554, 114 Stat. 2763.

320 L.A. Hagerman, G.L. Clark, and T. Hebb, *Investment Intermediaries in Economic Development: Linking Pension Funds to Urban Revitalization* (Labor and Worklife Program, Harvard Law School, 2007), 44–45.

321 T. Hebb, "Canadian Labour Sponsored Investment Funds: A Model for U.S. Economically Targeted Investments" (presentation at the Second National Heartland Labour-Capital Conference, Washington D.C., April 29–30, 1999), 5–7.

322 K. Damsell, "Labour Funds Wither as Crocus Wilts," *Globe and Mail,* April 7, 2005, B15.

342 | SOCIALLY RESPONSIBLE INVESTMENT LAW

Overall, tax incentive schemes provide a pragmatic tool for SRI by appealing to the bottom line. Some lessons can be gleaned from current schemes in order to improve them. The Dutch example has succeeded because of its relatively simple administrative structure. In particular, the criteria concerning the eligibility of projects are clear and strict. Because authorities must give certification, the Dutch government can help ensure that projects receiving finance provide concrete environmental benefits. Thus, the Dutch scheme points to possible solutions to the determination of criteria for SRI. The SRI funds should also adhere to rigorous transparency mechanisms (e.g., reporting requirements) to ensure that their activities are subject to scrutiny by investors and the wider general public. The French model of the "social enterprise" appears to be useful for this purpose. The label assures investors, consumers, and other stakeholders skeptical of the motives of private sector businesses that they are dealing with an enterprise presumably managed according to socially responsible standards.

2. Securities Transaction Taxes

EIs may also aid SRI by imposing costs on financial trading inimical to sustainable development. Securities transaction taxes (STTs) can discourage short-term, speculative trading often associated with causing market volatility. Some economists believe such volatility increases risk, and thereby the capital cost for real investment.[323] Short-term trading is also associated with panic buying and selling that divorce trading from market fundamentals. Raising the cost of such trading should reduce its incidence, potentially resulting in more efficient markets.

Financial market taxes have a long and somewhat contentious history. In 1972, Nobel laureate James Tobin famously proposed an international tax on currency trading in order to restrain dangerous market volatility and also to apply its revenue to address poverty and other issues plaguing developing nations.[324] Commentators and policy-makers have since debated the value of STTs in other contexts. STTs on the purchase and sale of stocks, bonds, and other assets have been proposed to reduce speculative trading.[325] Commentators have

---

323 L.H. Summers and V.P. Summers, "When Financial Markets Work Too Well: A Cautious Case for a Securities Transaction Tax," *Journal of Financial Services Research* 3 (1989): 261.

324 J. Tobin, "A Proposal for Monetary Reform," *Eastern Economic Journal* 29(4) (2003): 519; and see subsequent commentary, K.A. Erturk, "On the Tobin Tax," *Review of Political Economy* 18(1) (2006): 71.

325 J.E. Stiglitz, "Using Tax Policy to Curb Speculative Short-term Trading," *Journal of Financial Services Research* 3 (1989): 101.

also suggested graduated taxation of capital gains on trading, based on the length of the holding period.[326] Assets held for minimum periods could be exempt from an STT to encourage holding positions over the long term. In addition to their macroeconomic benefits, STTs could raise substantial revenue for long-term social and environmental investments.[327]

Conversely, some critics contend that STTs have negative effects on price discovery and liquidity, and may reduce the informational efficiency of markets.[328] For example, by making trading more expensive, an STT can hamper fund managers' ability to manage financial risks. This is supposedly because, if "investors cannot carry out their desired trades, their latent demands are not fully satisfied and resources are not allocated to their best use."[329]

Historically every major financial market imposed STTs or related charges at some point, and some still do.[330] STTs can take many forms; they can be applied broadly, or by exemption. Until 1965, the US federal government levied a stamp tax on issue and transfer of equities and bonds.[331] Britain continues to levy an STT on dealing in UK registered equities, which is paid by the buyer at 0.5 percent of the purchase price.[332] From 1984 to 1991, Sweden imposed a 50-basis-point tax on the purchase or sale of an equity security.[333] Japan's STTs were phased out during the late 1990s after its stock

326 R. Barber and T. Ghilarducci, "Pension Funds, Capital Markets and the Economic Future," in *Transforming the U.S. Financial System: Equity and Efficiency for the 21st Century*, eds G.A. Dymski, et al. (M.E. Sharpe, 1993), 287, 307.

327 D. Baker and A. Fung, "Collateral Damage: Do Pension Fund Investments Hurt Workers?" *Working Capital: The Power of Labor's Pensions*, eds A. Fung, T. Hebb and J. Rogers (Cornell University Press, 2001), 13, 36.

328 K. Habermeier and A.A. Kirilenko, *Securities Transaction Taxes and Financial Markets*, Staff Papers 50 (International Monetary Fund, 2003); P.H. Kupiec, "Noise Traders, Excess Volatility, and a Securities Transactions Tax," *Journal of Financial Services Research* 10(2) (1996): 115; P.H. Kupies, "A Securities Transactions Tax and Capital Market Efficiency," *Contemporary Economic Policy* 13(1) (1995): 101.

329 Habermeier and Kirilenko, ibid., 178.

330 M.G. Wrobel, *Financial Transactions Taxes: The International Experience and the Lessons for Canada* (Parliamentary Research Branch, 1996).

331 Ibid.

332 Oxera Consulting, *Stamp Duty: Its Impact and the Benefits of Its Abolition.* Prepared for ABI, City of London Corporation, IMA and London Stock Exchange (Oxera Consulting, May 2007), 3.

333 D. Waldesntrom, "Why are Securities Transactions Taxed? Evidence from Sweden, 1909–91," *Financial History Review* 9(2) (2002): 169.

market woes.[334] With the trend to financial market deregulation many STTs have been rolled back.[335] US regulators have even sought to reduce brokerage commissions and fees.[336] However, not all jurisdictions have abandoned STTs, and some have even introduced new ones. India introduced its first STT in October 2004.[337] China tripled its tax on stock transactions in May 2007, in an attempt to cool its booming share market.[338]

Research and modeling on the impact of STTs is inconclusive. Some studies suggest minimal effects on market turnover and price volatility.[339] Others conclude that appropriately designed STTs could substantially reduce trading volumes and encourage longer-term holdings.[340] One study estimated that a 0.5 percent STT on each stock sale (0.25 percent paid each by the buyer and seller) and comparable taxes on bonds and other financial assets in the US could potentially raise more than US$100 billion a year.[341]

While use of STTs has mostly contracted, governments retain other policy tools to encourage long-term investment and savings. Many governments subsidize institutional saving by exempting pension contributions and assets returns from taxation until withdrawn at retirement (at which time they

---

334 J.D. Malcolm, *Financial Globalisation and the Opening of the Japanese Economy* (Routledge, 2001), 318.

335 J.M. Schaefer, C. Hildebrandt, and D.G. Strongin, "The International Trend Away from Transaction Taxes: Lessons to Be Learned," *Securities Industry Trends* 20(4) (1994): 1 (incongruously, while the tax burden on financial markets has been reduced, governments continue to levy on households substantial taxes on the conveyance of real estate).

336 R.J. Shiller, *Irrational Exuberance* (Princeton University Press, 2000), 39.

337 *Indian Finance Act*, 2004; see Bank of India commentary at http://www. bankofindia.com/Home/faq/faqedu.asp.

338 "China Shares Fall After Tax Rise," *BBC World News Online*, May 30, 2007, at news.bbc.co.uk/2/hi/business/6703165.stm.

339 E.g., S.Y. Hu, "The Effects of Stock Transaction Tax on the Stock Market — Experiences from Asian Markets," *Pacific-Basin Finance Journal* 6 (1998): 347; V. Saporta and K. Kambon, *The Effects of Stamp Duty on the Level and Volatility of U.K. Equity Prices*, Working Paper (Bank of England, 1997).

340 B.H. Baltagi, D. Li, and Q. Li, "Transaction Tax and Stock Market Behaviour: Evidence from an Emerging Market," *Empirical Economics* 31 (2006): 393; I. Grabel, "Taxation of International Private Capital Flows and Securities Transactions in Developing Countries: Do Public Finance Considerations Augment the Macroeconomic Dividends?" *International Review of Applied Economics* 19(4) (2005): 477.

341 R. Pollin, D. Baker, and M. Schaberg, "Securities Transaction Taxes for U.S. Financial Markets," *Eastern Economic Journal* 29(4) (2003): 527.

would ordinarily be taxed at a lower marginal tax rate).[342] Canada and the UK are among those jurisdictions that offer these tax concessions. New Zealand, on the other hand, has relatively few occupational pension funds, precisely because it offers no such tax benefits.[343] There is some support in the financial sector for even stronger financial incentives for long-term investment. A 2005 survey of UK occupational pension funds found that 74 percent of respondents supported higher dividends for long-term investors (e.g., five years or more) and lower capital gains tax for long-term shareholders.[344] A longer-term perspective should have the corollary effect of institutional investors becoming more involved in corporate governance.

V. Environmental Liability of Financial Sponsors

A. THE BASIS FOR FINANCIERS' ENVIRONMENTAL LIABILITY

Environmental liability is a special type of EI. Liability instruments are at the "harder" end of the regulatory spectrum, therefore posing more controversy. Assigning liability to financiers can assist SRI by modifying the behavior of unseen polluters, traditionally oblivious to the environmental consequences of their loans and investments. An argument for liability could be made where financiers have advance knowledge of the development being capitalized, enabling them to assess and avoid possible future environmental and social impacts. Such a scenario would most likely arise in banks and project financing, but less so with equity investing. The nature of the stock market is such that investors do not actively scrutinize companies on social and environmental grounds. However, where environmental damage is considered inherent to the type of business, as in climate change and oil companies, an equity investor should understand the broader impacts of their investment.

Once law defines the conditions for liability, it is possible to quantify and account for the financial risk to lenders and investors. Avoidance of or

---

342 E. Whitehouse, *The Tax Treatment of Funded Pensions*, Social Protection Discussion Paper Series, No. 9910 (World Bank, 1999).

343 L. Marriott and C. Fowler, *From Social Policy to Economic Policy: Taxation Incentives for Retirement Income Savings in New Zealand (1910–2005)*, Working Paper No. 18 (School of Accounting and Commercial Law, Victoria University of Wellington, 2005), 22.

344 Gribben and Gitsham, note 141, 19–20.

compensation for these risks may be sought by increasing the cost of loans or by discounting the price of corporate securities and assets. As such, liability rules may improve capital allocation for sustainable development. The polluter pays principle, which informs the construction of environmental liability, has tended to focus on what damage ought to be paid for, rather than on who caused the damage. However, the traditional precept that liability should attach to those who "cause" the damage begs the question: what does it mean to "cause"? The extent of firms' reliance on external finance was examined in chapter 2. The analysis suggests that, without loans from banks or equity purchases from investors, some companies could not embark on new, potentially damage-causing, projects and developments. Plausibly, financial sponsorship is intimately etched into the "cause" of corporate activities harming the environment.[345]

Policy considerations for fixing environmental liability differ somewhat depending on the type of financial institution. Lending banks are in a better position than equity investors to monitor corporate behavior. Banks also have an advantage over bondholders. As with shareholders, corporate bond ownership is dispersed and fluid, and thereby hinders collective action. Another policy consideration weighing on the environmental liability mechanism is transaction costs. Reliance on case-by-case adjudication by courts as the principal means of determining liability is costly and time-consuming.[346] Further, the underlying liability standards, involving the simplistic cause-effect assumptions and individual assignment of culpability, may struggle to accommodate the complex and pervasive nature of many contemporary environmental problems.

Even if authorities spare financiers from direct liability, they may still experience indirect financial risks from environmental problems that pose a

---

345 Conceivably, one could extend this reasoning to consider also culpable any person or entity that facilitates the life of a company, such as its employees or consumers who buy its products. Yet, unlike financial markets, consumers and workers lack the commensurate ability to concentrate their economic power to discipline firms. Nor do they have access to the same level of resources to investigate and understand the impacts of firms. However, consumers and workers indirectly are implicated as they increasingly hold stakes in institutional investment funds, such as their occupational pension plans.

346 P. Menell, "The Limitations of Legal Institutions for Addressing Environmental Risks," *Journal of Economic Perspectives* 5(3) (1991): 93, 99–101.

financial hardship to a borrower or company in which they hold shares.[347] As studies canvassed in chapter 3 showed, companies that face regulatory sanctions and costly litigation can lose market value or become insolvent, with investors bearing the loss. Banks also face security risks where problems arise in individual sites which they hold as loan security. If contamination is discovered in such sites, the security may lose value. Creditors face an additional risk in insolvency law. In some jurisdictions, a company's expenses to remediate polluted lands may take priority over the claims of other creditors in insolvency proceedings.[348]

The following sections examine liability for lenders and shareholders, reviewing existing legal rules and further policy considerations for reform.

B. LENDER LIABILITY

1. Legislative Provisions

Definitions of "owner," "operator," "permits," or "causes" found in pollution control legislation may potentially implicate lenders. A bank may incur environmental liability where authorities deem it sufficiently close to the operations of a borrower, or where it has control over the borrower's assets.[349] Specifically, liability could arise when a bank takes title to the contaminated land pursuant to foreclosure proceedings. Currently, merely providing finance is generally not sufficient to incur liability.

Close involvement in a borrower's business management and operations theoretically may also generate lender liability. In some jurisdictions, a creditor

---

347 H.H. Li, "Finding Sustainable Profitability: The U.S. Financial Services Industry's Pursuit of Corporate Social Responsibility," *Corporate Governance Law Review* 2(3) (2006): 343, 362–63.

348 On the clash of public policy objectives at stake, see J.T. Losch, "Bankruptcy v. Environmental Obligations: Clash of the Titans," *Louisiana Law Review* 52 (1991): 137 (discussing US developments); P. Ellington and M. Steiner, "Environmental Issues in Insolvency under English Law," in *Environmental Issues in Insolvency Proceedings*, ed. J.A. Barrett (Kluwer Law, 1998), 93–134 (offering a UK perspective).

349 J. Lipton, "Project Financing and the Environment: Lender Liability for Environmental Damage in Australia," *Journal of International Banking Law* 11 (1996): 7; H. Thompson, "The Impact of Environmental Law on the Lending Industry in Canada," in *Environmental Law and Business in Canada*, eds G. Thompson, M. McConnell, and L. Huestis (Canada Law Books, 1993), 409.

could suffer liability if deemed a "shadow director."[350] British, Australian, and New Zealand company legislation contain provisions on shadow directors,[351] and courts have regarded banks as shadow directors in some situations: asserting influence by offering advice and giving instructions for the management of a business as an alternative to appointing an administrative receiver;[352] and engaging in soft receivership or intensive care missions.[353] Lender involvement in a client's environmental management has not yet been construed by courts as falling within the parameters of a shadow director.

So far, lender liability for pollution has materialized as a significant concern only in the US. With the *Comprehensive Environmental Response, Compensation, and Liability Act* (CERCLA) of 1980,[354] —also known as the "Superfund" law — a lender could face joint or sole liability to remediate contaminated sites.[355] The CERCLA provides mechanisms for funding and apportionment of liability to restore orphaned or uncontrolled hazardous waste sites. Although the legislation has established a cleanup fund (the Superfund) by assessing surcharges against groups of companies considered responsible for the contamination problem,[356] ultimate liability for individual cases remains with the owners and operators of the sites. The CERCLA authorizes the EPA or any other party that incurs cleanup costs to engage in court proceedings to recover their costs from a variety of parties other than current owners.

Initially, lenders considered themselves safeguarded under an apparent statutory exemption of a secured creditor acting as no more than the notional owner of contaminated property.[357] However, courts saw

350 N.R. Campbell, "Liability as a Shadow Director," *Journal of Business Law* (1994): 609; J. Millet, "Shadow Directorships, a Real or Imagined Threat to Banks," *Insolvency Practitioner* 1 (1991): 14.

351 E.g., *Corporations Act*, 2001 (Cth), s. 9; *Companies Act,* 2006 (UK), ss 250, 251.

352 See, e.g., *Re a Company No. 005009 of 1987 ex parte Copp.,* [1989] B.C.L.C. 13; 4 B.C.C. 424.

353 See, e.g., *Re Tasbian (No. 3),* [1991] B.C.C. 436; *3M Australia Ltd. v. Kernish,* (1986) 10 A.C.L.R. 371.

354 Pub. L. No. 96-510, 94 Stat. 2767.

355 D.R. Berz, "Lender Liability under CERCLA: In Search of a New Deep Pocket," *Banking Law Journal* 108 (1991): 1, 4; J. Norton, "Lender Liability in the United States: A Decade in Perspective," in *Banks, Liability and Risk,* ed. R. Cranston (Lloyds of London Press, 1995), 329.

356 On financing the Superfund, see K.N. Probst, et al., *Footing the Bill for Superfund Cleanups: Who Pays and How?* (Brookings Institution Press and Resources for the Future, 1995).

357 Note 354, s. 9601 (20(A)).

matters differently.[358] The *Fleet Factors Corporation* case was one of the most astonishing rulings.[359] It found the lender liable for environmental damages incurred during the foreclosure process while a hired firm was acting for the lender to sell the assets. The court reasoned that the lender's involvement in the financial management of the borrower gave it the "capacity to influence the corporation's treatment of hazardous waste," even though it was not involved in the actual operation of the firm.[360]

A diversity of rulings on the scope of lender liability followed *Fleet Factors*, creating considerable uncertainty for lenders.[361] The joint and several liability provisions of CERCLA as interpreted by the courts encouraged targeting the deepest pockets to restore contaminated lands.[362] This caused lenders to dramatically alter their practices in financing the big polluter industries.[363] According to a survey by the American Bankers' Association, 88 percent of the respondent banks altered their lending practices in order to protect themselves from CERCLA liability.[364] Specifically, nearly 63 percent of commercial

---

358 On the evolving position of lender liability under CERCLA, see S.R. Alexander, "CERCLA's Web of Liability Ensnares Secured Lenders; The Scope and Application of CERCLA's Security Interest Exemption," *Indiana Law Review* 35 (1991): 165; R. Tom, "Interpreting the Meaning of Lender Management Participation under Section 101(20)(A) of CERCLA," *Yale Law Journal* 98 (1989): 925.

359 *United States v. Fleet Factors Corporation*, (1990) 901 F. 2d. 1550 (11th Cir.).

360 Ibid., 1557–58; and see N.V. Toulme and D.E. Cloud, "The *Fleet Factors* Case: A Wrong Turn for Lender Liability Under Superfund," *Wake Forest Law Review* 26(1) (1991): 127.

361 See, e.g., *In re Bergsoe Metal Corp*, (1990) 910 F. 2d. 668 (9th Cir.) (contrary to *Fleet Factors*, determined that substantially higher level of creditor participation in management is necessary to impose lender liability under CERCLA); *Bancamerica Commercial Corp. v. Trinity Industries, Inc.,* (1995) 900 F. Supp. 1427 (D. Kan.) (liability required some actual management of the facility to impose liability and a secured lender does not participate in the management of a facility by taking actions related to the facility's financial operations).

362 Berz, note 355.

363 See generally, S.B. Clanton, "Fleeting Security: CERCLA Liability for Secured Creditors," *Emory Law Journal* 4(1) (1992): 167; M.L. Greenberg and D.M. Shaw, "To Lend or Not to Lend—That Should Not Be the Question: The Uncertainties of Lender Liability under CERCLA," *Duke Law Journal* 41(4) (1992): 1211.

364 American Bankers Association, Comment to EPA Rule, No. NCP-LL/DSB-2-206 (1991) (unpublished document, on file with EPA); see also R. Carter, "Lender Liability: Can You Bank on Insurance for Protection?" *AKO Policyholder Advisor* 4 (1995): 4, 6.

banks had rejected potential borrowers because of the possibility of environmental liability, and about 46 percent had discontinued financing to known hazardous sectors because of similar concerns. Concomitantly, escalating premiums for liability insurance or retraction of coverage in relation to contaminated lands illustrates the adverse response of another arm of the financial sector.[365]

Despite the evolution of more cautious lending practices, uncertainty surrounding the parameters of lender liability spurred the banking sector to mount campaigns to amend the CERCLA.[366] In 1996, a coalition of major banks succeeded in pressing Congress to create a safe harbor for lenders. The legislation clarified what actions lenders may take without becoming liable as an owner of contaminated property—the essential requirement being that the lender should not participate in the management of the facility causing the contamination and that the lender hold the property only as a security interest.[367] Court decisions have subsequently reassured lenders as to their much more truncated exposure to Superfund liability.[368] Although the CERCLA amendments did not dissipate lenders' potential liabilities stemming from other federal or state environmental laws, parallel amendments to some state mini-Superfund programs have since mostly assuaged lenders.[369] Some states have also introduced new legislation to provide exemptions to lenders in the context of brownfield cleanups, such as Pennsylvania's *Economic Development Agency, Fiduciary and Lender Environmental Liability Protection Act* of 1995.[370]

---

365 See R.N. Sayler and A.M. Cole, "The Mother of All Battles: The Dispute Over Insurance Coverage for Environmental Contamination in the US," *Environmental Liability* 1 (1993): 29.

366 Discussed in M. Murphy, "Brownfield Sites: Removing Lender Concerns as a Barrier to Redevelopment," *Banking Law Journal* 14(2) (1996): 440, 458–60.

367 *Asset Conservation, Lender Liability and Deposit Insurance Protection Act*, 1996, Pub. L. No. 104-208, 110 Stat. 3009; see further O. de S. Domis, "New Law Finally Limits Environmental Liability," *American Banker* 161(189) (1996): 3.

368 Discussed in R. Burke, "Sailing in Safe Harbors: Recent Developments Regarding Lender Liability under CERCLA," *Pace Environmental Law Review* 16 (1998): 143, 163–67; see also *Monarch Tile Inc. v. City of Florence*, (2002) 212 F.3d 1219 (11th Cir.); *United States v. Bestfoods*, (1998) 118 S. Ct. 1876; *Canadyne-Georgia Corp v. NationsBank, N.A. (South)*, (1999) 183 F. 3d 1269 (11th Cir.).

369 See J.D. Epstein, "Bankers Pressing for States to Legislate Shield from Cleanup Liability," *American Banker* 160(57) (1995): 16.

370 Pa. Laws 11 (1995).

The Superfund experience has been watched with interest by other jurisdictions where legislative regimes have been adopted to manage the treatment of contaminated lands, toxic substances management, and other hazards. Most OECD countries have introduced tough environmental impairment legislation providing for strict joint and several liability, usually with exceptions and protections shielding secured creditors not involved in corporate operations.

Aware of the US controversy, the EU's 2004 Directive on environmental liability did not include provisions that specifically target lenders.[371] The Directive covers types of environmental harm not normally addressed in environmental legislation, such as damage to biodiversity, soil, and water. By virtue of the definition of "operator" in the EU Directive, all the provisions of the Directive may apply to financial actors exerting operational control over the polluting facilities or sites.[372] This could potentially arise where a lender assumes control of a polluted industrial site upon foreclosure of the insolvent borrower.

Although extremely rare, environmental liability of lenders was possible in most EU member states even prior to the Directive.[373] In the UK, for instance, Midland Bank became directly liable for the cleanup of a site the bank had repossessed; the lender appeared unaware of the seriousness of the site's oil contamination until regulatory authorities issued it with a remediation notice.[374] Banks in the UK (like other common law jurisdictions) are more vulnerable to lender liability than banks in continental Europe, because in the UK, the lender normally enforces a security by taking possession or by appointing a receiver to do so. The receiver is technically an agent of the defaulting corporation, and not of the lender,[375] but the lender would incur liability for the mistakes of the receiver if the receiver acted on the directions of the lender.[376] By contrast, in

---

371 Directive 2004/35/EC of 21 April 2004, O.J. L. 143/56.

372 Article 2(6) of the Directive provides, in part: "'operator' means any... person who operates or controls the occupational activity or... to whom decisive economic power over the technical functioning of such an activity has been delegated....

373 EC, *Study of Civil Liability Systems for Remedying Environmental Damage — Final Report* (McKenna and Company, 1996), 168–78; Thompson, note 12, 244–45.

374 R. Lee and T. Egede, *Bank Lending and Environmental Liability*, Working Paper Series No. 30 (Centre for Business Relationships, Accountability, Sustainability and Society, Cardiff University, 2005), 12.

375 See V. Finch, *Corporate Insolvency Law: Perspectives and Principles* (Cambridge University Press, 2002).

376 Ibid., 415.

continental Europe, banks usually do not take possession because the procedure is administered by the courts of bankruptcy.[377]

Among other jurisdictions, Canadian lenders have similarly become much more attuned to pollution liability threats.[378] Under provincial and federal environmental legislation,[379] those holding title and those in possession or control of contaminated property or toxic substances may be held liable for any environmental damage caused by that property or substance.[380] But legislation generally does not target a lender who merely has a security over the land. There is, as yet, little Canadian case law on environmental liability of lenders,[381] and major Canadian banks do not regard the issue as a serious concern compared to the experience of US banks.[382] Some provincial environmental legislation attempts to create a safe harbor for lenders in specific contexts. This includes Ontario's *Brownfields Statute Law Amendment*,[383] and the federal *Nuclear Safety and Control Act* (amended in 2003 to exempt financing institutions investing in nuclear reactors from any environmental liability expense).[384] The legal situation is broadly similar in other common law jurisdictions such as Australia, where pollution control legislation that potentially threatens lenders has caused some commotion, but negligible case law or regulatory enforcement action appears to support such fears.[385]

2. Future Directions in Lender Liability

Depending on how environmental liability law evolves, banks may respond in various ways. First, they could become reluctant environmental police,

377 A.B. Coulson and V. Monks, "Corporate Environmental Performance Considerations Within Bank Lending Decisions," *Eco-Management and Auditing* 6 (1999): 1, 5.

378 See "Environmental Liability Scares Away Bank Loans," *Financial Post Daily*, June 19, 1992, 5; T. Reiman, "Lender Liability All the Rage," *Canadian Lawyer* 15(4) (1991): 33.

379 E.g., the *Canadian Environmental Protection Act*, R.S.C. 1999, s. 95; and *Fisheries Act*, R.S.C. 1985, ss 34–38.

380 See A. Szweras and R. Schwartz, "Lender Liability: Legal Update, Environmental Law," *Canadian Lawyer* 19(4) (1995): 39.

381 See, e.g., *Busse Farms Ltd v. Federal Business Development Bank*, [1996] S.J. No. 780.

382 Personal communication, James Evans, Senior Manager, Corporate Environmental Affairs, RBC (Toronto, September 20, 2007).

383 S.O. 2001.

384 S.C. 1997; and *Act to Amend the Nuclear Safety and Control Act*, S.C. 2003.

385 See e.g., *Contaminated Land Management Act*, 1997 (NSW), s. 12(1), s. 14(1)–(2); *Environmental Protection Act*, 1994 (Qld), s. 391(4).

scrutinizing borrowers to ensure compliance with set environmental criteria and denying loans to those that fail to meet them. In effect, lenders would act as surrogate environmental regulators. Certainly, most banks would loathe such a scenario, regarding themselves as lacking relevant environmental expertise and too remote from borrowers' operational decisions. Second, banks could cooperate with other businesses and governmental institutions to encourage borrowers to adopt sound environmental practices and provide them with information and advice to improve their risk management. This way, banks genuinely interested in sustainability could potentially take on a proactive environmental role. Some lenders already do so, such as the Co-operative Bank (UK) and UmweltBank (Germany). In this respect, they could target their financing to businesses that demonstrate superior environmental performance and even subsidize loans made to those firms. Yet without a more conducive regulatory framework and stronger incentives, most banks would shirk such a role.

Notwithstanding the sustainability imperatives to address the unseen polluters in this financial sector, blanket imposition of liability on lenders could be unwise. In the case of urban environmental improvements, if banks decline to finance redevelopment of brownfield sites owing to fears of cleanup liability, it may have the perverse effect of discouraging the recycling of urban land. It may also lead to displacing development pressures to greenfield lands,[386] while leaving brownfield sites orphaned and untreated.[387] Surveys of US banks have revealed concerns that brownfield sites carry greater financial risks than greenfield sites.[388]

Retroactive liability and joint and several liability standards, especially in the context of strict liability, pose the most complicated policy issues. Considerable theoretical difficulties inhere in designing an appropriate liability regime. It should create an appropriate balance for banks to stop funding environmentally contentious developments, without stifling socially valuable investment.[389]

---

386 E. Ward, "Working Together: Financing the Remediation and Redevelopment of Contaminated Properties," *UNEP Industry and Environment* 22(1) (1999): 20.

387 L. Morelli, "Cleaning Up Superfund: The State of Superfund Reauthorisation," *Environmental Liability* 6(2) (1998): 27, 32.

388 Bankers Roundtable, *Roundtable Survey: Environmental Liability of Secured Parties and Fiduciaries* (Bankers Roundtable, May 1995), 1.

389 R. Pitchford, "How Liable Should a Lender Be? The Case of Judgement-proof Firms and Environmental Risk," *American Economic Review* 85 (1995): 1171.

Strict or absolute liability standards[390] are problematic as they tend not to discriminate between enterprises according to their investment in safety measures and thus may discourage environmentally responsible behavior and concomitantly banks' willingness to finance such improvements. However, such a liability standard lessens the litigation burden of determining culpability; as Jeffrey Kehne asserts, "a strict liability standard probably makes claims more predictable than they would be under a negligence standard."[391] While the retroactive character of some environmental liability laws strengthens the objective of providing compensation, it hardly deters future unsustainable financing. Penalizing lenders for unforeseeable harm caused by past activities does little in itself to influence future lending practices, except to avoid taking possibly contaminated land as loan security.[392]

A standard of joint and several liability is also problematic. Allowing a plaintiff to recover all of the damages from any of the defendants in an action regardless of their individual share of damages can, in effect, function as a mechanism for mutual regulation encouraging dealings with only environmentally reputable parties and creating strong incentives to monitor one another's behavior.[393] However, the rule of joint and several liability conflicts with the polluter pays principle. The defending party with the deepest pockets, often lenders, will bear the greater burden, rather the party with the greatest culpability.[394] This can cause "over-deterrence" of financial parties and "under-deterrence" of less solvent parties (who may believe that no claims will be brought against them).[395] Allowing wealthier parties to recover

---

390 In some legal contexts, a distinction is made between strict liability (excusing actors who followed appropriate due diligence from liability) and absolute liability (no excuse if act proved), while sometimes strict liability is understood as not accommodating due diligence measures: see M.L. Larsson, *The Law of Environmental Damage: Liability and Reparation* (Kluwer Law, 1999).

391 J. Kehne, "Encouraging Safety through Insurance-Based Incentives: Financial Responsibility for Hazardous Wastes," *Yale Law Journal* 96 (1986): 403, 419.

392 J.J. Lyons, "Deep Pockets and CERCLA: Should Superfund Liability Be Abolished?" *Stanford Environmental Law Journal* 6 (1986): 271, 301.

393 G. Teubner, "The Invisible Cupola: From Causal to Collective Attribution in Ecological Liability," *Cardozo Law Review* 16(2) (1994): 429, 430.

394 T.H. Tietenberg, "Indivisible Toxic Torts: The Economics of Joint and Several Liability," *Land Economics* 65(4) (1989): 305.

395 M.J. Gergen, "The Failed Promise of the 'Polluter Pays' Principle: An Economic Analysis of Landowner Liability for Hazardous Waste," *New York University Law Review* 69 (1994): 624, 674.

contributions from joint tortfeasors in separate proceedings does not sufficiently mitigate the problem, because of the additional costs of further litigation and potentially, suing insolvent tortfeasors. No convincing solution has been proposed to these issues. Some law and economics theorists advocate a model of "partial" lender liability that essentially strikes the most economically efficient balance between the competing considerations.[396]

Regardless of all these considerations, lender liability remains structurally limited because it is tethered to the same environmental standards as the companies financed. A bank's liability ultimately arises because its borrower breached an environmental rule. This approach does not accommodate the necessity of sometimes subjecting financiers to higher standards of environmental accountability, as outlined in chapter 1. The unseen polluters of the financial sector exert an economic and environmental influence over the long-term that is often much more profound than their individual borrowers, requiring a higher level of accountability.

C. SHAREHOLDER LIABILITY

Apart from lender liability, an older and more heated debate is on shareholder liability.[397] The cardinal principle in Anglo-American systems of company law is that the company is a separate legal person from the members who comprise it.[398] A corollary principle is that, absent exceptional circumstances, shareholders in the company are not liable beyond the amount they invest.[399] As a separate person, a corporation is solely responsible for its juridical acts. For instance, in the words of the *Canada Business Corporations Act*: "[t]he shareholders of a corporation are not, as shareholders, liable for any liability, act, or default of the corporation...."[400] Thus, if the value of claims against a company exceeds the value of its assets, the shareholders' only risk is losing the amount of their investment.

This ceiling on shareholder liability is rationalized as serving several beneficial economic functions.[401] It encourages new business formation and improves the liquidity and efficiency of security markets. Also, by reducing

---

396 Pitchford, note 389.

397 On this debate, see F.H. Easterbrook and D.R. Fischel, "Limited Liability and the Corporation," *University of Chicago Law Review* 52 (1985): 89.

398 See, e.g., *Salomon v. Salomon and Co. Ltd*, [1897] AC 22.

399 Easterbrook and Fischel, note 397, 89.

400 R.S.C. 1985, s. 45.

401 Easterbrook and Fischel, note 397, 94.

investors' need to closely monitor corporate management, limited liability enables investors to compile a less risky and diversified portfolio of assets that should boost returns.[402]

Limited liability is controversial, and many commentators strongly contest its justifications.[403] Certainly, the crushing exertion of environmental liability would, in due course, force liquidation of a polluting enterprise,[404] but before its dissolution it may have caused unacceptable impacts on society. Limited liability interferes with the polluter pays principle to the extent that insolvent firms do not pay for the entire cost of their environmental impacts. By shielding companies from some of their environmental costs, limited liability hinders SRI. Imagine how much more seriously investors would pay attention to corporate sustainability performance if they were potentially liable for some of the environmental delinquencies of companies in their portfolio. Limited liability for shareholders is, in effect, a subsidy for investment, insulating shareholders from the environmental risks of their corporations, and thereby encouraging over-investment in hazardous activities.

To digress slightly, we can also examine investors' potential liability in the context of the relationship between beneficiaries and those who administer their funds. Consider for example a pension plan or mutual fund organized as a trust. A trust does not have legal personality or legal capacity, and therefore a creditor has no direct claim or remedy against the trust's assets and no direct claim against a beneficiary.[405] However, the trustees may be personally liable for torts and other causes of action.[406] If trustees, while acting within the terms of the trust, were liable in their capacity as shareholders or by some other means for environmental harm associated with the

---

402 See K.F. Forbes, "Limited Liability and the Development of the Business Corporation," *Journal of Law, Economics and Organisation* 2 (1986): 163; F. Easterbrook and D. Fischel, *Economic Structure of Corporate Law* (Harvard University Press, 1991).

403 See C. Stone, "The Place of Enterprise Liability in the Control of Corporate Conduct," *Yale Law Journal* 90 (1980): 1; J.A. Brander and T.R. Lewis, "Oligopoly and Financial Structure: The Limited Liability Effect," *American Economic Review* 76 (1986): 956.

404 A. Schwartz, "Products Liability, Corporate Structure, and Bankruptcy: Toxic Substances and the Remote Risk Relationship," *Journal of Legal Studies* 14 (1985): 689, 715.

405 *Worrall v. Harford*, (1802) 8 Ves. Jun. 4, 8; 32 E.R. 250; *Re Evans*, (1887) 34 Ch. D. 597.

406 A.J. Oakley, *Parker and Mellows: The Modern Law of Trusts* (Sweet and Maxwell, 1998), 676–77.

trust's investments, so too the beneficiaries might be affected. For such liabil-ities, the trustee has the right of indemnity out of the trust assets. The trustee also has in general a right to indemnification by the beneficiaries personally.[407] According to Guy Spavold, beneficiaries are "exposed to unlimited liability" unless the trust instrument provides that no right of indemnity exists, as it often would.[408] However, where a beneficiary instigated or requested a breach of trust in order to procure a personal benefit, or exercised a degree of control over the trustee to create an agency relationship, then "the beneficiaries can still become liable to indemnify the trustee even if the terms of the trust exclude the trustee's right of indemnity."[409]

Various mechanisms can overturn limited liability of companies. Piercing the corporate veil (i.e., disregarding the formalities of the corporation to look to the shareholders for personal liability) is available in a few contexts, includ-ing under-capitalization, misrepresentation, failure to follow corporate for-malities, failure to give effect to specific statutory policies, and above all, where the corporation is effectively an agent of the shareholder.[410] Veil pierc-ing is rare in environmental regulatory contexts.[411]

Among various academic proposals about where to strike the balance on the liability continuum, Nina Mendelson advocates a "capacity to control" test, explaining that "[c]ontrolling shareholders, in particular, may have lower information costs, greater influence over managerial decision-making, and greater ability to benefit from corporate activity."[412] As noted earlier, in rela-tion to lenders, Superfund liability was interpreted in the *Fleet Factors* case as extending to a bank where its involvement in the borrower's business gave it the "capacity to influence" certain decisions. Alternatively, Henry Hansmann

---

407 Ibid., 703–4; R.P. Austin, "The Role and Responsibilities of Trustees in Pension Plan Trusts: Some Problems of Trusts Law," *Equity Fiduciaries and Trusts*, ed. T. Youdan (Carswell, 1989), 111; *Hardoon v. Belilios*, [1901] A.C. 118.

408 G.C. Spavold, "The Unit Trust —A Comparison with the Corporation," *Bond Law Review* 3(2) (1991): 249, 269.

409 Ibid., 271.

410 See, e.g., C. Alting, "Piercing the Corporate Veil in American and German Law —Liability of Individuals and Entities: A Comparative View," *Tulsa Journal of Comparative and International Law* 2 (1995): 187; R.B. Thompson, "Piercing the Corporate Veil: An Empirical Study," *Cornell Law Review* 76 (1991): 1036.

411 C.A. Schipani, "Taking it Personally: Shareholder Liability for Corporate Environmental Hazards," *Journal of Corporation Law* 27 (2001): 29.

412 N.A. Mendelson, "A Control-based Approach to Shareholder Liability for Corporate Torts," *Columbia Law Review* 102(5) (2002): 1203, 1203.

and Reinier Kraakman argue for pro-rata, unlimited liability for corporate torts,[413] arguing that distributing liability pro-rata to all shareholders is the best way to encourage corporations to internalize risks that affect third parties while discouraging liability evasion.

For the foreseeable future, it appears unlikely that legislators or courts will embrace the proposition of unlimited liability for shareholders or even significant exemptions to limited liability. However, in order to prevent or reduce further corporate environmental abuses, disallowing a traditional corporate structure on environmentally hazardous projects may put lenders and investors on notice that liability will not be limited.

VI. Investment SRI Mandates and Restrictions

A. STATE AND PUBLIC SECTOR PENSION FUNDS

1. US State and Municipal Funds

Legislative directions as to how financiers should invest may garner more resistance than other reforms canvassed in this book. Such directions are not unprecedented, although uncommon given the political risks. Some jurisdictions have in discrete contexts obliged financiers to consider social and environmental issues in their investment policies.

So far, occurrence of such regulations has been confined mainly to government sector funds, which, since they are controlled by the state, present fewer political obstacles.[414] These mandates nonetheless attract controversy, as they are perceived as making it difficult to hold pension plan boards accountable for optimal financial returns.[415] Since the early 2000s, national pension schemes, notably in Sweden, Norway, New Zealand, and France, have been statutorily obliged to invest responsibly and ethically.[416] In 2007, the UNEPFI published a detailed survey of these and various public sector funds,

---

413 H. Hansmann and R. Kraakman, "Towards Unlimited Shareholder Liability for Corporate Torts," *Yale Law Journal* 100 (1991): 1879.

414 Of course, so long as such SRI-directed pension plans do not under-perform the market.

415 R. Pozen, "Arm Yourself for the Coming Battle over Social Security," *Harvard Business Review* 80(11) (2002): 52.

416 J. Myles and P. Pierson, "The Comparative Political Economy of Pension Reform," in *The New Politics of the Welfare State*, ed. P. Pierson (Oxford University Press, 2001), 305.

"highlighting a range of some of the most advanced and creative approaches to responsible investment."[417]

US public pension plans were the first to incur SRI-related legislative directions. Many state pension funds were already voluntarily investing responsibly and ethically in the 1980s before legislative standards.[418] Apartheid in South Africa became the issue that galvanized the first wave of reforms that required these funds to look beyond the financial bottom line when considering an investment. During the 1980s, various US states led by Connecticut[419] began to prohibit their public pension funds from investing in companies conducting business in South Africa unless the company adhered to the Sullivan Principles[420] and had been rated a good performer under its scoring system.[421] Massachusetts also directed its public pension funds to avoid investment in banks or other financial institutions that had outstanding loans to South Africa.[422] Similarly, some city governments enacted ordinances to give effect to the Sullivan Principles.[423] The validity of these US examples from a fiduciary law perspective was upheld in the *City of Baltimore* case (as discussed in the previous chapter).[424] The federal government also got involved pursuant to the *Comprehensive Anti-Apartheid Act* of 1986,[425] prohibiting new US investment in apartheid South Africa and requiring

417 UNEPFI Asset Management Working Group and UKSIF, *Responsible Investment in Focus: How Leading Public Pension Funds are Meeting the Challenge* (UNEPFI, 2007), 7.
418 K.F. Murrmann, J.D. Schaffer, and R.E. Wokutch, "Social Investing by State Public Employee Pension Funds," *Labor law Journal* 35 (1984): 360.
419 Conn. Pub. Acts 80-431 (1980).
420 The Sullivan Principles were drafted in 1977 by Leon Sullivan, a pastor and human rights activist, and posited voluntary labor standards for US companies operating in South Africa: H.J. Richardson, "Leon Sullivan's Principles, Race and International Law: A Comment," *Temple International and Comparative Law Journal* 15 (2001): 55.
421 P.M.C. Carroll, "Socially Responsible Investment of Public Pension Funds: The South Africa Issue and State Law," *Review of Law and Social Change* 10 (1980–81): 407; G. Jubinsky, "State and Municipal Governments React Against South African Apartheid: An Assessment of the Constitutionality of the Divestment Campaign," *University of Cincinnati Law Review* 54 (1985): 453.
422 Mass. Ann. Laws, ch. 32, (Supp. 1984), s. 23(1)(d)(ii).
423 Jubinsky, note 421.
424 (1989) 317 Md. 72; 562 A.2d 720.
425 Pub. L. No. 99-440, 100 Stat. 1086.

American businesses with more than twenty-five employees in South Africa to comply with the Sullivan Principles.[426]

Religious and political tensions in Northern Ireland became another social issue to attract investment restrictions. A number of US states legislated to apply the MacBride Principles,[427] prohibiting public pension funds from investing in corporations conducting business in Northern Ireland without promoting equal hiring practices and ensuring the security and safety of employees.[428] Over fifteen states and the federal Congress enacted MacBride legislation.[429]

Apart from the South African and Northern Ireland issues, pension funds have not been obliged to follow SRI policies. However, Connecticut state law provides that state pension fund fiduciaries *may* consider the environmental and social implications of investments.[430] The Connecticut Retirement Plans and Trust Funds (CRPTF) have chosen to consider such factors, and in relation to proxy voting their 2007 investment policy informatively states:

> The CRPTF will evaluate on a case-by-case basis [shareholder] proposals that request the company to cease certain actions that the proponent believes is harmful to society or some segment of society, with special attention to the company's legal and ethical obligations, its

---

426 Some US states have tried to impose other restrictions on investment of public funds. Texas law forbids state entities from investing in any company that owns at least 10 percent of a business that records or produces certain kinds of music deemed offensive by the statute (e.g., promotes illegal drug use and racially-motivated violence): N. Strauss, "Texas Bans Investment in Explicit Recordings," *New York Times*, June 21, 1997, s. 1, 13.

427 The MacBride Principles, proposed by Seán MacBride, an international human rights activist, are a US corporate code of conduct drafted in 1984 to combat discrimination against Catholics in Northern Ireland: K.A. Bertsch and H.E. Booth, *The MacBride Principles and U.S. Companies in Northern Ireland* (Investor Responsibility Research Centre, 1991).

428 See C. McCrudden, "Human Rights Codes for Transnational Corporations: What Can the Sullivan and MacBride Principles Tell Us?" *Oxford Journal of Legal Studies* 19(2) (1999): 167; N.J. Conway, "Investment Responsibility in Northern Ireland: The MacBride Principles of Fair Employment," *Loyola of Los Angeles International and Comparative Law Review* 24 (2002): 1.

429 K.A. Burke, "Fair Employment in Northern Ireland: The Role of Affirmative Action," *Columbia Journal of Law and Social Problems* 28 (1994): 1, 12.

430 Conn. Gen. Stat. (2002), s. 3-13d(a) (allowing the Treasurer to consider the "social, economic and environmental implications of investments of trust funds in particular securities or types of securities").

ability to remain profitable, and potential negative publicity if the company fails to honor the request.[431]

Among US state and municipal pension funds, many governing board members are political appointees and some are elected by plan members. This composition may help explain why these US public funds have been more active in corporate governance than private pension funds.[432] US public pension funds are more likely to manage their portfolios internally and, hence, more likely to vote their own shares. Even when they use external managers, they retain voting authority more frequently than private funds.[433] However, while some US public funds have strongly supported community investment,[434] it would be misleading to deduce that they are the vanguard of SRI. Some empirical research suggests they do not widely practice responsible financing beyond negative screening on a limited set of issues mandated by legislation, and the US funds generally lag behind European and Australasian financiers in incorporating ESG considerations.[435]

Beyond the pension sector, US lawmakers have also sought to promote socially responsible banking. The *Community Reinvestment Act* (CRA) of 1977[436] aims to make commercial banks and some other lenders invest a portion of their portfolio into their local economy, especially supporting historically marginalized groups. The legislation arose from concerns that banks' mortgage lending practices discriminated against minority communities and deprived neighborhoods, a practice known as "redlining."[437] Under the CRA, banks are examined annually by federal authorities and graded on their performance. Their ratings are made public, and their performance may affect government approval of bank mergers and access to the federal insurance program. For example, in 1989 the Federal Reserve denied on CRA grounds an application by the Continental Bank Corporation to acquire

431 State of Connecticut Office of the Treasurer, *Domestic Proxy Voting Policies* (adopted April 11, 2007), 32.

432 R. Romano, "Public Pension Fund Activism in Corporate Governance Reconsidered," *Columbia Law Review* 94 (1993): 795, 820–21.

433 Ibid., 832.

434 Hagerman, Clark, and Hebb, note 320.

435 D. Hess, *Public Pensions and the Promise of Shareholder Activism for the Next Frontier of Corporate Governance: Sustainable Economic Development*, Working Paper No. 1080 (Ross School of Business, University of Michigan, March 2007), 23–24.

436 Pub. L. No. 95-128, 91 Stat. 1147.

437 P.P. Swire, "The Persistent Problem of Lending Discrimination: A Law and Economics Analysis," *Texas Law Review* 73 (1995): 787.

Grand Canyon Bank.[438] The CRA has helped to create an entire sub-sector of community development financial institutions in the US, enhancing access to capital and credit to poor and disadvantaged communities, particularly for mortgage lending.[439] However, because of structural changes in the debt financing market, a substantial portion of credit is no longer subject to detailed scrutiny under the CRA, and consequently commentators have called for modernization of the legislation to maintain its relevancy.[440]

2. Swedish AP Funds

The Swedish pension system includes six "AP funds" that serve as buffer funds to assist during periods when the national pension reserve needs to make major disbursements, such as when the baby-boom generation begins to retire.[441] Although the funds operate under similar legislative standards, each is managed separately.

Under Sweden's *National Pension Insurance Funds (AP-Funds) Act* of 2000,[442] as amended in 2001, the AP funds must take "environmental and social considerations... into account without relinquishing the overall goal of a high return on capital."[443] Specifically, each AP fund must formulate an annual business plan, describing how it accounts for such factors in investment activities. The Swedish Finance Department is responsible for monitoring the funds' compliance with these provisions. While each AP fund has adopted its own investment strategy, the funds rely on international treaties ratified by the Swedish government as a normative basis for the standard to which they will hold companies responsible. The funds also generally apply corporate engagement rather than SRI screens to implement their mandate.[444]

---

438 G.L. Garwood and D.S. Smith, "The Community Reinvestment Act: Evolution and Current Issues," *Federal Reserve Bulletin* 79(April) (1993): 251.

439 W. Apgar and M. Duda, "The Twenty-Fifth Anniversary of the Community Reinvestment Act: Past Accomplishments and Future Regulatory Challenges," *Economic Policy Review* 9(2) (2003): 169.

440 Ibid.

441 See http://www.ap1.se; http://www.ap2.se; http://www.ap3.se; http://www.ap4.se; http://www.ap6.se, http://www.ap7.se.

442 *Lag om* allmänna *pensionsfonder (AP-Fonder)*, *Svensk författningssamling* (2000): 192.

443 Translated by Oxford Business Knowledge, *Recent Trends and Regulatory Implications of Socially Responsible Investment for Pension Funds* (OECD Roundtable on Corporate Responsibility, 2007), 21.

444 E.g., Trejde AP-fonden, *Third Swedish National Pension Fund: Annual Report 2004* (Trejde AP-fonden, 2005), 22.

Thus, to illustrate, AP2 has a corporate governance policy that avows to promote transparent and active use of shareholder rights as a means to reform corporate culture.[445] AP2 has also collaborated with Sustainable Asset Management to create a valuation model for ethical and environmental issues to assist its fund managers. In addition, AP2 has shown that it is prepared to divest if a company's response to consultation is unsatisfactory, as it did with Wal-Mart because of the chain's dubious labor practices.[446] The AP1 fund relies on similar techniques,[447] and it engaged with the Marriott hotel chain to improve the hotel's human rights policies to help combat child sex tourism.[448]

The first four AP funds co-operate though their joint Ethical Council, established in early 2007 to assess the ethics of the non-Swedish companies in their portfolios.[449] The Council comprises one representative from each of the AP funds, but lacks formal representation of outside interest groups. Any divestment decisions are ultimately made by each fund separately. The Ethical Council reviews some 3,500 overseas companies, and annually identifies about ten firms that have infringed international environmental or human rights standards to engage them in active dialogue.[450] These standards come from the UN Declaration of Human Rights, UN Global Compact (UNGC), OECD Guidelines for Multinational Enterprises, International Labor Organization conventions, and various environmental treaties. GES Investment Services was appointed by the Council to carry out the ethical screening work.[451] This collaboration does not include screening Swedish companies, as this assessment is left to the individual funds.

3. French Retirement Reserve Fund

The French Retirement Reserve Fund (Fonds de réserve pour les retraites),[452] set up to meet a predicted shortfall in the existing pay-as-you-go state pension scheme, is obliged by its enabling legislation to disclose how it takes into account environmental and social considerations in its

---

445 UNEPFI and UKSIF, note 417, 14–15.
446 Andra AP-fonden, "Second AP Fund Excludes Wal-Mart," Press release, September 7, 2006, at www.ap2.se/default.aspx?id=486.
447 See http://www.ap1.se/en.
448 "Sweden's AP Funds Unite to Monitor Ethics of Foreign Partners," *European Pension and Investment News*, February 12, 2007.
449 "AP Funds Team Up to Put Foreign Firms Under Ethical Microscope," *European Pension and Investment News*, February 28, 2007.
450 UNEPFI and UKSIF, note 417, 16.
451 Http://www.ges-invest.com.
452 Http://www.fondsdereserve.fr.

investment decisions.[453] The obligation to explain its consideration of such matters implies that the Funds should invest responsibly.

In April 2003, the Fund's supervisory board adopted an SRI policy including: a policy for proxy voting at shareholder meetings of its portfolio corporations, and inclusion of certain social and environmental considerations in the stock-research and selection criteria.[454] In a subsequent policy statement in June 2005, the Reserve Fund explained that its investment approach is multi-criteria, and that it does not apply ethical screens to exclude *a priori* certain economic sectors.[455] Instead, it advances SRI through a "best-in-class" method of stock selection, based on such standards as the UNGC. The Fund's policy on SRI emphasizes five themes: respect for international law and basic human rights; corporate environmental responsibility; employment creation; consumer rights and fair trade; and good corporate governance.[456]

The French Retirement Reserve Fund has concentrated on implementing its SRI policy mainly in European portfolios and some global portfolios. This is because it found few fund managers offering sufficiently appropriate investment portfolios to meet its social and environmental criteria.[457] In November 2006, the Fund initiated a process aimed at assessing its entire portolio to ESG analysis.[458] In reviewing corporate stocks for investment: it relies on EIRIS to assess compliance with international standards on basic human and labor rights; and retains Trucost, an environmental research organization, to assess the environmental grounds.[459] Overall, Eurosif has identified the Fund as providing crucial "leadership" for SRI among European institutional investors.[460]

---

453 The legislation states: "Il en rend compte régulièrement au conseil de surveillance et retrace notamment, à cet effet, la manière dont les orientations générales de la politique de placement du fonds ont pris en compte des considérations sociales, environnementales et éthiques": Loi No. 2001-624 *portant diverses dispositions d'ordre social, éducatif et culture* (July 17, 2001), art. L.135-8.

454 French Retirement Reserve Fund, Press release, April 2003, http://www.fondsdereserve.fr/spip.php?rubrique127.

455 French Retirement Reserve Fund, Press release, June 2005, http://www.fondsdereserve.fr/spip.php?rubrique127.

456 UNEPFI and UKSIF, note 417, 44.

457 Ibid., 43.

458 French Retirement Reserve Fund, Press release, November 2006, at http://www.fondsdereserve.fr/spip.php?rubrique127.

459 UNEPFI and UKSIF, note 417, 45.

460 Eurosif, *European SRI Study* (Eurosif, 2006), 7.

4. *New Zealand Superannuation Fund (NZSF)*

New Zealand, a country renowned for some of the most progressive environmental legislation in the world,[461] has also sought to promote SRI through its national retirement fund. The New Zealand *Superannuation and Retirement Income Act* of 2001 interestingly specifies that the Guardians of the NZSF, a public corporation entrusted to administer the Fund, must invest: "on a prudent, commercial basis, and in doing so... [avoid] prejudice to New Zealand's reputation as a responsible member of the world community."[462] Further, the Act requires the Guardians to publish a statement of investment standards and procedures that "must cover... ethical investment, including policies, standards, or procedures for avoiding prejudice to New Zealand's reputation as a responsible member of the world community,"[463] and the "retention, exercise, or delegation of voting rights acquired through investments."[464] The Fund must report annually on the implementation of its investment policy.[465]

Yet, while the NZSF must not do anything prejudicial to New Zealand's reputation internationally, active consideration of socially and environmentally responsible issues is not explicitly required. Moreover, the legislation does not give guidance as to what constitutes "prejudice to New Zealand's reputation," which is left to its Board of Guardians to decide.[466] These legislative provisions have been interpreted by the New Zealand Treasury staff as simply requiring the NZSF "to have a policy regarding ethical investment: it does not prescribe any particular approach to or emphasis on ethical investment."[467]

The Board of Guardians, appointed by the Minister of Finance, supervises the Guardians' SRI policy, and it has established the Responsible Investment Committee to oversee the development of the SRI policy, to monitor its performance, and to make recommendations to the Board. The Guardians' statement of investment policy is reviewed by the Board at least annually.

---

461 See articles in the *New Zealand Journal of Environmental Law*, at http://www.nzcel.auckland.ac.nz.

462 Section 58(2)(c).

463 Section 61(d).

464 Section 61(i).

465 Section 68(e)–(f).

466 Guardians of New Zealand Superannuation, *Statement of Investment Policies, Standards and Procedures* (NZSF, September 11, 2006), section 6, 21–23.

467 B. McCulloch and J. Frances, "Governance of Public Pension Funds: New Zealand Superannuation Fund," in *Public Pension Fund Management: Governance, Accountability, and Investment Policies.* eds A.R. Musalem and R.J. Palacios (World Bank, 2004), 157, 189.

The Guardians were slow to make SRI a priority, and by the close of 2005 apparently no investment had been blacklisted on ethical grounds.[468] During 2006, the NZSF changed its course and signed the UNPRI and the UNGC. The Fund states that it uses the UNGC as the benchmark against which it assesses corporate behavior.[469] The Fund then divested from Singapore Technologies Engineering, Textron Systems, and several other companies involved in the production of anti-personnel mines.[470] Like the Swedish funds, the Guardians prefer engagement and dialogue with problematic companies rather than divestment. According to its *Responsible Investment Policy*, published in June 2007:

> [I]f companies in the Fund are found to have corporate practices that breach the Guardians' [responsible investment] standards, the Guardians may consider engaging with the company, either directly, or in conjunction with other investors, and taking other shareholder action as appropriate. The Guardians believe they can, in most instances, have a greater impact on company practices through dialogue with company management in conjunction with others.
>
> There may be occasional circumstances where the Guardians may consider excluding a particular investment, or divesting the Fund's holding.[471]

Among the criteria determining engagement or divestment, the policy examines whether the "issue is contrary to New Zealand law and international agreements."[472]

Their reluctance for more extensive use of the divestment option has contributed to concerns expressed by the Green Party, a growing political force in New Zealand politics, and the New Zealand Council for Socially Responsible Investment. When the Green Party denigrated the NZSF for investing in ExxonMobil, a company down-playing climate change, then Chief Executive of the Fund, Paul Costello, explained that because the NZSF's policy was to divest from only those companies whose products or activities are illegal in New Zealand, there was no basis to divest from Exxon and its

---

468 Personal communication, Paul Costello, CEO, Guardians of the New Zealand Superannuation Fund (Auckland, December 14, 2005).

469 Guardians of New Zealand Superannuation, *Responsible Investment Policy, Standards and Procedures* (NZSF, June 27, 2007), 5.

470 See http://www.nzsuperfund.com/index.asp?pageID=2145844241, link to "activities."

471 Guardians of New Zealand Superannuation, note 469, 4.

472 Ibid.

quite legal petroleum business.[473] Robert Howell, head of the Council for Socially Responsible Investment, has criticized the weaknesses of the "international reputation" clause in the superannuation legislation as failing to prevent the NZSF and other Crown financial institutions from investing "in tobacco companies, and companies with unacceptable or questionable human rights behavior or environmental impacts, such as Nike, Wal-Mart, BJ Services (operating in Myanmar), and ExxonMobil."[474] Further, a report authored by Russel Norman, co-leader of the Green Party, examined the ethical nature of the NZSF's investments by comparing them to those of the Norwegian Pension Fund (considered below), which is viewed as the most progressive SRI fund among national pension plans.[475] He found that the NZSF had significant investments in twelve companies that the Norwegian Fund had divested from for ethical reasons including environmental damage and munitions production.[476]

In late 2006, a Private Member's Bill tabled in the New Zealand Parliament to strengthen the SRI criteria in the NZSF legislation and to apply a similar SRI standard to other New Zealand Crown financial institutions pointed to further concerns.[477] Its key provisions were that the investment policy of these institutions must be consistent with and governed by ethics promoting socially responsible and environmentally sustainable development; that their investment policy must take into account international norms and conventions supported or ratified by the New Zealand government; and that they must make annual reports regarding the investment policy criteria. While this Bill had not been adopted at the time of writing, the NZSF's SRI practices remain under political scrutiny.

5. Norwegian Public Pension Fund

The most recent example of a statutory SRI mandate concerns the Norwegian Government's Public Pension Fund,[478] the largest pension fund in Europe.

473 "Greens Urge Super Fund to Dump Exxon," *New Zealand Herald*, October 6, 2006.

474 R. Howell, "The New Zealand Crown Financial Institutions' Non-Financial Investment Criteria" (presentation to the Council for Socially Responsible Investment Conference, Reward, Risk and Reputation — Rethinking the Investment Role of Crown Financial Institutions in New Zealand's Growth, Auckland, December 2, 2005), 1.

475 R. Norman, *Betting the Bank on the Bomb* (Green Party of Aotearoa New Zealand, 2007).

476 Ibid., 3.

477 *Ethical Investment (Crown Financial Institutions) Bill*, 2006.

478 The Fund incorporated the existing Government Petroleum Fund and the National Insurance Scheme Fund, which already had some SRI policies.

368 | SOCIALLY RESPONSIBLE INVESTMENT LAW

Appointed by the government, the 2002 Graver Committee inquiry recommended ethical guidelines to govern the Fund, a stance apparently endorsed by 60 percent of Norway's population.[479] In November 2004, regulations were adopted to govern the Fund's international investment, and the government established a Council on Ethics to evaluate potential investments for compliance with the ethical guidelines. The *Act relating to the Government Pension Fund* of 2005 assigned the Fund's management responsibilities to the Norwegian Ministry of Finance and the operational control to Norges Bank, Norway's central bank. The Council on Ethics has five members, including three academics, and is presently chaired by Professor Gro Nystuen of the Norwegian Centre for Human Rights at the University of Oslo.

The Fund's ethical standards are based on two grounds. First, the Fund serves to ensure that a reasonable share of Norway's petroleum wealth benefits posterity. Those riches, derived incongruously from the fossil fuel industry, must be managed through sustainable development in order to provide reasonable returns in the long term. Second, the Fund should not make investments that would result in deleterious social and environmental practices. According to the ethical guidelines, the Fund:

> ... should not make investments which constitute an unacceptable risk that the Fund may contribute to unethical acts or omissions, such as violations of fundamental humanitarian principles, serious violations of human rights, gross corruption or severe environmental damages.[480]

In assessing investments on these grounds, the Fund refers to the UNGC and the OECD Guidelines for Corporate Governance and for Multinational Enterprises.[481] It uses a combination of screening and engagement strategies.

Based on recommendations of the Council on Ethics, the Fund has divested from companies dealing with cluster bombs (Lockheed Martin), nuclear weapons components (Boeing), breaches of human rights and labor standards (Wal-Mart), and environmental damage (Freeport). In March 2006, the Fund

479 I. Bay, *Valueless Money? The Petroleum Fund —the Road Towards Ethical Guidelines*, Report 1/2001 (Framtiden I Våre Henders Forskningsinstitutt, 2002).
480 Issued December 22 2005 pursuant to *Regulation on the Management of the Government Pension Fund*, 2004, at: http://odin.dep.no/fin/english/topics/pension_fund/p10002777/guidelines/bn.html.
481 UNEPFI and UKSIF, note 417, 47.

sold approximately US$416 million of Wal-Mart shares.[482] The Ministry of Finance evaluates the Council's recommendations and makes the final investment or divestment decisions. As of early 2007, the Fund had divested from twenty companies out of some 3,500 in its portfolio (corresponding to 1.8 percent of the Fund's benchmark portfolio for equities). Divestment usually occurred after dialogue and engagement strategies failed to change the targeted companies' behavior.[483] Of all the public sector pension funds, the Norwegian fund appears to have been the most earnest in implementing SRI.

6. SRI in Other Public Sector Funds

While it is encouraging to see examples of public pension funds mandated to pursue SRI, many of their peers still adhere to more traditional investment mandates. Most such funds consider SRI issues solely via corporate engagement and only where they are perceived as acutely material for the financial bottom line. The Dutch Stichting Pensioenfonds ABP reportedly even had an explicit policy as recently as 2000 which barred any SRI if such investments would compromise financial returns.[484] And Japan's Government Pension Fund has had a policy of avoiding shareholder activism.[485] In recent years, assets of public pension and other sovereign wealth funds have grown substantially, yet concern is arising about the lack of transparency and accountability in the management of some funds.[486]

Among the slightly better examples from an SRI perspective, in May 2006, the Belgian Government introduced a regulation requiring all public authorities' pension funds to invest at least 10 percent of their capital in SRI assets. They must also justify their choice of investment on an annual basis.[487] However, by restricting SRI to a mere "10 percent" of the portfolio, the implication that other investments can be made regardless of social and environmental concerns hardly makes the Belgian law a role model.

---

482 Ibid., 49.
483 Norges Bank Investment Management, *Annual Report 2006* (Norges Bank, 2007), section 4.2.
484 ABP Investment Policy Statement, reproduced in J. Carmichael and R. Palacios, "A Framework for Public Pension Fund Management," in *Public Pension Fund Management*, note 467, 1, 38.
485 OECD, *Recent Trends and Regulatory Implications in Socially Responsible Investment for Pension Funds* (OECD, 2007), 21.
486 E.M. Truman, *Sovereign Wealth Funds: The Need for Greater Transparency and Accountability*, Policy Brief (Peterson Institute for International Economics, August 2007).
487 "Belgian Funds Forced into SRI Investing," *Eurosif Newsletter*, June 2006.

Australia's Future Fund, which was established by the federal government in 2006 under the *Future Fund Act*, provides only modest scope for SRI.[488] The Future Fund is designed to meet unfunded superannuation liabilities forecast to arise from the demographic bulge of the retiring baby boom generation. The Fund's governing legislation makes no reference to consideration of ESG issues in its investment strategies. The Future Fund Board of Guardians must, by virtue of section 18(1) of the Act, "maximize the return earned on the Fund over the long term, consistent with international best practice for institutional investment," and subject to any directions given by the responsible Ministers.

The Government has issued investment mandate directions to the Future Fund.[489] In language redolent of the NZSF legislation, the official directions state that "the Board must act in a way that... is unlikely to cause any diminution of the Australian Government's reputation in Australian and international financial markets."[490] Further encouragingly, the Board is directed to "have regard to international best practice for institutional investment in determining its approach to corporate governance principles, including in relation to its voting policy."[491] In 2006, a parliamentary inquiry recommended that the Fund become a signatory to the UNPRI.[492] However, the Future Fund's investment policies, issued in 2007, make no reference to ESG considerations. They only mildly acknowledge a role for shareholder activism, stating: "[t]he Board will exercise its shareholder rights as a prudent investor seeking to maximize investment returns over the long term, while minimizing risk of loss."[493] Such a stance may change with the new Labor Party Government elected in November 2007, which has much stronger policies on social justice and environmental protection than its predecessor.

Similarly, Ireland's *National Pensions Reserve Fund Act* of 2000 provides that the investment mandate of the National Pensions Reserve Fund is strictly to "secure the optimal total financial return."[494] When drafting the legislation,

---

488 Http://www.futurefund.gov.au.

489 P.H. Costello and N.H. Minchin, *Future Fund Investment Mandate Directions* (May 3, 2006).

490 Ibid., clause 1(b).

491 Ibid., clause 1(c).

492 Parliamentary Joint Committee on Corporations and Financial Services, *Corporate Responsibility: Managing Risk and Creating Value* (Commonwealth of Australia, 2006), 77.

493 Future Fund, *Statement of Investment Objectives* (Future Fund, July 12, 2007), 21.

494 Section 19(1); see also A. Maher, "Public Pension Funds Accountability: The Case of Ireland," in *Public Pension Fund Management*, note 467, 125.

proposals for including SRI obligations were rejected in parliament.[495] In February 2006 a proposed amendment to incorporate an SRI mandate into the Fund's governing framework was also rejected.[496] The proposed amendment provided that: "[t]he Minister shall make regulations to require the National Pension Reserve Fund to adopt an ethical investment policy and to comply with such requirements and subject to such conditions as may be prescribed." The amendment was opposed on the basis that it would "politicize" the Fund's investment mandate and cause significant difficulties in its interpretation and implementation.

The absence of an SRI mandate has not hindered some funds from forging SRI policies. These include the Canada Pension Plan and the Australian VicSuper, as well as pension funds in developing countries, such as the Thai Government Pension Fund, and the Brazilian PREVI, the employees' pension fund of the state-owned Banco do Brasil.[497] This trend is perhaps not unexpected, given the evolution of the SRI discourse from an ethical or mission-based investing style to a prudent financial management method. In other words, environmental and social issues are reconstituted as financial risks rather than ethical imperatives.

VicSuper, one of Australia's largest public sector superannuation funds, has made SRI a central policy.[498] It sees its aim as one of "sustainable investing," which it defines as "investing in companies that identify and manage the risks and maximize the opportunities deriving from economic, social and environmental developments in their industry and, as a result, increase their profitability and long-term shareowner value."[499] It offers specialist SRI options, such as the Equity Growth Sustainability Option, for its most socially conscious members. Unusually, VicSuper has also signed a voluntary agreement with the Victorian Environment Protection Agency to collaborate on environmental protection measures in Victoria.[500] It calls the agreement a "sustainability covenant," which commits VicSuper to investigate new

495 A. Maher, "National Pensions Reserve Fund in Ireland" (paper presented at the conference on Public Pension Fund Management, Washington D.C., September 24–26, 2001), 13.
496 Select Committee on Finance and the Public Service, *Parliamentary Debates* 44 (February 23, 2006), 5.
497 UNEPFI and UKSIF, note 417, 50–53; 62–65.
498 Http://www.vicsuper.com.au.
499 VicSuper, "Sustainabily Investing," at http://www.vicsuper.com.au/www/html/1019-sustainability-investing.asp?intSiteID=1.
500 VicSuper and Environment Protection Agency Victoria, *Sustainability Covenant* (VicSuper, August 17, 2005).

investment in environmentally beneficial projects and services, to explore ways to reduce the ecological impact of VicSuper Fund investments, to develop procedures for assessing the environmental sustainability of VicSuper Fund's investment portfolio, and to issue a periodic Sustainability Report on its performance on these and other activities.

The Canada Pension Plan (CPP) is also incorporating an SRI envelope into its investment policies. The CPP is a contributory, earnings-related social insurance program, managed by the Canadian government.[501] The *Canada Pension Plan Investment Board Act* of 1997[502] established the CPP Investment Board to oversee the investment of CPP assets. For some time, it apparently showed little interest in SRI, and some of its investments engendered public criticism, such as tobacco stocks and armaments companies.[503] The Board issued its first SRI policy in 2002, which has been periodically revised. The current policy, of February 2007, states that the guiding investment principles include:

- Recognizing that the importance of environmental, social and governance (ESG) factors varies across industries, geography and time, responsible corporate behaviour with respect to ESG factors can generally have a positive influence on long-term corporate performance.
- Investment analysis should incorporate ESG factors to the extent that they affect long-term risk and return.[504]

The Investment Board's "overriding" responsibility however remains to "maximize investment returns without undue risk."[505] According to Brigid Barnett, a responsible investment advisor at the CPP, the Board "look[s] at environmental, social and governance (ESG) factors only as they affect the potential risk and return of investments."[506] The Board generally avoids

501 See http://www.sdc.gc.ca/en/isp/cpp/cpptoc.shtml.

502 S.O. 1997.

503 S. Cordon, "Critics Call for Halt to CPP Investments in Tobacco Companies," *Canadian Press Newswire*, December 5, 2002; P. Gillespie, "Your Pension Contributions at Work?" *Toronto Star*, December 23, 2005; T. Flynn, "War and Weapons Funded by Canada Pension Plan," *Alternatives Journal* 30(4) (2004): 16.

504 CPP Investment Board, *Policy on Responsible Investing* (CPP Investment Board, 2007), 2.

505 Ibid.

506 B. Barnett, "CPP Investment Board's Approach to Responsible Investing" (paper presented at the 2007 Canadian Responsible Investment Conference, Montreal, May 27–29, 2007).

applying exclusionary screens, and prefers cooperative engagement and dialogue with portfolio companies.[507] According to Donald Raymond of the
CPP Investment Board, "[e]ngagement is a more effective approach to bring
about positive change and enhance long-term financial performance."[508]
However, of some 2,000 firms in its portfolio, the CPP Investment Board
engages with only some ten to fifteen companies each year. In 2007, its priority issues for engagement were climate change, extractive industries, and
executive compensation. It is significant that the Investment Board has begun
to recognize the materiality of SRI issues without the necessity of any amendment to its legislative charter to compel it.

The Quebec pension plan (Caisse de dépôt et placement du Québec), the
second largest pool of capital in Canada after the CPP, also has an SRI policy.[509]
However, unlike the CPP's governing legislation, the Quebec pension plan is
mandated by its statute to invest "with a view to achieving optimal return on
capital within the framework of depositors' investment policies while at the
same time contributing to Québec's economic development."[510] This is a
mandate for a form of SRI that resembles "economically targeted investment." In January 2005, the Caisse de dépôt et placement du Québec introduced a new, responsible investing policy that, like the CPP policy,
emphasizes active engagement and exercise of proxy voting rights to promote
change.[511] It states that the "Caisse expects the companies in which it invests …
to take all measures necessary to respect and to protect the environment in
which they operate."[512]

In the US, CalPERS is one of the largest public pension plans in the world
in terms of assets under management.[513] It provides various retirement and
health benefit programs and services to California's public employees and
their dependants. CalPERS seeks to promote exemplary corporate governance

---

507 The Board's policy does at least explicitly preclude investment in companies
that manufacture anti-personnel landmines: CPP Investment Board, "Letter to
Ralph Goodale Regarding Possible Investments in Landmines," January 28,
2004.

508 D.M. Raymond, "Mainstreaming Responsible Investment: Our Approach"
(paper presented at GLOBE 2006, Vancouver, March 30, 2006), 5.

509 Http://www.lacaisse.com.

510 *An Act respecting the* Caisse *de dépôt et placement du Québec*, R.S.Q. 1977,
s. 4(1).

511 Caisse de dépôt et placement du Québec, *Policy on Socially Responsible
Investment* (Caisse de dépôt et placement du Québec, January 2005).

512 Ibid., 2.

513 Http://www.calpers.ca.gov.

in accordance with its Pension Plan Statement of Investment Policy for Global Proxy Voting and the CalPERS' Global Principles of Accountable Corporate Governance.[514] Periodically, it singles out a few companies with the most atrocious governance practices for concerted dialogue and engagement. Also, CalPERS has adopted a corporate governance environmental strategy to improve disclosure of environmental impacts and risks, such as those associated with climate change.[515] Like some other major institutional investors, CalPERS has signed the CDP, and it participates in the INCR. It also advocates for companies, particularly those in its emerging markets portfolio, to commit to a credible sustainability performance reporting protocol, such as the GRI.[516] It has dedicated US$500 million for investment in asset portfolios that use environmental screens, and a further US$200 million for clean environmental technology development,[517] although these commitments represent very small portions of its total portfolio, worth US$250 billion as of September 2007.[518]

Other countries appear likely to introduce national savings schemes to bolster their pension regimes, thereby potentially augmenting opportunities for state involvement in SRI. For instance, the UK Government is considering reforms for a national savings scheme including personal accounts, which could give contributing workers the right to choose from a menu of investment options including SRI portfolios.[519] More substantial measures to promote SRI in this sector are essential. At the very least, if governments expect private financiers to invest ethically with regard to social and environmental issues, public funds should set an example.

B. INVESTMENT RESTRICTIONS

Occasionally, governments outlaw investment in specific activities. Outright prohibitions serve to reinforce primary regulatory checks. Most governments have laws prohibiting the financing of terrorism, drug operations, and other illegal and socially undesirable activities.[520] It is politically difficult however

---

514 UNEPFI and UKSIF, note 417, 25.

515 Ibid., 26.

516 Ibid., 28.

517 Ibid., 29.

518 CalPERS, *Facts at a Glance: Investment Facts* (CalPERS, 2007).

519 H. Williams, "Personal Accounts Could Grow Green Investment Savings," *PensionsWeek*, February 12, 2007, 1.

520 E.g., M.S. Navias, "Finance Warfare as a Response to International Terrorism," *Political Quaterly* 73(1) (2002): 57.

to advance a case for investment restrictions on broader social and environmental grounds, which financiers might view as interference with legitimate economic goals. If an activity is perfectly legal or officially regulated, as commonly in the case of mining or automotive manufacturing to illustrate, on what basis could governments concomitantly prohibit financing of these activities? Usually (but not always) when it is an activity conducted in other jurisdictions that states wish to dissociate from.

Thus, several US states, including Illinois, Arizona, California, Louisiana, New Jersey, and Oregon, have adopted Sudan divestment laws.[521] Public funds in these and other states are reported to have shifted US$2 billion out of Sudanese linked-companies between 2005 and 2007.[522] A similar divestment campaign against companies doing business in Iran is now underway in the US.[523] Interestingly, lacking a foreign policy dimension, Massachusetts enacted legislation in 1997 that required state pension funds to sell their tobacco stocks within three years and barred future investments in the tobacco industry.[524]

Apart from these isolated examples, investment restrictions in the field of SRI are used primarily to bolster underlying legal prohibitions on certain activities. One example is the Belgian government's bans on investing in production and dealing of cluster bombs and anti-personnel mines, which are produced by foreign companies such as Lockheed Martin and Northrop Grumman.[525] The ban on financing anti-personnel mines was implemented in 2005 and, in 2007, similar measures for cluster bombs were adopted. The law prohibits banks and investment funds operating in the Belgian market from financing producers of cluster bombs. The ban also applies to purchase of bonds issued by these companies. Only investments through index funds, and financing of these companies' other projects clearly unrelated to

---

521 L.J. Dhooge, "Condemning Khartoum: The Illinois Divestment Act and Foreign Relations," *American Business Law Journal* 43(2) (2006): 245, 274.

522 A.H. Munnell, *Should Public Pension Plans Engage in Social Investing* (Centre for Retirement Research, 2007), 3.

523 R. Pichardo, "Divestment Focus Shifts to Iran," *Pensions and Investments* (May 28, 2007).

524 *An Act Requiring Divestment of Tobacco Stocks, Securities or other Obligations from Public Pension Funds*, Mass. Ann. Laws, Ch. 119 (October 15, 1997). Specifically, it provides in s. 1: "and no new investment of funds shall be made in stocks, securities, or other obligations of any company which derives more than 15 percent of its revenues from the sale of tobacco products."

525 Netwerk Vlaanderen, "Belgium Bans Investments in Cluster Munitions," Press release, March 2, 2007.

cluster munitions are allowed. The ban on cluster bomb financing emerged largely as a result of campaigning by the Belgian NGO Netwerk Vlaanderen.

VII. Conclusions

There are many governmental policy instruments deployed to promote SRI. They range from more remote transparency measures, able to be rationalized within the terms of conventional finance theory, to highly controversial controls, including lender liability and legislated investment directives. Most of these reforms have not been adopted explicitly to promote SRI. Rather, they were brought about to enable more informed decision-making, to reduce agency problems, and to generally achieve more "efficient" financial markets. But ethical investment mandates of state pension funds and taxation incentives for green investment show that at times SRI is the central purpose.

Practical implementation of these policy instruments has generally been under-whelming. Certainly, many pension funds have adopted SRI statements, companies have issued more environmental reports, and institutional investors have become less passive. But the measures are often ad hoc and perfunctory and, usually motivated by a business case rationale rather than ethical principles. The emphasis on disclosure-based regulation has not worked as effectively as reflexive law would predict, for "disclosure systems can employ flawed metrics, provide a partial picture of reality, or lack the resources for effective enforcement."[526] Policy instruments that leave financiers with less discretion, such as lender liability or mandatory investment rules, currently target only small sectors of the financial market in a limited range of jurisdictions.

States have sometimes chosen different regulatory paths to accommodate SRI, largely owing to their distinctive regulatory traditions and political cultures.[527] Thus, European countries especially the Netherlands have tended to favor taxation mechanisms, redolent of their heavy reliance on taxation policy to correct market failures. The UK and US, having moved further along the market deregulation spectrum, emphasize disclosure-based regulation.

---

526 M. Graham, "Is Sunshine the Best Disinfectant? The Promise and Problems of Environmental Disclosure," *Brookings Review* 20(2) (2002):18.

527 See generally R.E. Löfstedt and D. Vogel, "The Changing Character of Regulation: A Comparison of Europe and the United States," *Risk Analysis* 21(3) (2001): 399.

This includes the SRI disclosure statements required for pension funds (in the UK) and proxy voting disclosures for mutual funds (in the US and Canada). European countries, with a stronger tradition of command regulation and big government, have applied stronger SRI mandates to their national pension schemes (France, Norway, and Sweden) compared to the US where the mandates have tended to be confined to narrower foreign policy concerns (e.g., formerly South Africa and today Sudan).

Yet, the forces of globalization that have transformed financial markets have also influenced regulatory practices, resulting in some convergence of legal techniques. Thus, the UK's innovation in SRI disclosure for pension funds was copied by at least five continental European states and Australia. As the following chapter shows, emerging international codes of conduct, such as the UNPRI, are also helping to harmonize governance systems. Quite likely, therefore, future SRI regulation will increasingly be untethered from the mores of national legal systems, and shaped by the global dissemination and sharing of best practices and experiences wherever pioneered.

To improve SRI, reformers must entertain a wider range of policy instruments and pay attention to their optimal combinations.[528] In some cases, policy instruments may simply co-exist, while in other cases they may interact and influence each other. This depends on both their intrinsic qualities as well as their contexts. For instance, a restriction on investment in tobacco stocks or armaments producers has little or no bearing on other SRI regulations such as proxy voting disclosures. On the other hand, mandatory corporate sustainability reporting can enhance the impact of taxation incentive measures in enabling investors to assess corporate environmental performance. In some cases, policy instruments interactions can also be contradictory, such as where the state subsidizes polluting industries (e.g., the oil industry) while investors are expected to take into account and disclose climate change risks in their securities filings.

Therefore, the task of reforming regulatory policy to promote SRI requires a comprehensive approach, in which the impact of policy instruments is assessed holistically, rather than in isolation. Reflexive law instruments may provide front-line controls in some cases, while in other contexts financial markets may only respond to more assertive means of change such as environmental liability and mandatory investment directions. Whilst coercive approaches tend to alienate investors and thereby generate transactional and political costs, the softer alternatives are vulnerable to exploitation by

528 Gunningham and Grabosky, note 31, 125–32.

self-interested parties and to being undermined by free-riders. The "balance" between these approaches, according to Ian Ayres and John Braithwaite, is "responsive regulation." They conceptualize a regulatory pyramid, in which authorities respond with increasingly restrictive approaches until compliance with policy goals is achieved.[529]

The imperative of regulating the unseen polluters must also take into account the proliferation of non-state governance mechanisms, such as voluntary codes of conduct. The impact of official regulation is increasingly a result of its interaction with ordering systems provided by the market and civil society. Mobilizing third parties as a means of governance can sometimes improve public policy. The next chapter delves into this governance beyond the state.

---

529 Ayres and Braithwaite, note 29, 21.

CHAPTER 6

SRI Governance Beyond the State

I. Governing SRI Through Market Forces

A. INTRODUCTION

Governing the unseen polluters of the financial sector is no longer a simple matter of official regulation. Governance for SRI is now also becoming informed by the proliferating codes of conduct, management protocols, and reporting guides generated by market actors and other nongovernmental entities. This ensemble of multi-layered and fragmented regulation with little government input furnishes both substantive standards and procedures for potentially more transparent and accountable financial decisions.[1] While these mechanisms are mostly for voluntary application, for some financiers, the question now is no longer about whether or not to apply such mechanisms, but about which ones to apply and how. Of course, their rising popularity does not immediately imply radical changes in investment practices. Nonetheless, some commentators remain hopeful. Kate Miles, for instance,

---

1 See K. Miles, "Targeting Financiers: Can Voluntary Codes of Conduct for the Investment and Financing Sectors Achieve Environmental and Sustainability Objectives?" in *Critical Issues in Environmental Taxation, Volume 5, eds* K. Deketelaere, et al. (Oxford University Press, 2008), forthcoming; D. Leipziger, *The Corporate Responsibility Code Book* (Greenleaf Publishing, 2003); EC Employment and Social Affairs, *Mapping Instruments for Corporate Social Responsibility* (EC, 2003); O. Perez, *The New Universe of Green Finance: From Self-Regulation to Multi-Polar Governance*, Working Paper No. 07-3 (Bar-Ilan University, Faculty of Law, 2007).

explains that "voluntary codes for the financing sector are making a positive impact," including "through the rejection or modification of environmentally damaging projects, the raising of environmental awareness amongst the financing sector ... and the harmonization of lending standards. ..."[2]

While these initiatives essentially involve the private sector, formulated or implemented by the market or civil society institutions, they are not wholly separable from official regulation. The opportunities to apply these instruments of non-state governance for SRI are sometimes created by public institutions.[3] For instance, the US pension fund regulations of the 1980s restricted investments in companies with operations in apartheid South Africa or North Ireland, but they also incorporated exceptions for investment in those firms adhering to the Sullivan Principles or the MacBride Principles.[4] Similarly, as noted in the previous chapter, the French Retirement Reserve Fund's policy requires its managers to follow the UNGC principles in their investment decision-making. Incorporation of the accountancy profession's standards into financial reporting also illustrates the private sector's ability to impact and inform public regulations. The reverse effect is certainly also true, as public norms may inform private sector practices. For instance, "Convention Watch" of EIRIS assesses companies for their compliance with a wide range of international treaties, as well as soft law instruments.[5]

Governance theorists observe the increasingly collaborative nature of contemporary regulation, evidenced by formal and informal partnerships between states and private sectors.[6] Third-party conscriptions also arise, such as in states' obliging banks to report suspicious transactions to assist official money-laundering controls, requirements to obtain privately audited environmental assessment or certification, or obligations to carry environmental liability insurance. Then, in some cases, governments may simply cede significant autonomy to financial institutions to govern themselves, as it mostly does with CRAs.[7]

---

2 Ibid., 2.

3 H. Ward, *Public Sector Roles in Strengthening Corporate Social Responsibility: Taking Stock* (World Bank, 2004).

4 See discussion of these instruments later in this chapter.

5 Http://www.eiris.org.

6 L. Hancher and M. Moran, "Organizing Regulatory Space," in *Capitalism, Culture and Economic Regulation*, eds L. Hancher and M. Moran (Clarendon Press, 1989), 271; P. Grabosky, "Green Markets: Environmental Regulation by the Private Sector," *Law and Policy* 16(4) (1994): 419.

7 S.L. Schwarcz, "Private Ordering of Public Markets: The Rating Agency Paradox," *University of Illinois Law Review* (2002): 1.

A valuable feature of these new mechanisms is that they can apply to multi-jurisdictional contexts and target financial institutions operating in global markets.[8] The international business community has been an influential voice in this trend.[9] The drift to private-public rule-making internationally raises concerns about the adequacy of inclusiveness, transparency, and accountability of such standard-setting, particularly for NGOs[10] and disadvantaged peoples in the South.[11] While official regulation for SRI almost exclusively originates from national level reforms, the majority of the non-state SRI governance mechanisms have emerged from transnational institutions. Given the lacunae in international law in governing the social and environmental impacts of financial markets, the transnational sources and applications are of potentially critical importance. Technological advances and market deregulation have increased capital mobility, while concomitantly reducing states' ability to regulate capital markets.[12] National regulators face chronic deficiencies in capacity and information to supervise financiers engaged in complex trans-border commerce. Even within the EU, with its relatively sophisticated intergovernmental supervision of capital flows, few regulations touch on SRI.[13]

This web of SRI governance relies on a diversity of methods, structures, and objectives, broadly categorized into four types. First, normative regimes

---

8 R. Falkner, "Private Environmental Governance and International Relations: Exploring the Links," *Global Environmental Politics* 3 (2003): 72.

9 E.B. Kapstein, "The Corporate Ethics Crusade," *Foreign Affairs* 80 (2001): 105.

10 See generally eds, S. Khagram, J.V. Riker, and K. Sikkink, *Restructuring World Politics: Transnational Social Movements, Networks and Norms* (University of Minnesota Press, 2002).

11 Notably, K. Dingwerth, "The Democratic Legitimacy of Public-Private Rule Making: What Can We Learn from the World Commission on Dams?" *Global Governance: A Review of Multilateralism and International Organizations* 11(1) (2005): 65.

12 A. Walter, *World Power and World Money* (Harvester Wheatsheaf, 1993), 202–4; H.M. Kim, *Globalization of International Financial Markets: Causes and Consequences* (Ashgate Publishing, 1999); J. Braithwaite and P. Drahos, *Global Business Regulation* (Cambridge University Press, 2000), 7–8; and further S. Strange, *The Retreat of the State: The Diffusion of Power in the World Economy* (Cambridge University Press, 1996); M. Schaberg, *Globalization and the Erosion of National Financial Systems* (Edward Elgar Publishing, 1999).

13 R. Lastra, *Legal Foundations of International Monetary Stability* (Oxford University Press, 2006); On the EU, see R. Lastra, "The Governance Structure for Financial Supervision and Regulation in Europe," *Columbia Journal of European Law* 10(1) (2003): 49.

provide substantive principles and guidance toward desirable performance. In theory, normative frameworks set goals or benchmarks to move financiers from perpetuating or mere tinkering of existing unsustainable practices. Examples of these normative mechanisms include the Collevecchio Declaration on Financial Institutions and the UNPRI. Process standards, enabling evaluation and communication of performance, provide a second form of governance. They can help financiers to evaluate their potential environmental impacts, verify the effectiveness of their procedures for responsible financing, and publicize their performances in coherent terms. The GRI and the EPs are examples of process standards. Third, management systems, such as the 14001 standard of the ISO, provide integrated or issue-specific frameworks to guide ongoing management of environmental and social impacts. Management systems go beyond process standards by emphasizing operational procedures and mechanisms in incorporating sustainability considerations into corporate conduct. They may not however set actual performance standards. The fourth modality is comparative rating mechanisms. Unlike process standards involving self-assessment and self-disclosure of social or environmental performances, comparative evaluation involves third party evaluators and comparison of the results relative to peers or to normative benchmarks. These rating mechanisms include SRI stock market indexes such as the Dow Jones Sustainability Indexes and reports of SRI research and advisory bodies such as EIRIS and UKSIF. Their work often influences the composition of SRI portfolios.

This chapter examines these governance mechanisms: their demands of financial institutions, their implementation, and their adequacy as a form of governance for SRI.

The first-raised concern is that the current, market-based SRI governance is too ambiguous and open-ended in its expectations. The codes of conduct mostly lack substantive standards of socially just or ecologically sustainable outcomes. SRI thus becomes a matter of personal ethics, left to individual choice; or too complex to define precisely and meaningfully, and therefore best handled through the "objective" protocols of financial risk management. Thereby, the empirical reality of global warming or depletion of biodiversity is rendered as matters of "personal choices" or "financially material considerations" warranting action only to the extent they pose investment risks or opportunities. The closest approach to transformative SRI standards demanding substantive changes in the behavior of financial markets is the Collevecchio Declaration, a product of civil society institutions.

The concept of "financial materiality" also relates to a second constraint to voluntary SRI governance (as well as much official regulation). A pervasive assumption is that SRI should not diminish financial returns. Financiers accommodate SRI norms insofar as they bring environmental protection and profitable investment into harmony. Research suggesting that firms that adhere to global environmental standards enjoy the highest market values brings comfort to such social investors.[14] According to a recommendation of the WBCSD: "[s]hareholder value is a crucial yardstick for measuring economic success, and by taking the environmental and social aspects into account when conducting our business, we can reduce risks further improving our bottom-line and creating long-term value."[15] This is achievable because most social and environmental problems are shorn of their ethical implications and presented as challenges of financial risk management. In this view, for instance, climate change does not raise questions about the sustainability of capitalism. Instead, global warming to responsible financiers is just another guiding reason to steer clear of certain investments that pose financial risks, such as real estate developments in New Orleans; or it is an indicator to buy into certain assets promising lucrative returns, such as firms supplying wind and solar energy. Virtually everything is analyzed through the lens of financially materiality, and only those issues that meet this threshold warrant response.

The notion that environmental care and business success can be compatible is, of course, not inconceivable. The danger is how the optimism behind this synergy can become a pretext for standard business practices. A huge gap between a financial materiality model of SRI and an ecologically sustainable economy persists. That model does not guarantee cessation of resource depletion and environmental damage, because current financial market metrics cannot reflect all environmental values. Moreover, a potent business case continues for many environmentally tragic practices, such as the vacuuming of the oceans of marine life and the unabated oil fields exploitation despite looming climate change.

In place of transformative ethical standards, the assortment of voluntary mechanisms emphasizes procedural standards such as disclosure, reporting, and auditing. While these transparency measures have some beneficial effects, they appear unlikely to induce major changes in investors' underlying goals. Information on pollution or human rights violations must compete for attention in a crowded field abundant with often seemingly more pressing and tangible concerns. CSR and SRI voluntary codes can simply serve to defuse

---

14 G. Dowell, S. Hart, and B. Yeung, "Do Corporate Global Environmental Standards Create or Destroy Value?" *Management Science* 46(8) (2000): 1,059.

15 WBCSD, *Financial Sector* (WBCSD, September 2002), 2.

384 | SOCIALLY RESPONSIBLE INVESTMENT LAW

opposition while allowing corporate behavior to continue with largely cosmetic adjustments.[16]

Limited and fragile means of enforcement pose a source of further unease. Voluntary mechanisms typically lack credible sanctions or enforcement codes. Compliance with the voluntary standards depends on self-discipline of the market or effective NGO pressure. Investors who do not adhere to their commitments may incur reputational risks and consequential financial losses. Where formal sanctions exist, they commonly entail withdrawal of privileges (e.g., termination of membership or decertification) but not financial penalty or public denunciation. Without onerous consequences, the voluntary approach risks perpetuating business-as-usual. Ultimately, therefore, Robert Gibson believes economic actors will only commit to sustainability "not by the promise of gain but by the grind of obligation."[17]

However, the failure of states so far to endorse the UN Norms on the Responsibilities of Transnational Corporations illustrates the political obstacles to proposing norms that deviate too far from the status quo.[18] The UN Norms embody various labor standards, consumer protection, and environmental measures for TNCs to observe.[19] Equally significantly, the UN Norms also contain several procedural requirements for implementation and enforcement.[20] TNCs are to "apply and incorporate [the] Norms in their contracts or other arrangements and dealings,"[21] and where their contracting partners violate these terms, TNCs would have to "cease doing business with them."[22]

---

16 See K. Bruno and J. Karliner, *Earthsummit.biz: The Corporate Takeover of Sustainable Development* (Food First Books, 2002); N. Klein, *No Logo: Taking Aim at the Brand Bullies* (Vintage Canada, 2000).

17 R.B. Gibson, "Voluntary Initiatives, Regulations, and Beyond," in *Voluntary Initiatives: The New Politics of Corporate Greening*, ed. R.B. Gibson (Broadview, 1999), 239, 251–52.

18 UN Economic and Social Council (ECOSOC), Sub-Commission on Promotion and Protection of Human Rights, *Norms on the Responsibilities of Transnational Corporations and Other Business Enterprises with Regard to Human Rights*, UN ESCOR, 2003, UN Doc.
E/CN.4/Sub.2/2003/12/Rev.2. For an historical perspective of the Norms, see D. Weissbrodt and M. Kruger, "Norms on the Responsibilities of Transnational Corporations and Other Business Enterprises with Regard to Human Rights," *American Journal of International Law* 97 (2003): 901.

19 For instance, TNCs are to respect a societal "right to a clean and healthy environment": ibid., Commentary, s. 14(a).

20 Ibid., Part H.

21 Ibid., s. 15.

22 Ibid., s. 15(c).

Sanctions for non-compliance include compensation determined by national or international courts.[23] With these requirements, the UN Norms seek to supplement state authority by imposing international legal obligations directly on TNCs.

The UN Norms herald a radical departure from previous intergovernmental attempts to govern TNCs.[24] Corporate interests criticized the Norms as shifting the obligation to protect human rights and the environment from governments to private companies.[25] Unsurprisingly the UN Commission on Human Rights eventually declined to endorse the Norms.[26] A report by John Ruggie, UN Special Representative on Human Rights and Business, was critical of the form and the reach of the Norms, viewing the initiative as being "engulfed by its own doctrinal excesses" and creating "confusion and doubt" through "exaggerated legal claims and conceptual ambiguities."[27]

B. THE PATH TO VOLUNTARY ENVIRONMENTAL GOVERNANCE

Governance broadly refers to the decision-making processes that control and coordinate society and its organizations.[28] We commonly associate governance with official regulation—state-imposed obligations or constraints on private sector conduct.[29] In an international context, governance traditionally implies intergovernmental cooperation through treaties and other forms of cooperation among states. The shortfall of these notions based on agency or institution is that a government decision may be labeled as governance

---

23 Ibid., s. 18.

24 B. Krumsiek, "Voluntary Codes of Conduct for Multinational Corporations: Promises and Challenges," *Business and Society Review* 109(4) (2004): 583.

25 D. Kinley and R. Chambers, "The United Nations Human Rights Norms for Corporations: The Private Implications of Public International Law," *Human Rights Law Review* 6(3) (2006): 16.

26 UN ECOSOC, Sub-Commission on the Promotion and Protection of Human Rights, *Report of the United Nations High Commissioner on Human Rights on the Responsibilities of Transnational Corporations and Other Business Enterprises with Regards to Human Rights*, UN Doc. E/CN.4/2005/91 (2005).

27 UN, *Interim Report of the Secretary-General's Special Representative on the Issue of Human Rights and Transnational Corporations and Other Business Enterprises* E/CN 4/2006/97 (February 22, 2006), 15.

28 By way of introduction, see M. MacNeil, N. Sargent, and P. Swan, eds, *Law, Regulation and Governance* (Oxford University Press, 2003).

29 OECD, *Reforming Environmental Regulation in OECD Countries* (OECD, 1996).

regardless of whether or not it actually discharges regulatory functions. Conversely, private sector norms, sometimes more influential in controlling corporate behavior, are often overlooked.

In recent decades, legal theorists and policy researchers have advanced new understandings of governance emphasizing the impact of non-state institutions in policy-making, norm-setting, policy delivery, and other aspects of governance. Legal pluralism has assisted in conceiving of regulation as more than just the activities of the state;[30] contemporary governance commonly involves collaboration between the state, market, and civil societal interests.[31] Further, the tool-box of governance is becoming less coercive by including more information- and incentive-based techniques to facilitate desired behavior.[32] Private codes of conduct and other forms of market-generated accountability programs also feature in these new heterogeneous modes of governance.[33]

This transformation in environmental governance was shaped by several intertwined factors.[34] One factor concerned the restructuring of the state, particularly in OECD nations, under the aegis of neoliberal political philosophy and the globalization of the markets. Since the early 1980s, the costs and inefficiencies of administrative-based regulation and the welfare state have garnered increasing criticisms; environmental and other public regulations were pressured to downsize in favor of seemingly more flexible and economical market governance instruments.[35] Financial industry groups for instance have resisted social or environmental regulation on their activities, which they claim can "stifle innovation and creativity of companies."[36]

---

30 S. Merry, "Legal Pluralism," *Law and Society Review* 22 (1988): 869.

31 See M. Rein, "The Social Structure of Institutions: Neither Public nor Private," in *Privatization and the Welfare State* (Princeton University Press, 1989), 49; J. Jordana and D. Levi-Faur, eds, *The Politics of Regulation Institutions and Regulatory Reforms for the Age of Governance* (Edward Elgar Publishing, 2005).

32 G.I. Balch, "The Stick, the Carrot and other Strategies: A Theoretical Analysis of Governmental Intervention," in *Policy Implementation: Penalties or Incentives?* eds J. Brigham and D.W. Brown (Sage Publications, 1989), 43.

33 See Krumsiek, note 24.

34 S. Wood, "Voluntary Environmental Codes and Sustainability," in *Environmental Law for Sustainability*, eds B.J. Richardson and S. Wood (Hart Publishing, 2006), 229, 234–36.

35 See I. Ayres and J. Braithwaite, *Responsive Regulation: Transcending the Deregulation Debate* (Oxford University Press, 1992); D. Osborne and T. Gaebler, *Reinventing Government: How the Entrepreneurial Spirit is Transforming the Public Sector* (Addison-Wesley Publishing, 1992).

36 Australian Bankers Association (ABA), *Submission to the Parliamentary Joint Committee on Corporations and Financial Services Inquiry into Corporate Responsibility* (ABA, October 11, 2005), 10.

Also, ecological modernization doctrine as discussed in the previous chapter has been advanced as a means of reconciling the needs of the market with the demands of modern environmental management.[37] Ecological modernization applauds market efficiency, technological innovation, and managerial know-how as the way to get to the root of many problems, while still enhancing firms' competitiveness and profitability.[38] The notion that environmental improvement can enable cost savings and improve market competitiveness contributed to a new assumption that most companies would have an interest in voluntarily improving their sustainability performance, which will then enhance their profitability.

Another factor fueling voluntary approaches to environmental governance is the international renaissance of the CSR movement, in which the business sector is seen as a benevolent partner in society-wide efforts to promote sustainability.[39] Business enterprises were no longer cast simply as a source of environmental problems; but with their financial resources, acumen, and capacity for innovation, they became championed as a part of the solution. Civil society organizations have also pushed for greater corporate accountability beyond the letter of the law or beyond firms' bottom line.[40] Viewing corporations as potentially moral actors rather than purely economic calculators, John Braithwaite and Brent Fisse contend that market self-regulation is effective when corporations are sensitive about their reputations and where it may forestall "the less palatable alternative" of official regulation.[41]

These changes in governance resonate with "reflexive" forms of regulation, as noted in the previous chapter. Viewing modern societies as having evolved into a collection of distinct and semi-autonomous subsystems such as the market or the political spheres, Gunther Teubner contends that CSR is best articulated through governance techniques tailored to the idiosyncratic characteristics of the corporation and the market.[42] Rejecting regulatory

---

37 A.P.J. Mol, *Globalization and Environmental Reform: The Ecological Modernization of the Global Economy* (MIT Press, 2001); A.P.J. Mol and D. Sonnenfeld, *Ecological Modernisation Around the World: Perspectives and Critical Debates* (Frank Cass Publishers, 2000).

38 P. Shrivastava "The Role of the Corporation in Achieving Ecological Sustainability," *Academy of Management Review* 20 (1995): 936.

39 Reflective of such optimism, see J. Makeower, *Beyond the Bottom Line: Putting Social Responsibility to Work for your Business and the World* (Touchstone, 1995).

40 H.E. Daly and J.B. Cobb, *Redirecting the Economy Toward Community, the Environment and a Sustainable Future* (Beacon Press, 1997).

41 J. Braithwaite and B. Fisse, "Self-Regulation and the Control of Corporate Crime," in *Private Policing*, eds C.D. Shearing and P.C. Stenning (Sage, 1987), 221, 222.

42 G. Teubner, "Corporate Fiduciary Duties and their Beneficiaries," in *Corporate Governance and Directors' Liabilities*, eds K.J. Hopt and G. Teubner (Walter de Gruyter, 1985), 149.

compulsion, Teubner reasons that legal systems can best affect corporate behavior by targeting companies' internal organizational structures. For instance, requirements to disclose, inform, and consult with stakeholders should help ensure that company practices are isomorphic with external public policy demands. Reflexive regulation is not just a matter of redesigning government legislation or international treaties. It also arises through nongovernmental sources of governance; voluntary codes may also promote reflection and learning within the subject organizations, thereby inducing a superior organizational culture.[43]

If the trend towards voluntary SRI governance is to continue, ultimately such measures must also acquire sufficient legitimacy, not only within the market but among other affected constituencies. This shift in governance beyond the state raises conceptual and practical problems of how to legitimate the new norms and procedures.[44] The political legitimacy of states traditionally rested on the means by which authority was originally constituted (e.g., elections and other polyarchal processes), but increasingly has hinged on "outputs" associated with the modern state's preeminent role as an economic manager.[45] Today, democratically elected governments that preside over periods of economic stagnation typically have a truncated life. Globalization has strained considerably this basis to governmental authority as states find themselves increasingly less able to control the behavior and impact of transnational market forces.[46]

For private sector forms of governance, a similar dichotomy between origins and ends underpins the foundations of their legitimacy. In the context of SRI, whose governance is in a state of great flux, it is unclear how its legitimacy will ultimately be framed. While the acceptability of a given norm, actor, or decision depends not on "formulaic lists of requirements," but

43 J. Nash and J. Ehrenfeld, "Codes of Environmental Management Practice: Assessing their Potential as a Tool for Change," *Annual Review of Energy and the Environment* 22 (1997): 487 (considering five codes in terms of their generation of new environmental practices and facilitation of cultural change in participating organizations).

44 See S. Clarkson and S. Wood, *Governing Beyond Borders: Law for Canadians in an Era of Globalization* (Law Commission of Canada, 2006); M. Suchman, "Managing Legitimacy: Strategic and Institutional Approaches," *Academy of Management Review* 20(3) (1995): 571.

45 Conceptualized in A. Fraser, *The Spirit of the Laws: Republicanism and the Unfinished Project of Modernity* (University of Toronto Press, 1990), passim.

46 D. Devetak and R. Higgot, "Justice Unbound? Globalization, States and the Transformation of the Social Bond," *International Affairs* 75(3) (1999): 483.

"is highly contextual and contingent upon particular" circumstances,[47] some general principles for defining legitimacy in private governance exist.[48] SRI codes and other voluntary standards that were designed inclusively and openly with participation from key stakeholders should be better able to establish and hold their authority. Tom Franck and David Szablowski stress the importance of rule-making procedures (e.g., participation, transparency, accountability, and other indicators of good process) in generating legitimacy.[49] Alternatively, to the extent the financial sector remains a recalcitrant closed shop, it will depend on mobilizing informational and organizational resources to manipulate other stakeholders to accept its worldview. From the Gramscian perspective of "ideological hegemony,"[50] finance capitalism would have to devote more effort to greenwashing and deceiving societies of the integrity of their largely self-regulatory mechanisms.

However, if the gravity of our ecological and social problems worsens, and public agitation and protest grow, pressures for these regimes to swing towards conforming to the sustainability agenda will surely alter the basis of their legitimacy. The financial sector would need to show that it is actually reducing its ecological footprint, ameliorating social injustices, and decreasing economic inequalities. While SRI governance beyond the state is still fairly young, it faces an enormous task to make the financial sector more committed to the sustainability agenda.

C. VOLUNTARY STANDARDS FOR SRI

For now, without sufficient international or national regulation to promote SRI, much will hinge upon the willingness of financiers to voluntarily take appropriate action. By appearances, the voluntary approach to corporate

---

47 S. Bernstein, *The Elusive Basis of Legitimacy in Global Governance: Three Conceptions*, Working Paper GHC 04/2 (Institute on Globalization and the Human Condition, McMaster University, 2004), 18.
48 See especially S. Wood, "ISO Corporate Social Responsibility Standards and the Legitimation of Global Regulation beyond the State" (paper presented at the 2007 Law and Society Annual Meeting, Berlin, July 26–28, 2007).
49 T. Franck, *The Power of Legitimacy Among Nations* (Oxford University Press. 1990); D. Szablowski, *Transnational Law and Local Struggles: Mining, Communities and the World Bank* (Hart Publishing, 2007).
50 A. Gramsci, *Selections from the Prison Notebooks*, ed. and trans. Q. Hoare and G.N. Smith (International Publishers, 1971).

responsibility is thriving.[51] Voluntary standards, which take many forms, differ from governmental command regulation in two key ways. First, officially they are not mandatorily imposed upon companies; only firms that have opted into the regime are governed by it. Second, voluntary measures lack the administrative and criminal apparatus available to state regulators. Consequently, voluntary regimes rely upon informal sanctioning measures, such as dialogue and community pressure, or ostracism of delinquent firms from the regime by the sponsoring industry association.

The expansion of global commerce and finance has fuelled public debate over the appropriate and legitimate role of the private sector in responding to environmental and social problems. The industry increasingly participates in discussions concerning social equity and environmental protection, both as a cause and a solution to problems. Legitimation strategies that seek to reframe private actors, especially TNCs, from amoral, profit-seeking enterprises to "corporate citizens," have heightened public expectations of socially responsible behavior.[52]

This new social context to corporate conduct has engendered various forms of private governance to control market actors.[53] These systems of governance can arise in several ways:[54] by a company designing its own internal code of conduct specifically tailored to its individual operations; by cooperating with other firms to design regimes tailored to the circumstances of their particular industry;[55] and by adhering to standards set by third parties,

---

51 See generally, Wood, note 34, 229; A. Mol, V. Lauber, and D. Liefferink, eds, *The Voluntary Approach to Environmental Policy* (Oxford University Press, 2000); D. Leipziger, *The Corporate Responsibility Code Book* (Greenleaf Publishing, 2003); ed., P. ten Brink, *Voluntary Environmental Agreements: Process, Practice and Future Use* (Greenleaf Publishing, 2002), 37; Gibson, note 17.

52 J. Moon, "The Firm as Citizen? Social Responsibility of Business in Australia," *Australian Journal of Political Science* 30(1) (1995): 1.

53 Falkner, note 8.

54 K. Bondy, D. Matten, and J. Moon, "The Adoption of Voluntary Codes of Conduct in MMCs: A Three-Country Comparative Study," *Business and Society Review* 109 (2004): 449.

55 One renowned industry code is that of the chemical industry's "Responsible Care," which posits standards to reduce the environmental impact of its operations: see N. Gunningham, "Environment, Self-Regulation, and the Chemical Industry: Assessing Responsible Care," *Law and Policy* 17 (1995): 57. Concerning other environmental industry codes, note D. Fiorino, "Towards a New System of Environmental Regulation: The Case for an Industry Sector Approach," *Environmental Law* 26 (1996): 457.

governmental or nongovernmental. Each of these options present a particular set of considerations to both the companies and to society at large.[56]

In practice, a company's adherence to a voluntary code or similar mechanism is seldom, if ever, purely "voluntary." Christopher Wright and Alexis Rwabizambuga contend that "codes of conduct are primarily adopted by firms as signaling devices for demonstrating positive credentials, with the aim of strengthening corporate reputation and organizational legitimacy more generally."[57] Voluntary commitments may thus be driven by the prospect of increased competitiveness and profitability through an enhanced business reputation.[58] Environmental care can improve productivity and efficiency through less wasteful use of resources.[59] Pressure to heed voluntary standards may also arise from a threat of mandatory regulation, stakeholder perspectives, or the prospect of adverse publicity.[60] Finally, apart from social pressures in a firm's institutional milieu, there are also other company-specific motivations for voluntary commitments.[61] For instance, the choice of environmental management arrangements may be influenced by managerial attitudes and corporate culture. Whatever the motivations, voluntary

---

56 See H. Pitt and K. Groskaufmanis, "Minimizing Corporate Civil and Criminal Liability: A Second Look at Corporate Codes of Conduct," *Georgetown Law Journal* 78 (1990): 1559; N. Stoeckl, "The Private Costs and Benefits of Environmental Self-Regulation: Which Firms Have the Most to Gain," *Business Strategy and the Environment* 13 (2004): 135.

57 C. Wright and A. Rwabizambuga, "Institutional Pressures, Corporate Reputation, and Voluntary Codes of Conduct: An Examination of the Equator Principles," *Business and Society Review* 111(1) (2006): 89, 90.

58 See K. Lester, "Protecting the Environment: A New Managerial Responsibility," in *Green Reporting: Accountancy and the Challenge of the Nineties*, ed. D. Owen (Chapman and Hall, 1992), 39; I. Salzmann, A. Ionescu-Somers, and U. Stegers, "The Business Case for Corporate Sustainability: Literature Review and Research Options," *European Management Journal* 23 (2005): 27.

59 M.E. Porter and V. der Linde, "Green and Competitive: Ending the Stalemate," *Harvard Business Review* 73(5) (1995): 120.

60 M. Saha and G. Darnton, "Green Companies or Green Con-panies: Are Companies Really Green, or Are They Pretending to Be?" *Business and Society Review* 110(2) (2005): 117; see also E. Bergman and A. Jacobson, "Environmental Performance Review: Self-Regulation in Environmental Law," in *Environmental Law and Ecological Responsibility: The Concept and Practice of Ecological Self-Organization*, eds G. Teubner, L. Farmer, and D. Murphy (John Wiley and Sons, 1994), 208.

61 S. Sharma, "Managerial Interpretations and Organizational Context as Predictors of Corporate Choice of Environmental Strategy," *Academy of Management Journal* 43 (2000): 681.

standards remain "voluntary" to the extent that authorities do not formally enforce their adoption. However, while adoption of voluntary codes is not legally obligatory, they may have legal consequences if adopted.[62] For instance, they may generate legal consequences through contracts between participating firms (e.g., a loan covenant between a lender and borrower).

Corporate responses to voluntary standards vary considerably.[63] Generally, at one extreme, companies that actively address environmental issues view escalating pressures on their reputation as a strategic opportunity to enhance the business value by adopting new practices beyond the requirements of environmental law. Conversely, some companies react negatively, perceiving the pressures as a source of financial risk and liability, potentially detrimental to shareholder value. Indeed, most firms seek to avoid specific, and thereby conceivably constraining, standards. Yet, they are also averse to overly vague standards, as ambiguity can generate normative confusion, as well as the potential for "free-riding" by unscrupulous businesses.[64] The nature of a firm's stakeholder relationships influences how it conceptualizes challenges to its corporate reputation. For example, a project-lending bank closely monitored by NGOs may face relatively high reputational risks from irresponsible financing decisions. In contrast, a pension fund not directly involved in development financing decisions may face less societal scrutiny, and therefore fewer reputational risks.

Can voluntary mechanisms provide a viable means of governance for the environmental and social problems of the market?[65] Various empirical studies

---

62 OECD, *Voluntary Approaches for Environmental Policy in OECD Countries* (OECD, 1999), 19–20; A. Baranzini and P. Thalmann, eds, *Voluntary Agreements in Climate Policy* (Edward Elgar Publishing, 2004), 4.

63 See P. Bansal and K. Roth, "Why Companies Go Green: A Model of Ecological Responsiveness," *Academy of Management Journal* 43(4) (2000): 717; S. Sharma, A. Pablo, and H. Vredenburg, "Corporate Environmental Responsiveness Strategies: The Role of Issue Interpretation and Organizational Context," *Journal of Applied Behavioral Science* 35 (1999): 87.

64 Indeed, Tenbrunsel believes that ambiguous codes can foster self-interested and unethical behavior: A.E. Tenbrunsel, "A Behavioral Perspective on Codes of Conduct: The Ambiguity-Specificity Paradox," in *Global Codes of Conduct: An Idea Whose Time Has Come*, ed. O. Williams (University of Notre Dame Press, 2000), 128.

65 See A. Neale, "Organising Environmental Self-Regulation: Liberal Governmentality and the Pursuit of Ecological Modernisation in Europe," *Environmental Politics* 6 (1997): 1; I. Maitland, "The Limits of Business Self-Regulation," *California Management Review* 27(3) (1995): 132.

question their effectiveness.[66] Ideally, voluntary mechanisms create an institutional context through which firms can deploy their business acumen, managerial skill, and technological wizardry to further sustainable development. More commonly, however, voluntary measures tinker with such challenges, and lack transparency and accountability to other stakeholders.[67] In fact, they may even facilitate deliberate circumvention of official regulation and thereby forestall meaningful change.[68] In addition, negotiation and development of voluntary measures carry transaction costs vulnerable to incurring the perennial danger of free-riding.[69]

The credibility of voluntary mechanisms often depends on external verification of performance and sanctions for non-compliance.[70] Verification of performance may be sought via various avenues. Self-verification involves a company assessing and determining its own compliance. By contrast, second-party verification entails compliance assessment by another party with a commercial interest in the subject company (e.g., a bank verifying a borrower). Potentially strongest of all, third-party verification involves an independent, impartial party evaluating compliant performance.[71] Without these oversight mechanisms, NGOs or even government agencies may assume informal responsibility as watchdogs.

Finally, voluntary regimes have implications for power relations; their development, content, or implementation may disadvantage particular actors, such as developing countries, public interest NGOs or governments.[72]

---

66 E.g., M. Vidovic and N. Khanna, "Can Voluntary Pollution Prevention Programs Fulfill Their Promises? Further Evidence from the EPA's 33/50 Program," *Journal of Environmental Economics and Management* 53(2) (2007): 180; US Government Accountability Office (GAO), *Climate Change: EPA and DOE Should Do More to Encourage Progress Under Two Voluntary Programs* (GAO, April 2006); Agence France Press, "EU to Introduce Legislation as Car Makers Fail on Emission Targets" (November 2006); C. Woolfson and M. Beck, eds, *Corporate Social Responsibility Failures in the Oil Industry* (Baywood Publishing, 2005).

67 R.B. Gibson, "Questions about a Gift Horse," in Gibson, note 17, 6–7.

68 OECD, note 62, 31–38.

69 Ibid., 40–42, 99.

70 Wood, note 34.

71 Ibid.

72 See R. Krut and H. Gleckman, *ISO 14001: A Missed Opportunity for Sustainable Global Industrial Development* (Earthscan, 1998); N. Roht-Arriaza, "Shifting the Point of Regulation: The International Organization for Standardization and Global Lawmaking on Trade and the Environment," *Ecology Law Quarterly* 22(3) (1995): 479; R. Hillary, *Environmental Management Systems and Cleaner Production* (John Wiley and Sons, 1997).

We must therefore ask which actors and interests dominate and which actors are excluded or marginalized by such regimes. More involvement of community groups and NGOs in designing the voluntary measures may enhance their public legitimacy. The AccountAbility's AA1000 Assurance Standard for stakeholder engagement is thus significant, as it is overseen by an international multi-stakeholder council.[73] The council's representatives include NGOs and academics. Many SRI governance regimes however lack such a democratic imprimatur, thereby endangering their long-term legitimacy unless they can demonstrate real commitment to the sustainability agenda.

II. Normative Frameworks for SRI

A. INTRODUCTION

One governance mechanism for SRI involves normative codes designed by third parties, setting performance standards, which corporations or financial institutions are invited to implement. These third parties commonly include industry associations, international organizations such as the UN, and even NGOs.[74] The following table enumerates the international codes most relevant to SRI,[75] representing only a fraction of the plethora of CSR codes generally.[76]

None of the above codes are formal intergovernmental initiative.[77] Even with the two UN-sponsored codes, UNEP simply coordinates and facilitates the process for businesses and other nongovernmental participants.

---

73 Http://www.accountability.org.uk.

74 See T. Guay, J.P. Doh, and G. Sinclair, "Non-governmental Organizations, Shareholder Activism, and Socially Responsible Investments: Ethical, Strategic, and Governance Implications," *Journal of Business Ethics* 52(1) (2004): 99.

75 The full text of some of these codes is available in K. McKague, *Compendium of Ethics Codes and Instruments of Corporate Responsibility* (Schulich School of Business, York University, 2005).

76 In 2001, the OECD found 246 codes of conduct designed to promote global corporate responsibility. OECD, *Corporate Responsibility: Private Initiatives and Public Goals* (OECD, 2001), 33. See also G. Smith and D. Feldman, *Company Codes of Conduct and International Standards: An Analytical Comparison* (World Bank, 2003).

77 E. Morgera, "The UN and Corporate Environmental Responsibility: Between International Regulation and Partnership," *Review of European Community and International Environmental Law* 15(1) (2006): 93.

Table 4: Voluntary normative codes for SRI

Code of Conduct	Principal Sponsor
CERES Principles	Coalition for Environmentally Responsible Economies
Collevecchio Declaration	NGO coalition
Global Sullivan Principles	Reverend Leon Sullivan
London Principles of Sustainable Finance	UK Department of Environment and Corporation of London
UN Global Compact	United Nations
UN Principles for Responsible Investment	UN Environment Program Finance Initiative (UNEPFI)
UN Statement by Financial Institutions on the Environment and Sustainable Development	UNEPFI

Corporate leaders and governments appear to have encouraged the UN to provide a forum for these SRI mechanisms in order to stave off the much less palatable alternative of incorporating SRI into treaties governing international finance and trade. According to the International Chamber of Commerce:

> The multilateral trading system should not be called upon to deal with such non-trade issues as human rights, labour standards and environmental protection. To call on it to do so would expose the trading system to great strain and the risk of increased protectionism while failing to produce the required results. The right place for addressing these issues is the UN and its appropriate agencies.[78]

While the normative values espoused by voluntary codes have encouraged more reflection on the environmental impacts of finance, so far they have not engineered radical changes to financial markets. Their participants have downplayed ethical motivations to promote sustainability while accentuating considerations of financial risk and materiality.

---

78 International Chamber of Commerce (ICC), *World Business Message for the UN Millennium Assembly on the Role of the UN in the 21st Century* (ICC, March 2003), at http://www.iccwbo.org/home/statements_rules/statements/2000/millennium_assembly.asp.

B. UNEP FINANCE INITIATIVE (UNEPFI)

The UNEPFI envisions itself as a catalyst for bringing environmental issues to the attention of global financial markets.[79] Established in 1991, UNEPFI is a public-private partnership between the interests of businesses (the main participamts), NGOs, and governments.[80] It promotes governance standards, education, and research on SRI and its management tools.[81] In 1992, UNEPFI released its first code, the Statement by Banks on Environment and Sustainable Development, to help banks manage their environmental risks.[82] In 1995, UNEPFI sponsored a similar statement for the insurance industry.[83] In 1997, UNEPFI issued a more general umbrella code for all financiers, the Statement by Financial Institutions on the Environment and Sustainable Development.[84]

These early initiatives are notable given that before 2000 UNEPFI was a small operation with few staff and limited engagement with mainstream investors. Apart from its sustainable finance statements, UNEPFI served mainly to network environmental risk experts in the financial sector.[85] With many more staff and resources today, UNEPFI organizes training and work-shops, task force meetings, global roundtables, and themed conferences.[86] It facilitates various working groups targeting specific issues, which have pro-digiously published on numerous SRI issues.[87] The UNEPFI also convenes regional taskforces for banks and insurance companies in North America,

---

79 Http://www.unepfi.org.

80 See http://www.unepfi.org/about/index.html.

81 See e.g., UNEPFI, *2nd Annual General Meeting of the UNEP Financial Institutions Initiative* (September 1998); UNEPFI, "Managing Environmental Risks in Project Finance," Fact Sheet No.1 (UNEPFI, 1999).

82 UNEP, Advisory Committee on Banking and the Environment, *Statement by Banks on Environment and Sustainable Development* (UNEP, 1992).

83 See http://www.unepfi.org/signatories/statements/ii/index.html. For analysis, see C. Joly, "UNEP Insurance Industry Initiative on the Environment: Developments in 1996," *International Journal of Insurance Law* 3 (1997): 171.

84 Http://www.unepfi.org/signatories/statements/fi/index.html.

85 For a sample of its recent activities and achievements, see UNEPFI, *2006 Overview* (UNEPFI, 2007).

86 E.g., *Show Me the Money: Linking Environmental, Social and Governance Issues to Company Value* (UNEPFI, 2006); *The Materiality of Social, Environmental and Corporate Governance Issues to Equity Pricing* (UNEPFI, 2004); *Foreign Direct Investments: Financing Sustainability: Meeting Report* (UNEPFI, 2002).

87 E.g., Climate Change Working Group, Property Working Group, and the Asset Management Working Group.

the Asia-Pacific region, and other regions. All of these efforts essentially focus on creative ways to improve appreciation of the links between finance and sustainability.

Although the 1997 UNEPFI Statement lacks concrete specifics, it does provide some useful guidance for environmental risk assessment and public reporting of environmental policy and practice.[88] The Statement focuses on three areas of financiers' environmental performance: internal operations (e.g., energy consumption and resource use efficiency); identification and quantification of environmental risk; and promotion of financial products and services to enhance environmental protection. Appropriately, the Statement also targets the influence that financiers may exert over the environmental performance of their borrowers and clients. Among the more ambitious clauses, the Statement proclaims that signatories will "regard sustainable develop-ment as a fundamental aspect of sound business management," "support the precautionary approach to environmental management," and that they "will foster openness and dialogue relating to environmental matters with relevant audiences. ..."[89] As of early 2008, about 180 institutions had agreed to these commitments, including commercial banks, venture capitalists, and asset managers.[90] The UNEPFI signatories represent at least 15 percent of global capital assets under management.[91]

The UNEPFI Statement of 1997 has some shortcomings, and signatories' implementation has attracted criticism. Apart from its inherently nonbinding nature as a voluntary code, the Statement lacks an external verification mech-anism to assess the quality of implementation by its signatories. Some of the commitments in the Statement are, arguably, not very far-reaching or strongly worded. The lack of transparency, characteristic of most financiers' opera-tions, hinders assessment of the extent to which signatories actually meet their commitments. A 1998 survey of European financial institutions' imple-mentation of all of the UNEPFI statements found that a majority of the sixty-three respondents had a dedicated environmental unit and specific envi-ronmental policies and procedures for corporate credit and project finance.[92]

---

88 E.g., clauses 2.3 and 3.1.

89 Http://www.unepfi.org/signatories/statements/fi/index.html.

90 See http://www.unepfi.org/signatories.

91 Remarks, N. Purcell, Group General Manager, Westpac (UNEPFI Global Roundtable, Melbourne, Australia, October 24–25, 2007).

92 UNEPFI, *UNEP Financial Institutions 1998 Survey* (UNEPFI, 1999). While 60 percent of institutions had taken steps to integrate environmental risk into credit decisions, only 20 percent had done so for investment portfolio management.

It noted that environmental policies and procedures were relatively uncommon in the investment banking and insurance sectors. A 2007 survey by BankTrack of the credit policies of forty-five major international banks, including thirty UNEPFI signatories, found widespread grounds for concern. Evaluating the content, transparency, and implementation of the lenders' policies on sustainable development, BankTrack forlornly concluded that "voluntary standards and initiatives are no substitute for stringent policies developed by banks themselves."[93]

Other anecdotal evidence of signatories' implementation of UNEPFI standards reveals muted and patchy performance. The Bank of America has been a signatory of UNEPFI since 2001. Its web site contains information on the Bank's environmental initiatives, but appeared to make no mention of UNEPFI as of 2007.[94] Rather, the Bank explains its guidance by other norms, such as the World Bank's Pollution Control and Abatement Guidelines and the EPs. The YES Bank of India was the first Indian bank to become a signatory to UNEPFI, but its web site and public documents reveal virtually nothing about what it is doing to implement the initiative.[95] Similarly, the Wachovia Corporation, a US financial services company, is a UNEPFI signatory but does not explain on its "External Environmental Involvement" web site what it does in relation to UNEPFI.[96] More enlightening is Barclays Bank's disclosures. Its recent *Corporate Social Responsibility Report* discusses its involvement with UNEPFI, including its contributions to a new "toolkit" that provides UNEPFI members with "a set of guidance notes that would cover key aspects of environmental risk assessment."[97] Barclays also collaborated with UNEPFI to develop a human rights project that "aims to provide context, guidance, and an online reference tool for the financial services sector, primarily on how to identify and mitigate human rights risk in lending transactions."[98] In the absence of a mandatory reporting system for signatories, a comprehensive survey of the activities of UNEPFI members is overdue to assess more carefully the impact and effectiveness of this regime.

---

93 BankTrack, *Mind the Gap: Benchmarking Credit Policies of International Banks* (BankTrack, December 2007), xi.
94 Http://www.bankofamerica.com/environment/index.cfm?template =env_core_bpractices.
95 Http://www.yesbank.in.
96 Http://www.wachovia.com/inside/page/0,,132_10475_10524,00.html.
97 Barclays, *Corporate Social Responsibility Report: Responsible Banking* (Barclays, 2006), 25.
98 Ibid., 56.

C. UN PRINCIPLES FOR RESPONSIBLE INVESTMENT (UNPRI)

The UNPRI principally address institutional investors such as pension funds. They were developed under the auspices of UNEP, although advanced as an initiative of the UN generally. The Principles were adopted because the UNEPFI statements, focusing on banks and insurers, were not considered by the SRI community to provide an adequate normative framework for responsible financing in the institutional sector.

The UNPRI were drafted by a group of invited investment professionals, mainly from the pension fund sector, and supported by a seventy-person multi-stakeholder collection of experts from the investment industry, inter-governmental and governmental organizations, civil society, and academia. Friends of the Earth and WWF were among the NGOs involved. UNEP did not formally supervise the drafting of the UNPRI because its participation would have required adoption of a formal intergovernmental process that would have been too slow and politically complicated.[99] Thus, the UNPRI became an industry-led initiative, in which UNEP largely just coordinated the negotiations.

The UNPRI is a concise document of six core principles, each of which is illustrated by several "possible actions" to achieve them. They are intended for three types of institutions: asset owners (e.g., pension funds), investment managers, and professional service partners (e.g., stock exchanges). As of early 2008, over 250 institutions had signed the Principles, holding more than US$10 trillion in assets.[100] The Principles state:

1. We will incorporate environmental, social and corporate governance (ESG) issues into investment analysis and decision-making processes.
2. We will be active owners and incorporate ESG issues into our ownership policies and practices.
3. We will seek appropriate disclosure on ESG issues by the entities in which we invest.
4. We will promote acceptance and implementation of the Principles within the investment industry.
5. We will work together to enhance our effectiveness in implementing the Principles.

---

99 Personal communication, staff member of UNEPFI (December 6, 2005).
100 The signatories are drawn mainly from North America and Western Europe, see: http://www.unpri.org/signatories.

6. We will each report on our activities and progress towards implementing the Principles.[101]

The accompanying list of "possible actions" essentially amounts to a best practice guide. Concerning the second principle, for instance, the suggested actions to achieve active ownership include "exercise voting rights," "develop an engagement capability," and "file shareholder resolutions consistent with long-term ESG considerations."

As a normative framework for SRI, what can one expect of the UNPRI? From a business case perspective, the UN explains:

> Implementing the Principles will lead to a more complete understanding of a range of material issues, and this should ultimately result in increased returns and lower risk. There is increasing evidence that ESG issues can be material to performance of portfolios, particularly over the long term.
>
> PRI signatories are also part of a network, with opportunities to pool resources and influence, lowering the costs and increasing the effectiveness of research and active ownership practices. The Initiative also supports investors in working together to address systemic problems that, if remedied, may then lead to more stable, accountable and profitable market conditions overall.[102]

Apart from the narrowness of this orientation, the Principles have some specific shortcomings. Among the possible actions listed for the first principle, there is no stated expectation that investors actually incorporate ESG factors into their ultimate portfolio choices. The Principles do not require a signatory to demonstrate any particular SRI performance standards with regard to human rights or environmental protection. The second principle on active ownership focuses on participation in investee companies, while incongruously ignoring the imperative of democratizing decision-making within financial institutions themselves. Nor do the UNPRI insist on any independent audit or verification mechanism to assess the quality of signatories' implementation. Nor are prospective signatories expected to demonstrate preparedness to meet specific benchmarks. The UNPRI web site explains:

> There are no legal or regulatory sanctions associated with the Principles. They are designed to be voluntary and aspirational. There may be

---

101 Http://www.unpri.org/principles.
102 UNPRI, "Frequently Asked Questions": http://www.unpri.org/faqs.

reputational risks associated with signing up and then failing to take any action at all, but the commitments are, for most signatories, a work in progress and a direction to head in rather than a prescriptive checklist with which to comply. The initial focus is on innovation, collaboration and learning by doing. The annual PRI Reporting and Assessment survey will help you evaluate your progress. The minimum requirement to remain a signatory is participation in that survey and through that tool, demonstrating continual improvement.[103]

While Principle 6 expects signatories to "report on their activities and progress towards implementing the Principles," presently they do not need to disclose formally such information to the public. The UNPRI secretariat periodically surveys members on their implementation activities, and it has commissioned Mercer to consider a new reporting and assessment protocol for systematic reporting by all signatories. Regardless of the extent of reporting, rigorous oversight from the UNPRI governing board is not assured, because the board, a large majority of whose members are asset owners, is chosen from among the signatories.

Yet, despite or because of such limitations, the UNPRI will likely become one of the main benchmarks for SRI. They have been generally well-received by the finance sector, attracted to the Principles for the eminence of their sponsorship by the UN while still maintaining considerable latitude in the open-ended standards. The 2007 "Progress Report" on implementation of the UNPRI trumpets that they have "started to build a vibrant network for sharing information, best practices and engagement strategies."[104] The "UNPRI Engagement Clearinghouse" and the "UNPRI in Practice Implementation Blog" are innovative tools established to foster such networking.[105]

At an individual institutional level, the Progress Report and other evidence suggests that most signatories are at least formally acknowledging the UNPRI in their investment policies. For example, CalPERS, a signatory since April 27, 2006, states in its Investment Policy for Corporate Governance that: "[f]or Funds investing in developed and emerging markets, every effort will be made to apply the [UNPRI];" and "[t]actics employed to address under-performing companies, in developed and emerging markets, will be consistent with the [UNPRI]."[106] PGGM, a large Dutch pension fund and

103 Ibid.

104 UNEPFI and UNGC, *PRI Report on Progress 2007* (UNEPFI, 2007), 5.

105 Ibid., 7–8.

106 CalPERS, *Statement of Investment Policy for Corporate Governance Investments* (CalPERS, May 14, 2007).

UNPRI signatory also since April 27, 2006, explains that its responsible investment policy "has chosen the Principles for Responsible Investment as the central framework for its activities in the field of responsible investment."[107] The policy elaborates specific ways PGGM seeks to implement the UNPRI. No doubt, with the name of the UN behind it coupled with financiers' participation in its governance, the UNPRI will continue to exert significant influence over the SRI community.

D. COLLEVECCHIO DECLARATION

Critical of facile, business-friendly codes of conduct, civil societal groups have offered financial institutions an alternative standard. In 2003, a coalition of NGOs drafted the Collevecchio Declaration on Financial Institutions,[108] comprising six principles that stress accountability, transparency, and stakeholder rights. Prepared by groups outside of the financial sector, the Collevecchio Declaration presents itself as the more credible code untainted by business self-interest. On the other hand, this design also carries a disadvantage, as the Declaration has had little buy-in from the financial sector. As of early 2008, approximately one hundred organizations, mostly NGOs, have endorsed the Declaration,[109] but apart from the pension fund giant CalPERS, financiers have largely ignored it.

Going beyond a merely business case rationale for SRI, the Collevecchio Declaration requires financiers' commitment to: sustainability, "no harm," responsibility, accountability, transparency, and sustainable markets and governance. The accompanying Implementation Document outlines immediate steps that financial institutions should take, such as the adoption of internationally-recognized industry standards for credit, investing, and underwriting transactions.

The Declaration differs from other normative standards in its rigorous and detailed requirements. The ambitious "commitment to sustainability" principle obliges investors to:

> ... expand their missions from ones that prioritize profit maximization to a vision of social and environmental sustainability. A commitment to sustainability would require financial institutions to fully integrate the

---

107 PGGM Board of Trustees, *Responsible Investment Policy* (PGGM, November 2006), 5.

108 Http://www.foe.org/camps/intl/declaration.html.

109 Http://www.foe.org/camps/intl/endorsements.html.

consideration of ecological limits, social equity and economic justice into corporate strategies and core business areas (including credit, investing, underwriting, advising), to put sustainability objectives on an equal footing to shareholder maximization and client satisfaction, and to actively strive to finance transactions that promote sustainability.

Concomitantly, the Declaration emphasizes precaution and avoidance of harm, rather than mere mitigation of impacts, as implied by some other codes. The Declaration's "do no harm" principle entails an explicit commitment to categorical prohibitions for the most socially and environmentally egregious transactions.

It also seeks to strengthen financiers' accountability and transparency beyond the loose requirements of some other codes. On transparency, it expects financial institutions to be "responsive to stakeholder needs for specialized information" and that "commercial confidentiality should not be used as an excuse to deny stakeholders information." The Implementation Document usefully elaborates these principles and gives financiers specific guidance for promoting environmentally sound financing.[110] For example, concerning the Commitment to Transparency, it provides:

a) Corporate Sustainability Reporting
Financial institutions should publish annual sustainability reports according to an internationally recognized reporting format supported by civil society. Financial institutions should further include disclosure on the sustainability profile of the financial institution's portfolio, a breakdown of core business activity by sector and region, and the implementation of the financial institution's sustainability policies and objectives.

b) Information Disclosure
There should be an assumption in favour of disclosure of information. Particularly for compiled transactions, but also for those in the pipeline, financial institutions should publicly provide information on companies and significant transactions in a timely manner, and not hide behind the excuse of business confidentiality.

Unfortunately, the Collevecchio Declaration lacks the secretariat and financial resources of the UNPRI to enable its promotion. The Declaration's ethically-guided framework for SRI has been largely shunned by the financial sector.

---

110 See http://www.foe.org/camps/intl/declaration.html.

As this chapter shows later, in the case of banks, they favor the EPs to manage their social and environmental activities because these Principles, developed largely by the banking community, give lenders greater discretion and do not set the bar too high. But the Collevecchio Declaration retains its value as a benchmark to assess the ethical adequacy of other codes.

E. OTHER NORMATIVE STANDARDS RELEVANT TO SRI

Many other international voluntary codes set yardsticks for corporate environmental and social performance. While they are not all specifically aimed at the financial sector (e.g., UNGC), some financiers may still follow them. These codes may also appeal to the SRI industry when evaluating the performance of companies considered for investment. A company's adherence to a credible international standard can signal good sustainability performance. The following comments canvass just a few of these other governance codes.

1. CERES Principles

The Coalition for Environmentally Responsible Economies (CERES), a partnership of investors, foundations, trade unions, and environmental, religious, and other civil society groups, has sponsored two initiatives important for SRI. In 1989, it drafted the CERES Principles. Originally known as the Valdez Principles (in the wake of the Exxon Valdez oil spill disaster), they combine normative and procedural standards for corporate activities. CERES' second landmark achievement is the Global Reporting Initiative (considered later in this chapter). The CERES Principles furnish a ten-point, environmental code of conduct that commits signatories to protect the biosphere, use natural resources sustainably, reduce waste production, conserve energy, make safe products, provide safe services, and report to stakeholders on issues that affect them.[111]

The CERES Principles is a reasonably successful example of collaboration between corporate and NGO interests, suggesting that this approach may avoid the pitfalls of the business sector-designed codes, lacking in public credibility, and the wholly civil society-driven standards, often too abrasive or naive for the corporate community. In particular, they have helped to improve the substantive quality of environmental reporting. This is in part because a company cannot unilaterally endorse the CERES Principles.

---

111 Http://www.ceres.org/coalitionandcompanies/principles.php.

Instead, it must first engage the CERES Board of Directors and other stakeholders (including institutional investors) on how the Principles would specifically apply to the company.

Among its impacts, commentators believe that the CERES Principles were instrumental in igniting the movement to environmental auditing and reporting.[112] The Principles have also influenced some corporate engagement practices of SRI institutions. For instance, the American Federation of Labor and Congress of Industrial Organizations' Proxy Voting Guidelines include a reference to the CERES Principles.[113] Also, the New York City Pension Funds and CalPERS are founding and currently active members of the Board of the CERES. The Ontario Public Service Employees Union supports shareholder proposals concerning the CERES Principles as per its Proxy Voting Guidelines of 2005.[114]

2. OECD Guidelines for Multinational Enterprises

These OECD Guidelines, dating from 1976 and revised several times since, provide one of the most comprehensive codes on CSR.[115] The OECD Guidelines differ from other voluntary codes of conduct, primarily shaped by the private sector, in that governments were involved in their formulation. While companies are not obligated to follow the Guidelines, OECD member states must promote them to companies operating within their jurisdictions. The Guidelines address human rights, disclosure of information, anticorruption, taxation, labor relations, suppliers/subcontractors, environment, science and technology, and consumer protection. The environmental provisions require firms to adhere to a version of the precautionary principle, to establish an environmental management system, and to improve environmental performance on an ongoing basis. The OECD Committee on International Investment and Multinational Enterprises oversees the Guidelines.

---

112 S. Davis, J. Lukomnik, and D. Pitt-Watson, *The New Capitalists. How Citizen Investors are Reshaping the Corporate Agenda* (Harvard Business School Press, 2006), 161.

113 American Federation of Labor and Congress of Industrial Organizations' (AFL-CIO), *Proxy Voting Guidelines 2003*, at: http://www.aflcio.org/corporatewatch/capital/upload/proxy_voting_guidelines.pdf.

114 Ontario Public Service Employees Union Trust, *Proxy Voting Guidelines* (2005) at http://www.optrust.com/investments/proxy.pdf.

115 See http://www.ncp-pcn.gc.ca. See further H. Christiansen, P. Borkey, and C. Tébar Less, *Environment and the OECD Guidelines for Multinational Enterprises: Corporate Tools and Approaches* (OECD, 2005).

The OECD Guidelines are viewed by some as an "established part of the global architecture of standards for business,"[116] including SRI. The role of the Guidelines in promoting responsible financing was discussed at the 2007 annual OECD Roundtable on Corporate Responsibility.[117] Some investors advocate them in shareholder resolutions, in proxy voting guidelines, and also as benchmark criteria for SRI screens. For instance, the FTSE4Good Index Series (discussed later in this chapter) draws its corporate responsibility criteria from the OECD Guidelines.[118] However, the Guidelines lack universal legitimacy, as some interests perceive them as a product of OECD industrialized countries. The lack of clarity about how they apply to non-OECD members persists.[119]

Nevertheless, perhaps the most valuable feature of the OECD Guidelines is the complaint procedure for investigating alleged breaches. The designated "national contact point" (NCP) of each OECD country has established a "specific instance" procedure, to allow any person or organization to raise a specific complaint about the conduct of a multinational company.[120] The NCP must establish an advisory body representative of a broad range of interests to review the complaint, and if it deems that the matter has merit, it can consult with the concerned parties and facilitate mediation. A coalition of NGOs, called OECD Watch, monitors the operation of the NCPs.[121]

The specific instance procedure has been used to challenge financial institutions, albeit not always with satisfactory results. Between 2000 and 2005, a total of 106 complaints were filed with NCPs, of which ten concerned environmental issues.[122] For instance, in August 2006 the Australian Conservation Foundation and allied NGOs lodged a complaint with the Australian NCP

---

116 WBCSD, *Issue Management Tool* (AccountAbility, October 2004), 16.

117 OECD, *The OECD Guidelines for Multinational Enterprises and the Financial Sector: Summary of the Discussion* (Annual OECD Roundtable on Corporate Responsibility, June 18, 2007).

118 W. Oulton, "The Role of Activism in Responsible Investment: The FTSEFGood Indices," in *Responsible Investment*, eds R. Sullivan and C. Mackenzie (Greenleaf Publishing, 2006), 196, 198.

119 S.A. Aaronson and J.T. Reeves, *Corporate Social Responsibility in the Global Village: The Role of Public Policy* (National Policy Association, 2002), 11.

120 OECD, *Guidelines for Multinational Enterprises: Ministerial Booklet* (OECD, 2000), 32, 35–37.

121 Http://www.oecdwatch.org.

122 OECD, *OECD Guidelines for Multinational Enterprises: 2005 Annual Meeting of the National Contact Points: Report by the Chair, Meeting held on 15–16 June 2005* (OECD, 2005), 14.

against the ANZ Bank for allegedly breaching human rights and environmental provisions of the OECD Guidelines.[123] The complaint concerned the ANZ's provision of financial services to the Rimbunan Hijau consortium engaged in intensive forestry operations in Papua New Guinea. Their accusation was dismissed on the basis that the loans and financial services provided by the ANZ to Rimbunan Hijau did not constitute an "investment nexus" within the meaning of the OECD Guidelines.[124] Another pertinent example is the complaint filed to the Swedish NCP against Nordea Bank in 2006 for funding the construction of a controversial pulp mill in Uruguay.[125] Overall, the NCPs have yet to reach their potential. One study for the UN found that their performance was "uneven," and that "more uniform practices and greater public accountability would enhance the NCPs' currently modest contribution."[126]

3. London Principles of Sustainable Finance

In 2002, the UK Department for Environment and the Corporation of London issued the London Principles, advocating measures to improve financiers' engagement with sustainable development.[127] The Principles, which apply to all aspects of finance rather than just specific niches, comprise seven, quite brief, core norms. They include the expectation that signatories, "where relevant to the product and geographical scope of their business," will "reflect the cost of environmental and social risks in the pricing of financial and risk management products." Further, signatories should "provide access

---

123 Australian Conservation Foundation, et al., *Submission of Specific Instance under the OECD Guidelines for Multinational Enterprises to the Australian National Contact Point Concerning: Facilitation by the Australia and New Zealand Banking Group Limited of Illegal and Environmentally and Socially Destructive Forestry Operations in Papua New Guinea* (Australian Conservation Foundation, August 23, 2006).

124 M. Lee, "NGOs Find Novel Ways to Air Complaints of Alleged Environmental and Human Rights Breaches of Voluntary OECD Guidelines—ACF and Others v. ANZ Bank," *National Environmental Law Review* 2–3 (2006): 31.

125 OECD Watch, "Swedish OECD National Contact Point Accepts Complaint Against Nordea for Possible Financing of Controversial Botnia Pulp Mill Project in Uruguay," Press release, November 17, 2006.

126 J. Ruggie, *Interim Report of the Secretary-General's Special Representative on the Issue of Human Rights and Transnational Corporations and Other Business Enterprises* (February 22, 2006), E/CN 4/2006/97, 11.

127 Corporation of London and the Department for Environment, Food and Rural Affairs (DEFRA), *Financing the Future. The London Principles: The Role of UK Financial Services in Sustainable Development* (DEFRA, 2002), 7.

to market finance and risk management products to businesses in disadvantaged communities and developing economies." Like most other SRI codes, the London Principles lack mechanisms to ensure credible, independent verification or enforcement of performance.

For several reasons, the London Principles do not appear to have had much impact internationally. First, the finance sector had only limited input in the drafting of the Principles, unlike with some other codes, such as the EPs, in which the finance sector had a leadership role. Second, the release of the London Principles was timed with a view to giving the UK government something concrete to announce at the Johannesburg Earth Summit of 2002, rather than responding to issues that the financial sector thought were particularly pertinent at that time. Third, the government did not provide sufficient resources to facilitate implementation, promotion, and monitoring of the Principles. Finally, the close association of the "London" Principles in name and sponsorship to the UK likely diminished the Principles' standing as a universal code. The implication that "London knows best" may have been problematic for others in the international financial community.

Despite such constraints, the London Principles continue to retain a reasonable profile in the British SRI community, and groups such as Forum for the Future have been working to promote their implementation.[128]

4. UN Global Compact (UNGC)

The UNGC is a multi-stakeholder, voluntary initiative launched by the UN in 1999.[129] Its participants pledge adherence to ten principles distilled from key environmental, labor, and human rights agreements. The UNGC draws on key international instruments in these fields[130] and recasts them as corporate commitments. For example, on the environment, the UNGC obliges businesses to take a precautionary approach and to develop environmentally friendly technologies.

---

128 Forum for the Future, and Corporation of London, *The London Principles: Three Years on from Johannesburg* (Forum for the Future, 2005).

129 Http://www.unglobalcompact.org.

130 E.g., the Universal Declaration of Human Rights, G.A. Res. 217 (LXIII); ILO Declaration on Fundamental Principles and Rights at Work, 37 ILM (1998): 1233; and the Rio Principles of Environment and Development, 31 ILM (1992): 874.

While the UNGC enjoys the prestige of UN backing, it is still a non-binding instrument, vulnerable to perfunctory implementation.[131] It has no formal auditing and certification process. Companies sign up merely by sending a letter of support to the UN Secretary-General and publicly advocating its principles. However, unlike the UNPRI, signatories must file a "communication in progress" within two years of subscribing to the UNGC, or risk ejection from the UNGC's activities and loss of the right to display the official logo. Traditionally, these submissions were not evaluated or verified by the UNGC Office. Following criticisms about this process, in 2004 the UNGC was amended to include a mechanism for receiving complaints against allegedly non-compliant companies.

The value of the UNGC as a transformative tool for corporate responsibility is debatable. Rather than welcoming the UNGC as an attempt to extend international social and environmental norms directly to the corporate sector, some NGOs have been critical of the Compact. They view it as part of a wider dilution of the UN's mechanisms of public oversight and accountability in favor of voluntary forms of corporate self-regulation.[132] Conversely, Michael Barnett and Raymond Duvall herald the UNGC as ushering a new style of global governance, since it "engages the private sector to work with the UN, in partnership with international labor and nongovernmental organizations (NGOs), to identify, disseminate, and promote good corporate practices based on … universal principles that are found in various UN documents."[133] They also conceptualize the UNGC as forging a new "discursive space" in which various non-corporate actors acquire legitimacy to judge corporate behavior on human rights and other standards that inform the UNGC.[134]

Apart from major international companies that have pledged to the UNGC, some financial institutions have also signed up, including Deutsche Bank,

131 See G. Kell, "The Global Compact Selected Experiences and Reflections," *Journal of Business Ethics* 59(1) (2005): 69; L. Whitehouse, "Corporate Social Responsibility, Corporate Citizenship and the Global Compact: A New Approach to Regulating Corporate Social Power?" *Global Social Policy* 3(3) (2003): 299; W.H. Meyer and B. Stefanova, "Human Rights, the UN Global Compact, and Global Governance," *Cornell International Law Journal* 34 (2001): 501.
132 C. Raghavan, "TNCs, Global Compact and Davos Face Critical NGOs," *South-North Development Monitor*, January 25, 2001.
133 M. Barnett and R. Duvall, "Power in International Politics," *International Organization* 59 (2005): 39, 60.
134 Ibid., 61.

HSBC, and Morgan Stanley.[135] The New Zealand Government's Superannuation Fund has also subscribed to the "Global Compact Plus," a research tool pioneered by Innovest to rank companies based on their adherence to the UNGC principles.[136] In addition, Canada's Shareholder Association for Research and Education (SHARE) has included the UNGC as an international benchmark to guide Canadian pension funds in voting their shares in its "Model Proxy Voting Guidelines;"[137] the Ethical Guidelines of the Norwegian Government Pension Plan refer to the UNGC as a basis for evaluating CSR;[138] and the Guile European Engagement Fund is dedicated specifically to investment in companies aligned with the UNGC.[139]

The UNGC has sought to boost interest in the financial sector even further. In January 2004 a group of eighteen major financiers were invited to form a collaborative initiative under the auspices of the UNGC to develop guidelines and recommendations for integrating ESG issues in asset management and associated functions, and also to advise on ways financial actors such as stock exchanges and pension funds could consider ESG issues. This initiative led to their advisory report *Who Cares Wins: Connecting Financial Markets to a Changing World*. A 2005 report by the World Bank's International Finance Corporation (IFC) on implementation of *Who Cares Wins* found improvements in some areas, but also identified various gaps in the performance, including: lack of incorporation of ESG issues into pension fund trustees' mandates; insufficient research on the implications of ESG integration into different asset classes; and too few long-term investment products.[140] It also noted, however, encouraging progress in ESG related investment in emerging markets such as Brazil, South Africa, and Korea.[141] The IFC also found that the UNGC criteria were starting to inform SRI screening tools, such as one designed by Innovest.[142]

---

135 "Major Investment Houses Endorse Global Compact Initiative," *CSR Wire*, June 25, 2004, at: http://www.csrwire.com/PressRelease.php?id=2842.

136 Innovest Group, "Innovest Launches Global Compact Assessment Tool" (September 23, 2005), at http://www.innovestgroup.com/news.htm.

137 SHARE, *Proxy Voting Guidelines 2005*, at: http://www.share.ca.

138 See http://www.dep.no/fin/english/topics/pension_fund/p10002777/guide-lines/bn.html.

139 See http://www.guile.net/site.asp?dex=1&bkey=0&nid=53&lid=0.

140 IFC, *"Who Cares Who Wins": One Year On* (IFC, 2005), 11.

141 Ibid., 7, 15.

142 Ibid., 16–17.

III. Process Standards

A. EQUATOR PRINCIPLES (EPs)

1. Overview of the Standards

In the project finance market, the EPs provide lenders with a framework to manage their social and environmental impacts.[143] Project finance is loans for specific projects such as highways, dams, factories, and other economic investments that often have a substantial ecological footprint. Formulated primarily by the banking industry under the auspices of the World Bank's IFC, the EPs target private, commercial lending in developing countries and emerging economies where environmental regulation may be tenuous. While the EPs are categorized in this chapter primarily as process standards, they also include a normative framework through their incorporation of the IFC's Performance Standards.

The EPs arose under pressure from institutional investors such as the Calvert Group and Insight Investment, as well as by demands of NGOs including the WWF and Friends of the Earth.[144] The financing of the Chad-Cameroon oil pipeline was one catalyst for such pressure.[145] Motivated to evade both the criticisms for supporting the controversial project and the loss of business to less scrupulous lenders, a cohort of banks sought to establish a new level playing field for responsible project financing. The credibility of the standards was boosted by involving the IFC, the World Bank's private-sector lending arm with extensive hands-on experience in project finance, including application of environmental standards. Although NGO pressure was a seminal factor contributing to the creation of the EPs, apparently "the fast-track process of drafting the Equator Principles prevented meaningful input from stakeholders."[146]

The EPs are not entirely self-contained standards, but incorporate references to other standards, primarily the IFC's Safeguard Policies for social and environmental impact assessment (SEIA), forestry, dam safety, Indigenous peoples, and

143 T. O'Riordan, "Converting the Equator Principles to Equator Stewardship," *Environment* 47(4) (2005): 1.
144 Freshfields Bruckhaus Deringer (FBD), *Banking on Responsibility* (FBD, July 2005), 7.
145 M. Spek, *Financing Pulp Mills: An Appraisal of Risk Assessment and Safeguard Procedures* (Center for International Forestry Research, 2006), 53.
146 N. Affolder, "Cachet Not Cash: Another Sort of World Bank Group Borrowing," *Michigan State Journal of International Law* 14 (2006): 141, 156.

other topics. By focusing on social standards (e.g., human rights), in addition to environmental concerns, the EPs draw attention to a side of project financing due diligence that financiers had traditionally not systematically considered. The EPs were finalized in June 2003,[147] and then revised in July 2006, following the April 2006 revisions to the baseline IPC standards.[148] The revised EPs apply to upgrades or expansions of existing projects where additional environmental or social impacts are significant. All signatories pledge to provide loans only to borrowers who conform to the Principles.

Originally designed for banks, the Principles may accommodate other financial institutions connected to project financing. Its 2006 revisions reflect the belief that no qualifying criteria should limit membership, which led to endorsements of the Principles by export credit agencies and other types of financiers. The EPs presently apply to projects with a total capital cost of at least US$10 million (previously US$50 million). Since the threshold is cost-based, it is unrelated to the project's social or ecological impact. The EPs require lenders to rate projects that they plan to finance based on the magnitude of potential impacts and risks in accordance with the screening criteria of the IFC.[149] These criteria categorize projects as A, B, or C (high, medium, and low) depending on their potential environmental and social impacts. A or B project borrowers must undertake a SEIA based on IFC standards to address the issues identified in the screening process. Project financing banks must also prepare an Action Plan based on the conclusions of the SEIA.[150] For category C projects, no further assessment is required beyond the initial screening.

Lenders of category A and B projects must ensure that the borrower has consulted with affected local communities "in a structured and culturally appropriate manner."[151] This requirement falls short of the "prior informed consent" standard demanded by Indigenous peoples and other vulnerable communities, as reflected in some international legal instruments.[152] However, proponents must make the SEIA report and Action Plan publicly available in

---

147 Http://www.equator-principles.com.
148 See E. Morgera, "Significant Trends in Corporate Environmental Accountability: The New Performance Standards of the International Finance Corporation," *Colorado Journal of International Environmental Law and Policy* 18(Winter) (2007): 151.
149 Principle 1.
150 Principle 4.
151 Principle 5.
152 See C. Charters, "Indigenous Peoples and International Law and Policy," *Public Law Review* 18(1) (2007): 22.

a local language for a reasonable period to allow for public comment. These documents are also subject to independent expert review.[153] The revised EPs also require a borrower to establish a "grievance mechanism" to allow it to "receive and facilitate resolution of concerns and grievances about the project's social and environmental performance raised by individuals or groups from among project-affected communities."[154] Finally, prior to drawing on the loan, the borrower must covenant with the lender to: (i) comply with the environmental management plan in the construction and operation of the project, (ii) provide regular reports on compliance with the plan, and (iii) where applicable, decommission facilities in accordance with an agreed plan.[155]

Still, the Principles do not capture all financing activities of banks.[156] While Equator banks must not fund non-compliant projects, they may circumvent this standard if acting indirectly through financial intermediaries, such as an export credit agency (unless the latter itself has signed the EPs). Many banks have invested via their asset management arms in energy companies, mining firms, or other sectors commonly associated with project finance. Again, the Principles do not explicitly cover such investment. Notwithstanding the restricted scope of the EPs applying only to project finance, some signatories profess to apply the EPs or other general norms of responsible financing to other arms of their business. For instance, HSBC claims that it applies the EPs to "advisory work" on projects, in addition to financing.[157] Citigroup applies a EPs-derived policy to corporate loans and debt securities underwriting where the specific use of proceeds is known.[158] Even banks not in the project financing business face pressure from NGOs and other stakeholders to follow the spirit of the EPs.[159]

2. Implementation

Given the banking sector's hand in the design of the EPs, its embracement of the Principles is unsurprising. As of April 2008, some sixty banks and related financial institutions, accounting for over 85 percent the global

153 Principle 7.
154 Principle 6.
155 Principle 8.
156 G. Lambe, "Good Principles Hard to Live Up To," *The Banker*, March 5, 2007, 34.
157 HSBC, *2006 Corporate Responsibility Report* (HSBC, 2007), 19.
158 Citigroup, *Citizenship Report 2006* (Citigroup, 2007), 48.
159 J. Langton, "The Greening of Corporate Canada," *Investment Executive*, May 2, 2006.

project financing market, had signed the EPs.[160] Most of the signatories are North American or Western European banks. As project financing is often undertaken through banking syndicates, where lenders share the financial risks, the EPs potentially have even wider application where a syndicate includes some Equator signatories. A study by the British law firm Freshfields Bruckhaus Deringer concluded that the Principles' "impact on the financial market generally and their success in redefining banking considerations has been far greater than anyone could have predicted."[161]

The EPs have appealed to banks for several reasons, including that they counter stakeholder and NGO activism, protect market share, maintain a level field, incorporate voluntary standards, and minimize financial risks.[162] Through common standards and procedures for earlier and more granular risk assessment, the EPs have helped signatory banks to minimize the reputational risks associated with development projects that pose significant social and environmental disruption. Subscription to the EPs offers public relations benefits to deflect NGO's incessant scrutiny of lenders.[163] For instance, a 2005 shareholder proposal was filed to the Bank of Montreal by the Ethical Funds Company, but the resolution was withdrawn after the bank agreed to adhere to the EPs.[164] Similarly, the Rainforest Action Network was particularly successful in its "Global Finance Campaign," which led Citigroup (the world's largest bank by market capitalization) to revise its policies to avoid destructive investment in endangered ecosystems.[165]

The 2006 revisions to the EPs have improved their accountability, transparency, and enforceability, although not entirely to the satisfaction of all critics.[166] A lender's categorization of a project or the scope of an SEIA or

---

160 Listed at http://www.equator-principles.com.

161 Freshfields, note 144, 1.

162 Ibid., 50. The Freshfields study (at 65) also identified reasons why some banks reject the EPs: scepticism of their value, necessary internal management systems not in place, and fear of "contagion" (i.e., pressure could arise to apply the Principles to other arms of the bank's business).

163 See generally D.H. Schepers, "The Impact of NGO Network Conflict on the Corporate Social Responsibility Strategies of Multinational Corporations," *Business and Society* 45(3) (2006): 282.

164 Ethical Funds Company: http://www.ethicalfunds.com/do_the_right_thing/sri/shareholder_action/shareholder_resolutions_2005/03_bank_montreal.htm.

165 See http://www.ran.org.

166 B. Baue, "Revised Equator Principles Fall Short of International Best Practice for Project Finance," *Social Funds Sustainability Investment News*, July 12, 2006; A. Missbach, "The Equator Principles: Drawing the Line for

management plan cannot readily be challenged. The categorization of a project is crucial, for it influences the types of environmental standards and procedures that would subsequently apply, and normally, environmental legislation would allow interested persons to review and challenge such threshold decisions. However, under the EPs, while affected groups may publicly comment on a SEIA or a proposed management plan, they are not able to legally challenge their adequacy. Moreover, the Principles' language in parts is vague, such as one stipulation that the assessment of projects need only "refer to" the IFC standards.

Nevertheless, the EPs do require the lender to appoint an independent environmental expert to monitor all category A projects, and "as appropriate," all category B projects.[167] Further, unlike the UNPRI, Equator banks must, "at least annually," disclose to the public their "implementation processes and experience, taking into account appropriate confidentiality considerations."[168] While these measures should help to illuminate lenders' implementation efforts, the EPs lack a well resourced supporting secretariat comparable to the UNEPFI to coordinate oversight.

BankTrack, an umbrella organization of NGOs pooling their advocacy on financial issues, has put the spotlight on Equator banks. Its 2005 review of the Principles (before the revisions) concluded that the majority of lenders provided only limited reports of their implementation of the EPs.[169] BankTrack also noted hesitation among some of the Equator banks to disclose the details (e.g., names, locations, and facilities) of the projects they had financed or declined.[170] Conversely, a report by Freshfields Bruckhaus Deringer suggested, more optimistically, that the Principles have led some Equator banks "into more structured dialogue with stakeholders and NGOs about social and environmental aspects of their lending."[171]

On enforceability, the EPs disclaim that they confer "any rights in, or liability to, any person." Thus, while borrowers must adhere to environmental covenants included in the loan agreement, lenders are not contractually bound to comply with the EPs or to enforce the terms against their borrowers.

Socially Responsible Banks? An Interim Review from an NGO Perspective," *Development* 47 (2004): 78; Wright and Rwabizambuga, note 57.

167 Principle 9.

168 Principle 10.

169 M. Chan-Fishel, *Unproven Principles: The Equator Principles at Year Two* (BankTrack, 2005), 5.

170 Ibid., 6.

171 Freshfields, note 144, 10.

Theoretically, shareholders of an Equator bank might contend that they have relied on their bank's public statements that it abides by the EPs. In some jurisdictions this misleading communication could give cause to shareholder lawsuits where the bank's reputation (and therefore the business and shareholder value) has suffered because of a failure to implement the EPs.[172]

The banks' own corporate sustainability reports elucidate the manner of their implementation of the EPs. Barclays Bank, for example, discloses in its *Corporate Responsibility Report 2006* that it concluded thirty-six project financing deals that year (eighteen of which were category A and B projects) and it declined involvement in six projects.[173] Of the approved deals, Barclays explained that thirty were subject to changes to address environmental and social issues. HSBC boasts that in 2006 it rejected four of seventy-six projects (forty-two being category A or B projects) reviewed for compliance with the Principles.[174] The Royal Bank of Canada (RBC) disclosed that between 2003 and 2006 it reviewed fourteen projects against the EPs (including twelve category A or B projects) of which two were cancelled and one sought alternative financing.[175]

One of several major international infrastructure projects to have tested the credibility of the EPs is the Baku-Tbilisi-Ceyhan (BTC) pipeline project, running through Azerbaijan, Georgia, and Turkey to bring Caspian Sea oil to the West.[176] BankTrack contends that this project, funded by a consortium of financiers including some Equator banks, violates the EPs in regard to protection of Indigenous peoples and ecologically sensitive terrain. However, the pipeline development consortium has shown itself to have applied the EPs openly in other respects. The consortium created for instance a publicly accessible web site[177] for anyone to consult environmental assessments and related documents, many of which are published in local languages. The BTC case shows that an Equator bank may fund a development that many see as being unsustainable while still fully complying with the decision-making procedures of the Principles.

172 See R. Kraakman, et al., "When are Shareholder Suits in Shareholder Interests?" *Georgetown Law Journal* 82 (1994): 1733.
173 Barclays, *Corporate Responsibility Report 2006* (Barclays, 2007), 23.
174 HSBC, *2006 Corporate Social Responsibility Report 2005* (HSBC, 2007), 19.
175 RBC, *Towards Sustainability: Where Our Values Lead Us* (RBC, 2007), 20–21.
176 BankTrack, *Principles, Profit or Just PR?* (BankTrack, 2004); see also "BTC Project is the First Major Test of the Equator Principles," at http://www.equator-principles.com/btc.shtml.
177 See http://www.caspiandevelopmentandexport.com/ASP/Home.asp.

A further contentious project is the Sakhalin II oil and gas project, in Sakhalin Island, eastern Russia. Desperate for foreign investment at the time, Russian authorities approved the environmentally problematic pipeline in the 1990s. The project is financed by an international consortium including Credit Suisse First Boston (an Equator financier), as well as assistance from multilateral sources and export credit agencies. The project risks oil spills that could destroy rich salmon fisheries and endanger rare whales.[178] In June 2005 eight NGOs placed a full-page advertisement in the *Financial Times* urging Credit Suisse to abide by its EPs sustainability commitments and to sever its relationship as financial advisor to the Sakhalin II project.[179] The NGO advocacy has achieved some success in influencing the financiers and developers to modify the project, testifying to their watchdog capacity in the absence of effective official oversight.[180]

Another controversial project testing the credibility of the EPs is the Uruguayan pulp mills near the Rio Uruguay bordering Uruguay and Argentina. The mills, which pose many environmental hazards, have engendered a feisty dispute between the bordering countries that included litigation in the International Court of Justice (ICJ).[181] In November 2006, the IFC approved a US$170 million investment in one of the two mills, the Orion pulp mill, the majority of which is owned by Finnish company Oy Metsä-Botnia Ab.[182] Although some Equator banks have declined to join in, the IFC's endorsement opened the path for others such as Calyon (an EPs signatory) to invest in the pulp mills.[183] A report by the Center for International Forestry Research contends that the SEIA submitted by Oy Metsä-Botnia Ab

178 See CEE Bankwatch Network, at http://www.bankwatch.org/issues/oil-clima/sakhalin2/ main.html.

179 "Oil is Over. Fund the Future," *Financial Times*, June 30, 2005.

180 M. Bradshaw, "The 'Greening' of Global Project Financing: The Case of the Sakhalin-II Offshore Oil and Gas Project," *Canadian Geographer* 51(3) (2007): 255.

181 *Pulp Mills on the River Uruguay (Argentina v. Uruguay)*, Request for the indication of provisional measures, ICJ (July 13, 2006), in ILM 45 (2006): 1025. The ICJ issued a preliminary ruling against Argentina's request to halt construction of the paper mills, finding no grounds to order provisional relief. It has yet to adjudicate the substantive case against Uruguay.

182 IFC, "IFC and MIGA Board Approves Orion Pulp Mill in Uruguay: 2,500 Jobs to Be Created, No Environmental Harm," Press release, November 21, 2005.

183 D. Taillant, *ING Group Says it Would Not Finance Pulp Paper Mills if Argentina Did Not Agree to Investment* (Center for Human Rights and Environment, December 29, 2005).

"falls far short of what a proper assessment of the mill should consider."[184] It also faulted a belated environmental assessment process that began only after the projects were well advanced.

Given the structure of project financing, it is perhaps unrealistic to expect the EPs to revolutionize lending practices. The Principles would have minimal impact in developed country markets where major projects usually require an environmental assessment in any event to obtain the initial permits to undertake the project. In emerging markets—the intended domain for the EPs—environmental assessments are not routinely required, and consequently the Principles may create additional compliance costs for lenders. Project financers however have other reasons to pay attention to environmental issues, such as the impacts of reputational risks and financial hardship of borrowers incurring pollution fines.[185] Still, even a sufficiently motivated bank can have only limited leverage over a borrower, as banks are not often involved in a financing deal until after basic project choices and design decisions have been made.[186] Further, determined would-be borrowers have alternative ways to circumvent an Equator bank's demands—such as self-financing a project using shareholder funds or the bond market.[187] These considerations suggest that more comprehensive solutions to promote SRI are necessary.

Apart from imperfect implementation, the EPs' integrity can be undermined by signatory lenders maintaining other types of financial relationships with companies connected to social and environmental problems. For instance, JPMorgan Chase (JPMC) owns a small stake (approximately 5 percent) in an Australian company, Lafayette Mining, the primary owner and operator of an environmentally controversial polymetallic open mine in the Philippines. While JPMC has not provided project finance to Lafayette Mining,[188] BankTrack claims that the project contravenes the EPs because of local community opposition to the mine, and deficient environmental and social risk assessments.[189] Similar lacunae in the application of the EPs arise

---

184 M. Spek, *Financing Pulp Mills: An Appraisal of Risk Assessment and Safeguard Procedures* (Center for International Forestry Research, 2006), 57.
185 B.J. Richardson, "Environmental Liability and Banks: Recent European Developments," *Journal of International Banking Law* 17(10) (2000): 289, 290.
186 Freshfields, note 144, 11.
187 Ibid., 12.
188 Several EP signatory banks have provided project finance to the Lafayatte mine: BankTrack, "Dodgy Deals: Lafayette Mine, Rapu Rapu Island," at http://www.banktrack.org/?show=dodgy&id=26.
189 Ibid.

with regard to Calyon's financing of the controversial Uruguay pulp mill.[190] Calyon ignored a EPs Compliance Complaint filed against it in 2006 by nine international organizations.[191] Calyon officials contend that their involvement in the pulp mill is not a normal "project finance" arrangement, and thus beyond the scope of activities requiring compliance with the Principles.

What of the behavior of non-EPs signatories? Some maintain their own environmental standards, sometimes more stringent than the EPs. Some commercial and investment banks apply their own responsible financing standards. Some export credit agencies have not adopted the EPs, instead applying the OECD's 2003 Recommendation on Common Approaches on Environment and Officially Supported Export Credits.[192] At the other extreme, some NGOs express growing concern against the increasing involvement of Chinese banks in project financing, as they allegedly "have not yet adopted policies that are comparable to those of leading international lenders."[193] The seriousness of this situation is reflected in the former President of the World Bank, Paul Wolfowitz, criticizing Chinese banks for not following the World Bank's example in adhering to environmental and human rights standards when lending to infrastructure projects in Africa.[194]

In general, commentators suggest that "fears that there would be a significant amount of 'bottom feeding' (i.e. non-Equator local or regional banks offering sponsors a less stringent approach to social and environmental assessment), may be unproven, unfounded, or a little exaggerated."[195] Indeed, some anecdotal evidence suggests that, instead of firms being deterred from borrowing through an Equator bank because of their increased standards, companies

---

190 "Calyon to Support Controversial Botnia Pulp Mill Project in Uruquay," *BankTrack News Item*, January 15, 2007.

191 Center for Human Rights and Environment, et al., Equator Principles Compliance Complaint *Regarding Proposed Pulp Paper Mill Investment in Fray Bentos Uruguay* (Center for Human Rights and Environment, May 18, 2006).

192 See http://www.oecd.org/dataoecd/26/33/21684464.pdf.

193 M. Chan-Fishel, *Time to Go Green: Environmental Responsibility in the Chinese Banking Sector* (Friends of the Earth and BankTrack, 2007), 1.

194 Editorial, "Mr. Wolfowitz and the Bank," *New York Times*, January 2, 2007, s. 1, 16.

195 P.Q. Watchman, A. Delfino, and J. Addison, "EP2: The Revised Equator Principles: Why Hard-nosed Bankers are Embracing Soft Law Principles" (LeBoeuf, Lamb, Greene and MacRae, 2006), 25 (also published in *Law and Financial Markets Review* 1(2) (2007)).

actually seek to comply with the EPs so their projects become eligible.[196] Yet, among EPs signatories, pressures for perfunctory implementation lurk. Banks rarely exercise the covenants written into the loan agreement to recall the loan. While risk managers "may want to pull the plug[,] ... deal makers will do everything in their power to keep the whole thing afloat and to keep lines of credit open."[197]

B. SUSTAINABILITY REPORTING REGIMES

1. Global Reporting Initiative (GRI)

The GRI, launched by CERES and UNEP in 1997, is a multi-stakeholder process for an internationally applicable framework for reporting sustainability issues.[198] The GRI furnishes the reporting principles and the specific indicators to guide sustainability reports by companies and other organizations. The GRI Sustainability Reporting Guidelines (known as G3, being the third generation of guidelines) were issued in 2006.[199] They comprise Reporting Principles, Reporting Guidance, and Standard Disclosures. The Reporting Principles, which set the tone for the other components, include materiality, stakeholder inclusiveness, sustainability context, and completeness.

Appreciating the limits of a homogeneous reporting framework, the GRI has created sector-specific supplements, which contribute to its precision and comprehensiveness. The draft financial sector supplement focuses on unique environmental and social impacts associated with financial services and products.[200] In addition to indicators for direct environmental impacts, the reporting standards use thirteen indicators to cover the indirect impacts of financiers, such as "description of process[es] for assessing and screening environmental risks in core business lines" and "description of voting policy on environmental issues for shares over which the reporting organization

196 A. Hardenbrook, "The Equator Principles: The Private Financial Sector's Attempt at Environmental Responsibility," *Vanderbilt Journal of Transnational Law* 40 (2007): 197, 230.
197 Lambe, note 156.
198 Http://www.globalreporting.org.
199 Http://www.globalreporting.org/ReportingFramework/G3Online.
200 GRI, *Financial Services Sector Supplement: Environmental Performance. Pilot Version 1.0* (GRI, March 2005). The pilot version is being revised, see GRI and UNEPFI, *The GRI Financial Services Sector Supplement: Draft Version Proposed for Public Comment* (GRI and UNEPFI, 2007).

holds the right to vote shares or advise on voting."[201] Oren Perez believes that "[b]y proposing to integrate the environmental report with the traditional financial report, the GRI scheme seeks to revolutionise the cognitive frame in which corporations operate."[202] Another beneficial attribute of the GRI is its participatory governance structure which has enabled numerous stakeholders to influence the reporting guidelines. This consensus-making approach increases the GRI's legitimacy and applicability.

Through such measures, with the goal of bringing firms closer to sustainability, the GRI is arguably one of the world's most progressive CSR reporting standards. Surprisingly, its relative stringency has not dissuaded companies from adopting the standards, perhaps reflective of how the development of the GRI has included close consultation with the corporate sector, and the prestige associated with the involvement of UNEP. The number of S&P's 100 Index companies that report using GRI principles grew from twenty-six in 2005 to thirty-one in 2006, and in the S&P's 1200 index, the corresponding growth was from 256 firms in 2005 to 292 in 2006.[203] A KPMG analysis in 2005 of corporate reporting trends found changes in both the style and the scale of environmental reports.[204] First, perhaps reflecting the changes to the GRI Guidelines, the focus of reporting has evolved from primarily pure environmental issues (until the late 1990s) to sustainability issues (social, environmental, and economic). Second, on the scale of changes, sustainability reporting has become more popular among the majority of large companies surveyed.[205] Of the respondents interviewed, 40 percent noted that the GRI was determinative of the content of their company's sustainability report.[206] Other studies have also verified the increasing status of the GRI.[207]

---

201 Ibid., 4.
202 O. Perez, *Facing the Global Hydra: Ecological Transformation at the Global Financial Frontier—The Ambitious Case of the Global Reporting Initiative*, Working Paper No. 06-9 (Bar-Ilan University, Faculty of Law, 2006), 17.
203 NRTEE, *Capital Markets and Sustainability: Investing in a Sustainable Future. State of the Debate Report* (NRTEE, 2007), 19.
204 KPMG, *International Survey of Corporate Responsibility Reporting 2005* (KPMG, 2005).
205 Ibid., 4.
206 Ibid., 20.
207 S&P's, Sustainability, and UNEP, *Risk and Opportunity: Best Practice in Non-Financial Reporting* (S&P's, 2004), 38, 47.

Its status is evident in other ways. In South Africa, companies listed on the Johannesburg Stock Exchange must adhere to the King II Report.[208] The King II Code of Corporate Practices and Conduct refers to public sustainability reporting based on the GRI. Section 5 of the Code states: "[d]isclosure of non-financial information should be governed by the principles of reliability, relevance, clarity, comparability, timeliness and verifiability with reference to the [GRI] Guidelines...."[209] This is the first instance of a major stock exchange applying a sustainability reporting standard based on the GRI guidelines. The SRI community in other countries has sought to promote use of the GRI among financial institutions.[210] However, the quality of GRI reporting by some financial institutions has been disappointing; many simply report on their direct, in-house activities rather than on the broader environmental risks and impacts of their clients and borrowers.[211] Some financiers have found the GRI unhelpful to assessing environmental risks because it does not itself adequately enable succinct financial quantification of such risks.[212]

2. EUROSIF TRANSPARENCY GUIDELINES

Of the numerous sustainability reporting standards, apart from the GRI, that this chapter could explore, one worth noting is the Eurosif Transparency Guidelines. It was designed specifically for the SRI market.[213] Based in Paris, the European Social Investment Forum (Eurosif) is a pan-European association of institutions interested in the SRI market and governance. Its members include pension funds, financial service providers, academic institutes, and NGOs. Eurosif provides a forum to help institutions collaborate on SRI issues and convey ideas to European policy makers.[214]

---

208 King Committee on Corporate Governance, Secretariat (Mervyn King, Committee Chair), *King Report on Corporate Governance for South Africa* (Institute of Directors in Southern Africa, 2002).

209 Ibid., 35.

210 See A. Willis, "The Role of the Global Reporting Initiative's Sustainability Reporting Guidelines in the Social Screening of Investments," *Journal of Business Ethics* 43(3) (2003): 233.

211 See the GRI Register of all reports filed: http://www.corporateregister. com/gri.

212 Personal communication, James Evans, Senior Manager, Corporate Environmental Affairs, RBC (Toronto, September 20, 2007).

213 Eurosif, *The Eurosif SRI Retail Fund Transparency Guidelines* (Eurosif, 2004).

214 Http://www.eurosif.org.

The Eurosif Transparency Guidelines furnish a voluntary code intended for SRI retail funds to provide more disclosure and increased accountability to investors. Eurosif also admits that the Guidelines were introduced partly "to pre-empt potential regulation that could be enacted without the involvement of the greater SRI community."[215] Under the Guidelines, SRI funds should provide detailed information about their research processes and investment criteria, method for voting shareholder proxies, and their strategies for engaging corporations to improve CSR. Signatories to the Guidelines must make publicly available disclosures at least once annually. The Guidelines have directly informed reporting practices by some SRI institutions. For instance, the Ethical Funds Company in Canada and the Calvert group in the US have issued disclosure statements using the Eurosif guide as their template.[216]

The Guidelines may serve to empower investors in the retail market, particularly in the mutual fund sector, which traditionally has not offered opportunities for socially conscious investors to understand the intricacies of investment policy-making. On the other hand, the Eurosif Guidelines do not direct how institutions should invest, nor do they explicitly refer to any ethical motivations that should drive SRI.

C. ECO-LABEL STANDARDS

Companies that achieve environmental accreditation standards can usually market an approved label or emblem to advertise their environmental credentials. Eco-labels, as commonly known, have been widely promoted for decades to publicize environmental performance of producers or specific products. However, eco-labels remain less common for service providers.[217] Eco-labels for the financial sector should stimulate marketing and reward innovation in this area, particularly in the retail sector such as SRI mutual funds and banks offering green mortgages. They can provide assurance to investors about the quality of SRI products, which is needed in a market

---

215 Eurosif, note 213, 1.
216 Ethical Funds Company, *Eurosif Transparency Guidelines: Statement of Commitment from the Ethical Funds Company* (Ethical Funds Company, 2005); Calvert, *Eurosif Transparency Guidelines: Calvert Statement of Commitment* (Calvert, 2006).
217 Traditionally, eco-labels are applied to individual consumer products rather than services, for which the environmental impact is much harder to assess: see generally OECD, *Eco-Labelling: Actual Effects of Selected Programmes* (OECD, 1997).

where fungible standards and cheap marketing can confuse investors and deter them from investing ethically. In the consumer market, research suggests that nearly 30 percent of shoppers who do not buy eco-friendly products were skeptical of marketers' environmental claims.[218]

Most eco-label schemes do not however specifically target the financial sector, although some examples may indirectly benefit SRI. For example, green building certification schemes can help social investors in the real estate market.[219] The EU's official eco-label scheme can apply to financial services and products. The Eco-label Regulation was revised in 2000 to enable the awarding of eco-labels to "any goods and services" including, in theory, financial services.[220] Some national eco-label schemes already include financial services. The Austrian eco-label was amended to allow environmental funds to receive the Umweltzeichen label from the Ministry of Environment.[221]

Apart from these official schemes, the private sector has advanced a few dedicated SRI label schemes. Ethibel, a Belgian entity that researches companies for responsible investors, has designed one such scheme. It developed the Sustainability Label, in association with the Centre for Sustainable Development of the University of Ghent. Ethibel's label is awarded to European SRI funds that meet its specified social and environmental standards.[222] In France, a label scheme was devised by the Committee for Employees' Savings (Comité intersyndical de l'epargne salariale), established in 2002 by a group of trade unions to control the investment of employee salary savings schemes and to guide fund managers towards SRI choices.[223] The scheme applies only to employee savings funds. The label awarded by the Committee certifies that fund investment products have been screened according to SRI criteria, and that employee representatives hold the majority of seats on the fund supervisory boards. Finally, perhaps the most eminent SRI label is the scheme introduced in 2005 by Australia's RIAA.[224] Presently, it applies to four categories: fund managers, superannuation funds, dealer groups, and financial advisers. The certification scheme requires that investment institutions disclose their

218 R. Gardyn, "Eco-Friend or FOE," *American Demographics* 25(8) (2003): 12.
219 UNEPFI Property Working Group, "Responsible Property Investing," *CEO Briefing* (UNEPFI, October 2007), 8–9.
220 Council Regulation 1980/2000 of 17 July 2000 on a revised Community eco-label award scheme, O.J. L. 237/1.
221 See http://www.umweltzeichen.at.
222 Ethibel, "The Collective European Quality Label for Socially Responsible Investment Funds," at http://www.ethibel.org/subs_e /2_label/main.html.
223 Http://comite.cies.free.fr.
224 Http://www.eia.org.au.

SRI methodology, quality control processes, and asset holdings. The certification standard is thus based on the funds' decision-making procedures, rather than their substantive social or environmental investment goals.

IV. Management Systems

A. ENVIRONMENTAL MANAGEMENT SYSTEMS (EMSs)

Like reporting mechanisms, EMSs help financial institutions assess their own or their clients' environmental performance.[225] EMSs are formal structures of standards and processes for corporations and other organizations to adopt in order to improve their internal use of materials and energy. They are also frameworks enabling companies to identify, evaluate, and minimize environmental risks. Participation in an EMS can lead to production cost savings and better market reputation.[226] EMSs may harness a variety of management tools, notably, environmental accounting and auditing, life-cycle assessment, and environmental performance indicators. In theory, through EMSs investors and lenders are better able to gauge the environmental credentials of companies seeking finance, and financial institutions also benefit by being able to control their direct and indirect environmental impacts.

By summarizing environmental performance data, EMSs should assist efficient assessment of risks associated with companies that financiers support, thereby providing a "second-hand form of assurance," in which governance is based on controlling the procedural mechanisms and management protocols rather than on influencing the substantive goals of companies.[227] Insurance markets were the first to acknowledge the significance of EMS

---

225 See generally R. Sroufe and J. Sarkis, *Strategic Sustainability: The State of the Art in Corporate Environmental Management Systems* (Greenleaf Publishing, 2007); J. Voorhees, "Global Environmental Solutions: Management Systems and Synchronicity," *Stetson Law Review* 28 (1999): 1155; D. Monsma, "Sustainable Development and the Global Economy: New Systems in Environmental Management," *Vermont Law Review* 24 (2000): 1245.

226 See R. Fairley, "Environmental Policy and Audit—What's in It for Us?" *Environmental Law and Management* 7 (1995): 31.

227 M. Power, "Making Things Auditable," *Accounting, Organizations and Society* 21 (1996): 289.

accreditation when underwriting and determining coverage.[228] Some insurers offered significant discounts on environmental liability insurance premiums to chemical manufacturers subscribing to the Responsible Care EMS.[229] Some banks now offer preferential terms to EMS-certified borrowers.[230] Banks are particularly keen to see small business clients (normally subject to less onerous public reporting standards) certified to an established EMS that can outline a clearer picture about their environmental performance and risks.[231] Chris Davies suggests, "by looking for [EMS] registration in loan applications, banks can determine several facts relevant to the health of their loan portfolios."[232] Still, because EMSs tend to assess existing environmental performance, rather than future performance, ongoing monitoring is often also necessary.

While the propagation of corporate EMSs provides a salutary framework for reflexive management of environmental problems, it does have some limitations.[233] Some firms may decline to open themselves to an environmental audit for fear that regulators, insurers, or NGO activists will hold the disclosed information against them.[234] To accommodate such concerns, some governments offer evidentiary privilege for audit reports and partial immunities from self-identified regulatory violations.[235] Another concern is that

---

228 See "How to Open Pollution Coverage Market—Make Policy Contingent on Obeying Environmental Code Insurance," *Advocate* 108(14) (1997): 10.

229 See E. Rafferty, "Participants in Responsible Care Offered an Insurance Discount," *Chemical Engineering* 105(2) (1998): 48; D. Hunter, "Responsible Care Earns Discount on EIL-Premiums," *Chemical Week* 159(29) (1997): 11.

230 P.L. Stenzel, "Can the ISO 14000 Series Environmental Management Standards Provide a Viable Alternative to Government Regulation?" *American Business Law Journal* 37 (2000): 237, 272.

231 D. Dal Maso, C. Marini, and P. Perin, "A Green Package to Promote Environmental Management Systems Among SMEs," in *Sustainable Banking: The Greening of Finance*, eds J.J. Bouma, M. Jeucken, and L. Klinkers (Greenleaf Publishing, 2001), 56, 57.

232 C. Davies, "What ISO 14001 Means for the Banking Industry," *Canadian Banker* 106(3) (1999): 8–9.

233 J. Nash and J. Ehrenfeld, *Environmental Management Systems and their Roles in Environmental Policy* (National Research Summit on Environmental Management Systems, 1999), 3–4.

234 D. Hansell, "The Discoverability of Environmental Audits," *International Insurance Law Review* 3(8) (1995): 273.

235 See M.R. Harris, "Promoting Corporate Self-compliance: An Examination of the Debate over Legal Protection for Environmental Audits," *Ecology Law Quarterly* 23(4) (1996): 663.

a company's self-selected goals for its EMS may be superficial, so that it can achieve the desired standards at little inconvenience.[236] Such arrangements simply perpetuate business-as-usual. Thus, EMSs can become mere ritualistic documenting and certifying compliance with management protocols without any critical reflection on improving environmental performance.[237] Greater involvement of arms-length NGOs and other stakeholders in designing and overseeing EMS standards provides a way to enhance their credibility.[238]

B. ISO 14000 SERIES

Several internationally applicable management systems can aid SRI.[239] The most important are the International Organization for Standardization (ISO) 14000 series,[240] the EU's Eco-Management and Audit Scheme (EMAS),[241] AccountAbility's AA1000 Assurance Standard,[242] and Social Accountability International's SA8000 standard.[243] Each standard takes a distinct approach. For instance, AccountAbility's standards raise the bar for organizations' accountability to their stakeholders, including.stakeholder engagement and responsiveness. This following discussion canvasses only the ISO and EMAS standards, as illustrations.

---

236 Stenzel, note 230, 284 (discussing problems with the ISO 14001's environmental goals).
237 For example, auditing serves to certify the process, not the product, so that, for example, no distinction is made between a company producing solar powered technologies from one that produces industrial chemicals: G. Bbrüggemeier, "Enterprise Liability for Environmental Damage: German and European Law," in *Environmental Law and Ecological Responsibility*, note 60, 75, 90.
238 Stenzel, note 230, 279.
239 See J. Nash and J. Ehrenfeld, "Codes of Environmental Management Practice: Assessing their Potential as a Tool for Change," *Annual Review of Energy and Environment* 22 (1997): 487; D. Monsma, "Sustainable Development and the Global Economy: New Systems in Environmental Management," *Vermont Law Review* 24 (2000): 1245.
240 See generally R. Hillary, ed., *ISO 14001: Case Studies and Practical Experience* (Greenleaf Publishing, 2000).
241 Council Regulation 1836/93 of 29 June 1993 allowing voluntary participation by organizations in a Community eco-management and audit scheme, 1993 O.J. (L. 168).
242 Http://www.accountability.org.uk.
243 Http://www.sa-intl.org.

The ISO, an umbrella organization of a network of national standards institutes from over 155 countries, has produced numerous technical standards to facilitate technology exchange and trade.[244] The ISO structure is a good example of the hybrid governance networks increasing their presence in the market. Many of ISO's member institutes are government parastatals or quangos, while others are rooted in the private sector, having been established by industry associations.

The ISO's first EMS is the ISO 14000 series, encompassing management system principles, environmental auditing, and life cycle assessment. There is no official ISO standard for the financial services sector as such. All of the ISO 14000 series take the form of "guidance," with the exception of the ISO 14001, which is a certified standard,[245] requiring the participating organizations to develop an environmental policy statement, a corporate plan to achieve environmental goals and comply with legislation, as well as a monitoring system. It aims to provide businesses and other certified entities with a process for reflexive learning to identify and eliminate environmentally damaging activities.[246] Yet, while ISO compliance does indicate the existence of management controls, it does not necessarily signify an absolute level of performance. Commentators have expressed doubts about the extent to which ISO-certified firms have actually improved their environmental performance.[247]

Another relevant standard developed by ISO is the 14064 standard, released in March 2006. It seeks to promote consistency, transparency, and credibility in quantifying, reporting, and verifying GHG emissions, in order to facilitate trade in GHG allowances and credits, pursuant to the Kyoto Protocol and regional schemes. The ISO 14064 comprises standards for general guidance, for organizational and project level activities, and for validation and verification of allowances and credits.[248] It is complemented by

---

244 Http://www.iso.ch.

245 Certificates are issued independently of ISO by the various national and international certification or registration bodies operating around the world.

246 See generally R.A. Reiley, "The New Paradigm: ISO 14000 and its Places in Regulatory Reform," *Journal of Corporation Law* 22 (1997): 535.

247 D. Vogel, *The Market for Virtue. The Potential and Limits of Corporate Social Responsibility* (Brookings Institution Press, 2005), 137; D. Rondinelli and G. Vastag, "Panacea, Common Sense, or Just a Label?—The Value of ISO 14001 Environmental Management Systems," *European Management Journal* 18(5) (2000): 499.

248 ISO 14064-1: 2006, *Greenhouse Gases—Part 1: Specification with Guidance at the Organization Level for the Quantification and Reporting of Greenhouse Gas*

ISO 14065, detailing the requirements to accredit or recognize bodies that undertake the validation or verification work.[249] These initiatives reflect ISO's aims to distinguish itself as a key standard provider in government-created emissions and carbon credit markets. It also illustrates the growing interaction between public and private governance in financial markets.

The ISO is also designing a new voluntary standard for CSR, which may prove particularly beneficial for SRI. The guidance standard should be published in late 2008 as ISO 26000.[250] It will not, however, include specific requirements, and thus it will not serve as a certification standard such as ISO 14001. Rather, explains the ISO, "ISO 26000 will be a distillation of international expertise on Social Responsibility—what it means, what issues an organization needs to address in order to operate in a socially responsible manner, and what is best practice in implementing SR."[251]

The financial sector has taken some interest in ISO 14001.[252] Banks have been the most interested, and in 1997 the Swiss bank UBS became the first certified lender.[253] The Credit Suisse Group, also ISO 14001 certified, has spoken of its advantages, including that it "improves the marketing of the green and ethical funds we offer to our institutional and retail customers."[254] In asset selection, Credit Suisse explains that "it is much easier to select stocks of ISO 14001-certified companies for a green and/or ethical fund."[255] Where project financing involves material environmental risks, banks will generally take into account a prospective borrower's ISO certification (or other credible third party standard) in evaluating risks, although certification alone would

Emissions and Removals; ISO 14064-2: 2006, *Greenhouse Gases*—Part 2: *Specification with Guidance at the Project Level for the Quantification, Monitoring and Reporting of Greenhouse Gas Emission Reductions and Removal Enhancements;* ISO 14064-3: 2006, *Greenhouse Gases*—Part 3: *Specification with Guidance for the Validation and Verification of Greenhouse Gas Assertions.*

249 ISO 14065: 2007, *Greenhouse Gases—Requirements for Greenhouse Gas Validation and Verification Bodies for Use in Accreditation or other Forms of Recognition.*
250 ISO, *ISO and Social Responsibility* (ISO, 2006).
251 Ibid., 3.
252 E.g., S. le Clue, *ISO 14001: 2004. What Do Investors Need to Know?* Association *for Sustainable and Responsible Investment (ASrIA) Brief 003* (ASrIA, May 2005).
253 Discussed in B. Furrer and H. Hugenschmidt, "Financial Services and ISO 14001," *Greener Management International* 28 (1999): 32.
254 O. Bisang, "Green Banking—The Value of ISO 14001 Certification in the Financial Sector," *ISO 9000 + ISO 1400 News* 4 (2000): 7, 10.
255 Ibid., 11.

not normally be determinative of an evaluation.[256] In 2000, a group of German and Swiss financial institutions designed some environmental performance indicators for the financial sector based on the ISO 14031 guideline.[257] The indicators however focus on financiers' direct environmental activities and impacts, rather than their usually much more extensive indirect effects through their borrowers or other financial relationships.

C. ECO-MANAGEMENT AUDIT SCHEME (EMAS)

Adopted in 1993, EMAS differs from other governance standards considered in this chapter in that it is a product of EU legislation. It is a governmental standard rather than a private regime, although it relies on private sector auditors to implement it. Moreover, unlike traditional regulation, EMAS is a voluntary standard ceding significant responsibility to the private sector.

The EMAS differs from ISO 14001 in that it seeks continual performance improvements and public disclosure of environmental auditing findings.[258] Participating organizations voluntarily agree to install an EMS (usually for discrete physical sites) and prepare performance reports for verification by a certified environmental auditor at least once every three years. Those that attain the performance standards can market an approved emblem in their advertisements and promotions. The organizations must also formulate an environmental policy statement, also for verification by an auditor, made available to the public. The EMAS is considered a good example of reflexive environmental law because it encourages awareness-raising and the disclosure of environmental impacts within the industry.[259]

The EU amended EMAS in 2001 to broaden its scope to include financial services.[260] Previously, EMAS was limited to specific physical sites rather

256 Personal communication, James Evans, Senior Manager, Corporate Environmental Affairs, RBC (Toronto, September 20, 2007).
257 O. Schmid-Schönbein and A. Braunschweig, *EPI-Finance 2000; Environmental Performance Indicators for the Financial Industry* (E2 Management Consulting, 2000).
258 By way of introduction, see M. Palomares-Soler and P.M. Thimme, "Environmental Standards: EMAS and ISO 14001 Compared," *European Environmental Law Review* 5(8/9) (1996): 24.
259 E.W. Orts, "Reflexive Environmental Law," *Northwestern University Law Review* 89(4) (1995): 1227.
260 Council Regulation 761/2001 of 19 March 2001 allowing voluntary participation by organizations in a Community eco-management and audit

than the entire operations of an organization. Authorities could extend EMAS only to the service sector on an experimental basis, as Germany did for its banking and insurance industries.[261] The new focus of EMAS is the organization as a whole. This change was crucial for EMAS to encompass the financial sector. Further, under Annex VI of the revised EMAS, an organization can only be certified if it considers all environmental aspects of its activities, including "indirect environmental aspects" arising from "capital investments, granting loans and insurance services."[262]

These changes should be seminal. A financial organization's direct ecological footprint is markedly narrower from the more pervasive, cumulative impacts of its borrowers and customers. However, EMAS promotional material for the financial sector suggests that the present scheme primarily targets financiers' immediate footprint, including consumption of resources such as paper and energy, and possibly also financiers' supply chains.[263] Financial institutions with EMAS certification include UniCredito Italiano and Oesterreichische Nationalbank. The FTSE4Good market index, which helps investors pick leading companies on sustainability criteria, uses EMAS certification when evaluating corporate performance.[264]

Overall, EMAS has not attained the profile and success of ISO 14001 in terms of market penetration. A review of EMAS in 2005 reported that "[f]ar less than 0.1% of all companies in the EU are EMAS registered," and even suggested that the scheme should possibly close if it did not attract greater public and corporate support.[265] Little has changed since then. Government regulation could help improve the uptake of the EMAS among financial institutions and other economic sectors. Of the nearly 6,000 sites presently awarded EMAS certification, over one-third are in Germany, because the

scheme, O.J. (L. 114). The original EMAS scheme was promulgated by Council Regulation 1836/93 of 29 June 1993, O.J. (L. 168).

261 Detailed in German Association for Environmental Management in Banks, Savings Banks and Insurance Companies, *Time to Act: Environmental Management in Financial Institutions* (Federal Ministry for the Environment, Nature Conservation and Nuclear Safety, 1998), 4, 71.

262 Note 260, Annex VI, cl. 6.3(b).

263 W. Kahlenborn and D. Dal Maso, *The Eco-Management Audit Scheme: A New Opportunity for Financial Institutions* (EC, 2001).

264 FTSE, *FTSE4Good Index Series Inclusion Criteria* (FTSE, 2006),

265 IEFE—Università Bocconi, *Evaluation of EMAS and Ecolabel for their Revision. Report 1: Options and Recommendations for the Revision Process* (EC, 2005), 68.

German Government offers financial incentives to companies that adhere to the scheme.[266]

V. Rating Mechanisms

A. INTRODUCTION

One of the most dynamic areas of SRI governance is the proliferation of institutions offering services to evaluate and rank companies on their social and environmental performances. The most valuable of these services' many objectives is to assist investors construct SRI portfolios. A 2006 study identified at least seventy-one institutions worldwide providing CSR ranking services.[267] They include providers of securities indexes, such as the Dow Jones Sustainability Indexes;[268] in-house research centers that supply special CSR rating reports, such as EIRIS;[269] and general surveys provided by industry associations, such as SIF in the US.[270] While the latter bodies typically canvass a vast array of criteria, others concentrate on just a few, such as corporate governance, as in the case of GovernanceMetrics International.[271]

These rating providers apply diverse methodologies; some of the common characteristics include evaluation of both corporate production methods and life cycle impacts, stakeholder effects ensuing from corporate behavior, corporate governance practices, a broad range of social and environmental impacts, and integrated assessments that attempt to assess overall sustainability performance. A firm's initial rating is typically followed by monitoring, which aims to determine future changes in the company's behavior that may warrant an adjustment in its rankings.

The criteria and values that frame these CSR ratings predominantly reflect a business case model, although often with explicit reference to international

---

266 "EMAS Statistics: Evolution of Organisations and Sites," Quarterly Data (October 22, 2007); and see U. Steger, C. Schindel, and H. Krapf, "The Experience of EMAS in Three European Countries: A Cultural and Competitive Analysis," *Business Strategy and the Environment* 11(1) (2001): 32.

267 H. Schäfer, et al., *Who is Who in Corporate Social Responsibility Rating? A Survey of Internationally Established Rating Systems that Measure Corporate Responsibility* (Bertelsmann Foundation, 2006), 24.

268 Http://www.sustainability-indexes.com.

269 Http://www.eiris.org.

270 Http://www.socialinvest.org.

271 Http://www.gmiratings.com.

norms and conventions on human rights and the environment. Frequently, the evaluation focuses on the management of social and environmental risks to protect shareholder value, measures to improve eco-efficiency such as reduced use of raw materials or production of waste, and innovations including environmental technologies for improved market competitiveness and profitability.

The CSR rating mechanisms arose to fill a gap in the market not provided by credit rating agencies (CRAs). CRAs such as Moody's and S&P's assist financial markets by appraising the creditworthiness of corporations and states.[272] Credit ratings classify borrowers into risk classes according to their individual likelihood of default, and "[r]esults of the ratings influence the volume of capital flowing to different firms and, particularly, the terms on which capital is made available."[273] The weakness of these credit ratings is the inadequacy in accounting for social and environmental performances that have not materialized into concrete financial risks.[274] Moody's has specific rating methodologies for environmentally significant industries, such as for the chemical industry, but they only acknowledge environmental performance issues briefly.[275] Similarly, S&P's does not have a specific policy for rating sustainability, although it may be factored in indirectly. Its 2006 policy advises that "[p]roper assessment of credit quality [includes] vulnerability to technological change, labor unrest, or regulatory actions."[276] Furthermore, S&P's explains that it takes into account "environmental liabilities ... recognized on the balance sheet and otherwise."[277] Since the Enron scandal, the major CRAs have paid somewhat more attention to corporate governance as a key ingredient into their overall company ratings, and this should help SRI institutions.[278] Some CRAs are also starting to provide supplementary CSR rating mechanisms, as in the collaboration between S&P's

272 For introduction, see G. Majnoni and C.M. Reinhart, eds, *Ratings, Rating Agencies and the Global Financial System* (Kluwer Law, 2002).

273 Davis, et al., note 112, 41.

274 E.g., S&P's, *Corporate Ratings Criteria, 2006* (S&P's, 2006).

275 Moody's, *Rating Methodology: Global Paper and Forest Products Industry* (Moody's, June 2006); *Rating Methodology: Global Chemical Industry* (Moody's, February 2006).

276 S&P's, note 274, 24.

277 Ibid. This is particularly in the case of real estate finance involving contaminated land: S&P's, *S&P's Structured Finance Ratings Real Estate Transactions: Environmental Criteria* (S&P's, 1997).

278 Davis, et al., note 112, 39–41, 115.

and CRISIL, India's main rating agency, to establish an SRI index for Indian corporate securities.[279]

The comparative evaluation processes provided by rating mechanisms constitute a form of market governance that may help improve the integrity of the SRI market in three crucial ways. First, the methodologies to select and rank companies constitute a normative benchmark for the whole SRI market, including companies not formally included in any ranking survey or index. In turn, the rating providers may draw from the criteria for corporate responsibility of international codes of conduct, such as the UNGC, thereby amplifying the influence of these primary norms. Second, the rating mechanisms provide sustainability benchmarks to aspire to. Some companies have sought inclusion in the SRI indexes provided by the New York and London stock exchanges for "public recognition of their corporate virtue."[280] Responsible investors may rely on SRI indexes, for instance, both as a benchmark to compare the progress of their SRI portfolio to the sustainability index and as a means of choosing assets that comply with the investor's preferred sustainability criteria. Third, the ultimate membership selections and rankings presented by the rating mechanisms constitute an instrument of market ordering. Firms that seek competitive advantages by association with a prestigious rating provider should be more disciplined to adhere to the rating criteria. Each mechanism helps communicate the standards of social investors to corporations in an understandable format. Together, these characteristics afford rating mechanisms a unique potential for enforcing CSR standards, as removal from or down-grading in a rating mechanism would focus the attention of shareholders and management in a way that bad publicity or criticism by an institutional investor may less likely be able to do.

Although rating institutions constitute a means of SRI governance, they themselves lack government supervision or regulation. Therefore, their influence heavily depends on the credibility of their data and evaluations. A seminal difference between CSR rating and conventional credit rating is that, presently, nearly all CSR rating is conducted on an unsolicited basis, and therefore is less susceptible to the conflicts of interest that allegedly mire some CRA services.[281] On other hand, the plethora of rating institutions and their diverse methods can engender confusion among market participants

---

279 "S&P's Indian SRI Index Signals Wider Move into Emerging Markets," *European Pensions and Investment News*, November 6, 2006.

280 Vogel, note 247, 64.

281 S. Rousseau, "Enhancing the Accountability of Credit Rating Agencies: The Case for a Disclosure-Based Approach," *McGill Law Journal* 51 (2006): 618.

and thereby hinder the influence of CSR ratings.[282] The challenge is to have CRAs and mainstream investment research incorporate the methodologies and findings of CSR ratings, currently occurring only to a limited extent, such as in the work of the Enhanced Analytics Initiative.[283]

The following section provides a small, representative sampling of these rating mechanisms, focusing on those that have garnered considerable interest in the SRI community.

B. SUSTAINABILITY INDEXES

1. General Characteristics

Sustainability indexes are a special type of market index designed to assess and compare social and environmental performances of public companies. A market index is a statistical indicator that represents the total value of the securities constituting it. Stock market indexes serve to track the price movements of listed securities, thereby providing a barometer for the state of a given market. Securities index providers commonly involve stock exchange companies, such as London's Financial Times Stock Exchange (FTSE). Some specialist SRI research providers and investment groups have also established SRI indexes. A sustainability index is distinctive by including only the firms that meet specified environmental and social criteria, possibly in addition to demonstrating financial robustness. Each index has its own inclusion criteria and data collecting methods. The first primitive SRI index was developed by Good Money in 1976 as an alternative to the Dow Jones Industrial and Utility Averages.[284] The Domini 400 Social Index, launched by KLD Research and Analytics in 1990, was the first comprehensive equity benchmark for social investors, and is one of fourteen SRI indexes provided by KLD as of January 2008. The following table details some providers of major SRI indexes (the entire field of such indexes being far too numerous to list).

Apart from general SRI indexes that reflect corporate sustainability performance, some specialist SRI indexes cater to discrete environmental issues

---

282 Å. Skillius and U. Wennberg, *Continuity, Credibility and Comparability: Key Challenges for Corporate Environmental Performance Measurement and Communication* (International Institute for Industrial Environmental Economics, Lund University, 1998), s. 5.2.

283 Http://www.enhancedanalytics.com.

284 J.A. Brill and A. Reder, *Investing From the Heart: The Guide to Socially Responsible Investments and Money Management* (Crown Publishers, 1993), 388–89.

Table 5: Sample of major sustainability indexes as of 2008

Index provider	Country	Sustainability indexes	Year launch
SAM Group	Australia	Australian SAM Sustainability Index	2005
Calvert	US	Calvert Social Index	2000
Citizens Funds	US	Citizens Index	1994
Dow Jones (DJ) and SAM Group	US	DJ World Sustainability Indexes	1999
		DJ Sustainability Indexes	2001
		DJ Sustainability Index 40	2001
		DJ Sustainability North American Indexes	2001
		DJ Euro Sustainability Indexes	2001
E. Capital Partners	Italy	Ethical Index Euro	2000
		Ethical Index Europe Small Cap	2003
		Ethical Index Global	2001
Ethibel	Belgium	Ethibel Sustainable Index (ESI) Global	2002
		ESI Americas	2002
		ESI Europe	2002
		ESI Asia Pacific	2002
FTSE	UK	FTSE4Good Global Index	2001
		FTSE4Good U.S. Index	2001
		FTSE4Good Europe Index	2001
		FTSE4Good UK Index	2001
		FTSE4Good Japan Index	2004
Jantzi Research	Canada	Jantzi Social Index	2000
Johannesburg Stock Exchange	South Africa	JSE Socially Responsible Index	2004
Kemplen Capital Management; SAM Asset Management	Netherlands	Kempen SNS Smaller Europe SRI Index	2003
KLD	US	Domini 400 Social Index	1990
		KLD Large Cap Social Index	2001
		KLD Broad Market Social Index	2001
		Global Sustainability Index	2007
Morningstar Japan	Japan	Morningstar SRI Index	2003
Sao Paulo Stock Exchange	Brazil	Bovespa Corporate Sustainability Index	2005

Table 5: Sample of major sustainability indexes as of 2008—cont'd

Index provider	Country	Sustainability indexes	Year launch
Tel Aviv Stock Exchange	Israel	Maala Socially Responsible Investing Index	2005
Vigeo	France	ASPI Eurozone 2001	2001

and risks. The JPMorgan Carbon Beta Index, for instance, overweights securities judged to have relatively lower risk due to climate change, and underweights companies with higher climate risk exposure.[285]

Each sustainability index includes only those companies sourced from a specific investment universe, such as European equities or US equities. Most indexes also cap the number of constituents, so if one company is excluded it is replaced immediately with another. The Dow Jones specialist SRI indexes typically have between 100 and 350 companies each.[286] Companies of course must have publicly traded stocks to be eligible for inclusion in an index. This mandate excludes some socially responsible companies that are not public firms (e.g., Ikea). The composition of each index is also usually determined by a market capitalization weighted formula. Usually an index includes only large firms, by reference to the total value of their traded shares. Consequently, the sustainability performances of small and medium market capitalized companies are often overlooked. Kempen Capital Management, a Dutch investment bank, is one of the few providers of a small capitalization SRI index.[287] Avshalom Adam and Tal Shavit contend that because the methodologies employed by the SRI indexes exclude many firms from the eligible investment universe, the incentive for most of the excluded corporations to improve their sustainability performance is blunted.[288]

The following sections examine in detail two of the main sets of sustainability indexes—the Dow Jones Sustainability Indexes and the FTSE4Good

285 JPMorgan, *Introducing the JENI-Carbon Beta Index* (JPMorgan, February 2007).

286 Http://www.sustainability-indexes.com.

287 Http://www.kempen.com.

288 A.M. Adam and T. Shavit, "How Can a Ratings-based Method for Assessing Corporate Social Responsibility (CSR) Provide an Incentive to Firms Excluded from Socially Responsible Investment Indices to Invest in CSR?," *Journal of Business Ethics* (2008): forthcoming.

Index Series. These indexes, through their connection with major international stock exchanges in New York and London, have the profile and market influence largely unobtainable by rival SRI indexes. Both indexes also include many financial institutions, mainly banks and investment firms.[289]

2. Dow Jones Sustainability Indexes (DJSIs)

The DJSIs were launched in 1999 to track the financial performance of what the provider claims are the leading CSR-driven companies worldwide.[290] As the first index created in this family, the DJS World Index comprises over 300 companies that represent the top 10 percent of the leading sustainability companies drawn from the DJ Global Indexes. Other indexes added to the family include the DJS North American Index, the DJS United States Index, and the DJS European Index.[291] They are reputed to have financially matched or outperformed some general market indexes.[292]

All indexes of the DJSI family are constructed according to the same CSR criteria, including general and industry-specific criteria covering three areas: environmental, economic, and social performances.[293] The Swiss-based Sustainable Asset Management (SAM) makes the evaluations. Using a business case model of CSR, SAM examines how corporate sustainability performance creates both financial risks and opportunities, thus providing a "financial quantification of corporate sustainability performance."[294] The business case model is further evident in SAM's definition of "corporate sustainability," namely: "a business approach to create long-term shareholder value by embracing opportunities and managing risks deriving from economic, environmental and social developments."[295] The general SAM assessment criteria include corporate governance, financial robustness, environmental management and performance, human rights, supply chain management, and labor practices.

---

289 W. Baue, "Banks and Financial Service Providers Figure Prominently in FTSE4Good Attrition, DJSI Matriculation," *Social Funds Sustainability Investment News*, September 8, 2005.

290 Http://www.sustainability-indexes.com.

291 DJSIs, *Guide to the Dow Jones Sustainability North America Index and the Dow Jones Sustainability Index* (DJSIs, September 2005).

292 P. Cerin and P. Dobers, "What Does the Performance of the Dow Jones Sustainability Index Tell Us?" *Eco-Management and Auditing* 8 (2001): 123.

293 DJSIs, *Dow Jones Sustainability World Indexes Guide* (DJSIs, September 2005).

294 Ibid., 15.

295 DJSIs, "Corporate Sustainability," at http://www.sustainability-index.com/07_htmle/sustainability/corpsustainability.html.

Table 6: DJSI—Environmental and social assessment criteria[296]

Criteria	Weighting (%)
Environmental Performance (eco-efficiency)	7.0%
Environmental Reporting	3.0%
Industry Specific Environmental Criteria	Depends on the industry
Corporate Citizenship/ Philanthropy	3.5%
Labor Practice Indicators	5.0%
Human Capital Development	5.5%
Social Reporting	3.0%
Talent Attraction and Retention	5.5%
Industry Specific Social Criteria	Depends on the industry

This information is assimilated and verified to obtain an overall "corporate sustainability score." This score apparently enables identification of leading sustainability companies in each sector. SAM also applies some limited negative screens to the DJSI World to create subset indexes that exclude companies involved in production of tobacco, alcohol, gambling, armaments, and firearms.

The DJSIs have some methodological weaknesses. One drawback is the heavy reliance on questionnaires completed by companies to assess their inclusion in the indexes.[297] Self-assessment by companies is not a rigorous method of evaluation.[298] The DJSI's questionnaires apparently have a response rate of below 30 percent, and only respondents are eligible for inclusion in the index.[299] Other information, of lesser importance, includes miscellaneous corporate documents and reports, media commentary, stakeholder reports,

---

296 DJSIs, "Corporate Sustainability Assessment Criteria," at http://www. sustainability-indexes.com/07_htmle/assessment/criteria.html.

297 DJSIs, "Information Sources," at http://www.sustainability-indexes.com/07_ htmle/assessment/infosources.html.

298 Although some independent research suggests that the DJSI World companies perform strongly on CSR indicators: J.E. Ricart, M.A. Rodriguez, and P. Sánchez, "Sustainability in the Boardroom: An Empirical Examination of Dow Jones Sustainability World Index Leaders," *Corporate Governance* 5(3) (2005): 24.

299 A. Chatterji and D. Levine, *Breaking Down The Wall of Codes: Evaluating Non-Financial Performance Measurement*, Working Paper Series No. 14 (Center for Responsible Business, University of California, Berkeley, 2005), 16.

and occasional direct contacts with companies. While the criteria and methodology of the index are publicly available, the collected data determining the composition of each DJSI are not generally disclosed. Another methodological weakness is the emphasis on economic factors (about 30 percent of the weighting) relative to environmental factors (about 10 percent), which is difficult to reconcile with the claims that the DJSIs reflect the leading companies for environmental sustainability performance.[300]

Helpfully, to maintain the integrity of each index, a "Corporate Sustainability Monitoring" system purports to verify "a company's involvement and management of critical environmental, economic and social crisis situations that can have a highly damaging effect on its reputation."[301] Further, each DJSI is reviewed annually and quarterly to ensure accurate reflection of the leading sustainability companies in the eligible pool of companies.[302] There is also a constant review to respond to extraordinary corporate actions, such as mergers and takeovers, which would affect the index composition.[303]

The Design and Advisory Committees are critical to the DJSI governance. The former comprises two representatives from each DJSI and the SAM Group. This Committee is the one responsible for conducting the annual and quarterly reviews, as well as the ongoing review of all extraordinary corporate actions. The Committee also verifies the integrity of market data and, ultimately, decides on the composition of the index. The DJSI Advisory Committee has ten independent financial sector advisors and CSR experts. Its primary mandate is "to give advice on possible implications for sustainability-driven portfolio management and offer input regarding the methodology."[304]

3. FTSE4Good Index Series

The FTSE4Good Index Series was launched by the Financial Times Stock Exchange (FTSE) Group in July 2001 with the intention of raising funds for UNICEF by donating licensing fees from the index. By 2007, FTSE4Good had grown to a family of five indexes covering global and major

---

300 S.J. Fowler and C. Hope, "A Critical Review of Sustainable Business Indices and their Impact," *Journal of Business Ethics* 76(3) (2007): 243, 248.
301 DJSIs, note 291, 13.
302 Ibid., 22–23.
303 Ibid., 24.
304 Ibid., 31.

regional markets.[305] The FTSE4Good Indexes are derived from the parent FTSE All-Share Index (UK) or the FTSE Developed Index (Global).

Unlike the DJSI, the methodology of the FTSE4Good Indexes does not focus on recognizing companies' relative performance. Rather, it sets threshold standards for companies' inclusion in the index. The FTSE periodically revises the standards, constantly moving the member companies to respond to ever-higher levels of sustainability performance to maintain their status in its indexes. This progressive tightening of criteria can be seen in the new climate change standards.[306] The FTSE4Good also differs from the DJSI in that it has a policy of active engagement and dialogue with companies. It is more proactive than other SRI index providers in pushing companies to improve their sustainability performance.[307]

The FTSE4Good also uses a mix of positive and negative screens. It includes companies that satisfy requirements in five areas: the environment, climate change, human rights, supply chain labor standards, and bribery suppression. On the flip side, it excludes companies connected to tobacco, nuclear weapons, nuclear energy or uranium mining. However, the FTSE4Good Policy Committee may eventually replace such exclusion criteria with purely performance-based criteria.

The FTSE4Good team devised detailed criteria to define three dimensions of sustainability.[308] Environmental criteria (detailed in the table below) assign companies a low, medium, or high impact rating according to the industry sector. Higher impact sectors incur more stringent index inclusion criteria. These criteria cover corporate environmental policy, management systems, and reporting practices. For example, a company in a high impact sector is required to adopt a formal EMS, while a company in a low impact sector is exempt.[309] Further, high impact companies must publish regular reports on their environmental policies and practices, which lower impact sector companies, need not do.

305 FTSE, *FTSE4Good Index Series Factsheet* (FTSE, 2006). Currently the benchmark indexes are: FTSE4Good Global, FTSE4Good UK, FTSE4Good Europe, FTSE4Good US and FTSE4Good Japan: http://www.ftse.com/Indices/FTSE4Good_Index_Series/Constituents.jsp.
306 FTSE, *FTSE4Good Climate Change Criteria* (FTSE, 2006).
307 Oulton, note 118, 199, 203.
308 FTSE International, *FTSE4Good Index Series Inclusion Criteria* (FTSE, 2006).
309 Ibid., 3.

Table 7: FTSE4Good Indexes—industry sector impacts[310]

High Impact Sectors	Medium Impact Sectors	Low Impact Sectors
Agriculture	DIY and building supplies	Information technology
Air transport	Electronic and electrical equipment	Media
Airports		Consumer / mortgage finance
Building materials (includes quarrying)	Energy and fuel distribution	Property investors
Chemicals and pharmaceuticals	Engineering and machinery	Research and development
Construction	Financials not elsewhere classified (see right)	Leisure not elsewhere classified (gyms and gaming)
Major systems engineering	Hotels, catering and facilities Management	Support services
Fast food chains	Manufacturers not elsewhere classified	Telecoms
Food, beverages and tobacco	Ports	Wholesale distribution
Forestry and paper	Printing and newspaper publishing	
Mining and metals	Property developers	
Oil and gas	Retailers not elsewhere classified	
Power generation	Vehicle hire	
Road distribution and shipping	Public transport	
Supermarkets		
Vehicle manufacture		
Waste		
Water		
Pest control		

Like the DJSI, the FTSE4Good retains an SRI consultancy group, EIRIS, to gather data and assess companies according to the FTSE4Good criteria. EIRIS relies on questionnaires, direct contact, and company reports for its evaluations. A specialist FTSE committee retains the ultimate responsibility for decisions to include or exclude a company from the Indexes. The FTSE4Good Policy Committee, whose membership is drawn from corporations, academia, NGOs, and the financial sector, conducts semi-annual reviews of the FTSE4Good Indexes as well as oversees the design and approval of criteria revisions or introductions.

The FTSE4Good indexes appear influential because they provide the basis for regional and global SRI index tracker funds as well as for asset selection

310 FTSE, *FTSE4Good Index Series Inclusion Criteria* (FTSE, 2006), 3.

by actively managed investment portfolios. According to the FTSE, its SRI indexes help "investors to navigate through the plethora of corporate social responsibility (CSR) codes and standards around the world."[311] A 2004 study of the FTSE4Good's impact on corporate behavior suggests that it has affected the internal operations of listed companies, particularly their reporting strategies, policy decisions, and management systems.[312] As of early 2007, some twenty companies had been removed for not meeting the human rights criteria, and eighty-five excluded for not meeting the environmental criteria.[313] Another forty-one firms were removed under the semi-annual reviews of the FTSE4Good Indexes conducted during the remainder of 2007.[314]

C. SRI RESEARCH AND ADVOCACY FORUMS

A significant facet of the nongovernmental governance of the SRI market is the work of many research, consultancy, and advocacy bodies. These market and civil society institutions perform many functions, including sharing information, raising awareness, building consensus for action, disseminating best practice examples, and encouraging policy advocacy. They assist governance via many avenues: evaluating and ranking corporate sustainability performance for financial transactions; analyzing SRI market trends; disseminating information through conferences, web sites, and reports; and facilitating direct changes in behavior through protests and pressure tactics. The major SRI research and advocacy forums include:

- Association of Investors for Sustainable Development (Netherlands)
- Association for Sustainable and Responsible Investment in Asia
- Belgian Sustainable and Socially Responsible Investment Forum
- Council for Socially Responsible Investment (New Zealand)
- European Social Investment Forum
- German Sustainable Investment Forum
- Interfaith Center on Corporate Responsibility (US)
- Investor Responsibility Research Center (US)
- Italian Forum for Sustainable Finance

---

311 FTSE, *FTSE4Good Index Series Factsheet* (FTSE, 2006).
312 G. Cobb, et al., "FTSE4Good: Perceptions and Performance" (paper presented at the Seventh Alternative Perspectives on Finance Conference, Stockholm University, August 8–10, 2004).
313 FTSE, *FTSE4Good Index Series Factsheet* (FTSE, 2007).
314 FTSE, *Semi-annual Review of the FTSE4Good Indices* (FTSE, September 2007), 1; FTSE, *Semi-annual Review of the FTSE4Good Indices* (FTSE, March 2007), 1.

- Responsible Investment Association of Australasia
- Shareholder Association for Research and Education (Canada)
- Social Investment Forum (US)
- Social Investment Organization (Canada)
- Sweden Forum for Sustainable Investment
- UK Social Investment Forum

Most of these examples are member associations mainly for SRI professionals and investment institutions providing information resources, networking, and coordination for policy change advocacy. They provide annual surveys of the SRI markets in their jurisdiction, publish various reports on aspects of SRI, prepare submissions to government on policy reforms, and facilitate dialogue between SRI practitioners and the NGO community. The Australian association, the RIAA, even pioneered an SRI label scheme, as discussed earlier in this chapter. While they are not formal corporate ranking services, their work contributes indirectly to the evaluation and the rating of corporate social and environmental performance, and consequently SRI norm-building. The process by which companies collect and respond to questionnaires, surveys, and other information requests may help them to reflect upon their social and environmental performance, possibly with a view to making organizational and policy changes.

Some of these SRI research institutions have lobbied and pressured governments for reforms. For instance, Canada's SIO has campaigned to amend Canadian pension fund legislation to require SRI policies disclosure.[315] The SIO has also, along with the chief executive officers of some mutual fund companies, called on Canada's political parties to take action on climate change and introduce GHG reduction targets to meet Canada's Kyoto obligations.[316] Other national SRI associations have performed similar roles in their jurisdictions.

In addition to these SRI networks, market actors such as associations of institutional investors have collaborated to promote governance standards for SRI. These groups include the Canadian Coalition of Good Governance,[317] the Council of Institutional Investors,[318] and the International Corporate

---

315 B.J. Richardson, "Financing Environmental Change: A New Role for Canadian Environmental Law," *McGill Law Journal* 49(1) (2004): 145, 177.

316 D. Rolfe, et al., "An Open Letter to Prime Minister Stephen Harper, Liberal Leader Bill Graham, NDP Leader Jack Layton, Bloc Quebecois Leader Gilles Duceppe" (SIO, November 16, 2006).

317 Http://www.ccgg.ca.

318 Http://www.cii.org.

Governance Network.[319] Several investor coalitions have formed subsidiary groups targeting specific SRI concerns. Climate change is one example, in response to which investors have set up various protocols: the Carbon Disclosure Project[320] (gathering information from companies to assess the financial risks posed by global warming); the Institutional Investors Group on Climate Change[321] (for exchanging information on the material risks to and opportunities for businesses associated with climate change); and the Investor Network on Climate Risk (addressing financial risks implicated with climate change).[322]

Another facet is the specialist agencies providing SRI advice and research to investors. These include Mercer Management Consulting,[323] Innovest,[324] Enhanced Analytics Initiative,[325] EIRIS,[326] and KLD Research and Analytics.[327] Depending on their specific function, they may evaluate corporate environmental performance, research the state of the SRI market, or provide management tools for investors to integrate environmental, social, and governance factors into their financial decisions. Their influence can be significant when major investors use their services. For instance, the Norwegian Government Pension Fund's Council on Ethics appointed EIRIS, and the Swedish AP pension funds' Ethical Council appointed GES Investment Services, to help screen companies. These consultancy bodies are particularly crucial to enhancing the capacity of financial markets to measure the financial significance of corporate environmental performance and to incorporate such information into investment analyses. Some leaders in the SRI industry believe that the surveys, reports, and rankings of Mercer Consulting and similar bodies contribute to a form of "peer" regulation, which can be more influential than government policies in facilitating changes.[328]

Apart from industry-linked SRI associations and research providers, various civil society groups increasingly scrutinize financiers.[329] Some environmental

---

319 Http://www.icgn.org.

320 Http://www.cdproject.net.

321 Http://www.iigcc.org.

322 Http://www.incr.com.

323 Http://www.mercermc.com.

324 Http://www.innovestgroup.com.

325 Http://www.enhanced-analytics.com.

326 Http://www.eiris.org.

327 Http://www.kld.com.

328 Personal communication, Louise O'Halloran, Executive Director, Responsible Investment Association (Sydney, December 8, 2005).

329 WWF and BankTrack, *Shaping the Future of Sustainable Finance: Moving from Paper Promises to Performance* (WWF, 2006); C. Berger, *False Profits: How Australia's*

NGOs now demand from banks and pension funds the same level of account-ability and transparency they have long sought from governments and corpo-rations.[330] NGOs seek to change the behavior of companies by targeting their financial sponsors, by tarnishing companies' reputations, and mobilizing shareholder pressure against the management.[331] Notably, BankTrack dedi-cates itself specifically to financial sector issues, focusing particularly on the Equator banks.[332] The Belgium group Netwerk Vlaanderen has a campaign slogan "My Money—Clear Conscience?" and aims to demonstrate to finan-ciers what their responsibilities are.[333] In recent years, it has taken protest action, dialogue, and shareholder pressure against the Dutch bank Internationale Nederlanden Groug and other institutions for financing weap-ons manufacturers including the production of cluster bombs.[334] In the US, the National Community Reinvestment Coalition periodically publishes a survey that ranks US lenders according to their level of service to minorities and disadvantaged populations. One recent report ranks lenders based on the portion of home purchases and refinance loans made to the traditionally underserved communities while examining the general lending patterns in these metropolitan communities.[335]

Another example is the campaign in the late 1990s by the British student-run group, People and Planet, to get the UK Universities Superannuation Scheme (USS) to adopt a credible ethical investment policy and to use its shareholding power to encourage CSR.[336] The USS has since become one of the most progressive and responsible institutional investors in the UK, which Steve Waygood substantially attributes to the People and Planet campaign.[337]

Finance Sector Undervalues the Environment (Australian Conservation Foundation, 2006).

330 D.H. Schepers, "The Impact of NGO Network Conflict on the Corporate Social Responsibility Strategies of Multinational Corporations," *Business and Society* 45(3) (2006): 282.

331 S. Waygood, *Capital Market Campaigning: The Impact of NGOs on Companies, Shareholder Value and Reputational Risk* (Risk Books, 2006).

332 Http://www.banktrack.org.

333 Http://www.netwerkvlaanderen.be.

334 Netwerk Vlaanderen, *Explosive Investments: Financial Institutions and Cluster Munitions* (Netwerk Vlaanderen, February 2007).

335 Http://www.ncrc.org. Among its reports, see National Community Reinvestment Coalition (NCRC), *America's Best and Worst Lenders: A Consumers' Guide to Lending in 25 Metropolitan Markets* (NCRC, 2003); NCRC, *The 2005 Fair Lending Disparities: Stubborn and Persistent II* (NCRC, 2006).

336 Waygood, note 331, 90–106.

337 Ibid., 102–3.

Another successful example cited by Waygood is the WWF's campaign to protect the Arctic Wildlife Refuge from British Petroleum exploration by lobbying institutional investors with large shareholdings in this corporate behemoth to exert pressure on its management.[338]

In the US, the Rainforest Action Network has been one of the most active NGOs to campaign against financial institutions. In 2000, it targeted Citigroup in its Global Finance Campaign, blaming the global bank for destruction of tropical forests and disruption of the livelihoods of Indigenous peoples.[339] The Rainforest Action Network's campaign included site protest actions outside Citigroup offices. In 2004, Citigroup adopted a series of new environmental policy measures that the Network hailed as a vindication of its pressure.[340] More recently, the Rainforest Action Network has launched a campaign against major Wall Street financiers (e.g., Citibank, JPMorgan Chase, and Merrill Lynch) for supporting the Bush administration's plans to expand the coal-powered utility sector with scores of new power plants. The Network has also targeted Canadian banks (e.g., Scotiabank, and TD-CanadaTrust Bank) for financing energy and forestry operations in the northern boreal forests.[341]

These vignettes are merely a fraction of the examples of market and civil society institutions exerting pressure on the financial sector for responsible investment. Their research, ratings, advice, and advocacy assist with making SRI more transparent, accountable, and effective. It would be advantageous however if the major SRI codes and other standards, including official SRI regulations, gave such bodies greater formal standing in SRI governance. The limited involvement of nongovernmental institutions from the emerging economies is the other principal limitation of this valuable work. The SRI actors and networks mainly comprise developed country interests, which invariably creates some biases and blind spots to the possible detriment of peoples in the South.

VI. Verdict

Non-state actors play an increasingly influential role in SRI governance. Their mechanisms of governance include normative frameworks, process

---

338 Ibid., 106–36.
339 Http://ran.org/what_we_do/global_finance.
340 Http://www.citigroup.com/citigroup/environment/initiatives.htm.
341 See http://ran.org/what_we_do/global_finance/resources/canadian_banks.

standards, management systems, and rating systems. Normative frameworks furnish guidance on best practices and acceptable performance. Process guidelines enable an organization's performance to be assessed, verified, and communicated. Management systems guide the integration of corporate codes of conduct in strategic and day-to-day corporate management. Finally, rating mechanisms provide comparative evaluation of businesses to help SRI institutions' selection of assets and engagement with companies.

Is the fragmented, smorgasbord of norms and institutions the most effective way to achieve a more sustainable society through the financial sector? Presently the behavioral impact of these norms and institutions lacks comprehensive empirical verification, although there are reasons for concern. Many banks and investors have subscribed to codes of conduct, issued policy statements, established new organizational units, and changed their environmental risk assessment procedures. However, the impact of these changes on the companies that they finance is much harder to demonstrate.

Some reliance on private mechanisms of governance is inevitable given the available alternatives. Despite international agreements to liberalize financial services, governments have retained some authority to regulate at a national and international level the environmental and social impacts of investment. For instance, the GATS in regard to financial services includes a so-called "prudential carve-out" allowing states to enact public interest regulation to control unwelcome side effects of financial markets.[342] However, governments have been unwilling to use the prudential carve-out power to address issues related to the SRI market. Official laws and policies directed to SRI canvassed in the previous chapter leave various issues unresolved. Nor have governments been willing to cooperate to enact international financial agreements that would impose substantive standards for ethical and responsible financing. These lacunae in hard law—in both the national and international spheres—have thus been left to soft law standards to fill. Yet, these nongovernmental institutions and mechanisms are vulnerable to usurpation and co-option by the very market forces they should govern.

Voluntary governance mechanisms have hardly provided a total solution to the void in traditional regulation. Mechanisms such as the UNPRI and EPs have been relatively successful at asserting global norms for financiers' social and environmental conduct compared to competitor standards, such as civil society groups' Collevecchio Declaration. Yet, these regimes fare poorly on various criteria of good governance, such as inclusiveness, transparency,

---

342 L.E. Panourgias, *Banking Regulation and World Trade Law: GATS, EU and "Prudential" Institution-Building* (Hart Publishing, 2006).

stringency, monitoring, and enforcement. While the former codes enjoy growing support from the financial community, and states have not sought to challenge them, many NGOs have to be persuaded that they are worthy of support. Many people see "a substantial gap between discourse and practice with respect to virtually all codes and voluntary standards."[343] In the absence of a strong business case, firms may lag in their voluntary commitments, especially during times of economic hardship that compel belt-tightening. Voluntary mechanisms can thus amount to greenwash.[344] The gushing rhetoric about the burgeoning number of signatories to the UNEPFI or UNPRI deflects attention from the ultimate issues, namely, whether those signatories actually change their behavior and of those firms they finance.

So far, it is clear that the financial institutions that have committed to SRI standards are overwhelmingly from Western Europe, and to a lesser extent, from North America and Oceania. These are regions characterized by high levels of political and civil rights, mature markets, and active civil society organizations. Conversely, countries without these conditions lack a major impetus for their companies to adopt SRI codes of conduct.[345] Corporate policies and strategies are more likely to address environmental issues if this is demanded or induced by the institutional context.

But if only voluntary standards and codes are likely to be tolerated by financial markets and international policy-makers in the near future, what improvements can we realistically expect?

First, should the numerous standards be harmonized into fewer, comprehensive governance frameworks? The complexity and institutional diversity of financial markets with financiers pursuing different roles would favor the continued evolution of sector and function-specific governance mechanisms. And the number and diversity of separate codes and standards may also protect against their total evisceration by recalcitrant market forces. On the other hand, arguments for consolidation of governance tools include decreased confusion and costs for implementation by organizations. For example, the numerous, competing corporate rating tools use different methodologies. Further, the interrelationships between normative, process, and management

---

343 Vogel, note 247, 164.

344 S. Wood, "Green Revolution or Greenwash? Voluntary Environmental Standards, Public Law and Private Authority in Canada," *in New Perspectives on the Public-Private Divide,* ed. Law Commission of Canada (University of British Columbia Press, 2002), 123; G. Johnson, *Don't Be Fooled 2005: America's Ten Worst Greenwashers* (The Green Life, 2004).

345 Wright and Rwabizambuga, note 57, 90, 100–4.

system based governance mechanisms are poorly defined; they each perform distinct and valuable governance functions, but tend to interact randomly and incoherently. For instance, signatories to the EPs may be concurrent signatories to different normative codes that prescribe conflicting standards.

Second, the voluntary mechanisms are deficient in the implementation and enforcement side.[346] Market institutions such as stock exchanges could be better harnessed as surrogate regulators, such as by moving beyond the current sustainability indexes by requiring companies to meet environmental standards as a precondition for stock exchange listing. Public involvement should be expanded for monitoring and enforcing the codes of conduct such as the EPs and the UNEPFI statements. Signatories must publicly disclose their implementation of codes, and have their statements independently audited. Further, financiers should be accountable not only to their shareholders and other supporters, but also to the communities whose livelihoods are affected by the projects they finance. Creating mechanisms for community accountability such as the World Bank Inspection Panel or the IFC's Office of the Compliance Advisor/Ombudsman should be a priority for SRI codes.[347]

A third notable aspect of the current menu of SRI governance tools is their characteristic as primarily informational policy instruments. They serve to communicate, evaluate, and rank corporate environmental performance for interested responsible investors. Even the normative codes are mainly directed towards motivating financiers to become more transparent. Such information feeds the ethical concerns of investors, and may also influence the market value of businesses by disclosing other factors that affect earning and profitability, such as possible liabilities.[348] In this respect, they dovetail with trends in official regulation geared towards transparency measures. However, even as transparency measures several standards and codes lack mandatory disclosures, and virtually none promote more democratic decision-making in

---

346 A. Kolk, R. van Tulder, and C. Welters, "International Codes of Conduct and Corporate Social Responsibility: Can Transnational Corporations Regulate Themselves?" *Transnational Corporations* 8(1) (1999): 143, 167–70.

347 D. Hunter, "The Emergence of Citizen Enforcement in International Organizations," in *Proceedings of the Seventh International Conference on Environmental Compliance and Enforcement*, Volume 2 (International Network for Environmental Compliance and Enforcement, 2005), 229.

348 R. Repetto and D. Austin, *Coming Clean: Corporate Disclosure of Financially Significant Environmental Risks* (World Resources Institute, 2000); A. Campanale, "Green Investment: Incentive for Disclosure," *Review of European Community and International Environmental Law* 3(1) (1994): 43.

investment decisions. Taking steps in this direction should be central to the next generation of SRI governance regimes.

Finally, current SRI standards and codes have lamentably been deficient in emphasizing the ethical responsibilities of the financial sector. Apart from perhaps the Collevecchio Declaration, CERES Principles, and the GRI, the other SRI governance standards mostly reflect a business case approach to corporate responsibility. A clearer ethical commitment to sustainability, not routinely contingent on financial materiality or other business rationales, could be developed following the example of the Earth Charter.[349] In response to the UN's failure to adopt an Earth Charter at the 1992 Rio Summit,[350] the NGO delegates drafted their own Earth Charter based on ethical and "ecocentric" defined responsibilities to the planet.[351] The IUCN Draft International Covenant on Environment and Development takes a similar approach.[352]

The Earth Charter now provides a framework for a raft of initiatives promoted by civil society groups. It stresses interconnected issues of ecological integrity, human rights, poverty eradication, democracy, and other like fundamental concepts.[353] In relation to financial markets, however, the Earth Charter only vaguely requests "multinational corporations and international financial organizations to act transparently in the public good, and hold them accountable for the consequences of their activities."[354] Klaus Bosselmann argues that the progressive "Earth Charter thus illustrates the potential of the NGO sector to step ahead of states and forge new environmental norms," and that it "provides the values and principles for a sustainable future."[355]

---

349 See K. Bosselmann, "In Search of Global Law: The Significance of the Earth Charter," *Worldviews: Environment, Culture and Religion* 8(1) (2004): 62.

350 Substituted by the relatively tame Rio Declaration on the Environment and Development, ILM 31 (1992): 874.

351 Published in Pacific Institute of Resource Management, ed., *Commitment for the Future: The Earth Charter and Treaties agreed to by the International NGOs and Social Movement* (Pacific Institute of Resource Management, 1992).

352 Drafted in 1995 and revised in 2001 and 2004: IUCN Commission on Environmental Law, *Draft International Covenant on Environment and Development. Third edition: Updated text* (IUCN, 2004). Article 2 states: "Nature as a whole warrants respect: The integrity of the Earth's ecological systems shall be maintained and restored. Every form of life is unique and is safeguarded independent of its value to humanity."

353 Http://www.earthcharter.org.

354 Ibid., Principle 12.

355 K. Bosselmann, "Ecological Justice and the Law," in *Environmental Law for Sustainability*, note 34, 129, 162.

Despite the considerable limitations of the panoply of voluntary standards for SRI, they are not without merit. The drawbacks of alternate routes to international environmental regulation are well known. It was governments' inability or unwillingness to regulate financial institutions and corporate conduct that prompted civil society and responsible investor groups to take the lead. The failure of states to adopt the UN Norms on the Responsibilities of Transnational Corporations illustrates this shortcoming.[356] When governments fail to regulate international financial markets, the advantages of the current array of instruments become even more apparent, as they help to overcome the shortcomings of global politics where agreement on intergovernmental policies and regulations can take many years to happen. Over the long term, nonetheless, current SRI governance beyond the state is very likely to be insufficient to regulate the unseen polluters.

---

356 In early 2005 the UN Commission on Human Rights declined to endorse the Norms: UN Economic and Social Council, Sub-Commission on the Promotion and Protection of Human Rights, *Report of the United Nations High Commissioner on Human Rights on the Responsibilities of Transnational Corporations and Other Business Enterprises with Regards to Human Rights*, UN Doc. E/CN.4/2005/91 (2005).

CHAPTER 7

The SRI Agenda: Climate Change and Indigenous Peoples

I. Introduction

It is now time to look more closely at SRI in practice: to assess how and why financiers respond to specific social and environmental issues; and to illuminate how law shapes their behavior. Case studies help to explain financiers' attention to some SRI issues, and their disregard of others.

This chapter looks at Indigenous peoples and climate change, primarily for two reasons. First, these examples contrast the business and ethical drivers for SRI. Climate change garners much more interest than Indigenous peoples. This disparity is not merely because climate change is a global threat of potential concern to all, in contrast to the limited number of jurisdictions with Indigenous denizens. The divergent responses of social investors also derive from how markets more readily conceptualize global warming as a business case issue. In particular, climate change offers new financial opportunities to savvy investors in the renewable energy and environmental technology sectors. Conversely, Indigenous peoples do not offer the same financial upside, rather tending to be construed as primarily an issue of financial risk stemming from Indigenous land claims and protests on areas sought for resource development. Second, these case studies reveal SRI's dependency on good regulation. SRI will stagger along without regulatory drivers and controls. It cannot effectively address climate change without complementary governmental interventions, such as economic instruments for carbon trading and taxing. Likewise, without legal protocols to negotiate with and compensate affected communities, project financing will much less likely accommodate Indigenous peoples' concerns.

In contrast to the colossal attention given to climate change among some investors, evident in such pioneering initiatives as the CDP and the INCR, investors often treat Indigenous peoples as an ephemeral or marginal issue. While climate change certainly poses extremely grave threats, presently they are mostly distant and abstract concerns. Conversely, Indigenous peoples' interests have long spawned considerable litigation and conflict that often remains unresolved. Although Indigenous peoples comprise less than 5 percent of the world's population, they have a proportionately larger stake in land and environmental resources that amplifies their significance. In Australia, Aboriginal peoples comprise some 2.2 percent of the population and in 2006 owned or controlled 16 percent of the land.[1] In the US, in 2004 approximately 1.4 percent of the population was identified as American Indian or Alaskan Native,[2] and they hold about 5 percent of all land.[3] Moreover, according to the UN, some 80 percent of the planet's biodiversity is found within Indigenous communities' ancestral territories.[4]

Despite such presence, Indigenous peoples lack commensurate recognition as an SRI issue. Belatedly, a few investment circles have started to rectify this anomaly. Commendably, in the US, the SIF has established an Indigenous Peoples' Task Force to raise awareness among financiers about Native American peoples.[5] In Canada, the Ethical Funds Company has pioneered shareholder advocacy for Indigenous interests. Also, fears of climate change itself have drawn attention to the likelihood that Indigenous peoples will be among its first victims; living closest to nature, their subsistence livelihoods face ruin by the changing ecological conditions.[6]

---

1 Figures provided by the Australian Institute of Aboriginal and Torres Strait Islander Studies in "Native Title Resource Guide," at http://ntru.aiatsis.gov.au/research/resourceguide.

2 US Census Bureau, *The American Community - American Indians and Alaskan Natives: 2004* (US Department of Commerce, 2007), 1.

3 Remarks, R. Adamson, President of First Nations Development Institute (18th Annual SRI in the Rockies Conference, Santa Ana Pueblo, New Mexico, November 3–6, 2007).

4 UN Economic and Social Council, *Secretary-General's Note for the Multi-Stake Holder Dialogue Segment of the Second Preparatory Committee Addendum No. 3: Dialogue Paper by Indigenous People* E/CN.17/2002/PC.2/6.Add.5 (January 2002), 1.

5 Http://www.socialinvest.org/projects/indigenous.cfm.

6 See J. Hand, "Climate Change and Indian Tribes" (paper presented at the 5th Worldwide Colloquium of the IUCN Academy of Environmental Law, Paraty, Brazil, May 31 – June 5, 2007).

This chapter thus investigates financiers' responses to these SRI causes, leading to the conclusion that issues readily framed within the business case discourse are likely to garner the most interest. Conversely, ethical imperatives, such as claims to a fairer distribution of resources or moral arguments for cultural self-determination, are not so easily accommodated into the prevailing SRI discourse. This demonstrates, in part, the obstacles to quantifying the financial risks associated with ethical issues. In both cases, the legal system can sometimes play a crucial role in structuring how investors perceive and respond to SRI issues.

Case studies of specific SRI issues foster a deeper, nuanced understanding of the drivers for SRI and how the legal system shapes the market.[7] Research sponsored by UNEPFI on the sectoral challenges for SRI is among its most valuable contributions to the financial community. For example, UNEPFI's Biodiversity and Ecosystem Services Work stream is helping investors to identify and resolve the financial dimensions of loss of biodiversity and the degradation of ecological services.[8] Similarly, UNEPFI's Water and Finance Stream has published guidelines on the risks and financial opportunities in the water sector.[9]

Another stream of empirical research that is helping to illuminate SRI priorities and drivers is the cataloguing of SRI actions and surveys of the attitudes of social investors. Shareholder advocacy records indicate that corporate governance, product quality, and environmental management issues usually motivate SRI activists much more than human rights matters. Kathleen Rehbein and others found that shareholder activists file resolutions concerning product quality and corporate environmental performance more than other CSR issues.[10] Robert Monks and colleagues documented that, of the 671 shareholder proposals filed at large US corporations between 2000 and 2003, just over half concerned traditional corporate governance topics while the balance addressed various CSR topics.[11] Of the latter, climate change and renewable energy were among the main concerns. Another survey,

7 E.g., R. Holmstrom, ed., *Upscaling Social Investment: 50 Case Studies* (International Association of Investors in the Social Economy, 2000).

8 UNEPFI, "Biodiversity and Ecosystem Services: Bloom or Bust?" *CEO Briefing* (October 2007).

9 O. Jensen and C. Namazie, *Half Empty or Half Empty?* (UNEPFI, October 2007).

10 K. Rehbein, S. Waddock, and S. Graves, "Understanding Shareholder Activism: Which Corporations are Targeted?" *Business and Society* 43 (2004): 239.

11 R. Monks, A. Miller, and J. Cook, "Shareholder Activism on Environmental Issues: A Study of Proposals at Large US Corporations (2000–2003)," *Natural Resources Forum* 28 (2004): 317.

asking UK pension funds what factors would most likely affect market value, revealed the quality of customer relations and good corporate governance as having the greatest significance, and respect for community needs in developing countries as having the least.[12] An earlier survey by Marc Epstein and Martin Freedman concluded that investors are most interested in data on the quality of products and environmental performance, and least interested in social issues, such as charity donations, community involvement, and diversity policies.[13] These findings are broadly congruent with the arguments of this chapter about the relative importance of climate change (largely perceived as an environmental issue) and Indigenous peoples (mainly perceived as a social issue).

The following sections examine the different investment philosophies and methods applied to climate change and Indigenous peoples. They also explore how SRI governance mechanisms modulate the response of financiers. Hopefully, through these and other case studies, the potential and the limits of SRI as a means to regulate the unseen polluters can be better discerned.

II. Protecting Indigenous Peoples Through SRI

A. INDIGENOUS PEOPLES AND THE FINANCIAL ECONOMY

Indigenous peoples[14] share common experiences of subjugation, dispossession, exclusion, and discrimination.[15] There are some 300–500 million Indigenous peoples worldwide, dispersed in more than seventy countries, including Australia, New Zealand, and countries in North America and Scandinavia.[16]

---

12 C. Gribben and M. Gitsham, *Will UK Pension Funds Become More Responsible? A Survey of Trustees* (JustPensions, UKSIF, 2006), 6.

13 M. Epstein and M. Freedman, "Social Disclosure and the Individual Investor," *Accounting, Auditing and Accountability Journal* 7 (1994): 94.

14 They are also sometimes known as Aboriginal peoples or First Nations, among various descriptions.

15 E.I. Daes, "Standard-Setting Activities: Evolution of Standards Concerning the Rights of Indigenous People," UN ESCOR Sub-Commission on Prevention of Discrimination and Protection of Minorities, UN Doc. E/CN.4/Sub.2/AC.4/1996/2, P. 26 (1996), 69.

16 J. Burger, *The Gaia Atlas of First Peoples: A Future for the Indigenous World* (Doubleday Books, 1990), 18–19, 180–85; UN Permanent Forum on Indigenous Issues, *Indigenous Peoples, Indigenous Voices* (UN Department of Public Information, 2007), 12.

There are also substantial Indigenous communities in developing countries.[17] Aboriginal land and resource rights, self-government, and other familiar indicia of Indigenous self-determination have become insufficient to protect and revitalize their communities. Traditionally, Indigenous peoples have seen governments as the only significant power to reckon with.[18] Now, the growth of corporate power and financial markets has created another threat. Land rights lose some of their luster when Indigenous communities are starved of investments to build a local economy. Conversely, they may face pressure to accommodate environmentally and culturally inappropriate investments, such as large-scale mining and other resource projects financed by international banks.

Many peoples in the so-called "developing countries" suffered this fate, dashing their hopes for prosperity in the wake of decolonization. The inequalities of the global economic system denying them fair trade, equitable access to capital resources, and independent control over their economic policy have left many of these people destitute.[19] Post-colonial scholarship illustrates how formal political sovereignty may obfuscate ongoing oppression of the developing world under the guise of economic relations.[20] Likewise, Indigenous peoples are starting to appreciate that they must look beyond their relationship to the state to obtain recognition and protection of their cultural and legal interests. They must also reckon with the financial sector, which plays a pivotal role in sponsoring economic development of potential harm or benefit to them.

The finance sector affects Indigenous peoples in primarily two ways. First, it finances projects and companies that alter Indigenous livelihoods,

---

17 E.g., Ache (Paraguay), Mapuche (Chile), Miskito (Nicaragua), Batwa (Central Africa), Bushmen (Southern Africa), Cordillera (the Philippines), and Ami (Taiwan).

18 P. McHugh, *Aboriginal Societies and the Common Law* (Oxford University Press, 2004), 315–64.

19 See S. George, *A Fate Worse Than Debt* (Penguin Books, 1990); I. Wallerstein, "Dependence in an Interdependent World: The Limited Possibilities of Transformation within the Capitalist World Economy," *African Studies Review* 17 (1974): 1; S. Amin, *Unequal Development: An Essay on the Social Formations of Peripheral Capitalism* (Monthly Review Press, 1976); R.P. Buckley, "International Capital Flows, Economic Sovereignty and Developing Countries," in *Yearbook of International and Financial Law*, ed. J.J. Norton (Kluwer Law, 1999), 17.

20 See G. Rajan and R. Mohanram, eds, *Postcolonial Discourse and Changing Cultural Contexts* (Greenwood Press, 1995); P. Williams and L. Chrisman, eds, *Colonial Discourse and Post-Colonial Theory: A Reader* (Longman, 1994).

such as large infrastructure projects.[21] Tied to the land, Indigenous peoples are very place-based and therefore acutely vulnerable to ecological changes that disturb their homelands. They have been displaced by such intrusions as the Ok Tedi mine (Papua New Guinea), Freeport mine (Indonesia), Narmada dam (India), Jabiluka mine (Australia), and Sakhalin pipeline (Russia). The expansion of Freeport mine was, according to BankTrack, "only made possible by a massive capital raising campaign, in which banks underwrote new equity shares and bonds, and lent hundreds of millions of dollars in general purpose loans."[22] Too often, lenders only belatedly, and defensively, acknowledge the impacts of such ventures when protests and other actions create reputational risks and expensive delays for them.

The second way the finance sector threatens Indigenous peoples is less specific and difficult to quantify, involving the propagation of values controversial for them during the development process.[23] Aboriginal communities have a long history of participation in markets and trading,[24] often engendering costly and unwelcome cultural change.[25] Consider, for instance, the stark differences in the environmental values between Indigenous cultures and Western capitalist societies. In contrast to the instrumental and utilitarian views of nature in industrial capitalism, Indigenous peoples traditionally perceived themselves as part of the community of nature, being vulnerable to its ecological fluctuations, and thus aware that misuse of the environment

---

21 E.g., C. Ballard and G. Banks, "Resource Wars: The Anthropology of Mining," *Annual Review Anthropology* 32 (2003): 287; A. Gedicks, *The New Resource Wars: Native and Environmental Struggles Against Multinational Corporations* (South End Press, 1993).

22 BankTrack, *The Role of the Financial Services Sector in Respecting Human Rights* (BankTrack, 2006), 3.

23 J. Nash, "Indigenous Development Alternatives," *Urban Anthropology and Studies of Cultural Systems and World Economic Development* 32 (2003): 57; C.C. Chi, "Capitalist Expansion and Indigenous Land Rights: Emerging Environmental Justice Issues in Taiwan," *Asia Pacific Journal of Anthropology* 2(2) (2001): 135.

24 E.g., A.J. Ray, *Indians in the Fur Trade* (University of Toronto Press, 1974).

25 The resistance of many Indigenous peoples to the appropriation and commercialization of their traditional knowledge is one example. For instance, the 1993 *Mataatua Declaration on the Cultural and Intellectual Property Rights of Indigenous Peoples* (clauses 2.6–2.8) states: "Commercialisation of any traditional plants and medicines of Indigenous peoples must be managed by the Indigenous peoples who have inherited such knowledge. A moratorium on any further commercialization of Indigenous medicinal plants and human genetic materials must be declared until Indigenous communities have developed appropriate protection mechanisms": at http://www.ankn.uaf.edu/IKS/mataatua.html.

would inevitably reverberate and harm their livelihoods.[26] While their environmental track-record is certainly not untainted, Indigenous peoples have generally been much better environmental stewards.[27] As Indigenous lands and resources have become conscripted into economic development to service global needs, Indigenous peoples have become increasingly drawn into the world market to the detriment of their traditional values.[28]

The existing international laws concerning Indigenous peoples pay no attention to the financial sector. The International Labor Organization (ILO) Convention No. 169 (1989)[29] and the UN Declaration on the Rights of Indigenous Peoples (2007)[30] both disregard the financial and corporate sectors.[31] This is a curious omission for otherwise pioneering instruments that putatively recognize Indigenous peoples as having an international legal personality. By failing to impose responsibilities on businesses to respect Indigenous rights, the ILO Convention and UN Declaration conceptualize international legal obligations conservatively. They blithely assume that business behavior is an internal matter for state supervision and not a concern of international law-makers.[32] Evidence of the business community's lobbying of governments against adoption of the UN Declaration is one possible reason for this stance.[33]

---

26 See A. Dunning, *Guardians of the Land: Indigenous Peoples and the Health of the Earth* (Worldwatch Institute, 1992); ed., T. Inglis, *Traditional Ecological Knowledge: Concepts and Cases* (International Development Research Centre, 1993).

27 The historical record suggests some Indigenous peoples' contribution to ecological degradation: T. Flannery, *The Future Eaters* (Reed Books, 1995); and continuing concerns, see LM. Shields, "Are Conservation Goals and Aboriginal Rights Incompatible?" *Environmental Law and Practice* 10 (2000): 187.

28 B.J. Richardson and D. Craig, "Indigenous Peoples, Law and the Environment," in *Environmental Law for Sustainability*, eds B.J. Richardson and S. Wood (Hart Publishing, 2006), 195, 200.

29 ILO Convention Concerning Indigenous and Tribal People in Independent Countries, No. 169, June 27, 1989; ILM 28 (1989): 1382.

30 UN Doc. A/61/L.67, September 7, 2007.

31 The closest the UN Declaration comes to addressing financial issues is article 39, which provides: "Indigenous peoples have the right to have access to financial and technical assistance from States and through international cooperation, for the enjoyment of the rights contained in this Declaration."

32 Large TNCs can yield more economic resources and power than some nation-states: see D.C. Korten, *When Corporations Rule the World* (Kumarian Press, 1995); S. Beder, *Global Spin: The Corporate Assault on Environmentalism* (Chelsea Green Publishing, 1998).

33 D. Caluza, "MNCs Biggest Foes of Indigenous Peoples' Rights," *Inquirer.net*, August 14, 2007, at http://newsinfo.inquirer.net/breakingnews.

Indigenous peoples themselves at times also fail to appreciate the malevo-
lence of some financiers. Their protests typically do not lead them to the
boardrooms of international banks or pension funds. Instead, they vent their
concerns where threats physically materialize, such as mining sites, or they
petition government regulators naively perceived as being solely in charge.[34]
Angry communities took this approach in challenging the Sakhalin pipeline
construction in eastern Russia by blocking roads to the construction sites.[35]
However, reflective of more sophisticated tactics beginning to emerge, in
2007, Indigenous groups from Cambodia, Malaysia, Papua New Guinea, and
Guyana approached Credit Suisse for US$10 million compensation for acting
as a financial adviser to Samling, a controversial Malaysian timber company,
during its stock-market floatation.[36]

While parts of the SRI movement advocate respect for Indigenous rights,
Aboriginal peoples are typically not significant participants in that movement, let alone financial markets. Lacking significant assets of their own, or
unwilling to commercialize their resources, First Nations often can only hope
for SRI institutions to heed their concerns and interests.

B. SRI FOR INDIGENOUS PEOPLES

1. Opportunities and Constraints

Indigenous peoples should be a quintessential SRI cause, as they elicit both
social and environmental values. Indigenous land rights have cultural significance and relevance for environmental stewardship. Misuse of their land
can have severe social and ecological consequences for displaced Indigenous
denizens.[37] Their plight should therefore appeal equally to investors sensitive
to human rights and social justice, as well as to investors preoccupied by
ecological protection and sustainable development.

34 A. Gedicks, *Resource Rebels: Native Challenges to Mining and Oil Corporations*
(South End Press, 2001); B.J. Cummings, "Dam the Rivers; Damn the
People: Hydroelectric Development and Resistance in Amazonian Brazil,"
Earth and Environmental Science 35(2) (1995): 151.

35 "Sakhalin Indigenous People Blockade Oil Development," *Environment News
Service*, June 30, 2005, at http://www.ens-newswire.com.

36 I. Mulder, *Biodiversity, the Next Challenge for Financial Institutions?* (IUCN,
2007), 13.

37 R. Howitt, *Rethinking Resource Management: Justice, Sustainability and Indigenous
Peoples* (Routledge, 2001).

Socially responsible investors began to acknowledge Indigenous rights in the 1980s, coinciding with the birth of MDBs' policies to manage the impacts of their loans on tribal and other local peoples. Since then, Indigenous peoples have been of concern to investors primarily in the context of project financing. Compared to other SRI causes, however, Indigenous rights have rarely received any spotlight. They share a crowded and expanding field of causes spanning diverse matters, including climate change, armaments, child labor, and tobacco. Financiers may perceive Indigenous peoples as an idiosyncratic, country-specific concern rather than as one of global significance. Even in jurisdictions with Aboriginal denizens, investors have tended to treat Indigenous rights as a relatively low priority.[38] Indigenous peoples' concerns sometimes get subsumed within a broader SRI human rights agenda.[39]

Another constraint to SRI for Indigenous peoples is the lack of accurate and reliable information for investors to base investment decisions. According to William Baue:

> Accessibility to information is the biggest challenge in applying [Indigenous peoples'] rights screens. The areas are remote and getting accurate information is expensive and difficult. Even where information is available, there may be questions on the credibility or reliability of such information.[40]

Relatedly, a 2007 study by EIRIS and the Centre for Australian Ethical Research (CAER) on corporate relations with Indigenous peoples concluded that "[t]he quality of reporting is generally poor, with most companies providing a response to any allegations of breaches of indigenous rights but few report voluntarily on areas of noncompliance."[41]

Not only is information in short supply, investors also struggle in quantifying its financial significance. The risk of a pollution accident may be quantifiable in terms of monetary damages based on cleanup costs. Yet how does one calculate the impact of a protracted protest movement driven by Indigenous

---

38 J. Tippet, "Investors' Perceptions of the Relative Importance of Investment Issue," *Accounting Forum* 24(3) (2000): 278 (discussing the low profile of Aboriginal rights among Australian investors).

39 As evident for instance in UNEPFI's online "Human Rights Guidance for Financial Institutions": http://www.unepfi.org/work_streams/human_rights/index.html.

40 W. Baue, "The Emergence Story Behind Indigenous Peoples Rights Screens," *Social Funds Sustainability Investment News,* June 10, 2004.

41 EIRIS and CAER, *Indigenous Rights, Indigenous Wrongs: Risks for the Resource Sectors* (EIRIS, 2007), 2.

land claims? Similarly, a fund manager may apply a blanket exclusionary screen against tobacco stocks, but how would she go about determining the threshold for human rights transgressions to justify divestment?

Yet the potential financial risks and benefits that inhere in development affecting Indigenous peoples are manifold. Many financiers tend to perceive Indigenous peoples as posing only a downside for their investments, yet discounting how companies that respect human rights can gain reputational advantages and protect their brand image. Conversely, firms that exploit Indigenous knowledge and resources without consent risk conflict and litigation.[42]

The case of Platinex, a Canadian mining exploration company, epitomizes the risks to investors when their firms scorn Indigenous interests. Platinex suffered a costly setback in 2006 when it intimidated the Kitchenuhmaykoosib Inninuwug (KI) First Nation by suing them for a preposterous C\$10 billion and seeking to bar KI members from Platinex's drilling sites. In its ruling on the dispute, the Ontario Superior Court of Justice granted KI an interlocutory injunction prohibiting Platinex from exploration on areas subject to the Indigenous land claim.[43] Justice George Smith accepted the argument that Platinex's solvency would be jeopardized by the ruling, but he faulted the company for behaving unilaterally and authoring its own financial misfortune by understating to its investors the immense opposition to the drilling operations.[44]

Ethical compulsions to respect Indigenous peoples are similarly diverse and complex. The ICCR explains in its Principles for Global Corporate Responsibility (1999) that: "by virtue of their inherent rights, [Indigenous peoples] are entitled to full participation in the business decisions which pertain to their ancestral lands and their way of life."[45] Likewise, the preamble of the

---

42 E.g., I. Mgbeoji, *Global Biopiracy: Patents, Plants, and Indigenous Knowledge* (University of British Columbia Press, 2006); G. Manners, "Unresolved Conflicts in Australian Mineral and Energy Resource Policies," *The Geographical Journal* 158(2) (1992): 129.

43 *Platinex v. Kitchenuhmaykoosib Inninuwug First Nation*, (2006) 272 D.L.R. (4th) 727.

44 However, on May 22, 2007, in *Platinex v. Kitchenuhmaykoosib Inninuwug First Nation* (CanLII 20790), the Ontario Superior Court of Justice decided not to extend the injunction and imposed a protocol for future consultation, and also gave permission to Platinex to begin its drilling program subject to certain restrictions. The delays with the project nonetheless cost Platinex considerably.

45 Section 1.4P8, at http://www.bench-marks.org/downloads/Bench%20Marks %20-%20full.pdf.

UN Declaration on the Rights of Indigenous Peoples proclaims: *"Recognizing the urgent need to respect and promote the inherent rights of indigenous peoples which derive from their political, economic and social structures and from their cultures, spiritual traditions, histories and philosophies, especially their rights to their lands, territories and resources."*[46] The ethical case is thus rooted in notions of social justice and the right of vulnerable peoples to self-determination. They are values not contingent on a financial cost-benefit analysis. Social investors however may struggle to understand how to accommodate such seemingly broad and open-ended ethical standards.

The principal means advocated to fulfill such standards is to consult with and obtain the consent of affected communities, on the assumption that if an informed community freely consents to an investment project, it must be ethically acceptable. Obligations on states to consult with and sometimes obtain the approval of Indigenous peoples appear in some international environmental treaties, such as the Convention on Biological Diversity.[47] These stipulations are even more strongly enunciated in the ILO Convention and the UN Declaration.[48] The World Resources Institute argues in a pioneering report that private sector financiers and developers should also seek the "free and informed consent" of affected Indigenous and other local communities.[49] Such consent can bestow on companies a social license to complement any official permits. In practice, financiers have tended only to consult rather than additionally to obtain permission.

2. Multilateral Development Bank (MDB) Policies

The MDBs financing economic projects and programs in developing countries were the first financial institutions to adopt policies to address the impacts of their loans on Indigenous peoples.[50] The rationale of these policies was motivated both for the MDBs to deflect public criticisms about insensitive project

---

46 UN Doc. A/61/L.67, September 7, 2007.

47 Article 8(j), 31 ILM (1992): 881.

48 P. Tamang, "An Overview of the Principle of Free, Prior and Informed Consent and Indigenous Peoples in International and Domestic Law and Practices," *Australian Indigenous Law Reporter* 9(2) (2005): 36.

49 S. Herz, A. Vina, and A. Sohn, *Development without Conflict: The Business Case for Community Consent* (World Resources Institute, 2007).

50 See A. Gray, "Development Policy, Development Protest: The World Bank, Indigenous Peoples and NGOs," in *The Struggle for Accountability: The World Bank, NGOs, and Grassroots Movements*, eds J.A. Fox and L.D. Brown (MIT Press, 1998), 267.

financing to the detriment of Indigenous peoples, and also by the belief that these peoples, because of their isolation and acculturation status, are especially "vulnerable" in the development process. Therefore, the MDBs introduced procedures to help design projects that minimized adverse social impacts.

The World Bank took the lead with an operational policy on Indigenous peoples adopted in 1982.[51] This led to Operational Directive 4.20 (OD 4.20) in 1991, which was revised in 2005 in the form of Operational Policy and Bank Procedure on Indigenous Peoples 4.10 (OP/BP 4.10). The latter decrees a procedure to assess a proposed project's effects on Indigenous peoples, to consult with affected peoples, and to prepare a plan to minimize impacts.[52] Any consequential loan contract must incorporate the government borrower's obligations to adhere to measures relating to Indigenous peoples.[53] In some cases, OP/BP 4.10 contemplates that project financing may hinge on the legal recognition of Indigenous peoples' land rights, equitable sharing of the benefits of commercial development, and consent to the development of cultural resources and knowledge.[54] Although OP/BP 4.10 does not explicitly recognize Indigenous rights, the World Bank can influence states' treatment of Indigenous peoples through covenants included in loan agreements.[55] Apart from its operational standards, in 2003 the World Bank launched a Global Fund for Indigenous Peoples in developing countries. It supports implementation of culturally appropriate projects and programs for sustainable development, and it assists the operations of the UN Permanent Forum on Indigenous Peoples.[56]

In practice, implementation of the World Bank's Indigenous-related policies has been erratic.[57] Disagreements about the definition of Indigenous

51 World Bank, *Tribal Peoples in Bank-Finances Projects, Operational Manual Statement 2.34* (World Bank, February 1982); see F. McKay, "The Draft World Bank Operational Policy 4.10: Progress or More of the Same?" *Arizona Journal of International and Comparative Law* 22 (2005): 65.
52 World Bank, *Operational Policy and Bank Procedure 4.10 Indigenous Peoples* (World Bank, 2005), para. 1. McKay (ibid) provides an excellent summary of an earlier draft of this policy, and related concerns.
53 Ibid., para. 11.
54 Ibid., para. 8(a).
55 G.A. Sarfaty, "The World Bank and the Internalisation of Indigenous Rights Norms," *Yale Law Journal* 114 (2005): 1791, 1796.
56 See http://www.worldbank.org/indigenous.
57 Sarfaty, note 55, 1802, concludes that the World Bank Operations Evaluation Department report in 2003 "found that only 55 of the 89 projects (or about 62%

peoples and borrower resistance to what they see as interference in internal political affairs have impeded policy implementation.[58] Many World Bank and other MDB-financed projects such as dams, highways, and forestry projects have been implicated in the displacement of Indigenous communities and degradation of their environment.[59] Many Indigenous peoples remain skeptical of OP/BP 4.10's policy of "free and informed *consultation*," in contrast to their preferred standard of "free and informed *consent*."[60] The World Bank treats consultation as a means to assess whether a project has the "broad support" of affected communities. The World Bank's Extractive Industries Review specifically recommended that the Bank routinely require such "broad support" as a precondition to its funding of extractive industry projects.[61]

Other international banks, such as the Asian Development Bank and the Inter-American Development Bank, have also issued policies addressing Indigenous peoples.[62] The Asian Development Bank's Policy on Indigenous Peoples (1998) requires initial project assessments of impacts on Indigenous peoples. If it believes the impact to be significant, the policy requires development of an Indigenous peoples' plan to mitigate the impacts and/or to provide compensation.[63] The policy does not, however, require Indigenous peoples' free and informed consent to developments. The Inter-American Development Bank's Strategy for Indigenous Development (2006) contains

   of the projects) that could have potentially affected Indigenous peoples (as determined by the OED's application of the policy's stated criteria) actually applied OD 4.20."

58 Ibid.

59 Ed., C. McDowell, *Understanding Impoverishment: The Consequences of Development-Induced Displacement* (Berghahn Books, 1996); "Going Under: Indigenous Peoples and the Struggle Against Large Dams," *Cultural Survival Quarterly* 23(3) (1999) (special issue), at http://www.cs.org.

60 For an overview of the debates, see M. Satterthwaite and D. Hurwitz, "The Right of Indigenous Peoples to Meaningful Consent in Extractive Industry Projects," *Arizona Journal of Comparative and International Law* 22(1) (2005): 1.

61 World Bank, *Striking a Better Balance - The World Bank Group and Extractive Industries: The Final Report of the Extractive Industries Review, World Bank Group Management Response* (World Bank, 2004), 50.

62 See analysis in C. Charters, "Indigenous Peoples and International Law and Policy," *Public Law Review* 18(1) (2007): 22.

63 Asian Development Bank (ADB), *The Bank's Policy on Indigenous Peoples* (ADB, 1998), para. 37.

similar measures to avoid or mitigate the adverse impacts of its financed projects on Indigenous peoples.[64]

3. SRI Methods for Indigenous Peoples

A. SRI SCREENS

Relatively few investors explicitly screen companies for their stance toward Indigenous peoples. Domini Social Investments' policy explains:

> The value of the diversity that these groups bring is incalculable and its loss is irretrievable. Responsible corporations can help preserve unique cultural riches in our world that are all too easily destroyed in a rush to short-term profit. We evaluate such controversies with great care both because we respect the rights of indigenous peoples to preserve their cultures and because the effect of confrontations between companies and indigenous peoples can be so harmful to corporate reputations.[65]

The US-based Calvert Group, a large mutual fund family, is also commendable for having one of the most detailed screens of the kind. It states:

> We avoid companies that have a pattern and practice of violating the rights of Indigenous Peoples. We will not invest in companies for which we have verifiable or clear evidence of egregious practices towards Indigenous Peoples. We value companies that have adopted policies and programs respecting Indigenous Peoples. We invest in companies that positively portray all peoples, including indigenous or ethnic peoples and their religious and cultural heritage.[66]

These are not empty words. In 2000, Domini worked with Friends of the Earth and other groups to negotiate with Enron to modify a 345 wind-turbine project on sacred sites belonging to the Yakama Indian Nation in the US.[67] In 2004 Calvert ceased investment in Calpine, a US energy company, objecting to its plans to extract geothermal development in the sacred

---

64 Inter-American Development Bank (IADB), *Strategy for Indigenous Development* (IADB, 2006), para. 5.1.

65 Domini Social Investments (DSI), *Global Investment Standards* (DSI, 2006), 17.

66 See http://www.calvert.com/pdf/6132.pdf.

67 W. LaDuke, "The Wind that Blows over Our Ancestors," *Earth Island Journal* 16(3) (2001): http://www.earthisland.org/eiJournal.

Medicine Lake Highlands of California.[68] In 2002 Calvert also divested from Liz Claiborne, the sportswear company, citing complaints from Indians about the company's misuse of the name "Crazy Horse" (the famous Lakota Sioux chief) on some of its apparel. Calvert's divestment won applause from the American Indian Coalition on Institutional Accountability.[69] Unfortunately, like many SRI decisions, Calvert lacked sufficient market clout to influence Liz Claiborne, which continues to flaunt the Crazy Horse label.[70]

These examples are rare among investors. A 2001 study of investment criteria in fifteen Australian SRI funds noted that only one paid regard to Indigenous land rights, and only five funds referred to human rights criteria.[71] Most such funds singled out armaments, tobacco, alcohol and gambling, and uranium mining for screening.[72] According to the Natural Capital Institute's database of approximately 110 SRI funds in the US and Canada listed as of March 2007, eighty-one funds do not screen for Indigenous rights at all.[73] Other data from Canada, where Indigenous peoples have a relatively high political profile, showed that, in 2006 only ten of the eighty-four asset management firms sampled explicitly screened on "Aboriginal relations." In comparison, twenty-three funds screened on tobacco, twenty-two on armaments, and sixteen against pornography.[74] One would expect to find even lower levels of interest among investors in jurisdictions without Indigenous denizens.

In the absence of a specific Indigenous policy, incidental capture under a general human rights screen is the best prospect for Indigenous peoples. Thus, the Norwegian Government Pension Fund's Ethical Guidelines advise that the Fund: "should not make investments which constitute an unacceptable risk that the Fund may contribute to unethical acts or omissions,

68 M. LeBeau, "LeBeau: Protecting the Sacred Medicine Lake Highlands" (December 3, 2004), at http://www.indiancountry.com/content.cfm?id=1096409955.
69 International Indian Treaty Council, "Calvert's Divestment from Liz Claiborne Praised by Indigenous Leaders" (October 17, 2002), http://www.treatycouncil.org/new_page _524111.htm.
70 See http://www.lizclaiborneinc.com/ourbrands/brand_crazy.asp.
71 U. Trog, *Socially Responsible Investment - Integrating Personal Values and Societal Concerns with Investment Decisions* (Eco Design Foundation, 2001), 5–6.
72 Ibid., 6.
73 See http://www.responsibleinvesting.org/database.
74 SIO, *Canadian Socially Responsible Investment Review 2006* (SIO, 2007), 11 (overall, Aboriginal issues ranked 12th of 16th possible screens surveyed).

such as . . . serious violations of human rights. . . ."[75] On this basis, the Fund divested from Freeport in 2006, citing its involvement in the controversial Indonesian mining project on tribal lands in Irian Jaya.[76]

Some SRI stock market indexes screen with regard to treatment of Indigenous peoples. Responsible investors may rely on such indexes to identify companies complying with the index's policies on respect of Indigenous peoples. The FTSE4Good Index provides that a company must have "a stated commitment to respecting indigenous peoples' rights."[77] More narrowly, the DJSIs consider Indigenous peoples in the category of labor standards, assessing companies against: "Labor Practice Indicators; e.g., cases involving discrimination, forced resettlements, child labor and discrimination of indigenous people; workplace accidents and occupational health and safety."[78] The criteria of both indexes seem too restrictive or vague to guide behavior meaningfully. Nonetheless, some companies have been delisted for failure to meet standards; the FTSE4Good Index removed Freeport in 2005, citing the environmental impacts of its Indonesian operations.[79] According to the FTSE4-Good Index annual review, "[g]lobal resource companies have improved considerably on policies for indigenous peoples rights."[80] However, it is puzzling how some companies achieve listing. In September 2007, Barrick Gold, with a disquieting track record on Indigenous peoples, was added to the DJSI for its apparently exemplary "commitment to sustainability."[81]

B. SHAREHOLDER ACTIVISM AND ENGAGEMENT

Investors have occasionally applied shareholder pressure to encourage companies to respect the rights of Indigenous peoples. To illustrate, in 2006, the Ethical Funds Company of Canada filed a shareholder resolution against Enbridge, a natural gas supply firm. The resolution responded to Enbridge's plans to build a major pipeline in British Columbia through a

75 Issued December 22, 2005, pursuant to *Regulation on the Management of the Government Pension Fund* (2004), http://odin.dep.no/fin/english/topics/pension_fund/p10002777/guidelines/bn.html.
76 *Nordic Region Pensions and Investment News*, June 20, 2006, 12.
77 FTSE, *FTSE4Good Index Series: Inclusion Criteria* (FTSE, 2006), 5.
78 DJSI, *World Indexes Guide* (DJSI, August 2006), 14.
79 FTSE, *Semi-Annual Review of the FTSE4Good Indices* (FTSE, September 2005), 2.
80 FTSE, *Criteria Development and Company Engagement Programme* (FTSE, 2005), 1.
81 Barrick Gold, "Barrick Gold Named to Dow Jones Sustainability Index," Press release, September 7, 2007. On Barrick Gold's track record, see the website dedicated to documenting its behavior: http://protestbarrick.net.

territory subject to outstanding Aboriginal land claims. The resolution requested:

> The Board to prepare a report (at reasonable cost and omitting propri-etary information) by September 1, 2006 assessing the impacts of company operations on ecosystems claimed by First Nations. This report should describe:
>
> 1. Environmental impact assessment procedures, including assessment of cumulative impacts on biodiversity;
> 2. Risk assessments detailing how current and proposed company operations may be impacted by First Nations land claims;
> 3. Mechanisms to consult and provide compensation to affected First Nations.[82]

This shareholder resolution was eventually withdrawn after Enbridge man-agement agreed to address the concerns raised by Ethical Funds and the First Nations.[83] Where such resolutions are deliberated, even a failure to muster a majority does not render such efforts futile when they serve to prod corporate management into dialogue and, perhaps, effect an eventual policy change.

Another example is Trillium Asset Management, a US investment company, which pledges to avoid companies having "demonstrated a pattern of disrespect-ful or exploitative behavior" toward Indigenous peoples.[84] And, "if problems emerge at a company in which we are already invested, we will engage with management in dialogue to determine if the company is committed to changing its behavior and redressing past wrongs."[85] Trillium promises to divest as a "last resort, to be used only if dialogue and shareholder proposals fail to have a posi-tive impact upon corporate behavior."[86] Among examples, in 2001 Trillium filed resolutions for the annual meetings of BP, Chevron, and ExxonMobil call-ing for a modification of drilling in the Arctic National Wildlife Refuge that threatened the livelihoods of the Gwich'in and Inupiat communities.[87]

---

82 Http://www.amnesty.ca/campaigns/sharepower/enbridge_resolution.php.

83 Ethical Funds Company, *The Ethical Funds Company Focus List for the 2006 Shareholder Action Program*, at http://www.ethicalfunds.com/do_the_right_thing/sri/focuslist/General2006.asp.

84 Trillium Asset Management, *Indigenous Rights: Our Work on Social and Environ-mental Issues* (2003), at http://www.trilliuminvest.com.

85 Ibid.

86 Ibid.

87 Trillium Asset Management, *Arctic National Wildlife Refuge: at Risk* (2001), at http://www.trilliuminvest.com.

In Canada, Amnesty International has assisted the Grassy Narrows First Nation in Ontario to resist clear-cut logging on their ancestral lands by the forestry behemoth Weyerhaeuser. In an open letter to the company's investors, Amnesty garnered support for a shareholder resolution filed by Capital Strategies Consulting in 2007 requesting that Weyerhaeuser assess the feasibility of suspending its purchases of wood fiber derived from the disputed forestry area until Grassy Narrows gave informed consent to further logging.[88] The dispute has a long history, but previous tactics, such as site blockades and legal actions challenging licenses granted to Weyerhaeuser, have failed to halt the logging of the area's boreal forests.[89] While Weyerhaeuser attempted to muzzle activists at the April 2007 shareholder meeting, and the resolution attracted only 5 percent of the vote, the dispute simmers unabated.[90]

Similar wrangles between socially conscious investors and resource developers have flared. In May 2007, an alliance of NGOs and Aboriginal activists disrupted the Toronto shareholder meeting of Barrick, the world's largest gold mining company.[91] Barrick has a controversial record against Indigenous inhabitants of areas its mines in Australia, the US, Chile, and other jurisdictions.[92] Similarly, opposition from Indigenous peoples caused costly disruptions and delays to operations at Río Tinto's copper mine in Bougainville, Papua New Guinea, and a geothermal plant operated by the Philippine National Oil Company on the island of Mindanao in the Philippines.[93]

C. COMMUNITY FINANCE

Community finance, also known as microfinance, constitutes a third SRI process affecting Indigenous peoples. While the causes of poverty in Indigenous communities are complex and wide-ranging, one factor is insufficient access to capital for small business development and community economic endeavors.[94]

---

88 T. Scurr, "Open Letter from Amnesty International (Canada) to Socially Responsible Investors with Shares in Weyerhaeuser" (Amnesty International, April 11, 2007).

89 Further details at http://freegrassy.org.

90 Amnesty International, "Share Power: Weyerhaeuser Mills Wood Logged from Grassy Narrows without Consent," Press release, April 30, 2007.

91 Details at http://www.protestbarrick.net.

92 CorpWatch, "Barrick's Dirty Secrets: Communities Worldwide Respond to Gold Mining's Impacts" (CorpWatch, May 2007).

93 Herz, Vina, Sohn, note 49, 13–14.

94 Community Development Financial Institutions Fund (CDFiF), *The Report of the Native American Lending Study* (CDFiF, 2001); S. McDonnell and

Encouragingly, one solution is Indigenous-controlled, locally operated financial institutions (constituted as credit unions or community banks). They help connect Indigenous communities to the capital markets. One survey counted twenty-five community finance institutions dedicated specifically to Native Americans in the US in 2003.[95] They often serve as intermediaries between other social investors and tribal communities.[96] The Hopi Credit Association is one tribal credit union linking banks and tribal borrowers by raising funds from commercial lenders and administering loan selection and servicing.[97] Another is the Cherokee Nation's Micro-Enterprise Development Program to provide loans of up to US$25,000 for business ventures having less than five employees and operating in Cherokee Nation jurisdictional boundaries.[98] Also in the US, the Native American Bank was established in 2001 with the mission to assist Indigenous persons, enterprises, and tribal governments achieve "self-determination in economic investment and job creation" by enhancing their access to banking and financial services.[99] In Australia, a First Nations Australian Credit Union set up in 1999 serves a similar role.[100] In Canada, the National Aboriginal Capital Corporation Association assists its member institutions in providing customized financial products and services to Aboriginal business communities.[101]

Community financiers differ from mainstream banks in several ways. While they are market-sensitive, community finance institutions fill niches overlooked by other lenders. They offer credit to those neglected by conventional banks,[102] and provide services to help ensure that credit is used effectively. Among these are services that regular banks often see as too costly

N. Westbury, *Banking on Indigenous Communities: Issues, Options, and Australian and International Best Practice*, Working Paper No. 18 (Centre for Aboriginal Economic Policy Research, Australian National University, 2002).

95 S. Dewees, *Investing in Community: Community Development Financial Institutions in Native Communities* (First Nations Oweesta Corporation and First Nations Development Institute, 2004), 9.

96 S. Sarkozy-Banoczy and E. Meeks, "Investing in Ourselves: Native CDFis," *Indian Country* 23(49) (2004): A5.

97 Dewees, note 95.

98 Http://www.cherokee.org/services.

99 "About Native American Bank," at http://www.nabna.com/about.shtml.

100 McDonnell and Westbury, note 94, 15.

101 Http://www.nacca.net.

102 For example, much Indian land in Canada and the US is held in trust by the government, which hinders the use of land as collateral for loans, particularly housing loans.

to administer, such as financial literacy training and credit counseling to customers, and technical assistance to small businesses. Despite such salutary objectives, research suggests there are far too few effective microfinancing programs specifically for Indigenous communities.[103]

A few mainstream commercial lenders also provide banking services and credit somewhat tailored to the needs of Indigenous peoples. In Canada, the Bank of Montreal has operated an Aboriginal Banking Unit since 1992.[104] It opened branches on some Indian reserves, providing home ownership programs for reserve residents where conventional loan security cannot be readily provided, and banking products for Aboriginal businesses.[105] Similar Aboriginal banking units are operated by several other Canadian banks, including RBC[106] and Canadian Imperial Bank of Commerce.[107] In the US, Fannie Mae supports housing loans to Indians through its Native American Conventional Lending Initiative.[108] However, it should be borne in mind that such lenders might be less willing to assist First Nations were it not for government guarantees on some of these loans.

C. SRI GOVERNANCE FOR INDIGENOUS PEOPLES

1. International Codes of Conduct

Indigenous peoples are mentioned in the EPs and the UNPRI. As discussed in the previous chapter, the EPs provide a voluntary code of conduct for responsible project financing.[109] Banks that sign the EPs agree to implement measures to minimize the social and environmental harm of infrastructure

---

103 R.H. Tipton III, "Microenterprise through Microfinance and Microlending: The Missing Piece in the Overall Tribal Economic Development Puzzle," *American Indian Law Review* 29 (2004–2005): 173 (evaluating microfinance for Native Americans).

104 Bank of Montreal, "Aboriginal Business Unit," http://www4.bmo.com/aboriginalbanking.

105 C. McLaughlin, "BMO Relates to Aboriginal Goals," *Windspeaker Business Quarterly* Spring (2007): 22.

106 Http://www.rbcroyalbank.com/RBC:RbOeyY71A8UAA1-CYiA/aboriginal/init.html.

107 Http://www.cibc.com/ca/small-business/aboriginal/philosophy.html.

108 Http://www.fanniemae.com/homebuyers/findamortgage/mortgages/native.jhtml.

109 Http://www.equator-principles.com.

projects they finance.[110] In particular, the EPs expect project sponsors to assess and limit potential impacts on Indigenous lands and communities. For projects posing the most significant impacts (category A projects), signatory banks must ensure: "that the borrower or third party expert has consulted, in a structured and culturally appropriate way, with project affected groups, including indigenous peoples."[111]

If the project proceeds, the sponsoring bank must require borrowers to formulate a development plan for Indigenous peoples in accordance with the World Bank's IFC Performance Standard 7. This standard provides, in part:

> When avoidance [of adverse impacts] is not feasible, the client will minimize, mitigate or compensate for these impacts in a culturally appropriate manner. The client's proposed action will be developed with the informed participation of affected Indigenous Peoples and contained in a time-bound plan, such as an Indigenous Peoples Development Plan.... [112]

However, the EPs do not require borrowers to obtain the free, prior informed consent of any affected Indigenous communities, even though this standard has been recognized in international law. The lesser standard of "consultation" does not require developers to respond to and address the advice or concerns raised by Indigenous peoples. Unlike a consultation process, the consent standard implies a two-way, interactive negotiation that accords more input from the affected communities into the decision-making process, and it is more likely to advance culturally appropriate developments.

When adverse impacts are anticipated, the IFC Performance Standards expect borrowers to take the following steps.[113] First, the borrower will offer affected communities compensation (cash or in-kind) to those who hold full legal title to land under national laws, a standard that is unlikely to assist dispossessed Indigenous peoples. Further, the borrower must consider feasible alternative project designs to avoid the relocation of Indigenous peoples. If relocation is unavoidable, the borrower must not proceed with the project without having engaged in "good faith negotiations" with the concerned communities. This is the closest the IFC comes to an explicit free and informed consent-standard.

---

110 T. O'Riordan, "Converting the Equator Principles to Equator Stewardship," *Environment* 47(4) (2005): 1.

111 Principle 5.

112 IFC, *Performance Standard 7: Indigenous Peoples* (IFC, April 2006), clause 8.

113 Ibid.

Of approximately forty-five banks that had pledged themselves to the EPs as of late 2006, only five had policies that explicitly addressed Indigenous peoples, according to a BankTrack study.[114] It found JPMorgan Chase to have the leading policy, on the basis of its commitment to finance projects only where: the affected peoples support the project through free, prior informed consultation using customary institutions; they have been fully informed about the project; they have access to a grievance mechanism; and major Indigenous land claims have been appropriately addressed.[115] Commendable as these aims appears on paper, even JPMorgan Chase has been dogged by criticisms from some NGOs, such as for its participation in a financial syndicate to support a controversial oil pipeline through tribal lands in Ecuador.[116] Another EPs signatory, Bank of America, explains in its forest practices policy that it considers the direct and indirect impacts of projects on Indigenous peoples, and that it will not finance such operations unless the concerned peoples are represented and informed, and no unsettled land claims remain.[117] While this statement appears satisfactory, its application beyond forest-related projects such as mining developments is unclear.

The proposed UN Norms on the Responsibilities of Transnational Corporations also compel businesses, specifically TNCs, to respect Indigenous rights.[118] The Norms may apply to a range of firms including investment companies and other financial intermediaries. They address environmental standards, labor standards, and consumer protection. In contrast to the EPs, the UN Norms purport to be legally binding if adopted by individual states. The UN Norms posit safeguards for Indigenous peoples, particularly the

---

114 The banks are ABN AMRO, Bank of America, Citigroup, HSBC and JPMorgan Chase: A. Durbin, et al., *Shaping the Future of Sustainable Finance: Moving from Paper Promises to Performance* (WWF and BankTrack, 2006), 27.

115 JPMorgan Chase, *Environmental Policy* (undated), section 4, at: http://www.jpmorganchase.com/cm/cs?pagename=Chase/Href&urlname=jpmc/community/env/policy/indig.

116 "Ecuador: New Oil Pipeline Threatens Fragile Ecosystems and Communities from Amazon Rainforest to Pacific Coast," World Rainforest Information Portal: http://www.rainforestweb.org/pages/ocp.php.

117 Bank of America, *Forests Practices—Global Corporate Investment Bank Policy* (undated), at: http://www.bankofamerica.com/environment/index.cfm?template=env_workrel.

118 UN Economic and Social Council, Sub-Commission on Promotion and Protection of Human Rights, *Norms on the Responsibilities of Transnational Corporations and Other Business Enterprises with Regard to Human Rights*, UN Doc. E/CN.4/Sub.2/2003/12/Rev. 2.

strong guarantee of non-discrimination and the inclusion of a general commitment to respect cultural rights.[119] They stipulate that:

> [T]ransnational corporations and other business enterprises have the obligation to promote, secure the fulfilment of, respect, ensure respect of and protect human rights recognized in international as well as national law, including the rights and interests of Indigenous peoples.... [120]

The official Commentary on the Norms elaborates on how companies should consider Indigenous rights. They should respect the principle of free, prior and informed consent of affected communities.[121] The Commentary also advises companies not to evict communities lacking "recourse to, and access to, appropriate forms of legal or other protection pursuant to international human rights law."[122] The UN Norms also incorporate several procedural requirements to strengthen their implementation and to hold TNCs accountable.[123] Nonetheless, such an unprecedented attempt to govern TNCs has come at a price. The UN Commission on Human Rights in early 2005 declined to endorse the Norms,[124] following withering criticisms from the International Chamber of Commerce and other business groups who viewed the Norms as inappropriately shifting the obligation to protect human rights from governments to private companies.[125]

Some voluntary CSR reporting codes also refer to Indigenous peoples. The GRI requires signatories to disclose how they address Indigenous peoples under the "Management Approach."[126] One of the GRI's human rights performance indicators refers to the "total number of incidents of violations

---

119 Ibid., arts 10 and 12.
120 Ibid., art. A.1.
121 *Commentary on the Norms on the Responsibilities of Transnational Corporations and Other Business Enterprises with Regard to Human Rights*, UN Doc. E/CN.4/Sub.2/2003/38/Rev.2 (2003) at art. E.10(c).
122 Ibid.
123 Part H.
124 UN Economic and Social Council, Sub-Commission on the Promotion and Protection of Human Rights, *Report of the United Nations High Commissioner on Human Rights on the Responsibilities of Transnational Corporations and Other Business Enterprises with Regards to Human Rights*, 2005, UN Doc. E/CN.4/2005/91.
125 C. Hillemanns, "UN Norms on the Responsibilities of Transnational Corporations and Other Business Enterprises with regard to Human Rights," *German Law Journal* 10(4) (2003): 1065, 1068.
126 GRI, *Sustainability Reporting Guidelines* (GRI, 2006), 32.

involving rights of indigenous people and actions taken."[127] The GRI's
Mining and Metals Sector Supplement also asks signatories to: "[d]escribe
process for identifying local communities' land and customary rights,
including those of indigenous peoples, and grievance mechanisms used to
resolve any disputes."[128] The GRI financial sector supplement however does
not refer to Indigenous peoples.

2. National SRI Regulation

No state has any comprehensive legal mechanisms that specifically encourage
SRI for Indigenous peoples. However, broad references to human rights
or environmental policy in SRI laws and policies should encompass these
peoples.

Legislation in the UK, several other European countries, as well as
Australia, obliges pension fund administrators or trustees to disclose whether
they invest with regard to social and environmental standards.[129] The
Australian standard extends to various retail fund products. Anecdotal evidence suggests some funds' policies make reference to Indigenous peoples.
For instance, in Australia, the Catholic Super and Retirement Fund discloses
in its "product disclosure statement" (PDS) that it excludes investment in
companies that "do not appropriately consult on native title issues."[130] The
policy however sheds no light on how this standard is implemented. The
Australian Ethical Investments' PDS issued in 2007 is generally inclusive of
many social and environmental issues,[131] yet does not explicitly refer
to Indigenous peoples despite commenting in another publication that:
"[t]o get a mining company into the portfolio we would want to see a company
with... a good record of working with neighbouring communities—including
indigenous communities.... To date, we haven't found one that we like
enough to invest in."[132]

For banks, incurring joint liability for the social and environmental harms
of their borrowers can have a very sobering effect that encourages more

---

127 Ibid., 33.
128 GRI, *GRI Mining and Metals Sector Supplement Pilot Version 1.0* (GRI, 2005), 26.
129 B.J. Richardson, "Pensions Law Reform and Environmental Policy: A New
     Role for Institutional Investors?" *Journal of International Financial Markets:
     Law and Regulation* 3(5) (2002): 159.
130 Catholic Super and Retirement Fund (CSRF), *Allocated Pension Fund Product
     Disclosure Statement* (CSRF, 2006), 14.
131 Australian Ethical Investment (AEI), *Australian Ethical Investment Trusts:
     Product Disclosure Statement* (AEI, July 2007).
132 AEI Trusts, *Half-Year Report to 31 December 2005* (AEI, 2006), 2.

cautious lending. In the US, banks' lending practices were impinged by the *Comprehensive Environmental Response, Compensation, and Liability Act* (CERCLA) of 1980,[133] which created a potential for joint liability for lenders in cleanup costs of lands contaminated by the firms they financed. CERCLA treats government-recognized Indian tribes as states, giving them the same treatment as states with respect to notification, consultation on remedial actions, information collection, and capacity to assume primary enforcement responsibility of the legislation on tribal lands.[134] Many Indian lands have been subject to CERCLA decontamination programs. Among them are the Prewitt Abandoned Refinery, Navajo lands in New Mexico,[135] and the General Motors site, on the land of the St. Regis Mohawk Nation.[136] In each case, CERCLA was applied to obtain compensation for decontamination of tribal lands.[137] However, none of these efforts thus far have directly affected lenders, as cleanups were funded by CERCLA's Superfund levied on the chemical industry.

Another legal mechanism to encourage responsible banking is community financing legislation obligating lenders to help meet the financial needs of the local communities in which they are chartered. The US *Community Reinvestment Act* of 1977[138] aims to improve credit and low-cost banking services for households and small businesses in low-income and minority communities.[139] The Act also requires banks whose annual turnover exceeds a certain threshold to reinvest into registered community programs. The US *Community Development Financial Institutions Act* of 1994[140] is another community financing instrument, designed to provide government support to businesses that can revitalize distressed communities. Both statutes have helped resource Indigenous communities to finance economic development.[141] Governments have also encouraged private lending to Indigenous

---

133　Pub. L. No. 96-510, 94 Stat. 2767.

134　Sections 107 and 126; J.V. Royster, "Environmental Protection and Native American Rights: Controlling Land Use through Environmental Regulation," *Kansas Journal of Law and Public Policy* 1 (1991): 89, 94.

135　EPA, *Second Five-Year Review of Prewitt Superfund Site* (EPA, 2005).

136　EPA, *General Motors (Central Foundry Division) Site Description* (EPA, 2006).

137　E.g., *Berrey, et al. v. Asarco Inc. et al.* (2006) W.L. 401822 (10th Cir.).

138　Pub. L. No. 95-128, 91 Stat. 1147.

139　J.T. Campen, "Banks, Communities and Public Policy," in *Transforming the U.S. Financial System: Equity and Efficiency for the 21st Century*, eds G.A. Dymski, et al. (M.E. Sharpe, 1993), 221.

140　Pub. L. No. 103-325, 108 Stat. 2160.

141　McDonnell and Westbury, note 94, 19–20.

peoples by providing financial guarantees, thereby reducing or eliminating the risks and the attendant unwillingness to provide services.[142]

In sum, the regulatory framework internationally and domestically that touches on the interactions between financial institutions and Indigenous peoples does not appear to furnish strong incentives to take account of Indigenous rights and interests. It mainly comprises scattered due process requirements to consult with or notify Indigenous peoples, coupled with occasional tax breaks for proactive community financing. The status of Indigenous peoples in SRI more likely hinges on other legal measures, notably the extent to which they hold title to their ancestral lands and have negotiated self-government agreements, which give them some (although incomplete) leverage in their dealings with financiers. The capacity of Indigenous communities to mobilize protest actions against unwelcome developments also factors into this equation.

III. Finance in a Climate of Change

A. INTRODUCTION

Climate change will likely be the most complex and expensive environmental problem humanity has ever had to address. According to the Stern Review commissioned by the UK government, the cost of business-as-usual, not taking immediate action to mitigate climate change, will likely amount to between 5 to 10 percent of world GDP each year.[143] But the cost of measures to reduce GHG emissions and protect carbon sinks to avert dangerous climatic changes would reduce world GDP only by an average of 1 percent per year if we act now—still sizeable costs though.[144] Weaning off fossil fuels will entail pervasive changes to economic systems. GHG emissions, principally carbon dioxide (CO_2), have risen considerably

---

142 For instance, Canada's Department of Indian Affairs provides loan guarantees to help finance housing on Indian reservations: http://www.ainc-inac. gc.ca/ps/hsg/cih/hs/amm_e.html. There are more extensive loan guarantee programs in the US: M. Fogarty, "Bankers See Commercial Loan Opportunity on Reservations," *Indian Country Today*, July 25, 2006, at http://www.indiancountry.com.

143 N. Stern, *Stern Review on the Economics of Climate Change* (H.M. Treasury, 2007).

144 The Stern review focused on the feasibility and costs of stabilization of GHG concentrations in the atmosphere in the range of 450–550 parts per million.

since the beginning of the Industrial Revolution and may continue to balloon as China and other developing countries rapidly industrialize.[145] Credible government policy measures to reduce emissions are mostly still inchoate.[146]

Although the transition to a low carbon economy is a responsibility of all countries, the Kyoto Protocol of 1997 expects rich nations to take the lead. Acknowledging states' "common but differentiated responsibilities,"[147] the Protocol obliges developed nations to "provide new and additional financial resources to meet the agreed full costs incurred by developing country Parties"[148] and to "provide such financial resources, including for the transfer of technology, needed by the developing country Parties to meet the agreed full incremental costs of advancing the implementation."[149]

Given the scale of investments needed in alternatives to fossil fuels, financial markets hold a pivotal position, because public finance alone cannot create a low carbon economy.[150] The financial sector can help price climate risks and facilitate investment in renewable energy and efficient technologies. The investment community increasingly perceives climate change as posing various risks to their portfolios and borrowers, including tighter regulations, impairment of physical assets, reduced revenues, and reputational damage.[151] An IFC report assessed climate change as "a particularly powerful catalyst" for incorporation of ESG factors into investment decision-making.[152]

---

145 Among the more interesting books in the sizeable literature, see T. Flannery, *The Weather Makers* (HarperCollins, 2005); G. Monbiot, *Heat: How to Stop the Planet Burning* (Allen Lane, 2006).

146 F. Yamin and J. Depledge, *The International Climate Change Regime: A Guide to Rules, Institutions and Procedures* (Cambridge University Press, 2005); eds, M. Peeters and K. Deketelaere, *EU Climate Change Policy: The Challenge of New Regulatory Initiatives* (Edward Elgar Publishing, 2006); C. Redgwell, et al., eds, *Beyond the Carbon Economy* (Oxford University Press, 2008).

147 Kyoto Protocol, UN Framework Convention on Climatic Change, art. 10, ILM 37 (1998): 22.

148 Ibid., art. 11(2)(a).

149 Ibid., art. 11(2)(b).

150 S. Labatt and R.R. White, *Carbon Finance: The Financial Implications of Climate Change* (John Wiley and Sons, 2007).

151 A. Shell and M. Krantz, "Global Warming a Hot Spot for Investors," *USA Today Online*, February 27, 2007; J. Leggett, "Climate Change and the Banking Industry: A Question of Both Risk and Opportunity," *Bankers Magazine* 179 (1996): 25; CERES and World Resources Institute (WRI), *Questions and Answers for Investors on Climate Risk* (CERES and WRI, 2004), 3.

152 IFC, *"Who Cares Who Wins." One Year On* (IFC, 2005), 8.

Some analysts predict that "climate change due diligence... will soon become an indispensable facet of inquiry in any transaction."[153] A recent survey by the UK Association of Investment Companies found that 14 percent of its members felt climate change would definitely affect their investment decisions, and 48 percent said it might affect their decisions.[154] Given such anxieties, the financial sector is churning out numerous studies that underline the impact of global warming to portfolio value. Included among them are *The Business of Climate Change*,[155] *Energy Security and Climate Change: Investing in the Clean Car Revolution*,[156] and *Climate Change and the Financial Sector: An Agenda for Action*.[157]

However, such attitudes strain credibility in light of the flurry of investments in new oil fields, pipelines, and other infrastructure of the fossil fuel economy. Even many SRI funds continue to dabble in the fossil fuel industry. A study as recent as 2002 found that all but one of Australia's SRI mutual funds held stakes in at least one fossil fuel business (i.e., coal and oil firms).[158] Moreover, much of the attention of investors is focused on short-term weather risks rather than climate risks, evident in the growth of the weather derivatives market and other insurance techniques that harness the capital markets.[159] Seasonal weather changes particularly affect farm yields, as well as demand for residential heating fuels.

The significant long-term impacts of climate change, which should raise profound questions about the very sustainability of our economic models, are not so seriously debated in the mainstream financial community. More than in the case of financiers' treatment of Indigenous peoples, the paradigm of

---

153 J.A. Smith, "The Implications of the Kyoto Protocol and the Global Warming Debate for Business Transactions," *New York University Journal of Law and Business* 1 (2005): 511.

154 Association of Investment Companies, "Latest AIC Investor Confidence Index - Global Warming May Affect Nearly Two Thirds of Active Investors' Investment Decisions," Press release, March 14, 2007.

155 J. Llewellyn, *The Business of Climate Change: Challenges and Opportunities* (Lehman Brothers, 2007).

156 World Resources Institute (WRI) and Merrill Lynch, *Energy Security and Climate Change: Investing in the Clean Car Revolution* (WRI and Merrill Lynch, 2005).

157 WWF and Allianz, *Climate Change and the Financial Sector: An Agenda for Action* (Allianz, 2005).

158 N. Lansbury, *Socially Responsible Climate Change? Fossil Fuel Investments of the Socially Responsible Investment Industry in Australia* (Mineral Policy Institute, 2002), 30.

159 E. Mills, "Insurance in a Climate of Change," *Science* 309(5737) (2006): 1040.

financial risk management has overwhelmingly shaped investors' attention to global warming. It poses a technical and managerial challenge that can be optimistically resolved through the techniques of ecological modernization. Conversely, others suggest we need a shift in ethics to successfully address global warming.[160] Notably, Prue Taylor and Donald Brown argue that we need to reflect on the ethical issues raised by climate change to reach an urgently needed international consensus for action.[161] They also see ethical reflection as crucial to help lead the world toward an equitable sharing of the burdens and benefits of protecting the planet, as called for in the UN Framework Convention on Climate Change (UNFCCC).[162]

Even within an economic framework, the financial drivers continue to favor investment in fossil fuels. The business case for investment in fossil fuels remains far more potent than the business case for divestment. In an acknowledgement of the limits of current approaches, the WBCSD concedes that the transition to a low carbon economy requires government policy instruments to send the correct economic signals.[163] The market has failed to capture and reflect climate risks efficiently. These failures mean that financing renewable energy supplies and energy efficiency technologies "generally entail[s] higher risks and initial costs than conventional projects."[164] Government policies must therefore set a long-term value for carbon if the SRI market driven solely by the business case is to be a force for change.

B. CLIMATE CHANGE: RISKS AND OPPORTUNITIES FOR INVESTORS

Given its significance to the whole economy, climate change should be of major concern to any "universal investor." Cynthia Williams and John Conley believe that climate change could become a "wedge issue," by "drawing more institutional investors into the process of thinking about the consequences of

---

160 See the internet network at: http://www.climateethics.org.

161 D. Brown, *American Heat: Ethical Problems with the United States Responses to Global Warming* (Rowman and Littlefield, 2002); P. Taylor, *An Ecological Approach to International Law: Responding to Challenges of Climate Change* (Routledge, 1998).

162 Article 3.1, ILM 31 (1992): 849.

163 WBCSD, *Energy and Climate Change: Sharpening the Focus for Action - A Business Perspective* (WBCSD, 2005).

164 See Z.X. Zhang and A. Maruyama, "Towards a Private-Public Synergy in Financing Climate Change Mitigation Projects," *Energy Policy* 29(15) (2001): 1363.

long-term social and environmental issues for the value of their portfolios."[165] In the financial sector, institutional investors such as pension funds have vocalized most for action on global warming with the view that it poses wide-ranging and long-term risks to portfolio values.

Regulatory risk is the most immediate and certain concern as governments ratchet up controls on GHG emissions. Carbon taxes and emission limits, if widely adopted, will affect the competitive advantage of polluters including their investors. The Kyoto Protocol and the EU's Emission Trading Scheme are driving many of these and other initiatives. The UK's *Climate Change and Sustainable Energy Act* of 2006 and New Zealand's *Climate Change Response Act* of 2002 are among the flurry of climate laws providing a framework for GHG reductions.

Even in the US, where federal policy has been largely indifferent to global warming, several states have taken unilateral actions.[166] The *Global Warming Solutions Act* of 2006 caps GHG emissions at 1990 levels by 2020 in California. In addition, it also mandates a cap-and-trade system for controlling emissions state-wide by 2012.[167] In 2001, Massachusetts legislated to require designated power plants to reduce their CO_2 emissions by 10 percent from 1997–99 levels by 2006.[168] About twenty other states have adopted renewable portfolio standards that require utilities to use increasing amounts of electricity from renewable sources such as wind and solar power.[169] Some climate regulation at the federal level will also likely arise in the US in the near future, as the Supreme Court ruled in *Massachusetts v. Environmental Protection Agency*[170] that the *Clean Air Act* gives the EPA authority to regulate tailpipe emissions of GHGs. Polluting industries such as coal power utilities, oil and gas, manufacturing, and transportation should become competitively disadvantaged by such regulation if they do not change their ways. The World Resources Institute predicts such new regulatory measures could

---

165 C.A. Williams and J.M. Conley, *An Emerging Third Way? The Erosion of the Anglo-American Shareholder Value Construct*, Legal Studies Research Paper No. 04-09 (University of North Carolina, 2005), 55.

166 C. Carlarne, "Climate Change Policies an Ocean Apart: EU and US Climate Change Policies Compared," *Penn State Environmental Law Review* 14 (2006): 435.

167 California Health and Safety Code (2006), s. 38500.

168 Carlarne, note 166, 446–47.

169 B.G. Rabe, *Greenhouse and Statehouse: The Evolving State Government Role in Climate Change* (Pew Center on Global Climate Change, 2002).

170 (2007) 127 S. Ct. 1438.

cause shareholders in these sectors to lose up to 5 to 7 percent of their investment values.[171]

Litigation risks present further concern to some investors. A number of
lawsuits initiated in North America against major GHG emitting power
utilities and manufacturing giants have created fears of a litigation onslaught
reminiscent of the anti-tobacco campaign.[172] Big polluters could be liable
for damages associated with the physical effects of climate change (e.g.,
flooding, severe storm damage, droughts). In 2004, eight US states and
New York City filed an unprecedented lawsuit against five of the country's
largest power companies.[173] In a public nuisance claim, which they lost in
the first round of litigation, they sought damages associated with global
warming and an order enjoining the defendants to abate their nuisance by
reducing their CO_2 by a specified percentage for at least ten years. In *Lockyer
v. General Motors*,[174] California commenced a tort action against six automobile manufacturers contending that the defendants, by emitting CO_2 and
other GHGs, are causing both public nuisance and injury. The suit seeks
unspecified monetary damages. While some legal commentators believe
"the probability of legal victories against global warming is low,"[175] they
also concede that such litigation may create reputational risks and substantial legal fees.[176] The Inuit people of the Arctic have also brought an action
against the US at the Inter-American Commission on Human Rights claiming that harm from GHG emissions violates their rights articulated in the
American Declaration of the Rights and Duties of Man.[177] Climate justice

171 World Resources Institute (WRI), *Changing Oil: Emerging Environmental
Risks and Shareholder Value in the Oil and Gas Industry* (WRI, 2002).

172 K.J. Healy and J.M. Tapick, "Climate Change: It's Not Just a Policy Issue
for Corporate Counsel - It's a Legal Problem," *Columbia Journal of
Environmental Law* 29 (2004): 89; J. Gupta, "Legal Steps Outside the Climate
Convention: Litigation as a Tool to Address Climate Change," *Review of
European Community and International Environmental Law* 16(1) (2007): 76.

173 See e.g., *State of Connecticut, et al. v. American Electric Power Company, Inc.,
et al.* (2005) 406 F. Supp. 2d. 265 (S.D.N.Y.) (under appeal).

174 No. 3:06. Civ. 05755 (N.D. California, filed September 20, 2006).

175 M. Levinson, "Liability for Climate Change," *North American Corporate
Research* (JPMorgan Chase, November 29, 2006).

176 Ibid., 1.

177 *Petition to the Inter American Commission on Human Rights Seeking Relief From
Violations Resulting from Global Warming Caused by Acts and Omissions of the
United States* (Submitted by Sheila Watt-Cloutier, with the Support of the
Inuit Circumpolar Conference, December 7, 2005).

SOCIALLY RESPONSIBLE INVESTMENT LAW

litigation is spreading to other countries, including Australia[178] and Canada.[179]

Climate change also creates physical risks. Economic sectors dependent on precise climate conditions, such as agriculture, forestry, and tourism, face such threats.[180] The oil industry itself is vulnerable, as it was affected by Hurricane Katrina, which shut down many US refineries. The real estate finance sector is also exposed to damages from extreme weather events. Banks face a direct risk when making loans for property in areas that are vulnerable to changing environmental conditions, such as melting of permafrost or recurrent floods.[181] The insurance industry, which covers many of these risks, is also acutely exposed to global warming, given the industry's reliance on historical climate data for accurate risk assessment.[182]

High-profile companies that disregard climate change also face reputational risks. Fossil fuel corporations like ExxonMobil are favorite targets of consumer boycotts and shareholder pressure.[183] Civil society groups also target financial institutions associated with GHG emitting firms; a coalition of mostly US environmental groups started a campaign in 2006 that demanded banks cease lending for certain projects such as coal power plants.[184]

Conversely, companies that pioneer low carbon technologies and make efficiency innovations stand to gain financially.[185] Climate change offers new business opportunities for these investors, now stampeding into companies specializing in renewable energies, ethanol production, environmentally efficient technologies, and carbon offset projects.[186] Citigroup's 2007 list of "climatic consequences companies" identified seventy-four companies

---

178 *Australian Conservation Foundation v. Minister for Planning*, [2004] V.C.A.T. 2029, 23.

179 *Friends of the Earth v. Her Majesty the Queen, et al.*, 2007 (Notice of Application, Plaintiff), Court file no. T-1683-07, Federal Court of Canada.

180 See UBS, *Climate Change: Beyond Whether* (UBS, 2007).

181 ISIS Asset Management, *A Benchmarking Study: Environmental Credit-Risk Factors in the Pan-European Banking Sector* (ISIS Asset Management, 2002), 14.

182 M. Northrop, "Leading by Example: Profitable Corporate Strategies and Successful Public Policies for Reducing Greenhouse Gas Emissions," *Widener Law Journal* 14 (2004): 21, 32.

183 F. Barringer, "Environmental Groups Planning to Urge Boycott of ExxonMobil," *New York Times*, July 12, 2005, A14.

184 J. Donnelly, "Banks are Urged Not to Finance Coal Power," *Boston Globe Online*, January 16, 2007.

185 World Resources Institute (WRI) and CERES, *Questions and Answers for Investors on Climate Risk* (WRI, 2004), 23.

186 D. Berman, "Hot for Green Investing," *Financial Post*, February 19, 2007.

(across twenty-one industries in many countries) "that seem well positioned to benefit from these trends."[187] The creation of the Photon Photovoltaic Stock Index, ABN AMRO Biofuel Commodity Index, Wilder Hill Clean Energy Index, and the KLD Global Climate 100 Index, among various examples, enable investors to track the performance of companies in these sectors. The development of carbon emissions trading systems promises further lucrative spoils. Financiers who broker carbon allowance trading will benefit too. The World Bank estimated that the global carbon market reached US$30 billion in 2006, mostly in the EU's trading scheme.[188]

Yet, incongruously to this bandwagon of initiatives, the fossil fuel sector thrives. The gushing rhetoric in the financial industry about addressing climate change does not reflect the evidence in reality. The spree of investment in the world's new oil frontier, Alberta's oil sands, is just one example—the production there is expected to triple by 2015.[189] A 2007 study by the Ethical Funds Company of the booming oil sands industry documented that only four of the fifty companies assessed were cutting emissions.[190] Only a handful was taking appropriate measures, such as factoring carbon costs into capital allocation decisions and conducting GHG emission inventories. And few had invested in renewable energy production. Another indicator of the motivations of the financial sector is their response to the Extractive Industries Review, commissioned by the World Bank. The Review proposed that the Bank immediately withdraw from lending to the coal industry, and by 2008, also to the oil industry.[191] Eleven banks, signatories to the EPs, jointly wrote to the World Bank President in April 2004 urging him to reject the proposal on the incredulous basis that those loans provide revenue for developing countries to alleviate poverty.[192] This view was advanced despite the fact that the Extractive Industries Review had argued precisely that such intensive projects often do not help the most disadvantaged peoples. Thus, so long

187 Citigroup, *Climatic Consequences* (Citigroup Research, January 19, 2007), 1.
188 K. Capoor and P. Ambrosi, *State and Trends of the Carbon Market 2007* (World Bank, May 2007), 3.
189 R. Walker, Ethical Funds Company (presentation at the Canadian Responsible Investment Conference, Montreal, May 27–29, 2007).
190 Ethical Funds Company, *Head in the Sands? Climate Change Risks in Canada's Oil and Gas Sector* (Ethical Funds Company, 2007), 2–4.
191 E. Salim, *Striking a Better Balance: The World Bank Group and Extractive Industries*, Volume 1 (World Bank, 2003), 65.
192 D. Sevastopulo, "Banks Contest Ban Proposed for Coal and Oil Extraction," *Financial Times*, April 5, 2004, 6.

as fossil fuels remain a relatively cheap alternative and vested interests thwart change, SRI in the energy sector has rather constrained prospects.

New policy instruments will thus be required in order to mobilize investors to help finance the transition to a low carbon economy. While the public sector, alone, lacks the financial resources to achieve this economic restructuring, it must provide the correct alternation of carrots and sticks to motivate private financiers. A report by WWF and the Allianz Group in 2005 advised that: "banks and investors in particular need a clear regulatory framework on climate policy which they can adapt and base their investment and lending decisions."[193]

C. CLIMATE POLICIES TO HARNESS MARKET FORCES

Climate change poignantly illustrates SRI's dependence on public policy intervention to create conditions conducive to action by financial institutions. Emerging regulations to limit GHG emissions or to offer economic incentives to reduce them have been closely intertwined with the response of the financial sector to climate change. The regulatory and litigation risks are beginning to spur financiers to treat climate change as financially material. The SRI movement may appear to offer new norms for climate change abatement and mitigation, but it still takes its cues primarily from the public sector. We should thus examine the public regulation that shapes their responses.

At an international level, the Kyoto Protocol to the UNFCCC provides a framework for intergovernmental cooperation. The Protocol, which came into force in February 2005, sets binding limits on emissions of CO_2 and related GHGs[194] for the Protocol's Annex I countries (in the OECD and the former Soviet Union and Eastern European nations). To attain these goals, the Protocol provides several "flexible mechanisms" that harness market forces to achieve cost-effective emission reductions. They include trading emission allowances, earning emission credits by funding abatement efforts in other parties via the Clean Development Mechanism (for developing countries) or Joint Implementation (for Eastern Europe), and banking surplus carbon allowances for future use.[195] By exploiting the marginal cost differentials between countries, in theory these flexible mechanisms enable parties to achieve their GHG reductions at the lowest price. Economic analyses by the

---

193 WWF and Allianz, note 157, 9.
194 These gases are methane (CH_4), nitrous oxide (N_2O), hydrofluorocarbons (HFCs), perfluorocarbons (PFCs), and sulphur hexafluoride (SF_6).
195 D. Firestone and C. Strek, *Legal Aspects of Implementing the Kyoto Protocol Mechanisms: Making Kyoto Work* (Oxford University Press, 2005).

World Bank suggest that the overall costs of implementing the Kyoto commitments would be about ten times cheaper with full use of the flexible mechanisms.[196]

The Kyoto Protocol's flexible mechanisms also yield new market opportunities for financiers in several ways.[197] First, they should expand corporate lending opportunities for emission abatement technologies. Second, project finance will be stimulated in the Clean Development Mechanism and Joint Implementation sectors. Third, carbon emission trading creates a demand for brokerage services. Fourth, financial analysts will have additional work in factoring climate risks into equity and debt financing.

National level policies have included market-based instruments such as tradable pollution allowances, carbon taxes, and subsidies for clean energy investments.[198] This partiality to economic instruments reflects a broader evolution in environmental law systems worldwide, moving away from bureaucratic command-and-control regulation toward reflexive law instruments perceived as more congruent with the workings of the market.[199] Thus in 2001, the UK, once a staunch opponent of carbon taxation, introduced a climate change levy to tax non-renewable energy consumed by industry and public sector agencies.[200] Scandinavian countries have the most extensive energy taxes in the world.[201] However, because such taxes are sometimes perceived to erode market competitiveness, and potentially generate considerable political opposition, some governments have stumbled in advancing policy changes. The New Zealand government has twice clumsily backtracked on

---

196 Cited in M. Harmelink and P. Soffe, *Financing and Financing Mechanisms for Joint Implementation (JI) Projects in the Electricity Sector* (EcoSecurities, 2001), 25.

197 J. Janssen, "Implementing the Kyoto Mechanisms: Potential Contributions by Banks and Insurance Companies," *Geneva Papers on Risk and Insurance* 25(4) (2000): 602; J. Mandt, "Managing Risk in Kyoto Projects," *Environmental Finance* 1(2) (1999): 23; H. Hugenschmidt and J. Janssen, "Kyoto Protocol: New Market Opportunities or New Risks?" *Swiss Derivatives Review* 11 (1999): 22.

198 B.J. Richardson, "Climate Law and Economic Policy Instruments: A New Field of Environmental Law," *Environmental Liability* 12(1) (2004): 1.

199 D. Driesen, "Economic Instruments for Sustainable Development," in *Environmental Law for Sustainability*, note 28, 277.

200 B.J. Richardson and K. Chanwai, "The UK's Climate Change Levy: Is It Working?" *Journal of Environmental Law* 15(1) (2003): 39.

201 A. Bruvoll and B.M. Larsen, "Greenhouse Gas Emissions in Norway: Do Carbon Taxes Work?" *Energy Policy* 32(4) (2004): 493.

promises to tax carbon.[202] Denmark and Germany chose to assuage affected industries by allowing firms to negotiate tax exemptions for improved energy management.[203]

In this context, the cap-and-trade schemes have become the thoroughbred tool to tackle global warming emissions.[204] In addition to the Kyoto mechanism, various regional and local schemes have sprouted. The EU adopted a directive in 2005 for CO_2 emission allowance trading.[205] In the US, the Northeast Regional Greenhouse Gas Initiative of Northeastern and Mid-Atlantic states aims to stem CO_2 emissions through a multi-state cap-and-trade system.[206] In NSW, Australia, since 2003 an Energy Efficiency Certificates Trading Scheme allows electricity retailers and other parties to meet mandatory GHG emission reduction goals by trading in abatement certificates.[207] With Australia's belated ratification of the Kyoto Protocol in December 2007 a plethora of new climate policies initiatives will likely transpire under its Labor Government. Other trading schemes have been utilized in the Netherlands, the UK, and some states in the US to enhance investment in the renewable energy market.[208]

Government price support schemes have also boosted renewable energy. The guaranteed prices are a premium above the charges for non-renewable electricity and are set at a level to allow renewable electricity suppliers to flourish. Guaranteed feed-in tariff schemes have been a popular choice in Austria,

---

202 B.J. Richardson, "Economic Instruments and Sustainable Management in New Zealand," *Journal of Environmental Law* 10(1) (1998): 21; B. Fallow, "Carbon Tax: Fuel Rise Off, Power Hike On," *New Zealand Herald*, December 22, 2005.

203 M.M. Roggenkamp, et al., eds, *Energy Law in Europe* (Oxford University Press, 2001), 412–13.

204 See P. Koutstaal, *Economic Policy and Climate Change: Tradeable Permits for Reducing Carbon Emissions* (Edward Elgar Publishing, 1997); B. Hansjürgens, ed., *Emissions Trading for Climate Policy: US and European Perspectives* (Cambridge University Press, 2005).

205 Peeters and Deketelaere, note 146.

206 Http://www.rggi.org.

207 Http://www.greenhousegas.nsw.gov.au.

208 J. Drillisch, "Renewable Portfolio Standard and Certificates-Trading on the Dutch Electricity Market," *International Journal of Global Energy Issues* 14(2) (2000): 1; B.J. Richardson, "Taxing and Trading in Corporate Energy Activities: Pioneering UK Reforms to Address Climate Change," *International Company and Commercial Law Review* 14 (2003): 18; R. Wiser, K. Porter, and R. Grace, "Evaluating Experience with Renewables Portfolio Standards in the United States," *Mitigation and Adaptation Strategies for Global Change* 10(2) (2005): 237.

Denmark, and Germany.[209] Governments have also offered accelerated tax depreciation of energy-saving equipment expenditures and investments in renewable energy power.[210]

Some of these economic instruments have been designed with a role for the fifinancial sector in mind. In the UK, following representations from the renewable energy industry and investors, the government strengthened the existing incentives in December 2003 by extending the "Renewables Obligations" from 2010–11 to 2015–16 to give investors more confidence in long-term returns.[211] Under these Obligations, all electricity suppliers must source a certain percentage of their total sales from renewable energy sources.[212] Financial institutions will likely continue to shape further policy measures. Citigroup's 2007 statement on climate change declares: "[w]e believe that the United States must act now to create a national climate change policy to avoid the economic, social, and environmental damage that will result if GHG emissions are not reduced."[213] Other climate-related policies that directly target the financial sector will likely materialize soon. Indicative of the rapidly hardening attitudes of law-makers, in November 2007 the European Parliament passed with a resounding majority a resolution that calls for "the discontinuation of public support, via export credit agencies and public investment banks, for fossil fuel projects."[214]

D. FINANCIAL SECTOR RESPONSES TO CLIMATE CHANGE

1. Risk Management

The financial sector often appears effusive in its concern about climate change, but it is frequently taciturn in its actions. Most investors are a long way from

---

209 D.A. Fuchs and J. Maarten, "Green Electricity in the Market Place: The Policy Challenge," *Energy Policy* 30(6) (2002): 525.

210 E.g., New Zealand "Projects to Reduce Emissions" initiative: http://www.mfe.govt.nz/issues/climate.

211 N. Robins, "Shaping the Market: Investor Engagement in Public Policy," in *Responsible Investment*, eds R. Sullivan and C. Mackenzie (Greenleaf Publishing, 2006), 318.

212 P.M. Conner, "The UK Renewables Obligation," in *Switching to Renewable Power*, ed. V. Lauber (Earthscan, 2005), 159.

213 Citigroup, *Citi Position Statement on Climate Change* (February 2007), at http://www.citigroup.com/citigroup/environment/ climateposition.htm.

214 European ECA Reform Campaign, "European Parliament Passes Resolution to End Taxpayer Support for Fossil Fuels Projects," Press release, November 29, 2007.

490 | SOCIALLY RESPONSIBLE INVESTMENT LAW

integrating climate exposure of their assets into their investment strategies, let alone to making concerted efforts to divest from fossil fuel industries. Fund managers are generally not literate on climate issues, and they need to devote more resources to research, disclosure, and risk management. Most financiers conceptualize climate change issues in terms of minimizing financial risks and developing market opportunities, rather than as demanding to attain particular environmental goals of social value. While a minority of social investors may view climate change as a political or ethical issue, analogous to tobacco or armaments, most treat it strictly as a business case. Because a strong business case for investment in fossil fuel industries persists, SRI will likely be greatly hindered until government policy can correct the underlying market failures.

With diverse portfolios and long-term financial liabilities, large institutional investors are most exposed to climate risks. The UN convened an Investor Summit on Climate Risk in 2003 and 2005 to consider the implications of climate risk for long-term asset allocation, and to share best practices.[215] The first Summit launched the Investor Network on Climate Risk (INCR) for on-going dialogue and collaboration on these challenges.[216] As of early 2008, the INCR claimed a membership of over sixty institutional investors, collectively managing assets of some US$4 trillion. It organizes conferences and forums to educate fund managers about climate risks, and publishes various reports. Its members filed forty-two climate change-related resolutions with thirty-six US companies during the 2007 proxy season—a record.[217] Another association performing a similar collaborative role is the UK-based Institutional Investors Group on Climate Change (IIGCC).[218] The UN is also partnering with institutional investors through the UNEPFI's Climate Change Working Group. It raises awareness of climate issues in the financial sector and has been an advocate for public policy reform.[219]

Arguably, institutional investors' fiduciary duties extend to taking into account climate change risks. A guide for UK pension fund trustees co-sponsored by the IIGCC suggested that:

Climate risk can have a real impact on portfolio holdings. There is a growing case for trustees to attain some level of knowledge around

---

215 UNEP, "Global Finance Community Joins UN to Tackle Climate Change," UNEP News Centre, May 10, 2005.
216 Http://www.incr.com.
217 INCR, "Global Warming Shareholder Resolutions Pending in 2007 Proxy Season - Investor Summary," Press release, April 6, 2007.
218 Http://www.iigcc.org.
219 Http://unepfi.net/cc.

these issues, and to take steps to mitigate any negative consequences of not taking action.

In line with these definitions of fiduciary responsibility, we suggest that it is consistent with fiduciary responsibility to address climate change risk.[220]

Some institutions are heeding this message. In 2001, the UK pension fund giant, USS, issued a working paper examining climate change as a financial risk.[221] In the US, public sector pension funds have also taken the lead in identifying climate change as a long-term risk to portfolio companies.[222] The "Green Wave Initiative," launched in 2004 by the California State Treasurer with CalPERS and the California State Teachers' Retirement System (CalSTRS), commits these funds to invest millions in climate-friendly technologies and clean energy companies.[223]

Some funds in the retail sector have acknowledged climate change. Henderson Global Investors' Future Fund is marketed for its low carbon content.[224] Still, while climate change is used increasingly as a screening criterion for SRI funds, the screens tend to be rather crude. One exception is Inhance Investment Management, which became the first Canadian mutual fund company to take firms' management of climate risks into account in constructing investment portfolios.[225] Inhance's analysts assess companies in five key areas: participation in emissions trading, emission reduction targets, low carbon fuel production, risk management, and investment in research and development.

For banks, their primary concern with climate change is the risk it poses to a specific project, "rather than the risk that project financing poses to the

220 Mercer Investment Consulting (MIC), *A Climate for Change: A Trustee's Guide to Understanding and Addressing Climate Risk* (MIC, IIGCC and Carbon Trust, 2005), 18–19.

221 M. Mansley and A. Dlugolecki, *Climate Change—A Risk Management Challenge for Institutional Investors* (USS, 2001).

222 C.A. Williams and J.M. Conley, "An Emerging Third Way? The Erosion of the Anglo-American Shareholder Value Construct," *Cornell International Law Journal* 38 (2005): 493, 544–55.

223 J. Sandred, "Catching the Green Wave: Investment in Environmental Technology Gaining Momentum" *San Francisco Chronicle*, May 31, 2004.

224 Henderson Global Investors (HGI), *The Future is Low Carbon: The 2006 Carbon Audit of the Henderson Industries of the Future Fund* (HGI, June 2006).

225 Http://www.inhance.ca.

global environment."[226] Julia Philpott notes that: "there is not, at present, a standard approach within the international banking industry for transparency and accountability for the global warming performance of project finance."[227] A few banks profess to go beyond business as usual. In a potential harbinger of change, in its energy-lending portfolio, the Bank of America promises to reduce GHG emissions of projects it finances by 7 percent.[228] Yet, as recently as June 2007 the Bank of America was the target of protest actions for its continuing investments in the coal industry.[229] The HSBC unveiled its carbon management plan in December 2004, committing the bank to "carbon neutrality" from its operations globally.[230] Citigroup has announced that it will report all GHG emissions associated with projects it finances.[231] In its *2004 Corporate Citizenship Report*, Citigroup disclosed financing one power plant, and estimated the total implied CO_2 emissions as ranging from 2.7 million tons to 5.5 million tons of CO_2, depending on the life of the project. Citigroup declared itself "responsible" for a portion of this carbon based on the percentage of the loan it contributed.[232]

Financiers increasingly need to understand the implications of emissions trading for their portfolio companies. Financial risks for participants in cap-and-trade schemes include cash flow risks, such as increased expenditure for measures to reduce CO_2 or the purchase of emission allowances.[233] S&P's predicts that large European power utilities face heightened financial risks under such schemes.[234] To hedge such risks, firms may resort to various types

---

226 J. Philpott, "Keeping it Private, Going Public: Assessing, Monitoring, and Disclosing the Global Warming Performance of Project Finance," *Sustainable Development Law and Policy* 5 (2005): 45.

227 Ibid., 47.

228 Bank of America, "Bank of America Climate Change Position," at http://www.bankofamerica.com/environment/index.cfm?template=env_clichangepos.

229 "Activists Drape 50ft Banner Across From B of A Headquarters, Call on Bank to Stop Funding Dirty Coal," *Asheville Indymedia* (October 23, 2007), at http://asheville.indymedia.org/features/environment.

230 "HSBC Earns Credit for Being First 'Carbon Neutral' Bank," *GreenBiz.com*, December 7, 2004.

231 Citigroup, *Citizenship Report 2004* (Citigroup, 2005), 39.

232 Ibid.

233 UNEPFI Climate Change Working Group, *CEO Briefing. Emissions Trading* (UNEPFI, January 2004), 4.

234 S&P's, *Emissions Trading: Carbon Will Become a Taxing Issue for European Utilities* (S&P's, 2003).

of derivatives, such as forwards and options that allow future trading of emission allowances at a fixed price.[235]

Property and casualty insurers in fact were the first institutions in the financial sector to take heed of climate change.[236] Recent costly weather catastrophes, seen as a harbinger of global warming, have made some insurers uneasy, pushing them into climate policy debates.[237] These events undermine prediction of weather-related risks and can expose insurers to unexpected colossal losses.[238] Some insurance companies have responded by withdrawing coverage for certain risks, hiking premiums, imposing greater deductibles, and adopting physical risk management and other protective measures as a precondition to insurance.[239] Some also exert pressure on policy-makers, lobbying for regulatory action, and collaborating with public authorities on research and preventative measures,[240] although tending to fail to live up to the expectations of environmentalists.[241]

However, insurance cannot reduce the risks of global warming—though it may indirectly assist in dealing with them, by reducing the ensuing damage to those that implement mitigation measures, and by channelling compensation to victims of climate-change impacts. To play its part, insurers have pioneered new catastrophe risk mechanisms, such as catastrophe future and

---

235 UNEPFI Climate Change Working Group, note 233, 5.

236 Innovest, *Climate Change and the Financial Services Industry. Module 1 - Threats and Opportunities* (UNEPFI Climate Change Working Group, 2002), 16–17.

237 The cost of major weather disasters has increased astronomically in since the mid-1980s: UNEPFI Climate Change Working Group, *CEO Briefing. Adaptation and Vulnerability to Climate Change: The Role of the Financial Sector* (UNEPFI, 2006), 14.

238 See C. Flavin, "Storm Warnings: Climate Change Hits the Insurance Industry," *World Watch* 7 (1994): 10; D.G. Friedman, "Implications of Climate Change form the Insurance Industry," in *Coping with Climate Change*, ed. J.C. Topping Jr. (Climate Institute, 1989), 389.

239 A. Dlugolecki, "An Insurer's Perspective," in *Climate Change and the Financial Sector*, ed. J. Leggett (Gerling Akademie-Verlag, 1996), 64, 75; A. Abbott, "Insurance Company to Back Out of Some Climate-Linked Risks," *Nature* 372(6503) (1994): 212.

240 D.L. Kirk, "Insurers Voice Need to Combat Climate Risks," *Business Insurance* 33(45) (1999): 45; F.W. Nutter, "Global Climate Change: Why US Insurers Care," *Climatic Change* 42(1) (1999): 45.

241 M. Paterson, "Risky Business: Insurance Companies in Global Warming Politics," *Global Environmental Politics* 1(4) (2001): 18.

weather derivatives that tap into the deep resources of the capital markets.[242] The market for weather derivatives contracts is a new risk management option for hedging climate-related risks.[243] For example, if a disaster occurs, the insurer that issued the catastrophe bond would pay claims with the funds that would otherwise have gone to the bondholders. If good weather prevails during the bond period (typically a year), investors gain by the return of their principal plus interest payments.[244]

Yet, curiously, insurance companies often overlook the climate risks in their own investment portfolios. They commonly neglect to apply the lessons from their risk underwriting activities to their investment activities, evident for instance in the significant stakes some insurers retain in the oil industry. For example, Friends of the Earth has documented how major UK insurers retain large holdings in a range of environmentally problematic firms including fossil fuel industries.[245] Until they address these anomalies, insurers' warnings about global warming may lack credibility.[246]

Many investors remain hampered in their ability to assess and respond to the financial risks of global warming for many reasons.[247] Cognitive barriers contribute to financiers' limited understanding of and attention to climate change. These include the notions that climate change is too remote to affect a company's bottom line, that there are many seemingly more pressing issues that affect investment values, and that global warming is associated with NGO-led political sensationalism rather than tangible financial risks. Another hindrance to action is the difficulty in determining the implications of climate change and government policy responses for financial markets.

---

242 See further D.M. Jaffee and T. Russell, "Catastrophe Insurance: Capital Markets and Uninsurable Risks," *Journal of Risk and Insurance* 64(2) (1997): 205; S.P. D'Arcy and V.G. France, "Catastrophe Futures: A Better Hedge for Insurers," *Journal of Risk and Insurance* 59(4) (1992): 575.

243 See G. Chichilnisky and G. Heal, "Managing Unknown Risks," *Journal of Portfolio Management* 24(4) (1998): 85: see further R.E. Smith, E.A. Canelo, and A. DiDio, "Reinventing Reinsurance through Capital Markets," *Geneva Papers on Risk and Insurance* 22 (1997): 26.

244 See J.S. Tynes, "Catastrophe Risk Securitization," *Journal of Insurance Regulation* 19(1) (2000): 3.

245 FM Research, *Capital Punishment: UK Insurance Companies and the Global Environment* (Friends of the Earth, 2000), 47–49.

246 See G. Townley, "Insurance Industry Hit by Global Warming," *Pensions World* 23(7) (1994): 8 (arguing that insurers need to focus on ethical investment to help combat global warming).

247 Innovest, *Climate Change and the Financial Services Industry. Module 2 – A Blueprint for Action* (UNEPFI, 2002), 31–34.

For instance, there is insufficient research demonstrating the relationship between GHG emission regulations and investment returns. Key finance and insurance sector advisors often lack awareness of climate change, leading to insufficient analysis and information being provided to investment decision-makers. Basic data may also be too imprecise for practical decisions.

Political and market barriers also stall financiers.[248] The lack of agreement on GHG emission targets among nations obstructs setting a durable value for carbon reduction and climate adaptation measures. The reluctance of securities regulators to demand more corporate disclosure of material risks related to climate change similarly hinders carbon pricing. Market barriers are associated with the transactions for emission reduction credits, carbon offsets, and such. This is hampered by overly complex and seemingly inflexible regulations governing emissions trading, carbon taxation, the CDM, and other market instruments. The high overheads and transactions costs of such mechanisms deter some investors.

2. Climate Impact Disclosures

The absence of comprehensive, standardized methodologies for measuring and reporting emissions and carbon sequestration is an equally serious barrier to action within the financial sector.[249] Financial institutions are thus beginning to create new informational tools to overcome these cognitive and analytical barriers to action on global warming. If successful, they can help bring to account the unseen climate polluters.

Despite regulatory stipulations in some jurisdictions, companies facing material environmental risks still habitually fail to adequately disclose the pertinent information regarding climate change in their security filings and reporting to capital markets. In the US and various other jurisdictions, companies are expected to disclose climate change and other environmental issues with potential for current or future, direct or indirect effects on the entity's financial health, liquidity, or capital expenditures material to investors.[250] Many US-based multinational companies continue to under-report climate

---

248 Ibid.
249 PricewaterhouseCoopers (PWC) and International Emissions Trading Association (IETA), *Uncertainty in Accounting for the EU Emissions Trading Scheme and Certified Emission Reductions* (PWC and IETA, 2007), 15–16.
250 E.g., Canadian Institute of Chartered Accounts (CICA), *MD&A Disclosure about the Financial Impact of Climate Change and Other Environmental Issues: Discussion Brief* (CICA, October 2005).

change risks in their 10-K reports filed to the SEC.[251] Institutional investors have called on the SEC to improve the enforcement of its disclosure rules.[252] The Friends of the Earth noted in its 2006 annual review of climate change reporting to the SEC that such "reporting in general has steadily increased in quality and quantity," climbing to 49 percent of firms in the surveyed sectors compared to just 26 percent in 2000.[253] A recent international survey of businesses by the Economist Intelligence Unit showed that 32 percent do not monitor their carbon emissions and 46 percent have no plans to reduce their carbon impact.[254]

Apart from meaningful disclosure regulation, financiers also need enhanced metrics to measure and quantify companies' carbon footprints and risks. Presently, two voluntary standards, the Carbon Disclosure Project (CDP) and the Greenhouse Gas Protocol Initiative (GHG Protocol Initiative) provide the principal tools for investors. They generate the data that helps to facilitate dialogue between financial institutions and companies on addressing global warming.

The CDP is the coordinating secretariat for institutional investor collaboration on climate change disclosures.[255] Launched in December 2000, the CDP is a means by which investors can collectively sign a single global request for disclosure of information regarding companies' policies on climate change and emissions of GHGs, climate regulation impacts, physical risks of climate change, and their emission trading activities. These requests are made annually to an ever-larger pool of major companies. By 2007, some 2,400 corporations were asked to report to the CDP, on behalf of over 300 investment institutions. About half responded. However, 77 percent of the 500 largest companies globally answered the questionnaire, with 76 percent

251 J.A. Smith, "The Implications of the Kyoto Protocol and the Global Warming Debate for Business Transactions," *New York University Journal of Law and Business* 1 (2005): 511, 529.

252 CERES, "Thirteen Pension Leaders Call on SEC Chairman to Require Global Warming Risks in Corporate Disclosure," Press release, April 15, 2004; S. Mufson, "SEC Pressed to Require Climate-Risk Disclosures," *Washington Post*, September 18, 2007, D01.

253 M. Chan-Fishel, *Fifth Survey of Climate Change Disclosure in SEC Filings of Automobile, Insurance, Oil and Gas, Petrochemical, and Utilities Companies* (Friends of the Earth, October 2006), 1.

254 Economist Intelligence Unit, *A Change in the Climate. Is Business Going Green?* (UK Trade and Investment, May 2007), 8.

255 Http://www.cdproject.net.

of them reporting implementation of a GHG reduction plan.[256] Significantly, during 2007 the CDP began to widen its scope to solicit information about companies' emissions connected to their supply chains, thereby helping to provide a more comprehensive picture of GHG pollution.[257] The CDP now claims to be the largest registry of corporate GHG emissions data in the world, for the benefit of hundreds of climate-conscious institutional investors such as Credit Suisse Group and the Connecticut Retirement Plans and Trust Funds.[258] While the CDP creates a framework for dialogue between investors and companies on climate change, whether such disclosures and dialogue lead to changes in capital allocation and corporate behavior is entirely another matter yet to be demonstrated.

In contrast to the CDP's focus on better reporting, the GHG Protocol Initiative aims to improve the underlying methods of accounting for GHG emissions and climate impacts.[259] Developed by the WBCSD and the WRI, the GHG Protocol Initiative consists of two modules. The Corporate Accounting and Reporting Standard Module helps companies and other organizations to identify, calculate, and report GHG emissions. This module is limited in that it does not adequately address the position of financial institutions. They do not have to account for the GHG emissions of companies they fund—rather, the companies do this for themselves, as separate "legal entities." The second module is the Project Accounting Protocol and Guidelines, designed for calculating reductions in GHG emissions from specific projects and land use changes. The GHG Protocol provides the accounting framework for the EU Emissions Trading Scheme and other initiatives.

Some other disclosure regimes utilize the reporting frameworks of the CDP and GHG Protocol Initiative. The World Economic Forum's Global Greenhouse Gas Register (GHG Register), established in 2004, provides a global inventory of corporate emissions inventories and reduction targets, based on the GHG Protocol.[260] The GRI, the gold standard for sustainability reporting, contains directions on reporting relevant information regarding climate change.[261] The GRI's G3 Reporting Framework of October 2006

---

256 Innovest, *Carbon Disclosure Report 2007: Global FT500* (CDP, 2007).

257 Remarks by P. Dickinson, Chief Executive Officer, CDP (UNEPFI Global Roundtable, Melbourne, Australia, October 24–25, 2007).

258 US EPA, *New Developments in Corporate Climate Disclosure* (EPA Climate Leaders 5th Anniversary Meeting, March 2007), 1.

259 Http://www.ghgprotocol.org.

260 Http://www.weforum.org/en/initiatives/ghg/GreenhouseGasRegister.

261 See http://www.globalreporting.org.

introduced a specific reporting indicator on the "financial implications due to climate change." Adding to the proliferation of standards is the Climate Risk Disclosure Initiative, launched by CERES in May 2005. It guides corporate disclosures in various climate impact and risk themes by applying the CDP or other reporting methodologies.[262]

Another initiative also informed by the GHG Protocol is the ISO 14064 standard, released in March 2006. It aims to promote consistency, transparency, and credibility in GHG emission quantification, reporting, and verification, to thereby facilitate trade in GHG allowances and credits. The ISO 14064 comprises three standards for detailing specifications and guidance for the organizational and project levels, and also for validation and verification.[263] The ISO 14064 is complemented by ISO 14065, which specifies requirements to accredit or recognize bodies that undertake GHG validation or verification using ISO or other applicable standards.[264]

The accounting profession is also making contributions. Take for example the Climate Disclosure Standards Board, set up by the World Economic Forum in 2007.[265] The Board is a partnership of seven organizations, including the CDP, aiming to align information requests to businesses into a standard, universal format. The Board is preparing a set of Generally Accepted Carbon Accounting Principles for this purpose. The IASB, through its International Financial Reporting Interpretations Committee, has issued accounting guidance for carbon emission assets and liabilities.[266] The 2004 guidance seeks to establish financial values for these attributes. If companies produce GHG emissions, they must recognize a financial liability in the obligation

262 CERES, *Global Framework for Climate Risk Disclosure* (CERES, October 2006).
263 ISO 14064-1: 2006, *Greenhouse Gases—Part 1: Specification with Guidance at the Organization Level for the Quantification and Reporting of Greenhouse Gas Emissions and Removals*; ISO 14064-2: 2006, *Greenhouse Gases—Part 2: Specification with Guidance at the Project Level for the Quantification, Monitoring and Reporting of Greenhouse Gas Emission Reductions and Removal Enhancements*; ISO 14064-3: 2006, *Greenhouse Gases—Part 3: Specification with Guidance for the Validation and Verification of Greenhouse Gas Assertions*.
264 ISO 14065: 2007, *Greenhouse Gases—Requirements for Greenhouse Gas Validation and Verification Bodies for Use in Accreditation or Other Forms of Recognition*.
265 World Economic Forum, "New Consortium Created to Develop Standard Framework for Company Reporting of Climate Risks," Media release, January 26, 2007.
266 IASB, "IFRIC Issues Guidance on Accounting for Greenhouse Gas Emissions and Scope of Leasing Standard," Press release, December 2, 2004.

to retain allowances to cover those emissions. These accountancy standards should percolate into the financial accounting rules applied in individual countries.

3. Finance for Climate Abatement

In the corporate, retail, and project financing sectors, financial resources for climate abatement are being disbursed. They fund renewable energy technology development as well as infrastructure development arising from adaptation to climate change, and energy efficiency-related projects. Financiers are also acting as intermediaries in carbon markets such as emission allowance trading. The Kyoto Protocol's flexible mechanisms have created or facilitated some of these new financing roles.

The Kyoto Protocol's Clean Development Mechanism (CDM), which promotes collaboration between developing and developed countries in project financing, helps to overcome barriers to private lending. The sale of emission credits from CDM projects can offset the high upfront investment costs associated with climate-abatement projects. The Joint Implementation (JI) mechanism can provide a similar benefit. Conversely, CDM and JI, by their very design, tend to be very complex to implement and generate high transaction costs and risks,[267] as each project must secure approval and independent verification of the emission reductions. Some CDM projects are also subject to the Protocol's adaptation levy.[268] Partly because of such obstacles, private banks and investors have been slow to partake in CDM or JI projects until recently.[269] Private lenders usually take into account only the value of emission reductions units in the assessment of a CDM or JI project if a carbon purchase agreement has been concluded to provide a definite value. Therefore, the MDBs and individual governments have dominated the CDM and JI markets.

The UNFCCC requires developed countries to finance climate adaptation programs in the emerging economies.[270] It established several funds, including the Special Climate Change Fund and the Least Developed Countries Fund (both of which operate under the auspices of the Global Environment Facility),

267 UNEPFI Climate Change Working Group, CEO Briefing: Finance for Carbon Solutions (UNEPFI, January 2005), 5.
268 With the exception of projects in a "least developed country party": FCCC/CP/2001/13/Add.2, Decision 17/CP.7– Modalities and procedures for a clean development mechanism as defined in Article 12 of the Kyoto Protocol, clause 15(b).
269 UNEPFI, note 267, 1.
270 Article 4.4, ILM 31 (1992): 848.

and the Kyoto Protocol Adaptation Fund.[271] Besides these primarily intergovernmental funds, the World Bank has promoted co-financing arrangements with private lenders to remove some of the market and institutional barriers to their involvement in climate mitigation projects in emerging markets. Co-financing is leveraged through the Prototype Carbon Fund, BioCarbon Fund, and the Community Development Carbon Fund.[272] The World Bank's IFC also runs a Renewable Energy and Energy Efficiency Fund.[273] They have helped make projects viable; the World Bank's Prototype Carbon Fund increased estimated rates of return by over 5 percent through selling emissions credits.[274]

Apart from CDM or JI project contexts, investment banks are beginning to acknowledge climate change risks and opportunities in project finance. Several project finance and venture capital funds have been announced in recent years focusing on clean technology or carbon finance.[275] While the EPs—the main SRI standard for project financing—make no explicit mention of climate change risks, the IFC's revised Performance Standards (2006), informing the Principles, do so. Performance Standard 3 furthers the IFC's goal of advancing climate friendly investments by requiring clients to "promote the reduction of project-related greenhouse gas (GHG) emissions in a manner appropriate to the nature and scale of project operations and impacts."[276] For projects "that are expected to or currently produce significant quantities of GHGs,"[277] borrowers must quantify and monitor direct emissions from facilities owned or controlled within the physical project boundary, and also quantify the indirect emissions associated with the off-site production of power used by the project, on an annual basis. Borrowers must also evaluate technically and financially feasible options to reduce GHG emissions during project design and operation.

271 S. Huq, "The Bonn-Marrakesh Agreements on Funding," *Climate Policy* 2 (2002): 243.
272 See http://www.CarbonFinance.org.
273 E. Martinot, "Renewable Energy Investment by the World Bank," *Energy Policy* 29(9) (2001): 689.
274 Innovest, note 236, 20; see further S. Smith, "The Prototype Carbon Fund: A New Departure in International Trusts and Securities Law," *Sustainable Development Law and Policy* 5(2) (2005): 28.
275 E.g., KfW Foderbank's Carbon Fund, http://www.kfw-foerderbank.de; Axiom Venture Capital, http://ww.axiomvc.com; and Enviro Finance, http://www.envirofinance.com.
276 IFC, *Performance Standards on Social and Environmental Sustainability* (IFC, April 2006), 13.
277 Ibid.

Financial institutions are also jostling to take advantage of markets for trading in emission allowances and carbon off-sets.[278] One such player, the UK-based Carbon Capital Markets, buys and sells EU carbon allowances for companies.[279] It also invests private equity in CDM and JI projects. Another intermediary is EcoSecurities, which works with companies to create and purchase carbon credits from projects that do not produce emissions.[280] Presently, the GHG emission market remains immature and imperfect. Emission unit prices are too low, and the market lacks liquidity. In the most active carbon market, the EU trading scheme, the price of a ton of carbon collapsed to below one euro in early 2007 due to a glut of gifted emission allowances.[281] There are also voluntary trading schemes. The most successful is the Chicago Climate Exchange (CCX), initiated in December 2003. The CCX is a GHG emission allowance trading hub for emission sources and offset projects in the US and a growing number of other countries including Canada, Brazil, and Mexico.[282] CCX members, including household names such as Ford and IBM, make voluntary commitments to reduce their GHG emissions in 2010 by 6 percent below a baseline period of 1998–2001. As of November 2007, CCX had some 380 members including non-corporate members such as municipalities and universities.[283]

In the retail finance markets, banks have opened new product lines in "green" home loans and mortgages. The energy efficient mortgage developed by Fannie Mae in the US rewards buyers of energy efficient homes with more favorable mortgage terms.[284] A growing array of banks offers similar deals.[285] As an illustration, consider the Citizens Bank in Canada. Its green mortgage tempts borrowers with a "green savers home energy audit," complimentary compact fluorescent lights, and coupons for energy efficient products and services from local stores.[286] These schemes unfortunately do not directly penalize borrowers who acquire or build homes that generate additional climate costs.

278 See generally D. Stowell, *Climate Trading: Development of Kyoto Protocol Markets* (Palgrave Macmillan, 2005).
279 Http://www.carboncapitalmarkets.com.
280 Http://www.ecosecurities.com.
281 Figures from Carbon Market Europe: http://www.pointcarbon.com.
282 Http://www.chicagoclimatex.com.
283 Remarks, R. Sandor. CEO, Chicago Climate Exchange (18th Annual SRI in the Rockies Conference, Santa Ana Pueblo, New Mexico, November 3–6, 2007).
284 Http://www.fanniemae.com.
285 UNEPFI, *Green Financial Products and Services: Current Developments and Future Opportunities in North America* (UNEPFI, 2007), 17–19.
286 Http://www.citizensbank.ca.

4. Shareholder Activism

Environmental NGOs and some institutional investors use shareholder resolutions and dialogue to spur corporate management to act responsibly on climate change. In 1990, Friends of the Earth took the lead. With a mere 400 shares in Exxon, it called on the corporate behemoth to "reduce production of CO_2 emissions from its energy production plants and facilities."[287] These shareholder proposals commonly ask management to report on climate change risks and effects. They normally do not ask firms to adopt specific actions to mitigate their emissions, as in some jurisdictions that could be construed as a prohibited attempt to dictate managerial action. Even so, some firms have resisted such "interference" as encroaching upon the prerogatives of management. Yet others have reacted positively, by disclosing GHG emissions, setting emission reduction goals, making energy efficiency investments, and integrating climate risk into core business plans.

Shareholder proposals on climate issues have been relatively rare and garnered little open support until recently.[288] The vast majority of such resolutions have been filed in the US. A study of proposals filed in eighty-one US companies during the period 2002–2003 found that global warming resolutions attracted an average support of only 13 percent.[289] A survey by SIF documented twenty-five shareholder resolutions on climate issues in 2003, rising to thirty-five in 2005. The resolutions attracted an average of 16.7 percent support in 2003, which declined to 10.8 percent in 2005.[290] One resolution asking the ExxonMobil board of directors to comprehensively review how it would meet GHG reduction targets in countries subject to the Kyoto Protocol received a relatively high 28.3 percent support.[291] The 2007 proxy season in the US saw a further spike in climate change-related resolutions, with a record forty-three proposals filed with US companies.[292]

---

287 D.G. Cogan, *Unexamined Risk: How Mutual Funds Vote on Climate Change Shareholder Risk* (CERES, 2006), 7.

288 R. Monks, et al., "Shareholder Activism on Environmental Issues: A Study of Proposals at Large U.S. Corporations (2000–2003)," *Natural Resources Forum* 28 (2004): 317, 319.

289 Ibid., 321.

290 SIF, *2005 Socially Responsible Investing Trends in the United States: 10-Year Review* (SIF, 2006), 19 (in each year, some of the resolutions were withdrawn before the vote, usually because management agreed in advance to respond positively to the requests).

291 Ibid., 10.

292 CERES, "Investors Achieve Record Results in 2007 in Spurring Corporate Action on Climate Change," Press release, August 13, 2007.

Shareholder resolutions that went to a vote garnered a record high average voting support of 21.6 percent, including nearly 40 percent backing for a resolution filed with Allegheny Energy, the most ever for a global warming resolution in the US.[293] Public sector pension funds and faith-based investors are the most climate-conscious shareholders, instigating many of these resolutions.[294]

Mutual funds have traditionally been taciturn, although some commentators believe this will change in the US and Canada in the wake of securities regulation reforms requiring funds to disclose their proxy voting record.[295] The US mutual fund industry has tended to routinely side with management on shareholder resolutions. A report commissioned by CERES analyzed how the US's 100 largest mutual funds voted their shareholder proxies on climate change resolutions filed in 2005.[296] During that period, only three investment companies (Columbia, Franklin Templeton, and Neuberger Berman) had proxy voting guidelines allowing fund manages to support proposals for corporate disclosure on environmental issues such as climate change. Moreover, of votes actually cast, no mutual funds surveyed supported any climate change proposals filed.

Most funds have proxy voting policies that instruct their fund managers to oppose or abstain on many shareholder risk issues, climate change being one of them. For example, Excelsior Funds, which has issued Voting Guidelines on Social and Environmental Issues (adopted in October 2004), states:

> We do not believe that social and political restrictions should be placed on a company's business operations, unless determined as appropriate by management. While from an investment perspective we may consider how a company's social and political practices may affect present and prospective valuations and returns, we believe that proposals which prohibit companies from lines of business for social or political reasons are often motivated by narrow interest groups and not in the best interest of the broad base of shareholders of a company. We believe that management is in the best position to determine

293 Ibid.
294 SIF, note 290, 22.
295 C.A. Williams and J.M. Conley, "Corporate Social Responsibility in the International Context: Is there an Emerging Fiduciary Duty to Consider Human Rights?" *University of Cincinnati Law Review* 74 (2005): 75, 96.
296 Cogan, note 287.

these fundamental business questions. We will typically vote against such proposals.[297]

In the US, the SEC has arbitrated[298] over many shareholder resolutions on climate change, which the targeted companies challenged as being improper.[299] The Commission has tended to rule against resolutions if they raise "ordinary business" issues deemed a prerogative of management.[300] The SEC nonetheless has not always been apparently consistent in its rulings. In April 2003, the SEC allowed Xcel Energy to exclude a shareholder request for an evaluation of climate change risks to the market competitiveness of the company.[301] In March 2005, the SEC allowed an ExxonMobil shareholder proposal for the firm to "undertake a comprehensive review and publish a report on how it will meet the greenhouse gas reduction targets of those countries in which it operates which have adopted the Kyoto Protocol."[302] The SEC did not agree with ExxonMobil's management that the shareholders' request constituted an attempt to micromanage its business.

So far, while shareholder resolutions on climate change issues are relatively uncommon compared to traditional subjects of shareholder proposals (such as executive pay), it garners more shareholder proposals than virtually any other SRI environmental cause.[303] And companies may be willing to meet shareholder demands even if a proposal is defeated. Thus, Ford agreed to implement a failed resolution asking it to report on the business implications of reducing GHG emissions from its vehicles and manufacturing facilities.[304]

---

297 Cited in Cogan, note 287, 28.

298 The SEC typically does so via a "no-action letter," whereby it clarifies whether a particular action would constitute a violation of the federal securities law.

299 For a more detailed discussion, see S.H. Choi, "It's Getting Hot in Here: The SEC's Regulation of Climate Change Shareholder Proposals Under the Ordinary Business Exception," *Duke Environmental Law and Policy Forum* 17 (2006): 165.

300 Ibid., 178–79.

301 Xcel Energy Inc., "SEC No-Action Letter, 2003," *Lexis* 500, April 1, 2003, 1.

302 ExxonMobil Corporation, "SEC No-Action Letter, 2005," *Lexis* 466, March 23, 2005, 1.

303 SIF, note 290, 19 (only shareholder proposals on political contributions were more numerous among US investors in 2005).

304 Ford published its report on 2005, and claimed to have reduced CO_2 from its manufacturing facilities by 15 percent, with further reductions planned, and was adopting measures to improve the fuel efficiency of its cars:

IV. Comparisons

These case studies on climate change and Indigenous peoples help to illuminate how SRI works in practice—the way financiers respond to specific issues, the motivations that drive their behavior, and the way that regulation helps or hinders their engagement. Climate change may be a much "bigger" SRI issue, yet a study of the SRI sector's response to Indigenous peoples is just as enlightening of the potential and limitations of responsible financing.

Traditional legal measures to assist Indigenous peoples, such as land rights and self-government agreements, are insufficient in a world where economic development is mostly in the hands of the private sector. Yet, so far, these legal resources have provided Indigenous peoples with their principal strength to resist unwelcome developments. SRI-related regulation has not been particularly attentive to their plight. While the SRI movement is starting to champion Indigenous rights, it is largely a low-key aspect of the SRI market, mostly addressed within project financing or equity investments in the energy and resource sectors. Lenders have often contended with Indigenous interests in a confrontational rather than a cooperative manner. Only a handful of mutual funds such as Ethical Funds Company (Canada) and Calvert (US) have robust policies on Indigenous relations. Apart from community, microfinancing initiatives, the SRI sector's responses to Indigenous peoples are mainly defensive, as a form of risk management to protect business reputations and access to resources. Indigenous peoples as an SRI cause do not offer the same lucrative investment opportunities, such as in the biofuels and solar power sectors, which are igniting interest among climate-conscious investors.

The ethical questions concerning fair treatment of Indigenous peoples may find some expression within the business case framework. A pioneering study by the WRI suggests that there is a business case for community consent, and that projects should proceed only with consent rather than mere "consultation."[305] Based on several international case studies, it concluded that "the risks created by not obtaining community consent are significant and quantifiable."[306] Thus, the WRI recommended that:

Ford Motor Company, *Ford Report on the Business Impact of Climate Change* (Ford Motor Company, 2005), 3.

305 Herz, Vina, and Sohn, note 49.

306 Ibid., vi.

---

project sponsors and financiers incorporate community involvement and consent procedures and requirements into their project and investment decision making, planning, and operations at the very beginning, and that host governments incorporate such procedures and requirements into their permitting processes.[307]

The EPs do not meet this standard of consent. They merely require "good faith negotiations," and they repose too much discretion to financiers.

Community consent also has an ethical dimension, and that is one reason why financiers often struggle to deal with Indigenous rights and claims. It expresses the moral right of communities to oppose development that is culturally inappropriate, harmful to their environment, or of little economic benefit to them. Community consent is not merely based on legal property rights, which allow a landowner to eject a trespassing developer. Rather, it is fundamentally an ethical expression of a human entitlement for the self-determination of communities. This ethical imperative cannot readily be accommodated within an SRI discourse grounded in "financial materiality" and the demands of capital owners to have access to all affordable development space. Requiring financiers to consult with and obtain the consent of Indigenous communities affected by their investments is one area of potential reform for SRI regulation.

Climate change of course is potentially a vastly more environmentally and economically significant issue for peoples worldwide. It therefore arouses financial markets in a much wider array of contexts. Yet, climate change has also generated disproportionately more interest because it readily dovetails with business case drivers of SRI. Undoubtedly, climate change is also very much an ethical issue, as humanity's ability to tamper with the planet's entire climate raises profound questions about the relationship between humankind and nature.[308] Indeed, the UNFCCC proclaims as one of its core principles that: "[t]he Parties should protect the climate system for the benefit of present and future generations of humankind, on the basis of equity and in accordance with their common but differentiated responsibilities and respective capabilities."[309] The financial sector has been able largely to bypass such uncomfortable themes that might throw the very legitimacy of our economic system into doubt. Instead, the climate finance discourse has been carefully framed

---

307 Ibid., 3.
308 P. Taylor, "The Business of Climate Change: What's Ethics Got to Do With It?" *Global Business and Development Law Journal* 20 (2007): 161.
309 Article 3.1, ILM 31 (1992): 849.

around business risks and investment opportunities. There is nothing objectionable with investors financially benefiting from reducing their carbon footprint. The problem is that the business case will not always provide sufficient motivation for change, especially where a potent countervailing business case for investment in oil and other fossil fuels remains.

A second significant insight of climate finance is the growing dependency the sector has on government regulation. Regulation and litigation risks are major drivers for financiers to factor climate change into their investment choices. The prospect of carbon emission caps, carbon taxes, renewable energy subsidies, and mandatory corporate disclosures on climate impacts—all imposed by governments—are becoming crucial for the SRI market on climate finance. Such regulation is most relevant to the market pricing of GHG emissions, by creating incentives for their mitigation. Government policies on climate adaptation—concerning the impacts of global warming such as rising sea levels or more frequent droughts—are less important at this stage but will eventually assume similar importance for financiers. These facts should remind us of how heavily SRI often depends on market regulation. In this sense SRI presents a paradox, having emerged as a form of surrogate market regulation to compensate for the lacunae of official regulation, yet sometimes dependent on the state to set environmental standards necessary to stimulate the SRI market.

CHAPTER 8

The Path to Ethical Investment for Sustainability

I. Renewing the Promise of SRI

A. THE URGENCY OF OUR TIMES

The time has come to rethink some basic assumptions of our development path. Ecological problems, some long foreseen, are now cascading upon us. Not a week passes without alarming news of rapidly melting ice caps, poisoned food chains, and animal species being obliterated into extinction. In 2005, the Millennium Ecosystem Assessment Board warned that "human activity is putting such strain on the natural functions of the Earth that the ability of the planet's ecosystems to sustain future generations can no longer be taken for granted."[1] Such bleak predictions are echoed by many other international studies, such as UNEP's 2007 *Global Environmental Outlook* report.[2] With the developing world rapidly emulating an unsustainable economic model, ecological tipping points may be reached, with no apparent remedy.[3] At current population density and high consumption

---

1 Millennium Ecosystem Assessment Board (MEAB), *Living Beyond Our Means: Natural Assets and Human Well-Being. Statement from the Board* (MEAB, 2005), 5.

2 UNEP, *GEO Yearbook 2007: An Overview of Our Changing Environment* (UNEP, 2007); see also WWF, *Living Planet Report 2006* (WWF, 2006) for similar dire warnings.

3 S.R. Carpenter, et al., *Ecosystems and Human Well-being: Scenarios: Findings of the Scenarios Working Group,* Volume 2 (MEAB and Island Press, 2005).

rates, humankind would require several more Earth-like planets to sustain life.[4] Humankind has largely forgotten how environmental stresses have proved ruinous to older civilizations.[5] Current environmental threats and risks are much more serious.[6]

The capital-intensive global economy, driven increasingly by financial markets, both amplifies these threats and reduces the capacity of our governing institutions to stanch them. Despite the stream of evidence linking economic activity to impacts on the biosphere, most institutions seem stagnant in changing their course. Economic growth is the modern yardstick of human evolution, whether at the corporate level (measured by increasing earnings), the financiers' level (investment returns), or the nation-state level (GDP). In *The Cancer Stage of Capitalism*, John McMurtry likens this economic surge to a tumor, rather than the growth of a healthy organism.[7] Riane Eisler argues that economic indicators and resultant policies give little value to caring for the contribution of nature to overall wealth.[8] "Wealth" created by economic growth has at times delivered questionable gains even for its richest beneficiaries.[9] Economists have pioneered alternative measures of economic vitality and well-being, suggesting that the seemingly most prosperous nations do not necessarily enjoy the highest standard of living or contentment.[10]

---

4 W.E. Rees, "Consuming the Earth: The Biophysics of Sustainability," *Ecological Economics* 29 (1999): 23; W.E. Rees, and M. Wackernagel, *Our Ecological Footprint: Reducing Human Impact on the Earth* (New Society Publishers, 1995); C.W. Fowler and L. Hobbs, "Is Humanity Sustainable?" *Proceedings of the Royal Society of London, Series B: Biological Sciences* 270 (2003): 2579.

5 J.A. Tainter, *The Collapse of Complex Societies* (Cambridge University Press, 1990); J. Diamond, *Collpase: How Societies Choose to Fail or Succeed* (Viking Books, 2004).

6 U. Beck, *World Risk Society* (Polity Press 1999).

7 J. McMurtry, *The Cancer Stage of Capitalism* (Pluto Press, 1999).

8 R. Eisler, *The Real Wealth of Nations: Creating a Caring Economics* (Berrett-Koehler Publishers, 2007).

9 William Rees documents that recent increases in per capital expenditures on US healthcare have not improved the overall health of its population: W.E. Rees, "The End (of Growth) is Nigh" (paper presented at the Ecological Integrity and Sustainable Society Conference, Dalhousie University, Halifax, June 23–27, 2007).

10 H. Henderson, *Ethical Markets; Growing The Green Economy* (Chelsea Green Publishing, 2007). Consider, for example, alternative measures of prosperity, such as the "Genuine Progress Indicator," http://www.gpiatlantic.org,

Sustainable living requires moderating economic growth expectations. Sustainability implies any form of development that is careful not to undermine the long-term integrity of life-supporting ecosystems. Consequently, the use of renewable resources should not exceed their rate of regeneration; use of non-renewable resources should not exceed the rate at which renewable replacements for such resources are developed; and emissions should remain within the assimilative capacity of the environment.[11] Sustainability therefore values different methods of decision-making, entailing a more long-term perspective that includes public participation, environmental impact assessment, and an ethic of restraint.[12] Yet decades of debate on sustainable development since the Brundtland report of 1987, has not revolutionized economic models.[13] Markets systemically fail to account for much social and environmental degradation,[14] yet since Brundtland there has been more market deregulation, mass privatizations, and other neoliberal policies, intensifying market pressures.[15] The principal alternate economic model, associated with the command economy of socialism, proved equally addicted to senseless economic growth. The growth ethos is not solely responsible for humanity's unsustainable path, but is one of the most vital factors.

Current financial market governance tends to overlook the unseen polluters—lenders and investors who fuel and profit from unsustainable development. Herman Daly, a well-known environmental economist, stated that it is both a moral and economical wrong to "treat the earth as a business in liquidation."[16] Capitalism only seriously manages two kinds of capital—money and goods—while selling out an even more critical source of capital: nature.

"Index of Sustainable Economic Welfare," http://www.neweconomics.org, or the "Happy Planet Index," http://www.happyplanetindex.org.

11 For some of the most authoritative scholarship on sustainability, see H. Daly, *Beyond Growth: The Economics of Sustainable Development* (Beacon Press, 1997); R. Costanza, et al., eds, *Institutions, Ecosystems, and Sustainability* (CRC Press, 2000); C. Soskolne, ed., *Sustaining Life on Earth* (Lexington Books, 2007).

12 C. Brodhag, "From Rationality to Governance: The Decision Process of Sustainable Development," *International Journal of Sustainable Development* 2(3) (1999): 388.

13 World Commission on Environment and Development, *Our Common Future* (Oxford University Press, 1987).

14 See R. Costanza, et al., *An Introduction to Ecological Economics* (St. Lucie Press, 1997).

15 P. Arestis and M.C. Sawyer, *The Rise of the Market: Critical Essays on the Political Economy of Neoliberalism* (Edward Elgar Publishing, 2004).

16 Quoted in C. Cobb, T. Halstead, and J. Rowe, "If the GDP is Up, Why is America Down," *Atlantic Monthly* 276(4) (1995): 59.

It is reasonable to conclude that the financial sector shares responsibility in ensuring that development from its investments respect ecological constraints.[17] The debate is not whether the financial sector should be accountable; rather, it is about how to hold it accountable, which may require rethinking the basic foundations of economic governance. Flourishing societies are culturally agile—able to discard the sacred cows of obsolete values and capable of radical transformation for survival. Business organizations must also be agile enough to face this magnitude of change, along with parallel changes in the behavior of other organizations, governments, and individuals.

It appears that business case SRI has lacked this transformative capacity. Certainly, today far fewer people consider SRI to be a fringe movement. Mainstream SRI educates financiers of the salience of corporate social and environmental externalities, thereby helping to induce some beneficial changes in financial markets. Yet, unlike traditional social protest movements, SRI seeks solutions to capitalism's weaknesses within its very own transactional system. SRI relies on markets as the means of ordering—thus, few fund managers will tolerate significant sustainability objectives that do not lead to higher returns. Business case SRI is not the most effective way to alleviate ethical anxieties about the economy. But, in the absence of an entirely new economic model, one way to circumvent this mindset is through additional and smarter regulation. How, then, can we improve the governance of SRI?

B. MOVING BEYOND BUSINESS-AS-USUAL

SRI serves as both a warning and an opportunity to financial markets. It warns that our current patterns of investment often impair ecological health and social justice. It also presents an opportunity to reform investment practices to respect social and environmental values so essential to the long-term health of the economy. Despite the recent growth of SRI, most financial institutions have not heeded this message.[18] A business case model of SRI sanguinely transforms the tensions between environmental protection

---

17 See J. Rada and A. Trisoglio, "Capital Markets and Sustainable Development," *Columbia Journal of World Business* 27(3/4) (1992): 42; W.L. Thomas, "The Green Nexus: Financiers and Sustainable Development," *Georgetown International Environmental Law Review* 13 (2001): 899.

18 D.L. Owen, "Towards a Theory of Social Investment: A Review Essay," *Accounting, Organizations and Society* 15(3) (1990): 249, 259–64.

and profitable investment into a harmonious relationship. Of course, that environmental care and business success can be compatible is not an objectionable proposition, in principle. Financiers should benefit from companies that reduce their ecological footprint.

The problem lies in the fact that some financiers will just tinker with unsustainable modes of development. Tied to a concept of financial materiality, the business case can help to address some environmental problems through improved research and analysis. However, it cannot accommodate ecological issues not valued by the market, and existing strategies in this model struggle to transform investment "value" to incorporate other non-financial factors. Concomitantly, business reputational risk may provide a flimsy basis for assuring ethical conduct. One reason is that the marketplace has a short institutional memory; for instance, how many remember that Lee Iacocca was the man behind the Ford Pinto? Many corporate reputation-enhancing measures mask a different reality.[19] Thus, without demonstrated financial advantage, an investment analysis may advocate delaying or halting measures that mitigate pollution, especially in the absence of effective government regulation and stakeholder pressure. In fact, a countervailing business case for intensifying environmentally unsustainably practices will be evaluated. For example, despite the SRI industry's rhetoric about climate change risks, the fossil fuel industry has hardly changed. The flood of new investment dollars in Alberta's oil sands is one example.[20] Without an additional layer of ethical responsibility, many financiers lack incentive to take actions beyond those prescribed by a business case.

As ecological modernization theory suggests, financial markets will take note of changes in environmental behavior that capture financial benefits: more efficient use of resources leading to lower production costs, or the creation of new environmentally-friendly products answering specific market demands. But improvements in environmental behavior that capture no financial benefit for firms, and by implication their investors, will be largely discounted. A study of the North American finance sector in 2005 reported:

> [M]ainstream investment professionals are at best wary and at worst actively hostile to SRI. Rightly or wrongly, most have concluded that SRI approaches unnecessarily and arbitrarily restrict the set of

---

19 G. Pitcher, "Corporate Responsibility Isn't Always About Charity," *Marketing Week*, March 14, 2002, 33.

20 K. Makin, "High-stakes Battle Looms over Oil-Sands Pollution," *Globe and Mail*, August 15, 2007, A1.

investment opportunities and therefore jeopardize both financial returns and the money managers' exercise of their fiduciary responsibility. Even when purely financial arguments are made for including environmental information, these tend to be lost or overwhelmed by a general skepticism about its relevance.[21]

David Vogel suggests that those firms and investors that do pay attention to such issues are primarily motivated by "their corporate strategy and business identity: it is a way for them to differentiate themselves from their competitors."[22] Large, highly visible international firms may also pay more attention to their social and environmental conduct as a preemptive defense against NGO activists seeking to tarnish their brand name.[23] Even then, further reform is likely necessary. Paul Hawken once astutely observed that "if every company on the planet were to adopt the environmental and social practices of the best companies—of, say, the Body Shop, Patagonia, and Ben and Jerry's—the world would still be moving toward environmental degradation and collapse."[24]

Renewing the promise of SRI requires many changes, foremost of which is to reframe the core objective of financial institutions to an overarching responsibility for ethical investing for sustainability. The only permissible financial returns should be those achieved without unaccounted-for public costs to the environment and social welfare. This does not mean that financial returns are not important, but that the focus of the investment objectives be over the long term, so that even in the long-term interests of the financial market itself, natural and social "capital" is not degraded. The sustainability of the financial sector should be seen as depending ultimately on the sustainability of life.

Therefore, restoring the promise of SRI means that the business case approach must be bolstered by an ethical case: historically demonstrated through the Quakers' rejecting profiting from slavery, later through the divestment campaign against apartheid in South Africa. More recently,

21 S. McGeachie, M. Kiernan, and E. Kirzner, *Finance and the Environment in North America: The State of Play of the Integration of Environmental Issues into Financial Research* (Environment Canada, 2005), 8–9.
22 D. Vogel, *The Market for Virtue. The Potential and Limits of Corporate Social Responsibility* (Brookings Institution Press, 2005), 73.
23 S. Waygood, *Capital Market Campaigning. The Impact of NGOs on Companies, Shareholder Value and Reputational Risk* (Risk Books, 2006).
24 P. Hawken, "A Declaration of Sustainability," in *Environmental Philosophy*, eds M. Zimmerman, et al. (Prentice-Hall, 1998), 375, 376.

in 1992, some 1700 world scientists issued their "Warning to Humanity," advising that "[h]uman beings and the natural world are on a collision course."[25] To avert this disaster, these scientists called for "[a] new ethic[,] ... a new attitude towards discharging our responsibility for caring for ourselves and for the earth."[26] Yet, such calls for more ethical practices, on their own, will unlikely motivate reform as evidenced by inaction to this warning now sixteen years later. Given the current institutional and legal structure of capital markets, it is not at all surprising that the SRI movement has largely marginalized ethical motivations. Criticisms of banks or mutual funds should be equally directed to those responsible for their regulation.

Of course, a more comprehensive and progressive system of SRI is not the only ingredient for sustainable development. In particular, we need to retain prescriptive regulation on investment to protect critical ecosystems and to manage policy issues too complex for effective SRI analyses. For instance, environmental sustainability implies social equity (the principle of "intragenerational equity"), which is problematic for financial markets that invariably exacerbate inequalities. While investment fiduciaries may be able to effectively respond to discrete social problems, such as divesting from firms that exploit child labor or practice racially discriminatory hiring, fiduciaries can hardly address pervasive social and economic inequalities inherent in a capitalist economy.

Similar cognitive limitations in the financial sector arise in relation to environmental policy. For instance, legislated limits to GHG emissions to avoid dangerous climate change are necessary to delineate the boundaries of permissible investment to ensure that the integrity of the planet's climate is not transgressed. While financial institutions may help to mitigate and abate climate change, by financing demand for renewable energy or raising the cost of capital for polluters, financiers cannot together coordinate overall economic activity to keep GHG emissions within ecologically safe limits. There is no internal steering mechanism within the financial sector to coordinate and keep its growth within biosphere constraints. Only states can determine those limits, such as by capping carbon emissions. However, as explained earlier in this book, the limitations of strict command regulation imply that this style of governance should be reserved for strategic and critical policy issues involving stubborn market failures.

---

25 Union of Concerned Scientists, *World Scientists' Warning to Humanity* (1992), at http://www.ucsusa.org/ucs/about/1992-world-scientists-warning-to-humanity.html.

26 Ibid.

C. THE STATE OF SRI GOVERNANCE

Clearly, there is no SRI "global revolution," as prematurely proclaimed by one notable commentator.[27] More mutedly, SRI is gradually becoming a mainstream style of investment. But with mainstreaming, SRI's rebellious and activist side has softened; its critical edge, as well as its ideological strength, has diminished. SRI, once at odds with profit maximization, is now championed as a means to profitability. Yet, the SRI market remains small even with expansive definitions. While SRI funds appear to perform well financially, they have hardly affected polluters' cost of capital. Nor have there been profound changes at the governance level; no attempt has been made to design an overall governance *system* for SRI to promote cooperative interaction of policy instruments to engender real change.

Increased shareholder advocacy, growth of the SRI retail market, new SRI codes of conduct, and improved financial analysis of corporate environmental performance do show signs of hope. SRI suggests a new social economy that realigns the relationships between the state, market, and civil society, offering the prospect of new forms of citizen involvement in the economy in pursuit of socially responsible savings and financing. However this goal remains a distant dream for now, and SRI growth occurs unevenly. Public pension funds have tended to be among the most active shareholders, and most democratically run, while mutual funds lag considerably.[28] There is similar unevenness among various SRI causes. Climate change garners relatively abundant attention while issues that challenge the distribution of wealth and control of natural resources, as in the case of Indigenous peoples, are less commonly known.

While SRI's recent blossoming has coincided with the ascendancy of neoliberal inspired political and economic restructurings, other factors are also at work. Countervailing pressures from the anti-globalization movement, environmental NGOs, and growing public anxiety about the state of the environment have moderated the neoliberal agenda. Civil society groups have even sought to influence change through participation in financial markets, by buying shares in targeted companies.[29] SRI appeals to governments because it functions as quasi-regulation and oversight of areas where the state has ceded authority to the private sector.

---

27 R. Sparkes, *Socially Responsible Investment: A Global Revolution* (John Wiley and Sons, 2002).

28 R. Sullivan, "Public Pensions Leading the Way on SRI," *Financial Times*, May 21, 2007, 13 (surveys).

29 J. Emel, "An Inquiry into the Green Disciplining of Capital," *Environment and Planning A* 34(5) (2002): 827.

As an outcome of changing relationships between state and society, the movement from "government" to "governance" in SRI and other policy sectors has entailed replacing or complementing coercive regulatory instruments with softer instruments, be they incentive-based or informational.[30] Such "decentered" and pluralistic forms of governance are perceived by states to provide the policy process with a better mix of accountability and efficiency. This is preferable to the less politically attractive options of either wholesale deregulation associated with neoliberalism at one extreme or a return to heavy-handed command controls at the other. SRI governance thus sits very much within the realm of the regulatory "third way," between restrictive regulation and unbridled deregulation.[31]

Consequently, SRI's philosophy on governance rarely supports setting absolute standards or limits on investment behavior. Instead, it relies on voluntary standards and facilitative regulatory techniques to infuse transparency in financiers' social and environmental impacts. It fosters a learning process within financial organizations to manage such impacts. These transparency norms provide a feedback loop by which companies and investors should see the effects of their actions on stakeholders. In a global market, where environmental effects are displaced by time and space, more informed decision-making by financiers is crucial. Disclosure measures create an incentive structure that rewards financiers that minimize environmental impacts and penalize those which increase them. The enhanced availability and quality of information about the externalities of financial decisions provided to stakeholders (such as consumers, NGOs, workers) enable them to make more informed decisions on consumption and investment, and to apply pressure on financiers to change. In theory, such measures promote a dialogue between financiers and those who entrust them with their investments.

This preference for reflexive types of regulation based on disclosure, learning, and adaptation is evidenced by the growth of process standards, such as requirements to report SRI policies, proxy voting activities, and material environmental impacts. Such process standards enable assessment, verification, and communication of performance. Better reforms perhaps include the voluntary GRI and the CDP, the Australian SRI disclosure regulations, and

---

30 See J. Pierre and B.G. Peters, *Governance, Politics and the State* (Macmillan Press, 2000); J.A. Vogler, "Governance and the Environment," in *Negotiating Environmental Change: New Perspectives from Social Science*, eds F. Berkhout, M. Leach, and I. Scoones (Edward Elgar Publishing, 2003), 137.

31 A. Giddens, *The Third Way. The Renewal of Social Democracy* (Polity Press, 1998); eds, I. Hargreaves and I. Christie, *Tomorrow's Politics: The Third Way and Beyond* (Demos, 1998).

some environmental reporting rules in Europe. But process standards have rarely extended to creating rights to participate in investment policy-making, and have not disturbed the overall fiduciary duties of investment intermediaries. This is acceptable for business case style SRI, but is insufficient to facilitate ethically motivated SRI. Disclosure-based regulation gives investment institutions the option of choosing *not* to take social, environmental, and ethical matters into account, provided that this too is disclosed.

Normative standards are another type of SRI governance, providing substantive principles and guidance toward a target performance. In practice, the current menu of regimes lack concrete performance standards to assess progress. The UNPRI is heavily subscribed by financiers, but it is an accommodating voluntary regime, without compliance machinery and not expecting radical changes in the behavior of signatories. Among official regulation, it is largely those in relation to public pension funds in some states, such as Norway, that impose substantive obligations to invest responsibly and ethically.

Other types of policy instruments applied to financial markets include economic incentives (e.g., green investment tax concessions), corporate governance reforms to enhance shareholder advocacy, environmental liability rules for lenders, management systems (e.g., the ISO and AccountAbility standards), and comparative rating mechanisms (e.g., the DJSI). However, these and other similar mechanisms have enjoyed only modest success. If an instrument is too effective, such as Superfund environmental liability for lenders, it risks being rolled back. Conversely, taxation concessions gain appeal because they reward positive behavior rather than penalize harmful conduct. In most cases, the prevailing norms of financial materiality and risk management hinder the recognition of other forms of "value" not currently quantified as economic indicators. Overall, despite the primary rationale for their introduction, reflexive styles of governance do not appear to be any more effective than command-and-control forms of state regulation. Indeed, the paucity of command regulation, such as caps on GHG emissions, has directly hindered action by progressive-minded financiers who would likely take climate change more seriously if governments rigorously taxed or restricted carbon.[32]

Finally, despite its global expanse, SRI remains somewhat defined within nationally distinctive regulatory styles and pressures. History and geography still influence particular forms of finance capitalism.[33] The UK pioneered

---

32 S. Dunn, "Down to Business on Climate Change: An Overview of Corporate Strategies," in *The Business of Climate Change: Corporate Responses to Kyoto*, eds K. Begg, F. van der Woerd, and D. Levy (Greenleaf Publishing, 2005), 31, 43.

33 See especially G.L. Clark and D. Wójcik, *The Geography of Finance: Corporate Governance in the Global Marketplace* (Oxford University Press, 2007).

disclosure-based SRI regulation partly because it had some tradition and experience with relying on light-touch transparency regulation of markets. Canada and the US also favored disclosure based regulation to address mutual fund proxy voting for similar reasons. On the other hand, Scandinavian governments mandated their national pensions to invest ethically with regard to social and environmental factors, because in these jurisdictions states have traditionally played a more central role in economic management. The prospects for SRI thus remain substantially influenced by the legal and policy traditions of each sovereign nation.[34]

In a global marketplace, however, demand for regulatory convergence and harmonization will surely grow. There is already evidence that regulators learn from each other's experience; for example, a number of EU states, including Italy, Germany, and Belgium, imitated the UK's SRI disclosure regulation for pension funds. Conversely, the UK has taken some cues from continental Europe. Britain's new "enlightened shareholder value" approach to corporate governance evident in the *Companies Act* of 2006 has introduced elements of a stakeholder model traditionally associated with the rest of Europe.[35] Today, UK, Dutch, and other European financial institutions generally lead global finance in terms of awareness and advocacy for change on social and environmental problems such as climate change.[36] In 2006, 55 percent of the UNEPFI signatories were European institutions and only 11 percent were North American.[37] Emerging markets are also offering opportunities for social investors, and although they have not introduced the range of legal reforms found in Europe, they are learning from developed-country models.[38] Among emerging economies, the Asia-Pacific region has the most vibrant SRI market.[39]

---

34 See L. Albareda, J.M. Lozano, and T. Ysa, "Public Policies on Corporate Social Responsibility: The Role of Governments in Europe," *Journal of Business Ethics* 74(4) (2007) 74: 391 (discussing difference approaches among EU states to the promotion of CSR).

35 R.V. Aguilera, et al., "Corporate Governance and Social Responsibility: A Comparative Analysis of the UK and the US," *Corporate Governance and Social Responsibility* 14(3) (2006): 147, 151–52.

36 Dunn, note 32, 43; M. van der Westen, "SRI in the Netherlands: An Explosive Issue," *European Pensions and Investments News*, July 16, 2007, 1.

37 UNEPFI, *2006 Overview* (UNEPFI, 2006).

38 See M. de Sousa-Shields, ed., *Towards Sustainable and Responsible Investment in Emerging Markets: A Review and Inventory of the Social Investment Industry's Activities and Potential in Emerging Markets* (IFC, 2003),

39 See discussions at the session "Asia-Pacific: Sustainable Finance for a Dynamic Region" (UNEPFI Global Roundtable, Melbourne, Australia, October 24–25, 2007).

The flurry of international codes of conduct for SRI, such as the UNPRI, GRI, and the EPs, are also leveling the governance field. This trend demonstrates a positive side of globalization that quickens the dissemination of standards. But intergovernmental financial regulation has so far remained impervious to global sustainability standards, demonstrated by the unfortunate failure to include environmental risk management standards in the Basel II accord. The principal downside of the non-state codes is their lack of independent auditing or compliance review, and mechanisms for redress. Upholding the integrity of the voluntary mechanisms has largely defaulted to the NGO sector, which scrutinizes the behavior of financial institutions against the standards they pledge to follow. Notably, BankTrack actively monitors the Equator banks. Although the EPs are voluntary, they contribute to the emerging social license that financial institutions need to maintain if they are to protect their "reputation capital" and to avoid tightening legal requirements.[40]

In sum, the SRI market remains evolutionary rather than revolutionary. Imbued with a business case, present forms of SRI are unlikely to revolutionize financial markets. Current SRI tends to have an after-the-fact palliative function, rather than offering tough preventative prescriptions for change. For instance, the "best-in-class" investment criteria allow some among the careless polluters to be portrayed as generous environmental leaders. SRI is not likely to engender far-reaching change without the support of public authorities and civil society. A vast regulatory terrain of possible reform remains under-explored.

II. SRI—Adding Values, Not Just Value

A. PRELIMINARY CONSIDERATIONS

At the heart of SRI is the dire need to motivate the financial sector to invest with a view to protecting natural "capital."[41] Traditionally, under long-standing corporate and market structures, governments have assigned only limited responsibility to financiers for the social and environmental sequelae of the corporations they invest in. This arrangement has been widely seen either as a positive factor that encourages economically productive

---

40 N. Gunningham, R.A. Kagan, and D. Thornton, "Social License and Environmental Protection: Why Businesses Go Beyond Compliance," *Law and Social Inquiry* 29 (2004): 307, 319–20.

41 A.M. Janson, et al., eds, *Investing in Natural Capital* (Island Press, 1994); R. Costanza and H. Daly, "Natural Capital and Sustainable Development," *Conservation Biology* 6 (1992): 37.

investment or because of the passive nature of investment it justifies dis-
connecting financiers from the liability of capital financing decisions that
harm the environment. Thus, Roberta Romano insists that "there is still no
basis for mandating social investments by pension funds. It is preferable for
a state to fund these projects directly, from general revenues, rather than to
impose a hidden tax on pension fund assets through regulation."[42] In truth,
financial markets have been subsidized by the failure of governance systems
to require investors to internalize the social and environmental costs they
contribute to and profit from. Financiers have imposed a "hidden tax" on
posterity, which will have to pay for such costs.

The financial economy needs new rules for changing circumstances.
It is not a novel idea that economic actors' profit-making should be constrained to safeguard environmental and social well-being.[43] The novelty is in
encompassing the financial sector. While a business case has a role in SRI,
it must function within a broader ethical framework, so that financial imperatives for SRI become one of several means to an end, rather than the end in
itself. Societies and policy-makers have still not heeded the call of the world's
leading scientists for a new "ethic [to] motivate a great movement, convincing reluctant leaders and reluctant governments and reluctant people
themselves to effect the needed changes."[44] Such an ethic could help transform a financial economy, guided by long-term goals of sustainability and
environmental justice for all. Ethical decisions imply consideration of the
interests of an "other," in contrast to business case SRI which is primarily or
only concerned with the financial interests of the investor. The ultimate
objective should be to reach a position where financial institutions' "viability
rests on [their] conformance to community standards and appraisals of moral
action."[45]

---

42 R. Romano, "Public Pension Fund Activism in Corporate Governance
   Reconsidered," *Columbia Law Review* 93 (1993): 795, 814.

43 This idea was suggested as early as 1946 by P. Drucker, *The Concept of the
   Corporation* (Transaction Publishers, 1946). Drucker argued that while
   corporations should be allowed to profit from their activities, "[t]his does not
   mean that the corporation should be free from social obligations. On the
   contrary, it should be so organized as to fulfill automatically its social obligations in the very act of seeking it own best self-interest" (at 16–17).

44 Union of Concerned Scientists, note 25.

45 L. Sama, S. Welcomer, and V. Gerde, "Who Speaks for the Trees? Invoking an
   Ethic of Care to Give Voice to the Silent Stakeholder," in *Stakeholders,
   the Environment and Society*, eds S. Sharma and M. Starik (Edward Elgar
   Publishing, 2004), 140, 154.

522 | SOCIALLY RESPONSIBLE INVESTMENT LAW

Certainly, in the current regulatory milieu, the environmental high road must correspond to business case advantages to inspire most investors. There are entrenched self-interests and ingrained patterns of behavior. Financial institutions are not natural persons, therefore, they need formal rules to play the equivalent role that virtues play for individuals. Unfortunately, there are few governance precedents for guiding such changes in corporate behavior. Financial reforms in OECD countries and many developing nations have taken their cues from the "financial repression" thesis that rejects the heavy hand of the state.[46] Governments have mostly confined themselves to the seemingly more efficient approach of broad oversight and prudential regulation, intervening aggressively only in cases of destabilizing market abuse.[47]

In light of the drastic environmental challenges worldwide, governments can no longer continue to rely on existing environmental law techniques, targeting only the operations of the "front-line" businesses, such as mining and manufacturing firms. In a "perfect" regulatory market, front-line developers would account for all social costs and would render SRI largely unnecessary. Yet the history of social and environmental regulation suggests that disciplining only front-line businesses has not promoted sustainable development. Governments worldwide have a patchy record of such environmental regulation,[48] plagued with problems of inefficiency, enforcement issues, and slow reactions to new threats or changed societal expectations.[49] Despite several decades of relatively intensive international efforts to address biodiversity depletion, deforestation, atmospheric pollution, and other perils, that same period has been the most ecologically destructive era in human history.

Protecting the environment by regulating financial intermediaries and controlling the flow of capital to unsustainable activities is one credible solution, but how? The regulatory track record also inclines toward caution

---

46 E.S. Shaw, *Financial Deepening in Economic Development* (Oxford University Press, 1975); A. Singh, "Financial Liberalisation, Stockmarkets and Economic Development," *The Economic Journal* 107(442) (1997): 771.
47 W.A. Lee, "Modern Portfolio Theory and the Investment of Pension Funds," in *Equity and Commercial Relationships*, ed. P.D. Finn (Law Book Company, 1987), 284, 314–15 (arguing that "[p]ension funds belong to pensioners and to no one else[;]... [a]s a rule in the law of trusts a settlor may dispose of benefits as he thinks fit, since he has furnished the fund."
48 See especially eds, B.J. Richardson and S. Wood, *Environmental Law for Sustainability: A Reader* (Hart Publishing, 2006).
49 D.J. Fiorino, "Rethinking Environmental Regulation: Perspectives from Law and Governance," *Harvard Environmental Law Review* 23 (1999): 441.

against the potential of environmental law to successfully control the financial sector. SRI governance must use different techniques; for instance, banks would not be required to obtain pollution permits and install emission abatement technology. Rather, policy instruments promoting SRI must influence the cost of capital, as well as redefine the fiduciary duties of institutional investors, who may hold a portfolio comprising thousands of assets, unlike the narrower interests of an individual corporation.

Moving beyond front-line company regulation is also necessary because in a global economy shaped by global finance, governance systems must target "wholesale" decisions concerning allocation of capital that influence future, downstream development. Given the extent of cross-border investment, where financiers may invest in foreign markets with much weaker human rights and environmental standards, it is crucial to impose global sustainability standards on capital investment. Such a strategy could reduce the burden on front-line regulatory controls, as companies passing the rigors of SRI standards should be easier to regulate at an operational level. Also, if corporations are refused financing in an initial round, they may act voluntarily to comply with more stringent financing qualification standards, lessening the need for government's regulatory intervention.

B. ETHICS FOR ETHICAL INVESTMENT

1. Building an Ethical Consensus

An ethical approach to SRI raises questions about the fundamental qualities of the human character, our ability to cultivate new ethical values, and the capacity of our institutions to give effect to those values. Some people may refute the very possibility of ethical change, interpreting values as reflective of ingrained characteristics of human nature.[50] Others see human behavior as dynamic and motivated by many factors beyond narrow materialistic wants.[51] Marc Hauser argues in *Moral Minds* that human beings are endowed with a moral faculty that conveys judgments of right and wrong based on

---

50 See the populist work of evolutionary psychologists, A.S. Miller and S. Kanazawa, *Why Beautiful People Have More Daughters* (Perigee Trade, 2007).

51 See, e.g., H. Gintis, "Beyond *Homo Economicus*: Evidence from Experimental Economics," *Ecological Economics* 35 (2000): 311; J. Thøgersen, "Monetary Incentives and Recycling: Behavioural and Psychological Reactions to a Performance-Dependent Garbage Fee," *Journal of Consumer Policy* 26 (2003): 197.

unconsciously operative principles of action.[52] Drawing on Noam Chomsky's theory of generative grammar,[53] Hauser contends that all humans possess a universal moral grammar, hard-wired into the brain. While Hauser does not specifically discuss environmental ethics, major shifts in ethical values are not unprecedented in history, such as the abolition of slavery and the rising status of women in many countries.

A similar major ethical transformation has not yet occurred in the financial sector. The diversity of approaches to SRI partly reflects investors' different values regarding the relative importance of social, environmental, and economic considerations.[54] Hylton indicts a "persistent inability on the part of all participants in the debate to develop a simple, coherent definition" of SRI.[55] Even where responsible investors share specific goals, they may differ in how to achieve them.[56] For example, during the anti-apartheid campaign, social investors disagreed on whether to divest entirely, or to retain financial ties and seek change through dialogue and tactical pressure. In today's postmodern world of ethnic and cultural diversity, concepts such as "sustainable development" or "corporate responsibility" may be read differently, depending on the actors and their situation.[57] Thus, when the Irish Parliament in 2006 rejected a legislative amendment to require the National Pensions Reserve Fund to invest ethically, one parliamentarian reasoned:

> A major difficulty in deciding on ethical investment policy is where to draw the line in defining the parameters of the policy, given that there will inevitably be different opinions and intense debate on what constitutes ethical and socially responsible investment.... Furthermore, the list of what might be considered unacceptable investment is likely

---

52 M. Hauser, *Moral Minds* (HarperCollins, 2006).

53 N. Chomsky, *Language and Mind* (Harcourt Brace Jovanovich, 1968).

54 See C. Mackenzie "The Choice of Criteria in Ethical Investment" *Business Ethics* 7(2) (1998): 81; R. Sparkes, "Ethical Investment: Whose Ethics, Which Investment?" *Business Ethics: A European Review* 10 (2001): 194.

55 M. O'Brien Hylton, "Socially Responsible' Investing: Doing Good versus Doing Well in an Inefficient Market" *American University Law Review* 42 (1992): 1, 2.

56 M. Schwartz, "The 'Ethics' of Ethical Investing" *Journal of Business Ethics* 43 (2003): 195.

57 See J.S. Dryzek, *The Politics of the Earth: Environmental Discourses* (2nd edn, Oxford University Press, 2005).

to change in light of developments in the political, social and scientific spheres.[58]

Contemporary conceptions of government tend not to emphasize the cultivation of shared morality and virtue.[59] Neoliberalism premises that key players such as state and market should reinforce the motivation of individual self-interest, defined primarily as the perceived neutrality of economic interests.[60] The global consumer culture that has flourished in this climate is hardly receptive to values associated with ethical investment.[61] Ron Engel, a renowned commentator on ethics and sustainability, bemoans:

> ... [a] popular consumer culture, based on the widespread and largely unconscious assumption that we have unlimited wants, that the good life consists in the acquisition of ever more manufactured products and experiences. Can we expect biodiversity to be valued and preserved when our public spaces are filled with advertising images that pander to the crudest material appetites, and that glorify a lifestyle of excessive material affluence? In the United States today the metaphor of marketing pervades and corrupts virtually every facet of public, business and personal life.... "[62]

Under such conditions, the possibility of forging shared values for SRI seems distant.

Unanimity on ethical issues can be difficult to establish even within groups ostensibly sharing the same fundamental beliefs, such as among church-based investors. In the case of *Harries and others v. Church Commissioners*

---

58 Parliament of Ireland, Select Committee on Finance and the Public Service, *Parliamentary Debates* 44 (February 23, 2006), 5 (per Mr Cowen).

59 A. MacIntyre, *After Virtue: A Study in Moral Theory* (University of Notre Dame Press, 1981), 233–36; D. Harvey, *The Condition of Postmodernity: An Enquiry into the Origins of Cultural Change* (Blackwell, 1990), 220.

60 A. Saad-Filho and D. Johnston, eds, *Neoliberalism: A Critical Reader* (Pluto Press, 2005); D. Harvey, *A Brief History of Neoliberalism* (Oxford University Press, 2005).

61 See especially F. Jameson, "Post-Modernism and Consumer Society," in *The Anti-Aesthetic: Essays on Postmodernist Culture*, ed. H. Foster (Bay Press, 1986), 111; J. Baudrillard, "The Hyper-realism of Simulation," in *Art in Theory 1900–1990: An Anthology of Changing Ideas*, eds C. Harrison and P. Wood (Blackwell, 1990), 1049.

62 R. Engel, "The Moral Power of the World Conservation Movement to Engage Economic Globalization," *The George Wright Forum* 22(3) (2005): 58, 69.

for England,[63] the court observed that "different minds within the Church of England, applying the highest moral standards, will reach different conclusions" as to the merits of a particular investment.[64] Accordingly, the Church Commissioners were vindicated in their decision not to prefer one ethical view to another "beyond the point at which they would incur a risk of significant financial detriment."[65] This lack of an exogenous understanding of SRI has incented a business-as-usual tendency.

Nor, of course, can social investors simply set their moral compass by the law of the land, as legal rules may reflect the power of vested interests and, in a world of global finance, the legal standards of one jurisdiction may be incompatible with basic international legal norms. Thus, an economic activity that is ostensibly "legal" may not necessarily be appropriate for ethical investment. The tobacco industry is a classic example.

Some diversity within SRI philosophies is likely unavoidable in our complex, heterogeneous societies, where values constantly evolve in response to new information and understanding. Even Paul Hawken, who criticizes SRI for its lack of orthodoxy, concedes that "[w]hat constitutes environmental social responsibility depends on the times and the common knowledge of those times."[66] Thus, Peter Kinder, of KLD, cautions against trying to impose a single, authoritative standard of SRI:

> {a}n orthodoxy would restrict the debate with corporations, government and society at large from which progress may emerge. An orthodoxy would drive dissenters from the field and inhibit socially responsible investors' ability to grow in understanding. Hence, it is futile to try to enforce a single set of standards for what is "socially responsible" on the evolving ethical standards of diverse investors.[67]

However, the financial sector's responsibility to shoulder some of the responsibility to protecting ecological integrity must not be interpreted as a discretionary consideration. Environmental ethics is a deeply rooted tree, not a reed. The room for debate and opinion principally arises in how best to further such conduct. Understanding that, the challenge is to build an ethical framework for SRI that goes beyond the business case, creating

---

63 [1992] 1 W.L.R. 1241.
64 Ibid., 1251.
65 Ibid.
66 P. Hawken, *Socially Responsible Investing* (Natural Capital Institute, 2004), 22.
67 P.D. Kinder, *"Socially Responsible Investing": An Evolving Concept in a Changing World* (KLD Research and Analytics, 2007), 21.

enduring core principles while leaving space for a dynamic and creative movement democratically responding to the needs and concerns of investors and other stakeholders in local and specific contexts.

There is a greater likelihood that internalized values will effect change, more than those imposed externally. Therefore, governance processes should include space to nurture ethical values for sustainability from within the financial sector. This may lead to more buy-in to ethical investment and thereby it may become a more pervasive influence in the investment community. Allowing other stakeholders, such as NGOs and other civil society groups to participate in that process is also important. Social protest mobilizations such as the peace and environmental movements form the progressive side of postmodern culture, challenging the privileged narratives of capitalism and liberalism,[68] and making rival world views more mainstream.[69] The new "politics of inclusion" raises the possibility for a new ethical paradigm for SRI.[70] Coupled with legal procedures that require financiers to account for the wider social and environmental impacts of their investments, this should help to ensure that the values and resulting SRI practices of the financial community are isomorphic to the imperatives of sustainable development.

Apart from the challenges of building socially legitimate standards, an ethical investment discourse must also overcome obstacles against its dissemination through the economy. It is unnecessary to accept Niklas Luhmann's claim that the economy is functionally differentiated and semi-autonomous from other domains of modern society, to be acutely aware of

---

68 J. Guidry, M. Kennedy, and M. Zald, "Globalizations and Social Movements," in *Globalizations and Social Movements: Culture, Power, and the Transnational Public Sphere*, eds J. Guidry, et al. (University of Michigan Press, 2000), 13; A. Touraine, *The Voice and the Eye: An Analysis of Social Movements* (Cambridge University Press, 1981).

69 See D. Shelton, "Environmental Justice in the Postmodern World," in *Environmental Justice and Market Mechanisms,* eds K. Bosselmann and B.J. Richardson (Kluwer Law, 1999), 21.

70 See R. Shamir, "Between Self-Regulation and the Alien Tort Claims Act: On the Contested Concept of Corporate Social Responsibility," *Law and Society Review* 38 (2004): 635, 644–48 (explaining the development of a sociological "field" of CSR, and defining it as a struggle over both the meaning of the term and a struggle over what entities ought to have power to participate in defining the term).

market impediments to SRI regulation.[71] With money as its lingua franca, the economy has built up its own values and goals around competition, acquisition, growth, and profitability. Other considerations, such as biodiversity conservation, which are not factored in the values of the market tend to lack traction. The dominance of business case SRI precisely illustrates barriers to incorporate non-economic factors into financial market analysis. Ethically-driven investors struggle to influence the economic system, which may see their values as an irritant, only to receive consideration to the extent that such values can be articulated in monetary terms.[72]

Conceivably, individual actors may be guided by values that differ from the prevailing norms of the economy.[73] The Luhmann framework itself distinguishes between social systems (i.e., the economy, legal system, etc) locked in their idiosyncratic logic, and human agents and organizations.[74] Investors may co-mingle values from other spheres of life. Ethical investment by church-based investors shows how one group's participation in the economy is guided by values from beyond the market. Abundant other evidence of ethical motivations in the marketplace exist, including consumers who pay a premium for green products and workers who accept lower wages for altruistic employment or refuse to work for unethical firms.[75] In a case study of implementation of the ISO 14001 environmental management system, Oren Perez and others also show that organizations, like individuals, can pursue "multiple goals and varied routines that which will not be determined by (or limited to) the economic ethos."[76]

---

71 N. Luhmann, *The Differentiation of Society* (Columbia University Press, 1982).

72 See N. Luhmann, *Ecological Communication* (Polity Press, 1989).

73 See N. Luhmann, *Organisation und Entscheidung* (Westduetscher, 2000); R.R. Nelson and B.N. Sampat, "Making Sense of Institutions as a Factor Shaping Economic Performance," *Journal of Economic Behavior and Organization* 44 (2001): 31.

74 N. Luhmann, *Social Systems* (Stanford University Press, 1995), 97–99, 139–45.

75 D. Kahneman, J. Knetsch, and R. Thaler, "Fairness as a Constraint on Profit Seeking: Entitlements in the Market," *American Economic Review* 76 (1986): 728; R. Frank, "Can Socially Responsible Firms Survive in a Competitive Environment?" in *Codes of Conduct: Behavioral Research into Business Ethics*, eds D.M. Messick and A.E. Tenbrunsel (Russell Sage Foundation Publications, 1997), 95, 96.

76 O. Perez, Y. Amichai-Hamburger, and T. Shterental, "Between Public and Private Regulation: ISO 14001, Environmental Commitment and Organizational Civic Behavior" (Bar-Ilan University, 2007), 13.

2. Ecological Ethics

What kind of ethics could support an environmentally sustainable system of investment? The financial world as already documented generally treats nature instrumentally as a resource for short-term gain, owing no direct accountability to environmental law standards that are considered only an operational matter for the companies they invest in. Like the economic system generally, the environment is rendered primarily as a storehouse to be transformed into financial returns for human wealth and well-being.[77] This anthropocentric worldview is reflected in Western traditions that restrict moral significance to human beings while excluding other creatures.[78] Some environmental lawyers suggest that changing this ethos is critical to progressing toward sustainability.[79] In its 2002 statement on unsustainable patterns of resource use, the UN Economic and Social Council explained:

> The value systems reflected in these patterns are among the main driving forces which determine the use of natural resources. Although the changes required for converting societies to sustainable consumption and production patterns are not easy to implement, the shift is imperative.[80]

Ethics is a tool to help us understand and improve human behavior. Ethics can be viewed at several related levels: in "worldviews" or general philosophical approaches, or in ethical principles that guide behavior in specific contexts. Ethics can also be seen in terms of the deliberative process, which emphasizes social discourse as a means for developing values. Ethics not only

---

77 For a classic defence of anthropocentrism, see J. Passmore, *Man's Responsibility for Nature: Ecological Problems and Western Traditions* (Duckworth Publishers, 1980), and E.C. Hargrove, *Foundations of Environmental Ethics* (Prentice-Hall, 1989). For an overview of the main strands of environmental ethics, see A. Light and H. Rolston III, eds, *Environmental Ethics: An Anthology* (Blackwell, 2003); J.R. des Jardine, *Environmental Ethics: An Introduction to Environmental Philosophy* (Wadsworth Publishing, 1997).

78 White traces the "historical roots of our ecological crisis" to the attitude of nature domination engendered by Judaeo-Christian religion: L. White, Jr., "The Historical Roots of our Ecologic Crisis," *Science* 155 (1967): 1203.

79 P. Taylor, "The Business of Climate Change: Challenges and Opportunities for Multinational Business Enterprises: The Business of Climate Change: What's Ethics Got to Do With It?" *Pacific McGeorge Global Business and Development Law Journal* 20 (1997): 161.

80 UN Economic and Social Council, *Implementing Agenda 21: Report of the Secretary-General*, E/CN.17/PC.2/7 (2002), 5.

help to expose the basal values that spur unsustainable habits, it can also help societies redefine their relationship with nature.

Theorists have debated alternate ethical frameworks for this very purpose, focusing on broadening moral consideration for all living creatures and their ecosystems.[81] Such "biocentric ethics" emphasize the ecological reality of humankind as an integral and interdependent part of the "web of life."[82] A cognate aspect of this ethic recognizes the sanctity of all life forms for their "intrinsic value," regardless of their contribution to human needs and wants.[83] Such biocentric ethics feature to some extent in the traditional culture of some Indigenous communities.[84] That perspective does not deny humans entitlement to use other forms of life; "this is a condition of our existence as participants in the evolutionary process."[85] Yet while these values neither refute nor prioritize human needs, they do encourage thinking *beyond* exclusive human wants. In the sustainable development literature, the principles that to some extent contribute to this worldview are inter-generational equity (the responsibility owed to future life)[86] and "inter-species justice."[87]

Processes for ethical deliberation are instrumental in cultivating such virtues. Ethical investment will have no lasting impression on the financial sector if it is regarded simply as academic wisdom or regulatory prescription. Opening investment institutions to participatory, ethical deliberation may help forge legitimate values. Investment policy committees is a forum that could afford representation and voice to investors and other stakeholders to allow for deliberation and consideration of appropriate ethical courses of action. Decision-making processes that encourage participation, discussion,

---

81 For overviews, see P.W. Taylor, *Respect for Nature: A Theory of Environmental Ethics* (Princeton University Press, 1986); R. Eckersley, *Environmentalism and Political Theory: Towards an Ecocentric Approach* (State University of New York Press, 1992); C.S. Stone, *Earth and Other Ethics* (Harper and Row, 1987); D. Schmidtz and E. Willott, eds *Environmental Ethics: What Really Matters* (Oxford University Press, 2002).

82 F. Capra, *The Web of Life. A New Scientific Understanding of Living Systems* (Anchor Books, 1996).

83 Notably, P. Singer, *Animal Liberation A New Ethics for Our Treatment of Animals* (Random House, 1975).

84 A. Durning, *Guardians of the Land: Indigenous Peoples and the Health of the Earth* (Worldwatch Institute, 1992).

85 Engel, note 62, 62.

86 See J. Agyeman, R.D. Bullard, and B. Evans, *Just Sustainabilities: Development in an Unequal World* (MIT Press, 1993).

87 K. Bosselmann, "Ecological Justice and Law," in *Environmental Law for Sustainability*, note 48, 129.

and reflection can be instrumental to effective policy-making.[88] Without a democratic discourse, the ethics of SRI may merely reflect the views of the powerful without sufficient introspection to debate the moral merits of its habits and practices.

However, such "bottom-up" ethics should not be determinative. Within a global context of diverse cultures and values, an ethical framework fostering shared values to support collaboration across cultural divides is necessary. Some ethical principles to safeguard ecological integrity form universal standards, comprising "principles so fundamental to human existence" that all societies should adhere to them.[89] They determine the moral free space of societies or institutions serving to judge, and if necessary, to invalidate local practices and values derived from institutionally-specific processes of ethical deliberation.[90]

The Earth Charter evokes the kind of universal principles directed to ecological integrity that could support an ethically framed SRI.[91] The Charter emerged in the aftermath of the 1992 Earth Summit, and was finally adopted in 2002, after lengthy consultation mainly held among civil society organizations.[92] It built on the earlier achievement of the 1982 World Charter for Nature (adopted by the UN General Assembly), which articulated a range of principles including the statement that "[e]very form of life is unique, warranting respect regardless of its worth to man, and, to accord other organisms such recognition, man must be guided by a moral code of action."[93]

---

88 M.A. Hajer, *The Politics of Environmental Discourse: Ecological Modernization and the Policy Process* (Clarendon Press, 1995), 16–21; K. Litfin, *Ozone Discourses Science and Politics in Global Environmental Cooperation* (Columbia University Press, 1994); S. Jasanoff and M.L. Martello, eds, *Earthly Politics: Local and Global in Environmental Governance* (MIT Press, 2004); see also J. Habermas, *The Theory of Communicative Action I: Reason and the Rationalization of Society*, trans. T. McCarthy (Beacon Press, 1984); N.C. Crawford, "Postmodern Ethical Conditions and a Critical Response," *Ethics and International Affairs* 12 (1998): 121.

89 T. Donaldson and T.W. Dunfee, "Towards a Unified Conception of Business Ethics: Integrative Social Contracts Theory," *Academy of Management Review* 19 (1994): 252, 265.

90 T. Donaldson and T.W. Dunfee, *Ties That Bind: A Social Contracts Approach to Business Ethics* (Harvard Business School Press, 1999).

91 Http://www.earthcharter.org.

92 M. Vilela, "Building Consensus on Shared Values," in *The Earth Charter in Action: Toward a Sustainable World*, eds P. Corcoran, M. Vilela, and A. Roerink (KIT Publishers, 2005), 17.

93 Preamble, ILM 22 (1983): 455.

The essence of the Earth Charter is to unify peoples, organizations, and governments worldwide with a common ethical framework for action. Accordingly, its first four core principles, upon which the other supporting eleven principles are based, state:

1. Respect Earth and life in all its diversity;
2. Care for the community of life with understanding, compassion, and love;
3. Build democratic societies that are just, participatory, sustainable, and peaceful;
4. Secure Earth's bounty and beauty for present and future generations.

Other Charter principles particularly relevant for the business sector include:

6. Prevent harm as the best method of environmental protection and, when knowledge is limited, apply a precautionary approach.
7. Adopt patterns of production, consumption, and reproduction that safeguard Earth's regenerative capacities, human rights, and community well-being. . . .
10. Ensure that economic activities and institutions at all levels promote human development in an equitable and sustainable manner.

For the financial sector, such standards would require fund managers and investors to recognize that their responsibilities extend beyond the constraints of the prospectus and targeted returns on investment, encompassing the health and prosperity of the community of all life.

Still, the Earth Charter is not tailored to the financial sector, and its provisions are cast much too broadly to provide workable guidance. The Earth Charter International Council's "Business Initiative" is trying to increase its appeal to this group, explaining: "[t]he challenge is how to break out of the current 'business-as-usual' model, while maintaining the best of the private sector's entrepreneurial, technological and financial skills and innovative capacity."[94] So far, approximately 180 business organizations worldwide have endorsed the Charter, of some 3,000 endorsements.

The Collevecchio Declaration on Financial Institutions, discussed in chapter 6, is possibly the most useful ethically-related code for SRI.[95] The advantage of the Declaration is its direct engagement of the business sector,

---

94 A. Atkisson, *The Earth Charter and the Business Sector: How a Consensus on Global Values Can Add Values* (Stockholm: Earth Charter International, 2006), 5.
95 See http://www.foe.org/camps/intl/declaration.html.

particularly financial markets. It requires a commitment to six core principles: sustainability, "do no harm," responsibility, accountability, transparency, and the creation of sustainable markets and governance. So far, the financial sector has largely disregarded the Collevecchio Declaration, perceiving it as an abrasive, ideologically-driven NGO initiative. This reaction suggests that an ethical framework must be based on more than a *voluntary* code, and furthermore, that its standards should be developed with input from applicable institutions.

In order to achieve sustainability, some ethical positions for SRI will remain local issues specific to institutions and individuals, while other values will be common, such as imperatives to address climate change and save biodiversity. The outstanding question is how such ethical imperatives and processes may attain legal expression to steer SRI? In surveying future direction, neither a grandiose blueprint nor a laundry list of corrective measures is proposed, as others have attempted.[96] Rather, the following section canvasses a few high priority areas that target the core of the financial sector. Reframing fiduciary duties of investment decision-makers is arguably the most important of these tasks.

III. Governance Reforms

A. REGULATING THE CONTENT OR MEANS OF SRI?

Policy instruments to improve the governance of SRI essentially may seek to restructure the processes by which investment decisions are made, in the hope of inducing more enlightened outcomes, or limit financiers' discretion by prescribing substantive investment criteria. Combinations of these approaches are possible, such as by manipulating the fiduciary duties of financial institutions.

One approach to improving SRI is to regulate its substantive subject-matter. Avery Kolers argues that we must distinguish between investment activities that are passively permissible and those that should be actively encouraged.[97] A possible third category is investments that authorities should

---

96 World Economic Forum (WEF), *Mainstreaming Responsible Investment* (WEF, 2005); NRTEE, *Capital Markets and Sustainability: Investing in a Sustainable Future. State of the Debate Report* (NRTEE, 2007).

97 A. Kolers, "Ethical Investing: The Permissibility of Participation," *Journal of Political Philosophy* 9(4) (2001): 435, 452.

discourage or even prohibit. Governments have rarely sought to ethically improve the economy in these ways. In the prevailing neoliberal policy climate, there is little appetite for anything approaching a command economy, stigmatized by the socialist experiment of Eastern Europe. Even ardent social investors might disfavor mandatory investment codes, for such regulations could resemble a rigid laundry list of fashionable causes, contributing to external ethical conformism rather than internal ethical deliberation and commitment to SRI.

Among the few regulatory precedents for mandatory SRI is the public pension funds in Sweden and Norway obliged to invest responsibly with regard to social, environmental, and other ethical criteria. While their governing legislations do not dictate specific investment choices, each fund is guided by an ethics council. Referring to internationally recognized standards for human rights and sustainable development as their benchmarks, these councils illustrate how a mandatory SRI scheme could flexibly accommodate case-by-case evaluations of specific investments and thereby abjure an ethics that "become[s] standardised and reduced to a few abstruse ratios."[98]

International law and policy can be a crucial source of normative guidance. In setting up its ethics council, the Norwegian Government's Graver Committee proposed that exclusion of investments should be grounded primarily on constituting "a violation of international law for Norway,... of international standards in general and other grossly unethical corporate practices."[99] The Committee reasoned that, not only do "they provide a specification of what international consensus has defined as minimum requirements that should be imposed with respect to fundamental rights all over the world,"[100] but also that:

> the... Fund must be rooted in democratic values and enjoy legitimacy in the political community. Anchoring the guidelines in internationally recognised standards will provide a democratic basis, as will the pursuit of transparency and the promotion of public debate around the fundamental priorities that are set and the criteria on which ownership management is based.[101]

---

98 P.H. Dembinski, et al., "The Ethical Foundations of Responsible Investment," *Journal of Business Ethics* 48 (2003): 203, 213.

99 Graver Committee, *The Report from the Graver Committee* (Norwegian Ministry of Finance, 2003), s. 5.3.2.

100 Ibid., s. 4.2.

101 Ibid., s. 5.2.3.

International environmental and human rights instruments are providing some standardization for SRI in other contexts. In Canada, the Ethical Funds Company's screening policy is informed by the "international legal and policy framework," including the Convention on Biological Diversity and the Universal Declaration on Human Rights.[102] The governing legislation of the Guardians of the NZSF requires their investments to "avoid prejudice to New Zealand's reputation as a responsible member of the world community."[103] The Guardians' investment policy cites the UNGC as a key benchmark for its assessment of corporate behavior.[104] Further, the Guardians review whether specific corporate behavior "is contrary to... international agreements."[105] Another example in the UK is EIRIS, which runs a service for fund managers called "Convention Watch," scrutinizing companies for compliance with various international treaties and soft law instruments.[106]

International norms may not always provide a comprehensive solution for shaping SRI. First, many international environmental and human rights standards are vague, and cannot provide answers for specific cases. Second, not all international norms make a suitable yardstick, because various states' views on environmental policy and human rights do not always coincide. Developing countries, preoccupied by poverty alleviation and social justice, may sometimes conceive of sustainable development differently from developed countries.[107] Many human rights treaties reflect a Western liberal discourse. Collective rights, such as those associated with Indigenous peoples, have been shunned by some Western states; the UN Declaration on the Rights of Indigenous Peoples, of 2007,[108] and the International Labor Organization's Convention on Tribal Peoples, of 1989, were rejected by the US, Canada, and some other states with Indigenous minorities.[109] Yet, there are also some widely ratified international environmental and human rights treaties that may provide commonality. Among them are the Convention on

---

102 Ethical Funds Company, *How the Screens are Derived*, http://www.ethical-funds.com/do_the_right_thing/sri/ethical_principles_criteria.

103 *New Zealand Superannuation and Retirement Income Act*, 2001, s. 58(2)(c).

104 Guardians of New Zealand Superannuation, *Responsible Investment Policy, Standards and Procedures* (NZSF, June 27, 2007), 5.

105 Ibid.

106 EIRIS, *Convention Watch Briefing Paper* (EIRIS, undated).

107 N.P. Peritore, *Third World Environmentalism: Case Studies from the Global South* (University Press of Florida, 1999).

108 UN General Assembly, A/61/L.67, September 12, 2007.

109 ILO Convention Concerning Indigenous and Tribal People in Independent Countries, No. 169, ILM 28 (1989): 1382.

Biological Diversity[110] (adopted by approximately 190 states) and the Convention on the Elimination of All Forms of Racial Discrimination[111] (adopted by approximately 175 states).[112]

Governments have also sought to influence the substantive content of SRI in other ways, such as by banning certain undesirable investments as an adjunct to primary controls. This approach could define SRI by negative criteria: controversial products and services (e.g., pornography or pesticides), controversial production methods (e.g., child labor, animal testing, or genetic engineering), and problematic sectors (e.g., munitions or nuclear power). A rare example is Belgium's ban on investments (loans, purchase of shares, and bonds) in companies that produce, distribute, or in other ways are connected to cluster bombs.[113] Another example is the bans instituted by some US states on pension fund investments in Sudan.[114]

Alternatively, SRI regulation may reference positive criteria, to reward investors who finance perceived desirable activities. The Netherlands' Green Investment Directive takes this approach by offering tax concessions to investors contributing to specific environmental improvement projects, as set by government authorities.[115] Other jurisdictions provide various tax incentives to prop up specific types of SRI, such as accelerated capital depreciation allowances for investments in renewable energy and economically-targeted investment projects in disadvantaged communities.[116]

Some standardization of SRI practices is also unfolding from private sector governance. A huge industry has flourished for assessing and ranking CSR and for evaluating SRI products. It has brought some coherence to the SRI market, albeit within a business case framework. SRI stock market

---

110 ILM 31 (1992): 818.

111 ILM 5 (1966): 352

112 See D. Bodansky, J. Brunnée, and E. Hey, *The Oxford Handbook of International Environmental Law* (Oxford University Press, 2007); M. Hess, *International Human Rights: A Comprehensive Introduction* (Routledge, 2007).

113 Netkwerk Vlaanderen, "Belgium Bans Investments in Cluster Munitions," Press release, March 2, 2007, at http://www.netwerkvlaanderen.be.

114 L.J. Dhooge, "Condemning Khartoum: The Illinois Divestment Act and Foreign Relations," *American Business Law Journal* 43 (2006): 43.

115 M. Jeucken, *Sustainable Finance and Banking: The Financial Sector and the Future of the Planet* (Earthscan, 2001), 92–94.

116 V. Norberg-Bohm, "Creating Incentives for Environmentally Enhancing Technological Change: Lessons from 30 Years of U.S. Energy Technology Policy," *Technological Forecasting and Social Change* 65 (2000): 125; A. Lincoln, "Working for Regional Development? The Case of Canadian Labour-sponsored Investment Funds," *Regional Studies* 34 (2000): 727.

indexes are one source of such private standard-setting. The Dow Jones[117] and the FTSE[118] furnish international SRI market indexes, setting standards on human rights compliance, labor standards, environmental management, and corporate governance. Companies that lag in compliance to these standards risk expulsion from the index.[119] SRI think tanks and investor associations also furnish standards through policy guidance, recommendations, research, and other outputs.[120] The German Social Investment Forum has drafted standards for its members on topics such as SRI policy transparency and corporate sustainability assessment.[121] The UK's Institutional Shareholders' Committee[122] has formulated best practice recommendations for institutional shareholders to encourage shareholder activism.[123] SRI label schemes that certify retail funds also seek to standardize investment practices. Some labels focus on procedural standards, such as public disclosure, while others certify the environmental integrity of particular products or services.[124]

Regulators and market actors have generally preferred process standards to controls that imply or dictate specific investment choices. Prescribing specific investments on social or environmental grounds is a complex undertaking and politically controversial. Process standards do not require additional societal agreement concerning what is "ethical" or "socially responsible." Rather, they shape the way investments are made, providing for greater inclusiveness, transparency, and accountability to enhance good process. Such measures may thereby facilitate a discourse on ethics within the

---

117 Http://www.sustainability-indexes.com.

118 Http://www.ftse.com/Indices/FTSE4Good_Index_Series.

119 "DJSI Boots Out 54 Firms," *Environmental Finance*, September 23, 2005.

120 E.g., Caring Company, http://www.caringcompany.se; Sustainable Investment Research International, http://www.sirigroup.org; Fundacíon Ecologia y Desarollo (Spain), http://www.ecodes.org; and Oekom Research AG (Germany), http://www.okem.de; Ethical Shareholders of Europe United, http://www.ethicalshareholders.net.

121 Http://www.forum-ng.de.

122 Its members include representatives from the Association of British Insurers; the Association of Investment Trust Companies; and the National Association of Pension Funds.

123 Institutional Shareholders Committee, "Statement of Principles—The Responsibilities of Institutional Shareholders and Agents," at http://www.uksif.org/J/Z/Z/lib/2005/files/04/jp-trtk/ISC-SttmntofPrinciples.pdf.

124 See generally J.A. Grodsky, "Certified Green: The Law and Future of Environmental Labeling," *Yale Journal on Regulation* 10 (1993): 147; OECD, *Eco-Labelling: Actual Effects of Selected Programmes* (OECD, 1997).

financial sector or at least make financiers more mindful of the values of other interests affected by their investments.[125] Considerable theoretical literature supports such an approach.

Process-oriented legal scholarship and deliberative approaches to democracy both emphasize the potential of such procedures for engineering changes in values and practices.[126] Democratic theory suggests that participation can foster new values and provide a forum for civic education.[127] Participation in environmental decision-making has been linked to the cultivation of deeper, ethical concerns for nature,[128] and critical, environmental problem-solving.[129] A more open and democratic decision-making process wherein the implications of development choices are openly and critically debated may lead to more informative and environmentally acceptable decisions.[130] Open SRI policy-making is evident in such examples as the public inquiry on SRI conducted by Canada's NRTEE,[131] and the GRI's multi-stakeholder consultation process.[132] Similarly, reflexive law scholarship stresses that encouraging companies to reflect and learn about their ecological impacts may afford greater influence and legitimacy than regulating through

---

125 See R. Delgado, "Norms and Normal Science: Toward a Critique of Normativity in Legal Thought," *University of Pennsylvania Law Review* 139 (1991): 933.

126 A. Gutmann and D. Thompson, "Deliberative Democracy Beyond Process," in *Debating Deliberative Democracy*, eds J. Fishkin and P. Laslett (Blackwell Publishing, 2003), 31.

127 C. Pateman, *Participation and Democratic Theory* (Cambridge University Press, 1970); B. Barber, *Strong Democracy: Participatory Policies for a New Age* (University of California Press, 1984).

128 B. Boer, "Social Ecology and Environmental Law," *Environmental and Planning Law Journal* 1(3) (1984): 233.

129 J. Dryzek, *Rational Ecology: Environment and Public Participation* (Basil Blackwell, 1987), 204–5.

130 D.L. Van Nijnatten, "Participation and Environmental Policy in Canada and the United States: Trends Over Time," *Policy Studies Journal* 27(2) (1999): 267; N.P. Spyke, "Public Participation in Environmental Decision-making at the New Millennium: Structuring New Spheres of Public Influence," *Boston College Environmental Affairs Law Review* 26(2) (1999): 263; B.J. Richardson and R. Razzaque, "Public Participation in Environmental Decision-making," in *Environmental Law for Sustainability*, note 48, 165.

131 NRTEE, *Capital Markets and Sustainability: Investing in a Sustainable Future. State of the Debate Report* (NRTEE, 2007).

132 Http://www.globalreporting.org.

coercive or reward-based systems.[133] In this vein, the legitimacy of SRI and other forms of governance perhaps could rest on "democratic procedures rather than substantive principles."[134]

While process standards currently provide the bulk of SRI regulation, they are generally not comprehensive enough to excite true change. Thus, UK pension funds must disclose whether they invest ethically, while US and Canadian mutual funds must report proxy voting policies and records. Voluntary standards, such as the Eurosif Transparency Guidelines and the UNPRI, also emphasize information transparency and communication. In practice, however, mandated disclosures often entail vague, boilerplate statements that reveal little about the methodology behind SRI decisions or their implementation.[135] SRI funds seldom demonstrate the level of transparency and participation they demand of the corporations that make up their portfolios. External consultants and fund managers often enjoy much more influence than fund members in the policies of the SRI-industry. Often the most informative and critical SRI dialogue transpires in the civil society sector, such as the campaigns of BankTrack, rather than within the financial sector. Stronger reforms of decision-making processes in investment institutions, such as stakeholder representation and consultation, have yet to be widely adopted.[136]

Redefining the fiduciary duties of institutions provides a means by which changes to both substantive and process investment standards could be made. Fiduciary norms could be framed to set general investment goals for fund managers or pension trustees to promote sustainable development, without being overly prescriptive and rigid. Fiduciary standards may also influence

---

133 See G. Teubner, L. Farmer, and D. Murphy, eds, *Environmental Law and Ecological Responsibility: The Concept and Practice of Ecological Self-Organization* (John Wiley and Sons, 1994).

134 N.C. Crawford, "Postmodern Ethical Conditions and a Critical Response," *Ethics and International Affairs* 12 (1998): 121, 128; D. Szablowski, *Transnational Law and Local Struggles: Mining, Communities and the World Bank* (Hart Publishing, 2007), 17.

135 Schwartz, note 56, 199–200. There are exceptions of course, such as Ethical Funds Company, *A Guidebook to Sustainable Investing* (Ethical Funds Company, 2005).

136 See G. Frug, "The Ideology of Bureaucracy in American Law," *Harvard Law Review* 97 (1984): 1277; S. Bottomley, "From Contractualism and Constitutionalism: A Framework for Corporate Governance," *Sydney Law Review* 19 (1997): 277.

the means of decision-making, such as requiring consultation with a wide range of stakeholders, or ensuring environmentally-informed decisions.

B. FIDUCIARY FINANCE

1. *Accounting for Sustainability*

A. BEYOND FINANCIAL INTERESTS

In reframing financial institutions, a potential model for reform would be to expand fiduciary obligations beyond the investors they serve to a broader stakeholder community. This would require a redefinition of the law of fiduciary responsibility to require fiduciaries to promote the interests of an expanded concept of beneficiary with broader social interests for sustainability.

While the concept of financiers' "fiduciary duties" is typically tethered to institutional investors in common law jurisdictions, as a fiduciary or trust obligation is a common law concept developed in the courts of equity, this discussion deploys the concept in a broader sense to address various financial institutions in different legal systems. Functionally equivalent duties for various types of financiers often apply in other legal systems. It is imperative to improve SRI standards for all financial entities, including banks and mutual funds, so that they accommodate sustainable development impera-tives. While individuals may invest directly in the market without a financial intermediary, in recent decades the proportion of people who do so has dropped precipitously. In the UK, the amount of all shares held by individu-als fell from 54 percent in 1963 to below 13 percent in 2006.[137] Very occa-sionally individuals can be effective activists for change, such as Ralph Nader in the US or Yves Michaud in Canada. In general, however, a regulatory focus on financial institutions and intermediaries is wholly justified given their resources and leverage to influence the corporate sector.

The concept of fiduciary duties is old, but its content is adaptable. For instance, the rulings of British courts from over half a century ago prohibiting municipal authorities owing a fiduciary duty to their rate-payers from offering fair wages to employees or subsidizing public transport would not be supported today.[138] Likewise, fiduciary standards that condone unethical or unsustainable development are increasingly scrutinized by the

---

137 UK, Office for National Statistics (ONS), *Share Ownership: A Report on Ownership of UK Shares as at 31ˢᵗ December 2006* (ONS, 2007).

138 See *Roberts v. Hopwood*, [1925] A.C. 578; *Prescott v. Birmingham Corporation*, [1955] Ch. 210.

SRI community. They were first dissected in the 1980s when legal commentators considered the legality of the South African divestment campaign.[139] Today, the question is whether fiduciary duties can support a much wider sustainability agenda. A World Economic Forum report recommended that governments "[m]odify pension fiduciary rules which discourage or prohibit explicit trustee consideration of social and environmental aspects of corporate performance."[140] The Freshfields Bruckhaus Deringer study commissioned by UNEPFI optimistically saw little need for reform, as "integrating ESG considerations into an investment analysis so as to more reliably predict financial performance is clearly permissible and is arguably required in all jurisdictions."[141] Indeed, some legal commentators believe that "[i]nstitutional investors could face negligence claims unless the investors take account of environmental, social and corporate governance when making decisions."[142] But such conclusions assume business case SRI.

There is nothing innate in the fiduciary duty that requires casting the interests of beneficiaries in purely financial terms.[143] The duty of loyalty is owed to the whole person, not just her dissected financial interests. Conceivably, "best interests" should also encompass social and environmental preferences. Even if they were the stereotypical parody of *homo economicus*, investors attach values, external to the monetary price of their share holdings. Financial investors, as individuals, also wear other hats as members of communities with diverse concerns and motivations. There is a clear rationale for financial institutions' fiduciary duties to encompass a wider array of interests and goals beyond financial returns. The challenge is defining what those duties for sustainability should entail.

---

139 T.A. Troyer, W.B. Slocombe, and R.A. Boisture, "Divestment of South Africa Investments: The Legal Implications for Foundations, Other Charitable Institutions, and Pension Funds," *Georgetown law Journal* 74 (1985): 127.

140 World Economic Forum, note 96, 10.

141 Freshfields Bruckhaus Deringer, *A Legal Framework for the Integration of Environmental, Social and Governance Issues into Institutional Investment* (UNEPFI, October 2005), 13.

142 L. Gettler, "Big Funds Warned on Negligence," *The Age*, November 30, 2005 (commenting on the Freshfields report).

143 Rarely does legislation explicitly define beneficiaries' interest in financial terms. In Canada, British Columbia's pension fund legislation is anomalous in referring to a duty to act in the best financial interests of the beneficiaries: *Pension Benefits Standards Act*, 1996, s. 44(1).

They can be expressed in various ways. One example is a fiduciary standard centering on the concept of "ecological integrity."[144] Ecological integrity means the natural or unimpaired structure and functioning of the Earth's ecosystems to continue providing the environmental services that sustain *all* life. The concept implies that economic agents, along with other human actors, work to protect, enhance, and restore natural capital. The concept of ecological integrity captures the notion of human dependency on viable and healthy ecosystems including the maintenance of ecological services for the entire biotic community, for future generations. This means that environmental policies will sometimes prevail over economic goals. But what such a standard, or other formulation of the imperatives of sustainability, would mean for fiduciaries in practical terms requires policy-makers to provide further specification.

The precautionary principle is the environmental policy concept that most precisely epitomizes the value of ecological integrity. While some states have enshrined the principle in their environmental legislation,[145] and in international environmental treaties,[146] they have not applied it to the regulation of capital markets. There are various definitions of the precautionary principle arising out of academic and policy debates.[147] The IUCN's guidance on implementation of the precautionary principle is among various initiatives that make it more workable.[148] The Earth Charter's definition of the precautionary principle best gives effect to an ethic of care and respect for the planet.[149] Principle 6a of the Charter refers to taking "action to avoid the possibility of serious or irreversible environmental harm even when scientific knowledge is incomplete or inconclusive," and Principle 6b places

144 S. Woodley, K. Kay, and G. Francis, *Ecological Integrity and the Management of Ecosystems* (St. Lucie Press, 1993); D. Pimentel, L. Westra, and R.F. Noss, eds, *Ecological Integrity: Integrating Environment, Conservation and Health* (Island Press, 2000).

145 E. Hey, "The Precautionary Principle in Environmental Law and Policy: Institutionalising Precaution," *Georgetown International Environmental Law Review* 4 (1994): 303; E. Fisher, et. al., eds, *Implementing the Precautionary Principle: Perspectives and Prospects* (Edward Elgar Publishing, 2006).

146 UN Framework Convention on Climate Change, art. 3, ILM 31 (1992): 849.

147 See J. Cameron and J. Abouchar, "The Precautionary Principle," *Boston College International and Comparative Law Review* 14 (1991): 1; D. Bodansky, "Scientific Uncertainty and the Precautionary Principle," *Environment* 33 (1991): 4.

148 R. Cooney, *The Precautionary Principle in Biodiversity Conservation and Natural Resource Management* (IUCN, 2004).

149 Http://www.earthcharter.org.

"the burden of proof on those who argue that a proposed activity will not cause significant harm and make the responsible parties liable for environmental harm."

Financial institutions could be required to undertake environmental and social impact assessments of major proposed investments and loans, where the financed companies themselves have not undertaken such assessments, and allow a greater margin of error to accommodate any uncertainty regarding possible environmental impacts. The precautionary principle could require financiers to forego or modify investments harming critical natural capital in situations of significant uncertainty. The Collevecchio Declaration embodies some of these requirements.[150] Principle 2 of the Declaration, entitled the "Commitment to Do No Harm," states:

> FIs should commit to do no harm by preventing and minimizing the environmentally and/or socially detrimental impacts of their portfolios and their operations. FIs should create policies, procedures and standards based on the Precautionary Principle to minimize environmental and social harm, improve social and environmental conditions where they and their clients operate, and avoid involvement in transactions that undermine sustainability.

Thus, the precautionary principle places a higher burden of justification for financing on those engaged in potentially harmful activities. It does not deny the rights to own, use, and manage natural resources, but rather, it crystallizes associated ethical responsibility in preventing ecological harm. Thus, it helps to define the limits of investment rights in complex situations where lack of scientific certainty of long-term environmental risks are undervalued as against competing "hard" and short-term economic values.

How, then, should law-makers redefine financiers' fiduciary duties to achieve such aims? The spectrum of possibilities is considerable, and may also depend somewhat on the nature of the type of financial institution, with variable standards to accommodate the particular functions of banks, mutual funds, and other financiers. Before canvassing possible legal formulae, the instruments for defining environmental goals and tracking performance must be identified. The critical challenge is to develop meaningful sustainability performance benchmarks with which to clothe fiduciary duties. Social accounting and sustainability indicators provide metrics that should assist here.

---

150 Http://www.foe.org/camps/intl/declaration.htm.

B. SOCIAL ACCOUNTING

Such a fiduciary standard implies that fiduciaries must take into account the "returns" to society and the environment, in addition to investors' financial returns.[151] In part, this would require new metrics quantifying social and environmental returns.[152] Some scholars are pioneering new models of "social accounting" attempting to capture collateral benefits (e.g., job creation, public infrastructure, and environmental protection) and collateral costs (e.g., damage to natural resources and intensification of social inequalities) of economic activity.[153] In the US community investment sector, social metrics are being advanced to enable investors to quantify non-financial returns.[154]

Social accounting differs from conventional methodologies associated with GAAP and IFRS. It focuses on community and environmental impacts rather than on other factors exclusively related to corporate financial health. Similar models being pioneered to measure economic activities in their entirety provide alternatives to GDP accounting's egregious methodology, which discounts the costs of natural resource exploitation.[155] Ecological economists have also pioneered vital research on measuring the economic value of ecosystems and biodiversity.[156]

151 See S. Lydenberg, "Universal Investors and Socially Responsible Investors: A Tale of Emerging Affinities," *Corporate Governance* 15(3) (2007): 467.

152 M. Power, "Constructing the Responsible Organization: Accounting and Environmental Representation," in note 133, 369.

153 J. Unerman, J. Bebbington, and B. O'Dwyer, eds, *Sustainability Accounting and Accountability* (Routledge, 2007); D.B. Rubenstein, "Bridging the Gap Between Green Accounting and Black Ink," *Accounting, Organizations and Society* 17(5)(1992): 501; A. Vanoli, "Reflections on Environmental Accounting Issues," *Review of Income and Wealth* 41(2) (1995): 113; J. Quarter, L. Mook, and B.J. Richmond, *What Counts: Social Accounting for Nonprofits and Cooperatives* (Prentice Hall, 2003); M.R. Mathews, "Twenty-five Years of Social and Environmental Accounting Research: Is there a Silver Jubilee to Celebrate?" *Accounting, Auditing and Accountability Journal* 10 (4) (1997): 481.

154 E.g., Community Development Venture Capital Alliance (CDVCA), *Measuring Impacts Toolkit* (CDVCA, 2005).

155 R. Repetto, et al., *Wasting Assets. National Resources in the National Income Accounts* (World Resources Institute, 1989); K.A. Brekke, *Economic Growth and the Environment: On the Measurement of Income and Welfare* (Edward Elgar Publishing, 1997); S. El Serafy, "Green Accounting and Economic Policy," *Ecological Economics* 21(3) (1997): 217.

156 J. Farley and H.E. Daly, *Ecological Economics: Principles and Applications* (Island Press, 2003); A.M. Jansson, et al., eds, *Investing in Natural Capital: The Ecological*

Social accounting must not be mistaken as an extension of business case SRI. While it seeks to recognize social and environmental impacts in financial terms and to incorporate that information into investment parameters, it differs from business case SRI in that its focus is on quantifying social welfare rather than merely furthering corporate needs. Properly supported with an appropriate fiduciary standard, social accounting has the potential to go further by assessing investment portfolio contributions to the welfare of society through a healthy environment. Such information could support an ethical investment standard requiring a fiduciary to ensure that financial returns are sufficiently adjusted to reflect the true costs and benefits of production.

However, while several decades of research on social accounting have helped to advance the measurement of companies' social and ecological footprints,[157] social accounting metrics have hardly influenced conventional financial accounting regimes. GAAP and IFRS rules primarily measure expenses and income associated with past, not future, market transactions of discrete entities. Accounting for the disparate and often ethereal externalities of firms in a financier's portfolio, through accounting reforms at the levels of corporate reporting and investment institutions' reporting, would require fundamental changes to this model.

Practically, social accounting has mostly influenced the propagation of satellite, narrative reporting schemes, for instance voluntary sustainability reporting as well as more informative "management discussion and analysis (MD&A)" sections in corporate financial statements. Such adjunct reporting, if properly executed, can influence investors despite its being apart from core accounting and reporting frameworks. Investment analysts seeking to predict future financial health of a corporation should thoroughly research all information at their disposal, beyond that reflected in financial accounting statements.

But what if social accountants or ecological economists cannot appropriately valuate social or environmental impacts? If unquantifiable, may these impacts be ignored, as occurs in business case SRI? Alternatively, what if predicted financial returns outweigh diminution in social or natural capital?

Economics Approach to Sustainability (Island Press, 1994); M. Common and S. Stagl, *Ecological Economics: An Introduction* (Cambridge University Press, 2005).

157 See R. Gray, D. Owen, and C. Adams, eds, *Accounting and Accountability: Changes and Challenges in Corporate Social and Environmental Reporting* (Prentice Hall International, 1996); D. Owen and B. O'Dwyer, "CSR: The Reporting and Assurance Dimension," *The Oxford Handbook of Corporate Social Responsibility*, eds A. Crane, et al. (Oxford University Press, 2008).

There is also the problem of how to enable investors to capture the benefits of any positive social returns derived from investment in environmental leading businesses. These questions raise legitimate concerns about the social accounting model. It faces onerous methodological problems in accurately measuring the economic costs and benefits of environmental performance. Further, as a form of "accounting," it may imply an instrumental and exploitative cost-benefit paradigm that does not ensure the maintenance of ecological integrity sometimes required at any cost. The Ford Pinto case, where managers used a cost-benefit analysis to conclude that costs of correcting a defective fuel system design on one of the company's cars outweighed the expected litigation costs of deaths and/or injuries, highlights the concern with reliance on instrumental economic calculations.[158]

While the cost-benefit calculus may seem controversial to some environmental ethicists, the calculus would apply only to *how* to achieve an ethical standard rather than to *whether* to follow that standard. Accounting systems subordinate to ethically driven SRI would vault financial analysis to a much more comprehensive process of reckoning for all costs and benefits, thereby helping to ensure sustainability. As Daniel Bromley puts it, "[s]ustainability is about the world to be inherited by future persons . . . [rather than] what would be efficient ... for the present generation to bequeath to the future."[159]

C. SUSTAINABILITY INDICATORS

Sustainability indicators (SIs) are essentially a means by which progress towards sustainability based on certain social, environmental, and other markers can be tracked over time.[160] They provide an additional policy tool to steer fiduciary investors towards investments compatible with ecological integrity; to assist decision-makers by translating ecological, economic, and social data into performance standards; and to warn of impending problems. While SIs can be just as methodologically complex to determine

---

158 D. Birsch and J. Fielder, *The Ford Pinto Case: A Study in Applied Ethics, Business, and Technology* (State University of New York Press, 1994). However, a social accounting model would presumably have placed a heavier price on the value of a human life, and led to a different cost-benefit decision in the Pinto case.

159 D. Bromley, "Environmental Regulations and the Problem of Sustainability: Moving Beyond 'Market Failure'," *Ecological Economics* 63 (2007): 676, 678–79.

160 See generally OECD, *Towards Sustainable Development: Indicators to Measure Progress* (OECD, 2000); S. Bell and S. Morse, *Sustainability Indicators: Measuring the Immeasurable* (revised edition, Earthscan, 2008).

as social accounting metrics, SIs do not per se require financial quantification. And they do not dictate *how* underlying performance standards be met. Therefore, from an ethical investment perspective, they may provide a better means of informing financiers. With further development, they can potentially replace shareholder value as a measure of corporate wealth.

As the term suggests, SIs "indicate" a situation. They tend to simplify numerous complex factors and are therefore required to selectively determine important criteria. They differ from traditional indicators of social, economic, and environmental progress. Traditional indicators—such as air quality, waste recycling, and life expectancy—measure changes in one domain as if they were entirely independent variables. SIs are more complex in that they reflect interconnections among such metrics enabling a more systemic, comprehensive, and multidisciplinary perspective. Some useful proxy indicators of sustainability have been pioneered, the "eco-footprint" concept being the most promising.[161] Mathis Wackernagel and others have proposed "ecological footprint accounts," aggregating ecological impacts of human economic activities.[162]

Indicators as a policy tool are not new. Classic indicators include inflation rates or unemployment levels, such powerful and recognizable indicators of economic performance that they may bring governments down. SIs certainly have not yet acquired such eminence, although efforts to design sustainability metrics have occurred at various scales, ranging from the global level down to the local community, company, and project levels.[163] In 1996 the British government published its first set of official sustainability indicators,[164] which it continues to revise and improve.[165] The UN's Commission on Sustainable

161 M. Wackernagel and W. Rees, *Our Ecological Footprint: Reducing Human Impact on the Earth* (New Society Publishers, 1996).

162 M. Wackernagel, et al., "Tracking the Ecological Overshoot of the Human Economy," *Proceedings of the National Academy of Sciences of the United States of America* 99(14) (2002): 9266.

163 J.J. Keeble, S. Topiol, and S. Berkeley, "Using Indicators to Measure Sustainability Performance at a Corporate and Project Level," *Journal of Business Ethics* 44(2–3) (2003): 149.

164 See, e.g., UK, Department of Environment, Transport and the Regions (DETR), *Indicators of Sustainable Development for the United Kingdom* (DETR, 1996).

165 E.g., UK, National Statistics, *Sustainable Development Indicators in Your Pocket 2007* (National Statistics and Department for Environment, Food, and Rural Affairs, 2007).

Development has assumed lead responsibility for formulating indicators for sustainability as part of its obligation to monitor implementation of Agenda 21.[166] Much work on designing sustainability metrics has focused on eco-efficiency indicators, including the work of the WBCSD.[167] So far, these indicators do not appear to have led to substantial shifts in national or international policy.

Indicators for sustainability have also been advanced for the corporate and financial sectors. Indicators at business-unit levels are complicated as their robustness requires an account of supply-chain and product life-cycle effects.[168] Ratings of corporate social and environmental performance have become crucial for the SRI industry, providing the basis for portfolio screens, best-in-class asset selections, and dedicated SRI market indexes such as the DJSIs. A vast research industry has mushroomed in recent years to develop corporate sector SIs, to evaluate corporate performance against them, and to translate them into investor advice.[169] They provide a normative benchmark and means of market ordering to the extent that firms are interested in SRI-portfolio inclusion. However, their competitive proliferation and lack of regulatory oversight and coherence have hindered their reliability.[170]

A further weakness of current approaches is that SIs for financial institutions' portfolios as a whole have not been adequately developed. There may be an inappropriate assumption that if individual firms are acceptable enough to form part of a sustainable portfolio that it follows that the financial institution is also acting sustainably. Erroneously, this assumption would not reflect aspects of a financial institution's management systems relevant for

166 UN Commission on Sustainable Development (CSD), *Indicators of Sustainable Development: Guidelines and Methodologies* (CSD, 2001).
167 H.A. Verfaillie and R. Bidwell, *Measuring Eco-Efficiency: A Guide to Reporting Company Performance* (WBCSD, 2000).
168 D. Tanzil and B.R. Beloff, "Assessing Impacts: Overview of Sustainability Indicators and Metrics," *Environmental Quality Management* 15(4) (2006): 41.
169 H. Schäfer, et al., *Who is Who in Corporate Social Responsibility Rating? A Survey of Internationally Established Rating Systems that Measure Corporate Responsibility* (Bertelsmann Foundation, 2006).
170 Å. Skillius and U. Wennberg, *Continuity, Credibility and Comparability: Key Challenges for Corporate Environmental Performance Measurement and Communication* (International Institute for Industrial Environmental Economics, Lund University, 1998), s. 5.2.

ethical investment, such as the democratic quality of its decision-making. If many companies are rated by the SRI industry for the quality of their corporate governance, so too should their financial sponsors. Those decision-making systems are important indicators of future performance, whereas most SIs are lagging indicators tracking only historic impacts.[171] Further, because financiers typically have a wider stake in the economy than individual firms, and often have longer-term financial liabilities, from a sustainability perspective financiers should be accountable to higher standards of environmental care.

In 2000, a consortium of German and Swiss banks created a set of environmental indicators targeted specifically at the financial sector.[172] Their report sets a common set of management and operational performance indicators considered relevant. Environmental effects associated with financial transactions were not addressed, as the report explained:

> The ecological impacts associated with an investment credit of a bank client, whose project for example leads to pollution of drinking water, cannot yet be measured through indicators by financial institutions. Firstly, there remains the methodical problem of a standardised worldwide measurement of such changes to the environment. Secondly, financial institutions play an important role but are not crucial in realising such environmentally relevant investments. It is the client's primary responsibility to document these changes to the environment within its own environmental management system.[173]

The GRI provides a more useful starting point for designing robust SIs and consequential performance standards for the financial sector. Although intended as a template for corporate environmental and social reporting, the GRI has a financial sector supplement broadly including social and environmental variables that financiers should report.[174]

---

171 M.J. Epstein and P.S. Wisner, "Using a Balanced Scorecard to Implement Sustainability," *Environmental Quality Management* 11(2) (2001): 1.

172 O. Schmid-Schönbein and A. Braunschweig, *EPI-Finance 2000; Environmental Performance Indicators for the Financial Industry* (E2 Management Consulting, 2000).

173 Ibid., 12.

174 GRI, *Financial Services Sector Supplement: Environmental Performance. Pilot Version 1.0* (GRI, March 2005).

Sustainability indicators are already starting to help the financial sector to measure its impact. One of the most innovative attempts to quantify one important externality of an entire investment portfolio is Trucost's annual "carbon counts" survey, which measures and ranks UK investment funds according to the carbon intensity of their portfolios.[175] Its recent evaluation of 185 investment funds on the carbon footprint of their portfolios found that one-quarter of the SRI funds polluted more than industry benchmarks.[176] A portfolio's carbon footprint is one of the most important indicators of sustainability.

2. The Spectrum of Fiduciary Duties for SRI

A. DISCRETIONARY STANDARDS

Fiduciary duties create a legal framework to give effect to the foregoing policy goals. The minimalist option, redolent of business case SRI, would expressly allow fiduciaries to take into account ESG factors where in good faith they consider them to be financially material. Fiduciaries could thus act despite the absence of an explicit mandate from their investors. For example, trustees of a pension fund investing for the long term may respond to climate change risks by including more emerging renewable energy and clean technology firms in their portfolio. Arguably, this materiality threshold test is already allowed, indeed essential if ESG-related risks jeopardize investments.[177] But with such a reform the matter would surely be put beyond doubt.

Already some jurisdictions authorize SRI as a legitimate adjunct consideration. Legislation in the state of Connecticut already provides that controllers of the Connecticut Retirement Plans and Trust Funds *may* consider the environmental and social implications of investments.[178] Its latest 2007 investment policy contains various provisions which suggest that it prioritizes such factors when selecting assets, voting proxies, and other similar actions.[179] Two Canadian provinces, Manitoba and Ontario, provide

---

175 Trucost, *Carbon Counts 2007: The Carbon Footprint Ranking of UK Investment* (Trucost, 2007).

176 Discussed in H. Williams, "News: Carbon Footprint Casts Doubt on SRI Products," *PensionsWeek*, July 23, 2007, 1.

177 E.g., J. Ambachtsheer, et al., *Fiduciary Guide to Toxic Chemical Risk* (Rose Foundation for Communities and the Environment, and the Investor Environmental Health Network, 2007).

178 Conn. Gen. Stat. (2002), s. 3–13d(a).

179 State of Connecticut Office of the Treasurer, *Investment Policy Statement for the State of Connecticut Retirement Plans and Trust Fund* (State of Connecticut

further examples. In 1995, Manitoba's *Trustee Act* was amended to permit trustees to consider non-financial criteria in their investment policies, so long as "the trustee exercises the judgment and care that a person of prudence, discretion and intelligence would exercise in administering the property of others."[180] In 2005, a similar provision was introduced into Manitoba's pension legislation.[181] Ontario's former *South African Trust Investments Act* of 1988 permitted a trustee to divest or reject investments in companies doing business in South Africa despite any effect on investment returns, without infringing their fiduciary duty.[182]

In a corporate context, the Supreme Court of Canada has endorsed a similar reformulation of directors' fiduciary duties to the company. *Peoples Department Stores v. Wise* was a suit brought by the trustee in bankruptcy representing various trade creditors who argued that an arrangement agreed to by defendant directors concerning two firms under their control had violated a statutory duty to trade creditors.[183] The Court interpreted the phrase "best interests of the corporation" in section 122(1) of the *Canada Business Corporations Act* as being distinguishable from the best interests of shareholders. Accordingly, it ruled that it was appropriate for directors to consider factors beyond the maximization of shareholder value, including "employees, suppliers, creditors, consumers, governments and the environment," which may affect the corporation.[184] Likewise, constituency statutes in the US attempt to achieve similar effects through explicit legislation.[185]

The principal constraint of fiduciary discretion is that it does not *oblige* consideration of societal interests. Nor does it allow affected outsiders to enforce their interests. In the case of *Peoples Department Stores*, the Court stressed the difference between taking the interests of various parties into account and *owing a duty* to those parties. In this case the duty of loyalty that a director owes remains to the corporation itself, not to other parties.[186] This makes the legal recognition and protection of other interests functionally unenforceable. While the Supreme Court's ruling erodes shareholder

---

Office of the Treasurer, 2007) (see e.g., Appendix B: Domestic/Global Proxy Voting Policies, at 32).

180 *Trustee Act*, S.M., 1995, s. 79.1.

181 *Pension Benefits Amendment Act*, S.M., 2005, s. 28.1(2.2).

182 R.S.O. 1990, (repealed in 1997).

183 [2004] 3 S.C.R. 461; 2004 S.C.C. 68.

184 Ibid., para. 42.

185 J.J. Hanks, Jr., "Playing with Fire: Nonshareholder Constituency Statutes in the 1990s," *Stetson Law Review* 21 (1991): 97.

186 [2004] 3 S.C.R. 461, 2004 S.C.C. 68, para. 43.

primacy, by restricting shareholders' ability to reproach directors who favor other constituencies, it does not offer much recourse for any other constituencies.

Perhaps the main advantage of a discretionary approach is that it enables fiduciaries to respond proactively, rather than reactively, to the social and environmental impacts of investment. Fiduciaries should confidently initiate steps to promote sustainable development, rather than merely react as material environmental risks and liabilities arise.

B. PROCESS STANDARDS

Alternatively, legislation could prescribe *procedures* to improve the likelihood that fiduciaries would consider the social and environmental impacts of their investment decisions.[187] To date, lawmakers have preferred transparency regulation, involving light-touch disclosure rules such as having financiers publicly reporting any SRI policy in place. In practice, this should be considered a first generation of procedural reform, because it has merely tinkered with the problems of unseen polluters.

A wide range of more ambitious procedural reforms short of actually mandating SRI are possible. The most obvious immediate step is to significantly bolster disclosure regimes. Regulatory standards for mandatory social disclosures can compel companies and their financial sponsors to disclose both positive and negative aspects of financial performance, as well as enable comparisons between institutions. Financiers should be obliged not only to disclose their policies on SRI, but also their investment methodology and implementation efforts, and where applicable, they should explain why they have not adhered to specified best practices. Authorities must also devote more resources to enforcing disclosure obligations. Financiers' disclosures on SRI should be audited independently, and industry rankings publicized to allow for comparative assessment of financiers' performance. Some of the plethora of private sector initiatives for sustainability reporting, such as the GRI, could be incorporated.

Moving along the spectrum of procedural reforms, authorities could also allow outside stakeholders to have a voice in financial institutions' governance, as representatives of particular social and environmental interests or constituencies. For large pension funds, this could involve stakeholder representatives sitting on governing boards. Less prominently, fiduciaries

---

187 G. Teubner, "Corporate Fiduciary Duties and Their Beneficiaries," in *Corporate Governance and Directors' Liabilities*, eds K.J. Hopt and G. Teubner (Walter de Gruyter, 1985), 165, 166.

could be required to consult with and consider the interests of specific stakeholders who do not have formal representation in fund management. For instance, the EPs require Equator bank signatories to ensure that in planning projects they finance, local communities who may be affected are consulted.

One rationale for such a reform is that the governing boards of pension trusts, investment funds, and banks are typically drawn from a narrow socio-economic segment of society. They commonly lack expertise on SRI issues and do not adequately understand modern social and environmental challenges. For instance, research on UK pension fund trustees reveals widespread ignorance on SRI issues among that group, despite several years of experience with the SRI disclosure law since 2000.[188] Representatives of various social and environmental constituencies could strengthen the ethical envelope of investment. Even nature itself could have a voice, in a manner analogous to Christopher Stone's suggestion for authorities to appoint guardians to represent the interests of ecosystems.[189] All stakeholder representatives of course could not have voice without being accountable. They too would need to be bound by fiduciary obligations. More representative governing boards may be better informed of the challenges of aligning private investment with public responsibilities to ensure sustainable development. They provide a means to democratically diversify the range of perspectives that inform SRI policy, and thereby bolster the social legitimacy of ethical investment decisions.

This stakeholder approach already appears, to a limited extent, in the practice of requiring independent or outside directors on corporate boards.[190] Stakeholder representation, for employees, was most strongly established as a traditional feature in the German system of corporate governance, and it has been retained there despite some gravitation to the Anglo-American model.[191] In several jurisdictions, proposals for CSR legislation have been tabled to

---

188 C. Gribben and M. Gitsham, *Will UK Pension Funds Become More Responsible: A Survey of Trustees* (JustPensions, UKSIF, 2006).

189 C. Stone, "Should Trees Have Standing? Toward Legal Rights for Natural Objects," *Southern California Law Review* 45 (1972): 450.

190 J. Wang and H.D. Dewhirst, "Boards of Directors and Stakeholder Orientation," *Journal of Business Ethics* 11(2) (1992): 115; A.J. Hillman, G.D. Keim, and R.A. Luce, "Board Composition and Stakeholder Performance: Do Stakeholder Directors Make a Difference?" *Business and Society* 40(3) (2001): 295.

191 C. Lane, "Changes in Corporate Governance of German Corporations: Convergence to the Anglo-American Model?" *Competition and Change* 7(2–3) (2003): 79.

include stakeholder rights. The UK's Corporate Responsibility Bill, which failed to pass in the House of Commons, called for annual reporting on a comprehensive set of performance indicators, social, environmental, and economic; it had also required consultation of and response to opinions of stakeholders potentially affected by any proposed projects.[192] The Bill also devised an extraterritorial control scheme enabling affected international communities to seek damages arising from human rights and environmental abuses committed by UK companies or their overseas subsidiaries. Similarly ambitious CSR laws have been proposed in the US[193] and Australia[194] in recent years without success so far.[195]

Advancing SRI in these ways may have various limitations.[196] The potential multitude of interests runs counter to arguments that efficient institutions are endowed with clear, single-purpose functions, where governance procedures are not compromised by competing considerations.[197] Where a fiduciary must consider numerous interests without owing a specific obligation to any of them or by owing a specific obligation to all of them, any decision taken that is not blatantly self-interested becomes defensible. Because of the extreme breadth of interests to "balance," no stakeholder could plausibly argue that the fiduciary was derelict in the duty to consider their interests. The fiduciary relationship crumbles where her loyalty splinters among multiple parties or stakeholders whose interests may not coincide. A report of the Corporations and Markets Advisory Committee of the Australian Government cautioned against widening fiduciary duties by concluding that too much fiduciary discretion would be detrimental to all

---

192 UK, House of Commons, *Corporate Responsibility Bill*, 2003, Bill 129.

193 *Corporate Code of Conduct Act*, 2000, H.R. 4596, 106th Congress.

194 *Corporate Code of Conduct Bill*, 2000 (Cth).

195 A. McBeth, "A Look at Corporate Code of Conduct Legislation," *Common Law World Review* 33 (2004): 222.

196 For a sample of the literature from the CSR perspective, see R.E. Freeman and D.L. Reed, "Stockholders and Stakeholders: A New Perspective on Corporate Governance," *California Management Review* 25(3) (1983): 88; T. Donaldson and L.E. Preston, "The Stakeholder Theory of the Corporation: Concepts, Evidence, and Implications," *The Academy of Management Review* 20(1) (1995): 65; C. Driver and G. Thompson, "Corporate Governance and Democracy: The Stakeholder Debate Revisited," *Journal of Management and Governance* 6(2) (2002): 111.

197 See M. Jensen, *A Theory of the Firm: Governance, Residual Claims, and Organizational Forms* (Harvard University Press, 2000).

parties to whom obligations are owed.[198] More democratic procedures within financial institutions could mitigate some of these problems and help build agreement or at least a majority view on some SRI issues.

Alternatively, the financial sector could accommodate a voice for stake-holders in an external entity, such as a national ethics council responsible for setting general standards for SRI. The state could establish a body with suitably qualified representatives from key constituencies to devise standards for ethical investment (and other economic activities) for sustainable development. Fiduciaries would receive guidance in addressing various perspectives on difficult ethical questions, enabling them to avoid trial and error. For instance, such an ethical council could target countries or corporate sectors and decree that no financier invest in a country whose government is complicit in human rights atrocities or mandate additional investment in renewable energy production.

This option may be more acceptable for public financial institutions (e.g., public investment funds, national savings schemes, export-credit agencies, and foreign aid) as it may be considered too controlling for private sector investments. Sweden and Norway have established ethics councils to guide their public pension funds according to international environmental and social standards. In 2001, Germany also established a National Ethics Council to serve as a forum for dialogue on ethical issues, and to provide government bodies and society with opinions and recommendations.[199] The private sector might tolerate an ethics panel with a more restrained mandate. For instance, it could set general guidance and voluntary standards. Investment institutions would be free to follow its advice, or not. Some might well choose to comply for the added legitimacy it could provide to invest-ment choices or as a measure of the reasonable administration of fiduciary obligation. Already, for instance, the Belgian fund Portfolio 21 claims to base its SRI screening decisions on the recommendations of the Norwegian Council of Ethics.[200]

C. PERFORMANCE STANDARDS

An alternative or additional means to ethical investment could be legislating a positive fiduciary duty to act for sustainable development, without reference to

---

198 Corporations and Markets Advisory Committee, *The Social Responsibility of Corporations Report* (Commonwealth Government, 2006), 111–12.

199 See http://www.ethikrat.org. So far, the work of the National Ethics Council has focused on bio-ethics.

200 See http://www.portfolio21.be/index.asp?LID=3.

any specific constituency. Designing a credible, functional standard with suffi-cient clarity would be a challenge; an undefined duty "to have regard to" or "to promote" sustainable development would not suffice. Like the sustainability discourse itself, such a vague yardstick subject to discretionary interpretations would perpetuate business-as-usual and allow trade-offs that compromise ecological integrity. Its legal formulation requires supplementary rules defin-ing the standard of care and determining to whom duties are owed.

Certainly, investing in an ostensibly lawful activity would not necessarily satisfy fiduciary standards by this approach. In other words, an emission license does not necessarily shield a polluter from other legal actions such as tort suits (e.g., public nuisance action).[201] Further, no simple distinction between a permissible and prohibited activity exists in this area. Typically, corporate activities or products are controlled, subject to impact assessments, permits, and other regulatory checks. In some countries with rudimentary systems of environmental law, even an expressly permissible activity may run afoul of elementary international sustainability standards.

Mandatory legislation for CSR in the context of corporate or financial regulation is not unprecedented. Among sparse examples, the UK's *Companies Act* of 2006 comes "close to a stakeholder model of director's duties" according to some legal commentators.[202] The applicable part, section 172(1), states:

> A director of a company must act in the way he considers, in good faith, would be most likely to promote the success of the company for the benefit of its members as a whole, and in doing so have regard (amongst other matters) to—
>
> (a) the likely consequences of any decision in the long term. . . .
>
> (d) the impact of the company's operations on the community and the environment. . . .

When this provision was being debated in the House of Commons, the then Minister for Industry and the Regions, Margaret Hodge, explained its significance:

> The clause does codify and bring into law for the first time duties around corporate social responsibility. I do not run away from that;

---

201 See, e.g., the cases of *Mandrake Management v. Toronto Transit Commission*, (1993) 102 D.L.R. (4th); *Wheeler v. J.J. Saunders Ltd*, [1995] 3 W.L.R. 466.
202 C.A. Williams and J.M. Conley, "Triumph or Tragedy: The Curious Path of Corporate Disclosure Reform in the UK," *William and Mary Environmental Law and Policy Review* 31(2) (2007): 317, 354.

it is a deliberate act by the Government. That is at the heart of the Bill. For me, one of the key issues is how we can marry the commercial success of individual companies and the resulting benefits to, and growth and prosperity of, the economy, with sustainability and social justice.[203]

While the British reform affects regular corporations, rather than financial institutions, it is significant that such steps have occurred in a key international financial hub. Breach of this duty could make a transaction voidable and result in civil liability for directors. However, its practical effect is yet to be judged by the courts, and legal commentators speculate that the discretion reposed in directors may well render the provision unenforceable.[204] Yet, because of directors' concurrent obligations under section 417 of the *Companies Act* to include a report of the company's environmental performance in their annual business review, fiduciary obligations will surely not be handled perfunctorily.

The UK reforms do not include nonshareholder interests in actual corporate governance, yet oblige directors to consider how environmental and social impacts affect corporate success. Applied to financial institutions, such as pension funds, such a standard could help to redefine fiduciary duties along the lines of the "universal owner" thesis.[205] The financial success of institutional investors, who have a stake in much of the economy, is even more likely to be affected by wider social and environmental interests than that of a single corporation operating in a particular industry sector.

From a sustainability policy perspective, obliging universal owners to consider social and environmental issues to the extent that they affect investment returns has certain limitations. The focus remains on profitability of the financial institution and, ultimately, its beneficiaries. Without other measures, this approach to fiduciary duties could still suppress ethical, social, and environmental considerations. Most fundamentally, while universal owners may respond to externalities of individual companies that create costs elsewhere in the economy, universal owners may be blind to externalities of

---

203 House of Commons, *Hansard Parliamentary Debates* (6th series), (July 11, 2006), 592, cited in Williams and Conley, ibid., 355.

204 P. Yeoh, "The Direction and Control of Corporations: Law or Strategy?" *Managerial Law* 49(1/2) (2007): 37.

205 J.P. Hawley and A.T. Williams, *The Rise of Fiduciary Capitalism* (University of Pennsylvania Press, 2000); S. Davis, J. Lukomnik, and D. Pitt-Watson, *The New Capitalists: How Citizen Investors are Reshaping the Corporate Agenda* (Harvard Business School Press, 2006).

the market as a whole. Moreover, the tendency to delegate investment management to specialist fund managers, with short-term performance targets, coupled with reliance on corporate valuation models that do not measure economic factors holistically, further undermines universal sustainable investing. Additional reforms are required to align universal owners with sustainable development.

With improvements to social accounting, the fiduciary's obligation could remain to serve the interests of its beneficiary investors, but only so long as returns to beneficiaries are adjusted to reflect environmental costs and benefits. This standard could allow, for instance, for more economically targeted investment generating locally positive externalities.[206] It would also require ecological cost deductions for applicable investments.[207] With the spread of economic instruments ascribing monetary value to environmental behavior, such as carbon taxes and tradable emission permits, quantification of some externalities can improve. Others, in the social realm, may require new accounting metrics. GAAP guidelines for social and environmental accounting could be fashioned, for international use.[208]

Alternatively, SIs could be prescribed by regulation and effectively set fiduciary performance benchmarks, such as the carbon footprint of a portfolio and other seminal indicators enabling a full view of environmental performance. Fiduciaries would not be required to account monetarily for social and environmental costs and benefits of investments under this approach. Rather, they would be required to ensure that the overall portfolio adheres to indicators of sustainability by whatever means they choose. Advantages of performance standards based on SIs are that they can set clear benchmarks for financiers while avoiding prescribed methods for arriving at set results.

By these means, the fiduciary standard would effectively prioritize ecological integrity over private investment returns. Either through social accounting or performance standards based on indicators, the computation of

---

206 E.A. Zelinsky, "The Dilemma of the Local Social Investment: An Essay on 'Socially Responsible Investment'," *Cardozo Law Review* 6 (1984–85): 111, 130–31.

207 K. Herbohn, "A Full Cost Environmental Accounting Experiment," *Accounting Organizations and Society* 30(6) (2005): 519.

208 The accounting profession is increasingly attentive to the challenge of aligning financial reporting metrics with corporate sustainability performance: see, e.g., Association of Chartered Certified Accountants (ACCA), *Industry as a Partner for Sustainable Development* (ACCA and UNEP, 2002); J. Desjardins and A. Willis, *Environmental Performance: Measuring and Managing What Matters* (Canadian Institute of Chartered Accountants, 2001).

returns must account for social and environmental impacts and benefits. While investors could nominally continue as sole beneficiaries of such fiduciary duties (but implicitly also owed to the state to safeguard the public interest), diminishing sustainability would no longer be a viable means of obtaining financial gain. Additional social benefits accrue to beneficiaries, not only in their capacity as investors but also as members of society. Steven Lydenberg, who argues that universal investors should favor such a broader concept of social returns, astutely observes: "[t]he measurement of the value of corporations to society solely on their stock price and their ability to raise that price is not only a narrow expression of the value of corporations to society, but a potentially dangerous one. . . ."[209]

Practical problems obstructing implementation of these recommendations are not trivial. However, failing to identify these difficulties as an excuse for maintaining the status quo is no longer an option. While some values and practices, particularly in areas such as human rights, may defy measurement in social accounting or simplification into sustainability indicators, supplementary means, such as duties to conduct social impact assessments and consult with affected stakeholders may provide some breakthroughs. For the near term, the most actionable recommendation is to provide for some discretionary fiduciary standards, coupled with more rigorous process reforms improving the quality of disclosures and enhancing consultation, and initially reserving the imposition of SRI performance standards for public sector institutions. Over the long term, more ambitious and wide-ranging changes will likely be necessary.

C. COLLATERAL REFORMS

2. Policy Levers for Change

While the reformulation of financiers' fiduciary duties can underpin a new ethical approach to SRI, other collateral measures are also imperative. While the following measures certainly could be construed as tools for furthering the business case for SRI, they also provide the means to enable financiers to more readily achieve fiduciary standards for safeguarding ecological integrity.

---

209 S. Lydenberg, "Universal Investors and Socially Responsible Investors: A Tale of Emerging Affinities," *Corporate Governance* 15(3) (2007): 467, 476.

Economic instruments, such as pollution taxes, emission allowance trading, and discrete subsidies, can strengthen SRI by pricing social and environmental externalities into the cost of development capital. In conjunction with social accounting reforms, economic instruments can attribute quantified negative and positive externalities to firms, for reflection in their earnings, competitiveness and, ultimately, share prices and other financial indicators. This in turn should influence the allocation of capital, making polluters competitively disadvantaged.

While a system of SRI governance nurturing ethical investment cannot rest only on a system of monetary incentives, economic rewards for changed behavior are the most politically viable reforms and can bolster adjunct measures such as new fiduciary standards. The Netherlands' tax incentive for green project investments has catalyzed the Dutch SRI market, accounting for about half of all its SRI.[210] Taxes can also reward long-term investment by targeting appropriate financial transactions. Meaningful taxes on short-term gains on trading shares, applied on a decreasing scale as the holding period lengthens, must be assessed. Concomitantly, investors who hold an ownership stake for a qualifying period (e.g., five years) could receive access to more complete information about a company's financial position and prospects than that which is disclosed publicly.

Related to economic policy instruments, financier liability provides another means to penalize creditors or shareholders for the environmental and social harms connected to companies or projects they fund. Liability could arise where an institutional shareholder alone or acting in concert was in a position to exert influence, or where a lender disregarded due diligence requirements such as assessing the adequacy of a borrower's environmental safeguards. Faced with such risks, fiduciaries must factor the costs of the potential liability into their investment decisions. This would implicitly redefine fiduciary duties, as fiduciaries could maximize returns only in so far as they account for any environmental and social liability risks.

However, as a reactive and adversarial tool, liability should not be the primary route to ethical investment. Many social and environmental problems are so numerous, diffused, and intertwined that the individual causal linkages between acts and damages are too remote to impose liability according to evidential rules in courts. Further, while institutional investors collectively own the majority of the stock market, a single pension fund will typically own only a small percentage of stock in each of possibly thousands

---

210 B. Scholtens, "What Drives Socially Responsible Investment? The Case of the Netherlands," *Sustainable Development* 13 (2005): 129.

of companies in their portfolio. For example, the Canada Pension Plan holds shares in some 2,000 companies worldwide, and the Norwegian Government Pension Fund has over 3,500 companies in its portfolio.[211] In such cases, an institutional investor cannot practically track the myriad environmental practices of firms in its portfolio, let alone exert influence over those practices unless acting in concert with other financiers.[212] Such problems with liability standards motivated Teubner to argue for legislative imposition of "an overarching cupola of quasi-collective responsibility for ecological damages," whereby financiers would be jointly liable on a pro rata basis.[213] Before adopting such a system, vastly improved corporate environmental reporting systems must be implemented to enable financiers to monitor firms.

Another limitation of the liability model is that it assumes that the environmental standards applicable to corporations should be suitable for their financial sponsors. In other words, so long as a firm acts according to the applicable environmental standards, there would be no recourse against its investors. Sometimes such standards may be acceptable, but at other times higher standards of care for financiers are appropriate. As investment institutions typically hold a broad portfolio of stocks and have long-term financial liabilities, it is important even from a business case that they be attentive to long-term or wide-ranging environmental risks and trends. Ethical investment for sustainability demands going beyond traditional legal standards applied to corporations to address such threats. Further, in any event, the liability model assumes that governments can create a comprehensive system of command regulation capturing and appropriately penalizing all costly externalities of front-line companies. This is unlikely as financiers invest globally and have lucrative opportunities in countries lacking the regulatory capacity to protect the environment. Governments would need to create laws of extra-territorial application, as does the US's *Alien Tort Claims Act*,

---

211 J.A. MacNaughton, "The Canadian Experience on Governance, Accountability and Investment," in *Public Pension Fund Management*, eds A.R. Musalem and R.J. Palacios (World Bank, 2004), 107, 119; B. Powell, "Sovereign Funds to the Rescue," *Time Magazine*, December 6, 2007.

212 Similar complexities could also be said to arise for fiduciaries obliged to account for the social and environmental impacts of their investment portfolios under a social accounting standard or via sustainability indicators. However, those complexities would be greatly reduced when the accounting burden falls primarily on individual firms, reporting in turn to financiers.

213 G. Teubner, "The Invisible Cupola: From Casual to Collective Attribution in Ecological Liability," *Cardozo Law Review* 16(2) (1994): 429, 430.

making financial institutions accountable for their behavior in foreign jurisdictions.[214] Problems remain in policing offshore activities of financiers.

Among other potential collateral reforms, government authorities should also collaborate with the private sector. One area for cooperation is through stock exchanges that perform a gatekeeping function. Already, specific SRI market indexes such as the DJSI provide a form of market selection on the basis of CSR performance. The next logical step would be for securities regulators, in conjunction with stock exchanges, to incorporate CSR criteria as a condition of stock market listing. Companies would have to adhere to more rigorous criteria to access capital markets and, be subject to delisting if they fail to meet required standards. Such criteria could range from providing periodic disclosure of CSR performance to adherence to more substantive sustainability performance standards. However, this is not a foolproof means of SRI governance, as there are alternative, less regulated sources of capital available. Moreover, as stock exchanges depend on the listing fees of members, they would need to be compensated by some means to ensure their motivation to remove or deny listing to companies that lag on performance standards.

There have been tentative steps in this direction in some jurisdictions. Since July 2004, listed companies in Australia must comply with the Australian Stock Exchange's (ASX) Principles of Good Corporate Governance. The ASX requires listed firms to adopt its Code of Conduct and Ethics indicating how they intend to deal with stakeholder concerns and interests.[215] In 2007, the ASX Corporate Governance Council proposed that listed companies should go further and report to shareholders about all material business risks they face, including environmental and ethical conduct-related risks.[216] Stock exchange listing requirements on corporate governance have also been introduced in several emerging markets, such as the Johannesburg Securities Exchange which requires listed companies to follow a specific code of corporate practices and to report on GRI indicators.[217]

---

214 S.A. Aaronson, "'Minding Our Business': What the United States Government Has Done and Can Do to Ensure That U.S. Multinationals Act Responsibly in Foreign Markets," *Journal of Business Ethics* 59 (2005): 175.

215 ASX Corporate Governance Council, *Principles of Good Corporate Governance Practice and Best Practice Recommendations* (ASX, 2003); J. McConvill and J. Bingham, "Comply or Comply: The Illusion of Voluntary Corporate Governance in Australia," *Company and Securities Law Journal* 22 (2004): 208.

216 S. Washington, "We Need to Keep Our Secrets," *Sydney Morning Herald*, February 19, 2007.

217 UNEPFI, *Sustainability Management and Reporting: Benefits for Financial Institutions in Emerging Economies* (UNEPFI, 2006), 18.

Finally, among possible collateral reforms for SRI, at an international level a new treaty dealing directly with social and environmental standards for global finance could be added to the "wish list." The existing range of voluntary standards such as the UNPRI fall short of the exacting standards required, on both substantive performance standards and procedural controls including public disclosures, auditing, and grievance mechanisms. Reforms to fiduciary duties outlined earlier in this chapter could be set as international standards for governments worldwide to adopt in their domestic legislation.

Ethical investment must be informed by internationally acceptable values. With foreign ownership of stock markets increasing and capital pouring into booming emerging economies, SRI governance cannot hinge solely on national standards.[218] International environmental law and human rights law instruments, including voluntary global codes, are already informing SRI practices, such as in the screening policies of mutual funds and portfolio selection of national pension plans mandated to invest ethically. International financial market regulation has advantages. For one, it would help to prevent a race to the bottom, as similar standards would preclude capital fleeing to the most regulatorily benign markets.[219] Institutional investors in global markets may even welcome standardization of SRI governance norms, as opposed to having to comply with different rules in different markets.

The UN Norms on the Responsibilities of Transnational Corporations, as discussed in chapter 6, illustrate what such an international instrument could look like.[220] Such norms could set benchmarks for assessing and reporting environmental impacts, participating in investment governance, promoting

---

218 For example, in the UK, foreign investors held only 7 percent of the stock of UK listed companies in 1963, but a staggering 40 percent by the close of 2006: National Statistics, *Foreign Investors Hold Two-fifths of UK Shares: Share Ownership 2006* (National Statistics, July 12, 2007); D.S. Doering, et al., *Tomorrow's Markets—Global Trends and their Implications for Business* (World Resources Institute, WBCSD, and UN Development Program, 2002), 54.

219 S.R. Umlauf, "Transaction Taxes and the Behavior of the Swedish Stock Market," *Journal of Financial Economics* 33 (1993): 227 (noting that when Sweden introduced a securities trading tax in 1984, foreign investors reacted by moving their trading offshore while domestic investors responded by reducing the amount of their equity trades).

220 UN Economic and Social Council, Sub-Commission on Promotion and Protection of Human Rights, *Norms on the Responsibilities of Transnational Corporations and Other Business Enterprises with Regard to Human Rights*, UN ESCOR, 2003, UN Doc. E/CN.4/Sub.2/2003/12/Rev.2.

sustainable development financing, and including enforcement mechanisms. Yet, given the corporate hostility to the UN Norms, as well as earlier attempts to muzzle UN plans to regulate TNCs, such a treaty would face acute political obstacles.[221] Typically, reaching an agreement on inter-jurisdictional reforms is more challenging than advancing reforms in a single jurisdiction. Potentially, the assortment of international voluntary standards such as the UNPRI helps to create a more receptive climate for the gradual entrenchment of sustainability standards for global finance. Certainly, the present course is towards more, not less, international accountability.

2. Public Sector Finance

Public sector finance must also set an example for SRI, as well as help SRI to achieve the critical mass necessary to exert market influence. David Hess heralds public pension funds as "a potentially powerful catalyst for change" towards sustainable development.[222] Short of a command economy, states should at least mobilize public capital to address strategic social and environmental issues, as occurs to some extent in the national pension plans of Scandinavia, France, and New Zealand. Other options for strengthening public savings schemes for sustainable investment have been canvassed. For example, Roberto Unger proposes unifying all private pension plans into a single national scheme, from which revenue would be channeled into "social investment funds" to meet social and economic needs marginalized by the market.[223] Jim Stanford advocates a public venture capital investing system for SRI, funded partly by a levy on private financiers.[224]

Beyond empowering public pension funds as SRI leaders, states could also influence capital allocation through central banks, giving preferential treatment to environmentally critical industries. Central banks in France, Japan, and South Korea have historically been assertive in addressing national, economically strategic sectors through loans and interest

---

221 T. Rathgeber, *UN Norms on the Responsibilities of Transnational Corporations*, Occasional Paper 22 (Friedrich-Ebert-Stiftung, 2006), 7–9.

222 D. Hess, *Public Pensions and the Promise of Shareholder Activism for the Next Frontier of Corporate Governance: Sustainable Economic Development*, Working Paper No. 1080 (Ross School of Business, University of Michigan, March 2007), 42.

223 R. Unger, *Democracy Realised: The Progressive Alternative* (Verso Books, 1998).

224 J. Stanford, *Paper Boom: Why Real Prosperity Requires a New Approach to Canada's Economy* (Canadian Centre for Policy Alternatives, 1999), 334–36.

rate subsidies.[225] Even the most neoliberal-minded states, such as the US, have retained a planned economy for military spending. Now faced with a growing environmental crisis, public finance could play similar strategic roles.

In an international context, foreign aid and multilateral development investment provide further nodes for sustainable development financing.[226] While catering to emerging economies, intergovernmental finance can sometimes set an example for private financiers, as done by the World Bank Group's environmental policies incorporated into the EPs. The Global Environment Facility also channels funds for sustainable development projects in strategic sectors unable to raise sufficient private capital.[227]

Co-financing arrangements offer a novel way by which governments can guide private financiers to behave more responsibly. Partnerships between public and private institutions may offer benefits for all parties. Public financial resources are often insufficient, while private financiers are too risk-adverse. A synergy can arise by using public funds to complement private investment in environmental projects by reducing initial barriers and implementation costs.[228] Environmentally conditioned public finance on preferential terms could bridge the cost gap between what private financiers wish to commit and what is necessary for sustainable development investments.

Sadly, development co-financing at a bilateral level has been mired in controversy. Bilateral export credit agencies (ECAs) have incurred criticism

225 R. Pollin, "Public Credit Allocation through the Federal Reserve: Why It Is Needed; How It Should Be Done," in *Transforming the U.S. Financial System: Equity and Efficiency for the 21st Century*, eds G.A. Dymski, et al. (M.E. Sharpe, 1993), 321, 323.

226 Among the literature, see F. Tarp, *Foreign Aid and Development: Lessons Learned and Directions for the Future* (Routledge, 2000); R.O. Keohane and M.A. Levy, *Institutions for Environmental Aid: Pitfalls and Promise* (MIT Press, 1996); G. Handl, *Multilateral Development Banking: Environmental Principles and Concepts Reflecting General International Law and Public Policy* (Kluwer Law, 2001).

227 Global Environment Facility: Instrument Establishing, ILM 33 (1994): 1273.

228 See H. French, *Investing in the Future: Harnessing Private Capital Flows for Environmentally Sustainable Development* (Worldwatch Institute, 1998); R.J. Pelosky, Jr., "Private Co-Financing: New Capital for Development," *Multinational Business* 2 (1983): 8; OECD, "The Growing Importance of Co-Financing in Funding Development Projects," *OECD Observer* July (1982): 31.

for lagging on environmental standards.[229] Export financing involves an assortment of financial and risk management services, including the provision of export credits. ECAs' role has been pilloried as "to enrich their countries' corporations by making it easier for poor countries to buy their products and services, regardless of any environmental and social disruption such purchases may cause."[230] Examples of ECA financing that inspire such denigrating remarks include the Three Gorges dam in China and the Ilisu dam in Turkey.[231] In the US, Friends of the Earth sought to enjoin two federal ECAs, the Overseas Private Investment Corporation and the Export-Import Bank, from providing loans or other aid to activities contributing to global warming without prior environmental impact assessments.[232] The OECD and the G-8 belatedly drafted environmental standards for ECAs, complementing national reforms in some jurisdictions:[233] for instance, the Dutch government's requirement for companies to adhere to the OECD Guidelines for Multinational Enterprises.[234] ECAs often participate in project financing syndicates, where lenders rely on the EPs, and the ECA takes special responsibility for overseeing management of social and environmental risks.[235]

Development co-financing through multilateral institutions perhaps has a better record. The World Bank Group is taking a lead role among MDBs to manage trust funds for co-financing climate change mitigation projects in developing countries and economies-in-transition.[236] These funds include the Community Development Carbon Fund, Renewable Energy Efficiency Fund, and the BioCarbon Fund. They typically support microfinance projects,

---

229 See Center for International Environmental Law (CIEL), *Export Credit Agencies and Sustainable Development*, Issue Brief for the World Summit on Sustainable Development (CIEL, 2002).

230 B. Rich, "Exporting Destruction," *The Environmental Forum* September/October (2000): 32, 32.

231 J.W. van Gelder, et al., *The Impacts and Financing of Large Dams* (WWF, 2002).

232 M. Levinson, "Liability for Climate Change," *North American Corporate Research* (JPMorgan, November 29, 2006), 3.

233 OECD, *Recommendation on Common Approaches on Environment and Officially Supported Export Credits* (OECD, 2003); see further coverage of developments at http://www.eca-watch.org.

234 S.A. Aaronson and J.T. Reeves, *Corporate Social Responsibility in the Global Village: The Role of Public Policy* (National Policy Association, 2002), 12.

235 Personal communication, Yolanda Banks, Senior Corporate Social Responsibility Advisor, Export Development Canada (Toronto, September 29, 2007).

236 World Bank Carbon Finance, at http://www.CarbonFinance.org.

where contributing private investors receive marketable GHG emission reduction credits while the World Bank shoulders the financial risks. The EBRD and the European Investment Bank concentrate on concessional and co-financing arrangements for sustainable energy investments in Eastern Europe.[237] Lines of credit and equity investment are provided, as well as financial guarantees, subject to projects meeting specified environmental and commercial standards. These examples point to the potential for expanding public-private financial partnerships for SRI.

IV. Finale

This book has been written by an environmental lawyer to highlight the role of some financiers as unseen polluters. Limiting the focus to regular companies can block some of the pathways to sustainability. The financial sector finances the future, yet often acts as though tomorrow will never come. Incessant demands of investors and fund managers have fueled too much short-term investment, sometimes of specious social value.[238] Financial institutions should not be considered innocent suppliers of capital, without knowledge of or control over the use of the capital they provide. At times, such funding contributes to and exacerbates many environmental and social ills.

The SRI movement's growth in recent years has yielded hope for a more environmentally responsible and socially just financial sector. SRI flags issues long ignored or marginalized by the market. But the dyadic nature of "mainstream" SRI creates tensions that ultimately threaten its very rationale. Too much SRI focuses on serving the financial interests of investors rather than prioritizing the social and environmental values that it is meant to champion. Claiming that business case SRI is responsible for the surge in SRI growth is irrelevant if it fails to promote true sustainability. The ultimate measurement of SRI's success should not hinge on whether it delivers market

---

237 C. Wold and D. Zaelke, "Promoting Sustainable Development and Democracy in Central and Eastern Europe: The Role of the European Bank for Reconstruction and Development," *American University Journal of International Law and Policy* 7 (1992): 559; J. Guiseppe, "Assessing the 'Triple Bottom Line': Social and Environmental Practices in the European Banking Sector," in *Sustainable Banking: The Greening of Finance*, eds J.J. Bouma, M. Jeucken, and L. Klinkers (Greenleaf Publishing, 2001), 96, 102–3.

238 See M. Tonello, *Revisiting Stock Market Short-Termism* (Conference Board, 2006).

advantages, but rather primarily on whether it improves corporate behavior. An industry fetish with financial returns confuses means with ends and diverts attention from critical SRI issues.

The SRI community must return to its roots of *ethical* investment, and focus on the purpose of sustainable development. Ethics give reasons and motivations to act when financial cues are absent. As a priority, SRI should evaluate companies with reference to enhancing sustainability and invest in those leading companies irrespective of short-term bottom line results. Investors' commitment to sustainability should not hinge merely on the question of financial materiality or the bottom line. The only exception to investing in companies that do not meet high sustainability standards should be where an investor is prepared to commit the resources to actively influence corporate behavior and monitor results.

Ethically-driven investment however cannot address all sustainability challenges, as some are too complex to be packaged into social accounting metrics or sustainability indicators for SRI governance purposes, or are simply better managed directly through state protective legislation. This book's case studies on Indigenous peoples and climate change highlight some of the challenges which inhere in specific SRI issues. Moreover, on the institutional side, some financiers will remain better placed than others to champion SRI. Public sector pension plans, cooperative banks, credit unions, and some religious groups will likely continue to set the pace. Because of the importance of ties to civil society as a variable in explaining why some financiers are more committed to SRI, the more closely financial institutions can build relationships with the NGO sector and local communities, the more likely they are to invest ethically.

Even with better SRI governance, the business case will likely prevail for a while, as reform takes time. It has made some contribution to responsible financing. It has emboldened some institutional investors and fund managers to incorporate ESG criteria into investment decision-making without fear of adverse legal or market repercussions. While the challenge now is to move beyond the business case to the ethical case for sustainability, cultivating new ethics for investment will also take time. Although an economic actor reacts quickly to new environmental taxes that affect its bottom line, changing the culture of financial decision-making is a much slower and tentative process. Having financiers merely accede to the Earth Charter or Collevecchio Declaration would hardly revolutionize SRI values. It requires a lengthy process of participation, dialogue, and formulation of workable standards. The pressing need to address problems such as global warming currently necessitates some reliance on business case strategies. However, over the long-term, the business case must be subsumed within a broader ethical framework for investment.

Booming emerging markets pose further crucial challenges to SRI. In November 2007, PetroChina surpassed the US energy behemoth ExxonMobil as the world's largest corporation measured by market capitalization.[239] PetroChina's investments in Sudan and other contentious places have angered human rights and environmental activists.[240] However, SRI is largely a Western-inspired phenomenon, and will likely require fresh ideas and techniques to gain traction outside of the OECD group. Worldwide sustainability is impossible unless SRI can speak to the concerns of communities and investors in the developing world. SRI networks such as ASrIA in Asia and increasingly UNEPFI will thus be crucial for pioneering SRI in emerging markets.[241] But they must do so in ways that do not reflect the imposition of Western standards. Even the most exemplary SRI-relevant standards, such as the GRI, have been questioned for such biases.[242] SRI must evolve into a global dialogue addressing the concerns of communities worldwide.

A robust framework for such ethical investment necessitates many changes to SRI governance. Markets do not exist in a state of nature; while they may behave as a discrete system, driven by internal operational codes, economic activity is also very much a product of government decisions. Likewise, SRI's success depends on sound public policies and laws, as well as robust non-state codes of conduct and other mechanisms. Solutions will not inhere in any particular regulatory tool, and reformers must ensure that the many tools of governance work synergistically. In engineering change, regulation should not simply be about imposing limits to behavior but about sustaining long-term motivation for financing sustainable development.

Among the menu of reforms, the reformulation of fiduciary duties is crucial. They define the core goals and processes of decision-making within

---

239 D. Greenlees and D. Lague, "PetroChina Shares Triple Value in Record IPO," *International Herald Tribune*, November 5, 2007.

240 See the session on "The China-Sudan Connection: Options for Concerned Investors" (18th Annual SRI in the Rockies Conference, Santa Ana Pueblo, New Mexico, November 3–6, 2007); A. Aslam, "U.S./Sudan: Activists Ask U.S. Funds to Divest from PetroChina," *Global Information Network*, September 6, 2007, 1.

241 See http://www.asria.org.

242 K. Dingwerth, "Private Environmental Governance in the South" (paper presented at the 2005 Berlin Conference on the Human Dimensions of Global Environmental Change, Germany, December 2–3, 2005).

financial institutions. Through fiduciary duties we can redefine the traditional concept of "benefit" to investors, and thereby steer financiers toward sustainable development. If combined with new forms of social accounting and sustainability indicators and performance standards, such fiduciary standards could bring us much nearer to a system of ethical investment that respects ecological integrity.

The ideas expressed in this book will be controversial to many people in the financial sector, even to seasoned practitioners of SRI. However, if we cannot resolve environmental degradation with the best current practices and structures, more radical solutions may have to be implemented if we wish to secure our future.[243] Reforming the economic structures and mechanisms of capitalism alone may well prove insufficient. If financial markets continue to fail to align themselves with sustainability, available choices for action will be limited. Timothy Flannery, in *The Weather Makers*, warns of a hypothetical "carbon dictatorship," where an "Earth Commission for Thermostatic Control" takes over the economy to safeguard a looming climate crisis.[244] William Ophuls has long warned of the specter of highly authoritarian rule to impose constraints on a rapidly depleting planet.[245] Ethical investment, if practiced widely, could help avert such far reaching and bitter alternatives. It offers an ounce of prevention to avoid the heavy pound of cure for the sustainability of the planet.

---

243 See the suggestions of M. Jacobs, *The Green Economy: Environment, Sustainable Development and the Politics of the Future* (Pluto Press, 1991), 45; H. Henderson, *Paradigms in Progress: Life Beyond Economics* (Adamantine Press, 1993); J. Lovelock, *Gaia: A New Look at Life on Earth* (Oxford University Press, 1979); R. Nash, *The Rights of Nature: A History of Environmental Ethics* (University of Wisconsin Press, 1990).

244 T. Flannery, *The Weather Makers* (HarperCollins, 2005), 290–95.

245 W. Ophuls, "Leviathan or Oblivion," in *Toward a Steady State Economy*, ed. H.E. Daly (W.H. Freeman, 1973), 215.

INDEX

A

ABN AMRO, 81, 100, 126, 148
ABN AMRO Biofuel Commodity
 Index, 485
ABN AMRO Groen Fonds, 338
ABP, 88, 138
AccountAbility, 394, 427
Accountability. *See* Regulation and SRI
Accounting
 and climate change, 498–99
 delayed liability for pollution, 11
 GAAP, 328–29, 331, 544, 545, 558,
  558n. 208
 and long-term investing, 143
 mark-to-market approach, 143
 rules and transparency, 328–32
 social accounting, 26, 331, 544–46
 for sustainability, 540–46
Accounts Modernization Directive
 (EU), 323, 323n. 214
Active investing, 218–19
Act on the Certification of Retirement
 Arrangement Contracts (Belgium),
 305
Act relating to the Government Pension
 Fund (Norway), 368
AIG, 75
Alberta, Canada, 485, 513
Alcan, 88, 114

Alcohol, 78, 84, 85, 90, 117, 118, 133.
 See also Intoxicants
Alien Tort Claims Act (US), 5, 217,
 561–62
Allegheny Energy, 503
Alliance of Religions and Conservation,
 119
Alliant Energy Corporation, 154
Allianz Group, 75, 486
American Declaration of the Rights and
 Duties of Man, 483
American Indian Coalition on
 Institutional Accountability, 467
Amnesty International, 96, 112, 119,
 470
Anglo-American economies. *See also*
 specific countries
 bond market in, 59, 62
 fiduciary duties in, 227
 model of corporate governance, 67,
  68, 234–37, 255–62, 256n. 348,
  314, 355–56, 553
Animal liberation, 35, 82, 84, 318
Annuities, 66
Anti-globalization movement, 285,
 298, 516
ANZ Bank, 407
Apartheid. *See under* South Africa
Arctic National Wildlife Refuge, 469

Ariel Fund, 131
Armaments and munitions, 35, 84, 88, 90, 117, 122, 366, 367, 368–69, 375–76
Asia, 60, 81, 125, 194, 194, 222, 226, 334, 519, 569
Asian Development Bank, 465
Asia Pulp and Paper, 94
ASIC (Australian Securities and Investments Commission), 306–7, 309
ASrIA. See Association for Sustainable and Responsible Investment
Asset management firms, 17, 45, 50–51, 69–71
Asset managers
 compensation, 142
 delegation to, 11, 65, 69–71, 251
 and pension fund sector, 65, 151, 265
 power of, 24, 155–56, 266
 short-term investments, 17
 and technological advances, 70–71
 and UNEPFI, 397
Asset smoothing techniques, 143
Associated Students of the University of Oregon v. Oregon Investment Council, 231
Association for Sustainable and Responsible Investment (ASrIA), 81, 125, 130, 569
Association of Investment Companies, 480
Association of Superannuation Funds of Australia, 226
Auditing, 109, 201, 301, 308, 380, 383, 405, 425–32, 501, 552
Australia
 bank loans, 75
 and climate change, 488
 collaborative initiatives, 154
 credit unions, 77
 economic instruments, 334
 faith-based investors, 119
 Future Fund, 370
 Indigenous peoples in, 454
 investment company assets, 47
 legislation. See specific legislation
 mining in, 18n. 79, 132, 470
 pension plans, 6, 65, 225–26, 267–68, 273, 306, 370, 375
 public opinion, 128
 regulation, 189, 306–9, 312, 517–18, 554–55
 and screening criteria, 467
 and shareholders, 182, 259, 259n. 373
 specialist SRI funds, 78
 SRI market, 20–21, 38, 78, 123
Australian Conservation Foundation, 312, 406
Australian Council of Super Investors, 258, 312–13
Australian Ethical Investments, 476
Australian Securities and Investments Commission (ASIC), 306–7, 309
Australian Stock Exchange's (ASX) Principles of Good Corporate Governance, 562
Austria, 305, 424, 488
Autopoiesis, Luhmann's theory of, 288–89, 294
Azad funds, 118

B
Balfour Beatty, 97
Banca Etica, 75
Banco do Brasil, 371
Bangladesh, 81, 100
Bank for International Settlements (BIS), 200, 248
Bank of America, 398, 474, 492
Bank of Montreal, 313, 414, 472
Banks and banking sector. See also specific institutions
 overview, 67–68
 bond market, 43–44
 central banks, 44, 564–65
 cooperative, 13, 34, 75–76, 98, 152n. 288, 568
 defensive banking vs. sustainable development, 75, 147, 147n. 262
 deregulation, 46, 60, 67
 EPs. See Equator Principles

ESG risk assessment, 93–94, 125–26, 147

ethical investing in, 23

fiduciary duties, 238–41

globalization of, 68

green mortgages, 75, 100–101, 126, 501

and Indigenous peoples, 471, 471n. 102, 472

investment vs. commercial banking, 66

lender liability, 6, 347–55, 560–61

linked deposit SRI products, 101

loans, 55–56, 59, 61, 171, 171n. 389

MDBs. *See* Multilateral development banks

microlending, 172. *See also* microfinance

policy accountability statements, 313

regulation, 238–41, 361

reputational risk, 19, 126

retail banks and SRI mutual funds, 157

shadow directors, 347–48

and small firms, 61

and UNEPFI, 397–98

universal banks, 67

worldwide assets of, 46, 67

BankTrack

on banks and EPs, 82, 126, 415–16, 418, 446, 474, 520

on democratic processes, 25

on Freeport mine, 458

importance of, 539

on voluntary standards, 398

Barclays Bank, 94, 398, 416

Barclays Global Investors, 70

Barrick Gold, 468, 470

Basel Committee of Banking Supervision, 44, 200, 201–2, 248, 520

Belgium. *See also* Europe

ethical screening, 555

investments and cluster bombs, 375–76, 536

legislation. *See specific legislation*

pension plans, 369, 519

tax concessions and social economy, 339

Ben and Jerry's, 514

Bendigo Bank, 101

Bentham, Jeremy, 85

Best-in-class method, 91–92, 95, 129, 133, 150, 364

BHP Billiton, 132

BioCarbon Fund, 500, 566

Biocentric ethics, 22, 530

BIS (Bank for International Settlements), 200, 278

BJ Services, 367

Blankenship v. Boyle, 232–33

Board of Trustees of Employee Retirement System of the City of Baltimore v. City of Baltimore, 231–32, 359

Body Shop, 514

Boeing, 368

Bond market

in Anglo-American economies, 59, 62

and banking industry, 43–44, 46

capitalization, 49–50, 68

and credit quality, 61

debt finance, 55–56, 172

institutional investors, 48

Boreal Initiative, 139

Bounded rationality, 11–12, 17–18, 27

Boycotts, 83, 166, 170, 484. *See also* Shareholders, advocacy and activism

BP (British Petroleum), 447, 469

Brand name, reputational risk, 18–19. *See also* Goodwill

Brazil, 125, 269, 371, 410, 501

Bretton Woods Agreement, 197

Britain, 138, 154–55, 189. *See also* United Kingdom

British Airways, 117

British Broadcasting Corporation, 311

British Columbia Ministry of Environment, 178

British Petroleum (BP), 447, 469

Brownfield sites, 350, 353

Brownfields Statute Law Amendment of 2001 (Ontario, Canada), 352

Brundtland, Gro Harlem, 12

Brundtland Commission, 12, 511

BT Financial Group, 132, 154

Burma, 84
Business case motivated SRI.
  achievement of "alpha," 14, 165
  climate change, 453, 481, 490,
    506–07
  costs of unsustainable development,
    17–18, 567
  financial materiality, 13, 19–20,
    29–30, 74–75, 92–93, 150, 167,
    438
  financial motivations, 14–15, 79–89,
    110, 161–62, 185, 298, 326
  homo economicus view of individuals,
    13, 213, 252–53, 541
  Indigenous peoples, 505
  quantifying of ethical issues, 18–19,
    121, 163, 246, 335, 545
  regulation, 212, 234, 284, 337, 400,
    451
  structural limitations, 19–20, 186,
    512–13, 520–22, 528
Business judgment rule, 236–37, 236n.
  264

C
CAER (Centre for Australian Ethical
  Research), 461
California Public Employees'
  Retirement System (CalPERS)
  beneficiary-elected trustees, 264
  and CDP, 374
  and CERES Principles, 405
  and Collevecchio Declaration, 402
  corporate governance policies, 373–74
  divestment, 168
  fiduciary activism, 138
  Green Wave Initiative, 491
  shareholder activism, 97–98, 180,
    182, 184, 270
  and UNPRI principles, 401
  voluntary codes of conduct, 259
California State Teachers' Retirement
  System (CalSTRS), 491
Calmeadow, 172
CalPERS. See California Public
  Employees' Retirement System

Calpine, 466–67
CalSTRS (California State Teachers'
  Retirement System), 491
Calvert Group, 411, 423, 466–67, 505
Calvert Social Index Fund, 95, 96, 132,
  224
Calyon, 417, 418–19
Cambodia, 460
Canada
  case law, 214–15
  and climate change, 501
  collaborative networks, 139
  corporate fiduciary duties, 235n. 258,
    236
  corporate polluters and stock values,
    178, 179n. 437
  credit union sector, 23, 77, 277–78
  fungible standards and screening,
    132–33
  Indigenous peoples of, 467–68,
    535–36
  investment company assets, 47
  labour-sponsored investment funds,
    98–99, 341
  legislation. See specific legislation
  lender liability, 352
  mission-based investors, 113–14, 119
  mutual funds, 156, 519, 539
  oil sands, 485, 513
  pension plans, 65, 137–38, 211, 264,
    267–69, 371, 372–73
  proxy voting, 314, 315, 316, 318
  public accountability statements,
    307–8, 313
  public opinion, 128
  regulation, 189, 274, 307–8, 327,
    328, 519
  research, 40, 74–75, 88, 157,
    271–72
  retained earnings, 59
  and shareholders, 259, 259n. 374, 301
  specialist SRI funds, 78
  SRI market, 123–24
  tax concessions, 345
  universal banks, 67
  venture finance, 127

Canada Business Corporations Act (Canada), 355–56, 551

Canada Pension Plan (CPP), 95n. 309, 124, 371, 372, 561

Canada Pension Plan Investment Board (CPPIB) Act, 372–73

Canadian Coalition of Good Governance, 444–45

Canadian Imperial Bank of Commerce, 472

Capital-intensive sectors, 61–62

Capitalism. *See also* Finance capitalism
   accountable, 157–58
   business and policy-making, 292–93, 292n. 47
   and ecological modernization, 295–99
   nature, economic valuation of, 104–8, 104n. 4
   and social obligations, 521n. 43
   stakeholder, 80–81, 260
   steady-state economy vs., 16–17

Capital Strategies Consulting, 470

Carbon Capital Markets, 501

Carbon Disclosure Project (CDP)
   and CalPERS, 374
   establishment of, 36, 154–55
   faith-based signatories, 119
   GHG emission disclosure, 183, 321
   and investor coalitions, 445, 454, 496–97, 517
   reflexive regulation vs., 498
   shareholder resolutions, 183

Carbon emissions. *See* Greenhouse gas emissions

Carbon markets, 76, 321, 486, 499–501

Car loans, green, 100, 101

Case law, pension funds and SRI, 228–34

Caisse d'économie solidaire, 158

Catholic Church, 88, 117, 476

Catholic Super and Retirement Fund, 476

CCX (Chicago Climate Exchange), 501

CDP. *See* Carbon Disclosure Project

Centre for Australian Ethical Research (CAER), 461

CERCLA (Comprehensive Environmental Response, Compensation, and Liability Act) (US), 348–50, 477

CERES Principles, 395, 404–5, 451, 498, 503. *See also* Global Reporting Initiative

Challenges and impact of SRI. *See also* Shareholders
   overview, 103–4
   capitalism and nature, 104–8, 104n. 4
   collective action problems, 150–55
   corporate social responsibility, 108–11
   economy-wide investors, 133–39
   faith-based investment, 111–20
   financial analysis, 146–50
   financial institutions, 155–58
   financial performance, 173–86
   fungible standards, 129–33
   investment horizons, 139–46
   market expansion, 120–29
   universal owners, 133–37
   virtue vs. prosperity, 159–86

Charitable trusts, 220

Charities Act (UK), 220

Charity sector, 76–77, 90

Cherokee Investment Partners, 270

Cherokee Nation Micro-Enterprise Development Program, 471

Chevron, 469

Chicago Climate Exchange (CCX), 501

Chile, 470

China
   ECA financing, 566
   human rights and Africa, 419
   labor and human rights practices, 154
   one SRI fund, 125
   predatory lending of banks, 196
   securities transaction taxes, 344
   Three Gorges Dam project, 152, 203

Chittendon Bank, 101

Christian Centre for SRI, 119

Church of England, 115, 116–17, 525–26

Church of Sweden, 117

CISs. *See* Collective investment schemes

Citigroup
    on climate change, 489
    EP based policies, 413
    GHG emissions reporting, 492
    list of climatic consequences
        companies, 484–85
    microfinance facilities, 100
    and Rainforest Action Network, 414,
        447
Citizens Bank, 501
Civil society investors. See also
    Collevecchio Declaration of Financial
        Institutions; Earth Charter
    advocacy and influence, 298, 387,
        443, 484, 516
    CERES Principles vs., 404
    compatibility with SRI, 13
    and economic instruments, 336
    ethical principles, 23–24, 34–35
    and faith-based investors, 119
    and globalization, 197
    microfinance, 99
    and retail ethics, 251–52
    sustainability reports, 403
    voluntary codes of conduct, 31
Clean Development Mechanism (CDM),
    36, 499–501
Climate Action Network, 119
Climate change. See also specific countries
    and legislation; and Greenhouse gas
    emissions
    and accounting, 498–99
    climate impact disclosures, 495–99
    climate justice litigation, 483–84
    climate policies and market forces,
        486–89
    disclosure regulation, 139, 321, 328,
        377, 496
    and EPs, 500
    finance for climate abatement,
        499–501, 566
    financial sector responses to climate
        change, 489–504
    and fiduciary duties, 216, 490–91
    fossil fuel investments, 173, 485,
        513

global warming
    carbon emissions reduction,
        23, 75, 182, 515, 518
    renewable energy, 36, 76, 550
    and insurance sector, 243, 292n. 47,
        493–94
    investment risks and opportunities,
        36, 82, 93, 301. 335, 383, 437,
        481–86, 491
    and investor coalitions, 14, 23, 97,
        138, 155, 216, 258, 445
    natural capital, 20, 105–6
    research on, 480
    risk management, 489–95
    shareholder activism, 114, 183,
        502–4
    and sustainability indexes, 441
    and universal owners, 134
Climate Change and Sustainable Energy
    Act (Canada), 482
Climate Change Capital, 76
Climate Change Response Act
    (New Zealand), 482
Climate Group, 138–39
Climate Risk Disclosure Initiative, 498
Coalition for Environmentally
    Responsible Economies. See CERES
    Principles
Coca-Cola, 133
Codes of conduct. See Voluntary codes of
    conduct; specific codes
Collaborative networks, 97, 113,
    138–39, 150–55
Collective investment schemes (CISs),
    62–73. See also Mutual fund sector
    hedge funds, 63, 146
    private equity funds, 64
    regulation of, 243–45, 272–76
    retail, 63
    worldwide assets, 63
Collevecchio Declaration of Financial
    Institutions, 23–24, 382, 395,
    402–4, 448, 451, 532–33, 543, 561,
    568
Colonial First State's Managed
    Investment Fund, 312

Command-and-control regulation, 28, 285, 287–88, 300, 333, 377, 390, 487, 515–18
Commission on Human Rights (UN), 385, 475
Commission on Sustainable Development (UN), 547–48
Committee on Payment and Settlement Systems, 201
Committee on the Global Financial System, 200
Community Development Banking and Financial Institutions Act (US), 341, 477
Community Development Carbon Fund, 500, 566
Community investing, 23, 76–77, 81, 470–72. See also Economically targeted investments
Community Reinvestment Act (US), 174, 240–41, 361–62, 477
Community Renewal Tax Relief Act (US), 341
Companies Act (UK), 236, 259, 316–17, 323, 323n. 215, 519, 556–57
Comprehensive Anti-Apartheid Act (US), 359–60
Comprehensive Environmental Response, Compensation, and Liability Act (CERCLA) (US), 348–50, 477
Confederation of British Industry, 317
Connecticut Retirement Plans and Trust Funds, 138, 497, 550
Constituency statutes (US), 236–37
Consumer liability, 346, n. 345
Continental Bank Corporation, 361–62
Control and Transparency in Business Act (Germany), 261
Convention on Biological Diversity, 535–36
Convention on Elimination of All Forms of Racial Discrimination, 535–36

Cooperative banking sector, 13, 34, 75–76, 152n. 288, 568
Co-operative Bank (UK), 23, 69, 75–76, 101, 353
Cooperative Credit Association Act (Canada), 277
Corporate financing, overview, 52–61. See also specific types
Corporate Governance International, 158
Corporate greenwash. See Greenwash
Corporate Library, 318
Corporate Reputation Index (Fortune), 164
Corporate social responsibility (CSR)
   chart of international codes, 395
   globalization, 50–51, 387
   impact of SRI and, 108–11, 536
   industry domination in US, 72
   ISO voluntary standards, 429
   OECD Guidelines, 405–7
   proposed legislation for, 554
   ratings agencies, 150
   ratings mechanisms, 432–35
   S&P's ratings on, 72, 433–34, 492
   values-based investors, 13
Corporations, 10, 45, 45n. 11, 60, 165–71. See also specific corporations
Corporations Act (Australia), 244–45, 327
Cost-benefit analysis, 463, 546
Council of Institutional Investors, 155, 444–45
Council on Ethics (Norway), 368–69, 534, 555
Cowan v. Scargill, 228–29, 304
CPP. See Canada Pension Plan
Credit counseling, 69, 471–72
Credit rating agencies (CRAs), 61, 71–73, 148, 300, 433, 435
Credit Suisse First Boston, 149, 417
Credit Suisse Group, 429–30, 460, 497
Credit Union Membership Access Act (US), 277
Credit union sector
   overview, 68–69

democratic process in, 69, 276–78
ethical investing in, 23, 76–77
and Indigenous peoples, 471
microfinance, 99–100
regulation, 276–78
CRISIL, 434
Critical natural capital, 105
CSR. *See* Corporate social responsibility

D
Data, financing, 58–60
Debt finance, 52–53, 55–56, 60, 71,
75, 171–72. *See also* Banks and
banking sector
Declaration of Human Rights (UN), 363
Declaration on the Rights of Indigenous
Peoples (UN), 459, 459n. 31, 463,
535
Defined Benefit Corporate Pension Law
(Japan), 227
Defined benefit vs. defined contribution
plans, 146, 266–67, 267n. 419
Defined contribution (DC) retirement
plans, 81, 146
Defined Contribution Pension Law
(Japan), 227
Democratic process
in credit unions, 69, 276–78
ethical deliberations, 24, 25, 187,
249, 253, 276
participation and change, 538–39, 555
and public pension funds, 516
regulation and participation, 246–50
Denmark, 269, 324, 488, 489
Deontological investing, 20, 85
Deregulation. *See also* Neoliberalism
and banking sector, 46, 60, 67
and credit unions, 278
finance capitalism, 5, 46, 60, 511
financialization of economy, 45, 190,
192
and insurance sector, 66
international markets, 30, 60,
192–94, 279, 381
investment regulation, 30, 187, 376
liquidity of capital, 193–94, 381

securities transaction taxes, 344
state control of economies, 30, 381,
517
Desjardins Ethical Canadian Balanced
Fund, 132
Deutsche Bank, 75, 99, 409–10
Disadvantaged groups. *See also*
Emerging markets; Indigenous peoples
community investing, 23
and credit unions, 69, 77
environmental harm to, 19
microfinance, 99
Diversification of portfolios, 162–63,
168–69, 217
Divestment campaigns
Burma, 84
and Green Party, 368–69
Indonesia, 468
Iran, 375
by Netherlands, 88–89
by New Zealand, 366–67
South Africa, 4–5, 22, 74, 113–14,
115, 167–68, 224–25., 230–32,
269, 359–60
Sudan, 84, 375
Wal-Mart, 363
Dividend distribution, 52
DJSIs. *See* Dow Jones Sustainability
Indexes
Dodge v. Ford Motor Company, 214
Domini 400 Social Index, 435
Domini Social Equity, 90
Domini Social Investments, 23, 90,
132, 275, 466
Donovan v. Walton, 213–14
Dow Chemicals, 74
Dow Jones Industrial and Utility
Averages, 94, 118, 435
Dow Jones Sustainability Indexes
(DJSIs), 33, 95, 110n. 42, 169, 174,
382, 432, 437, 438–40, 468, 537,
548, 562
Dutch Association of Investors
for Sustainable Development, 338–39
Dutch Stichting Pensioenfonds ABP,
369

E

Earth Charter, 119, 451, 531, 532, 542–43, 568

Eastman Kodak, 95–96

EBRD (European Bank of Reconstruction and Development), 76, 202, 567

Eco-label Regulation (EU), 424

Eco-label standards, 423–25, 423n. 217

Ecological citizenship, 85–86

Ecological integrity, 26, 29, 86, 139, 451, 526, 531, 542, 546, 556–58

Ecological modernization, 14, 108, 286–87, 295–99, 302, 333, 387, 481, 513–14

Eco-Management and Audit Scheme (EMAS) (EU), 427, 430–32

Economically targeted investments (ETIs), 98–100, 339, 373, 536, 558

Economic and Social Council (UN), 529

Economic Development Agency, Fiduciary and Lender Environmental Liability Protection Act (Penn., US), 350

Economic incentives. *See* Incentives

Economic instruments (EIs), 332–45
    financial sector implications, 335–37
    as means of SRI, 332–34, 560
    securities transaction taxes, 342–45
    tax concessions, 28, 337–42

Eco-savings deposits, 100

EcoSecurities, 501

Ecuador, 474

Ecumenical Council of Corporate Responsibility and the Church Investors Group, 118–19

Efficient market theory, 163–64, 176

EIRIS. *See* Ethical Investment Research Service

EIs. *See* Economic instruments

Ekobanken, 69

EMAS (Eco-Management and Audit Scheme) (EU), 427, 430–32

Emergency Planning and Community Right to Know Act (US), 324–25

Emerging markets. *See also specific countries*

corporate finance, 39

external financing, 60

finance capitalism, 45

long-term vs. short-term investment, 145

microcredit institutions, 81, 99

pecking order hypothesis, 58

social investor expansion into, 125, 519

SRI indexes, 95

and UNEPFI, 569

Employee Retirement Income Security Act (ERISA) (US), 213–14, 223–24, 242, 265–66, 270

Employees' Pension Insurance Law (Japan), 227.

Enbridge, 468–69

Energy efficiency, 36, 76

Energy Efficiency Opportunities Act (Australia), 327

Engagement strategies, 95–98, 95n. 309, 182, 233–34, 268, 310, 313, 362, 372–73, 468–70

Enhanced Analytics Initiative, 149, 445

Enron, 11, 72, 180, 192, 328, 466

Environment Agency (UK), 93

Environmental, social and governance (ESG) issues. *See also* Regulation and SRI
    asset managers' responsibilities for, 70
    business case for, 12–13, 14–15, 19, 87, 98
    client demand for, 80, 183
    in financial analysis, 80–81, 88–89, 90, 92–94, 146–50
    performance reporting, 303
    rating mechanisms, 32–33
    research industry use of, 150
    risk assessment, 92–94
    screening for. *See* Exclusionary screens

Environmental law, 1–12, 182, 189, 194, 281–98, 350, 392, 430, 487, 522–23. *See also specific legislation*

Environmental Liability Directive of 2004 (EU), 351, 351n. 372
Environmental Management Act (Netherlands), 324
Environmental management systems (EMSs), 18, 32, 109, 177–78, 313, 382, 425–32, 448, 518, 528, 549
Environmental Protection Act (Denmark), 324
Environmental Protection Agency (EPA) (US), 147, 178, 326, 348, 482
EPA. See Environmental Protection Agency
Episcopal Church, 113
EPs. See Equator Principles
Equator Principles (EPs)
  BankTrack survey of banks, 82, 126, 446, 520
  climate change, 500
  compared to UNEPFI, 415
  governance initiatives, 196, 382, 411–20, 565
  Indigenous peoples, 37, 506
  local communities, 553
  mining industry, 418
  as process standards, 32
  voluntary codes and standards, 203, 472–74
Equity finance, 54–55, 92, 95, 165–71
ERISA. See Employee Retirement Income Security Act
ESG. See Environmental, social and governance (ESG) issues
Ethibel, 150, 339, 424
Ethical Council (Sweden), 363, 534, 555
Ethical Funds Company
  on Alcan, 88
  collaboration to protect Canadian boreal forests, 139
  and Eurosif Transparency Guidelines, 423
  Indigenous peoples, 454, 505
  member surveys, 275
  on oil sands industry, 485

screening policies, 91–92, 535
shareholder advocacy and activism, 414, 468–69
voting disclosure, 318
Ethical Investment Association, 20–21, 123 See also Responsible Investment Association of Australasia
Ethical investment for sustainability. See also Sustainability; and Exclusionary screens
  accounting for sustainability, 9, 540–46
  beyond business-as-usual, 512–15
  civil society, 34, 119, 298, 382, 387, 404, 443–45, 452, 484, 516, 527, 539, 568
  discretionary standards, 129–31, 550–52
  ecological ethics, 529–33
  ethics consensus for, 29, 523–28
  ethical motivations and SRI, 18–24, 83–89, 159, 515
  fiduciary duties, 550–59
  fiduciary finance, 540–59
  governance reforms, 25–27, 533–67
  governance systems, 516–20
  performance standards, 555–59
  policy instrument content, 533–40
  policy levers for reform, 559–64
  process standards, 552–55
  protection of natural capital, 520–23
  public sector finance reform, 564–67
  religious investors, 111–20.
  social accounting, 544–46
  sustainability indicators, 546–50
  urgency of, 509–12
Ethical Investment Research Service (EIRIS)
  Convention Watch, 380, 535
  and French Retirement Reserve Fund, 364, 380
  and FTSE4Good, 442
  establishment, 112
  on Indigenous peoples, 461
  on North American financial community, 146

rating mechanisms, 150, 163–64, 382, 432
as research organization, 149, 445
scope of, 79
screening tools, 410
on UK pension funds, 309
Ethics
biocentric, 22, 530
defined, 84–85, 524–26
deliberative process, 24, 249, 527, 538
deontological, 20, 85
ecological ethics, 86, 481, 529–33
human values, 523–24
as responsible investment, 21, 79, 87–88, 119, 363, 367–68, 382, 555, 568
retail, 131, 251–52, 276, 279
teleological, 20, 85–86
virtue vs. prosperity, 159–86
ETIs. *See* Economically targeted investments
Europe. *See also specific countries*
corporate governance and stakeholders, 237, 262
environmentally responsible lending, 75–76, 125
EU regulation. *See specific initiatives*
financing sources, 59
investment company assets, 38
mutual funds, history of, 63
pension plans, 64–65, 226, 269, 273
policy disclosure measures, 308
proxy voting, 316
relationship banking, decline of, 68
shareholders, 316
SRI market, 122–23
stakeholder capitalism, 80–81, 260
universal banks, 67
venture finance, 127
European Bank of Reconstruction and Development (EBRD), 76, 202, 567
European Commission. *See specific legislation and initiatives*
European Investment Bank, 567
European Social Investment Forum (Eurosif)

overview, 130
as collaborative network, 155
on French Retirement Reserve Funds, 364
on investment research, 122on pension and insurance sector, 122
Transparency Guidelines, 316, 422–23, 539
European Union. *See specific legislation and initiatives*
Eurosif. *See* European Social Investment Forum
Evangelical Christian investors, 118
Excelsior Funds, 503–4
Exclusionary screens. *See also specific screening issues*
best-in-class methods vs., 133
engagement strategies vs., 95–98, 95n. 309, 182, 233–34, 310, 313, 362, 372–73
ERISA on, 223–24
faith-based investors, 114–15
and fiduciary duties, 218
impact on performance, 109, 176, 176n. 419
for Indigenous peoples, 466–68
integrated assessment vs., 88
legal issues, 191, 272
methodologies, 29, 84, 131–33, 410
norms-based screens, 90
and portfolio diversification, 162–63, 165, 217–18
as proprietary information, 173
shareholders, 95, 131
social screens, 89–91, 176n. 419
SRI indexes, 95
Executive pay, 57–58, 57n. 83, 58n. 85
Export credit agencies (ECAs), 30, 203, 419, 565–66
Export-Import Bank, 566
ExxonMobil, 326, 366–67, 469, 484, 502, 504, 569

F
Fair Pensions, 310, 313
Fair trade, 35, 84, 117, 364, 457

Faith-based investment. *See* Religious
institutions
Fannie Mae, 472, 501
Federal Council of Churches, 112
Federal Credit Union Act (US), 277
Federal Reserve, 361–62
Fidelity, 156
Fiduciary duties
in Anglo-American economies, 227
in banking sector, 238–41
in Canada, 235n. 258, 236
and climate change, 216, 490–91
corporate, 234–38, 235n. 258
and ethical investment, 550–59
in financial sector, 29–30, 205–20,
550–59
and human rights, 216–17
in insurance sector, 241–43
in pension funds, 221–34
investors' passivity, 251, 265–67, 279
prudent person rule, 191, 191n. 13,
207, 223, 244
reform of, 25, 539, 550–59
scope of and governance, 34
and screens, 218
UNEPFI report on, 206, 414, 415,
541
in US, 235n. 258, 236
Finance capitalism, 43–51
as defined by Marxist economists, 44
deregulation, 5, 46, 60, 511
ideological hegemony, 389
market context of SRI, 43–48
social and environmental
implications, 48–51, 247
Finance theory, 162–71
Financial Accounting Standards Board,
143
Financial analysis, 80–81, 88–89,
146–50
Financial Instruments and Exchange
Law (Japan), 227
Financialization of the economy, 45,
190, 192, 284–85
Financial literacy training, 69
Financial materiality

and climate change, 445
and corporate governance, 80,
382–83
enhanced analysis and, 89
globalization and, 80
myopic views of, 19–20
as prime standard, 29–30, 252
SRI and, 74–75, 92–93
tangible vs. intangible, 13
Financial Modernization Act (US), 192
Financial planners, 69–71, 157, 158
Financial repression thesis, 522
Financial sector and institutions.
See also specific institutions
overview, 43–44
and environmental law, 1–9
environmental policies, 51
and globalization, 30–31, 35, 49–50,
68, 193–97
intermediaries of, 17, 69–73
internal governance, 155–58
investment companies, 62–73
money laundering controls, 8, 240,
282–83, 380
redefining fiduciary duties, 29–30,
550–59
social accounting, 26, 331, 544–46
social license of, 83–84, 329–30
and steady-state economy, 16–17
as surrogate regulators, 8, 282–83,
380
as universal owners, 16–17, 133–37,
139, 217, 246, 262, 557–59
Financial Services Action Plan (EU), 204
Financial Services and Market Act
(UK), 189, 247
Financial Services Reform Act
(Australia), 306
Financial Times, NGO sponsored
advertisement, 417
Financial Times Stock Exchange.
See FTSE4Good
First Nations, 139, 460, 469, 470, 471,
472. *See also* Indigenous peoples
First Nations Australian Credit Union,
471

Fitch, 72
Fleet Factors Corporation; United States v.,
   349, 349n. 359, 349n. 361
Foley v. Hill, 238
Ford Motor Co., 214, 501, 504, 504n.
   304, 546
Foreign Exchange and Foreign Trade
   Control Act (Japan), 192
Forestry development, 37, 94, 139,
   292, 407, 417–18, 442, 447, 460,
   465, 470, 474, 484, 522
Fortune, on Corporate Reputation Index,
   164
Framework Convention on Climate
   Change (UNFCCC), 481, 499–500,
   506–7. *See also* Kyoto Protocol
France. *See also* Europe
   central banks, 564–65
   corporate governance, 262
   diversity of ESG criteria, 131
   eco-labels, 424
   economic instruments, 340
   pension plans, 25, 358, 363–64, 380,
      564
   policy disclosure measures, 305, 324,
      324nn. 222–23
   relationship banking, decline of, 68
   retained earnings, 59
Freeport mining project, 368, 458, 468
French Retirement Reserve Fund,
   363–64, 380
Freshfields Bruckhaus Deringer report,
   206, 414, 415, 541
Friends of the Earth
   criticisms of ECAs, 566
   on insurance sector, 494
   negotiations with Enron, 466
   shareholder activism, 83, 411, 502
   stock purchases and influence, 97
   studies on climate change risk
      disclosure, 327, 496
   and UNPRI principles, 399
Friends Provident's Ethical Funds, 112
FTSE4Good (Financial Times
   Stock Exchange) Index, 95, 150, 169,
   431, 406, 435, 440–43, 468, 537

Fund management. *See* Asset
   management firms
Fund managers. *See* Asset managers
Future Fund Act (Australia), 370

G
GAAP (Generally Accepted Accounting
   Principles), 328–29, 544, 545, 558,
   558n. 208
Gabčikovo-Nagymaros Project, 2
Gambling, 35, 84, 85, 86, 90, 117, 133
Gates Foundation, 77
General Agreement on Tariffs and Trade
   (GATT), 81–82
General Agreement on Trade in Services
   (GATS), 198–99, 448
General Board of the National Council
   of Churches, US, 74
General Motors, 113, 477
Germany. *See also* Europe
   bank loans, 59, 75
   and climate change, 488, 489, 549
   co-determination system, 260
   corporate governance and
      stakeholders, 237, 260–62, 553
   Corporate Governance Code, 260,
      260n. 386
   credit unions, history of, 68
   EMAS certification in, 431–32
   insurance industry, 241
   investment company assets, 47
   legislation. *See specific legislation*
   pension funds, 226–27, 519
   regulation, 189, 304–5, 519
   relationship banking, decline of, 68
   retail banks and SRI mutual funds,
      157
   retained earnings, 59
   tax concessions, 334
GES Investment Services, 363, 445
GHG. *See* Greenhouse gas emissions
GHG Register, 497
Glass-Steagall Act (US), 190
Global Compact (UNGC)
   overview, 408–10
   and best-in-class criteria, 364

as form of new governance, 195
French pension plan adherence to,
 380
and Norwegian Public Pension Fund,
 368
and NZSF, 366, 535
and Swedish AP Funds, 363
Global Fund for Indigenous Peoples,
 464, 464n. 57
Globalization of markets
anti-globalization movement, 285,
 298, 516
civil society investors, 197
conglomerates, 35
CSR standards, 50–51, 387
and democratically elected
 governments, 388
in finance sector, 30–31, 49–50, 68,
 193–97
financial materiality, 80
Global Reporting Initiative (GRI)
overview, 420–22
climate change indicators, 497–98
democratic processes, 538–39
human rights indicators, 475–76
as process standard, 32, 382, 517
social and environmental variables,
 549
Western bias of, 569
Global warming. See Climate change
Global Warming Solutions Act
 (California, US), 482
Globe and Mail awards, 124
GlobeScan, 157
Goldcorp, 124
Good Money, 94, 435
Goodwill, corporate, 18–19, 92, 147,
 329–30
Governance, nongovernmental
CERES Principles, 404–5, 420–22
Collevecchio Declaration, 382, 395,
 402–4, 448, 532–33, 543, 568
Dow Jones Sustainability Indexes,
 382, 432, 438–40
eco-label standards, 423–25, 423n.
 217

environmental management systems,
 425–27
EPs, 382, 411–20
Eurosif Transparency Guidelines,
 316, 422–23, 539
FTSE4Good Index Series, 406, 431,
 440–43
Global Reporting Initiative, 382,
 420–22
ISO 14000 series, 382, 427–30
London Principles of Sustainable
 Finance, 407–8
management systems, 425–32
market forces, 379–94
normative frameworks, 394–410
OECD Guidelines for Multinational
 Enterprises, 363, 368, 405–7, 566
rating mechanisms, 432–47
research and advocacy forums,
 443–47
sustainability indexes, 435–43
sustainability reporting regimes,
 420–23
UNEPFI, 396–98
UNGC, 408–10
UNPRI, 382, 399–402
voluntary environmental governance,
 385–89
voluntary standards, 389–94
Governance, overview. See also
 Regulation and SRI
government policies, 27–31
issues and response to, 35–37
market-based regulation, 27–29
private rule-making, 31–33
voluntary controls, 35–37
GovernanceMetrics International, 149,
 184, 432
Governance Research and Engagement
 (Regnan), 154
Government. See also specific countries
cross-border financial activities, 31
ethical pension fund investing,
 25, 30
interests of posterity, 140n. 219
international laws, 25, 31

state and municipal fund regulation, 358–62

state control of economies, 30, 381

state-market realignments, 287–91

wealth, 46

Grameen Bank, 81, 100

Grameen Foundation, 100

Grand Canyon Bank, 361–62

Grassy Narrows First Nation, 470

Green Century Funds, 78

Greenfield sites, 353

Greenhouse gas emissions (GHG). *See also* Climate change

CDP and disclosures, 183, 321, 496–97

command regulation, 515, 518

costs of reducing or not, 478, 483, 489

emissions trading, 36, 334, 428, 482, 486–88, 501, 567

and banks, 492, 500

and insurance companies, 75, 495

reporting of, 328, 428, 492, 497–98

shareholder activism, 484, 502–4

Greenhouse Gas Protocol Initiative, 496–98

Green Investment / Project Directive (Netherlands), 337–38, 536, 560

Green mortgages, 75, 100–101, 126, 501

Green Party (New Zealand), 366–67

Greenpeace, 101

Greenwash, 25, 33, 110–11, 129, 320–21, 389, 449

GRI. *See* Global Reporting Initiative

Groupe Investissement Responsible, 79

Group of 8 (G-8), 566

Group of 10 (G10), 197, 200

Growth, infinite, 5, 5n. 16

Guaranteed investment contracts, 66

Guidelines for Multinational Enterprises (OECD), 363, 368, 405–7, 566

Guile European Engagement Fund, 410

Guyana, 460

H

Harries and others v. Church Commissioners for England, 228, 525–26

Harvard Corporation, 128

Hedge funds, 63, 146, 243

Henderson Global Investors' Future Fund, 491

HESTA Eco Pool, 91

High net worth individuals (HNWI) market, 71, 79, 157

Holocaust survivors, 4

Home Depot, 182

Homo economicus view of individuals' interests, 13, 213, 252–53, 541

Hopi Credit Association, 471

Hostile takeovers, 57, 235, 256

Household wealth, 46

Housing, 23, 98, 338, 341, 471n. 102, 472

HSBC Group, 126, 410, 413, 416, 492

Human rights

Amnesty International on, 96

Catholic Church on, 117

corporate views on, 385

and fiduciary duties, 216–17

and FTSE4Good, 443, 468

GRI on, 475–76

ICCR on, 154

of Indigenous peoples, 467–68, 535–36

public opinion, 128

and risk mitigation in lending, 398

TCCR on, 114

Huntington Life Sciences, 82

Hurricane Katrina, 484

Hybrid securities, 52n. 53

Hyper-regulation, 288

I

IBM, 501

Incentives

ecological tax reform, 333–34

economically targeted investments, 98–100, 339, 373, 536, 558

lender liability for pollution, 28

securities transaction taxes, 342–45

tax concessions
    in Belgium, 339
    in Canada, 345
    EIs, 337–42
    in Germany, 334
    for green investment, 26, 28,
      518
    insurance interest income
      deferment, 66
    in Japan, 334
    in Netherlands, 101, 337–38
    and regulatory standards,
      282–83
    in UK, 340–41, 345
    in US, 331
India, 81, 125, 192, 398, 434, 458
Indigenous peoples. *See also* Equator
  Principles; *specific countries*
  and banking sector, 471, 471n. 102,
    472
  casino gambling and faith-based
    ethics, 86
  commercialization of traditional
    knowledge, 458, 458n. 25
  community investing, 470–72
  and credit union sector, 471
  IFC Safeguard Policies and, 411–12,
    473
  land rights of, 35, 84, 454
  markets and trading, 458–59
  natural resource projects vs., 37, 462,
    468
Indigenous peoples and SRI agenda,
  453–78, 505–7
  community finance, 470–72
  demographics, 456–57
  governance, 472–78
  human rights, 467–68, 535–36
  Indigenous peoples and the financial
    economy, 456–60
  international codes of conduct,
    472–76
  MDB policies, 463–66
  national regulation, 476–78
  opportunities and constraints,
    460–63

  protection of Indigenous peoples,
    456–78
  screens, 466–72
  shareholder activism and engagement,
    468–70
Indonesia, 458, 468
Industrial Revolution, 44, 479
Informational mechanisms, 303–32.
  See also Regulation and SRI
ING Bank, 75, 101, 446
Inhance Investment Management, 491
Innovest, 79, 146, 149, 164, 410, 455
  Insight Investment, 98, 405
Institutional investing, overview,
  45–49. *See also* Financial sector and
  institutions; *and* Universal investing
Institutional Investors Group on
  Climate Change (IIGCC)
  on climate change material risks,
    445
  goals of, 14, 23, 138–39, 216,
    490–91
  as investor coalition, 258, 490
Institutional Shareholder Services, 149,
  158
Insurance Business Law (Japan), 241
Insurance sector
  overview, 66–67
  and climate change, 75, 493–94
  collective action in, 151
  deregulation, 66
  environmental risks and costs, 82,
    146
  fiduciary duties, 241–43
  interest in SRI, 75
  worldwide assets, 66
Insurance Supervision Act (Germany),
  304–5
Inter-American Commission on Human
  Rights, 483
Inter-American Development Bank,
  465–66
Interfaith Center on Corporate
  Responsibility (ICCR)
  establishment, 119
  Global Working Group, 23

mission-based collaboration, 97, 113, 115, 154, 155
Principles for Global Corporate Responsibility, 462–63
Internal equity, 52–53, 52n. 54
International Accounting Standards Board (IASB), 201, 319, 329–30, 498–99
International Association of Deposit Insurers, 201
International Auditing and Assurance Standards Board, 201
International Chamber of Commerce (ICC), 395, 475
International Cooperative Alliance, 276
International Corporate Governance Network, 155, 259, 444–45
International Court of Justice (ICJ), 2, 417, 417n. 181
International Finance Corporation (IFC). *See also* Equator Principles (EPs)
on climate change, 479
on lenders' use of ESG issues, 126
Office of the Compliance Advisor/Ombudsman, 450
Performance Standards (2006), 473, 500
Renewable Energy and Energy Efficiency Fund, 500, 566
Safeguard Policies and indigenous peoples, 411–12, 473
Who Cares Wins report, 410
International Financial Reporting Standards (IFRS), 329–30, 331, 544, 545
International Forestry Research, 417–18
International Interfaith Investment Group (3iG), 115, 154
International Investors' Group on Climate Change, 97
International Labor Organization (ILO), 459, 463, 535
International Monetary Fund (IMF), 44, 285
International Network of Pension Regulators and Supervisors, 201

International Organization for Standardization (ISO)
14000 series, 427–30
14001 standard, 32–33, 382, 428, 430, 528
14031 standard, 430
14064 standard, 428–29, 498
14065 standard, 498
International Organization of Securities Commissions (IOSCO), 201, 248, 248n. 317
International Union for Conservation of Nature (IUCN), 15, 136, 451, 542
Intoxicants, 78, 84, 85, 90, 117, 118
Investment Advisers Act (US), 315–16
Investment Company Act (US), 244, 245, 273, 315
Investment Funds Institute of Canada, 272
Investment Management Association, 141, 144
Investment Modernization Act (Germany), 244
Investment regulation obstacles, 187–280
overview, 187–88
banks and fiduciary duties, 238–41
case law, 228–34
collective investment schemes, 243–45, 272–76
corporate fiduciary duties, 234–38, 235n. 258
corporate governance and participation, 254–62
credit unions, 276–78
duty of care, 208–9
duty of loyalty, 210–12
EU initiatives, 203–5, 223, 226–27
fiduciaries and beneficiaries, 205–8
fiduciary duties in pension funds, 221–34
fiduciary duties of institutional investors, 205–20
fiduciary obligations and SRI policies, 217–20, 550–59
fiduciary standards, 208–20

of financial markets, 188–205
globalization of finance, 193–97
global-level governance, 197–203
insurance firms' fiduciary duties,
   241–43
methods and trends, 188–93
non-financial benefits, 212–17
participation in investment
   management, 246–78
pension fund governance, 262–72
pensions regulation, civil law, 226–28
pensions regulation, common law,
   222–26
Investor Network on Climate Risk
   (INCR), 36, 155, 374, 445, 454, 490
Investor Responsibility Research Center
   (IRRC), 314–15
Investor's Circle, 64
Investors Group, 128
Investor Summit on Climate Risk
   (UN), 490
IOSCO (International Organization of
   Securities Commissions), 201, 248,
   248n. 317
Iran, 375
Ireland, 360, 370–71, 524–25.
   See also Europe
IRRC (Investor Responsibility Research
   Center), 314–15
Irving, In re, 214–15
Islamic churches, 118
Islamic Market Sustainability Index,
   118
ISO. *See* International Organization for
   Standardization
Israel, 211–12
ISS Proxy, 158
Italy, 75, 269, 305, 305n. 114, 519.
   See also Europe
IVIS, 158

J
Jantzi Research, 149
Jantzi Social Index, 94
Japan
   bank loans, 59

central banks, 564–65
corporate governance and
   stakeholders, 237
insurance industry, 241
investment company assets, 47
keiretsu system, 261–62
market penetration, 81, 125
pension plans, 65, 227–28, 369
regulation, 189, 192
relationship banking, decline of, 68
retained earnings, 59
securities transaction taxes, 343–44
shareholder advocacy, 182, 369
specialist SRI funds, 78
stakeholder capitalism, 260
tax concessions, 334
voluntary reporting, 328
Job creation, 23, 98, 471, 544
Johannesburg Stock Exchange, 81, 125,
   422
*John Hancock Mutual Life Insurance Co. v.
   Harris Trust and Savings Bank,* 242
Joseph Rowntree Charitable Trust, 112
JPMorgan Chase (JPMC), 149, 418,
   437, 474
Junk food, 84
Juridification, 288
JustPensions (UKSIF), 309–10

K
KAIROS (Canadian Ecumenical Justice
   Initiatives), 114, 119
Kant, Immanuel, 85
Keiretsu system, 261–62. *See also* Japan
Kempen Capital Management, 437
Kitchenuhmaykoosib Inninuwug (KI)
   First Nation, 462, 462n. 44
KLD Global Climate 100 Index, 485
KLD Research and Analytics, 90, 169,
   435
Kok Report, 205
Korea Corporate Governance Service,
   158
KPMG, 338–39, 421
Kyoto Protocol
   and Canada's SIO, 444

Clean Development Mechanism (CDM), 36, 499–501
climate policies, 482, 486–88, 502
expectations of rich nations, 479
and ExxonMobil, 504
and ISO, 428
Joint Implementation (JI) projects, 499–501
Kyoto Protocol Adaptation Fund (UNFCCC), 500

L

Labour-sponsored investment funds (LSIFs), 98–99, 341
Lafayette Mining, 418
Latin America, 60, 125, 179, 322. *See also specific countries*
Law of Accounts of 1999 (Sweden), 324
Law of Trusts, The (Scott), 210
Least Developed Countries Fund (UNFCCC), 499–500
Legal pluralism, 31, 40, 291, 386, 517
Lender liability. *See* Banks and banking sector.
Life insurance companies
overview, 34, 45
defined benefit vs. defined contribution retirement plans, 146
investment types, 66
long-term savings, 65, 139–40, 140n. 215
Lisbon Strategy (EU), 204–5
Liz Claiborne, 467
Lockheed Martin, 368, 375
Lockyer v. General Motors, 483
Logging. *See* Forestry development
London Principles of Sustainable Finance, 395, 407–8
Long-term vs. short-term investment, 139–46
LSIFs (Labour-sponsored investment funds), 98–99, 341
Luhmann, Niklas, 288–89, 294, 527–28
Lutheran churches, 117

M

MacBride Principles, 360, 360n. 427, 380
Malaysia, 125, 460
Managed Investments Act (Australia), 273
Mandela, Nelson, 168
Marathon Club, 140–41
Market capitalization, 49, 57, 165, 414, 437, 569
Market failures, exploitation of, 9–10, 106
Market forces and governance, 379–94
overview, 379–85
voluntary environmental governance, 385–89
voluntary standards, 389–94
Market indexes for SRI, 17–18, 32–33, 70, 81, 90, 94–95, 435–43. *See also* specific indexes
Market surveys, 120–27
Mark-to-market accounting, 143
Marriott hotel chain, 363
Martin v. City of Edinburgh District Council, 228, 230–31
Massachusetts v. Environmental Protection Agency, 482
Materiality. *See* Financial materiality
McDonald's, 133, 182
MDBs. *See* Multilateral development banks
Mecu, 77, 101
Media coverage of pollution and stock losses, 178–79
Mercer Investment Consulting, 79, 80, 158, 401, 445
Meritas Jantzi Social Index Fund, 94
Meritas Mutual Funds, 90
Merlin Ecology Fund, 78
Methodist Church, 117, 119
Mexico, 194, 501
Michaud, Yves, 540
Microcredit institutions, 81, 99
Microfinance, 81, 99–100, 172, 470–72
Midland Bank, 351

Millennium Ecosystem Assessment Board (UN), 20, 509
Mining, 19, 132, 368, 418, 458, 462, 468, 470
Missionary Oblates of Mary Immaculate, 88
Mission-based investment (MBI), 13, 20–24, 112–19, 154, 155
Modern portfolio theory (MPT), 162–63, 209
Money laundering controls, 8, 240, 282–83, 380
Moody's, 72, 433
Moral values, 15, 21–23. *See also* Civil society investors; Religious institutions
Morgan Stanley, 410
Morningstar's Stewardship Grade for Funds, 158
Mortgages, green, 75, 100–101, 126, 501
Motivations of SRI
  business case, 12–20, 84–89
  ethical investment, 20–24, 84–89
  strengthening policies, 24–27
Multilateral Agreement on Investment (OECD), 197
Multilateral development banks (MDBs). *See also* World Bank
  CDM and JI markets, 499
  emerging economies, 202–3
  environmental impact assessment, 6, 82
  and Indigenous peoples, 463–66
  standards and local communities, 76
Mutual fund sector
  collective action in, 151, 249, 253
  ethical investing in, 23, 37, 78, 82, 466, 505
  history of, 63, 77–78
  internal governance of, 137, 156, 158, 188, 243–45, 252, 272–76
  investment management, 133, 164, 176, 184, 246, 480, 491
  long-term vs. short-term investment, 145, 151, 184–85

overview, 62–64
regulation, 208, 243–46, 274, 306, 315–16, 539
retail investors, 71n. 118, 157, 164, 188, 276, 279
shareholder voting, 6, 156, 314–15, 317–18, 503
worldwide number of, 63
Myners Review (UK), 141–42, 219, 258

N
Nader, Ralph, 540
NAFTA (North American Free Trade Agreement), 198, 199
Nathan Cummings Foundation, 77
National Aboriginal Capital Corporation Association, 471
National Association of Pension Funds (NAPF), 141, 144
National Australia Bank (NAB), 99
National Community Reinvestment Coalition, 446
National Ethics Council (Germany), 555
National Pension Insurance Funds Act (Sweden), 362
National Pension Reserve Fund Act (Ireland), 370–71
National Round Table on the Environment and Economy (NRTEE) (Canada), 74–75, 206, 247–48, 283–84, 538
National Westminster Bank, 75
National Wildlife Federation, 112
Native American Bank, 471
Natural capital, 105–6, 520–23
Natural Capital Institute, 29, 133, 176, 467
Natural Step, 76
Nature, economic value of, 104–8, 104n. 4
Negotiated relationships, 31–32, 109, 298
Neoliberalism. *See also* Organization for Economic Cooperation and

Development
  economic instruments vs., 333
  ideology, 525
  influence of, 84, 190, 193–94,
    284–85, 511, 517, 534
  smart regulation vs., 298
  in US, 565
Netherlands. *See also* Europe
  bank loans, 75
  and climate change, 488, 560
  divestments, 88–89
  green project directive, 337–38, 536,
    560
  linked deposit SRI products, 101
  market expansion, 122
  pension plans, 88–89, 138, 269, 313,
    369
Netwerk Vlaanderen, 376, 446
New York City Pension Funds, 405
New York State Teachers Retirement
  System, 138
New Zealand
  and climate change, 487–88
  company legislation, 348
  economic instruments, 334, 345
  investment trusts, 244
  long-term vs. short term investment,
    145
  market reforms, 293–94
  pension plans, 25, 30, 82, 345, 358,
    365–67, 410, 564
New Zealand Council for Socially
  Responsible Investment, 366, 433
New Zealand Superannuation Fund
  (NZSF), 365–67, 410, 535
NGOs (Nongovernmental
  organizations). *See also specific
  organizations*
  affinity credit cards, 75, 100, 101
  campaign for environmental impact
    assessment, 6
  environmental NGOs and faith-based
    investment, 83, 119
  on ethical investing, 23–25, 376, 568
  influence on companies, 94, 97, 470,
    474, 514

influence on market behavior, 8, 182,
  194, 285, 392, 527
leadership of, 82, 299, 313
SRI funds of, 97
SRI governance, 381, 384, 388,
  393–96, 399, 402, 404, 406, 409,
  411, 414–19, 426–27, 446–47,
  451, 502, 520, 533
Nigeria, 19
Nike, 367
Nordea Bank, 407
Norges Bank, 368
Norms on the Responsibilities of
  Transnational Corporations (UN),
  384–85, 452, 474–75, 563–64
North American Free Trade Agreement
  (NAFTA), 198, 199
Northrup Grumman, 375
Norway
  on investor complicity, 4
  pension plans, 4, 25, 46, 358,
    367–69, 410, 445, 467–68, 518,
    534, 555, 561
  regulation, 189
Norwegian Government Public Pension
  Fund, 4, 367–69, 410, 445, 467–68
Norwegian Petroleum Fund, 4, 368
NRTEE. *See* National Round Table on
  the Environment and Economy
Nuclear power generation, 90, 132,
  292, 536
Nuclear Safety and Control Act
  (Canada), 352

O
Occupational Pension Schemes
  (Investment) Regulations (UK), 214
Occupational Pensions Directive (EU),
  214, 223, 226–27, 305
Oceania, 125, 449
OECD. *See* Organization for Economic
  Cooperation and Development
Oesterreichische Nationalbank, 431
One Percent Campaign, 85n. 254
Ontario Municipal Employees
  Retirement System, 137–38

Ontario Public Service Employees Union, 137–38, 405
Ontario Teachers' Pension Plan, 212–13, 271–72
Organization for Economic Cooperation and Development (OECD)
and deregulation, 60
on financial institutions' lack of environmental policies, 51
financial repression thesis, 522
Guidelines for Multinational Enterprises, 363, 368, 405–7, 566
Multilateral Agreement on Investment, 197
national contact points, 406–7
and neoliberalism, 386
pecking order hypothesis, 58
Principles of Corporate Governance, 259, 363, 368
Recommendation on Common Approaches on Environment and Officially Supported Export Credits, 419
regulation, 188, 190, 192–93, 203, 259, 267, 278, 351, 566
Overseas Private Investment Corporation, 566
OWW Consulting Responsibility Malaysia SRI Index, 95
Oxfam, 101
Oy Metsä-Botnia Ab, 417–18

P
Papua New Guinea, 407, 458, 460, 470
Parmalat, 11, 255
Parnassus Fund, 90
Patagonia, 514
Pax World Funds, 15, 78, 117, 133
PDS (product disclosure statement), 306, 476
Pecking order hypothesis of financing, 53, 58
Pension Benefits Act (Ontario, Canada), 269
Pension Fund Association (Japan), 227

Pension fund sector. See also specific funds
access to plans, 249–50
asset smoothing, 143
case law on, 228–34
collective action in, 151
defined benefit vs. defined contribution plans, 146
environmental liability of workers, 346n. 345
ethical investing in public funds, 23, 25, 75, 182
fiduciary duties in, 221–34
history of, 64–65
and life insurance companies, 66
mandated thresholds of return, 34
plan administrators, 65
regulation, 222–28, 262–72, 358–69
risk assessment, 93
shareholders, 24, 185, 253
suitability for SRI, 74–75, 80
types of plans, 65
worldwide assets, 64–65
Pension Protection Act (US), 143
Pensions Act (UK), 156–57, 222–23, 268, 304
Pensions Benefits Standards Act (Canada), 268–69
People and Planet, 83, 446
People's Bank of China, 39
Peoples Department Stores v. Wise, 215, 236, 551–52
Peru, 152
PetroChina, 128, 569
PGGM, 88, 401–2
Pharmaceutical Shareowner Group, 97, 153–54
Pharma Futures project, 153–54
Philanthropy
alignment to SRI, 74, 77
compared to SRI, 1–2, 21, 77, 85, 85n. 254
venture financing by HNWI, 79
Philippines, 418, 470
Photon Photovoltaic Stock Index, 485
Piercing the corporate veil, 357
Pioneer Fund, 77–78, 114

Platinex, 462, 462n. 44
Politics of inclusion, 527
Pollution
    accounting and delayed liability for,
        11, 255
    economic instruments, 332–36, 487,
        560
    lender liability for, 28, 347–48, 352,
        561
    market reaction, 164, 178-79, 302,
        418, 437, 461, 513
    regulation of corporate polluters, 10,
        244, 324, 329, 523
    social problems as result of, 4–5
Pornography, 21, 38, 84, 85, 90, 112,
    116–17, 335, 467, 536
Portfolio 21, 555
Postbank Groen, 338
Postmodern, 254, 524, 527
Poxinvest, 158
Precautionary principle, 26, 296, 318,
    297, 405, 408, 532, 542–43
Prewitt Abandoned Refinery, 477
PricewaterhouseCoopers' survey, 110
Principles for Global Corporate
    Responsibility (ICCR), 462–63
Principles for Responsible Investment
    (UNPRI)
    overview, 127–28, 399-400
    critique of, 25, 401
    and Friends of the Earth, 399
    and globalization, 40, 196, 290
    governance issues, 50, 290, 377, 382,
        399–402, 415, 520, 564
    as normative standards, 32, 382, 448,
        563
    and NZSF, 366
    signatories, 127, 370, 399, 449, 518
    transparency, 539
    voluntary codes and standards, 42,
        203, 563
Private equity market, 54–55, 64, 68,
    78, 136–37. See also Venture capital
    finance
Private property interests, 26, 104
Private rule-making, 31–33

Product disclosure statement (PDS),
    306, 476
Promotion of Access to Information Act
    (South Africa), 327
Property and casualty risk sector,
    66–67
Property law, bundle of rights structure,
    251
Prototype Carbon Fund, 500
Proxy voting
    Calvert Group on, 96
    CERES Principles on, 405, 503
    regulation, 274, 314–16, 503–4
    shareholders, 79, 156, 266
    UNGC principles on, 410
Public Sector Pension Plan Act
    (B.C., Canada), 269
Public Service Employees' Union Pension
    Act (Ontario, Canada), 269

Q
Quakers, 73, 112, 514
Quarterly performance reports, 11, 144,
    273

R
Rabobank, 75, 101, 126
Racial discrimination, 113, 536
Rainforest Action Network, 414, 447
RBC (Royal Bank of Canada), 172, 313,
    416, 472
Reflexive law / regulation, 28–29,
    286–87, 290–91, 301–3, 332, 337,
    376–77, 387–88, 430, 517–18, 538
Regional Greenhouse Gas Initiative,
    488
Regnan, 154
Regulation and SRI See also Investment
    regulation obstacles
    accountability, 281–87
    and ecological modernization,
        286–87, 295–99, 387
    economic instruments, 332–45, 560
    environmental governance, 283–87
    environmental liability of financial
        sponsors, 345–58, 560–61

financial incentive mechanisms, 332–45
investment mandates, 358–74, 564
investment restrictions, 374–76, 533–34
lender liability, 345–55, 560–61
policy reforms, 299–302, 533–67
political economy of environmental governance, 291–95
public sector pension funds, 358–74
regulatory design for sustainability, 287–302
reporting regulations, 322–28
shareholder liability, 355–58, 560
state and pension funds, 358–69, 534, 564
state-market realignments, 287–91
transparency regulation, 28, 42, 245, 250, 252, 275, 279, 303–32, 383, 450, 517, 537, 552
Relationship banking, 68
Religious institutions
deontological ethics, 20, 85
ethical investing, 22–23, 73, 84–85
faith-based investment, 83, 111–20
investor networks, 115
shareholder resolutions, 88
Renewable energy, 36, 76
Renewable Energy and Energy Efficiency Fund (IFC), 500, 566
Reporting, environmental. *See under* Sustainability
Reputational risk, 18–19, 21, 89, 94, 180, 329-30, 384, 392, 414, 458, 483–84, 513
Research
and advocacy forums, 443–47
on biodiversity, 454
on climate change, 480
industry, 79, 83, 149–50
methods, 40, 121
pension plan studies, 270, 271
Residential financing. *See* Housing
Responsible Investment Association of Australasia (RIAA)
overview, 130

eco-labels, 424–25
financial planner certification, 158
on growth of SRI in Australia, 123, 123n. 123
renaming of organization, 20–21
on retail SRI, 312
Restructurings, corporate, 49–50
Retail investment market, 63, 71, 71n. 164, 77–78, 131, 157, 312
Retained earnings, 58–59
Return on investment, 46
Rhodesia, 114
RIAA. *See* Responsible Investment Association of Australasia
Rimbunan Hijau consortium, 407
Rise of Fiduciary Capitalism, The (Hawley and Williams), 16
Risk, in financial management, 73–74, 92–94. *See also under specific financial institutions*; *and* Climate Change
Royal Bank of Scotland v. Skinner, 238–39
Russia, 417, 458, 460

S
St. Regis Mohawk Nation, 477
Samling, 460
S&P's. *See* Standard and Poor's
Sarbanes-Oxley legislation (US), 192, 325
Scotland, 230–31. 238. *See also* Europe
Screens. *See* Exclusionary screens
Second Banking Directive (EU), 204
Securities and Exchange Board of India Act, 192
Securities and Exchange Commission (SEC)
climate change risk disclosure, 139, 321, 495–96, 504
legislative oversight of, 244, 274, 315–16
reporting standards, 325–26
shareholder advisory resolutions, 7
Securities transaction taxes (STTs), 342–45
SEIA (Social and environmental impact assessment), 411–13, 414–15, 417–18

Shadow director, 347–48
Shareholder Association for Research
and Education (SHARE), 410
Shareholders. *See also* Investment
regulation obstacles
advisory resolutions, 7, 88, 96–97,
183, 259–60, 414
advocacy and activism
overview, 33, 139, 180–85,
468–70, 502–4
and active management, 70
civil rights, 74
compared to consumer
boycotts, 83
engagement vs. screens,
95–98, 95n. 309, 182,
233–34, 310, 313, 316,
362, 372–73
environmental vs. social
issues, 455
faith-based investors, 114
on global warming, 502–4
Indigenous peoples, 468–70
in Japan, 227–28
methods of, 96, 96n. 312
motivations of, 455–56
SIF on, 122
bondholders vs., 61
democratic decision-making, 24
diversity of social values among,
21–22
dividend distribution, 52
executive stock options, 57–58, 57n.
83
governance structure and wealth, 98
insurance companies, 66
member nominated representatives,
25, 156
passivity and lack of knowledge, 258,
258n. 360, 265–67
pecking order hypothesis, 53
polluters and stock losses, 178
protection of interests of, 8, 16, 49,
50–51
proxy voting, 79, 96, 156, 266,
274

regulation and liability, 10–11,
355–58
voluntary codes of conduct, 16
vote disclosure, 6
Shari'ah (Islamic law), 118
Shell, 19
Sierra Club, 97
SIF. *See* Social Investment Forum
Singapore Technologies Engineering, 366
Sin stocks. *See specific types*
SIO. *See* Social Investment Organization
Small business, 54, 60–61, 69, 70–71
Smart regulation, 289, 298
Social Accountability International, 427
Social accounting, 26, 331, 544–46
Social and environmental impact
assessment (SEIA), 411–13, 414–15,
417–18
Social Creed of the Churches, The (Federal
Council of Churches), 112
Social Investment Forum (Germany),
537
Social Investment Forum (SIF) (US),
121–22, 130, 183, 247, 454, 502,
502n. 290
Social Investment Forum (UKSIF), 6–7,
83, 130, 158, 186, 189, 309–10,
313, 382
Social Investment Organization (SIO),
6–7, 123–24, 130, 318, 444
Social license of financial institutions,
83–84, 329–30
Socially responsible investing (SRI),
overview, 1–3, 88n. 272, 130–31
Social Sciences and Humanities
Research Council (Canada), 40
Social security systems, 44, 46, 65
South Africa
apartheid and worldwide divestment
campaigns, 4–5, 22, 74, 113–14,
115, 167–68, 224–25, 230–32,
269, 359–60
market expansion, 125
SRI indexes, 81
Sullivan Principles in, 113
UNGC principles in, 410

South African Trust Investments Act
(Ontario, Canada), 224–25, 269, 551
South Korea, 158, 179, 410, 564–65
South Sea Company, 208
Special Climate Change Fund
(UNFCCC), 499–500
SRI movement,
advocacy and engagement, 95–98,
460
best-in-class methods, 91–92, 95,
129, 133, 150, 364
drivers and future directions, 79–84,
250, 567
economically targeted investment,
98–100
ethical motivation, 84–89, 159, 515
financial motivation, 84–89, 159,
337
financial risk management, 73–74,
92–94
historical advances, 73–79
index tracking, 94–95
products and services, 100–101
social screens, 89–91
terminology, 29
Stakeholder capitalism, 80–81, 260
Stakeholders and corporate governance,
234–38, 235n. 259, 260–61, 262,
519, 553
Standard and Poor's (S&P's)
CSR ratings, 72, 433–34, 492
S&P 100 Index, 421
S&P 500 Index, 169, 175, 183–84
S&P 1200 Index, 421
Standards
discretionary standards and ethical
investing, 550–52
eco-label standards, 423–25, 423n.
217
fiduciary standards, 212–20
fungible, 129–33
performance standards, 555–59
process standards, 552–55
reporting standards, 144
reputational advantage, 197, 197n. 43
universal, 21

Staples, 182
State. See Government
State and municipal funds, regulation
(US), 358–62
State-market realignments, 287–91
Statement by Financial Institutions on
the Environment and Sustainable
Development of 1997 (UNEPFI),
396, 397
State Street Global Advisors, 70
Steady-state economy, 16–17
Stern Review on the Economics of Climate
Change, 478–79, 478n. 144
Stock prices, 56–58, 57n. 83, 166,
166n. 357
STTs (Securities transaction taxes),
342–45
Sudan, 84, 128, 375, 536, 569
Sullivan, Leon, 113
Sullivan Principles, 113, 359–60, 359n.
420, 380
Superannuation and Retirement Income
Act (New Zealand), 365
Superannuation Industry Act
(Australia), 225, 268
Superannuation Legislation
Amendment Act (Australia), 225–26,
268, 306, 306n. 122
Superfund liability (US), 6, 177,
348–50
SustainAbility, 321
Sustainability. See also ethical
investment for sustainability
corporate behavior, 17, 95, 110, 382,
387
corporate reporting, 26, 150, 284,
303, 319–32, 374, 377, 403,
420–25, 497
ecological integrity, 29
defined, 2, 38, 86, 295, 511
ethics, 9, 206, 395, 451, 514, 521,
525, 527, 529, 533, 561
financial markets, 5, 9, 16, 19,
23v24, 51, 76, 80, 91, 105, 129,
172–80, 186, 194, 353, 389, 480,
514–15

financial performance, 83, 90,
    146–47, 158, 397, 512
fiduciary duties, 540–59
regulation, 282, 287–99, 338, 384,
    402, 420–25
sustainability indexes, 435–43
SRI, 20, 103–05, 234, 434, 567
sustainability indicators, 30,
    546–50
Sustainability indexes. *See* Market
    indexes for SRI
Sustainable Asset Management (SAM),
    150, 438–39, 440
Sustainable development, 2-3, 9–12,
    21–25, 37, 39, 43, 51, 75–77,
    80–81, 86, 99, 104, 118, 126, 134,
    139–40, 202, 249, 284, 295–98,
    332. *See also* sustainability
Sustainable Investment Research
    International, 148, 149, 150
Swedbank, 101
Sweden. *See also* Europe
    banking sector, 69, 101
    Ethical Council, 363
    faith-based investors, 117
    pension plans, 25, 264, 358, 362–63,
        445, 534, 555
    regulation, 189
    securities transaction taxes, 343
Switzerland, 189, 269, 549. *See also*
    Europe

T
Taskforce on the Churches and
    Corporate Responsibility (TCCR),
    114
Tax concessions. *See under* Incentives,
    and Economic instruments
Teachers Insurance and Annuity
    Association, College Retirement
    Equities Fund (TIAA-CREF), 156,
    264
Technological advances
    and asset managers, 70–71
    and energy efficiency, 36
    and finance capitalism, 46

and risk assessment, 92
and venture capital, 78–79
Teleological ethics, 20, 85–86
Textron Systems, 366
Thai Government Pension Fund, 371
Thailand, 371
3iG. *See* International Interfaith
    Investment Group
3M Company, 154
Timothy Plan funds, 118
TNCs. *See* Transnational corporations
Tobacco, 21, 35, 78, 84, 90,
    116–18, 122, 131–32, 168, 367,
    372, 375, 375n. 377, 439–42,
    461–62, 467, 483, 490, 526.
    See also Intoxicants
Tobin, James, 342
Toxics Release Inventory (TRI), 164,
    178
Trade-off theory of financing, 53
Trade unions and pension plans, 65, 75,
    185, 264, 268, 271
Transnational corporations (TNCs), 194,
    201, 384–85, 390, 474–75, 564. *See also*
    Norms on the Responsibilities of
    Transnational Corporations (UN); *specific
    corporations*
Transparency
    accounting rules, 328–32
    corporate sustainability reporting,
        319–28
    Eurosif guidelines, 316, 422–23,
        539
    implementation of disclosure reforms,
        309–13
    legislative standards, 303–9
    proxy voting disclosure, 314–18
Trillium Asset Management, 469
Triodos Bank, 75, 76
Triodos Groenfonds, 338
Trucost, 120, 364, 550
Trustee Act (Manitoba, Canada), 224,
    551
Trusts, 10, 62, 65, 207–8, 215, 220,
    230, 243, 245, 265, 316
Turkey, 566

U

UBS, 70, 149, 429
UK National Association of Pension
    Funds, 311–12
UKSIF. *See* Social Investment Forum
Umweltbank, 23, 75, 353
UNEP. *See* Global Reporting Initiative;
    Principles for Responsible
    Investment; United Nations
    Environment Program Finance
    Initiative
UNFCCC. *See* Framework Convention
    on Climate Change
UNGC. *See* Global Compact
UNICEF, 440
UniCredito Italiano, 431
Union of Concerned Scientists, 515
United Kingdom (UK). *See also* Europe
    arm's length banking relations, 68
    bond market, 59
    and climate change, 488, 489
    economic instruments, 334, 340–41,
        345
    environmentally responsible lending,
        75, 76
    investment company assets, 47
    legislation. *See specific legislation*
    London Principles of Sustainable
        Finance, 395, 407–8
    long-term vs. short-term investment,
        140–42, 145
    market reforms, 293–94
    market-tracking index funds, 70
    mission-based investors, 112,
        115–16, 118–19
    pension plans, 6, 23, 65, 222, 223–24,
        249, 264, 267–68, 320, 539
    public opinion, 128
    regulation, 189, 309–11, 518–19,
        554
    retained earnings, 59
    securities transaction taxes, 343
    shareholder activism, 139, 537
    SRI market, 123
    SRI network success in, 6–7
    sustainability indicators, 547

United Nations. *See specific initiatives*
United Nations Environment Program
    Finance Initiative (UNEPFI).
    overview, 32, 154, 186, 395–98
    biodiversity research, 454
    Climate Change Working Group, 490
    collaborative mechanism, 154, 396,
        569
    on consumer awareness in North
        America, 126
    emerging markets, 569
    EPs compared to, 415
    Freshfields Bruckhaus Deringer study,
        206, 414, 415, 541
    and Indigenous peoples, 37
    on integration of ESG, 14–15
    and Mercer Investment Consulting, 79
    on public sector funds, 358–59
    regulatory role of, 50, 203, 290, 449
    signatories, 80–81, 519
    on SRI research, 174, 186, 455
    voluntary codes and standards, 42,
        203, 395
*United Paperworkers International Union
    v. International Paper Company,* 317
United States
    arm's length banking relations, 68
    banking industry, 6
    bond market, 59
    case law, 213–14, 231–33
    and climate change, 482, 483, 488
    corporate fiduciary duties, 235n. 258,
        236
    credit unions, decline of, 69
    economic instruments, 334
    Indigenous peoples of, 454, 467, 471,
        472, 472n. 102, 535–36
    industry domination by CSRs, 72
    insurance industry, 241, 242
    investment company assets, 38,
        47–48
    legislation. *See specific legislation*
    long-term vs. short-term investment,
        145
    market reforms, 293–94
    market-tracking index funds, 70

military spending, 565

mining, 470

mission-based investors, 112, 113, 117

mutual fund sector, 6, 77–78, 244, 274, 519, 539

pension plans, 64–65, 81, 213–14, 223–24, 269–70, 359, 360–62, 405, 536

proxy voting, 314–16

regulation, 189, 192–93, 358–62, 519

retained earnings, 59

securities transaction taxes, 343

shareholders, 259–60

SRI market, 121–22

tax incentives, 341

universal banks, 67

venture finance, 127

Universal investing, 18, 88, 93, 282, 481

Universal owners, 16–17, 133–37, 139, 217, 246, 262, 557–59. *See also* Pension fund sector

Universities and responsible investing, 74

Universities Superannuation Scheme (USS)

on climate change as financial risk, 491

collaboration with pharmaceutical industry, 153–54

and People and Planet, 83, 446

policy statements of, 311

responsible investing of, 23, 138

shareholder advocacy, 182

UNPRI. *See* Principles for Responsible Investment

Uranium industry, 132

Urban Strategy American Fund, 270

Uruguay, 407, 417, 419

USS. *See* Universities Superannuation Scheme

V

Valdez Principles. *See* CERES Principles

Values-based investing. *See* Mission-based investment; Religious institutions

VanCity, 23, 77, 101

Venture capital finance (VCF)

environmental technologies, 78–79

market expansion, 127, 127n. 151

private equity funds, 54, 64, 136–37

risk assessment, 93

and small firms, 54, 61

Verdun v. Toronto Dominion Bank, 266

Vice Fund, 168

VicSuper, 371–72

Vietnam War, 74

Voluntary codes of conduct

chart of international codes, 395

and civil society investors, 31

and EPs, 203, 472–74

governance issues, 7–8, 35–37, 389–94

and Indigenous peoples, 472–76

institutional investors, 259

shareholder expectation of, 16

and UNEPFI, 203, 395

and UNPRI, 203, 563

W

Wal-Mart, 133, 363, 367, 368–69

WBCSD. *See* World Business Council for Sustainable Development

Weather, 493–94

Web of life, 21, 530

Westpac, 75, 101

Weyerhaeuser, 470

Wharton Business School, 99

Whole-life insurance policies, 66

Wilder Hill Clean Energy Index, 485

Withers v. Teachers Retirement System, 232

WMC Resources, 132

World Bank. *See also* International Finance Corporation

co-financing with private lenders, 152, 500, 566–67

in emerging economies, 202, 203

environmental impact assessment, 6, 81–82

Extractive Industries Review, 485–86

financialization of the economy, 285

on global carbon market, 485

and Indigenous peoples, 37, 464–65
Inspection Panel, 450
World Business Council for Sustainable
Development (WBCSD), 108–9, 383,
481, 497, 548
World Charter for Nature (UN), 531
Worldcom, 11, 72, 192
World Economic Forum, 140, 497,
498, 541
World Resources Institute (WRI), 19,
326, 463, 482–83, 497, 505–6
World Trade Organization (WTO),
197, 198, 199
World Wide Fund for Nature (WWF),
82, 83, 101, 126, 399, 411, 447, 486

WRI. *See* World Resources Institute
WTO (World Trade Organization),
197–99
WWF. *See* World Wide Fund for
Nature

X
Xcel Energy, 504

Y
Yakama Indian Nation, 466
Yamashita, Miwaka, 178
YES Bank of India, 398
Young Women's Christian Association
(YWCA), 113–14